Handbook of Research on Human-Computer Interfaces and New Modes of Interactivity

Katherine Blashki
Victorian Institute of Technology, Australia

Pedro Isaías
The University of Queensland, Australia

A volume in the Advances in Computational
Intelligence and Robotics (ACIR) Book Series

Published in the United States of America by
IGI Global
Engineering Science Reference (an imprint of IGI Global)
701 E. Chocolate Avenue
Hershey PA, USA 17033
Tel: 717-533-8845
Fax: 717-533-8661
E-mail: cust@igi-global.com
Web site: http://www.igi-global.com

Library of Congress Cataloging-in-Publication Data

Names: Blashki, Kathy, 1961- editor. | Isaias, Pedro, editor.
Title: Handbook of research on human-computer interfaces and new modes of
    interactivity / Katherine Blashki and Pedro Isaias, editors.
Description: Hershey, PA : Engineering Science Reference, an imprint of IGI
    Global, [2020] | Includes bibliographical references and index.
Identifiers: LCCN 2018056284| ISBN 9781522590699 (hardcover) | ISBN
    9781522590712 (ebook)
Subjects: LCSH: User interfaces (Computer systems)
Classification: LCC QA76.9.U83 H874 2020 | DDC 005.4/37--dc23 LC record available at https://lccn.loc.gov/2018056284

This book is published in the IGI Global book series Advances in Computational Intelligence and Robotics (ACIR) (ISSN: 2327-0411; eISSN: 2327-042X)

British Cataloguing in Publication Data
A Cataloguing in Publication record for this book is available from the British Library.

The views expressed in this book are those of the authors, but not necessarily of the publisher.

For electronic access to this publication, please contact: eresources@igi-global.com.

Advances in Computational Intelligence and Robotics (ACIR) Book Series

Ivan Giannoccaro
University of Salento, Italy

ISSN:2327-0411
EISSN:2327-042X

MISSION

While intelligence is traditionally a term applied to humans and human cognition, technology has progressed in such a way to allow for the development of intelligent systems able to simulate many human traits. With this new era of simulated and artificial intelligence, much research is needed in order to continue to advance the field and also to evaluate the ethical and societal concerns of the existence of artificial life and machine learning.

The **Advances in Computational Intelligence and Robotics (ACIR) Book Series** encourages scholarly discourse on all topics pertaining to evolutionary computing, artificial life, computational intelligence, machine learning, and robotics. ACIR presents the latest research being conducted on diverse topics in intelligence technologies with the goal of advancing knowledge and applications in this rapidly evolving field.

COVERAGE

- Fuzzy Systems
- Natural Language Processing
- Neural Networks
- Computational Logic
- Cognitive Informatics
- Adaptive and Complex Systems
- Computational intelligence
- Artificial Life
- Intelligent control
- Brain Simulation

IGI Global is currently accepting manuscripts for publication within this series. To submit a proposal for a volume in this series, please contact our Acquisition Editors at Acquisitions@igi-global.com or visit: http://www.igi-global.com/publish/.

Titles in this Series

For a list of additional titles in this series, please visit: www.igi-global.com/book-series

Computational Intelligence in the Internet of Things
Hindriyanto Dwi Purnomo (Satya Wacana Christian University, Indonesia)
Engineering Science Reference • copyright 2019 • 342pp • H/C (ISBN: 9781522579557) • US $225.00 (our price)

Artificial Intelligence and Security Challenges in Emerging Networks
Ryma Abassi (University of Carthage, Tunisia)
Engineering Science Reference • copyright 2019 • 293pp • H/C (ISBN: 9781522573531) • US $195.00 (our price)

Emerging Trends and Applications in Cognitive Computing
Pradeep Kumar Mallick (Vignana Bharathi Institute of Technology, India) and Samarjeet Borah (Sikkim Manipal University, India)
Engineering Science Reference • copyright 2019 • 300pp • H/C (ISBN: 9781522557937) • US $215.00 (our price)

Predictive Intelligence Using Big Data and the Internet of Things
P.K. Gupta (Jaypee University of Information Technology, India) Tuncer Ören (University of Ottawa, Canada) and Mayank Singh (University of KwaZulu-Natal, South Africa)
Engineering Science Reference • copyright 2019 • 300pp • H/C (ISBN: 9781522562108) • US $245.00 (our price)

Advanced Metaheuristic Methods in Big Data Retrieval and Analytics
Hadj Ahmed Bouarara (Dr. Moulay Tahar University of Saïda, Algeria) Reda Mohamed Hamou (Dr. Moulay Tahar University of Saïda, Algeria) and Amine Rahmani (Dr. Moulay Tahar University of Saïda, Algeria)
Engineering Science Reference • copyright 2019 • 320pp • H/C (ISBN: 9781522573388) • US $205.00 (our price)

Nature-Inspired Algorithms for Big Data Frameworks
Hema Banati (Dyal Singh College, India) Shikha Mehta (Jaypee Institute of Information Technology, India) and Parmeet Kaur (Jaypee Institute of Information Technology, India)
Engineering Science Reference • copyright 2019 • 412pp • H/C (ISBN: 9781522558521) • US $225.00 (our price)

Novel Design and Applications of Robotics Technologies
Dan Zhang (York University, Canada) and Bin Wei (York University, Canada)
Engineering Science Reference • copyright 2019 • 341pp • H/C (ISBN: 9781522552765) • US $205.00 (our price)

Optoelectronics in Machine Vision-Based Theories and Applications
Moises Rivas-Lopez (Universidad Autónoma de Baja California, Mexico) Oleg Sergiyenko (Universidad Autónoma de Baja California, Mexico) Wendy Flores-Fuentes (Universidad Autónoma de Baja California, Mexico) and Julio Cesar Rodríguez-Quiñonez (Universidad Autónoma de Baja California, Mexico)
Engineering Science Reference • copyright 2019 • 433pp • H/C (ISBN: 9781522557517) • US $225.00 (our price)

701 East Chocolate Avenue, Hershey, PA 17033, USA
Tel: 717-533-8845 x100 • Fax: 717-533-8661
E-Mail: cust@igi-global.com • www.igi-global.com

Editorial Advisory Board

List of Contributors

Table of Contents

Detailed Table of Contents

Section 1
Design and Methodology

Chapter 1

Dominik Hagelkruys, University of Vienna, Austria
Renate Motschnig, University of Vienna, Austria

Designing for people with special needs, especially cognitive and affective needs, can be challenging. Human-centered design (HCD), which inherently promotes user-inclusion and promises products that fit the users' needs, seems to be an optimal solution for such tasks. But can an HCD-approach be easily applied with special needs users? How much adaptation is necessary to perform classical HCD-techniques with users affected by certain difficulties? This chapter discusses the insights gathered and strategies adopted while applying human-centered design in the LITERACY-project, a project of the European Union aiming at improving social inclusion of youth and adults with dyslexia, by creating an interactive web-portal. Hopefully, this case study provides insight on and gives courage for inclusion of end-users even though—or particularly because—they have special needs.

Chapter 2

Abhishek Dahiya, Indian Institute of Technology Delhi, India
Jyoti Kumar, Indian Institute of Technology Delhi, India

Personas are a rich source of user information that assists designers at various stages of the design process. HCI designers use personas to help them explicate the understanding of their target users. Design literature advocates that personas are not only a source of information about users but also a tool to empathize with them. This chapter reports observations from an experimental study done on novice designers on how empathizing with persona affected their design solutions. A total of 50 novice designers participated in this study. Participants were asked to solve a graphical design problem for the persona. The data collected was analyzed through expert rating on design solutions on the basis of directness of illustration of persona information and verbal protocols. On the basis of direct illustration of persona information on design solutions, it was observed that empathizing with persona helped designers to iterate more on design thinking.

This chapter shares a protocol for reviewing games and documents the process in which it was used by an educational game design team for evaluating existing games to inform the design and development of new games for early algebra. While the design team has used their own learning games design model to develop several games—all of which included some kind of immersive learning and review activity—there has been no documentation provided on the specific processes used to review games as part of that immersion. Observations offer structured means for assessing existing games in a particular space and are thus valuable to identify how best to pursue the alignment of learning objectives with teaching content and game mechanics in the development of educational games.

Chapter 4

Detecting flow in games is key for successful adaptation processes. Until now, the method of choice to measure flow in games is the usage of questionnaires, such as flow short scale or game experience questionnaire. Because of the shortcomings of these methods, the theoretical model of flow is enhanced by the concept of immersion to propose a unified flow/immersion model. In combination with this more fine-grained model of immersion, player experience may be measured in a more detailed fashion. The enhancement of the theoretical model and the altered experiment procedure are presented. In conclusion, a perspective towards performing the experiment and future data recordings is given.

Churches have a long tradition using technology to grow their audience and to connect worshippers. Technologies used in Christian service are not even perceived as such: consider architecture, the organ, and light. Yet, faith-based organizations have always been critical of new technologies. The authors used design science research methodologies to develop an artifact of the Eucharist of a Catholic service. "Instant Church" is an interactive machine that guides visitors through the service and creates an individualized wafer with a laser-engraved QR-code that points to a random Tweet with a hate message that invites a moment of thought. Over 700 visitors saw that exhibit. A qualitative evaluation showed a high positive acceptance by users under40 while older visitors had a negative perspective. The artifact proved to be a highly suitable tool to invite a critical discourse and at the same time serves as a learning tool about the service. Interactive intelligent solutions reach the generation of digital natives and enable the discourse on the relationship between technology and faith.

Chapter 6

Norman G. Vinson, National Research Council, Canada
Heather Molyneaux, National Research Council, Canada
Joel D. Martin, National Research Council, Canada

The opacity of AI systems' decision making has led to calls to modify these systems so they can provide explanations for their decisions. This chapter contains a discussion of what these explanations should address and what their nature should be to meet the concerns that have been raised and to prove satisfactory to users. More specifically, the chapter briefly reviews the typical forms of AI decision-making that are currently used to make real-world decisions affecting people's lives. Based on concerns about AI decision making expressed in the literature and the media, the chapter follows with principles that the systems should respect and corresponding requirements for explanations to respect those principles. A mapping between those explanation requirements and the types of explanations generated by AI decision making systems reveals the strengths and shortcomings of the explanations generated by those systems.

Section 2
Applications

Chapter 7

João Antonio de Menezes Neto, University of the Region of Joinville, Brazil
Victor Rafael Laurenciano Aguiar, University of the Region of Joinville, Brazil

This chapter details the redesign process of the bank reconciliation interface of ContaAzul, an online cloud-based financial management software for small businesses in Brazil. The reconciliation is a feature that allows the user to import bank account statements and easily register them into the software, generating automated reports that help companies achieve their financial control. The research problem was motivated by use cases that were not covered in the studied version of this feature, as well as by recent technological advances. Interaction design was chosen as the project approach and Garrett's five planes as the methodology. As the final deliverable, a prototype was composed of static, bitmap screens, elaborated from a participatory design perspective. This research was developed as a course conclusion project in the Master's degree in Design Program of University of the Region of Joinville, Brazil. The first author of this chapter is also a design coordinator at ContaAzul.

Chapter 8

Takumi Shida, Kanagawa Institute of Technology, Japan
Hiroshi Sugimura, Kanagawa Institute of Technology, Japan
Moe Hamamoto, Kanagawa Institute of Technology, Japan
Masao Isshiki, Kanagawa Institute of Technology, Japan

The authors propose an interface for home energy management system (HEMS). This interface is aimed at raising the energy-saving consciousness of users who have little knowledge of energy saving. A possible reason for the low level of consciousness of such users is that HEMS does not provide information which helps users in energy-saving planning. To help users who have insufficient knowledge of energy saving, the interface visualizes power consumption and operational information obtained from network home appliances. In order to show which appliances have potential for significant energy-saving effects, the interface uses icons that visually represent high-power appliances whose power consumption exceeds 400 W, along with their operation periods. By viewing the screen, users can easily recognize how to operate appliances for energy-saving planning as well as which appliances have high energy-saving effects. The authors have developed a tool with a built-in interface and have evaluated it by questionnaire.

Chapter 9

Pedro Henrique Roscoe Lage de Oliveira, Minas Gerais State University, Brazil
Carlos Alberto Silva de Miranda, Minas Gerais State University, Brazil
Joao Victor Boechat Gomide, Universidade FUMEC, Brazil

This chapter proposes and experiments alternatives to replace or optimize the use of the game design document (GDD). The creation and development of a game is accomplished by relying on the GDD, which contains all the information, such as the script, mechanics, and relevant details, so the team can use as a guide. There is no exact formula for creating a GDD, and several formats are proposed and used nowadays. Information misinterpreted or misunderstood at different levels of responsibility can create irreparable problems after the start of production. This chapter proposes the use of analog prototyping associated with benchmarking techniques and agile development as efficient alternatives to GDD, which are tested in the development of the game Forsaken Dungeons, created by one of the authors.

Chapter 10

Conrado Ruiz Jr., De La Salle University, Philippines
Juan Lorenzo Simeon, De La Salle University, Philippines
Kingston Anthony Koa, De La Salle University, Philippines
John Israel Domingo Caingles, De La Salle University, Philippines
Anne Marielle Bagamaspad, De La Salle University, Philippines

LEGO structures are generally constructed by following an instruction manual in paper or digital form, which shows the LEGO model at different stages of assembly. Some instructions can be very complicated and difficult to illustrate on paper. Augmented reality (AR) is a technology that superimposes 3D models onto the physical world. This chapter explores the use of AR for assembly through a mobile application for Android devices that serves as an assembly guide for LEGO structures. The system can recognize the current step of the LEGO assembly using data captured via Microsoft Kinect while providing visual feedback through a mobile application. To identify the current step, the system obtains the color and depth data from the Kinect camera and converts the data into a point cloud, which is compared to stored LEGO model data. The system was evaluated based on the accuracy of the recognition, latency of the feedback and the assembly time of the user.

Chapter 11

Marisardo Bezerra de Medeiros Filho, Universidade Federal de Pernambuco, Brazil
Farley Fernandes, UNIDCOM IADE, Portugal & Universidade da Beira Interior, Portugal
Felipe Matheus Calado, Universidade Católica de Pernambuco, Brazil
André Menezes Marques Neves, Universidade Federal de Pernambuco, Brazil

This chapter presents an ARM (acquisition, retention, and monetization) framework for F2P (free-to-play) mobile games to be used as to support game design practice and research. ARM strategies are dispersed throughout various sources such as websites, papers, and books, hampering the work of researchers and practitioners in this field. The aim of this framework is to list and organize these strategies into a single source. A literature research about ARM strategies in F2P mobile games was conducted to identify and select elements. Based on surveys with game development professionals, some of these elements were polished, merged, or removed. Finally, these elements were organized into a single framework, consisting of 3 main categories (acquisition, retention, and monetization), 8 subcategories, and 59 specific elements.

Chapter 12

Isabel Araújo, Instituto Politécnico de Viana do Castelo, Portugal
Pedro Miguel Faria, Instituto Politécnico de Viana do Castelo, Portugal

From an early age, young people use mobile devices and are known as a "native digital generation," who constantly access information through mobile devices. Thus, educational practices are not indifferent to this reality. Consequently, several online platforms supporting the teaching-learning process have been developed. Additionally, several higher education institutions have a weekly attendance time, where teachers seek to clarify student's doubts physically in the institution. However, oftentimes, the students do not use that attendance time. In order to seek to improve this issue, a collaborative mobile web platform was developed: Higher M@t-EduTutor. This chapter starts by introducing a theoretical framework and then presents a broad study on collaborative web platforms in order to better relate them with the developed platform. This specific platform, to be used in mobile devices, with the objective of promoting students learning, allows students to clarify doubts with their teachers, collaboratively, in real time and at distance.

Chapter 13

Julie Ann Acebuque Salido, De La Salle University, Philippines & Aklan State University, Philippines
Conrado Ruiz Jr., De La Salle University, Philippines
Nelson Marcos, De La Salle University, Philippines

Melanoma is a severe form of skin cancer characterized by the rapid multiplication of pigment-producing cells. A problem on analysis of these images is interesting because of the existence of artifacts that produces noise such as hair, veins, water residue, illuminations, and light reflections. An important step in the diagnosis of melanoma is the removal and reduction of these artifacts that can inhibit the examination to accurately segment the skin lesion from the surrounding skin area. A simple method for artifacts removal for extracting skin lesion is implemented based on image enhancement and morphological operators. This is used for training together with some augmentation techniques on images for melanoma detection. The experimental results show that artifact removal and lesion segmentation in skin lesion images performed a true detection rate of 95.37% for melanoma skin lesion segmentation, and as high as 92.5% accuracy for melanoma detection using both GoogLeNet and Resnet50.

Section 3
User Experience and Usability Studies

Chapter 14

Hsiu-Feng Wang, National Chiayi University, Taiwan

This experiment examined children's visual aesthetics and learning motivation with regard to websites. It applied Berlyne's theory of aesthetic preference to these websites. The experiment explored the relations between visual complexity, visual aesthetics, learning motivation, and children's age, and their effect on websites. A total of 150 children between 10 and 12 years old were involved. The children were asked to rate websites of different levels of perceived visual complexity in terms of visual aesthetic and learning motivation. The results showed that the children preferred websites that displayed a medium level of perceived visual complexity to those that displayed a high or low level of perceived visual complexity. Thus, the results supported Berlyne's theory. However, when aesthetic preference was analyzed with respect to age-related differences, it was found that older children preferred a medium level of perceived visual complexity and younger children preferred a high level of perceived visual complexity.

Chapter 15

Brayan Mauricio Rodriguez, Universidad Icesi, Colombia
Carlos Arce-Lopera, Universidad Icesi, Colombia
Ana M. Arboleda, Universidad Icesi, Colombia
Javier Diaz-Cely, Universidad Icesi, Colombia
Julian Correa, Musicar SAS, Colombia
Pablo Montoya, Musicar SAS, Colombia

The authors describe the importance of music design for background instrumental music and the effect on task performance. Three instrumental music conditions that differ in tempo, articulation, mode, and musical meter were tested using a complex task scenario. The task was performed using a complicated web-interface that required users to focus their attention and perform several specific interactions for successfully finishing the task. All the interactions with the interface were recorded. Moreover, a mixed assessment of the emotional state, perceived task performance, and music perception was asked to participants upon task completion. Experimental results revealed that music design has complex effects on task performance and emotion. Also, the results revealed important trends that can help design music environments to control frustration when confronted to complex and cognitively demanding tasks.

The main objective of this research is to provide a procedure set, oriented by a clear and rigorous protocol that allows the replication of results regarding the accessibility claims of products and systems available for the blind community, thus validating their robustness. The goal during the experiment was to compare user preferences and effectiveness when performing tasks with the voice synthesizers JAWS and DOSVOX and a braille keyboard. The adopted evaluation protocol includes the following methods: usability testing, focus group, and user satisfaction survey. The study developed with the proposed protocol investigates assistive technology adequacy to target users. The tasks performed by 30 users were categorized as activities of entertainment, learning, and social inclusion. It is considered that the main contribution of this chapter is to provide the protocol and methodology, adapted for use in evaluations of accessibility products and devices.

Chapter 17

The process of game development is constantly evolving in order to meet the different demands of players as well as the need to adapt to the employment of new technologies and trends in the gaming market. The game design thinking methodology that adds quality to the game development once is focused on the game design and development based on design thinking, an interactive design process focused on collaboration between developers and users to propose user-centered solutions. The challenge-based learning methodology presents to the learners (and future professionals) a challenge scenario asking them to think about a number of possible solutions using a variety of interactive tools. This chapter proposes to combine both game design thinking and challenge-based learning methodologies into the process of game development in order to assist the game learners and professionals to be able to integrate different aspects necessary to the proposal of a game, considering its multidisciplinary nature and understanding the human needs involved.

Mindfulness is constantly increasing in popularity, having demonstrated benefits for psychological health and cognitive performance. Not only current psychotherapies have integrated mindfulness, but also digital technology for the general public such as mobile apps and games strive to incorporate mindfulness either explicitly (as mindfulness solutions) or implicitly (by training factors associated with mindfulness). The goal of this chapter is to clarify how mindfulness can be used in the context of HCI and provide practical insights for researchers and developers on how to create positive digital experiences. After a brief introduction of the intersection between those two fields, this chapter focuses on the challenge of operationalizing mindfulness and how it can be measured in HCI. Two review studies are presented, along with design recommendations, which are then applied in a case study. Results and implications are discussed.

Chapter 19

Naveen Kumar, Indian Institute of Technology Delhi, India
Jyoti Kumar, Indian Institute of Technology Delhi, India

Cyber-physical production system (CPPS) is being envisioned as the fourth major paradigm shift in the way industrial production happens. This chapter argues that though information technology-enabled automation will be used in CPPS, human intervention for production supervision would be required especially in critical scenario and human cognitive load would continue to affect the industry efficiency. The complexity of HCI-based control panel design would increase in CPPS due to task complexities and type of information presented through HCI systems. Also, the design methodologies for HCI systems have remained mostly technology centric and have not been able to include the cognitive load measurement caused by the design as a necessary consideration in the design process. Therefore, this chapter proposes user's cognitive load centric methodology for HCI based control panel design in context of CPPS. Cognitive load measurement should become a pivot for the HCI design process. In support of that, this chapter presents a case study using proposed UCLCD4 methodology.

Chapter 20

Ahmad Hashim Aal-Yhia, Aberystwyth University, UK & University of Baghdad, Iraq
Bernard Tiddeman, Aberystwyth University, UK
Paul Malcolm, Norfolk Norwich University Hospital, UK
Reyer Zwiggelaar, Aberystwyth University, UK

Groupwise non-rigid image alignment is a difficult non-linear optimization problem involving many parameters and often large datasets. Previous methods have explored various metrics and optimization strategies. Good results have been previously achieved with simple metrics, requiring complex optimization, often with many unintuitive parameters that require careful tuning for each dataset. In this chapter, the problem is restructured to use a simpler, iterative optimization algorithm, with very few free parameters. The warps are refined using an iterative Levenberg-Marquardt minimization to the mean, based on updating the locations of a small number of points and incorporating a stiffness constraint. This optimization approach is efficient, has very few free parameters to tune, and the authors show how to tune the few remaining parameters. Results show that the method reliably aligns various datasets including two facial datasets and two medical datasets of prostate and brain MRI images and demonstrates efficiency in terms of performance and a reduction of the computational cost.

Chapter 21

Marian McDonnell, Dun Laoghaire Institute of Art Design and Technology, Ireland
Hannah O'Sheehan, Dun Laoghaire Institute of Art Design and Technology, Ireland
Irene Connolly, Dun Laoghaire Institute of Art Design and Technology, Ireland

This research project evaluates Let's Be Safe, an e-learning application. This application aims to educate young adults with intellectual disability about cyberbullying—an issue prevalent among this population—and cybersafety. Twenty-two individuals with mild to moderate intellectual disability took part in the research. The study employed a mixed-methods design including observational and inquiry methods of usability evaluation as well as focus groups. The evaluation investigated the relationships between perceived aesthetics, emotional response, and usability for the application. The focus group gathered information from the participants regarding their knowledge and experience of cyberbullying and cybersafety. The analyses found no significant relationships between aesthetics, emotional response, and usability for this user group. However, the research gathered data, which will contribute to the development of Let's Be Safe. The findings of the focus group revealed that cyberbullying is an issue among this population.

Chapter 22

Ana Rita Teixeira, Polytechnic of Coimbra, Portugal
Anabela Gomes, Polytechnic of Coimbra, Portugal
Joao Gilberto Orvalho, Polytechnic of Coimbra, Portugal

As reported by the World Health Organization, an estimated 253 million live with visual impairment that cannot be corrected with glasses or contact lenses. It's necessary to bring awareness and understanding of the challenges blind people face and help to motivate research into new technology to answer those questions. This chapter starts to identify the challenges people with visual disabilities face in their life. The problem of navigation and orientation as well as the different possibilities to deal with the locomotion situation is also addressed. It describes the traditional navigational solutions as well as other which involves more sophisticated technological devices and their multimodal interfaces. The chapter ends with the description of the BlueEyes project, consisting in a solution using beacons to help blind people moving in a city. The phases of the project are described, and the actual research situations is also slightly explained.

Preface

Can you imagine a future where interfaces are not only interactive but truly immersive? A future where you only need to speak, or even think, with the technology in order to "interact". Recent shifts in the way in which we interact with technology has brought us closer to this future. Portable devices such as smartphones, tablets and smartwatches have substantially altered the interaction between humans and technology. Voice activated interactions have a firm grip on the daily life of many users, and commercial predictions anticipate that over the next 5 years the adoption rate of speech recognition will exceed 80%. Apple's Siri supplants the role of personal assistant, capable of completing a multitude of tasks by using simple voice command. Whilst initially astonishing, we are now accustomed to this new interaction and look even further into the future as devices grow smaller, their features more substantial and their popular, cultural cache exponentially increases. Augmented/virtual reality developments over the last few years promise take us where we imagined the Holodeck might, as headsets such as Oculus, Magic Leap and Hololens become increasingly popular. Whilst the current prices are not prohibitive, they still remain out of the reach of most users.

With these substantial developments in technology, new and unique ways of interacting will emerge and the Human Computer Interaction specialist will need to be equipped with the skills and knowledge to design, develop and implement immersive interfaces for individualised use.

This book has been developed with both the learner and the experienced professional in mind. A first-year undergraduate will gain insight into the breadth of the field and importantly, understand its importance to the ways in which we use technologies. The experienced HCI practitioner will find the specificity and depth in a wide-ranging variety of topics and tertiary educators will find a variety of exemplars for use as case studies, etc.

As technology continues to hold a steady course into an increasingly machine-driven future, the work of the Human Computer Interaction practitioner has never been so important.

The future is one in which we will be more closely bound to the technologies we use.

This is the future that those of us working in HCI have long envisioned, a future where the user and their specific needs take precedence over technological requirements. We have imagined a future where an interface and its technologies are adaptive to a user's need.

Until now, users have been bound to a screen for interaction; pushing, poking, swiping their way through an interface in order to utilise the benefits of their chosen technology. Our researchers have imagined a future where, rather than the interface merely being contained by a screen external to the user, the technology is integrated into daily life.

Whilst much of this imagined future may seem to be in experimental stages, assimilating voice, VR and wearables in our lives is no longer the domain of fantasy. We are looking to a future where humans and computers are integral to the functioning of each other.

However, building any system that is designed for interactive use by humans involves both a complexity and a multidimensionality that requires a wide range of roles. Nowhere is this more important than at the interface between the user and the machine. It is at this interface where the HCI practitioner is the mediator and strives to further the user experience with design processes, tools and methodologies to assist the user in their interactions. In this volume of collected research, scholars from across the globe showcase their explorations into this role of mediator.

We have brought together a community of scholars in this book, all of whom are exploring a range of innovative methodologies, processes, technologies, tools and techniques for the design, development and support of interactivity between humans and machines. The reader will readily discern the diversity and breadth of the research presented here, from medical applications to educational games. Much of this innovative research is already in use and adapted to current user populations. Other more challenging research and experimentation promises to pose some interesting conundrums for our future

We have so much to look forward to in the future of interactivity at the user interface.

This book is divided into three sections: Section 1 – Design and Methodology; Section 2 – Applications; and Section 3 – User Experience and Usability Studies. Each section is further divided into individually authored chapters in which authors share their experiences and explorations into Interactivity and the Human Computer Interface.

SECTION 1: DESIGN AND METHODOLOGY

In this section, the reader is offered a number of observations, reflections and experiences on the choices made in both design and methodology. Designing for specific users poses further challenges for any HCI practitioner and in Chapter 1, "Application of Direct and Indirect Human-centered Design Techniques With Dyslexic Users," the authors discuss the insights gathered, and the resulting strategies adopted, in the LITERACY-project of the European Union. The authors detail the processes involved in creating an interactive web portal with the express aim of promoting and improving social inclusion for people with dyslexia. The authors invite us to reflect on the inclusion of end-users with special needs in the design process and not merely because it constitutes robust Human-centred design thinking. Chapter 2, "Observations on Design Thinking in Novice Designers While Empathizing With Persona," offers insights on design solutions observed during an experimental study with novice designers. In Chapter 3, "A Protocol for Reviewing Off-the-Shelf Games to Inform the Development of New Educational Games," the authors share their protocols for use in the development of educational games and the process for reviewing the alignment of learning objectives with teaching content and game mechanics. The authors of Chapter 4, "Surveying Games With a Combined Model of Immersion and Flow," have also focused their research on games and discuss a methodological approach for measuring flow. In an effort to improve the player experience, the authors have developed an immersion model, designed to offer a more detailed measurement of the flow.

The authors of Chapter 5, "Deus ex Machina: The Automation of a Religious Ritual in a Data-Driven Machine – Design, Implementation, and Public Reception," discuss the development of their "Instant Church", an interactive artefact that guides the user through a Catholic service and creates an individualized wafer with a laser-engraved QR-code that points to a random Tweet inviting reflection by the user

In Chapter 6, "Explanations in Artificial Intelligence Decision Making: A User Acceptance Perspective," the authors relate the process of AI decision making to the impact on the real-world decision making that affects society. The authors offer principles that might be used to guide the use of AI decision making systems.

SECTION 2: APPLICATIONS

From the world of high finance, to the critical care of disease, to the playful worlds of lego and games, Section 2 offers the reader the work of scholars developing specialist applications that require specialist interaction.

The authors of Chapter 7, "Redesign of the Bank Reconciliation Interface of the ContaAzul Software," present the prototype of a reconciliation interface enabling increased financial control. For the project, the authors worked with businesses in Brazil to redesign a cloud-based finance management software interface.

In Chapter 8, "Development of Interface for Assisting Energy-Saving Utilizing Information From Network Home Appliances," the authors propose an interface for a Home Energy Management System (HEMS) that aims to raise the consciousness of users in ways of saving energy. To assist the user, the interface visually represents power consumption and ways to reduce energy output. The authors of Chapter 9, "Applied Alternative Tools and Methods in the Replacement of the Game Design Document," experiment with alternatives to the Game Design Document used as the primary project document in the development of games.

Chapter 10, "Using Augmented Reality to Aid in Lego Construction: A Mobile Application," describes the use of augmented reality to offer instructions for constructing Lego models. The authors discuss the use of a mobile application through which the user is enabled to interact with the Lego successfully. The authors of Chapter 11, "An ARM Framework for F2P Mobile Games," also focus on games however their discussion centres on the development of a framework specifically designed to support game design practice and research.

In Chapter 12, "Introduction to a Collaborative Mobile Web Platform: Higher M@t-EduTutor," the authors discuss the development of a collaborative mobile web platform. The authors intend that the platform will promote increased engagement for higher education students. In Chapter 13, "Lesion Boundary Segmentation With Artifacts Removal and Melanoma Detection in Skin Lesion Images," we move away from games and education into the field of medicine. The authors discuss the use of image enhancement and refinement in the diagnosis and treatment of melanoma. If the treating doctor has access to high resolution quality images, the detection rate can be as high as 92.5%.

SECTION 3: USER EXPERIENCE AND USABILITY STUDIES

In Section 3, the reader is presented with a wide variety of applications developed for specific users ranging from children, adults with intellectual disabilities and users with visual impairments. In the work here before the reader, the user is always considered paramount to the design and application.

The author of Chapter 14, "Think of the Children! The Relationship Between Visual Complexity, Age, Visual Aesthetics, and Learning Motivation With Regard to Children," presents us with an exploration of children's visual aesthetic preferences and their motivation to engage with the learning material offered.

In Chapter 15, "Instrumental Music Design: Influence on Task Performance," we take the reader from the visual world to the auditory. The authors discuss the effects of instrumental music on complex task performance and emotional state, suggesting that their results reveal important factors in the design of music environments. In Chapter 16, "Impact of Evaluating the Usability of Assisted Technology Oriented by Protocol," the authors discuss the development of a protocol and methodology for evaluating the adaptability of assistive technologies claiming accessibility for the visually disabled community. The authors of Chapter 17, "The Convergence Between Challenge-Based Learning and Game Design Thinking Methodologies: Exploring Creativity and Innovation in the Game Development Process," explore the combination of methodologies for the game development process arguing that the multidisciplinary nature of the game development team requires the use of a variety of interactive tools and techniques. Chapter 18, "Mindfulness and HCI," moves us from the field of task analysis to the integration of mindfulness and digital technologies in order to ensure positive user experiences. The author provides insights into the ways in which researchers and developers might utilise mindfulness, both explicitly and implicitly, to enhance user experience. The authors of Chapter 19, "Proposal of a User's Cognitive Load-Centric Methodology for HCI-Based Control Panel Design," argue for an increased awareness of user centric approaches in the automation of industrial production. This chapter also discusses appropriate design methodologies for revisioning the, often technology-centric, processes of production. In Chapter 20, "Groupwise Non-Rigid Image Alignment Using Few Parameters," the reader is presented with a discussion on optimisation strategies when dealing with large datasets. The authors argue that despite the complexity of an image, simplicity in the optimisation can be successfully achieved both in terms of the computational value and more importantly in terms of the ease of interaction for the user.

Chapter 21, "Evaluating an E-Learning Application to Protect Vulnerable Users from Cyberbullying," explores the use of multiple design methodologies in assessing the impact of cyberbullying on young adults with an intellectual disability. Our final work, Chapter 22, "BlueEyes: A Pilot Project and a New Way to See the World," identifies some of the many challenges faced by people with visual disabilities. In particular, the authors explore a variety of possibilities for navigation and orientation in moving throughout daily life.

We know that readers will find much in this volume that is innovative and may perhaps prompt further explorations into the fields of interactivity and human-computer interaction. The journey forward promises to be both challenging and exhilarating as technology continues to change our lives.

The editors would like to acknowledge the help of all the people involved in this project and, more specifically, to the authors and reviewers that took part in the review process.

The editors would like to thank each of the authors for selecting this book to share their work with the world. Each author contributed their time and expertise and without their support, this book would not have become a reality. In addition, the editors wish to acknowledge the invaluable contribution of the reviewers, each of whom contributed to improving the quality, coherence, and content of each chapters, each section and the book as a whole.

Katherine Blashki
Victorian Institute of Technology, Australia

Pedro Isaías
The University of Queensland, Australia

Section 1
Design and Methodology

Chapter 1
Application of Direct and Indirect Human–Centered Design Techniques With Dyslexic Users

Dominik Hagelkruys
University of Vienna, Austria

Renate Motschnig
University of Vienna, Austria

ABSTRACT

Designing for people with special needs, especially cognitive and affective needs, can be challenging. Human-centered design (HCD), which inherently promotes user-inclusion and promises products that fit the users' needs, seems to be an optimal solution for such tasks. But can an HCD-approach be easily applied with special needs users? How much adaptation is necessary to perform classical HCD-techniques with users affected by certain difficulties? This chapter discusses the insights gathered and strategies adopted while applying human-centered design in the LITERACY-project, a project of the European Union aiming at improving social inclusion of youth and adults with dyslexia, by creating an interactive web-portal. Hopefully, this case study provides insight on and gives courage for inclusion of end-users even though—or particularly because—they have special needs.

INTRODUCTION

In this chapter, the strategies applied and the experiences gathered while designing an interface for the LITERACY-portal, a web-portal for users with dyslexia, are described. For this purpose, dyslexic users were included already in the early phases of the human-centered design (HCD) process and functioned as active resources and frequent participants throughout the design-process. The inclusion of end-user is a critical success factor because the acceptance of any software-tool hinges on the degree to which the design-team manages to meet the (special) needs of the primary target groups. Therefore, the human-centered design process makes an optimal fit for the goals this project is trying to achieve.

DOI: 10.4018/978-1-5225-9069-9.ch001

Before users could actively be included into the process, the initial steps of the human-centered design process needed to be applied. Starting with analyzing the future users, by studying articles, looking at existing web-applications targeted at them, and personally talking to dyslexic persons the design-team already was in contact with. Based on this information potential tasks that might be performed on the LITERACY-portal were extracted and described. These tasks were generated by applying three of the core elements of the HCD process: personas, context analysis and task analysis.

The main **strategy** was to get in contact with people with dyslexia already in the early stages of the design. Through this interaction with the targeted audience, the research team tried to generate insights, not only regarding the special needs of the targeted user group, but also regarding special strengths of people with dyslexia. These initial contacts were followed up with literature research and preparation of key questions such as to be knowledgeable partners in the dialogue, but otherwise as open as possible to learn from their life stories and experiences. Following this mindset, it was considered to be most beneficial to engage in semi-structured interviews with dyslexic persons in various stages of life, and to gradually focus on some of their core issues that crystallized from the interviews such as finding work, using the internet, interacting in/with educational institutions, etc. The interview-partners also provided information regarding their individual preferences for screen designs and what terms they found relevant or interesting to look for on the LITERACY-portal.

Furthermore **experience** became a key factor during the design-process. Therefore, one goal for this chapter is to highlight issues worth specific consideration in order to share gathered experiences with interested peers, thus making the applied process reusable in the community of interface designers. In a nutshell, getting in contact with users with special needs may need special provisions, contacts with counseling centers, more time than talking to "ordinary" users, and an adaptation of methods and/or tools and procedures to accommodate for the particular special needs.

This chapter is structured as follows: the subsequent section discusses the background in which this research was conducted and provisions that were taken to maximize end-user inclusion in all aspects of the design process. Additionally, related work and studies that influenced different aspects of the research design are mentioned. Following the applied design strategies and the process of including people with dyslexia into the various design-steps through individual direct and indirect means of end-user inclusion are described. The particular experiences of included dyslexic users will be highlighted throughout this section. The final sections summarize the conducted research and experiences so far and give an outlook on further work. The contribution intends to confirm that the inclusion of end users in early stages of web-design is essential and that it should be done regardless of whether end-users have special needs or not. Furthermore, the chapter illustrates some concrete techniques and steps to include end-users with dyslexia and thus can serve as an example or inspiration on how to accomplish and exploit end-user inclusion for increased usability of a web-portal.

BACKGROUND AND RELATED WORK

The context in which HCD was applied is the **LITERACY-project**, a European-wide research endeavor funded by the European Commission in the area of ICT under the FP7 program. Its aim was to create an advanced online **portal**, the LITERACY-portal, which enables dyslexic youth and adults to acquire learning skills, accommodation strategies and methods for succeeding at literacy related tasks at work and at home. The portal provides personalized e-learning programs, useful tools and methods for helping people with dyslexia to improve their abilities in reading and writing. It also provides entry to an accessible online community of peers. A specialized interface and Community Zone with programs and services to improve the skills of the users, drastically simplifying otherwise complicated tasks. This is achieved by utilizing novel tools, which are integrated with both existing and adapted ICT tools and hardware. Dyslexic users are able to access the LITERACY-portal independently and receive real-time feedback on their progress (LITERACY Project, 2018).

The targeted user group of the web-portal are users with **dyslexia**. The British Dyslexia Association defines dyslexia as a "specific learning difficulty that mainly affects the development of literacy and language related skills". The British Dyslexia Association further states, that dyslexia "is likely to be present at birth and to be life-long in its effects. It is characterized by difficulties with phonological processing, rapid naming, working memory, processing speed, and the automatic development of skills that may not match up to an individual's other cognitive abilities" (British Dyslexia Association, 2019). The World Health Organization (WHO) defines dyslexia in its International Classification of Diseases (ICD) in similar fashion: "Developmental learning disorder with impairment in reading is characterized by significant and persistent difficulties in learning academic skills related to reading, such as word reading accuracy, reading fluency, and reading comprehension" (World Health Organization, 2018). The positioning of dyslexia within the ICD also connects it to other developmental learning disorders concerning impairments in written expression, mathematics and further impairments in learning. This connection is supported by dyslexia experts working on the LITERACY-project who state, that dyslexia often comes with other difficulties such as dyscalculia – numerical and math problems, dysgraphia and dysortographia – cognitive and motor writing difficulties, dyspraxia – coordination problems, and also attention deficit hyperactivity disorder (ADHD). These comorbidities are also mentioned in other relevant sources, e.g. These tend to be resistant to conventional teaching methods, but their effect can be mitigated by appropriately specific intervention, including the application of information technology and supportive counseling. Due to differences in languages and approaches of local bodies to defining and assessing dyslexia, it is hard to specify the prevalence of dyslexia in the population. Experts collaborating on the LITERACY-project suggest 10% and more, which would make more than 70 million people - in Europe only. Other sources confirm this number, e.g. Sprenger-Charolles et al (2011), Dyslexia International (2014) or the European Dyslexia Association (2014), with some even providing slightly higher estimates.

Human-centered design (HCD) is a specific design approach, which sets the focus on the users of a product. The HCD-process is standardized (ISO 9241-210:2010) and follows the philosophy that a product can only be good if it suits the needs of the people who use it. The HCD-process is inclusive and iterative and therefore heavily relies on the inputs, comments and suggestions of target groups. Other than the often used and easier to plan top-down (waterfall) approach, in which the users do not see the product before it is in an advanced stage, human-centered design already includes target groups in the early stages of the development. This early and constant inclusion makes it possible to take the requirements and needs of the users into account, thus enabling suitable design choices. Human-centered design and its techniques are described in various sources, like for example the The Field Guide to Human-Centered Design (IDEO, 2015), Seffah et al (2009) or Thimbleby (2008).

There exists a variety of quality work that influences different aspects of this article or discusses related topics. A source of information that was certainly used throughout various design steps was the book "Interaction Design: Beyond Human-Computer Interaction" (Rogers et al, 2011). It offers a broad variety of topics that not only focus on design aspects but also describes interaction processes or cognitive aspects. Therefore, it served as a handy lecture while setting up testing sessions for the special target groups. Another source that provided great insight and helpful tips on how to assess users with special needs is the book "Assessing Learners with Special Needs: An Applied Approach" (Overton, 2012). The information provided by Overton was helpful while setting up tests and for interpreting their outcomes.

Although there already exist standards about HCD, like ISO 13407 and its successor ISO 9241-210, there are also other great sources on this topic. Noteworthy Harold Thimbleby's article "Understanding User-Centred Design (UCD) for People with Special Needs" (Thimbleby, 2008), which offers valuable insights into the complex topic of human-centered design in a special needs context. It served as an initial stepping stone in the preparatory research phase. Another relevant area is the adaptation of HCD-techniques for application in special needs settings. For this purpose, the paper "Expanding Personas: How to improve knowledge about users" (Masiero, 2013), although it does not directly examine applications with special needs users, provided helpful insights and provided guidance regarding how to extend/adapt HCD-techniques. Furthermore, Thimbleby (2008) needs to be named again within this context.

There are various works that describe projects or relevant topics, like interface design for people with dyslexia or special needs in general. Notably there is the article "Web Accessibility: Designing for dyslexia" (Bell, 2009), which focuses on web-accessibility and interface design for people with dyslexia. Additionally, there is the article "Multimedia Software Interface Design for Special-Needs Users" (Lányi, 2009), focusing on interface design for people with special needs in a more general way. The paper "Designing with users, How?" investigates user involvement tactics for effective inclusive design processes (Lee, 2008) and describes the inclusive design processes on a general level. These papers and articles, among others, were a great source for designing the web-portal, as they provided insights and valuable tips.

Lastly there exists relevant material generated by other special needs projects. The information discovered while studying these other projects helped estimating the work necessary and identify potential problems. Notable examples are: "A mobile application concept to encourage independent mobility for blind and visually impaired students" (Liimatainen et al, 2012), "Under Watch and Ward at Night: Design and Evaluation of a Remote Monitoring System for Dementia Care" (Schikhof and Mulder, 2008), "Designing with Vulnerable Children: A Researcher's Perspective" (Culén, 2014) and the AGID-Project, which creates web-based training for professionals on three topics of ageing and intellectual disability by using a person-centered approach (AGID-Project, 2018).

DESIGN STRATEGIES AND INCLUSION OF USERS

Strategies in the Design of the Literacy-Portal

To achieve the goal of creating a successful online portal that suits the needs of its future users, it was decided to use methods and strategies that will support the ideas of the design team as well as the specific requirements of the target groups.

An important part of this strategy was to apply the human-centered design approach, which heavily includes users already in early design stages. Through this approach it was possible to learn about the specific needs and preferences of the future users and subsequently eliminate potential problems before they surface. The iterative process decreased the cognitive load continuously and simultaneously enhanced the user experience.

While interacting with dyslexic users, they were not only provided with different screen design variations but also specific pieces of content for people with dyslexia. This included for example theoretical input about dyslexia or different ways to increase social inclusion of dyslexic youth and adults in the real world as well as in the virtual world. Assisting dyslexic users in adjusting to daily life problems is one of the core goals of the portals content. The LITERAC-portal provides a variety of means to support its users, like for example tips, life stories, e-learning, training and ways for community building. These means help people with dyslexia dealing with problematic everyday situations, encourage them to work on their weaknesses, self-empower them and give them the possibility to get in contact with peers.

Another important part of the design-strategy is a strength-based approach. The web-portal should not only tell its users where they are weak and what they need to improve, it should emphasize their strengths and encourage them to use them. This strength-based approach is transported through **person-centered communication** (Motschnig and Nykl, 2014) and **appreciative inquiry** (Barret and Fry, 2005) in all contacts and dialogues. This means that all communication between the portal and the users is done in a way that fits the needs of the targeted groups, makes navigation as easy as possible, reduces the cognitive load and leaves them with a feeling of appreciation and motivation. The LITERACY-portal facilitates transparency and personalization and tries to make the users feel respected through inclusion and participation.

The inclusion of users into the design process of the online portal according to the HCD process was achieved through different ways, which could be roughly classified into **indirect** and **direct methods**.

Indirect Inclusion

Indirect methods include a series of different steps in the design process. Initially the topics of dyslexia and users with special cognitive and affective needs were researched through online-sources, specialist literature and relevant studies. This provided the design-team with basic ideas and guidelines for the design. The bandwidth of sources and literature gathered through this process is quite broad and extensive. It ranges from specialist websites, like the website of the British Dyslexia Association (British Dyslexia Association, 2019), over national organizations to papers and articles, like for example "What we know about dyslexia and Web Accessibility: A research review" (McCarth and Swierenga, 2009) to relevant expert literature like "Interacton Design: Beyond Human-Computer Interaction" (Rogers, Sharp and Preece, 2011). Parts of it can be found as sources of this article and in the "further reading" section. The life stories collected in the process of research provided valuable insight and proved to be essential in later tasks of the HCD, like for example the task analysis. Based on this research specific accessibility and design criteria to guide further steps in the design of the online portal were created and supplemented by other sources, like the "Dyslexia Friendly Style Guide" (British Dyslexia Association, 2018).

Subsequently the initial steps of the human-centered design process, personas, task analysis and context analysis, were applied.

Personas are a commonly used technique in human-centered design. They are fictional characters that represent real users during the design process. Their description is based on important user-groups and their specific characteristics, motivation and expectations. Personas were already used in many IT-projects and various adaptations for special needs applications and revisions of the concept itself were proposed, such as in the paper "Revisiting Personas: The Making-of for Special User Groups" (Moser et al, 2012), which describes a decision diagram for the creation of personas for elderly and children. For the purpose of the LITERACY-project a similar approach was chosen. To create suitable personas, information was gathered through online resources and literature as well as interviews with dyslexics and experts. In the end ten different personas were identified, which covered a wide range of users and included different types, like students, parents or professionals. Based on the criteria provided by these personas actual dyslexic users were contacted and invited to participate in the project and its testing sessions to create a suitable design for the LITERACY-portal.

The **task analysis** describes different use cases of users from their specific points of view. This is beneficial for the design process, because they describe what the users want to do and how the web-portal has to be designed to make it possible. By identifying major tasks that will potentially be done on the portal the design team gets a better idea of how the interface should look like and how it should respond. The collected tasks were stored in a database, in which they were organized in different categories and subcategories. Every task consists of a short description, an example, parameters for frequency and priority, ideas for implementations and comments from different reviewers.

The **context analysis** represents a mixture of indirect and direct inclusion, as it is partly based on feedback from potential users and experts as well as research and the intended functionality of the portal. It showed that the LITERACY-portal will be used in different environments and that the current state of mind of a user will have a huge impact on the reception of the information. Three important contexts were identified: assessment, everyday life and work. Every one of these three contexts describes different usage conditions, which heavily affect the users in various ways and therefore result in shifting levels of cognitive load. The results of this analysis provides the design team with valuable information that has to be considered when planning the portal.

The ISO Standard 9241-210 (ISO 9241-210:2010) describes the techniques "Personas", "task analysis" and "context analysis" under the headline "Context of use". Other sources also emphasize the close relation of these techniques (Stone, Jarrett, Woodroffe, & Minocha, 2005) (Courage & Baxter, 2005). It is a characteristic of HCD that all techniques influence each other, and outputs directly affect subsequent techniques and design steps. This is even more true for personas, task analysis and context analysis. Therefore, in the case of the LITERACY-portal, "Context of use" was applied as one big concept:

- The context analysis functions as the foundation for the other techniques. It serves as the background for personas and tasks identified within the project and helps describe and define them in more detail.
- Personas therefore can be embedded into multiple contexts, which adds additional facets to them and helps in analyzing their needs in different situations.
- Tasks can be connected to contexts as well, as some tasks may only occur in specific contexts. Furthermore, they can be linked to one or multiple personas. On the other hand, they do not necessarily have to be connected to all personas.

The result is a complex matrix of contexts, personas and tasks that can be mapped into a database and analyzed through various means.

Applying such a "Context of use" analysis benefits the project in multiple ways. Initially the combination of the three techniques enables the researchers to gradually improve their respective outputs. Embedding tasks within different contexts and linking them to personas for example helps in discovering potential difficulties and finding suitable solutions. On the other hand, it is easier to identify what is to be expected of the future users.

Applying these initial steps of human-centered design allowed the project team to outline target groups, set the main focus and identify potential problem areas.

Direct Inclusion

The next step after acquiring knowledge about people with dyslexia and their challenges from indirect sources, was to approach the users directly. The further steps of the human-centered design process chosen were interviews, simple prototypes of screen designs and card-sorting. All of these activities were done with the help of experts from the Psychological and Pedagogical Counseling Center in Brno. They shortlisted a number of their current and past clients, then contacted them via email, personally or even through television, to which 30 out of 40 invited persons responded positively. Through additional support of other partners in Hungary and Israel it was possible to conduct interview-sessions with a total number of 88 dyslexic-users. After a small workshop in Brno that set a common vision of the planned means of direct inclusion, the experts carried out interview-sessions and participated in the analysis of the results. The help of psychologists and special pedagogues was essential for reaching people with dyslexia, mainly because dyslexia is a sensitive matter, often concealed and not admitted. The experts assisted in picking people who were open to sharing their experience. The interview-sessions are described in more detail in the following sub-sections.

Interviews and Their Evolution

The first mode of the end user inclusion was dialogue in the form of an interview. The main strategy was to apply appreciative inquiry: try to find the strengths of an interviewee, look for the conditions in which the strengths express themselves and search how to replicate these conditions. Adoption of person-centered approach (Rogers and Roethlisberger, 1991; Motschnig and Nykl, 2011) and including active listening (Rogers and Farson, 1957), resulted in the creation of an atmosphere that was non-judgmental, empathic and open.

The interview-sessions started with one prototypical unstructured interview with N., a manager of technical support, formerly a teacher of computer science for pupils with special needs. In the search for strengths and motivations also the struggles and challenges he encounters came up and the design team was able to gather important insights for future sessions.

Then, based on this experience, a guide to interviewing was created and reviewed by doc. PhDr. Věra Vojtová, an associate professor of special pedagogy. This enabled scaling to a bigger number of interviews at the same time and supported data consistency. The guide summarized the strategy for interviewing, which consisted mainly of a non-judgmental approach, active listening and non-directive questioning. It also provided an outline of topics (school life, work life, internet usage, hobbies) and examples of questions, as can be seen in Appendix A.

Among the outcomes of the interviews was a collection of problems that adults with dyslexia encounter in their daily lives. They were mainly related to text in any form and medium. The top 12 problems as identified and reported by adults with dyslexia were that they:

- Read slowly
- Have difficulties reading small letters
- Get lost in text

- Do not understand what they read or have to focus too hard to understand
- Have problems moving to the next line
- Do not see numbers or other data in text
- Are unable to identify keywords in text thus evaluate it differently
- Detest the amount of text they have to read in their job
- Cannot focus deliberately
- Miss important information in emails
- Cannot write grammatically correct emails, yet these are requested by their employers
- Form sentences differently – these make sense to them, not to others

Following an example for such difficulties from a person working in a logistic firm, concerning misidentifying numbers in emails, can be read:

I sent a lorry to load the goods at a wrong hour. It could be forgiven once, but it kept happening. My boss had to let me go. I never told anyone about my dyslexia because I was afraid I would lose my job.

Furthermore, it was discovered that the majority of the respondents use the internet daily because they need it either for work or to study. They prefer sites relevant to their professions. Two thirds of the respondents use Facebook and more than a half have Google Chrome set as the default browser, the rest choosing Internet Explorer, Mozilla Firefox or Opera. Electronic diaries or schedulers and Skype came up in their lists of used tools only sporadically. Half of the respondents use office suites such as MS Office or Open Office, often criticizing the abundance of functions as unclear. Two respondents use Google Translator, three respondents are working with a text-to-speech tool and 2 adjust texts to their needs. Some did not know that an adjustment of a text could help them read.

The troubles that adults with dyslexia have when interacting with the internet are:

- Advertisement
- Too much text
- Low contrast
- Too many homepage sections
- Moving text
- Flashing text

Some of them described screen-readers and video tutorials as life-changers and shared various tricks they developed over time. The importance of a loving and willing parent or teacher as well as the fact that motivation from interests and hobbies can be transferred into reading, was stressed.

The insights gathered through these interview-sessions, resulted in a collection of the most useful questions into a simple yes-no questionnaire, which was shared online among the research team and contributing experts and continuously expanded. (For the final version of the questionnaire, see Appendix B).

Most importantly, through these interviews, it was possible to achieve a main goal of human-centered design requires - stepping into the shoes of a person with dyslexia and getting to know and understand the end-users first-hand. (Norman, D. A., 2002)

As it can be seen in the evolution of the interview, the iterative nature of the human-centered design was integrated into the interview-process itself. This might be helpful in cases such as the LITERACY-project, when the end users have distinctly different, sometimes counter-intuitive mental models.

Excursion to a Class With Dyslexic Students

An important opportunity for direct inclusion was a visit to a school in Budapest organized by dyslexia-experts from the Hungarian Academy of Science. A design-team, consisting of 8 experts from different fields of expertise, was invited to sit in on an English class at K-12 level of 12 pupils between 17 and 19 years of age, each having a special need. After mutual introductions, where the pupils openly shared the challenges they face, space for questions was given.

The questions focused mainly on the pupils' internet-usage habits. The result was that they all use Facebook and can cope with it, but with variations. Some spend 5 minutes only to check agreements with friends, reading as little as possible, others browse for 5 hours. They hardly ever use discussion boards, reading in any form consumes too much of their energy.

Interestingly, one young lady was asked how she experiences reading transport schedules and responded that it would be better if they were pink. This showcases the difference of the mental models that the designers have to bridge. Furthermore, most of the students stated that they are creative and motivated to express themselves in other than textual ways and claimed that they like photographing, dance, music, fine arts and sports. Just as in the case of the interviews, this encounter served as a way of understanding of daily life of people with dyslexia with focus on their internet usage.

Extending Interviews by Screen Design Choice

By the time the interview-sessions started, 5 screen design options were created. Each of them showed a different menu structure and three steps of going through it: the initial (home) screen, category choice and sub-category choice. Three of them, utilized buttons arranged in a grid and were suggested by Dr. Gyarmathy, an expert on dyslexia, and supported by Dr. Beránek, an IT specialist, both members of the LITERACY-consortium. The fourth is a more modern coverflow menu and the last one is a common vertical expanding menu. The menu-styles can be seen in the following figure:

Especially in the beginning of the interview-sessions it was difficult to get in touch with dyslexic users and arrange meetings. Therefore, it was decided to join more activities of human-centered design together to generate more data and insights. During each conducted interview the participants choose the screen design that they deemed the most suitable for them. If they picked one, 2 points were assigned to it, and if they also had a second choice it was assigned 1 point. This made it possible to see how the users reacted to the initial design-proposals and decide how to proceed with subsequent prototypes. The results pointed to the vertical menu, which was chosen by the majority of the respondents. However, there is a difference between the genders. Whereas female participants strongly favored the vertical expanding menu (73%), the analysis of male participants on the other hand shows an even outcome.

Although the vertical expanding menu is still the overall preferred choice, the three button menus combined (34%) and the coverflow menu (31%) are very close. There was also disparity between age-groups of users. Whereas respondents over the age of 20 preferred the vertical menu, the younger users seemed to be used to different styles of menu such as the coverflow-menus and button-grids used on tablets and smartphones.

Figure 1. The five different screen designs, each showing the menu with main categories

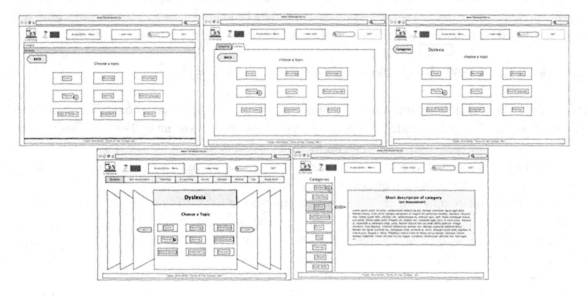

Figure 2. Overall Screen design choice and gender preferences

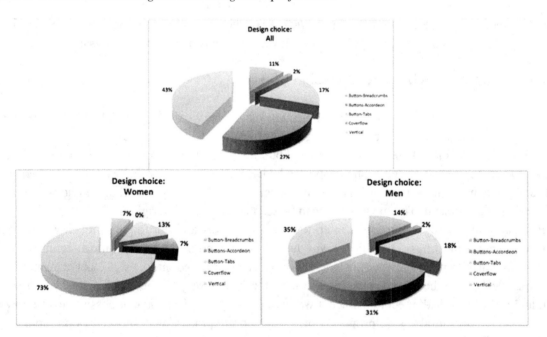

Extending Interviews by Card Sorting

The next step in the design process of the LITERACY-portal, which was also executed at the interview meetings described in previous sub-sections, was card-sorting. It is a simple activity which yields complex results. A broad offer of content and functions of the LITERACY-portal was assembled and transcribed onto 60 paper cards. The interviewees were told to go through them, ask for clarifications, create their own cards if necessary and then sort any chosen cards into their own menu structure. The results were photographed, noted in an Excel spreadsheet and analyzed by an application called xSort[1]. In total 30 card-sortings were performed by dyslexic users.

A cluster tree generated by xSort identified 8 main categories, which represent content and functions of the LITERACY-portal. Furthermore, the design team also received clues regarding the naming of the (sub)categories and learned that 60 cards is not too much for people with dyslexia to handle cognitively. Quite on the contrary, they accepted the task with engagement and enjoyed the creative work. Similarly, to the interviews, the card-sorting process was also iteratively improved.

The card-sortings also evaluated each function or piece of content planned for the portal. The respondents were free to omit any cards they would not want on the portal. The top 20 chosen to stay were Tests (27 votes), Dyslexia, Learning methods (26), Signs of Dyslexia, Reading (25), E-learning, Contact, Games (24), Second Language, Memory, ADHD, Complex aids, Tutorial (23), Training, Forum, Theories, Learning, Study aids (22) and Tips (21 votes). Based on these choice sums, the content-design team was informed regarding which specific content and function they should focus on. More details about these improvements and extended results of the card-sorting are published in (Motschnig et al., 2013).

SOLUTIONS AND RECOMMENDATIONS

So far, carrying out the preparatory research and applying methods of direct user-inclusion such as interviewing, prototyping and card-sorting have generated 4 main results.

First of all, a deeper level of **understanding** of people with dyslexia, the future end users, was reached. The design team experienced how differently they think, how this difference intertwines with their school-, work- and personal life and how they use the internet. For example, inquiries into internet usage helped realizing that people with dyslexia mind long texts, prefer sans-serif fonts, and require consistency throughout a website. Implementing screen-reading is necessary and other tools and guides to using them are also welcome. Moreover, due to the variability of thinking styles and of manifestations of dyslexia, a high degree of personalization for a tool such as the LITERACY-portal seems to be critical. These and other findings not only support the design process and mandate an open-minded style of thinking, but also showcase the potential of the user-group of people with dyslexia. To unfold their potential and utilize their strengths it is essential to consider direct inclusion.

Secondly, the design team was able to collect **specific ideas** that will be implemented in the next phases of the design process of the LITERACY-portal. Together with the future users, the vertical expanding menu-design was chosen as the most suitable menu style. Furthermore, the content of the portal was organized into 8 main categories and their names were optimized through the feedback of the participants. One example is the renaming if the "Assistive technology" sub-category into "Helping tools".

Thirdly, the design team learned about the **procedures of the HCD** process in the case of users with special needs. Interviews evolved, and a successful guide was created. Furthermore it was discovered, that 60 cards in the card-sorting procedure was an appropriate number and it was not necessary to develop a lighter version with fewer cards. With the willingness and cooperativeness of the interviewees on one hand and the appreciative as well as the person-centered approach on the other, these procedures went smoothly. All combined into one session they took up to 2 hours per person (plus more time for preparation and then processing and analysis). However, some flexibility should be built into each plan, whereas people with dyslexia vary in thinking and approach the questions and tasks they are given creatively. For example, the generated interview guide focuses more on strategy of asking and suggests some topics, rather than providing a rigid structure of questions.

Furthermore, performing the initial indirect and direct techniques led to three guiding concepts that would prove to be essential for all follow-up research and design efforts as well as the final product itself: "Keep it simple (for everyone)", "Make it accessible" and "Make it fun". These three key principles helped the design team in preparing and conducting testing sessions with special needs user groups and generating valuable feedback and data.

- *Keep it simple (for everyone):*
  - *Cognitive load: The cognitive load describes the amount of information and interactions that need to be processed by a user. Keeping the cognitive load low needs to be a main-goal, as it directly affects many other design-related goals. If the cognitive load is too high, the user will not be able to process the important information. Therefore, everything besides the information (e.g. the navigation, content, etc.) needs to be as simple as possible. The improvements regarding this goal will be directly affected by the achievements of the other goals.*
  - *Consistency: An easy (but also important) way to reduce the cognitive load is to be consistent regarding the design of the portal. This includes a clear navigation which is easy to use and understand but also a color-design that stays consistent throughout the whole portal and provides a "secure and known frame" the user can rely on.*
- *Make it accessible*
  - *Retrieving information: It is always important to provide a simple and easy design for the users. In the case of the LITERACY-portal it is necessary to keep it simple for different types of users, but especially for dyslexics. But the user-group of dyslexics is not very consistent itself, so it is necessary to provide content and services for a very wide range of potential users. One way of making this possible is to allowing users to access content and services through different types of communication channels. A first step will be to provide alternative methods to retrieve information. This could mean to provide text-alternatives for images or a voice-recording for a paragraph of textual information. Furthermore, the whole portal should adhere to the main requirements of accessibility to make it usable with different types of assisting technologies.*
  - *Responsive Design: Choosing a responsive design approach for the portal makes it accessible for a wide variety of devices while not affect the "normal" desktop-version of the portal-design in any way.*
- *Make it fun*
  - *User-autonomy: Users should be able to use the portal by themselves without any outside instruction and constrictions. This also includes the visual appearance of the portal. The user should be able to alter the visual elements of a webpage (i.e. color-themes, font, etc.). Furthermore, it would be ideal if the user could rearrange buttons and menus to fit them to the way he uses them.*
  - *Human-computer interaction: The communication and interaction between the system and the user will be a very important part of the design of the portal. The output of the system needs to be clear and easy to understand as well as motivational and encouraging. On the*

other side the user needs adequate possibilities to interact with the system and to provide his input. A thought-trough way of communication will make the portal fun and easy to use and will essentially improve the success of the users while using the portal. (Martín-Roldán Pérez & Ehrman, 2012, pp. 21-22).

The final outcome of this phase of human-centered design is that the design team started to build a **relationship** between the future users and the LITERACY-portal. Being a valued part of the design-process of the portal and seeing that they are listened to and their ideas are implemented or at least seriously considered for the portal, will make the adoption of the final product and spreading of the word among people with dyslexia more probable.

FUTURE RESEARCH DIRECTIONS

One of the outcomes of the LITERACY-project should be a "person-centered" portal, or, in other words, an online portal designed with focus on empathic understanding and acceptance of its end-user. Further research should specify a person-centered portal in more detail, inquire how the person-centered approach overlaps with human-centered design, how does a final product of such design process function and whether it promotes authenticity, inclusion and affective needs of its user. This research could be further augmented by analyzing the effect of person-centered communication (Motschnig and Nykl, 2014) and appreciative inquiry (Barret and Fry, 2005) within such contexts.

Another interesting research question is how HCD-techniques, and maybe also the HCD-process itself, could be better applied with special needs user groups. Interacting with dyslexic users showcased how different such user-groups behave and that testing-sessions need to be planned and performed accordingly. Finding strategies and similarities between special needs user groups could help improve design processes and generate better products that fit the users' special needs.

Lastly, preparation of the LITERACY-portal's piloting in four different languages and two alphabets inspires to delve deeper into the language-specific strengths and weaknesses of ICT usage in case of people with dyslexia. Extension of the portal to Spanish and German mutation for more comprehensive research in this direction is envisioned, too.

CONCLUSION

This chapter illustrated various design decisions, techniques and steps of including dyslexic youth and adults in the early design stages of the LITERACY-portal, an interactive web-application that is intended to support the social inclusion of users who are struggling readers. Two forms of end-user inclusion were applied, an indirect one in which the design team studied the special cognitive and affective habits of dyslexic users from literature, web-resources and by talking to experts from pedagogy and psychology and a direct one in which dyslexic users were asked about key aspects of the portal. The latter employed procedures such as semi-structured interviews, screen design choice and card-sorting. The results and sample data gathered through these various means not only helped generating a better understanding of how an optimal interface for the specific user group should look like but also how testing sessions need to be adapted to generate the best results. The findings of each individual design-step influenced subsequent ones and therefore helped in creating more suitable testing scenarios as well as estimate the limits of cognitive capabilities more closely or incorporate the creative tendencies of dyslexic users, which heavily influenced design decisions, into the testing sessions. These gradual improvements were only possible thanks to the help of experts of various fields of expertise within the LITERACY-consortium.

Future design-steps will focus on direct inclusion in the form of icon testing, refined screen design choice, users' estimation of experience regarding the portal's usability, and thinking-aloud based task testing.

So far the design team:

- Developed a deeper understanding of a person with dyslexia,
- Pinpointed the most recurring difficulties people with dyslexia encounter online and designed ideas for next phases of portal design,
- Learned about dyslexia-specific aspects of human-centered design procedures,
- Identified guiding design principles,
- And started building relationships with future users.

In this way, the portal has a higher chance of being accepted by its users, promoting inclusion of people with dyslexia and other reading difficulties and providing insights into human-centered design and person-centered communication with people with special cognitive and affective needs.

REFERENCES

AGID-Project. (2018). *About the Project*. Retrieved February 18, 2019, from http://agid-project.eu/index.php/en/project/about-the-project

Balharová, K., Motschnig, R., Struhár, J., & Hagelkruys, D. (2013). A Case Study of Applying Card-sorting as an Initial Step in the Design of the LITERACY – Portal for People with Dyslexia. In *Proceedings of the Conference Universal Learning Design*. Brno: Masaryk University.

Barret, F. J., & Fry, R. E. (2005). *Appreciative inquiry: a positive approach to building cooperative capacity*. Chagrin Falls, OH: Academic Press.

Bell, L. (2009). *Web Accessibility: Designing for Dyslexia*. Retrieved October 15, 2013, from http://lindseybell.com/documents/bell_dyslexia.pdf

British Dyslexia Association. (2016). *Dyslexia Friendly Style Guide*. Retrieved February 17, 2019, from http://www.bdadyslexia.org.uk/common/ckeditor/filemanager/userfiles/About_Us/policies/Dyslexia_Style_Guide.pdf

British Dyslexia Association. (2019). *Dyslexia Research Information*. Retrieved February 20, 2019, from http://www.bdadyslexia.org.uk/about-dyslexia/further-information/dyslexia-research-information-.html

Courage, C., & Baxter, K. (2005). *Understanding Your Users: A Practical Guide to User Requirements Methods, Tools, and Techniques*. San Francisco, CA: Morgan Kaufmann Publishers.

Culén, A. L., & Karpova, A. (2014). Designing with Vulnerable Children: A Researcher's Perspective. In P. Isaías & K. Blashki (Eds.), *Human-Computer Interfaces and Interactivity: Emergent Research and Applications* (pp. 118–136). Hershey, PA: IGI Global. doi:10.4018/978-1-4666-6228-5.ch007

Dyslexia International. (2014). *Duke Report*. Retrieved February 18, 2019, from https://www.dyslexia-international.org/wp-content/uploads/2016/04/DI-Duke-Report-final-4-29-14.pdf

European Dyslexia Association. (2014). *Dyslexia in Europe*. Retrieved February 18, 2019, from https://www.eda-info.eu/dyslexia-in-europe

IDEO. (2015). *The field guide to human-centered design*. San Francisco: IDEO.org / Design Kit. Retrieved February 18, 2019, from https://www.ideo.com/post/design-kit

ISO 9241 (2010). Ergonomics of human-system interaction – Part 210: Human-centered design for interactive systems.

Lányi, C. S. (2009). Multimedia Software Interface Design for Special-Needs Users. In M. Khosrow-Pour (Ed.), *Encyclopedia of Information Science and Technology* (2nd ed.; pp. 2761–2766). doi:10.4018/978-1-60566-026-4.ch440

Lee, Y. (2008). Designing with users, how? In *Investigate users involvement tactics for effective inclusive design processes. Design Thinking: New Challenges for Designers, Managers and Organizations*. Cergy-Pointoise.

Liimatainen, J., Häkkinen, M., Nousiainen, T., Kankaanranta, M., & Neittaanmäki, P. (2012). A mobile application concept to encourage independent mobility for blind and visually impaired students. In *ICCHP'12 Proceedings of the 13th international conference on Computers Helping People with Special Needs* (vol. 2, pp. 552-559). Berlin: Springer Verlag. 10.1007/978-3-642-31534-3_81

LITERACY Project. (2018). *About LITERACY*. Retrieved February 18, 2019, from http://www.literacy-portal.eu/en/info/about-literacy.html

Martín-Roldán Pérez, S., & Ehrman, B. (2012). D1.2 Report on the mapping the planned functional Portal. Deliverable of the LITERACY-Project, Madrid.

Masiero, A. A., Carvalho Destro, R., Curioni, O. A., & Aquino, P. T. Junior. (2013). Expanding Personas: How to Improve Knowledge About Users. In *Proceedings of the IADIS International Conferences Interfaces and Human Computer Interaction and Game and Entertainment Technologies* (pp. 103-109). Praga: IADIS.

McCarthy, J., & Swierenga, S. (2010). What we know about dyslexia and Web accessibility: A research review. *Universal Access in the Information Society*, 9(2), 147–152. doi:10.100710209-009-0160-5

Moser, C., Fuchsberger, V., Neureiter, L., Sellner, W., & Tscheligi, M. (2012). Revisiting personas: the making-of for special user groups. CHI '12 Extended Abstracts on Human Factors in Computing Systems.

Motschnig, R., & Nykl, L. (2011). *Komunikace zaměřená na člověka: rozumět sobě i druhým*. Prague: Grada.

Motschnig, R., & Nykl, L. (2014). *Person-centred Communication Theory, Skills and Practice*. Maidenhead, UK: McGraw Hill.

Norman, D. A. (2002). *The design of everyday things*. New York: Basic Books.

Overton, T. (2012). *Assessing Learners with Special Needs. An applied approach*. Boston: Pearson Education.

Rogers, C. R., & Farson, R. E. (1987). Active Listening. In R. G. Newman, M. A. Danziger, & M. Cohen (Eds.), *Communication in Business Today*. Washington, DC: Heath and Company. (Originally published 1957)

Rogers, C. R., & Roethlisberger, F. J. (1991). Barriers and Gateways to Communication. *Harvard Business Review*.

Rogers, Y., Sharp, H., & Preece, J. (2011). *Interaction Design: beyond human-computer interaction*. New York: Wiley.

Schikhof, Y., & Mulder, I. (2008). Under Watch and Ward at Night: Design and Evaluation of a Remote Monitoring System for Dementia Care. In *USAB '08 Proceedings of the 4th Symposium of the Workgroup Human-Computer Interaction and Usability Engineering of the Austrian Computer Society on HCI and Usability for Education and Work*. Berlin: Springer Verlag.

Seffah, A., Vanderdonckt, J., & Desmarais, M. C. (2009). *Human-Centered Software Engineering: Software Engineering Models, Patterns and Architectures for HCI*. London: Springer Verlag. doi:10.1007/978-1-84800-907-3

Sprenger-Charolles, L., Siegel, L. S., Jimenez, J. E., & Ziegler, J. (2011). Prevalence and reliability of phonological, surface, and mixed profiles in dyslexia: A review of studies conducted in languages varying in orthographic depth. *Scientific Studies of Reading*, *15*(6), 498–521. doi:10.1080/10888438.2010.524463

Stone, D., Jarrett, C., Woodroffe, M., & Minocha, S. (2005). *User Interface Design and Evaluation*. San Francisco: Morgan Kaufmann Publishers.

Thimbleby, H. W. (2008). Understanding User Centred Design (UCD) for People with Special Needs. In K. Miesenberger, J. Klaus, W. L. Zagler, & A. I. Karshmer (Eds.), *ICCHP* (pp. 1–17). Berlin: Springer Verlag. doi:10.1007/978-3-540-70540-6_1

World Health Organization. (2018). *ICD-11 for Mortality and Morbidity Statistics*. Retrieved from 6A03.0 Developmental learning disorder with impairment in reading: https://icd.who.int/browse11/l-m/en#/http://id.who.int/icd/entity/1008636089

ADDITIONAL READING

Edmondson, W. H. (2001). *A Taxonomical Approach to Special Needs Design in HCI* (pp. 909–913). New Orleans, LA: Universal Access in Human-Computer Interaction.

Goldsmith, S. (2007). *Universal Design*. Taylor & Francis. doi:10.4324/9780080520209

Spencer, D. (2009). *Card Sorting: Designing Usable Categories*. Brooklyn, NY: Rosenfeld Media.

KEY TERMS AND DEFINITIONS

Accessibility: Accessibility describes the extent to which persons with special needs or people who use assistive technologies can use a product, like for example software.

Card Sorting: Card sorting is an interactive activity in which the participants choose cards from a set number of options with a specific goal in mind, like for example elements of a menu.

Dyslexia: Dyslexia can be characterized as a learning deficiency, which expresses itself in form of reading and writing difficulties.

Human-Centered Design: Human-centered design (HCD) is an iterative design approach that puts the focus on the users. A central part of HCD is the constant inclusion of end-users into the different steps of the design process.

IT for Inclusion: IT for inclusion means the use of information technologies to support the social inclusion of specific user groups, such as users with special needs.

Personas: Personas are fictional characters that represent a certain user group. They comprise certain characteristics that are representative for this user group.

Screen Design: Screen design includes all visual elements of an interface, including positioning of objects, color-schemes, fonts, styles, etc.

Social Inclusion: Social inclusion depicts a form of inclusion that helps people to take part in social activities, like for example social media or different forms of communication.

Task Analysis: Task analysis depicts the process of assessing and describing potential tasks that users need, have or want to perform with the product.

Usability: Usability describes the extent to which a product, like for example software, can be used to achieve specific goals in an effective, efficient, engaging, error-tolerant, and easy-to-learn way.

User Analysis: User analysis is the process of assessing users of a product regarding a variety of different aspects (e.g., age, knowledge of the product, skill level, etc.).

ENDNOTE

[1]   See https://xsortapp.com/

APPENDIX

A. Interviewing

Strategy

- According to the appreciative inquiry – discover strengths, discover under which circumstances they prevail and how it would be possible to get into those circumstances more often
- According to the person-centered approach – being open, trying to understand, empathize and no judging.
- Stating the purpose of the project – e.g. empowering struggling readers online, strengthening social inclusion, interest in their personal experience and us wanting them to become a part of the project
- Stating that the interviewee can ask for a pause whenever he feels like it and also the interview can be ended anytime.
- The interview is semi-structured, going around certain topics. If the interviewer feels that the natural flow of interview is going to a different topic, let it happen and go for it, but keep in the overall goal in mind and return to a topic if necessary
- Firstly, try to acquire uninfluenced ideas from the interviewee and only after that present ours, e.g. prototypes
- If the interviewer knows something more about the interviewee, adjust questions to that knowledge to make the flow of interview more interesting for him or her

Sample Questions

- What type of student were you? What did you study? What did you like at school? What tricks did you invent to make learning easier for you? What would you like to have at school so that it was more interesting for you and why? Were there any mentors you liked? What were they like?
- What do you like about your work-life? What do you do? Which activities do you like most? Could you take a few moments and name your strengths? What could you do to use them more? How do you imagine a better workplace?
- Do you use internet? How often? How does it help you? What kind of webpages do you prefer? Do you use social networks? How would you imagine an improved social network, e.g. Facebook? Do you use any other tools? Can you describe how do you use them? What tools would you like to have? How about you and speech recognition? And text-to-speech?
- Do you read? What kind of texts? Which ones do you read with passion? Who or what lead you to reading? Do you like to use any reading tools (text-to-speech, e-readers)? Could you imagine something that would make reading easier or more enjoyable?
- Do you have any particular hobbies? How do you usually motivate yourself?

Note: In the first interview, the positive form of questions lead not only to discovery of various strengths, but many problems and issues as well. If the interviewer has a feeling that this is not happening, he or she can of course continue with questions on complications and problems as well.

B. After-Interview Questionnaire

I read slowly.

    Yes

    No

I read small letters with difficulties.

    Yes

    No

I get lost in text.

    Yes

    No

I don't understand what I read.

    Yes

    No

    Partially (I can when I focus really hard)

It is hard for me to go to a next line in a text.

    Yes

    No

I forget last letters, making it harder for me to understand.

    Yes

    No

I forget or don't see numbers and other data in a text.

    Yes

    No

Colouring numbers in a text helps.

    Yes

    No

I cannot recognize keywords.

    Yes

    No

I mind the amount of text I have to read in my job.

    Yes

    No

Deliberate focus is a problem for me.

    Yes

    No

I easily miss important information in an email.

    Yes

    No

I don't process details when reading, even when they are important.

    Yes

    No

I have to write grammatically correct emails at work.

    Yes

    No

I have problems writing in proper grammar.

    Yes

    No

I form sentences differently.

    Yes

    No

Online, I mind:

    Adverts.

        Yes

        No

    Too much text.

        Yes

        No

    Low contrast.

        Yes

        No

    Totally similar subpages (I get lost).

        Yes

        No

    Too many sections on the homepage.

        Yes

        No

    Moving text.

        Yes

        No

    Unclear text.

        Yes

        No

    Flashing text.

        Yes

        No

Chapter 2
Observations on Design Thinking in Novice Designers While Empathizing With Persona

Abhishek Dahiya
Indian Institute of Technology Delhi, India

Jyoti Kumar
Indian Institute of Technology Delhi, India

ABSTRACT

Personas are a rich source of user information that assists designers at various stages of the design process. HCI designers use personas to help them explicate the understanding of their target users. Design literature advocates that personas are not only a source of information about users but also a tool to empathize with them. This chapter reports observations from an experimental study done on novice designers on how empathizing with persona affected their design solutions. A total of 50 novice designers participated in this study. Participants were asked to solve a graphical design problem for the persona. The data collected was analyzed through expert rating on design solutions on the basis of directness of illustration of persona information and verbal protocols. On the basis of direct illustration of persona information on design solutions, it was observed that empathizing with persona helped designers to iterate more on design thinking.

INTRODUCTION

Persona creation has been argued as one of the crucial steps in User Centered Design (UCD) process (Hong 2009) (Norman 1988). Persona creation helps the designers to keep a focus on the users' needs and helps in making crucial design decisions from a users' perspective (So, C., & Joo, J. 2017). Often arguments about "what might be 'friendly' or 'easy' to one user versus another" emerges in the design discussions (Corry, Frick, and Hansen 1997) (Nielsen 1994). The root cause of these differences has been argued to be the difference in 'mental models' of designer's and various users (Norman 1988) (Carroll

DOI: 10.4018/978-1-5225-9069-9.ch002

2003). Often user research is conducted to understand the users before creation of persona. Various user research methods have been suggested by design practitioners and researchers for HCI design (Steen and Kuijt; Landauer 1988). Different user research methods provide different types of user information which are documented and presented in different formats (Pruitt and Adlin 2006). Often text is used to report observations from user research while pictures, documentary videos etc. are also used complimentarily. Some systematic methods of summarizing the user data have also evolved in the HCI field like personas, scenario, stories, case studies, use cases, user experience charts, emotional maps etc. Persona has been one of the most prominent and frequent forms of user data presentation in HCI design process (Nielsen, L. 2018). Personas has been defined as a "fictitious, specific, concrete representations of target users" (Pruitt & Adlin, 2006). A persona represents target users who share common behavioral characteristics (i.e., is a hypothetical archetype of real users) (Pruitt & Adlin, 2006). Introduced by Alan Cooper, personas were integrated into the design processes to help designers in developing useful and usable designs (Cooper 1999; Pruitt John 2003; Caballero, Moreno, and Seffah 2014). Persona has been used by design community for audience prioritization, organization of research data, making the user understanding explicit, within team communication aid, facilitator of innovative thinking etc. It has been argued that persona helps in empathizing with the user i.e. "creating an understanding of and emotional identification with the users/customers" (Miaskiewicz and Kozar, 2011). While role of empathy in design process has been often argued (Köppen, E., & Meinel, C. 2015), how the designer's ability to empathize with persona has an effect on the designer's design thinking and subsequently on the design outcomes has not been discussed much in literature. There is very little research available on how increased level of empathy with persona affects the design outcomes. There is a need to study the design thinking in light of empathy with persona as this may seriously affect the HCI design processes.

Design thinking has been seen as a highly complex process which involves knowledge from various disciplines to synthesize for a solution to solve a problem (Newell Allen, 1988). Of late design thinking is getting attention from various design researchers, practitioners and design philosophers. Various methods have been used in literature that aim to understand the design thinking in designers. One of the more popular approaches to understand design thinking has been by analysis of designer's approach to solution generation (Cross, 2001). Several studies using this approach has been reported where difference between expert and novice designer's thinking processes were observed. Novice designers were observed to have difficulty in analyzing scope of the design problem (Atman et al. 1999) (Cross, 2001). Also, novice designers have showed less 'cognitive actions' during design thinking (Kavakli and Gero 2001) and used more 'hit and trial method' for solution generation instead of systematic thinking (Ahmed, Wallace, and Blessing, 2003). While these studies are helpful in understanding the evolution and development of design thinking strategies in designers, they also indicate the development of 'expertise' in the designers by way of increase in 'cognitive actions'. Probably growth in expertise also means a greater reflection on the users' perspective intuitively. It is argued here that greater 'cognitive actions' are an indication of more self-reflection on each design thought and more self-reflections in turn are likely to be guided by internalized information on the users' perspective. In the light of above argument, it is posited here that the observed design thinking behavior of expert designer's in terms of more detailed 'cognitive action' can also be attributed to their greater empathy levels. This chapter reports observations on designers' design thinking when they undergo empathy exercise versus when they do not to infer role of empathy on design thinking process.

BACKGROUND

In order to explore the influence of empathy with persona on design thinking, several different sources of literature may be useful to study. To start with, details on user centered design, role of empathy in design, use of persona in HCI and its influence on design thinking are well reported in literature. Also, several different perspectives on how design thinking happens and methods to study it is available in literature. All these different sources of information make a good background information for investigating the role of empathizing with persona in design thinking.

User Centered Design

One of the methodologies for developing design solutions has been User Centered Design (UCD) which argues that the design process be 'centered' on the 'users' through iterative steps. Norman defined UCD as "a philosophy based on the needs and interests of the user, with an emphasis on making products usable and understandable" (Norman Donald A. 1988; Corry Michael D et al. 1997). Another definition of UCD says, "the active involvement of users for a clear understanding of user and task requirements, iterative design and evaluation, and a multi-disciplinary approach" (Vredenburg Karel et al. 2002). Overall, understanding the users is the central theme in UCD methodology (Koskinen and Battarbee 2003, Sleeswijk Visser et al. 2005). Participatory design is another design methodology that shares similar ideology of involving users in design process. Both the methodologies agree to the fact that there is a need to understand the user before providing solutions to a design problem. The difference is in the way users play a role in both methodologies. User centered design involves various tools and techniques that help in understanding and documenting user's behaviors, motivations, needs etc. by the design team. On the other hand, participatory design process argues for a more direct involvement of users at every stage of design process, even at solution generation stage.

Designers practicing UCD methodology have developed various tools and techniques that can help obtain user information related to design problem. These methods involve studying and observing the users and understanding their relation with the design product. Expert designers have tacit knowledge of observing and simultaneously producing solutions that would work in user's scenario. Novice designers, on the other hand require training to observe and understand their users and come up with novel ways to solve the design problem. As the tools and techniques for understanding users are widely used by novice designers, it becomes necessary to investigate how each tool influences their empathy towards the users.

Empathy in Design

The word 'empathic' in relation to design was introduced in the late-1990s (Battarbee and Koskinen 2005) when the design fraternity realized that users cannot be fully understood on the basis of questionnaires and response sheets (Leonard and Rayport 1997, Sanders and Dandavate 1999). Empathetic design (Kouprie, M., & Visser, F. S. 2009), helps designers to get a deeper look at the aspirations, motivations and beliefs of the users for which the product is being designed. Design practitioners advocate the need to inform designers about user experiences and their context (Leonard and Rayport 1997, Buchenau and Fulton Suri 2000). A number of tools and techniques are reported in literature that helps designers to empathize with their users (Fulton Suri 2003). Ickes (1997) has mentioned that empathy is a complex form of psychological inference in which observation, memory, knowledge, and reasoning are combined to yield insights into the thoughts and feelings of others. Therefore, empathy is an innate quality of a designer through which he/she is able to sense and develop an understanding of their users in various contexts (Ickes 1997). Expert designers over the time practice empathizing with their users and develop it as a tacit skill which help them to understand their users deeply. Novice designers on the other hand need to learn to empathize with their users. Although personas and scenarios are used frequently in UCD, studies on how empathizing with persona actually influences the design thinking of novice designers.

Persona as an Empathy Tool for HCI Design Thinking Process

Need to empathize with users in design process has been well argued (Gasparini, A. 2015). Persona as a tool to empathise with users has also been argued (Nielsen, L. 2018), (Miaskiewicz and Kozar, 2011). However, the effectiveness of persona as a tool in design has been doubted in absence of a proper training to use persona (Matthews, Judge, and Whittaker 2012). Cooper (1999) defines persona as "A precise description of our user and what he wishes to accomplish". Calde, Goodwin & Reimann (2002) describe persona as "fictional, detailed archetypal characters that represent distinct groupings of behaviors, goals and motivations observed and identified during the research phase". Personas are therefore "abstractions of groups of real consumers who share common characteristics and needs" (Pruitt & Adlin, 2006). Persona descriptions include demographic information, socioeconomic status, occupations, likenesses, possessions etc. of the users. Descriptions in persona helps designers to form an understanding of their target audience which can assist them in design decisions (Cooper, 1999; Manning; 2003; Pruitt & Adlin, 2006). Pruitt (2006) emphasizes on using rigorous user studies to create foundational documents of persona. Personas are therefore a consolidated plot of various user information and understanding developed by user researchers. Generally speaking, persona narratives: (1) aims to provide explicit information and the needs of the users to designers in context of the product to be designed (Long, F. 2009) and (2) help designers to empathize with the fictional character and make sense of user's affective and cognitive states (Miaskiewicz and Kozar, 2011). However, it has been argued that in absence of proper training of using persona, designers could not benefit from using persona in design process (Matthews, Judge, and Whittaker 2012). Thus, while persona has been argued to help HCI designers in design process as they inform about users (Cooper & Reimann, 2002; Grudin & Pruitt, 2002, Caballero, Moreno, and Seffah 2014), help empathize about users (Miaskiewicz and Kozar, 2011) and empathy with users is an important factor in success of design (Pruitt & Adlin, 2006; Nielsen, 2013) but in absence of appropriate empathy with persona, the design process suffers (Matthews, Judge, and Whittaker 2012).

According to Cooper, human beings are able to predict behavior and mental conditions of other human beings (Cooper 1999). This ability helps designers to envision how users will behave and respond to their design in any situation (Grudin, J., 2006). Development of persona as a user understanding tool is based on the fact that people tend to characterize other people in terms of traits. Traits are broad dispositions that predict or explain much of people's behavior. Grudin further argues that "actions and behaviors are predicted by building an internal model of the person. This ability to engage with models of real people is also applicable to the models of fictional people" (in this case, personas). According to Cooper "the more specific the persona is, the more effective they are as design tools" (Cooper,1999,). With more specific, idiosyncratic details, the persona becomes a "real" person in the minds of the developers. Working with persona can be as realistic as working with real users (Grudin, J.,2006). Hence, representation of user data as fictional people can be as engaging as models of real people.

It is helpful to take a note of how persona are typically developed and used in design process. In UCD, different data collection methods are used. The different methods of data collection from users can be divided into two groups, i.e. primary user data and secondary user data. Here, by primary user data, user data collected directly from the users by designers themselves is meant. On the other hand, secondary user data is the information about the users that is not directly collected by designers. Instead, user's notes, user research done by other teams, statistical information about the users from web server, call centers, help desk etc. are used as sources of information about the users. Persona is created from these various sources of data that reached the design team. Discrete user data collected from various sources is thus personified in form of a persona. Creating persona is an iterative process which includes assimilating and analyzing user data from various user research methods (Pruitt & Adlin, 2006). Typically, multiple personas are created for a design project. Once persona is developed, various designers in the design team use this persona to understand and empathize with the user and to keep the mutual design goals aligned. Individual designers in design teams use their imagination to submerse themselves into the persona and try to look at the problem from the persona's perspective while they generate design solutions. Persona thus developed helps designers to make design decisions while ideating for solutions. In order to empathize more with the persona, scenarios are also generated. The role of scenario is to help designers visualize the conditions in which user performs certain tasks using the product. Figure 1 illustrates a flowchart of how persona is developed and used in HCI design process.

Design Thinking Models and Methods of Observation

Literature on design thinking has used several different terms like creative thinking, design cognition, imaginative thinking etc. which mean the same intent of understanding how a designer goes about thinking of a design solution. Despite various views and definitions of these terms, we do not have an explicit definition of the construct 'design thinking' (Buchanan, 1992). Several different models and theories have been proposed that aim to explain design thinking process on the basis of empirical or theoretical studies. These theories and models for design thinking provide fundamental explanations for such a complex phenomenon as design thinking. Following are some of the theoretical models that have tried to explain design thinking process from various perspectives.

One of the attempts to model design thinking has been through the nature of problems that design thinking solves (Newell Allen, 1988). Simon has argued that design is an ill-defined problem solving activity, where design problems are open ended or loosely structured (Newell Allen, 1988). Design problems have been argued to be ill-defined because they have ambiguity in specification of goals, lack

Figure 1. Flowchart illustrating typical process of development and usage of persona in design process

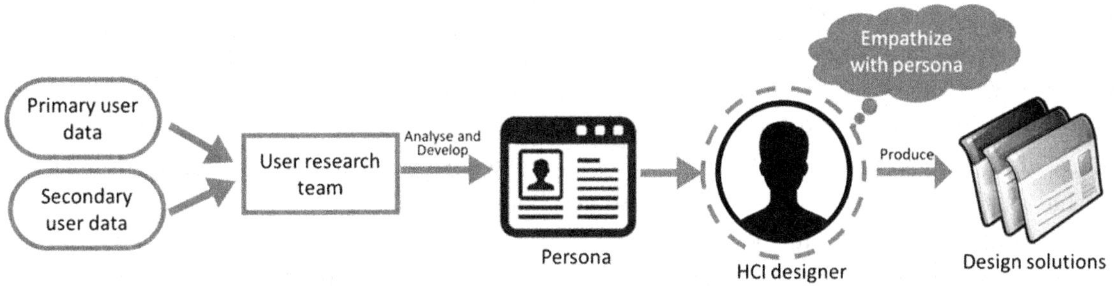

resolute solution path, and require knowledge from various domains. A similar analogy was provided by Goel and Pirolli (1992). They explained design activity as solving many degrees of freedom, consisting only of intentions, having limited and delayed feedback from the real world, generation of artifacts as outputs that must function independently of the designer, and creation of answers that tend to be neither right nor wrong, only better or worse (Goel and Pirolli 1992).

Another model of design thinking process has been in terms of the method of solution generation. Simon in his theory on information processing in problem solving proposed the idea of problem space (Newell Allen, 1988). This problem space is a representation of problem situation in the mind of problem solver. According to Simon, problem solving happens in problem space. Simon proposed that structure of problem space is crucial in thinking process as solution generation will depend on it. In other terms, structure of problem space will determine the possible design thinking strategies that can be adopted by a design thinker.

Plucker and Dow described the process of design thinking from the perspective of schema development (Plucker 2004). Plucker and Dow argue that design thinking is basically "interconnections of ideas that grow into complex, organized mental structures of information." According to Lubart, design process refers to a sequence of thoughts and actions leading to a novel, adaptive production (Lubart 2001).

The different models of design thinking process have also influenced the experiments to understand the design thinking in specific contexts. A number of experiments have been reported in literature which use the model of design thinking process as a problem solving process. The ill-defined problem that the designer has first requires development of a problem space with different attributes of problems mapped in the space. User's needs create one set of such problem space attributes. The designer iteratively considers each aspect of the problem space and generates partial solutions. The idea of schema of interconnected ideas also supports the same analogy of design thinking process. Designers use creativity in opportunistic selection of such interconnectedness to generate solutions. Creative outcomes in design process are influenced by cognitive applications and combinations (Bonnardel, 2000). The ill-defined problems in design typically present indefinite criteria and constraints, which makes it difficult to track cognitive steps in design thinking (Cross, 2001). There have been various attempts in literature to understand the design thinking steps.

Verbal protocol studies have been frequently used in various experiments to examine thinking processes (Cross, 2001). In verbal protocol reports, researchers provide extracts of protocols, and explain how a segment is encoded along with the meaning of the encoded behaviors (Kim and Kim, 2015). Since using think aloud protocol to study design thinking faces certain challenges on validity of gathered data (Someren, 1994), retrospective verbal accounts (i.e., recalling what one was thinking recently) have also been used (Cross 2001). Verbal protocols are often reported using frequencies of encoded items and presented in form of tables/charts and matrices.

Another method has been used to study design thinking by Valkenburg and Dorst who used different shapes to represent different types of design thinking steps and represented the relationships between them using arrows and boxes (Valkenburg and Dorst, 1998). Yet, another recent popular method called Linkograph was introduced by Goldschmidt (Goldschmidt 1990) which studies design thinking process by observing combination of sequential 'design moves', and links between them. Other, design researchers have also analyzed design thinking processes using sketches developed by designers while ideating for solutions (Tversky and Suwa 2009; Cardoso and Badke-Schaub, 2011).

To sum up, the oft used methods of study of design thinking process have been verbal protocol (concurrent as well as retrospective verbalizations on personal design thinking), observations on design sketching activities in process of concept generation and analysis of the design outcomes. These methods have been used in different context of design thinking process. In the context of this chapter, it will be useful to discuss about studies which have looked at how novice designers go about design problem solving as we aim to understand how empathizing with persona affects design thinking in novice designers.

It has been reported that novice designers tend to perform less cognitive actions during design thinking as compared to experts while solving design problems (Kavakli, M., & Gero, J., 2001). Another study presented by Dahiya & Kumar (2018) argues that designers working user data collected by themselves tend to generate less creative solutions and show more fixation on ideas while design thinking (Dahiya, A., & Kumar, J., 2018a). If we agree that the design thinking is the type of problem solving activity where the problems are not well defined and the problem spaces do not have rigid boundaries, the designers in the process of generating solutions often expand or shift the boundaries of the problem space opportunistically using his /her creativity as and when an interconnection of ideas emerge. This dynamic organization of thoughts and ideas to generate multiple complex structures of information in mind can also be observed through the iterative generation of concepts at artifact level. Novice designers are often observed to 'jump to conclusions' very early in solution generation which could be due to lack of rich interconnection of ideas through iterative shifting of the problems space using creativity and self-reflection in light of the various forms of internal or external data. User data may be one of such types of data which contributes to the interconnected ideas while generating solutions. Further, it has been reported that design thinking includes information retrieval from memory (Dominowski, R.L., & Dallob, P.,1995). The direct retrieval of information from memory has also been argued to be a sign of unoriginality of ideas (Runco, 1995). For the ideas to be creative, some manipulation of information upon being retrieved from, memory must be involved. The investment of the designer's self to engage into more sophisticated network of thoughts before producing new design ideas thus would require several cognitive steps on the memory based information. Such cognitive manipulation of original information retrieved from memory may be required for an idea to become a 'creative' idea.

As discussed above, in light of several such studies where the designers' design thinking process has been observed using verbal protocols, the produced artifact and analysis of designed concepts, the question that this chapter raised was how the user data and empathizing with user persona influences the design thinking process. Next section presents an experimental study which was conducted to observe how empathizing with persona influences the design thinking

AN EXPERIMENT TO STUDY IMPACT OF EMPATHY ON DESIGN

A total of 50 industrial design students participated in a study where they had to solve a design problem for a given persona and a problem related to the persona. Participants were given a persona description on a printed sheet of paper where an image of the person in context of work surroundings along with a description of person's demographics, psychographics and work profile etc. was provided. Also, a design problem relevant to the persona was given. The participants had to read about the persona and internalize the needs of the person being described. Thereafter they had to sketch a solution for the given problem that will work with the persona.

The participants in control group were given the persona description and the design problem and were given 30 minutes' time to submit their work. The participants in experiment group underwent an empathizing exercise with persona before they started synthesizing solutions. The research design was to test whether the empathy exercise had any effect in empathizing with persona and whether the same was observable in the designed artifacts by the designers.

In this experiment, the effect of empathizing with persona on design solutions was studied using multiple methods, namely, analysis of solutions generated by the participants, verbal protocols and expert rating on design solutions. It may be noteworthy that all the participants were novice designers who were in the starting their design education.

Design solutions created by participants were analyzed for 'cognitive actions' taken by designers during the design activity. Retrospective verbal protocols were used for personal description of the design activities. The 'direct illustration of user information' given in persona description used in design solutions has been considered as a marker of less 'cognitive actions' in the analysis. The difference in 'cognitive actions' between control and experimental groups has been analyzed to understand the impact of empathizing with persona on design thinking.

EXPERIMENT METHODOLOGY

As the experiment was aimed to understand how empathizing with persons affects design thinking in novice designers, like other similar studies in design literature (Cross, 2001), this study also observed the solution generation approach to a design problem by novice designers. Participants who were novice designers were given a graphical design problem where they were asked to read the given description of the persona before ideating for solution. Then participants were asked to design the graphical illustration for the person they just read about. Participants were divided into two groups. Each participant worked independently on the design exercise. One group of participants (control group, 25 participants) were given persona description and were asked to design solutions for the problem. The participants in other group (experiment group, 25 participants) underwent a 10-minute empathy exercise along with persona description before they were asked to design solutions. This empathy exercise was same for all the participants in experiment group. The empathy exercise (described in further section) was conducted one on one for each participant individually. After the empathy exercise, the participants in experiment group were asked to ideate for solutions on their own working alone in an isolated room. Both the groups were given equal time for designing their graphical illustrations. Design solutions produced by both the groups were collected. The verbal protocols of each participant were recorded one participant at a time where they were asked to describe the design thinking process during the solution generation. The recorded verbal protocol was transcribed and analyzed to assess the influence of empathy on design outcomes.

Persona Description

Participants were provided a persona before the design task was given to them. The design task was given after the participants had thoroughly read the persona. After 10 mins of persona reading the participants were given the design task in a printed format. The idea of introducing persona before design task was to ensure that participants do not carry any biases or fixations towards the first design ideas they upon reading the design problem. The persona was made very realistic with lots of details of person whose design problem was being given. Persona included a profile picture of the user and text describing about the user's demographics, interests, hobbies, habits, work profile and family background. The personas provided to the participants is shown below. In control group, out of 25 participants, 13 participants (P1

Figure 2. Experiment process for Control group and experiment group

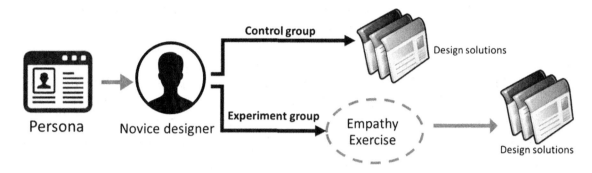

to P13) were provided first persona and next 12 participants (P4 to P25) were provided second persona. In experiment group, out of 25 participants, 13 participants (P26 to P38) were provided first persona and next 12 participants (P39 to P50) were provided the second persona. In the experiment, two personas were used instead of one for ease in generalizing the findings and to cancel out any specific influence of the specific persona that may have on the study. The idea was to observe if the design problem related to both personas got influenced by empathy exercises similarly. This was also important to study as it was posited that empathy may be easier with one type of persona versus another type due to easier connect of the designer with one persona than another. In case both the persona got similar influence from the empathy exercise, the effect of persona type will thus be negated. One of the persona was deliberately made stereotypical of the socio-cultural context while the other was a rare occurrence in the society, thus ensuring that while one persona may enable easier emotional connect by the designer due to prior experience of having met a similar person the other would be a rare occurrence. The two persona created were almost similar in their description structure, but were different in content of information. The text in the two personas are provided below for ease of reading as follows:

Persona 1: *Suchitra Basin is 29-year-old girl in Kanpur. She is a school teacher (6-8th class Mathematics) and stays with her husband, who is an entrepreneur, and her in-laws. Suchitra also takes evening tuitions at her home for children as a top up for her meager salary. Suchitra enjoys reading and writing and she is also interested in cooking. Often she invites relatives for get together at her home and enjoys testing new recipes with them.*

Persona 2: *Pallavi Sharma is 32-year-old Delhi girl. She is a dietitian and part time gym instructor. She got married 4 years ago. She has a son who is about to be 3 in a month's time. She lives with her husband who works in an IT company in NOIDA (close to Delhi). Pallavi had been sports enthusiast since her childhood and won many state level prizes in tennis and basketball during her school and college years. Pallavi smartly balances her home and professional life. Pallavi is also passionate about travelling in general and off road biking in particular.*

Empathy Exercise

Participants in experiment group were subjected to a 10-minute empathy exercise after 10 minutes of reading the persona description. The aim of this empathy exercise was to help designers take time to think about the users that they are designing for. The empathy exercise included narrations of some scenarios around the persona and discussions on some tasks that the persona within the given scenario is likely to perform. There is a dearth of literature on how empathy exercises help designers envisage user's actions and behaviors. Moreover, there is not much literature available on how empathy could be evoked using empathy exercises. The exercise developed in this study was created after many creative iterations and couple of pilot studies. The intent of designing the empathy exercise in such a way was to help the participating novice designer use personal visualization and imagination to get a firm mental grip on the details of the persona so that the understanding of the person created a memory from which the designer could fetch the interlinked ideas for designing the solution when one started sketching the solutions. Following paragraph captures, the exercise that was done with the experiment group:

Please close your eyes. Imagine yourself as the persona you just read about. Recall what are the things you like, work you do and activities that interests you. Imagine it is Saturday afternoon and you've just returned to home from your work. Now picture yourself in your (Suchitra/Pallavi) living room. Take your time to look around and see the interiors and objects placed near you. Take a look at the wall clock right in front of you, the photo frame kept on the table next to you, your water bottle, your bag, the painting on the side wall, see the design of on the carpet, lamp on the side of the bed, take a look at the wardrobe, open the wardrobe and go through the dresses you have. Try to observe details of your room for next 10 minutes

Design Task

Participants were asked to design "graphical composition for smart phone back cover" for the given persona using stickers of various geometric shapes. The idea of using shapes to design the graphical compositions was to minimize individual differences in ability of sketching/drawing. For example, a participant with low sketching/drawing competency might restrain his/her design ideas due to his/her inability to illustrate the idea. All participants were given equal set of materials required for the task. Participants were instructed to use the provided materials only for final solution. Participants were free to use colors over the stickers provided to express their design ideas. Materials provided to the participants were: 1. Persona description and design problem with instructions, 2. A4 size template of printed smart phone back cover, 3. Stickers: 24 circles, 12 squares, 6 rectangles, 6 rounded rectangles, 6 trapeziums and 6 triangles of various sizes, 4. Rough sheets, 5. Sketch pens, 6. Pencil, eraser and cutter.

Participants

Participants who volunteered to participate in this experiment were post-graduate students who were starting their Industrial Design education. A total of 50 students participated in the study. Participants constituted 27 males and 23 females with age ranges between: 23-27 yrs. (average age: 25.3 yrs., Std. dev.: 1.23 yrs.).

Experimental Procedure

Experiments were conducted in a controlled environment. Participants were given an isolated desk in a room which was free from any visual cues relevant to problem at hand. It was ensured that there were no visual or auditory disturbances. Participants were first given the persona to read followed by design task followed by instructions. Next, control group participants were provided an envelope consisting of materials required for the task and asked to ideate for solutions after the instructions. Whereas, experiment group participants were subjected to 10-minute empathy exercise after the participants had completed reading persona. Materials required for the task for experiment group participants were provided after empathy exercise session. Participants of both groups were given 40 minutes to ideate and design solutions. Participants were not allowed to use of any sources of inspiration like pictures form internet, magazines, books etc. while designing the graphical composition.

After the design task, participants were given 10-minutes break. Lastly, the experiment was followed by retrospective qualitative interview of the participants explaining how they went about designing the graphical composition.

ANALYSIS METHOD

The design solutions created by participants were analyzed for 'directness in application' of persona descriptions. As discussed in section titled 'design thinking models and methods of observation' earlier in this chapter, a 'direct illustration of user information' into design solutions has been reported to be a marker of less 'cognitive action' by novice designers. In this experiment, the 'directness of application' or 'direct illustration' of persona elements into design outcome was judged by three expert designers independently. One of the three experts was practicing industrial designer for five years, the second one was a design researcher for five years and the third expert was associated with design academics for more than seven years.

Experts were first asked to read the two personas. Next, the experts were asked to rate the design solutions on the basis of 'directness of illustration' in the designed solution given by the participating novice designer with respect to the relation of the textual descriptions written in persona. For example, a sample of directness of illustration from this experiment is illustrated in table 1. For persona one, description

Table 1. Examples of directness of illustration

Information from persona description	Graphical illustration
She is a dietitian and part time gym instructor	
She is a school teacher(6-8th class Mathematics)	

mentioned persona as 'gym instructor', and the designer illustrated gym equipment in design outcome. This is a direct illustration of persona information. Similarly, for second persona, it was mentioned that the user is a 'mathematics school teacher', illustrations of a school classroom or arithmetic operations in design is a marker of direct illustration of persona information.

The ratings were recorded on a 9 point Likert scale ranging from 1(indirect illustration) to 9 (direct illustration). Judges were kept blind to the existence of the different experimental conditions. Also, the design solutions from the two groups were mixed randomly and presented in a random order to the experts. The inter-rater reliability of judges' ratings was computed using the Cronbach alpha coefficient. In this experiment the inter rater reliability was found to be 0.920 which is highly significant.

OBSERVATIONS AND RESULTS

One of the most prominent observation from the experiment was that participants who had undergone empathy exercise had more 'cognitive actions' during design thinking. This section discusses in detail the findings leading to this observation. It was also observed that most of the design solutions generated by participants in control group (without empathy exercise) illustrated the information presented in persona descriptions directly. These illustrations were very direct visual depiction of words or phrases in the persona description. Verbal protocols from retrospective verbalizations also showed that participants of the control group were more influenced by words in persona description (Table 2).

Participants in experiment group who were subjected to empathy exercise did not show the tendency to illustrate the persona information directly into their designs as often as the control group had. Designs of experiment group participants were more focused on what the user might "like" rather than what is written in the description of the persona directly. Also, from the verbal protocols it was evident that the experiment group participants made more attempts to imagine the user's aesthetic taste before creating solutions. From these observations, it is inferred that participants in experiment group analyzed the persona information more deeply and reflected upon it using one's own imagination than the control group. This finding is a strong clue to how the persona can be used more effectively in the design process. Earlier, in literature, the concern about the design process suffering due to lack of sufficient empathizing with persona (Matthews, Judge, and Whittaker 2012) has been raised which this finding from the experiment gives some respite as to how more appropriate usage of persona can be encouraged by design teams.

Further, it was observed through the verbal protocol that all participants took the information given in the persona description as cues to identify the nature or character of the person and tried to depict it through visual graphics. This was evident through verbal protocols as participants used words like "traditional", "soft", "floral", "girly" for persona 1 and "rugged", "masculine", "bold", "tough", "strong", "sporty" etc. for persona 2, while explaining their designs. Further, designs generated by the participants in experiment group did not have depictions of motorcycle, food, books, classroom, gym or sports equipment. Graphical design made by the participants in experiment group were more abstract than that made by the control group. The control group had used more of realistic objects likely to be present in the environment of the persona given to the participants. Presence of greater abstraction level also shows more indirect depiction of the persona descriptions and therefore greater sophistication in the design thinking process (Runco, 1995).Table 3 shows the designs generated by the participants in experiment group along with their verbal protocols from retrospective verbalization sessions.

Table 2. Graphical illustrations by the participants (control group) along with verbal protocols

Phrases from persona	Examples from design solutions	Verbal Protocols from interview
"Pallavi is also passionate about travelli ng in general and off road biking in particular"		P9: "when I read the information...it was bike only that came out in my mind" P11: "So, for the first persona liked bike so I made a bike using stickers" "if she loves biking then bike must be there in her cover" P14: "because she was a biker... so it should look like that this is mountain and this is bike"
"She is a dietitian and part time gym instructor" "had been sports enthusiast"		P10: I would make something that the user could relate to herself, she has always been a sporty lady so I made lots of balls using the circles" P13: "...and it was written that she is basketball player, so I tried to show a basketball at the centre...."
"She is a school teacher"		P3: "teacher was something that came out to me first so I decided to go with teaching" P4: "being a teacher, I thought she should love to have kids around her... so I decided to show a classroom with lot of kids" P6: "what I made was I made clock, classroom so it shows that I am doing it for an education kind of thing"
"Suchitra enjoys reading and writing"		P6: For the teacher may be a simple design is what she might like, because that's how teachers are ... simple...quite.
"She is also interested in cooking"		P7: "she enjoying testing new recipes reinforced my idea of her being a creative lady" P8: "...as she enjoys cooking so I tried to make a chef's hat so that she could relate it to herself"

Graphical designs made by the participants in both the groups were also evaluated by three experts on the basis of "directness of illustration" of persona information into the designs. Scores obtained through experts rating were analyzed through two tailed t-test at 95% confidence interval. T-test results indicate that participants in control group (without empathy exercise) illustrated the information provided in persona more directly than the experiment group (with empathy exercise) ($f = 24.321$, $p < 0.01$). It is also evident from the boxplot (Figure 3) that median of control group is much higher than experiment group. This means that majority of the participants in control group illustrated the information provided in persona more directly than participants of experiment group. Therefore, a higher degree of directness of illustration of control group shows that novice designers in absence of empathy perform less cognitive actions as compared to the experiment group.

Table 3. Graphical illustrations by the participants (experiment group) along with verbal protocols

Phrases from persona	Examples from design solutions	Verbal Protocols from interview
"Pallavi is also passionate about travelling in general and off road biking in particular"		P38: "she is an adventurous lady, who is tough that's why I chose stronger lines in her design" P46: "rugged and bold design for her as she have a masculine personality"
"She is a dietitian and part time gym instructor" "had been sports enthusiast"		P47: I tried to show achievement in her design… she has been an achiever in her life" P39: "…to keep the design simple was the main idea as she would not want too many cluttered things in her design…" P49: "as she is more into sports, I tried to give the design a sporty look"
"She is a school teacher… she stays with her in laws…"		P26: "she is surrounded with lots of people in her life. I tried to show a sense of togetherness in the design" P29: "her life is mostly sorted; I gave more of a simplistic look to the design" P32: "as a teacher herself, she would love to keep things in order, I tried to show an order…an arranged pattern that I think she would like"
"Suchitra enjoys reading and writing"		P36: I think she is soft hearted, she reads much that means she can interpret meanings, I tried to make a flower, she would love flowers as I can guess from her nature". P37: "I thought that more fluidic, or soft or curvy design she would like… but with details"

Table 4. Results of t-test measuring directness of illustration

Groups	N	Mean	Std. Dev	Std Error Mean	F value	Sig.
Control Group	25	5.74	1.39	.246	24.321	0.001
Experiment Group	25	2.69	.811	.139		

CONCLUSION

While persona description has been known to aid the design thinking process, the design teams may not be using the persona effectively in design thinking process (Matthews, Judge, and Whittaker 2012). The way the designers empathize with persona to arrive at design solutions may be the reason for the non-effective use of persona in design thinking process. This chapter has argued for the role of empathizing with persona in design process and has reported an experiment to understand the influence of empathizing with persona in design thinking process. The design outcomes, verbal protocols and expert evaluations have together suggested that novice designers when using empathy exercise along with persona description were able to generate higher 'quality' of design thinking (more cognitive actions).

Figure 3. Overall comparison of directness of illustration scores

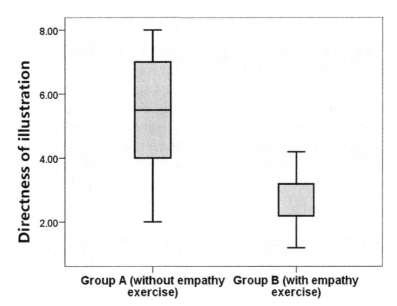

Figure 4. Persona wise comparison of directness of illustration scores

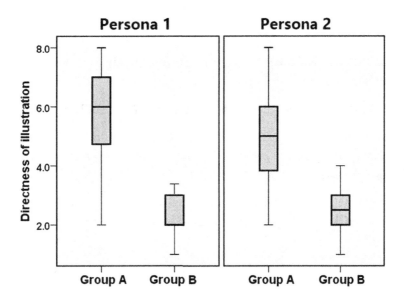

These observations were in line with another study presented by Dahiya & Kumar (2018) where novice designers were depicting the user information directly into their design solutions (Dahiya, A., & Kumar, J., 2018b). In light of above results from the experimental study reported in this chapter, it can be argued here that there is a need to train design teams in empathy exercises in order to effectively use the persona in a design process. This finding also implies that there is need to accommodate empathy exercises in the professional design practices along with user research and persona depictions.

LIMITATIONS AND FUTURE WORK

The present study was limited to analysis of design solutions on the basis of directness of illustration of user information on design solutions. Further studies studying design thinking can analyze other aspects of design thinking processes like creativity, novelty, fixation etc. which has not been studied in this exercise. Inclusion of other aspects of 'quality' of design thinking will create a more holistic framework to understand role of empathy in quality of design outcomes. Further, this study has reported effects of empathy exercise on design thinking. However, this research has not measured the degree of improvement of empathetic ability due to the empathy exercise on different designers. The present study is limited to observation of the effect of empathy on novice designers, further studies with professional designers may give useful benchmarks for comparison of design thinking and empathetic abilities.

REFERENCES

Ahmed, S., Wallace, K. M., & Blessing, L. T. (2003). *Understanding the differences between how novice and experienced designers approach design tasks.* Research in Engineering. doi:10.100700163-002-0023-z

Atman, C., Chimka, J., Bursic, K., & Nachtmann, H. (1999). A comparison of freshman and senior engineering design processes. *Design Studies*, *20*(2), 131–152. doi:10.1016/S0142-694X(98)00031-3

Battarbee, K., & Koskinen, I. (2005). Co-experience: User experience as interaction. *CoDesign*, *1*(1), 5–18. doi:10.1080/15710880412331289917

Bonnardel, N. (2000). Towards understanding and supporting creativity in design: Analogies in a constrained cognitive environment. *Knowledge-Based Systems*, *13*(7–8).

Buchanan, R. (1992). Wicked problems in design thinking. *Design Issues*, *8*(2), 5–21. doi:10.2307/1511637

Buchenau, M., & Suri, J. F. (2000, August). Experience prototyping. In *Proceedings of the 3rd conference on Designing interactive systems: processes, practices, methods, and techniques* (pp. 424-433). ACM. 10.1145/347642.347802

Caballero, L., Moreno, A. M., & Seffah, A. (2014). Persona as a Tool to Involving Human in Agile Methods: Contributions from HCI and Marketing. In Human-Centered Software Engineering (pp. 283–290). Springer Berlin Heidelberg.

Calde, S., Goodwin, K., & Reimann, R. (2002). SHS Orcas: the first integrated information system for long-term healthcare facility management. In Case studies of the CHI2002|AIGA Experience Design FORUM on - CHI '02 (pp. 2–16). AIGA. doi:10.1145/507752.507753

Cardoso, C., & Badke-Schaub, P. (2011). The Influence of Different Pictorial Representations During Idea Generation. *The Journal of Creative Behavior*, *45*(2), 130–146. doi:10.1002/j.2162-6057.2011.tb01092.x

Carroll, J. M. (2003). *HCI models, theories, and frameworks: Toward a multidisciplinary science.* Morgan Kaufmann.

Cooper, A. (1999). *The Inmates Are Running the Asylum: Why High-Tech Products Drive Us Crazy and How to Restore the Sanity.* Sams Publishing.

Corry, M. D., Frick, T. W., & Hansen, L. (1997). User-centered design and usability testing of a web site: An illustrative case study. *Educational Technology Research and Development*, *45*(4), 65–76. doi:10.1007/BF02299683

Cross, N. (2001). Design Cognition. In Design Knowing and Learning: Cognition in Design Education (pp. 79–103). Academic Press. doi:10.1016/B978-008043868-9/50005-X

Dahiya, A., & Kumar, J. (2018a). Do Design Outcomes Get Influenced by Type of User Data? An Experimental Study with Primary and Secondary User Research Data. In *International Conference on Human Systems Engineering and Design: Future Trends and Applications* (pp. 191-197). Springer.

Dahiya, A., & Kumar, J. (2018b). How empathizing with persona helps in design thinking: An experimental study with novice designers. *12th International Conference on Interfaces and Human Computer Interaction*.

Dominowski, R. L., & Dallob, P. (1995). Insight and Problem Solving. In R. Sternberg & J. Davidson (Eds.), *The nature of insight* (pp. 33–62). Cambridge, MA: MIT Press.

Gasparini, A. (2015). Perspective and use of empathy in design thinking. In *The Eight International Conference on Advances in Computer-Human Interactions* (pp. 49-54). ACHI.

Goel, V., & Pirolli, P. (1992). The structure of design problem spaces. *Cognitive Science*, *16*(3), 395–429. doi:10.120715516709cog1603_3

Goldschmidt, G. (1990). Linkography: assessing design productivity. In R. Trappl (Ed.), *Cyberbetics and System '90* (pp. 291–298). Singapore: World Scientific.

Grudin, J. (2006). Why personas work: The psychological evidence. *The Persona Lifecycle*, 642-663.

Hong, S. M. (2009). User Research and User Centered Design; Designing, Developing, and Commercializing Widget Service on Mobile Handset. In Human Centered Design (pp. 854–861). Academic Press.

Ickes, W. J. (Ed.). (1997). *Empathic accuracy*. Guilford Press.

Kavakli, M., & Gero, J. (2001). The Structure of concurrent cognitive actions: A case study of novice and expert designers. *Design Studies*.

Kim, E., & Kim, K. (2015). Cognitive styles in design problem solving: Insights from network-based cognitive maps. *Design Studies*, 40.

Köppen, E., & Meinel, C. (2015). Empathy via design thinking: creation of sense and knowledge. In *Design thinking research* (pp. 15–28). Cham: Springer.

Koskinen, I., Battarbee, K., & Mattelmäki, T. (2003). *Empathic design: User experience in product design*. IT Press.

Kouprie, M., & Visser, F. S. (2009). A framework for empathy in design: Stepping into and out of the user's life. *Journal of Engineering Design*, *20*(5), 437–448. doi:10.1080/09544820902875033

Landauer, T. K. (1988). Research Methods in Human-Computer Interaction. In Handbook of Human-Computer Interaction (pp. 905–928). Elsevier. doi:10.1016/B978-0-444-70536-5.50047-6

Leonard, D., & Rayport, J. F. (1997). Spark innovation through empathic design. *Harvard Business Review, 75*, 102–115. PMID:10174792

Long, F. (2009). Real or imaginary: The effectiveness of using personas in product design. In *Proceedings of the Irish Ergonomics Society Annual Conference* (vol. 14). Irish Ergonomics Society.

Lubart, T. I. (2001). Models of the creative process: Past, present and future. *Creativity Research Journal, 13*(3-4), 295–308. doi:10.1207/S15326934CRJ1334_07

Manning, H., Temkin, B., & Belanger, N. (2003). The power of design personas. *Forrester Research.* Retrieved from http://www.forrester.com/ER/Research/Report/0,1338,33033,00.html

Matthews, T., Judge, T., & Whittaker, S. (2012). How do designers and user experience professionals actually perceive and use personas? *Proceedings of the 2012 ACM annual conference on Human Factors in Computing Systems.* 10.1145/2207676.2208573

Miaskiewicz, T., & Kozar, K. A. (2011). Personas and user-centered design: How can personas benefit product design processes? *Design Studies, 32*(5), 417–430. doi:10.1016/j.destud.2011.03.003

Newell & Simon. (1988). The theory of human problem solving. *Readings in Cognitive Science*, 33–51.

Nielsen, J. (1994). *Usability Engineering*. Morgan Kaufmann.

Nielsen, L. (2013). *Personas - User Focused Design*. Springer London. doi:10.1007/978-1-4471-4084-9

Nielsen, L. (2018). Design personas- New ways, New contexts. *Persona Studies, 4*(2), 1–4.

Norman, D. A. (1988). *The Design of Everyday Things/Emotional Design/Design of Future Things*. Basic Books.

Plucker, J. A., Beghetto, R. A., & Dow, G. T. (2004). Why isn't creativity more important to educational psychologists? Potentials, pitfalls, and future directions in creativity research. *Educational Psychologist, 39*(2), 83–96. doi:10.120715326985ep3902_1

Pruitt, J. S., & Adlin, T. (2006). *The Persona Lifecycle*. Elsevier. doi:10.1016/B978-012566251-2/50003-4

Runco, M. A. (1995). Cognition and Creativity. *Contemporary Psychology, 44*(6), 554–555. doi:10.1037/002141

So, C., & Joo, J. (2017). Does a persona improve creativity? *The Design Journal, 20*(4), 459–475. doi:10.1080/14606925.2017.1319672

Steen, M., & Kuijt, L. (1988). *Early user involvement in research and design projects–A review of methods and practices*. Academic Press.

Suri, J. F. (2003). The experience of evolution: Developments in design practice. *The Design Journal, 6*(2), 39–48. doi:10.2752/146069203789355471

Tversky, B., & Suwa, M. (2009). Thinking with Sketches. In Tools for Innovation (pp. 75–84). Oxford University Press. doi:10.1093/acprof:oso/9780195381634.003.0004

Valkenburg, R., & Dorst, K. (1998). The reflective practice of design teams. *Design Studies*, *19*(3), 249–271. doi:10.1016/S0142-694X(98)00011-8

Van Someren, M. W., Barnard, Y. F., & Sandberg, J. A. C. (1994). *The think aloud method: a practical approach to modelling cognitive*. Academic Press.

Visser, F. S., Stappers, P. J., Van der Lugt, R., & Sanders, E. B. (2005). Context mapping: Experiences from practice. *CoDesign*, *1*(2), 119–149. doi:10.1080/15710880500135987

Vredenburg, K., Mao, J. Y., Smith, P. W., & Carey, T. (2002, April). A survey of user-centered design practice. In *Proceedings of the SIGCHI conference on Human factors in computing systems* (pp. 471-478). ACM.

Chapter 3
A Protocol for Reviewing Off–the–Shelf Games to Inform the Development of New Educational Games

Ruth Torres Castillo
New Mexico State University, USA

Sara Morales
New Mexico State University, USA

ABSTRACT

This chapter shares a protocol for reviewing games and documents the process in which it was used by an educational game design team for evaluating existing games to inform the design and development of new games for early algebra. While the design team has used their own learning games design model to develop several games—all of which included some kind of immersive learning and review activity— there has been no documentation provided on the specific processes used to review games as part of that immersion. Observations offer structured means for assessing existing games in a particular space and are thus valuable to identify how best to pursue the alignment of learning objectives with teaching content and game mechanics in the development of educational games.

INTRODUCTION

A number of design process models specify methods for developing educational games, highlighting unique design concerns in this space (Chamberlin et al, 2012; De Freitas and Neumann, 2009; De Freitas and Oliver, 2006; De Freitas and Routledge, 2013; Dormann and Biddle, 2008; Groff, J. et al, 2015; Gunter, G.A. et al, 2008; Kiili, K. et al, 2012; Mislevy and Haertel, 2006). In some of these models, a design step is to review existing games, not only to understand the market space, but also to identify design principles and good pedagogy (Chamberlin et al, 2012; De Freitas and Routledge, 2013; Dormann and Biddle, 2008). Existing game review models (Petri, G. et al, 2016; Lucero, A. et al, 2014; Sweetser

DOI: 10.4018/978-1-5225-9069-9.ch003

and Wyeth, 2005) evaluate games based on the player's experience, or analyze them from the perspective of a learning theory, such as flow (Csikszentmihalyi, 1996). While it is important to review games for design purposes, little information is given regarding the structure of the process and the ways this process differs from reviewing games for other reasons.

Game review is often a way to assess games for use in a classroom, curate a list of educational games, or identify what games are available in a content area for a certain age group. While it is important to review games to identify those that are of value for a specific type of player, it is also critical to review games as a way of identifying gaps in content and pedagogy. This type of game review can identify the need for new games, dictate what types of new games are needed, and might suggest ways in which games can present content in novel ways.

As part of a design process, the performance of game review serves another purpose when done collaboratively: it engages the design team in a deeper level of pedagogical understanding about the content and design of the games. Effective educational game design teams should represent diverse backgrounds and disciplines (Chamberlin et al, 2012), and it is important that all team members be well played (Being "well played" refers to game literacy, like being "well read": having a diverse knowledge and experience of playing games) (Davidson, 2009). Further, the process brings the team together in articulating a shared expertise vision for addressing game content, identifying valuable game mechanics, and deciding the best approaches for how a game should work. When interdisciplinary design teams review games with a variety of design lens, they: a) look at the overall quality of a game; b) identify gaps in content or pedagogical approach; c) continually reframe the problem; d) constantly question the underlying assumptions during the design process; and e) establish their own framework to guide the design of new games.

In this chapter, the authors contribute the description of a protocol for game review used to evaluate existing educational games to inform the development process of new mathematics games. In the present research, a design team at a non-profit, educational game studio is developing new games for early algebra. As part of their design process, the team reviewed games with related content (e.g., pre-algebra, algebra, patterns, ratios, properties, functions, expressions, equations), games for similar audiences (i.e., students in grades 4–6), and games with similar pedagogical approaches (i.e., inquiry-oriented problem solving). In the remainder of this chapter, the steps of the protocol are presented in the context of the team's learning approach and the game design model implemented in the research. Next, the outcomes from the group's review of the algebra games are tied as a discussion piece. The final section focuses on future work that the research team will work on. The authors expect this process to be valuable to other development teams as a structured way to review games with the purpose of informing their own design process.

BACKGROUND

The investigators have been developing multimedia-learning tools to enhance mathematics learning for more than 15 years. The research team is in the process of designing a new suite of games to enhance early algebra learning. The learning goals include the following mathematics topics: patterns, relationships between quantities, and expressions. The present research is grounded in constructivist learning principles for building knowledge and uses human-centered design to develop the games.

The team aims to connect the affordances (see definitions section) of games for learning to what they know about how people learn (Donovan et al, 1999) and how teachers can stimulate that learning through inquiry-based practices (Edelson, 2001; Gonzalez, 2013). The main goal of the design team is to develop products that use innovative design and pedagogical skills to build in depth knowledge of specific content.

The research team, which includes math educators, game designers, instructional designers, and mathematicians, prioritizes an inquiry-oriented approach to learning mathematics, which is based on constructivist principles (Edelson, 2001) as well as knowledge building (Scardamalia and Bereiter, 2008). Keeping the principle that knowledge should be constructed by the learner, rather than transmitted; the design team intends to provide games in which mathematical concepts are learned as a natural means to a strategic end.

The fundamental scheme for the team's mathematics education research and game production work is to base development of learning resources on documented gaps in mathematics content and pedagogy for which digital games and inquiry could be useful. Thus, this design team focused on design research that produces a contribution of knowledge (Zimmerman et al, 2007).

Effectiveness of Games in Mathematics Learning

Game use in the mathematics classroom has played an important role as a new learning strategy, providing teachers and students with more options and flexibility in their teaching practices. Thus, the use of games requires the development of specific strategies and game design mechanics to engage in the learning practice. Once engaged, learning takes place naturally within the storyline of a well-designed game (Shute, 2011).

Current theory-based pedagogy supports metaphors that consider the *construction* of knowledge rather than the *transmission* (Greeno, Collins, & Resnick, 1996; Van Meter & Stevens, 2000). The development resources in this research, connect all of these theories by developing engaging games with additional inquiry-based hands-on and socially mediated activities in classrooms that provide further applications of concepts first introduced in games. Additionally, games in mathematics offer multiple approaches to solving problems.

General Game Design Models

Critical to the design process is contributing new opportunities to learn content, rather than replicating existing tools or games. Educational game designers need an understanding of how to create games that enable interaction, provide ongoing feedback, grab and sustain attention, and have appropriate levels of challenge (Gee, 2003; Malone, 1981; Paras, 2005; Schell, 2014).

Research in game development includes different models of educational game design (e.g., Learning Games Design Model (LGDM) (Chamberlin et al, 2012); Exploratory Learning Model (ELM) (De Freitas and Neumann, 2009); Four Dimensional Framework (4DF) (De Freitas and Oliver, 2006; Groff et al, 2015); E-Leadership and Soft Skills Educational games design model (ELESS) (De Freitas and Routledge, 2013); affective walkthrough model (Dormann and Biddle, 2008); Relevance Embedding Translation Adaptation Immersion and Naturalization model (RETAIN) (Gunter et al, 2008); flow experience framework (Kiili et al, 2012); and Evidence-Centered Design (ECD) (Mislevy and Haertel, 2006).

Some studies on game design models, which provide attention to assessing existing games, offer insight to the research community on the value of game review as part of the design process. For instance, Dormann et al. (2008) outline an approach to designing games especially for affective learning, by identifying the key principles, creating a repository of effective learning game patterns, and using methods to contextualize gameplay. De Freitas et al. (2013) add the ELESS model for designing by analyzing game environments for leadership and soft skills. The LGDM (Chamberlin et al, 2012) encourages research in identifying existing tools before developing a new game, and brings team members with diverse expertise to the design table.

The three game design models mentioned above encourage reviewing games as a main step of the design process, yet there are no specifications on how to review a game, nor recommended processes for design teams to use in the reviewing process.

General Game Review Models

Some models do exist for reviewing games toward different analytical ends. These models – the Model for the Evaluation of Educational Games (MEEGA) (Petri et al, 2016); Playful Experiences (PLEX) framework (Lucero et al, 2014); and the GameFlow model (Sweetser and Wyeth, 2005) – generally address player experience and enjoyment in gameplay.

Savi and Ulbricht (2008) defined a quality educational game when pointing to the MEEGA framework (Petri et al, 2016) as a tool for evaluating software designed to teach computing engineering. The model compares stated objectives of the software to the experience of the learner and perceptions of learning. The PLEX framework is designed to evaluate general games, not necessarily educational or serious games. It is a categorization of playful experiences based on previous theoretical work on pleasure, game experiences, emotions, elements of play, and the reasons why people play (Lucero et al, 2014). The GameFlow model (Sweetser and Wyeth, 2005) consists of eight elements – concentration, challenge, skills, controls, clear goals, feedback, immersion, and social interaction – used to review and understand how players achieve enjoyment in games. These criteria are a useful tool to develop a concrete understanding of what constitutes good design and what issues affect player enjoyment in real-time strategy games.

The Content and Pedagogy Gaps From Game Review Models

Despite the success of the existing review models, game development teams with pedagogical needs and motivations in reviewing games as part of the design process may need different approaches to support their aims. For example, the review process for mathematics games should identify gaps regarding games of the proper content, as well as the quality of games and the approaches that are used to teach the content.

When reviewing off-the-shelf games, the research team noticed specific necessities that its interdisciplinary crew has identified as essential for learning mathematics through the use of games. Based on each person's expertise the reviewing protocol yielded questions about the overall high quality of games. These questions were the starting point for the presented protocol and will be describe in further detail subsequent sections.

The Research Team Defined Learning Games Design Model (LGDM)

The team had been implementing the LGDM (Chamberlin et al, 2012) to develop educational games over the past 5 years. The model facilitates collaboration between the development team, content experts and final clients. The combination of diverse perspectives provides the deep knowledge needed to build learning games.

The implementation of the LGDM involves all of the design team in asking guiding questions about the proposed design, reflecting on expected evidence of learning, and brainstorming engaging and meaningful learning experiences. Production continues through an iterative process, brainstorming, developing, testing with learners and teachers, and revising until a full working prototype is available. The resulting games reflect the team's conceptual framework for how games lead to learning.

Using the LGDM, game designers work with content specialists to articulate educational learning goals, identify the types of activities that move players through those goals, and then use game mechanics to engage players in those activities. The LGDM includes three phases: Pre-Development, Development, and Final Stage. Figure 1 shows the initial Pre-Development phase, as it relates to the steps of this research. Remaining phases can be referenced from the model authors' paper (Chamberlin et al, 2012).

Pre-Development Phase of the LGDM

During the Pre-Development phase of the LGDM, the client and the development team establish the learning objectives of the game as the first step. Then, all team members are engaged in understanding the educational content to be produced, the traditional approaches that are used to teach that content, and the learning problems that students usually encounter when learning the content area. To develop a better understanding of the content and how the game mechanics can be integrated into it, the team is involved in an immersion step.

During the immersion step of this phase, the team engages themselves in the world of the game player. This involves reviewing the ways in which content is currently taught to the audience and how games and other technologies address the content or meet other needs of the audience. It is during this phase that the reviewing of games, the focus of the present document, takes place. Evaluating existing games helps the design team understand the different ways that content can be transmitted to the players effectively or not.

After the immersion step, the development team members collaborate in discussion meetings to brainstorm, share knowledge, redefine objectives, and prepare design documents and prototypes for the anticipated product. They may re-frame the initial ideas about how the final game will look and what game mechanics would take the game to the final stage.

MAIN FOCUS OF THE CHAPTER

The 5-Step Protocol to Review Games Designed by the Research Team

The established protocol includes five steps through which different team members identify the criteria they will use to review and narrow the breadth of games, ultimately reviewing the most valuable games

Figure 1. The first phase of the Learning Games Design Model (LGDM). After the team works together to define what is going to be learned by the game and how is it going to be demonstrated, the Pre-Development phase concludes with brainstorming ideas of possible game options and characteristics that will meet the learning outcomes. Figure adapted from (Chamberlin et al, 2012), ©2012, IGI Global. Used with permission of the publisher and authors.

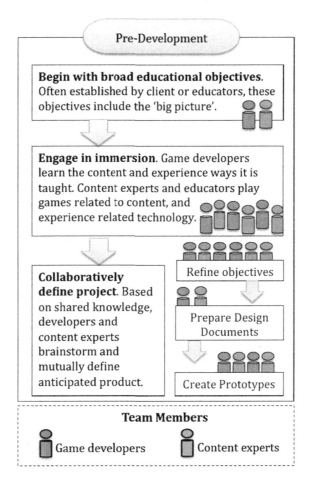

as a team. In the LGDM, this game review would take place during the Pre-Development phase, working with a proposed game that has established learning goals.

Step 1: *Establish Quality Criteria in Content Area.* It is important to define specific criteria to look for within a game to assess the proposed learning goals. Content areas are different among them, and so too are their quality criteria. The criteria can be established based on the learning objectives, the gameplay objectives, or the general goals for the game. The establishment of these criteria is a landmark and serves to identify content and pedagogy gaps that new development should address. The quality criteria could also evolve around guiding questions that the team has agreed upon (e.g.) a) What do all selected games have in common? b) What is easily adaptable to our own games? c) What does not relate to our learning objectives or is not needed? d) What needs to be modified to better fit the new game? e) How can our team of designers enhance the good qualities of the reviewed games? f) What are the limitations for the newly develop game?)

Step 2: *Identify Existing Games.* The next step is to identify games and/or apps that introduce or teach the same content area of development, utilize a similar learning pedagogy, and/or use similar game mechanics as the proposed game. Doing this comprehensive search can take an extensive amount of time. Its feasible scope may differ for each development team, depending on the hours designated for this work, the number of people assigned to it, and a team's access to resources.

Step 3: *Play Identified Games, Measure Criteria.* Once quality criteria are established, along with an identified corpus of games, team members should play the games and rate them according to the criteria. Because the corpus is likely large, this is a distributed task, with team members delegated to play certain games. Ideally, multiple team members play each game, but, depending on the size of the corpus and team, this may not be possible. It is worth noting that each game can take one or more hours to play through sufficiently to judge – and that team members have tasks other than gameplay.

Step 4: *Refine Game Selection.* Results from Step 3 feed into Step 4 to enable the team to refine the game selection, focusing on the games that best fit the criteria. The team should then focus on the best-rated games, which need to be re-distributed. At this point, all team members should play a subset of the top-rated games. It is worth noting, again, that this process is time-consuming, since each game likely needs at least one person-hour for assessment.

Step 5: *Review Top-Rated Games as a Team.* Once the top-rated games have been played by the team, it is possible to engage in team discussion about them. This gives the team the opportunity to deeply discuss the features of those games and how they should relate to the proposed game.

How an Interdisciplinary Development Team Applied the 5-Step Protocol

In the implementation presented in this section, the research team was aiming to develop new early algebra education games. The team consisted of two mathematicians, two math educators, three educational researchers, one learning scientist, one instructional designer, and three game developers. The proposed project would develop a suite of games and teaching resources for 4th-6th graders in those areas which mathematics education research suggests are critical for gaining foundations for later formal algebra: understanding patterns and relationships between quantities; properties of operations; and expressions. All developed products would be grounded at the early levels in numerical and visual environments and move toward more abstract and symbolic understanding as students advance in their game play. The proposed products would not be the drill and practice products or illustrated lectures found in many mathematics tools; these products would provide structured and interactive learning environments that facilitate inquiry-led exploration.

An in depth description of how the research team applied the 5-step protocol is following. Particular focus is given to steps 1 and 5 of this protocol, as these seem to bring new insights to the development process.

Step 1: The whole design team identified areas for quality criteria in the content area of early algebra. The research team aimed to identify:

a. Games that taught the same content as the proposed games (pre-algebra, algebra, patterns, properties, functions, expressions and equations)
b. Games that had the same pedagogical approach (inquiry based learning reflecting a constructivist framework), and
c. Game mechanics that lend themselves to learning (exploration versus simple practice).

The full integration of the interdisciplinary team in the process provided the opportunity to incorporate three core lenses (content, pedagogy, and game mechanics) in the development of a better game (see Figure 2).

Based on findings from their previous developments, the design team identified seven principles of game characteristics that demonstrate a connection to mathematics learning. These characteristics proved to be successful for making connections to math learning during the first developed suit of games. Since the same conceptual framework is being utilized in the new development for pre algebra games, the research team decided that these seven principles were required for the new game to be considered high quality. Table 1 describes the established criteria to evaluate games vis-a-vis these principles. As it can be noted, the seven principles integrate the three lenses that the experts in the team will focus on. Embedded vocabulary and multiple representations were targets for content. The inquiry-based approach and easy entry high ceiling as well as external resources were part of the pedagogical lens. Immediate feedback and limited instructions were part of what game mechanics support in games.

Step 2: To identify existing games, the design team asked eight graduate students from a Technology and Critical Thinking class, two research assistants, and two faculty members from the College of

Figure 2. The team should review games that are similar to the game they wish to create. This includes games that are similar in content, pedagogical approach, or have game mechanics that match the proposed game.

Connection of three lenses to consider in game review

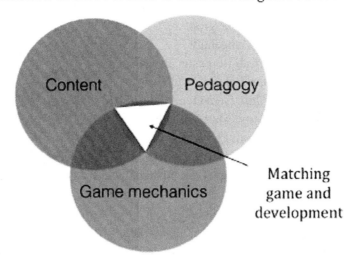

Table 1. Seven Principles: Characteristics used to evaluate educational games. Experience from previous development demonstrated that implementing these criteria into games will led to effective development of mathematic skills in the player. Factor G was rarely encountered in the evaluated games, but its implementation can enhance the acquired learning strategies.

A) an inquiry-based approach in learning
B) an embedded vocabulary
C) multiple representations of numbers and operations
D) easy entry to play, high ceiling to mastery
E) limited "instruction"
F) immediate and helpful feedback
G) resources to expand learning from game to other learning environments

Education to look for commercial off-the-shelf algebra games that appeared relevant to this project. The graduate students group identified 25 algebra games from multiple sources (Appendix).

Step 3: As the next step, the research team tasked the graduate students with playing the 25 algebra games and at the same time to evaluate each game using the specific criteria (Table 1). To review the collection of 25 games against the criteria previously established by the team, researchers created an adherence measure where each player could rank the characteristics of each game on a Likert scale from 1 (not present) to 5 (highly prevalent). The questions assessed each of the characteristics described in Table 1 in each game (item G was excluded because it was rarely encountered). Results from this Adherence Likert scale will be later shared in the discussion section.

Step 4: To fully immerse the math educators, researchers, and designers in the Pre-Development phase, the team refined the list of games to the top nine based on survey scores and planned a second analysis of them. These top nine games either scored well in their initial rubric, or the research team noticed there was something particularly valuable about that game based on her/his deep domain knowledge. The games that were chosen for a second revision were:

a. *DragonBox Algebra 5+* from WeWantToKnow AS
b. *Lure of the Labyrinth* from Learning Games to Go (LG2G) project
c. *Algebra Puzzle* from Math Playground
d. *Algebra Meltdown* from Mangahigh
e. *Hands on Equations 1* from Borenson and Associates
f. *Furry Math Friends* from Johannes Metzler
g. *Agent X: Algebra and Math* from Overpass Limited
h. *The Factor Tree Game* from Math Goodies
i. *Math Planet Grade 5+* from Playpower Labs

Step 5: After narrowing the selection to the 9 top rated-games, the development team focused the discussion using the three lenses of expertise: mathematicians assessing content; educators focusing on pedagogy; developers paying attention to game mechanics. From this conversation, the three mathematical key concepts that would be included in the games were finalized. With the help of the research team, a set of questions was agreed upon to guide the development of the new game aligned to variables, expressions and patterns. Table 2 documents these questions. These guiding questions were at the forefront of every discussion related to decisions about the new game.

It is important to note that when the team was playing the top rated games each expert will look at different features mostly related to their field of expertise. For example mathematicians will not pay attention to graphics but will pay attention to what type of mathematics is being addressed. Mathematics experts will also pay attention to whether or not the math is too easy or difficult for students. The education experts will notice what types of strategies are being used to teach that content. A graphic designer will mainly focus on the transitioning from level to level. The educators focused on the learning targets being addressed by both the game and the mathematics. Even when each expert will focus on specific points, the combination of the multiple perspectives is what produces a high quality educational game. To take advantage of each member's expertise, the team's engagement in a deep discussion about the features of the top rated games was a critical point. Resulting questions from this discussion (Table 2) are examples of specific contributions to post-production stages of the game design process. As every design team may have different requirements, the list of guiding questions described in Table 2, as well as the answers to them, may vary in importance and flexibility from team to team. Furthermore, these are only some guiding questions that can lead to further and deeper discussion.

DISCUSSION

Analysis of the initial evaluation results yielded some assumptions about the state of art of the reviewed off-the-shelf algebra games. Some findings showed differences between evaluated games and the desired constructivist approach, in areas prioritized by the design team, particularly related to mathematic pedagogy. These differences included:

Table 2. New design questions that will be applied in future work to evaluate games. After a rich discussion, the design team developed this set of questions, planning to use them as guidance. These questions can also be used to establish new criteria for the quality of games.

How does the game visually represent the content?
Does it have none, some, or too many instructions at the beginning?
Can the player skip levels in order to move ahead?
Can there be different correct answers or ways to solve the game?
Does the game offer feedback when you succeeded or failed?
Does the player recognize she/he is learning while playing?
Does the game have an easy entry and scaffold the learning?
Does the game offer extra support material besides just playing?
Can the game be played using different capabilities of a device?
Can the player track her/his progress?

1. The game did not offer the player enough exposure to mathematics vocabulary (low rating for characteristic B);
2. Many games lacked multiple representations (characteristic C), using simple text representations of numbers and operations without a visualization;
3. Games did not provide problems that could be solved in multiple ways, requiring players to accomplish tasks in exactly one specific way (characteristic C);
4. The game consists of a typical drill and practice experience (characteristic A);
5. The game uses typical pedagogical approaches, as it offered more of a quiz and reward structure;
6. Very few games gave some kind of explanation at the end as to why or what are you doing (characteristic F) only one game introduces the player into the concepts with an inquiry-based approach in learning by solving equations balancing the number of objects on each side of the game screen.

Final results from the Adherence Likert scale (from Step 3) showed that most of the games demonstrated incorporation of good strategies in teaching content through game design: characteristics A, D, E, and F. Two main characteristics scored low among all of the games: B and C. Figure 3 presents the scores from the adherence measure.

The cross-disciplinary team involvement proved true during the review progress. When content experts, game designers and educators were all involved in reviewing the games, the resulting discussion was richer because of the multiple perspectives on why a game was valuable or not. All design team members were immersed in the content, pedagogy and game mechanics useful for encouraging learning in pre algebra. Some of the findings from this discussion were:

Figure 3. Prevalence of the six used characteristics (Table 1) across all games. The deficiency of adherence of games to specific criteria shows the gaps in content and pedagogy from the evaluated games. The graph demonstrates which criteria measured low among all games –Embedded vocabulary and Multiple representation.

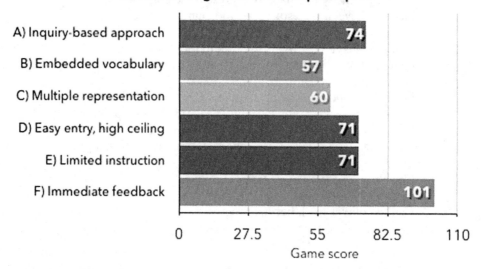

Content as a Major Factor

The *DragonBox* games showed the greatest similarity to content proposed in the new game design. *DragonBox* 5+, for children 5 to 10 years, and *DragonBox* 12+, for children 9 years and older, incorporated important algebra concepts such as addition, division, and multiplication of numbers and variables integrated by multiple visual forms of representation. The games also gave some kind of explanation at the end as to why or what are you doing (see Figure 4). They also introduce the player into the concept of solving equations by balancing the number of objects on each side of the game screen. Figure 5 shows a screen shot of how the game represents balanced equations.

Pedagogy as a Major Factor

After reviewing a different game than *DragonBox*, the team found they disagreed with the pedagogical approach of the game, as it offered more of a quiz and reward structure. This game destroys the physical obstacles presented to the main character depending on the correct answer for a question, and placed a time-limit on giving the answer. From the team's perspective, this meant that the lack of knowledge is a punishment for the player. In addition, simple rewards were brought for providing the correct answer. For instance, clicking on the box containing the correct value of x in the equation $-4 + x = -7$, will delete one of the many obstacles that block a pathway to walk. Again from the team's perspective, it did not provide a context in which the learning was meaningful to the student or in which the content was applied in a way beyond "solving the math problem." This game brought important discussion to the

Figure 4. DragonBox feedback. After a level is finished, the game offers a feedback screen describing what the players have done to gain the star scores. This feedback reminds the players about the core moves that are expected to be performed by them.

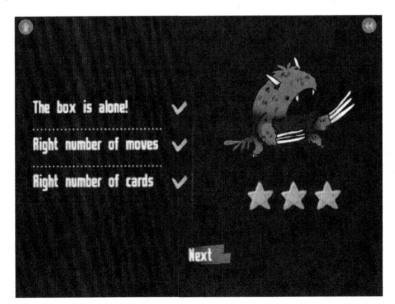

Figure 5. DragonBox content-based design. A split-screen game mechanic is used to represent balancing equations. After the player makes a certain number of moves, the left side of the screen is similar or has the same amount of objects than the right side. There are different ways to balance the equation, in this case dragging two same objects together or dividing by the same object will destroy both of them.

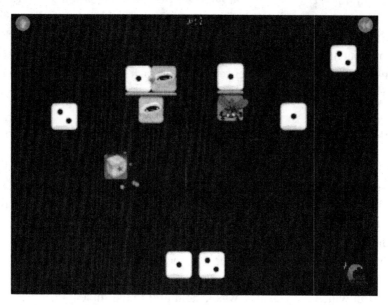

design team, in seeking to change the common "solve for *x*" approach to algebra, and led the team to understand new ways to help the learner see the meaning behind variables, rather than just the process for solving the equations.

Game Mechanics as a Major Factor

Though the initial review process was completed at the beginning of the design process, the team continues to engage in design and production of the games even after the pre-development phase. Because the team had common experiences in reviewing this core group of games, they have a valuable frame of reference (future design questions output from step 5) for discussing other games during the rest of the development process. As the team continues the progress on developing two early algebra games (one is a creation game where players collect different items and build a scene, the other a problem-solving puzzle game), they frequently reference specific items (Table 2) from the games they reviewed, and point one another to new games. Because the game mechanics to be used in a game are not entirely clear during the early design process, it is important to note that the game review process must continue during development. To this end, the design team must be encouraged to play games regularly and share games they have found with each other. This design team has iPads (so that they share a common game platform) and hold weekly gameplay sessions. They are encouraged to share apps and games with each other, and are given the opportunity to purchase apps to see different mechanics. While the initial review of games shaped the specific content and pedagogical approach of the games in development, the continuing review extends the understanding of how different game mechanics work effectively.

FUTURE RESEARCH DIRECTIONS

After this stage of the development process, the research team will continue working on building supplemental activities that support the new games. These supporting materials are usually hands on activities that accompany a lesson plan. To design engaging activities, the research team needs to look for and evaluate paper-based game-related tasks that teachers can integrate while games are being implemented in the classroom. The presented protocol can be utilized as the basis for this new evaluation stage of the project.

When testing the games and the supplemental activities in the classroom, the research team can also utilize some steps from this protocol. From the different game play and testing sessions, embedded data is going to be captured. Once enough data has been collected, the team will need to analyze and evaluate the different outcomes from these sessions. By revisiting step 1: *Establish Quality Criteria in Content Area* and step 5: *Review Top-Rated Games as a Team*, the team can compare the outcomes from the developed and tested games with the initially established learning goals and quality criteria, to make sure that the developed products are targeting the project goals.

CONCLUSION

While the core team had been working collaboratively on mathematic games for several years, newer members had not worked through the process and did not fully understand some of the specifics related to learning theory and mathematics content. This process of early exploration of algebra games yielded two potential benefits for the game design team presented in this observation: (1) content and information useful for game development, and (2) a process for reviewing games in terms of content, pedagogy and game mechanics gaps. For game designers, this protocol was helpful to review their framework and see the gaps among existing games. The process helped new members of the project to understand how games meet the design team's goals in different ways. By reviewing existing games, the investigators were better able to understand the team's pedagogical approach to games. In addition, the team was collaboratively immersed in the design and development process of the newly proposed games. This process suggested the protocol for game review as an effective model to inform the design of a game development project among a multidisciplinary research team.

ACKNOWLEDGMENT

Math Snacks materials were developed with support from the National Science Foundation (1503507). Any opinions, findings, and conclusions or recommendations expressed in this material are those of the author(s) and do not necessarily reflect the views of the National Science Foundation. Principal investigators for the Math Snacks project include: Wanda Bulger-Tamez, PhD STEM Outreach Director, College of Education; Theodore B. Stanford, PhD Associate Professor, College of Arts and Sciences; and Barbara Chamberlin, PhD Extension Instructional Design & Educational Media Specialist, Associate Professor Educational Media Productions.

REFERENCES

Chamberlin, B., Trespalacios, J., & Gallagher, R. (2012). The learning games design model: Immersion, collaboration, and outcomes-driven development. *International Journal of Game-Based Learning, 2*(3), 87–110. doi:10.4018/ijgbl.2012070106

Csikszentmihalyi, M. (1996). *Flow: Creativity and the psychology of discovery and invention.* Academic Press.

Davidson, D. (Ed.). (2009). Well Played 1.0: video games, value and meaning. Lulu.com.

De Freitas, S., & Neumann, T. (2009). The use of 'exploratory learning' for supporting immersive learning in virtual environments. *Computers & Education, 52*(2), 343–352. doi:10.1016/j.compedu.2008.09.010

De Freitas, S., & Oliver, M. (2006). How can exploratory learning with games and simulations within the curriculum be most effectively evaluated? *Computers & Education, 46*(3), 249–264. doi:10.1016/j.compedu.2005.11.007

De Freitas, S., & Routledge, H. (2013). Designing leadership and soft skills in educational games: The e-leadership and soft skills educational games design model (ELESS). *British Journal of Educational Technology, 44*(6), 951–968. doi:10.1111/bjet.12034

Donovan, M. S., Bransford, J. D., & Pellegrino, J. W. (1999). How people learn. Academic Press.

Dormann, C., & Biddle, R. (2008), November. Understanding game design for affective learning. In *Proceedings of the 2008 Conference on Future Play: Research, Play, Share* (pp. 41-48). ACM.

Edelson, D. C. (2001). Learning-for-use: A framework for the design of technology-supported inquiry activities. *Journal of Research in Science Teaching, 38*(3), 355–385. doi:10.1002/1098-2736(200103)38:3<355::AID-TEA1010>3.0.CO;2-M

Gee, J. P. (2003). What video games have to teach us about learning and literacy. *Computers in Entertainment, 1*(1), 20–20. doi:10.1145/950566.950595

Gonzalez, J. J. (2013). My Journey With Inquiry-Based Learning. *Journal on Excellence in College Teaching, 24*(2).

Greeno, J. G., Collins, A. M., & Resnick, L. B. (1996). Cognition and learning. Handbook of Educational Psychology, 77, 15-46.

Groff, J., Clarke-Midura, J., Owen, V. E., Rosenheck, L., Beall, M. (2015). *Better learning in games: A balanced design lens for a new generation of learning games.* Academic Press.

Gunter, G. A., Kenny, R. F., & Vick, E. H. (2008). Taking educational games seriously: Using the RETAIN model to design endogenous fantasy into standalone educational games. *Educational Technology Research and Development, 56*(5-6), 511–537. doi:10.100711423-007-9073-2

Kiili, K., De Freitas, S., Arnab, S., & Lainema, T. (2012). The design principles for flow experience in educational games. *Procedia Computer Science, 15*, 78–91. doi:10.1016/j.procs.2012.10.060

Lucero, A., Karapanos, E., Arrasvuori, J., & Korhonen, H. (2014). Playful or gameful?: creating delightful user experiences. *Interactions, 21*(3), 34-39.

Malone, T. W. (1981). Toward a theory of intrinsically motivating instruction. *Cognitive Science, 5*(4), 333–369. doi:10.120715516709cog0504_2

Mislevy, R. J., & Haertel, G. D. (2006). Implications of evidence-centered design for educational testing. *Educational Measurement: Issues and Practice, 25*(4), 6–20. doi:10.1111/j.1745-3992.2006.00075.x

Paras, B. (2005). *Game, motivation, and effective learning: An integrated model for educational game design.* Academic Press.

Petri, G., Von Wangenheim, C. G., & Borgatto, A. F. (2016). MEEGA+: an evolution of a model for the evaluation of educational games. *INCoD/GQS, 3*.

Savi, R., & Ulbricht, V.R. (2008). Educational games: benefits and challenges. *Revista Novas Tecnologias na Educação–Renote, 6*.

Scardamalia, M., & Bereiter, C. (2008). Pedagogical biases in educational technologies. *Educational Technology*, 3–11.

Schell, J. (2014). *The Art of Game Design: A book of lenses.* AK Peters/CRC Press.

Shute, V. J. (2011). Stealth assessment in computer-based games to support learning. *Computer Games and Instruction, 55*(2), 503-524.

Sweetser, P., & Wyeth, P. (2005). GameFlow: A model for evaluating player enjoyment in games. *Computers in Entertainment, 3*(3), 3–3. doi:10.1145/1077246.1077253

Van Meter, P., & Stevens, R. J. (2000). The role of theory in the study of peer collaboration. *Journal of Experimental Education, 69*(1), 113–127. doi:10.1080/00220970009600652

Zimmerman, J., Forlizzi, J., & Evenson, S. (2007, April). Research through design as a method for interaction design research in HCI. In *Proceedings of the SIGCHI conference on Human factors in computing systems* (pp. 493-502). ACM. 10.1145/1240624.1240704

KEY TERMS AND DEFINITIONS

Affordances: The qualities or properties of a game/tool that define its use or purpose as they are perceived on the way users see and experience the game/tool.

Content Expert: A person with special knowledge or skills in a particular subject area or learning topic who informs content and pedagogical decisions during research and development.

Game Artist: A person with art training who creates art for games.

Game Designer: A person who oversees the production of tools, guides formative product testing and leads the design process. Often a game designer is also its developer (as is the case for this study), so may be referred to as a game developer.

Game Developer: A person who fleshes out the details of a game's design, oversees its testing, and revises the game in response to player feedback.

Researcher: A person, who performs systematic investigation, oversees internal research and often serves as lead author on reports and articles. This person will also direct development of instruments and lead validation of research.

Embedded Data: Any gameplay information that would likely be recorded through logging systems.

APPENDIX

This appendix denotes the list of games that were evaluated in the first steps of the process.

1. Barron's Educational Series Inc. Mobile. 2011. *Painless Pre-algebra challenge.* Game [iOS]. (2011). Barron's Educational Series Inc., Hauppauge, NY. Retrieved from: https://itunes.apple.com/us/app/painless-pre-algebra-challenge/id449448476?mt=8.
2. Blue Duck Education Ltd. 2012. *Algebra Meltdown.* Online game [FLASH]. (2012). Blue Duck Education Ltd., London, England. Retrieved from: https://www.mangahigh.com/en-us/games/algebrameltdown.
3. Borenson and Associates, Inc. 2013. *Hands on Equations 1.* Game [iOS & Android]. (2013). Borenson and Associates, Inc., Allentown, PA. Retrieved from:http://www.borenson.com/tabid/1594/Default.aspx.
4. Brian West. 2012. *Algebra Champ.* Game [iOS]. (2012). Brian West. Retrieved from: https://itunes.apple.com/us/app/algebra-champ/id398873050?mt=8.
5. CYBERCHASE. 2015. *Stop the machine.* Online game [FLASH]. (2015). CYBERCHASE, Public Broadcasting Service. Retrieved from: http://pbskids.org/cyberchase/math-games/stop-machine/.
6. Doina Popovici. 2008. *One Step Equation Game.* Online Game [FLASH]. (2008). Math-play. Retrieved from: http://www.math-play.com/One-Step-Equation-Game.html.
7. Doina Popovici. 2010. *Math Racing - Subtracting Integers Game.* Online Game [FLASH]. (2010). Math-play. Retrieved from: http://www.math-play.com/math-racing-subtracting-integers-game/math-racing-subtracting-integers-game.html.
8. Futonge Nzembayie Kisito. 2011. *Algebraic Expression Football Game.* Online Game [FLASH]. (2011). Algebra4children. Retrieved from: http://www.algebra4children.com/Games/games-2/Algebraic-expressions/football-algebraic_expressions.html.
9. Gabriele Cirulli. 2014. *2048.* Online Game [FLASH]. (2014). Coolmath-games, New York, NY. Retrieved from: http://www.coolmath-games.com/0-2048.
10. Gisele Glosser. 2014. *Prime Factors Game.* Online game [FLASH]. (2014). Math Goodies, Colchester, CT. Retrieved from: http://www.mathgoodies.com/factors/prime_factors.html.
11. Hotmath. 2000. *Algebra vs the Cockroaches.* Online Game [FLASH]. (2000). Hotmath, Kensington, CA. Retrieved from: http://hotmath.com/hotmath_help/games/kp/kp_hotmath_sound.swf.
12. Johannes Metzler. 2013. *Furry math friends.* Game [iOS]. (2013). Johannes Metzler. Retrieved from: https://itunes.apple.com/app/furry-math-friends-mathematics/id742285981?mt=8.
13. Math Advantage. 2014a. *Algebra Puzzle* . Online Game [FLASH]. (2014). MathPlayground, Wellesley, MA. Retrieved from: http://www.mathplayground.com/algebra_puzzle.html.
14. Math Advantage. 2014b. *Algebraic Reasoning.* Online Game [FLASH]. (2014). MathPlayground, Wellesley, MA. Retrieved from: http://www.mathplayground.com/algebraic_reasoning.html.
15. Math Advantage. 2014c. *Otter Rush.* Online Game [FLASH]. (2014). MathPlayground, Wellesley, MA. Retrieved from: http://www.mathplayground.com/ASB_Otter_Rush.html.
16. MathNook. 2014. *Math Tank Run.* Online Game [FLASH]. (2014). MathNook, Spring, TX. Retrieved from: http://www.mathnook.com/math/math-tank-run-algebra.html

17. MIT Educational Arcade. 2015. *Lure of the Labyrinth*. Online Game [FLASH]. (2015). MIT Educational Arcade, Cambridge, Massachusetts. Retrieved from: http://labyrinth.thinkport.org/www/index.php.

18. Monterey Institute for Technology and Education. 2003. *HippoCampus*. Web page [FLASH]. (2003). Monterey Institute for Technology and Education, Marina, CA. Retrieved from: http://www.hippocampus.org/HippoCampus/.

19. Overpass Limited. 2014. *Agent X: Algebra & Math*. Game [iOS]. (2014). Overpass Limited, Oxfordshire, United Kingdom. Retrieved from: https://itunes.apple.com/us/app/agent-x-stop-rogue-agent-by/id693048176?mt=8.

20. Paw Apps LLC. 2011. *Math Overflow*. Game [iOS]. (2011). Paw Apps LLC. Retrieved from: https://itunes.apple.com/us/app/math-overflow/id482486011?mt=8.

21. Playpower Labs LLC. 2015. *5th Grade Math Planet*. Game [iOS]. (2015). Playpower Labs LLC. Retrieved from: https://itunes.apple.com/us/app/5th-grade-math-planet-fun/id892208395?mt=8.

22. Softschools. 2005. *Absolute Value Equation*. Online Game [FLASH]. (2005). Softschools. Retrieved from: http://www.softschools.com/math/absolute_value/equations/.

23. Sulan Dun. 2006. *Line Gem 1*. Online Game [FLASH]. (2006). FunBased Learning. Retrieved from: http://funbasedlearning.com/algebra/graphing/lines/default.htm.

24. Tardent Apps Inc. 2016. *Algebra Game with Linear Equations*. Game [iOS]. (2016). Tardent Apps Inc. Retrieved from: https://itunes.apple.com/us/app/algebra-game-linear-equations/id904192350?mt=8.

25. WeWantToKnow AS. 2013. *DragonBox Algebra 5+*. Game [iOS]. (2013). WeWantToKnow AS, Olso, Norway. Retrieved from: http://dragonbox.com/algebra#5.

Chapter 4
Surveying Games With a Combined Model of Immersion and Flow

Ehm Kannegieser
Fraunhofer Institute of Optronics, System Technologies, and Image Exploitation, Germany

Daniel Atorf
Fraunhofer Institute of Optronics, System Technologies, and Image Exploitation, Germany

Josua Meier
Karlsruhe Institute of Technology, Germany

ABSTRACT

Detecting flow in games is key for successful adaptation processes. Until now, the method of choice to measure flow in games is the usage of questionnaires, such as flow short scale or game experience questionnaire. Because of the shortcomings of these methods, the theoretical model of flow is enhanced by the concept of immersion to propose a unified flow/immersion model. In combination with this more fine-grained model of immersion, player experience may be measured in a more detailed fashion. The enhancement of the theoretical model and the altered experiment procedure are presented. In conclusion, a perspective towards performing the experiment and future data recordings is given.

INTRODUCTION

Digital Game-Based Learning concepts should enable the player to fully immerse into a fictional world and story. All learning objectives should be integrated and not abstracted from real life, making the game feel like an entertainment title, but implicitly allowing to accomplish learning objectives with high learning motivation, resulting in a better and sustainable learning outcome (Deci & Ryan, 1985; Krapp, Schiefele, & Schreyer, 2009).

The ability to measure flow (Atorf, Hensler, & Kannegieser, 2016), would provide a valuable input to adaptation processes that try to improve the attractiveness of the game, especially regarding its po-

DOI: 10.4018/978-1-5225-9069-9.ch004

tential of reaching a positive intrinsic motivational effect. Questionnaires, the standard method of flow evaluation until now (Nordin, Denisova, & Cairns, 2014), only provide the means to answer whether a flow state is reached or not. A more fine-grained analysis of player experience would enable earlier adaptation, thus improving the quality of the game.

The method explained in this paper expands upon the flow model (Csikszentmihalyi, 1991) by adding the definition of immersion by Cairns, Cox, Berthouze, Jennett and Dhoparee (2006). Cairns et al. (2006) establish immersion as a three-level construct, which is assumed as precondition for reaching the state of maximized intrinsic motivation. Figure 1 shows this hierarchical model and its three levels. It is proposed that a clear relationship between both immersion and flow can be established and linked into one unified model, thus improving the ability to detect flow and its precursors.

If the thesis of the combined model is correct, the incorporated immersion questionnaires will tend towards total immersion during identified phases of flow.

In addition to testing our combined model, the proposed experiment records physiological measurements of players during gameplay. Current methods to measure flow and immersion rely on questionnaires and as such lack objectivity and the capability to measure these states in real time. Using physiological measurements, our goal is to create a system that can measure flow and immersion automatically.

BACKGROUND

The three levels of immersion by Cairns et al. (2006) are elicited by the immersion questionnaire, published by Cheng, She and Annetta (2015). While flow is considered the psychology of optimal experience, immersion is known as the psychology of sub-optimal experience (Cairns et al., 2006). As such, these concepts appear to be linked by definition. However, the exact nature of this link is still unclear. Georgiou and Kyza (2017) define flow as part of the most extreme state of immersion, which puts it into the total immersion category of Cairns' model.

Existing methods used to elicit flow focus on questionnaires. These questionnaires are based on the definition of immersion employed in these studies. Csikszentmihalyi (1991) described flow as the optimal experience of an action, as a state of extreme focus on an activity. Flow is achieved when the individual becomes engrossed in the activity to a point, at which their surroundings no longer appear relevant. Csikszentmihalyi (1991) considers this the optimal experience, the optimal way to enjoy an action. He links this with the idea of an autotelic personality, a personality that performs actions for the enjoyment derived by the action itself, instead of external gains. This assertion is made based on the theory of intrinsic and extrinsic motivation, which divides motivations for actions into those motivated by external gains, such as money or rewards, and internal motivation. In this context, the idea of intrinsic motivation and an autotelic personality is special because it means that enjoyment can even be derived from work and other taxing activities. It is achieved when a balance between challenge and skill of the subject is struck.

The concept of flow was later mapped to games in the form of the GameFlow questionnaire (Sweetser & Wyeth, 2005). Games are useful for researching flow, as they are not played due to extrinsic motivation, but rather due to intrinsic motivation, for the enjoyment of the game itself. This makes it possible to reach the flow state when playing games. The GameFlow questionnaire was later further adapted by Fu, Su and Yu (2009) into the EGameFlow questionnaire for use with Serious Games.

For their study related to flow experiences in sports, Rheinberg, Vollmeyer and Engeser (2003) designed the Short Flow Scale. It was designed for use either alongside other flow elicitation questionnaires or to be used multiple times. It contains ten questions. While originally designed for a study related to sports, the questions are phrased in a way that the questionnaire can be used for general purpose flow elicitations.

The problem when defining immersion is that immersion is used to refer to two different things known as spatial immersion and emotional immersion. The definition of spatial immersion is synonymous with the definition of presence. As such, it refers to the psychological sense of perceiving a virtual reality as real while being physically located in another (Zhang, Perkis, & Arndt, 2017). The model proposed in this paper concerns itself with emotional and engagement-based immersion. This type of immersion deals with the intensity of user engagement with a task.

Ermi and Mäyrä (2005) analyze immersion in games as part of gameplay. While analyzing how players become immersed in virtual environments, they defined three important components of the gameplay experience. The first dimension is called sensory immersion and refers to the audiovisual perception players have of the game. For example, a game with greater audio and better visuals will generally invoke a greater sense of immersion in players than games with lower audiovisual quality. As such, this becomes a measurable quantity for determining how much immersion a game may provide. The second dimension they identify is the dimension of challenge-based immersion. Challenge-based immersion is equivalent to the definition of flow, as it describes the balance of skill and challenge. Challenge-based immersion increases when a balance is struck between personal ability and the challenges presented by the game. It does not make any statements about apathy, the state present in the flow model by Csikszentmihalyi (1991) when both skill and challenge are too low. The final dimension is called imaginative immersion and considers the story and world of the game as a reason for the immersion experienced by the player. As such, the model includes both game-centric aspects of measuring immersion, such as audiovisual quality and narrative structure, and player-centric aspects like the flow state.

In their series of papers, Cairns et al. (2006) and Jennett et al. (2008) define engagement-based immersion as a three-level construct. The first level is called engagement. It is automatically achieved when the subject interacts with a task. As such, its entrance barrier is "time". The second level, engrossment, is achieved when the subject becomes emotionally involved in the activity. It is synonymous with the feeling of the controls becoming invisible. The highest stage of immersion is referred to as "total immersion". In this state, the subject is completely cut off from reality and experiences both spatial real world dissociation as well as loss of a sense of time.

Based on this definition, Cairns et al. (2006) developed a questionnaire to measure immersion. They define five main factors: Cognitive involvement, real world dissociation, challenge, emotional involvement and control. Many of these factors overlap with flow. The main difference between flow and immersion is that immersion may be a sub-optimal experience. Cheng et al. (2015) improved upon the model of immersion by Cairns et al. (2006) by adding dimensions to the three layers. Engagement is broken into Attraction, Time Investment and Usability.

Engrossment, the second level of the immersion levels by Cairns et al. (2006) can be broken down into emotional attachment of the user to the task and decreased perceptions of time and spatial surroundings. The final level of the immersion model, "total immersion", has two components: The first refers to the loss of spatial awareness, and is identified by Cheng et al. (2015) as "presence", the feeling of being physically present in a virtual reality. Cheng et al. (2015) define the second term as "empathy", the state in which the player relates to their avatar on an emotional level and shares the character's emotions.

CONSIDERING A COMBINED MODEL OF FLOW AND IMMERSION

Georgiou and Kyza (2017) notice that term and define it as synonymous with "flow". This fits well with the definition of immersion as the "psychology sub-optimal experience" (Cairns et al., 2006), while flow is referred to by Csikszentmihalyi (1991) as the "psychology of optimal experience". This would make "flow" the highest state in the multi-level immersion model by Cairns et al. (2006).

The multi-level immersion model by Cairns et al. (2006) is employed at the base of the proposed model. On top of that, the model by Cheng et al. (2015) is used to extend the multi-level immersion model. The flow model of optimal experience by Csikszentmihalyi (1991) comes into play as part of the highest level of the immersion model, "total immersion". When looking at the two-dimensional eight-channel model of flow, flow is defined as the upper-right corner. It depicts an increase in flow along the diagonal. Given this diagonal increase, the lower levels of immersion, engagement and engrossment are situated at the lower left corner of the model.

Looking at the components of flow and immersion, a large overlap can be seen. Challenge and control are a part of both flow and immersion. Real world dissociation is also found as part of both immersion and flow, both as temporal dissociation and spatial dissociation (when interacting with virtual environments). The flow state's concentration aspect is synonymous with the most extreme version of cognitive involvement of immersion. Table 1 provides a comparison between the components of flow and the components of immersion.

Contrary to immersion, flow does not identify emotional involvement. With this knowledge, it can be useful to take a closer look at what emotions are and how they can be modeled.

Emotions are not necessarily discrete states. Overlap between emotional states exists. As such, models were introduced that can be used to define emotions in a three-dimensional space. The first such model is the model introduced by Wundt (1987). It defines the three dimensions pleasurable/unpleasurable, arousing/subduing and strain/relaxation. The first dimension defines the subjective feeling of the current situation's perceived attractiveness. In this context, the term valence is also important, as it also refers to the attractiveness of a situation. The second dimension refers to the strength of the emotion experienced. The final dimension refers to the attentiveness towards the experienced emotion.

Based on these dimensions, an alternate emotional model is given by Mäntylä, Adams, Destefanis, Graziotin and Ortu (2016). The Arousal-Valence model maps emotional states to a two-dimensional space defined by arousal and valence. Valence describes how attractive an experienced situation appears to the subject, similarly to the pleasurable/unpleasurable dimension in the model by Wundt. Arousal

Table 1. Comparison between flow and immersion

Flow	Immersion
Task	The Game
Concentration	Cognitive Involvement
Skill/Challenge Balance	Challenge
Sense of Control	Control
Clear Goals	Emotional Involvement
Immediate Feedback	-
Reduced Sense of Self and of Time	Real World Dissociation

refers to the strength of the experience and as such represents the second Wundt dimension, arousing/subduing. This is in so far interesting, because arousal and the flow model's challenge can be directly mapped to each other. Looking at the eight-channel flow model developed by Csikszentmihalyi (1991), boredom and arousal are already parts of the model. Arousal increases together with challenge. As such, measuring perceived challenge becomes synonymous with measuring arousal.

However, unlike arousal and challenge, skill and valence do not allow for such a direct mapping. On the eight-channel flow model, the skill axis is represented by the two opposing emotions of worry and feeling in control. As such, Mäntylä et al. (2016) suggested replacing valence with dominance for a mapping to skill. Dominance refers to the emotional dimension of feeling in control of a situation. This mapping is possible because the skill dimension refers to the level of perceived skill, which directly conforms to the definition of dominance. Measuring such an emotional dimension would be an interesting field of research by itself, so it was not a part of this experiment.

Flow is also strengthened by direct feedback from the interaction, which is not required in order to become immersed in an activity. This can be explained with flow being an extreme version of immersion. As thus, our model proposal can be summed up as a unification of flow and immersion, which treats flow as the most extreme state of immersion. Figure 2 displays this combined model by overlaying the three hierarchical levels of the immersion model over the 8-channel flow model. It must be noted that immersion levels are not influenced by the skill/challenge balance like flow, as the diagram is meant to visualize immersion turning into flow.

Physiological Measurements

The physiological measurements used in our study were chosen based on the idea that they should not interrupt the state of concentration the player is in while playing the game. Additionally, measures were used in a way that they do not impede gameplay.

Figure 1. Cairns' 3-level immersion model

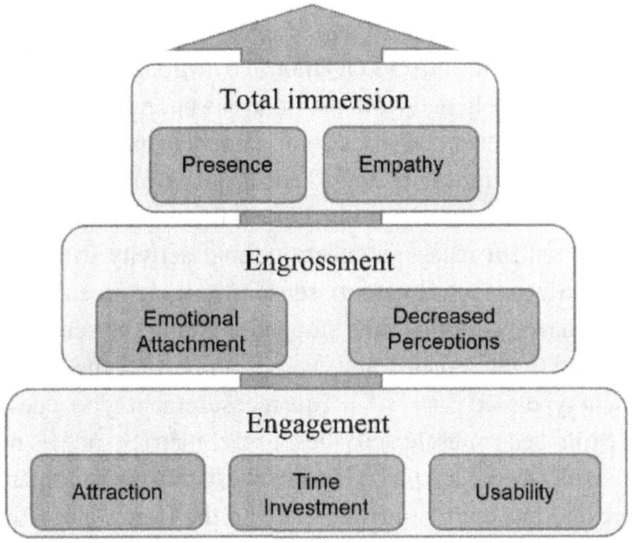

Figure 2. Combined 8-channel flow/immersion

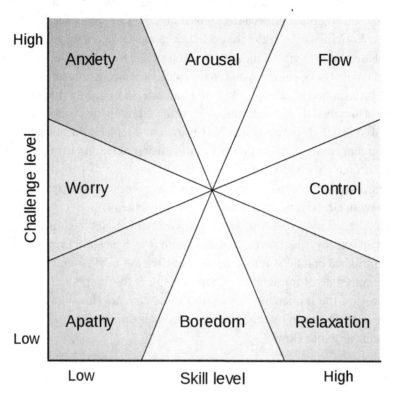

The first measure used is galvanic skin response. GSR uses electrodes to measure skin conductance. This has proven useful in emotion analysis, as skin conductance has been found to change in direct relation to arousal (Gravenhorst, Muaremi, Tröster, Arnrich, & Grünerbl, 2013), which is the strength of the emotion perceived, either positive (such as excitement) or negative (such as fear). Measuring skin conductance in the hand region would lead to both a loss of recording precision and a constraint on player movement. To prevent this, the electrodes are placed on the inside of the participant's foot, based on the measurement method outlined in (Gravenhorst et al., 2013). Two sensors are used to measure GSR in this study. The first sensor is the NAOS GQ mouse by Mionix, which has a built-in GSR sensor. However, test runs showed that data elicited from the mouse is not reliable. Measurement is taken at the lower palm of the hand using the mouse. During actual gameplay, participants often lift their hands or make slight adjustments to grip the mouse better. These types of movement lead to wrong or missing measurements, making it problematic for the study. Due to this, a more reliable sensor was employed, the Shimmer3 GSR+ sensor unit. It measures electrodermal activity in the skin using the electrode placements described above. Since it is a Bluetooth sensor, there are no cables to hinder gameplay, and participants during test runs have noted that they stopped noticing the sensor while playing the game. The Mionix mouse is still used to elicit data, and acts as a support for the shimmer sensor.

The second measurement type used is an ECG. This measurement type measures heart muscle activity from different angles. From heart muscle activities, useful metrics such as heart rate and changes in heart rate can be derived. As electrodes are placed on the chest, this measurement type may interrupt the player's focus on the game and prevent them from reaching the flow state. However, test runs showed that participants were not disrupted from playing the game by the recording equipment and did not actively notice it below their clothes. Data is measured using a Shimmer3 ECG measurement unit. Data is measured using five electrodes placed on the chest, while the sensor unit itself is placed near the stomach region on a belt. Clothes can be worn above the sensor electrodes without disrupting the measurement. Additionally, heart rate is also measured using the Mionix Naos QG. As explained in the GSR section, measurements from the mouse are unreliable and used in a supporting fashion.

Eye tracking is used to track gaze position on the screen. Eye movement can be differentiated into two different categories, movement and rest points. The amount of rest points has been found to be related to concentration (Jennett et al., 2008), making it an interesting metric for analysis in the study. Eye tracking does not interfere with players, making it useful for measuring immersion states. The eye tracker used in this study is a Gazepoint GP3 eye tracker. This eye tracker is useful, as it is cheap and can track eye movement reliably enough to derive information about rest points and the areas participants looked at. The sensor itself must be calibrated before use for each participant.

Finally, web cam footage of the player is recorded during gameplay. This gameplay footage can be used to analyze emotions displayed by a player. Its drawback is that it can only interpret expressed emotions, so if the player is feeling happy, but looks unhappy, the analysis would misidentify the emotion as unhappy. Like eye tracking, video recording does not disturb players playing the game. An alternative to using video footage is measuring face muscle activities using electrodes placed on the face. This approach can measure micro movements of face muscles and measure emotion felt and displayed more reliably. It was not chosen for this experiment, as placing electrodes on the face of players was found to be a strong distraction during gameplay.

Another relevant measurement type for eliciting reactions in players is an electroencephalogram (EEG). An EEG measures brain wave activity by means of electrodes placed on the head of the participant. EEGs come in different forms, for example some use caps, some use raw electrodes and other measurements use bands fastened to the head. The main problem is that less invasive measurements, such as headbands with a small amount of electrodes, measure brain activity less reliably than more complex measurement methods. Figure 3 shows one of those measurement methods. In order to measure the data the study wants to gather, a cap with a large amount of electrodes would have to be used. That is why, like with the facial EMG, EEG measurement was not chosen for the experiment, as it was found to distract players from getting immersed into the game.

Figure 4 portrays the measurement devices used in the study.

CONCEPT OF MEASURING FLOW AND IMMERSION

The procedure of evaluating our proposal consists of a gaming phase and an assessment phase. Figure 5 presents an overview over the different phases of the experiment, as well as an additional setup phase during which the experiment is set up. Test runs showed that 30 minutes were enough time to reach a relatively high state of immersion; accordingly, the gaming phase was set to 30 minutes of gameplay. The game can be selected freely; this choice was made in order to make it easier for test subjects to reach high states of immersion. Players chose from a variety of game genres: Action shooter (Overwatch, Counter Strike, Metal Gear), Rougelike (FTL, Curious Expedition), 4X-Strategy (Civilisation V), Artillery (Angry Birds), Adventure (Portal, The Wolf among us), Simulation (Kerbal Space Program) and Puzzle (Human Fall Flat). During the gaming phase, game play and player footage are recorded along

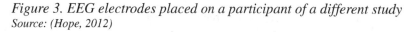

Figure 3. EEG electrodes placed on a participant of a different study
Source: (Hope, 2012)

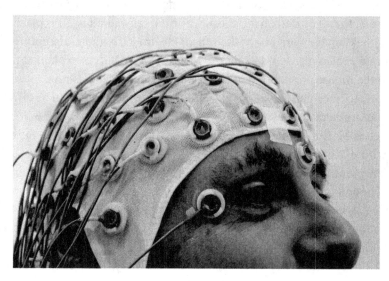

Figure 4. Experiment setup showcasing the GSR+ sensor, ECG sensor, eye tracker and measurement mouse used in the study. © 2018 Ehm Kannegieser. Used with permission.

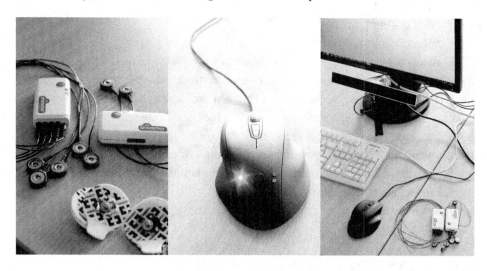

with physiological measurements. During the following assessment phase, the player watches the previously recorded gaming session and answers flow and immersion questionnaires periodically. These questionnaires elicit the player's flow state at the specified time in the video recording.

The questionnaires are shown multiple times in a three level hierarchical fashion, throughout the footage evaluation at differing time intervals:

The first level of questionnaires is measuring which level of immersion the player is currently in. It is based on the immersion questionnaire by Cheng et al. (2015), which adds multiple dimensions to the definition of immersion by Cairns et al. (2006) and is presented every three minutes. The original questionnaire contains 24 questions and was too long to be asked every three minutes. For this reason, the immersion questionnaire was split into two individual questionnaires. One questionnaire is used at the very beginning of the assessment phase and intends to elicit "immersive tendency" in players, another iterative questionnaire contains the seven questions Cheng et al. (2015) found most contributive to the questionnaire results of the different dimensions in their CFA.

The second level of questionnaires measures flow, based on the Flow Short Scale questionnaire (Rheinberg et al., 2003) and is presented every six minutes. This questionnaire was chosen because it is short and was designed to be used multiple times in succession.

The final level of questionnaires is presented at the end of the game footage playback. It is based on the Game Experience questionnaire (IJsselsteijn, de Kort, & Poels, 2013) and entails a complete elicitation of flow, immersion and related experiences. The Game Experience Questionnaire is used to elicit more general information concerning participants. Using data gathered in the questionnaire, links between game enjoyment, immersion and flow can be found.

This way, the theory that flow is an extreme version of immersion can be tested by comparing phases of immersion, identified in the first and third level (Immersion/Game experience questionnaire) to corresponding phases of flow, identified in the second and third level (Flow Short Scale/Game experience questionnaire).

The questionnaires were rewritten into past tense for consistency, additionally; some points were rewritten for clarity. As it was unclear to participants, they were also altered to reflect which span of time they refer to.

CONCLUSION AND PERSPECTIVE

The work in progress presented proposes a unified model of flow and immersion. The model will be verified by data elicited by flow and immersion questionnaires in the context of serious games. If the model is proven, a qualitative evaluation and steps towards an adaption process are enabled.

Figure 5. Phases of the experiment

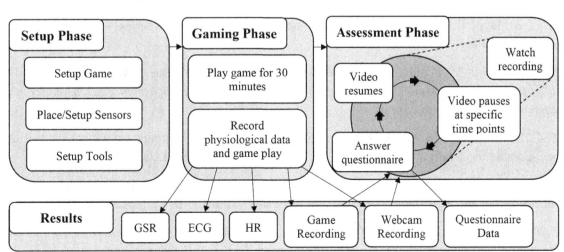

Furthermore, the approach will enable experiments towards establishing a method for measuring player flow/immersion levels automatically through physiological measurements. The list of physiological measurements proposed for the experiment is given in this work. These experiments will be about whether physiological parameters correlate during identified phases of flow or immersion, allowing a less intrusive, less biased and more automated analysis of player experience, during the activity under test.

REFERENCES

Allen, C. (2014, July 22). *The Proficiency Ladder. Life With Alacrity.* Retrieved July 22, 2014, from http://www.LifeWithAlacrity.com

Atorf, D., Hensler, L., & Kannegieser, E. (2016). Towards a concept on measuring the flow state during gameplay of serious games. In *European conference on games based learning (ecgbl)* (pp. 955–959). Paisley, UK: ECGBL. Retrieved from http://publica.fraunhofer.de/documents/N-438328.html

Bach, D. R., Friston, K. J., & Dolan, R. J. (2010). Analytic measures for quantification of arousal from spontaneous skin conductance fluctuations. *International Journal of Psychophysiology, 76*(1), 52–57. doi:10.1016/j.ijpsycho.2010.01.011 PMID:20144665

Cairns, P., Cox, A., Berthouze, N., Jennett, C., & Dhoparee, S. (2006). Quantifying the experience of immersion in games. Cognitive Science of Games and Gameplay workshop at Cognitive Science.

Cheng, M.-T., She, H.-C., & Annetta, L. (2015). Game immersion experience: Its hierarchical structure and impact on game-based science learning. *Journal of Computer Assisted Learning, 31*(3), 232–253. doi:10.1111/jcal.12066

Csikszentmihalyi, M. (1991). *Flow: The psychology of optimal experience.* New York, NY: Harper Perennial. Retrieved from http://www.amazon.com/gp/product/0060920432/ref=si3_rdr_bb _product/104-4616565-4570345

Deci, E., & Ryan, R. (1985). *Intrinsic motivation and self-determination in human behavior.* Academic Press.

Ermi, L., & Mäyrä, F. (2005). *Fundamental components of the gameplay experience: Analysing immersion.* Academic Press.

Ezzeldin A. Bashir, M., Gyu Lee, D., Akasha, M., Yi, G., Jong Cha, E., Bae, J.-W., . . . Ryu, K. (2010). *Highlighting the current issues with pride suggestions for improving the performance of real time cardiac health monitoring.* Academic Press.

Fu, F.-L., Su, R.-C., & Yu, S.-C. (2009). Egameflow: A scale to measure learners' enjoyment of e-learning games. *Computers & Education, 52*(1), 101–112. doi:10.1016/j.compedu.2008.07.004

Georgiou, Y., & Kyza, E. A. (2017). The development and validation of the ari questionnaire. *International Journal of Human-Computer Studies, 98*(100), 24–37. doi:10.1016/j.ijhcs.2016.09.014

Gravenhorst, F., Muaremi, A., Tröster, G., Arnrich, B., & Grünerbl, A. (2013). *Towards a mobile galvanic skin response measurement system for mentally disordered patients.* Academic Press.

Hope, C. (2012). *Volunteer Duty Psychology Testing*. Retrieved from https://www.flickr.com/photos/tim_uk/8135755109/

IJsselsteijn, W. A., de Kort, Y. A. W., & Poels, K. (2013). *The Game Experience Questionnaire*. Eindhoven: Technische Universiteit Eindhoven.

Jennett, C., Cox, A. L., Cairns, P., Dhoparee, S., Epps, A., Tijs, T., & Walton, A. (2008). Measuring and defining the experience of immersion in games. *International Journal of Human-Computer Studies*, *66*(9), 641–661. doi:10.1016/j.ijhcs.2008.04.004

Krapp, A., Schiefele, U., & Schreyer, I. (2009). *Metaanalyse des Zusammenhangs von Interesse und schulischer Leistung. postprint*. Institut für Philosophie.

Mäntylä, M., Adams, B., Destefanis, G., Graziotin, D., & Ortu, M. (2016). Mining valence, arousal, and dominance: Possibilities for detecting burnout and productivity? In *Proceedings of the 13th international conference on mining software repositories* (pp. 247–258). MSR '16. doi:10.1145/2901739.2901752

Nordin, A. I., Denisova, A., & Cairns, P. (2014). *Too many questionnaires: Measuring player experience whilst playing digital games*. Academic Press.

Rheinberg, F., Vollmeyer, R., & Engeser, S. (2003). Die Erfassung des Flow-Erlebens. In *Diagnostik von Motivation und Selbstkonzept* (pp. 261–279). Göttingen: Hogrefe.

Sweetser, P., & Wyeth, P. (2005). Gameflow: A model for evaluating player enjoyment in games. Comput. Entertain., 3(3), 3–3. doi:10.1145/1077246.1077253

Wundt, W. (1897). *Outlines of Psychology*. Academic Press.

Zhang, C., Perkis, A., & Arndt, S. (2017). Spatial immersion versus emotional immersion, which is more immersive? In *2017 9th International Conference on Quality of Multimedia Experience (QoMex)* (pp. 1–6). Academic Press. 10.1109/QoMEX.2017.7965655

KEY TERMS AND DEFINITIONS

Challenge: Level of difficulty presented when performing an activity. In the context of games, it refers to the difficulty of reaching the game's targets.

Control: Sense of being able to consciously influence outcomes when performing an activity. Within games, control refers to controlling the game's avatar using the inputs presented by the game.

ECG: Short for electrocardiography. During an ECG, heart muscle activity is recorded using electrodes placed on the chest. Heart muscle activity is gathered from multiple angles. It can be used to measure heart rate as well as the amplitude of the heart signal.

Flow: Optimal experience of an activity. Flow is used to describe a state of complete concentration, during which all senses are focused on the activity performed.

GSR: Short for galvanic skin response. Used to measure skin conductance using two electrodes placed on either the hand or the feet. Galvanic skin response signals consist of two signals, one baseline signal, which changes over minutes and a signal that changes quickly in reaction to stimuli. GSR can be used to measure emotional arousal.

Immersion: The sub-optimal experience of an activity. Describes a loss of spatial awareness and temporal awareness as focus is increased on the activity performed.

Player: Person controlling the game. Games can be controlled by multiple people at the same time, but for the experiment, only one person at a time will be playing the game.

Presence: Sense of feeling as if physically present in a virtual environment. Immersion is often used as a term when describing presence, but for the study presented here, immersion and flow describe two different phenomena.

Questionnaire: Collection of questions answered by participants in a study. Questionnaire questions can either be answered freely without guidance, answered by selecting from a possible range of given answers, or answered by means of a Likert scale. A Likert scale provides a range of equally distributed answers ranging from "strongly disagree" to "strongly agree" in response to a question. Likert scale questionnaires are the type of questionnaires used in the study.

Spatial/Temporal Awareness: Awareness of time and the surrounding environment while performing an activity that needs concentration. During immersion and flow, this awareness is usually reduced.

Video Game: Interactive software used for entertainment purposes. Games used for other purposes, such as education, are called serious games.

Chapter 5

Deus ex Machina:
The Automation of a Religious Ritual in a Data–Driven Machine – Design, Implementation, and Public Reception

Michael A. Herzog
https://orcid.org/0000-0002-7597-2272
Magdeburg-Stendal University, Germany

Danny Schott
Magdeburg-Stendal University, Germany

Carsten Greif
Magdeburg-Stendal University, Germany

Dominik Schumacher
Magdeburg-Stendal University, Germany

Florian T. Brody
Magdeburg-Stendal University, Germany

Sinah Herrklotsch
Magdeburg-Stendal University, Germany

ABSTRACT

Churches have a long tradition using technology to grow their audience and to connect worshippers. Technologies used in Christian service are not even perceived as such: consider architecture, the organ, and light. Yet, faith-based organizations have always been critical of new technologies. The authors used design science research methodologies to develop an artifact of the Eucharist of a Catholic service. "Instant Church" is an interactive machine that guides visitors through the service and creates an individualized wafer with a laser-engraved QR-code that points to a random Tweet with a hate message that invites a moment of thought. Over 700 visitors saw that exhibit. A qualitative evaluation showed a high positive acceptance by users under 40 while older visitors had a negative perspective. The artifact proved to be a highly suitable tool to invite a critical discourse and at the same time serves as a learning tool about the service. Interactive intelligent solutions reach the generation of digital natives and enable the discourse on the relationship between technology and faith.

DOI: 10.4018/978-1-5225-9069-9.ch005

INTRODUCTION: MOTIVATION AND CONTEXT OF THE PROJECT

Any sufficiently advanced technology is indistinguishable from magic.— Arthur C. Clarke. Third Law.

Technology and religion have been in a more or less close contact over the centuries. Often derided as evil, technology has always also served as a way to bring people to church. From architecture to the printing press, elaborate stained glass windows and complex organs to psychoactive substances, technological solutions have provided ways and means to provide spiritual guidance and bring to the church. The domains of spirituality, metaphysics and supernatural worlds gained a new quality in the age of digital media. (Hjarvard, 2008, p. 10) Technology per se has become a religion for many over the centuries and established religious practices, especially Christian churches have always strived to distance themselves from magical practices.

The interdependence between church and technology has always been a relevant driver how people perceived spiritual practice to increase church attendance as well as to maintain influence and uphold the power of the church. In parallel, technical development is also a strong inhibitor. "Thus, mediatization of religion may be considered a part of a gradual secularization: it is the historical process in which the media have taken over many of the social functions that used to be performed by religious institutions." (Hjarvard, 2008, p. 11) Christian churches for example, experience a steady decline in membership. In Germany, in 2017 alone, 270,000 Catholics and 390,000 Protestants left one of the two big Christian churches, mainly based on demographic changes.

Fifty-four percent of the German population belong to one of the two big Christian churches in 2017, compared to 62 percent in 2005 (SZ, 2018). The main reasons for people to leave their church being alienation from faith as well as a lack of commitment to the church as an institution. (Riegel et al., 2018). German religious sociologists see no fault in the offerings of the church and find the reasons for a decline in socio-cultural changes, urbanization, individualization and the growing recreational offerings. American consultants to the church identify clear issues "Why Churches Stop Growing and Decline Into Impotence", among them broken hospitality, neglect of the core mission that Jesus has given the church, comfort in the status quo, and others (Finkelde, 2016).

The diocese of Essen in cooperation with the University of Siegen investigated motivations for church exits since March 2017. Interviews conducted for this study reveal how active and former church members perceive the church today:

The church needs to open up and invite modern ideas. God wants us to love everybody and lead our lives the way we choose to (Catholic, 41-60 years, Duisburg) – I do not need a parish festival with sausages, I want to learn about faith, but nobody has time for this (Catholic male, 41-60 years, Bochum)

Leaving the church seems to be a drawn-out process, explains Riegel, driven by alienation, a loss of sense for the community, a growing disillusionment with the church, the disconnect between personal faith and the institution church, and others. Church taxation and scandals are often only the famous "final straw" (Qualbrink, n. d.).

The big churches are in denial of cultural changes and oblivious to the need for the spiritual guidance today's world is looking for. People are looking for spiritual grounding and community. This explains why Buddhism as well as Islam and community-oriented sects that care for their community gain memberships. Within a society driven by technology, comfort, and digital communication, the question arises if technology can create an incentive for young people to participate in a church.

Social services significantly benefit from an Internet-based solution. Advances in digital communication and social media provide break-through solutions in medical services worldwide. (Hagemann, 2017). Similar opportunities are available for religious organizations when correctly deployed. Technology needs to develop beyond imitation and provide a valuable experience that resonates with people.

Religious practice and the function of the church need to adapt to the life of its community continuously. This has been an ongoing process of hundreds of years and with the recent development of digital technology, social media, and interactive machines it seems as if the church can no longer keep pace. Can technology support religious practice today and is there a place for interactive machines in the church? "Engaging in social communication through the most innovative platform is a great start, but without awareness of the particular form, mode, and content intelligible in the digital age, this could lead to a frustrating experience." (Zsupan-Jerome, 2014). Implementing new technologies requires a structured design process that takes into consideration a clear identification of the problem to be addressed, a definition of the objectives to be accomplished, effective design and development, as well as a clear demonstration and evaluation of its features and applicability in order to communicate the product effectively to all stakeholders.

The Magdeburg-Stendal University in collaboration with the Cathedral of Saints Catherine and Maurice in Magdeburg, the oldest Gothic cathedral in Germany, built in 937, initiated a project that explores technological solutions that impact traditional interaction and communication models in a church setting. Interaction designers and engineers of multiple university departments developed a range of products that addressed different aspects of church activities.

The project opens up many theological questions of the quality of a sacred act, ordination, the role of the priest as an intermediary between human and God and at the center of this project: transubstantiation, a mystery that cannot be replicated by a machine.

RELATED WORK

A wide range of digital solutions exists to facilitate religious and spiritual practice, to make Bible texts more accessible, support the religious practice, facilitate meditation and other practices as well as managing church communities. The technologies of movable type and developments in printing initiated by Gutenberg and the printing of the 42-line bible allowed for a wider availability of religious texts, a development not always welcomed by church circles. Exploring the impact of the printed word on church and religion goes beyond the scope of this paper. As Francis Robinson points out, the printed book not only challenged religious authority and drove the Protestant Reformation, it was also "at the heart of the Catholic counter- offensive" (Robinson, 1993, p. 232) and was heavily controlled "through the machinery of the Papal Index and the Papal Imprimatur" (ibid).

Digital media and hypertext are useful to make religious material, especially the Old and New Testament, more accessible. YouVersion is a Bible App offering "1803 Bible versions in 1253 languages for free, and without advertising". It is a good example of a religiously-oriented technology solution that benefits from the free availability of a wide range of text versions to offer digital media for evangelical means. (Hutchings, 2014, p. 14). The digital version with a distribution of over 345 million makes references and sources much more accessible than on paper. YouVersion "is a case study in how technology can change behavior when it couples the principles of consumer psychology with the latest in analytics." (Eyal, 2013). The success of YouVersion shows a positive integration of Christian values and social media. Yet to some "the idea that pastors might become dependent on a mobile app has caused some resistance from Christian observers" (Hutchings 2014, p. 22) may seem controversial. The perceived dangers of media technology have been raised earlier, only in that earlier event a god gave the technology of writing to a king for his people, as retold by Socrates (Plato, 370 B.C.).

The church as an institution has the opportunity to continue the path taken since its beginnings to use the word to reach its community – be it with the integration of text and images in the Biblia pauperum, be it with Twitter. The 140-character limitation of a Tweet is well suited for Bible verses (Cheong, 2010, Hutchings, 2014, p. 23), to reach a younger generation and this will obviously meet the resistance of an older audience: "Have I not commanded you? Be strong and courageous. Do not be afraid; do not be discouraged, for the LORD your God will be with you wherever you go." (Joshua 1:9) (111 characters).

Technological innovations that support the Christian understanding and interpretation of the Bible were mostly accepted by the church. (Hutchings, 2014, p. 26). Faith-Based Design is an approach to develop and design products that help maintain traditional faith and religious practices. Christians are using modern technologies to communicate with friends and family or to measure their workday. Similar technologies are used to receive the word of the Lord daily for example bible verses (Gorman, 2009, p. 18). When LaserCard Corporation developed the first memory cards in business card size with 8 MB storage in 1989, a sect commanded to always carry the Bible was a major customer. No reading devices were available, which did not matter as they knew the text by heart anyway.

"Whatever one's religion, using a ringing, beeping electronic device that one carries on one's body – as opposed to an inert book or calendar that sits ignored on the shelf – is a new means of remembering, affirming and reflecting on belief." The availability of a wide range of hardware and software makes it more accessible to the practice of Christian rituals (Gorman, 2009, p. 19).

Research during the design process explored the role that technology has always played an integral part in religious rituals, both in Christian and in other faith-based practices. Technologies serve to provide a spiritual experience, facilitate practice, and communicate the message of the church. While none of this is new, digital technologies provide more diverse and flexible solutions. "By the fourteenth century, Nicolas of Lyra listed three reasons justifying the institution of images for religious purposes in his Praeceptorium." (Ess, 2004, p. 216) The second reason he gives is that the "the sluggish emotions of all people could be more powerfully moved to devotion by things seen than merely heard".

Social media provide another way of extending access to religious messages. Digital communication technologies allow to "listen in" on prayers and some of the hopes and wishes can actually be fulfilled by humans. "The Messenger" (Kim, 2011, p. 88), a project by design students at Art Center College of Design in Pasadena, CA, explored how prayers can be stored in a database. Wishes could actually come true: "Scientific and faith-based organization can listen in and try to provide help where it is needed, such as water in a draught, or medicine for the sick."

The object "Prayer Companion" (Gaver, 2011, p. 87) is a highly specialized communication device developed for the Poor Sisters in a monastery in the UK "with a very explicit purpose: It alerts the nuns to issues that need their prayers". This unique communication device solves the issue to integrate the nuns' vow of enclosure with very limited communication with the outside world with their wish to "keep prayers pertinent" to issues in the world while "minimizing its distracting potential" through an "understated and unobtrusive" design.

The object "Ticker Cross" (Kison, 2008) juxtaposes the duality of a mission of poverty and giving to the poor with the riches and the stock portfolio of the Catholic church by running a stock ticker atop the initials INRI on the holy cross. As a critical design object, it invites the audience to think about the invisible discrepancy between the mission to help the poor and the accumulation of money for the benefit of the organization.

Other products in the space of automation in the church include BetBox a vending machine for rosaries and bracelets that meets little resistance. (Kath.net, 2013) It follows the tradition of selling candles, booklets and postcards for the benefit of the church and does not create a discourse about faith and religious practice.

On the occasion of the 500th anniversary of the Reformation, the Protestant Church in Hesse and Nassau, Germany, in collaboration with Alexander Wiedekind-Klein, a robotics developer, created BlessU-2, a "robot pastor" that can bless you in seven languages and the local dialect. "in the same way Luther used the emerging technologies of his day, the church's robot has sparked conversation and debate; this time, addressing the relationships between humans and machines." (Miller Mc Farlan, 2017) A local TV station covered the product under the title "this extremely creepy robot priest will bless you and follow you into your dreams" (Henke, 2017). An earlier version of a mechanical cleric was developed in sixteenth-century Spain. "Driven by a key-wound spring, the monk walks in a square, striking his chest with his right arm, raising and lowering a small wooden cross and rosary in his left hand, turning and nodding his head, rolling his eyes, and mouthing silent obsequies." (King, 2002). A robot developed by Softbank was introduced as a cheaper alternative to human priests for funerals in Japan at a funeral industry convention in Tokyo in 2017. Dressed in the robes of a Buddhist priest, the robot chants sutras and taps a wooden drum and a bell (Gibbs, 2017).

Looking at present-day technology projects in the religious space the same issues arise as in the 500 years before. The independence of machines and faith at the border between technology, magic, superstition, and faith as always reflects on the socio-cultural setting. Poorly understood complexity of technology always posed a challenge, especially to the church. Father Athanasius Kircher, SJ "projected dancing shadows or phantasmagoric images onto sheets of cloth", (Ess, 2014, p. 216f) which entertained his fellow monks "until Kircher projected an image of the devil and his cohorts onto a cloud of smoke. Then suddenly, this marvel of the magic lantern was seen to be the "workings of the devil". (ibid) The core of the discourse remains the same as the topic Pope Francis addressed the World Economic Forum on the issue of Artificial Intelligence (AI) (Jenkins, 2018). Sister Ilia Delio, a Catholic nun and head of the science-and-theology focused Omega Center, points out that "The difficulty with the church is that technology, like everything else, runs on the principles of evolution [and] [e]volution runs on the principle of greater complexification, and that's where the church is resistant." Kircher defended himself against the "impending threat of exorcism or clerical torture" by publishing scholarly work, Ars Magna lucis et umbrae (Kircher, 1646). Kircher describes in a chapter "De Metamorphosi, seu transformatione catoptrica" (p. 1038) how images are created and morphed through the use of lenses and mirrors. This technology was as poorly understood at the time as AI is misunderstood today, and the church has similar challenges in putting the technology in its place. Kircher was the head of the museum of the Collegio Romano that held a wide range of "prodigies, exotic animals, relics, obelisks and bizarre machines" (Vermeir, 2007, p. 363) and the collection held many devices whose practical value remains unclear. Vermeir (ibid) tried to decode the meaning and practicality of many of these as described in the Ars Magna (Kircher, 1646) and concluded that some of them served for the inter-medial mixed-media spectacles, "the markedly sensual and visual Spiritual exercises of their [the Jesuits] founding father Ignatius of Loyola, to the elaborate stage plays they performed in order to retrieve lost souls" (Vermeir, 2007, p. 363). An in-depth analysis of Kircher's "multimedia" machines and explorations goes beyond the scope of this paper and extensive scientific literature is available.

While images create a deep impression both on an intellectual and emotional level, the word is what people believe to be the message. "In the beginning was the word" (John 1:1) and it is the word that builds belief systems. Joseph Weizenbaum developed Eliza a natural language system at the MIT media lab 1964-1966. (Weizenbaum, 1966) The system simulated person-centered psychotherapy. The method developed by the psychologist Carl Rogers was especially well suited to run on an extremely small set of rules and a very limited vocabulary to convince users that the machine deeply relates to them. Automated blessing works on the same underlying structures. Weizenbaum in his later work provides critical analysis of systems that create unclear boundaries in the human-computer interface (Weizenbaum, 1976) In a conversation during Ars Electronica Weizenbaum mentioned regarding the truth value of statements: "My father used to say it is written (in the holy scriptures), today we say the computer said" (Brody, 1984).

The position of machines is constantly changing and the quest into their relationship with religion, faith, and the church provides a highly fruitful testbed for design developments in communications and human-machine interaction. "Instant Church" provides a prototype into the investigation of the core of communication the Catholic faith: Holy Communion. The focus on Christian faith was largely driven by the partnership with the team of the Magdeburg Cathedral.

RESEARCH CONCEPT AND ITERATIVE DEVELOPMENT

"Instant Church" is the prototype of a machine developed through a rigorous scientific research process. Main objective of the project was to investigate and develop a critical perspective on the development of how the church embraces technology. Churches of all denominations always used technology for a wide range of applications from growing their reach to creating a spiritual experience as well as to establish their power. Monasteries were the center of education and research. They held the biggest libraries and with this had the largest group of people who could read and had time to think. Churches were built to serve a double purpose for astronomical research. A small hole in the roof allowed the sun to shine on very specific points to calculate the date and ensure that Easter fell on the first Sunday after the first full moon after the spring equinox (Manaugh, 2016). Churches were built as virtual reality spaces to create a truly mystical experience that must have deeply impressed the church community at a time where the most exciting color images were stained glass windows. With images, the sound from the organ, the smell and smoky clouds of frankincense with its intoxicating aromas, the church created a spiritual experience not to be missed. 4K television as entertainment and a wide range of spiritual practices that connect much more personal with its members lead to attrition of attendance. Jesuits have a long tradition to use a wide range of spectacles, including machinery such as Kircher's laterna magica to bring people back to the church as much as the church looks to technology today to reach its herd. "Kircher characterized his magical instruments as serving both entertainment and utilitarian purposes" (Vermeir, 2007, 373) and some of his machines such as one "consisting of a large crystalline globe full of water representing the resurrection of the Savior in the midst of the waters" (Sepibus, 1678, p. 3 quoted after Vermeir, 2007, p 374) or "a Christ walking on water, and bringing help to Peter, who is gradually sinking, by a magnetic trick" (ibid) may be considered heresy similar to the responses received for the Instant Church project.

For the development of this project Design Science Research (Hevner, 2004) provided the methodological foundation. To provide a means for further research, the team developed an interactive artifact to be presented in a public space. The development team used the Design Science Research Methodology model (DSRM) developed by Peffers et al. (2007) and adjusted it for this specific research process (Figure 1).

During the initial project phase, several workshops brought together public relation professionals of the Magdeburg Cathedral with researchers and students in the fields of human-computer interaction, interaction design, and electrical engineering at Magdeburg-Stendal University. The overall project was divided into two phases: The objective of the first phase was the exploration of the potential of innovative interaction techniques in a religious context. These projects were developed within five weeks by ten interdisciplinary teams and then presented to members of the Magdeburg Cathedral to encourage discourse and feedback.

Over its 1000 years of history the cathedral saw different religions at the church and continuous development of services and rituals, all of which left their signs in the space. The iterative development of the church over the centuries left its marks that even today impact the religious service and can be seen by everyone visiting. In a similar iterative approach, the project provided access to the different layers present in the relationship between technology and religious practice and a deep understanding of how technology is perceived from a faith-based perspective. The project addressed the question of how the highly interactive experience of a church service can benefit from digital interactive technologies.

These several shorter prototypes (Figure 2) were explored in different aspects of technological solutions in a religious space. The findings of these benefitted the development of the "Instant Church" project.

1. **"Night Sky"** ("Nachthimmel") is a video projection installation at the Magdeburg Cathedral of Saints Catherine and Maurice. The visual effects generated by five video projectors by the organ music captured in real-time by microphones. After initial mock-ups in Adobe Photoshop, the video installation was optimized inside the church and presented on May 4th, 2018 on the occasion of the tenth anniversary of the new organ that replaced the instrument destroyed during WWII. Over 1000 guests enjoyed the performance in two concerts.

Figure 1. Design science research methodology model applied to the instant church project

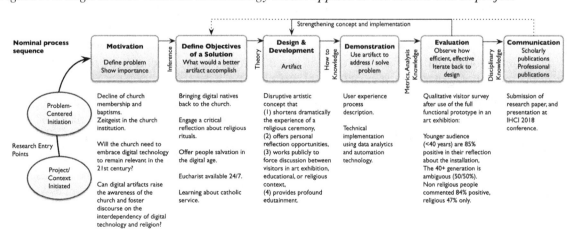

Figure 2. A: Night Sky; B: touchable music; C: condle; D: Tooth of time; E: hidden tombs; F: Let off steam

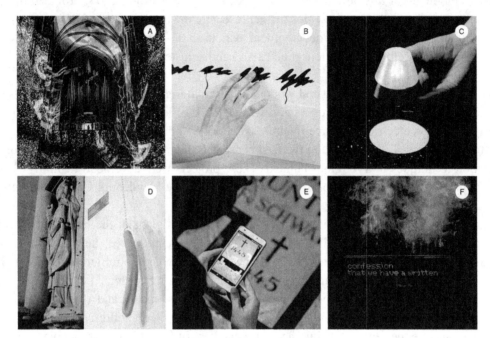

2.   **"Touchable Music"** ("Musik zum Berühren") allows visitors at the Cathedral to experience organ music. Several sequences of the contemporary music piece Riff-Raff were available for interpretation. The sequences were visualized with conductive ink and could be explored in a haptic way by visitors, allowing them to create and experience music without the need to attend a concert or a church service.

3.   Lighting a candle is a traditional spiritual act that implies gratefulness and a prayer. The digital prayer candle **"Condle"** expands the power of the candle by adding a highly personal message. The product was developed with a haptic interface that scans the heartbeat and converts it into a personal flicker rhythm as well as a second version that controls the flickering of the candle with the voice, delivering a message encoded into the ritual of lighting a candle.

4.   **"Tooth of time"** ("Zahn der Zeit" – German "for ravages of time") revitalizes the ancient artifact of a walrus tusk inside the cathedral and brings attention to this inconspicuous object. Its story almost lost in time is revitalized through a minimalistic intervention. A replica of the tooth is put into a pendulum motion, and its history is told via an audio track that is synchronized to the movement of the pendulum and activated via a motion sensor.

5.   **"Hidden tombs"** ("Versteckte Gräber") makes otherwise inaccessible information visible through a combination of tape art and QR Codes. The church serves as the final resting place of many historical figures, the founder of the Holy Roman Empire, Otto the Great and while some tombs are visible, many have been covered up by stones through construction over the centuries. This project makes them visible again and allows visitors to access information about the deceased via digital media.

6.   **"Let off steam"** ("Dampf ablassen") brings the confession back to the church. While multiple Internet platforms offer confession in a private way or a public setting for everyone to read, the Catholic faith requires confession in the church. This project takes confessions out of the virtual and onto a display inside the church. Then the device emits steam to let the sins free symbolically.

The projects were on display to visitors of the Cathedral had the opportunity to see the exhibits over four days during and to provide feedback through a survey that also contained open-ended questions.

The visitors perceived the projects mostly positively and were fascinated by the wide range of different solutions and modern technology interpretations. The audience valued the in-depth exploration of religious topics. Especially the young audience found the projects very inspiring, especially as cutting-edge technical solutions are rarely associated with the church.

The project "Let off steam" found critique as it represented a Catholic practice in a protestant church. Visitors were also concerned about the randomness of the selected Tweets and their relevance of religious practice.

While most visitors accepted the introduction of new technologies and innovative ideas into the church, a critical and open discussion is only possible in a very limited way.

In the second phase, three teams further developed the concepts of the first phase. First weekly concept meetings, then monthly reflection meetings for 16 weeks helped to iterate the DSRM cycles based on several creativity techniques (Figure 3). The consultation with the professional design and engineering community of the projects mentioned above and an exhibition with interim presentations involving the cooperation partner helped to iterate the design process and improve the concepts as the designed and programmed artifact. Multiple brainstorming meetings and sketching sessions produced additional ideas and concepts on religion and technology (Figure 4).

Figure 3. Design process: discussion in a concept meeting

Figure 4. An intermediate concept of the instant church as a "slot machine" in a vertical version

The insights from these projects served as the foundation for the design of the "Instant Church" project. The team of professional designers and engineers explored additional ideas for the "Instant Church" in regular meetings over several months. An exhibition of various stages of the project provided additional input for the design process and the DSRM cycles.

Results from Phase One showed a higher than expected acceptance of technology in the realm of religion. Feedback from churchgoers in individual qualitative interviews was consistently positive. The acceptance of the two projects "Let off steam" and "Condle", focusing on the digitization of church rituals, provided motivational input for Phase Two and the development of "Instant Church".

The Catholic Service provided a foundation for the Instant Church project as it offers a well-documented procedural structure. Well-documented processes with a large group of involved stakeholders offer themselves for automation and work-flow management. In Phase Two the team pursued an approach to automate the religious service and present it in form of a mechanical vending machine.

We defined design objectives to serve as a starting point for further evaluation in the process:

1.   Bringing digital natives back to the church.

Digital technology is becoming increasingly important in the lives of millennials. We intend to explore which aspects of technology are best suited to invite people back to the church.

2.   Engage a critical reflection about religious rituals.

Goal of the project was to engage the visitor in a critical reflection on questions of religious practice and rituals. In which ways can an automated system contribute or replace elements of a church service?

3.　Eucharist 24/7.

A technical solution could offer access to religious service at any time.

4.　Learning about catholic service.

Can digital artifacts raise the awareness of the church and foster discourse on the interdependency of digital technology and religion?

In order to further explore the defined goals in the critical design process (Dunne 2013), the ritual was represented as a physical design artifact in the form of an automation. The fully automated machine can serve for self-guided learning of religious rituals and presents the religious service as a process in a well-defined and shortened form. The approximation to a final prototype – presented and evaluated in a four-day public exhibition – resulted in a total workload of approximately 1000 working hours.

USER EXPERIENCE AND FINAL DESIGN

"Instant Church" is a digital design artifact that stages essential elements of the Catholic liturgy (opening, the liturgy of the Word, the celebration of the Eucharist, dismissal). It provides interactive access as well as an aesthetic and a spiritual approach.

Figure 5 visualizes the six steps of the interactive process as it relates to the Catholic service.

1.　**Greeting** The shortened and digitized Eucharistic celebration starts at Instant Church with the insertion of a coin (Figure 6). As a greeting a bell sounds, the playing of organ music marks the

Figure 5. Process overview shows the analogies of Catholic worship (duration about 60 minutes) with the vending machine in use (duration about 12 minutes)

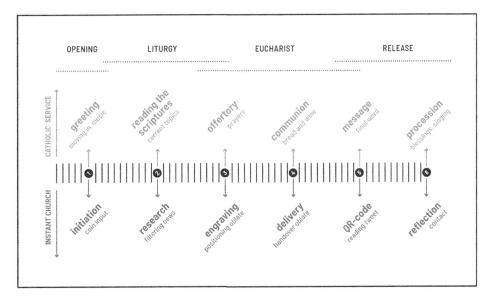

Figure 6. The user inserts a coin and starts the process of Eucharistic celebration

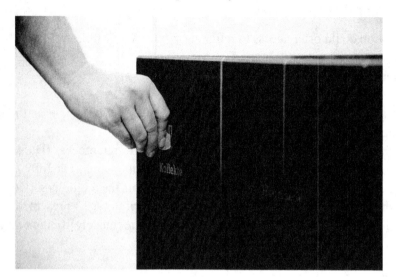

beginning of worship. The so-called opening (Entry, Confession, Kyrie, Gloria and Daily Prayer) stands as an accompanied entry into the church with the church choir.

2. **Reading the Scriptures**. After the opening, the next part of a Catholic service is the Liturgy of the Word (Old Testament readings, response psalms, Gospel readings, preaching, creeds, and intercessions). The automaton translates the part of the sermon with the start of animation on the whole semitransparent base plate on which the conveyor belt and all other elements are mounted. The animation visualizes how the software uses unique algorithms to analyze the social network Twitter for current political issues and to filter out hate tweets. The realization of this is explained in more detail in the Section Technical Implementation.

3. **Offertory**. Next comes the most critical part of the Catholic service, the actual eucharistic celebration (giving of gifts, high prayer, Lord's Prayer, peace greeting, Agnus Dei, Communion). Instant Church translates the gift preparation as the positioning of the wafer from the lavishly lit tabernacle (acrylic glass tube) on the conveyor belt (Figure 7). The conveyor belt transports the wafer into the black box by holding a laser engraving machine. A QR code is generated with a URL to a Tweet and engraved by Laser onto the wafer and visualized by a light animation. The Laser also emits smoke, and its smell is a reminiscence of incense.

4. **Communion** The conveyor belt begins to move again after the laser process and conveys the engraved wafer to a funnel through which the wafer rolls in an inclined rail to the ejector. The user could now take in the holy bread for him that represents the body of Christ (Figure 8). The experience of the Catholic worship by the automaton does not end at this point, but, like the actual service, has been extended by the announcement of the so-called dismissal.

5. **Message** The dismissal (announcement, blessing, dismissal, an excerpt with singing) starts at Instant Church with the scanning of the QR code on the wafer (Figure 9). With the smartphone, the user is now linked directly to the hate tweet on the Twitter platform and could read the message. Since it is not just a tweet, but a particular hate tweet, it is the user's job to form an opinion.

Figure 7. The wafer is transported from the tabernacle to the conveyor belt

Figure 8. (left) The user is getting the Holy Bread out of the box

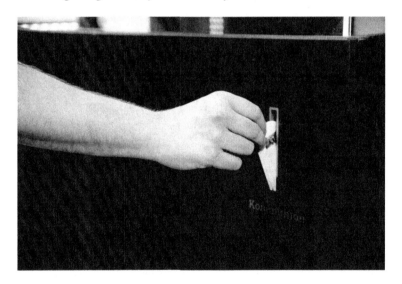

6. **Procession** The dismissal or excerpt, in the figurative sense, is now to contact the author of the tweet or to respond in a different way to the hate tweet. This act is thought-provoking, calling for action and promoting greater communication and freedom of expression in the global community. Finally, the user can absorb the body of Christ and complete the Communion. The user of an indulgence acted to receive the purification. The process ends with the eating of the sacramental bread, and this closes the Holy Communion.

An appropriate design has been applied, in order to motivate the user to approach the interactive object (Figure 10). The aesthetics of a mobile automaton serves as an allegory for the drastic reduction,

Figure 9. (right) Scanning the engraved QR code, which referenced the posting on Twitter

Figure 10. (left) General view of the data-driven slot machine Instant Church

Figure 11. (right) QR-Code generated by Machine with a link to a video demonstration

Figure 12. The engraving process of the wafer realized with microcontrollers and laser technologies

compression, and digitization of the service and is intended to underpin the critical theoretical provocation visually. The designers have created an appealing aesthetic for attention with various Christian design attributes like crosses, precious metal elements, animated lights and created a visual bridge to the topic of religion and digitization. Essential design elements to attract the attention of users include the small golden cross on the cover of the engine in front of the tabernacle (representing the donation in church), the conspicuously illuminated cross on the box containing the laser (representing the consecration). The acrylic cover (representing the church window) protects the precious and sacred elements and is fully illuminated by an animated light installation. The edges of the acrylic glass, both before and during the ceremony, are effectively "enlightened". During operation, the process is visually accompanied by a projection from below onto the internal surface. The user can observe in real time the workings of the machine as it indicates its steps relative to the Catholic service.

Figure 13 summarizes the technical process of "Instant Church." After a coin is inserted, the machine starts (1) playing church organ music and a light show (2). An algorithm searches Twitter for hate speech and selects one Tweet (3). In the next step, the machine visualizes the stations of the Catholic service, projecting it on its surface (4). The mechanism on the bottom of the acrylic tube representing the tabernacle moves a wafer onto the conveyor belt towards the laser inside the black box (5). The box is protection against Laser emission. With the wafer in the correct position under the Laser, the link to the hate tweet is converted into a QR Code and encoded onto the wafer (6). Upon completion of this step, the conveyor belt moves the wafer to the delivery slot (7). As the user removes the wafer, the music fades, and the lights darken. As the last step, the user has the option to scan the QR code and read the Tweet with the option to contemplate and react.

Figure 13. the technical process of "Instant Church"

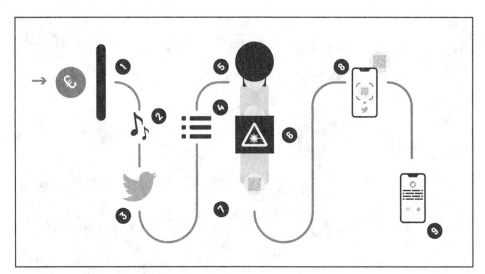

TECHNICAL IMPLEMENTATION AND PRACTICAL ISSUES

A functional prototype of the Instant Church project is built with rapid prototyping methods using latest generation microprocessors. The project consists of a software part, written in Java and the hardware of the machine. A real-time algorithm calls the Twitter API to request a pointer to a Tweet based on the selection criterium. The URL of the Tweet s is stored in temporary memory and converted to a QR code. The QR Code is converted to G-code, a numerical control programming language executable by a laser-cutter. Commonly problems in software development arise at the interaction of different interfaces and algorithms. This created a significant challenge in the development of the conversion of the Twitter URL into a vector-based QR code and then G-Code. The most reliable solution was to use proven open source frameworks. The program checks each pixel and transfers it to a pixel array which is then converted into a G-Code file. Identifying the optimal image structure required experimentation with different pixel variants. Elliptical points turned out to be best suited as they held the shape during lasering, were faster to generate with fewer errors. Correct positioning under the laser was critical and required multiple development steps with the conveyor belt. An optical sensor solved this issue. Isolating the laser with its dangerous emission was a particular challenge in an exhibition environment (Figure 14 J). Figure 12 shows the laser process that cannot be observed from the outside.

The process of technical lasering, as focused divine energy, is an excellent metaphor. (Professor, age 42)

Setting the correct laser power required extensive tests. Setting energy and duration too high resulted in faded contours and made the QR Code unreadable. Experiments with 3D printing on the wafer did not result in readable codes. Test series with different wafer types based on composition and thickness led to the best material for this purpose. A positive encoding result is shown in Figure 14 L with multiple failures in Figure 14 K.

Figure 14. (G to L) Iterations of technical realization

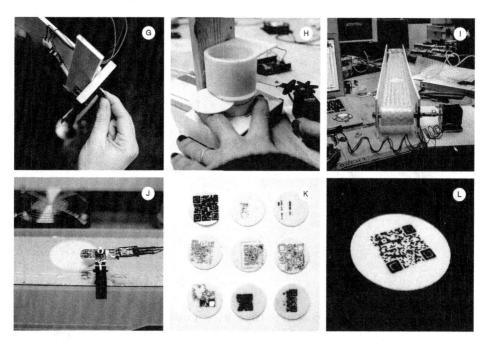

After iterative development and tests of the separate mechanical parts of the project, the sensors, and motors needed to be integrated with the microprocessor which turned out to be a rather complicated process. Rapid prototyping produced a range of solution approaches that were created in 3D printing. The coin acceptor consisting of a button with an extended lever was first designed with paper prototypes to ensure that the coin falls into the container. (Figure 14 G). The mechanism of delivering the wafer was rather complicated and created with 3D printing. Figure H shows an early variation of the ejection mechanism. The conveyor belt with its stepper motors and a conveyor made out of refractory material durable enough to withstand the laser process required fine-tuning to ensure it would deliver the wafer to the correct position under the laser. (Figure 14 I).

USER EVALUATION

The presentation during a four-day art and design exhibition in February of 2018 at the Forum Gestaltung exhibition space in Magdeburg and the Cathedral, allowed over 700 international visitors to experience the different projects. A wide range of interested attendees, from academia, as well as grade-school and college students, members of the church as well as people with no religious practice explored the "Instant Church".

Visitors from Germany, Great Britain, Romania, and Italy participated in semi-structured interviews and multiple open discussions about Instant Church. Thirty-one interview records were qualitatively evaluated and categorized by criteria for socio-demographic and religious affiliation. The statements were evaluated as positive, negative or neutral regarding subjective opinion and segmented by age group or church affiliation (Figure 15).

Figure 15. Comparison of categorized qualitative statements from the memorandum (n=31)

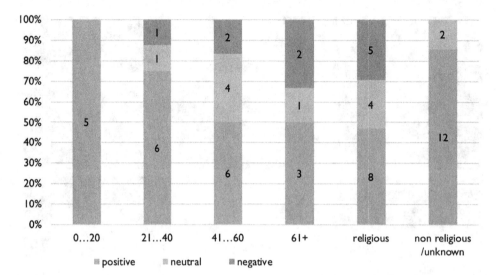

Participants interviewed for the project in the age bracket under 40 showed an 85% positive reflection about the experience and mindset of the installation, grade-students were 100% positive in their perception of the project.

"Perhaps not quite serious but nevertheless an interesting approach to getting young people excited about the church." (Chorus singer, female, 19 years old, religious) – If this would happen anywhere, then I would often participate in the church. (Student, 16, non-religious) – The installation emphasizes the zeitgeist of the constant availability of information. (Student, 19, unknown religious orientation)

Visitors in the age bracket 40+ showed a 50/50 distribution in their perception of the project in acceptance and rejection without strong negative responses

"The machine opens up a novel approach to the church, especially for non-religious people. (Catholic School Teacher, 62, religious) – That's pure blasphemy! (Church member, 68, religious) – The church committees would never tolerate such a thing! (Theist, High church official, 66, religious)

86% of the reviewed non-religious people had a favorable impression compared to 47% of people identifying as religious. Negative responses came from almost 30% of the group identifying as religious.

IMPLICATIONS AND OUTCOME

The artifact caused controversy and discussion regarding religion in the target group, especially with young and non-religious participants. As shown in the study "Now the Bible is an App" participants show affection for the use of digital technologies in the context of religion, which can be used as an entry point and intermediary to the younger generation, as demonstrated in our study. The related project "Nightsky," created in the same context, had a similar effect and reached an untapped target group for the church. Usually, an organ concert attracts about 100 visitors of an older target group. The two performances were sold out, attracting 1,200 visitors – a mostly younger audience – with classical music from the 20th century.

Over 700 visitors saw the Instant Church exhibit during the four-day exhibition and triggered controversial discussions (see the evaluation in Figure 15).

The prototype was recognized as a learning device that explains the Eucharist procedure to visitors who are not familiar with it. It demonstrates some parts of its meaning, its context, and metaphors quickly and attractively. In the same breath, it triggers questions and discussion. The authors planned it as a mediating learning technology in the sense of Bloom's taxonomy (Anderson, 2001, see Figure 16) that addresses not only remembering and understanding but also transfer-aspects like analysis and evaluation in the education process, triggered by the presented machine (Table 1).

As the learning function of Instant Church was particularly demanded at the exhibition by school teachers and students, this aspect could be extended in future development.

Even an active member of the church could not explain the process of the Eucharist celebration so precisely. (Journalist, 26, non-religious).

Despite an initial negative impression of the often-religious participants, it was possible to build up emotional access to this critical topic after further explanations, which increased the acceptance of the artifact. Real physical products, such as Instant Church, can also support the practice of faith as outlined in "religion on demand: faith-based design" (Gorman, 2009) and "using sketching to support design research in new ways." (Wyche & Grinter, 2012)

Figure 16. Learning objectives from Benjamin Bloom's taxonomy

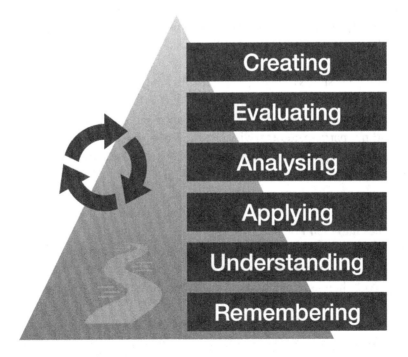

Table 1. Educational goals of "Instant Church" according to Bloom's Taxonomy

Remembering	The "Instant Church" machine performs the Eucharist and visitors watch the service, allowing them to learn about the different steps and gaining the ability to repeat them.
Understanding	Some aspects of the Eucharist are displayed on different levels with several metaphors to the learner. This helps understanding the meaning of the ritual due to its compactness, the multimedia explanations, and access to its core values.
Applying	Knowing about the ritual invites people back to the church.
Analyzing	Experts compare the "Instant Church" with their theoretical and experimental knowledge about the Eucharist. Knowing rituals from other religions also encourages the analysis of this technologically enhanced short version of the service.
Evaluating	Visitors were challenged to evaluate the project in multiple ways depending on their background, demographics, and spiritual affiliation. The evaluation shows that people had an unequivocal opinion about the project.
Creating	Encouraging members of the church to explore new ways to use digital technology to grow audience, educate, and provide access to the rituals.

The acceptance level by participants of this study as well as other research show that the church as an institution needs to explore new technologies to connect with different target groups.

Few documented projects were identified that describe interactive objects in the context of religion. This study shows the potential of using interactive technologies to attract a larger audience – especially younger people without religious affiliation. This offers an opportunity for churches to use digital media and technology to grow their audience, better connect with their members, and keep up with the newest developments in digitization. This research illustrates the opportunity, with Instant Church taking up only a small part of the ritual, the Eucharist. There is however always a risk of misunderstanding: Instant Church was in some cases interpreted as blasphemy. The automated process of the Eucharist may not work as a simple solution for current Church problems such as member attrition.

While the interest in the project was significant during the exhibition, the data collected did not show a clear indication that a system such as Instant Church would increase participation in church activities. Digital natives had the strongest interest in the specifics of the machine as well as its integration in critical social media processes.

The technical perspective shows a clear opportunity for automated systems to augment and contribute to religious rituals. The actual process will have to be defined by liturgy and the church interested in integrating machines into their practice. Providing 24/7 access to religious services will increase access for people who could not participate otherwise. At the same time, it opens the question if the church service inherently requires a group of church members. This question allows further research in collaboration with theological experts.

From a technical perspective there is a clear opportunity for automated systems to contribute and augment religious rituals. The actual process will have to be defined by liturgy and the church interested in integrating machines into their practice.

Providing 24/7 access to religious services will increase access for people who otherwise would not be able to participate in a service. At the same time, it opens the question if the church service inherently requires a group of church members. This question allows further research in collaboration with theological experts.

While all four segments of the initial critical design process could be completed, the critical reflection process can be considered as the most successful in reaching the goals of the objective. The quantitative and qualitative evaluation showed a highly diverse set of opinions with an almost positive response in the groups up to the age group up to 40 years of age.

However, it serves as an attempt through a vision of the future to encourage people to go new ways. Even if the audience understood the whole process of the automated Eucharist, the last and meaningful step of engraving a hate tweet on the oblate turned out to be a hardly understandable metaphor.

Why do you tattoo the Body of Christ? (Professor, 42, unknown religious orientation)

A different version of Instant Church can provide a different focus and step back to the original religious ceremony of just giving the oblate to the user, but in an automated and digitized form of blessing

Concerning the central questions of this research project: "Can a church ritual be digitized?" and "How do people react to that?" two general approaches could have been used to approach the objectives Religion and Digitization:

7. **Content focused**: Coming from Religion as a topic, analyzing rituals and cultural techniques leads towards an augmentation with technology. (E.g. Whispering Table, Recipe Trace).
8. **Technology focused**: Using and testing existing and new interaction techniques in a religious context will result in new applications. This analysis discovers interaction methods that are particularly suitable for religious practice.

FUTURE RESEARCH AND OUTLOOK

This project started with a content-focused approach, and then also explored the technology focus within the context of a Design Science Research Methodology. The Catholic faith was a focus in the process to get a particular way of realization. The authors analyzed other rituals and cultural techniques, covering non-Christian religious traditions and found many similarities. These similarities and differences could be represented in further development of this project.

The project also examined the extent to which **Augmented Reality** can be integrated into the concept. Finally, the realized data projection in and on the machine offers a comparable augmentation as that available through other AR technologies. This allows multilingualism, customization, expansion of content, etc. to be realized with little effort.

Sensor technology, the **Internet of Things** (IoT), and **Artificial Intelligence** would enable individual communication with the user. Responding to emotions (emotion tracking, such as Noldus FaceReader), detecting and using movements in front of the exhibit, recognizing single or group context would result in a more personal way of communication to the visitor.

A true 24/7 availability could be built and provide a range of product design variants that reflect different approaches to liturgy. A 24/7 solution will have to be completely self-explanatory. Other versions could include a live interaction with an ordained priest through a video conference or holographic representation, offering an individual exchange with a priest or through a networking system a point-to-multipoint connection for remote participation in a service. The system could be extended in the future to offer other rituals such as baptism and marriage. Once installed in a public place such a system could offer access to multiple denominations and religious belief systems.

In one variant this can allow remote access to a service held by a priest in church, in another it can become a fully autonomous product - can it augment and remotely connect to a priest or replace a priest?

Connecting on **Social Media** and generating personality profiles for individual addressing using AI algorithms (Bachrach, 2014) were identified as additional possibilities for extensions of this prototype.

This type of further research will raise a critical question: Will the society in the 21st century accept a highly personalized religious service and interaction and at what price? In former times, the village pastor knew almost everything from the conversations or confessions of the parishioners and used this for the binding of his sheep to the institutional church. Today, social media provide unavoidable transparency about each user. The church only uses this binding function in a few approaches yet (Eyal, 2013). It remains questionable whether acceptance for it arises or whether religious digital transparency is ethically justifiable.

Future research will have to include the question if laser-printing a QR code on a wafer represents "tattooing the Body of Christ" depending whether it is the unconsecrated host or the sacrament and if this is acceptable or even desirable as a sign of our age, which will have to be answered by theological experts that could not be answered in the scope of this project. Other research topics include how a system can give guidance and offer a wider range of tasks beyond reacting to a hate tweet. These tasks can also include communal services and study. Feedback showed that the integration of a step of critical review of social media hate messages was considered important by those interviewed and the service presented in the Instant Church prototype was definitely of interest. The question if a digital artefact has the potential to offer a path to salvation goes beyond the scope of this paper and needs to be referred to theologians and experts in ecclesiology.

The fascination of technical instruments, machines, and automata was always used by churches to impress its members and attract new audience. The digitization of religious rituals can be accomplished today both from a technical and a design perspective. This can include virtual interaction and communication spaces as well as social media and smart technology. Theological and ecclesiastical understanding and the relationship to the information society will determine the role of digital technology in the understanding, acceptance, and practice of religion in daily life. Technology can thus be a significant force in the perception of religious practices in society. A digital dimension can be integrated into religious action and thought, whether it catalytically reinforces the trend towards the church or turning away from religious institutions and beliefs, thus providing a moral compass.

ACKNOWLEDGMENT

The "Instant Church" project and this paper would not have been possible without the support of the members of the Magdeburg Cathedral project, Simon Frübis and Veronika Weiß for the project "Nachthimmel", Alina Kalacheva for the project "Musik zum Berühren", Sinah Herrklotsch and Thomas Gagelmann for the project "Zahn der Zeit", Nicole Rüde and Jenny Miosga for the project "Verborgende Grabstätten" and the many collaborators and supporters not listed here. A special thank you goes to Jürgen Häberle for internal support and Isabell Tönniges and Barry Jordan from Magdeburg Cathedral for the collaboration and supervision of the projects.

REFERENCES

Anderson, L. W. (2001). *A taxonomy for learning, teaching, and assessing: A revision of Bloom's taxonomy of educational objectives, abridged edition.* White Plains, NY: Longman.

Bachrach, Y., Graepel, T., Kohli, P., Kosinski, M., & Stillwell, D. (2014). Your digital image: factors behind demographic and psychometric predictions from social network profiles. In *Proceedings of the 2014 international conference on Autonomous agents and multi-agent systems.* International Foundation for Autonomous Agents and Multiagent Systems.

Cheong, P. H. (2010). Faith Tweets: Ambient Religious Communication and Microblogging Rituals. M/C Journal, 13(2).

de Sepibus, G. (1678). *Romani collegii Societatis Jesu musaeum celeberrimum.* Amsterdam: Janssonius van Waesberge.

Ess, C. M. (2004). *Critical Thinking and the Bible in the Age of New Media.* Lanham, MD: University Press of America.

Eyal, N. (2013). The App of God. *The Atlantic.* Retrieved from http://www.theatlantic.com/technology/archive/2013/07/the-app-of-god/278006/

Finkelde, J., & Finkelde, F. (2016). *Grow a healthy church.* Retrieved from https://www.growahealthychurch.com/7-reasons-why-churches-stop-growing-and-decline-into-impotence/

Gaver, B. (2011). Prayer Companion 2010, Interaction Design Studio, Goldsmith, University of London. In Talk to Me: Design and Communication between People and Objects. New York: The Museum of Modern Art.

Gibbs, S. (2017, August 23). The future of funerals? Robot priest launched to undercut human-led rites. *The Guardian.*

Gorman, C. R. (2009). *Religion on demand: Faith-based design. Design and Culture, 1(1),* 9–22.

Hagemann, T. (2017). Digitalisierung und technische Assistenz im Sozial- und Gesundheitswesen. In *Gestaltung des Sozial- und Gesundheitswesens im Zeitalter von Digitalisierung und technischer Assistenz* (pp. 9–18). Baden-Baden, Germany: Nomos Verlag. doi:10.5771/9783845279435-9

Henke, N. (2017). Dieser enorm gruselige Roboter-Priester segnet dich – und verfolgt dich bis in deine Träume. *Gallileo TV.* Retrieved from https://www.galileo.tv/tech-trends/dieser-enorm-gruselige-roboter-priester-segnet-dich-und-verfolgt-dich-bis-in-deine-traeume/

Hevner, A. R., March, S. T., Park, J., & Ram, S. (2004). *Design science in information systems research. MIS Quarterly, 28(1),* 75–105.

Hjarvard, S. (2008). The mediatization of religion: A theory of the media as agents of religious change. *Northern Lights, 6*(1), 9–26. doi:10.1386/nl.6.1.9_1

Hutchings, T. (2014). *Now the Bible is an app: digital media and changing patterns of religious authority. In Religion, Media, and Social Change* (pp. 151–169). Oxford, UK: Routledge.

Jenkins, J. (2017). The (holy) ghost in the machine: Catholic thinkers tackle the ethics of artificial intelligence. *Religion News Service*. Retrieved from https://religionnews.com/2018/05/22/the-holy-ghost-in-the-machine-catholic-thinkers-tackle-the-ethics-of-artificial-intelligence/

Kath.net. (2013). *Originell: Weltweit erster Automat für Rosenkränze*. Retrieved from http://www.kath.net/news/41705

Kim, J. Y., Chien, T. Y., Liao, S., & York, D. (2011). The Messenger. 2010. In Talk to Me: Design and Communication between People and Objects. New York: The Museum of Modern Art.

King, E. (2002). Clockwork Prayer: A Sixteenth-Century Mechanical Monk. Blackbird. *An Online Journal of Literature and the Arts, 1*(1), 1–29.

Kircher, A. (1646). *Ars magna lucis et umbrae in decem libros digesta: Quibus admirandae lucis et umbrae in mundo, atque adeò universa natura, vires effectus[que] uti nova, ita varia novorum reconditiorum[que] speciminum exhibitione, ad varios mortalium usus, panduntur*. Roma: Scheus.

Kison, M. (2007). *Ticker Cross, European Media Art Festival, Osnabrueck, Germany*. Retrieved from http://www.markuskison.de/

Manaugh, G. (2016). Why Catholics Built Secret Astronomical Features into Churches to Help Save Souls. *Atlas Obscura*. Retrieved from https://www.atlasobscura.com/

Miller Mc Farlan, E. (2017). Blessing robots: Is a technological reformation coming? *Religion News Service*. Retrieved from https://religionnews.com

Peffers, K., Tuunanen, T., Rothenberger, M. A., & Chatterjee, S. (2007). A design science research methodology for information systems research. *Journal of Management Information Systems, 24*(3), 45–77. doi:10.2753/MIS0742-1222240302

Plato. *(370 bc). Phaedrus 274e–275b. In Plato: Complete Works* (J. M. Cooper, Ed.).

Qualbrink, A. (n.d.). *Zukunftsbild im Bistum Essen: Initiative für den Verbleib in der Kirche*. Retrieved from https://zukunftsbild.bistum-essen.de/

Riegel, U., Kröck, T., & Faix, T. (2018). *Warum Menschen die katholische Kirche verlassen. Eine explorative Untersuchung zu Austrittsmotiven im Mixed-Methods Design*. Etscheid-Stams.

Robinson, F. (1993). Technology and religious change: Islam and the impact of print. *Modern Asian Studies, 27*(1), 229–251.

SZ. (2018). *Data provided by Evangelische Kirche in Deutschland (EKD) and Deutsche Bischofskonferenz (DBK)*. Retrieved from https://www.sueddeutsche.de/

Vermeir, K. (2007). Athanasius Kircher's magical instruments: An essay on science, religion and applied metaphysics. *Studies in History and Philosophy of Science Part A, Elsevier, 38*(2), 363–400. doi:10.1016/j.shpsa.2007.03.008

Weizenbaum, J. (1966, January). ELIZA—A computer program for the study of natural language communication between man and machine. *Communications of the ACM, 9*(1), 36–45. doi:10.1145/365153.365168

Weizenbaum, J. (1976). *Computer Power and Human Reason: From Judgment to Calculation*. W H Freeman & Co.

Wyche, S. P., & Grinter, R. E. (2012). Using sketching to support design research in new ways: a case study investigating design and charismatic Pentecostalism in São Paulo, Brazil. In *Proceedings of the 2012 iConference*. ACM. 10.1145/2132176.2132185

Zsupan-Jerome, D. (2014). *Connected Toward Communion: The Church and Social Communication in the Digital Age*. Collegeville, MN: Liturgical Press.

ADDITIONAL READING

Dunne, A., & Raby, F. (2014). *Speculative everything: Design, fiction, and social dreaming*. Cambridge, Mass.: MIT Press.

Ess, C. M. (2004). *Critical thinking and the Bible in the age of new media*. Dallas, TX: University Press of America.

Herzog, M. A., Wunderling, J., Gabele, M., Klank, R., Landenberger, M., & Pepping, N. (2016). Context Driven Content Presentation for Exhibition Places. Four Interaction Scenarios Developed for Museums. Electronic Imaging & the Visual Arts Conference EVA 2016, St. Petersburg.

Iglhaut, S., Kapfer, H., & Rötzer, F. (2007). *What if?: Zukunftsbilder der Informationsgesellschaft*. Hannover: Heise Zeitschriften.

Kantor, D. (2007). *Graphic Design and Religion: A Call for Renewal*. Gia Publications.

Klanten, R. (2011). *A touch of code interactive installations and experiences*. Berlin: Die-Gestalten-Verl.

Zielinski, S. (2006). Deep time of the media. Toward an Archeology of Hearing and Seeing by Technical Means, Cambridge Mass.

Chapter 6

Explanations in Artificial Intelligence Decision Making:
A User Acceptance Perspective

Norman G. Vinson
National Research Council, Canada

Heather Molyneaux
National Research Council, Canada

Joel D. Martin
National Research Council, Canada

ABSTRACT

The opacity of AI systems' decision making has led to calls to modify these systems so they can provide explanations for their decisions. This chapter contains a discussion of what these explanations should address and what their nature should be to meet the concerns that have been raised and to prove satisfactory to users. More specifically, the chapter briefly reviews the typical forms of AI decision-making that are currently used to make real-world decisions affecting people's lives. Based on concerns about AI decision making expressed in the literature and the media, the chapter follows with principles that the systems should respect and corresponding requirements for explanations to respect those principles. A mapping between those explanation requirements and the types of explanations generated by AI decision making systems reveals the strengths and shortcomings of the explanations generated by those systems.

INTRODUCTION

Artificial Intelligence (AI) systems are moving out of the laboratory and into the real world at an extremely rapid pace. As they do, the decisions they make affect people's lives in diverse domains such as medical treatments and diagnoses, hiring and promotions, loans and the interest rates borrowers pay, prison sentences and so on (Pasquale, 2015; Roshanov et al., 2013; Wexler, 2018). This adoption has produced a corresponding increase in ethical concerns about how these decisions are made, and for

DOI: 10.4018/978-1-5225-9069-9.ch006

good reason, as these decisions can be inaccurate or unacceptable (Guidotti et al., 2018). Such concerns have led to calls for AI systems to explain their decisions (Campolo, Sanfilippo, Whittaker, & Crawford, 2017; Edwards & Veale, 2017; Guidotti et al., 2018; Molnar & Gill, 2018; Wachter, Mittelstadt, & Russell, 2018). In this context, this chapter provides testable principles to which such explanations should conform to be acceptable to users of AI systems; both to the people who use the AI systems to generate decisions and to those who are subject to the decisions. If users do not find AI decisions-making system explanations acceptable, they will either not use the systems to generate decisions or refuse to comply with, or protest those decisions (Guidotti et al., 2018)[1].

Because the acceptability of AI explanations to users is a nascent area of research, the authors did not perform a systematic review of the topic. Rather, the authors searched broadly for journal articles and grey literature that might be relevant to the issue, using keywords such as "ethic*", "explanation*" and "artificial intelligence". Backward snowballing (Wohlin, 2014) led to other relevant articles. A review of the articles resulted in the proposal of three principles to which AI decision-making systems (AIDMS) should conform to support user acceptance. The principles were formulated to be testable, that is, to allow experiments to reveal whether explanations that conform to these principles are preferred by users, and/or are sufficient for users to accept the corresponding decisions. These proposed principles are fairness, contestability, and competence.

Fairness requires the equitable treatment of various groups of people and reasonable processing of relevant data. Contestability refers to the ability of a person about whom a decision is made to contest that decision. Competence requires the AIDMS' decision-making performance to meet a certain quality threshold. While these principles do not refer directly to AIDMS explanations, they do generate requirements for such explanations to respect the principles. To illustrate how the principles relate to explanations, the principles are coupled with real world cases identified through backward snowballing (Wohlin, 2014) of the articles and reports collected and through Google searches. Such case-based illustrations are a common educational approach in many fields (Johnson et al., 2012).

These three testable principles constitute this chapter's primary contribution to the field. The authors make a secondary contribution through their discussion of the varying potential of different AIDMSs to adhere to the proposed principles, showing that not all so-called black box (Guidotti et al., 2018) AIDMSs are equally opaque.

Philosophical investigations of the nature of explanations (e.g. Tuomela, 1980) were not examined, neither were the ways in which people generate explanations themselves (e.g. Hilton, 1990). Psychological research on explanation was also not examined. On the whole, psychology has focused on how people explain other people's behavior (Malle, 2011), the conditions that induce people to make cause and effect inferences (e.g. Subbotsky, 2004), the extent to which people's explanations of events are consistent with scientific ones (Kubricht, Holyoak, & Lu, 2017), and the formation of mental models about real-word events (Battaglia, Hamrick, & Tenenbaum, 2013). It is not that that this research is irrelevant to the issue, but it is just not as directly applicable as material that is specifically about AIDMS explanations and concerns.

The chapter continues as follows: Context is provided via an introduction to three commonly used types of AIDMSs. The features of explanations that users prefer to receive from recommender systems, another type of AIDMS, are then described. This is followed by a discussion of the concerns that have been raised about the effect of AI decision-making on people's everyday lives. These perspectives are then combined to propose principles and concrete requirements that AIDMS explanations should respect to (potentially) increase user acceptance. This leads into an assessment of the ability of the AI systems introduced earlier to adhere to those principles and requirements.

BACKGROUND

AI Decision-Making Systems

The purposes of this section are to provide a brief layman's introduction of AIDMSs and to explain how some AIDMSs are more amenable to providing explanations than others. These differences underlie the systems' abilities to meet the explanation requirements described later.

Artificial Intelligence (AI) is the subfield of computer science concerned with the simulation or creation of intelligent behavior in computers. AI systems increasingly rely on machine learning (ML) to generate intelligent behavior. For example, an AI system for bank loan approval could be built by applying an ML algorithm to a dataset of a large number of past loans and their outcomes. In the language of ML, this system is *supervised* and would learn a *model* to relate *inputs*, characteristics of the customer in this case, to an *output* prediction about whether the customer would default on the loan, or to a decision about whether the customer should receive a loan. The supervision in this case is the pairing of prior inputs to their corresponding outputs, providing the examples from which the system learns.

The decisions made by ML-based AIDMSs are often difficult to explain because the software developer does not specify how the system makes decisions; the developer does not encode decision rules in the software. Instead, the developer builds a system that *learns* to make the desired decisions. This learning is incorporated into a *model* (not the original software written by the developer) that makes the decisions. Testing an ML system does not typically involve verifying *how* it makes decisions but is instead limited to ensuring that it makes the same decisions that people made in the past. This provides an assurance that the system's decisions are consistent with decisions a human would make, and so, presumably are acceptable (Hulten, 2018; Junker, Hoch, & Dengel, 1999). Of course, this is not very explanatory and may only be palatable when the accuracy is extremely high. Moreover, explanatory information can be extracted more readily from some AIDMS models than others. The most commonly used AIDMSs, automated linear regression, decision trees, and neural networks, are introduced below with specific emphasis on the relative difficulty of extracting explanations for their decisions.

Automated Linear Regression

Automated linear regression is a basic form of ML (Goodfellow, Bengio, & Courville, 2016). It is considered ML because the system learns a model that can predict outcomes (predicted values of the variable y) based on inputs (the values of various variables x_1, x_2, etc.) For example, one could attempt to predict the sale price of a house (y) based on the number of rooms (x). A linear regression model would take the form an of equation such as (1)

$$\text{Predicted price of house} = \beta_0 + \beta(\text{number of rooms})_i + \varepsilon_i \qquad (1)$$

where β_0 is a constant representing the price of a theoretical house with no rooms; β is a coefficient representing the importance of the number of rooms in determining the price of the house; and ε is an error term representing the difference between the model's predicted house price and the actual house price (Field, 2000). This model is often represented graphically (see Figure 1).

In this model, each additional room is predicted to increase the price of a house by $50,000, though the errors (ε_i) show that is only an approximation. This $50,000 is the value of the coefficient β associated to the number of rooms.

Clearly, there is more to house prices than just the number of rooms. The reputation of the neighborhood school is probably a factor, as well as the age of the house, its location, and so on. All of these additional inputs are potential xs to be added to the model, so that the model can end up looking like equation (2) (Field, 2000).

$$Y = \beta_0 + \beta_1 x_1 + \beta_2 x_2 + \beta_3 x_3 + \ldots + \beta_n x_n + \Sigma \varepsilon_i \tag{2}$$

Here, x_1 is the number of rooms, x_2 is the reputation of the school, x_3 is the age of the house, and so on.

Linear regression produces a model that only includes the inputs that actually affect the price of a house, excluding the inputs that do not affect it. Moreover, the size of each input's influence on the price is given by the size of its associated β coefficient. In this model, one additional room will raise the predicted price of a house by $50,000. However, it is possible that one additional year in the age of the house lowers its predicted price by $2,000. The number of rooms would consequently have much more influence than age on house prices. More generally, linear regression allows us to assess the influence of

Figure 1. Data with linear regression model. The line represents the model's predicted y values for any input value x. The model is not perfect because for each value x_i there is a difference (ε) between the actual value of y_i, shown as a dot, and the predicted one, shown by the line. There is also a non-zero intercept β_0.

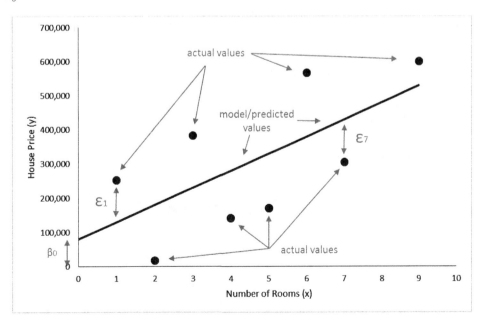

each input on decision-making (or predicted outcomes) (Field, 2000). The explanation for the predicted price of a house is the combination of influential inputs and their relative influence on the predicted price. For example, a house might cost about $400,000 because it has 8 rooms, a big yard, and is 10 years old. In contrast, the presence of a swimming pool may have little bearing on the predicted price, so the pool would not be part of the explanation for the predicted price. Of course, whether such an explanation is acceptable to users remains an unanswered empirical question.

Decision Trees

A decision tree (DT) is a simple branching structure that organizes sequential decisions to reach a final decision or a prediction; an output (Guidotti et al., 2018; Russell & Norvig, 2003). For example, a bank might use a DT to decide if a customer should receive a loan. The first branching question could be based on the loan value. For example, if the value exceeds $10,000, one branch is followed. If the value is less than $10,000, another branch is followed. Once the first question is answered, a second branching question must be answered, and the system continues on to other branches until it reaches a final decision. Further branching questions might include the requested payment schedule, the loan applicant's payment history, etc. The sequence of questions and branching answers can be drawn as a tree of possibilities with final decisions at the ends of the multiple sequential paths through the tree (see another example in Figure 2) (Russell & Norvig, 2003).

Figure 2. A decision tree on the probability of surviving the Titanic sinking. A decision tree showing the survival of passengers on the Titanic ("sibsp" is the number of spouses or siblings aboard). The figures under the leaves show the probability of survival and the percentage of observations in the leaf. Your chances of survival were good if you were (i) a female or (ii) a male younger than 9.5 years with less than 2.5 siblings
Source: Adapted from Milborrow (n.d.). The authors do not warrant the accuracy of the displayed information.

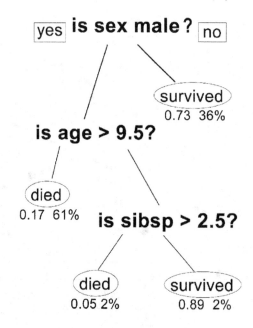

DT ML algorithms consider multiple different tree structures with different sequences of questions and answers. Top performing trees are constructed through supervised learning: the algorithms use a collection of inputs and their corresponding outcomes to score each tree. These algorithms then propose the DT structure that is most likely to lead to correct decisions (Russell & Norvig, 2003).

An explanation for a single DT decision is generated by following the sequence of questions and answers that led to the decision. Differing decisions can be easily explained by identifying the first branching question that produced different answers. (Russell & Norvig, 2003). An overview of a large collection of decisions can be summarized by using the tree as a visualization, possibly with edge thickness representing the number of decisions that followed each of those edges.

In practice, DTs are often combined to increase the system's accuracy. These combinations are known as *random forests*. For example, when determining if a customer should receive a loan, one DT might ask about collateral first, a second tree might ask about loan value first, etc. The ultimate decision might be the one provided by the majority of the DTs. In this more complicated representation, there is no longer a simple explanation about single decisions, for comparing two different decisions, or for summarizing a collection of multiple decisions (Russell & Norvig, 2003).

Neural Networks

Another type of popular ML system is the neural network (NN). In general, it is a layered graph in which each layer contains a set of nodes. The nodes in one layer are fully connected to those in the layer above, except for those of the top layer for which there are no nodes above. The first layer represents the inputs, and the last represents the outputs (see Figure 3) (Goodfellow et al., 2016).

There is a wide variety of NNs with different arrangements of nodes and different learning algorithms (Rumelhart & McClelland, 1986). However, at a very abstract level, a commonly used NN type is similar to regression. Each node represents a single number and each connection between nodes has a weight. The numbers in the input nodes represent a particular input. The numbers in each hidden and

Figure 3. A neural network

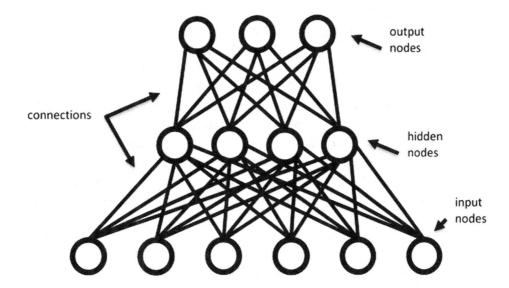

output node are a function of the numbers represented by the units connected to it, as y is to the xs in a regression model. The connection weights correspond to the regression model's coefficients. Learning proceeds through adjustments in the connection weights, such that the output units eventually represent the decisions corresponding to each input (Goodfellow et al., 2016; Rumelhart, Hinton, & Williams, 1986).

NNs are opaque because the effect of any input on the outputs is distributed throughout the system. Consider that the extremely simple NN shown in figure 3 contains seven linear-regression-like models of the form shown in equation (2), all of which interact with each other to produce the various outputs. NNs also typically contain additional transformations of the outputs of those regression-like models (Goodfellow et al., 2016). Moreover, individual inputs, like house prices, can be encoded over several input nodes. Consequently, even if one could identify one input *node* as being important, it is not clear how this would relate to the importance of the input *as a whole*.

Automated linear regression, DTs (and random forests), and NNs are perhaps the more commonly used AIDMSs. However, there are many more AIDMSs (see e.g. Russell & Norvig, 2003). Researchers have also developed a large number of techniques to generate explanations from various AIDMSs (Alonso, Castiello, & Mencar, 2018; Guidotti et al., 2018). However, the focus is this chapter is not on methods to generate explanations from AI systems but on what features those explanations should have for users to find them acceptable. These features have been investigated in the context of recommender systems, and the related findings are reviewed in the next section. The subsequent section contains descriptions of the controversies and concerns that have arisen as the use of AIDMSs has spread.

Recommender System Explanation Features Preferred by Users

The review described in the introduction revealed that research had been conducted on the type of explanation features preferred by users of recommender systems. Recommender systems are AI systems that recommend various products, services, articles, or social connections to users. Recommendations are typically personalized in reference to the user's personal profile. However, recommender systems do not all rely on the same AI technique. Instead, their commonality lies in their purpose: to recommend items of interest (Bilgic & Mooney, 2005).

The study of explanations in recommender systems is complicated by the diversity of the research questions (Nunes & Jannach, 2017), which can represent multiple different dimensions that are not always clearly identified, including transparency, trust, effectiveness, etc. (Al-Taie, 2013). Some studies experiment on the presentation of the explanations (with visualizations for example) in addition to the features of the explanations themselves. In many studies, researchers obtain inconsistent results across several dimensions such that one explanation feature performs best on one dimension, but not an another (e.g. Gedikli, Jannach, & Ge, 2014). Interpretation of the findings is further complicated by whether researchers examine satisfaction with the explanations or satisfaction with the recommended item, and again multiple metrics are used to measure satisfaction. This heterogeneity led the authors to cast a wide net by first searching for review articles of recommender systems focusing on user preferences or explanations, acceptance and trust. Where the review articles presented relevant findings, the authors accessed the primary sources. This procedure uncovered the information regarding the users' preferred explanation features.

Zanker (2012) found that explanations about spa recommendations increased users' perception of the system's usefulness, which would promote system adoption (Davis, 1989). For example, one explanation could be that a recommended spa was "family friendly" for users with families. The important aspect of this explanation is that it is personalized (Bilgic & Mooney, 2005; Tintarev & Masthoff, 2012): it relates one of the user's characteristics to a feature of the recommend product. However, users preferred more complex explanations involving several matching characteristics (Gedikli et al., 2014; Muhammad, Lawlor, & Smyth, 2016), or tradeoffs between items and profile features, indicating for example, that a spa may be family friendly, but also more expensive (Pu & Chen, 2007), or explicitly drawing relationships between matching characteristics (e.g. luxurious *therefore* expensive) (Zanker & Schoberegger, 2014).

Complexity has its limits, such that users do not often prefer the most complex explanations (Herlocker, Konstan, & Riedl, 2000; Pu & Chen, 2007; Zanker & Schoberegger, 2014). The preference for complexity seems to arise mainly when the users' expectations are violated (Kizilcec, 2016) or when the topic is important to them (Pu & Chen, 2007). Even in those situations, however, there is a limit to preferred complexity (Kizilcec, 2016). Similarly, users typically show less interest in the decision-making process, unless the decision is important to them or violates their expectations (Gedikli et al., 2014; Kizilcec, 2016).

The two recurring themes in this body of research are that explanations should relate the recommended item's characteristics to the user's personal characteristics and that they should neither be too simple nor too complex. However, research on recommender systems typically involves topics that have little impact on peoples' lives. It is therefore unclear to what extent these findings can be generalized to settings in which AIDMS decisions have more serious consequences, such as employment, criminal trials, immigration, and discrimination.

CONCERNS OVER AI DECISION-MAKING

AIDMSs are now being used in sensitive areas such as criminal sentencing (Wexler, 2018) and immigration (Molnar & Gill, 2018). This has led to calls to freeze the adoption of new AIDMSs in such areas (Molnar & Gill, 2018), or even to suspend their use altogether (Campolo, Sanfilippo, Whittaker, & Crawford, 2017).

This section includes a categorization of the concerns that have been expressed over AI decision-making. These categories are illustrated with real cases of controversial AI decisions where possible. Other examples are fictitious, but could reasonably occur given the use made of such systems (Pasquale, 2015).

The authors categorized the identified concerns as:

- Fairness
- Contestability
- Competence

It is important to note that this categorization is only intended to provide context for, and lead to, a set of testable principles about explanation acceptability. It is not intended to serve as a definitive taxonomy of concerns about AIDMSs. Moreover, this list is limited to concerns most germane to features of explanations. Other concerns, such as the loss of employment due to automation (Campolo et al., 2017), are unrelated to explanations. Accordingly, no claim is made that any AI system that addresses these concerns will receive widespread user acceptance. Finally, whether addressing these concerns will satisfy users still remains to be verified empirically. In the following sections, these categories of concerns are each discussed in turn, and illustrated with examples.

Fairness

In this section, the fairness of decision-making processes and their outcomes is addressed.

Bias

One aspect of fairness in decision making is ensuring that identifiable groups of people are not intentionally or accidentally disadvantaged (Hacker & Wiedemann, 2017; Zemel, Wu, Swersky, Pitassi, & Dwork, 2013). Fairness is not only a concern for users, but also, in some jurisdictions, for the authorities. In these jurisdictions, fairness is a legal requirement in that some personal characteristics (such as race or gender) cannot be used as a basis for selecting people (Edwards & Veale, 2017). Consequently, fairness is of concern not only to those about whom decisions are made, but also to those who rely on AIDMSs, and to the authorities. Such legal protections may be why fairness has dominated discussions on the ethics of AIDMSs (Edwards & Veale, 2017). Below, the concern for fairness is illustrated with a few specific cases.

Cases

The *Test-Achats* legal case is often used (for example by Edwards & Veale, 2017) to illustrate the issue of fairness in AIDMSs, even though it seems likely that the decisions resulted from actuarial calculations rather than AI. In this case, the plaintiffs challenged the practice of charging different insurance premiums to women and men, arguing that it was discriminatory and, as such, violated the EU directive on equal treatment of men and women. The defendants argued that this practice was permitted under Article 5 of the directive, which allows different premiums if there is actuarial evidence that risk differs according to sex. However, the *Cour constitutionnelle* (Constitutional Court) of Belgium ruled that the provision allowing this discrimination was intended to be temporary and, as a result, the *Cour* invalidated the provision (Association belge des consommateurs *Test-Achats* ASBL and others v. Conseil des ministres, 2011).

In this case, discrimination was intentional as it was based on a prohibited characteristic (sex). This discrimination was nonetheless allowed by an existing regulation that the judges struck down, thus making the discrimination illegal from then on.

Discrimination can also occur *unintentionally* through proxy variables. This is illustrated by Amazon's introduction of a free same-day delivery service. Obviously, this service could not be offered everywhere due to logistical constraints, so some urban neighborhoods in several cities were excluded. Unfortunately, many of those excluded neighborhoods had a characteristic in common: a majority of the residents were African-American. Since Amazon does not collect race data, it was not aware of the relationship between the racial composition of a neighborhood and Amazon's neighborhood selection process. This relationship was discovered through a Bloomberg news analysis that relied on race data from the census bureau. Understandably, this exclusion upset the people living in those neighborhoods, resulted in negative publicity for Amazon, and scrutiny from elected officials. Elected officials demanded that Amazon expand its free delivery areas, and Amazon quickly complied (Ingold & Soper, 2016). The decision to exclude certain neighborhoods was unfair but unintentional. It only occurred because neighborhood was an effective proxy variable for race.

Even worse, ML can perpetuate existing biases and discrimination by learning from a data set that incorporates them (Kiritchenko & Mohammad, 2018). For example, Bertrand and Mullainathan (2004) found that employment applicant CVs with white-looking or sounding names generated 50% more call-backs for interviews than CVs with African-American looking or sounding names. A ML model built with such CVs and callback data would incorporate the same racial bias without anyone knowing.

The Decision-Making Process

While discrimination against identifiable groups receives much of the attention in the discussion on fairness of AIDMSs, there is more to fairness than non-discrimination. One aspect of fairness relates to the ways in which the inputs are evaluated, transformed, combined, and incorporated as part of the decision-making process. For example, a user may believe that some inputs are more important than others and wish to confirm that the decision-making process weighted the inputs accordingly. The case described below illustrates this issue.

Kizilcec's (2016) study was motivated by a real-world situation involving the grading of class assignments. One teaching assistant for the class had graded assignments more harshly than the other. Understandably, this upset the students who received lower grades. To increase fairness, the instructor adjusted the grades to remove the teaching assistants' systematic differences. Kizilcec's (2016) experiment involved a similar grading situation in which the subjects were provided with different explanations about the grading process. One explanation stated that the grades were adjusted statistically to correct for the graders' systematic biases and accuracy. Kizilcec (2016) found that people preferred to see this explanation when their grades were lower than expected, but required no explanation when the grades matched their expectations.

Contestability

If governments require that some decisions be free of discrimination, then it stands to reason that they would allow decisions to be contested on the grounds that they are discriminatory (as in the *Test-Achats* case discussed above). Contestability, therefore, follows from fairness. Generally, contestability can be viewed as the opportunity for people who are affected by a decision to have it reviewed and its outcome potentially changed. Government decisions, in particular, can often be contested through internal mechanisms (Brewer, 2007). Moreover, the courts sometimes serve as a last resort (as in *Test-Achats*). Even judicial decisions can be appealed to a higher court.

In the legal literature, authors have expressed concerns that the ability to contest decisions in court is severely limited by the protection of the intellectual property embedded in AIDMSs (Edwards & Veale, 2017; Wachter, Mittelstadt, & Floridi, 2017; Wexler, 2018). Wexler (2018) notes that even a death penalty defendant for whom critical DNA evidence was produced by forensic software was unable to access the software's source code because it was protected as a trade secret. This is particularly troubling given the less-than-perfect accuracy of such systems (Butler, Kline, & Coble, 2018).

Competence

In this context, competence refers to the AIDMS' performance relating specifically to the quality of its decisions (as opposed to decision speed, for example). Organizations that employ AIDMSs should be particularly interested in competence because poor decision-making will hinder the organization's ability to reach its goals. Users about whom the decisions are made should also, of course, want the AIDMS to be competent. Consider, for example, the accused in the death penalty trial noted by Wexler (2018).

A recent decision by Amazon provides another example. Amazon recently discontinued a program to use an AIDMS for screening job applicants (Dastin, 2018). Reuters claims that the system performed poorly. While an Amazon spokesperson was quoted as saying that the tool "was never used by Amazon recruiters to evaluate candidates", Amazon declined to discuss the system's performance. If the tool did indeed perform poorly, it would *not* have been in Amazon's interest to use it to automatically select less-than-ideal job applicants. It is in Amazon's interest to ensure the screening tool performs competently before it is used in practice.

Several concerns over AI and other algorithmically derived decisions have been expressed in the media and the literature. Three of the important concerns are fairness, contestability, and competence. *Transparency* is also often mentioned (e.g. Edwards & Veale, 2017). However, in this chapter, transparency is viewed as a means of responding to all three of the above concerns.

SOLUTIONS AND RECOMMENDATIONS

The concerns reviewed above as well as the preferred features of recommender system explanations are re-formulated into proposed principles for AIDMS explanations to follow to increase their acceptability to users. Of course, these principles are only hypothetical in that their effect on acceptance remains to be empirically tested. In the subsequent section, the principles are related to the explanatory abilities of the three types of AIDMSs presented in the background section.

Principles and the Requirements for Respecting Them

Respect for User Preferences

The first principle and its accompanying requirements derive from the review of recommender systems' explanations.

- Principle 1: AI decisions should respect user preferences. Requirements:
  ○ The system should provide the inputs that are influential in making a specific decision about a specific individual.
  ○ The system should provide a rationale for why those inputs are relevant to that decision.

The review on recommender systems indicated that users prefer explanations that contain the recommended item features that matched their personal profile features. In more abstract terms, these are the inputs to the system with the greatest influence on the decision. These matching features also provide a rationale for why the item was recommended. For example, a recommender system might produce the following explanation for users expressing a preference for nearby activities: "This spa is recommended because it is near your residence". Hence, this explanation meets the second requirement. The review suggested that users were typically not interested in the decision making process. Finally, note that these requirements relate only to a specific decision about one individual, rather than to the whole body of decisions over all inputs.

Fairness

The second principle corresponds to the first concern: fairness. To be fair, AI decisions should not discriminate on the basis of proscribed characteristic. This requires an inspection of the inputs and a description of the way in which they are processed over the whole body of decisions. This contrasts to the respect of user preferences whose requirements only apply to individual decisions.

- Principle 2: AI decisions should be fair. Requirements:
  - The system should not receive inputs that are considered discriminatory given the context (e.g. gender, or age).
  - The system should not receive inputs that are known proxy variables for discriminatory characteristics.
  - The system should provide the inputs that are influential over all the decisions.
  - The system should provide descriptions of the way in which the input data is processed to arrive at decisions.
  - Organizations that rely on AI decision-making should provide data to ensure the absence of hidden proxy variables and biases:
    - The input data set.
    - The corresponding decision set.

Fairness is, in reality, more complicated than was depicted earlier. The definition of fairness that was presented requires non-discrimination. However, there are many other ways to define fairness and measure it mathematically. Worse even, some fairness measures are inversely related, such that modifying a decision-making system to improve fairness on one measure reduces it on another and vice-versa. Consider, for example, a high school football coach who implements *group* fairness for the age of his players. To attain an equal representation of players of each age, he selects 10 players of each of three ages: 16, 17, and 18 years. However, there are likely 18 year olds who were *not* selected, but are better football players than the younger players who *were* selected. Had the coach not applied group fairness, those 18 year olds would have been selected for the team. Therefore, one could argue that group fairness is unfair to them. The coach's increase in group fairness reduced *individual* fairness. Note also that attaining group fairness required the coach to discriminate on the basis of age in selecting his players (Chouldechova, 2017; Hacker & Wiedemann, 2017; Zemel et al., 2013). Such discrimination violates the fairness requirement adopted above. In specific situations, fairness requirements can therefore differ from those presented in this chapter depending on what type of fairness is sought.

One requirement states that AI systems should simply not have discriminatory inputs, such as age, gender, race, etc. However, the particular personal characteristics that are considered discriminatory often depend on context. For example, children are typically required to have a particular age to enter grade school. In this case, age discrimination is considered acceptable. However, using age discrimination in hiring is often considered unacceptable. Consequently, it is necessary to consider the context to identify the specific characteristics that are considered discriminatory.

Because discrimination can accidentally creep into an AI system via correlations of inputs with prohibited characteristics or biases implicit in the training data, users (and perhaps regulators) should be able to inspect the influential inputs and even obtain the input and decision data, including the training data, the test data, and the production data of AI decisions in real cases. This will allow the users (or regulators) to test for hidden biases. Bias testing will also often require additional data that reveals the correlations between prohibited characteristics and the decisions. In some cases, this data is collected by the government, as with the distribution of racial groups across neighborhoods. In other cases, the data would have to be collected directly from people. However, some people suffer discrimination at the hands of the very companies and organizations requesting their personal information. It therefore seems unlikely that many such individuals would be willing to provide this information, for fear it would be used against them.

Some have called for companies to test their systems and their data sets for fairness (Campolo et al., 2017) and others have called for independent, third party fairness verification (Molnar & Gill, 2018). However, without the correlational data mentioned above fairness cannot be adequately verified.

There exists computer science approaches for preventing discriminatory AI decisions. For example, input data bias can be reduced by adjusting the inputs or the decisions in the training corpus such that no group is disadvantaged (Hacker & Wiedemann, 2017; Zemel et al., 2013). Another approach involves incorporating equity as an objective for the ML mechanisms (Zemel et al., 2013). However, both these approaches require that the discriminatory input variable (e.g. race) be in the data set.

Finally, the decision-making process should also be described because it can have an impact on fairness. As illustrated in the grading case, a grade-adjusting algorithm reduced the bias that was present in the raw grades, the input data. Similarly, AI techniques that attempt to increase fairness have been developed (Hacker & Wiedemann, 2017; Zemel et al., 2013). Users should be interested in reviewing these techniques, particularly since different types of fairness can be involved in trade-offs, as noted above.

Contestability

As discussed earlier, contestability follows from fairness. Consequently, contestability incorporates the fairness requirements. It also incorporates the requirements for respecting user preferences.

- Principle 3: AI decisions should be contestable. Requirements:
    - The system and the organization using it should respect user preferences and ensure fairness.
    - The system should provide a description of the decision-making process for a specific decision.

As with fairness, the ability to contest a decision requires that the inputs forming the basis of the decision be revealed. The relevance of the inputs should be described in the explanation. A petitioner can then argue that the inputs are irrelevant to the decision, or that those inputs are discriminatory (as in the *Test-Achats* case). Again, the weight given to each input must be known. This issue of weight can arise in criminal sentencing during which the various mitigating and aggravating factors are considered to customize the sentence to the particular individual (Baldus, Pulaski, & Woodworth, 1983). An explanation of the decision-making process can increase user satisfaction and trust in the system (Kizilcec, 2016), thus deflecting a potential appeal. Of course, if users disagree with the process, they can appeal the decision on that basis.

Competence

As defined here, competence does not require an explanation per se, but some evidence of competence should be provided to the users. In situations with important outcomes, users may want access to the data so that they can measure the system's competence themselves.

- Principle 4: AIDMSs should be competent. Requirements:
    ○ The system should provide evidence of decision-making accuracy and/or,
    ○ The organization using the system should provide the input and decision data sets so that accuracy can be verified by a third party.

Testing for competence is usually not challenging. Typically, the system is trained on a set of data to learn to associate inputs with corresponding decisions that have already been made. This is known as the training set. A similar set of input/decision data is used to test the system. Not surprisingly, this is referred to as the test set. Unlike the training set decisions, the test set decisions are not shown to the system. Instead, the system processes the test set input data and generates the corresponding decisions itself. The system's decisions are then compared to the test set's decisions to determine how well they match. A competent system will correctly reproduce the test set decisions (Goodfellow et al., 2016).

While this approach is fairly common and standard, it still suffers from some limitations. Perhaps the major limitation is that test validity is limited by the representativeness of the test set sample. If the test sample is very representative of the cases that will be subsequently submitted to the system, then the system's degree of competence will generalize to the new data. If the test set is not representative, then the system's competence with the new data cannot be predicted from the test results (Goodfellow et al., 2016). This is one reason for calls for on-going performance monitoring (Campolo et al., 2017).

In this section, the authors specified requirements for AIDMSs to respect the principles of respect for user preferences, fairness, contestability, and competence. The following section contains a review of the extent to which the three types of AIDMSs introduced earlier can meet these requirements.

AI Decision-Making Systems' Abilities to Meet the Explanability Requirements

The features that explanations must have to meet the principles were specified above. This section provides a brief examination of the extent to which each type of AIDMS can meet those requirements (see Table 1). This examination focuses on the systems' native—*out-of-the-box*—explanatory abilities. The intent is to illustrate differences in system explanability; not review the very large body of work on the topic (Alonso et al., 2018; Guidotti et al., 2018).

Delivering the data to users (R1, R2), applying various techniques to remove bias from the data (R3), and computing system accuracy (R4) do not depend on the type of AIDMS used.

Differences between the systems appear with the other requirements. DTs meet nearly all of the other requirements, while linear regression meets fewer, and NNs meet only one. In a DT, all of the influential inputs (R5) can be identified by inspecting the whole tree (see Figure 2). Moreover, it is easy to follow a single path from the root down to the decision for an individual case, thus identifying a single decision's important inputs (R6). The description of the decision-making process is simply the traversal of the tree leading to the decision (R8, R9). However, it is not clear whether users would find this satisfactory.

Table 1. Explanation requirements met by the AI decision-making systems

	Requirement	Linear Regression	Decision Trees	Neural Networks
1	Provide input data set*			
2	Provide corresponding decision set*			
3	Do not use discriminatory input data	These requirements are not a function of the type of AIDMS		
4	Provide evidence of accuracy (or the data to compute it)			
5	Provide inputs with overall influence	Y	Y	N
6	Provide influential inputs for a single decision	Y	Y	N
7	Provide a rationale for why inputs are relevant to a single decision	N	N	N
8	Provide a description of the (overall) decision-making process.	Y**	Y**	Y**
9	Provide a description of the decision-making process for a single decision	N	Y**	N

Y = meets the requirement; N = does not meet the requirement; * Training, test, and production data. ** May not satisfy users.

Similarly, the rationale relating the inputs to the decision is that they are all on the same branch (R7). Again, this seems unsatisfactory. A more satisfactory explanation would describe the relationship between the input and the decision by referring to real-world requirements. For example, fitness level may be a requirement for a certain job *because the job is physically demanding*. The latter explanation goes beyond a mere statistical relationship between fitness and job performance by providing a job-related reason for the fitness requirement.

If simple statistical relationships between inputs and decisions are insufficient explanations for users, then most modern AIDMSs will fall short. Indeed, none of the three types of systems described herein can generate rationales relating inputs to decisions (R7) that refer to real-world relationships. Instead, people would have to provide such rationales. The inputs for which a rationale could be not provided could be culled from the model, thus, increasing its explanability, but reducing its competence.

Like DTs, linear regression models also reveal the inputs that contribute to their decisions (R5). These inputs are the terms in the model, in particular, those with larger coefficients, whether positive or negative (refer to equation 2). For a decision about a single case, the influential inputs are the case's inputs that match the model's inputs, like the price of the house (R6).

In contrast, in NNs, the influential inputs (R5, R6) are unknown, unless one applies an explanatory technique to the NN, such as approximating it with a DT (Guidotti et al., 2018).

Linear regression and NNs also have difficulty providing a satisfactory description of the decision-making process for an individual decision (R9) because all decisions are generated through a weighted combination of the inputs. Weighted combination is also the overall decision-making process (R8). While it is possible to understand linear regression models to some extent, the non-linearities and multiple layers in NNs make them almost impossible to understand without the application of an explanatory technique (Guidotti et al., 2018).

It is generally recognized that DTs are the most transparent AIDMSs (Guidotti et al., 2018), and this is borne out in the comparison presented above. However, like most modern AIDMSs, DTs are based on statistical regularities between the inputs and the decisions. These statistical systems share a fundamental limitation in that they cannot describe the relevance of an input to a decision beyond their statistical relationship. This poses a problem if people expect decisions to be based on real-world relevance rather than just statistical regularities.

FUTURE RESEARCH DIRECTIONS

There are three areas in which additional research could have a substantial impact on user acceptance of AI decisions. First, research on how AI systems can provide better explanations should continue. Second, research is required to improve user interfaces for interactive exploration of AI decisions and AI system performance. Finally, there should be more research on the features of explanations that support user acceptance. These last two areas of research, user interfaces and features of explanations, should be of interest to Human-Computer Interaction (HCI) researchers.

Future research in user interfaces could examine, for example, the way in which visual representations and images can complement text. Another user interface research topic is the customization of explanations to each user and to different contexts (Tintarev & Masthoff, 2007). Explanation exploration could involve interaction with the set of explanations, as in critique-based recommender systems (Chen & Pu, 2012). This topic could also include adjustments to the input values, allowing the user to create "what-if" questions. Even in a simple spa recommendation case, where a particular spa is recommended because it is family friendly, adjusting input values could be crucial because the user may not be bringing his family to the spa, in which case the original recommendation would be irrelevant. Moreover, information visualization approaches could be applied to the presentation of such information. Visualization of cases similar to the user's would be a fruitful area of research for HCI.

In terms of which features of AI explanations support user acceptance, there is a need to test the principles and requirements of explanations proposed here to confirm their validity and to understand the context in which the various principles and requirements apply. Research could also delve into the issue of the features of process descriptions that are acceptable to users, and specifically whether simple statistical associations between inputs and outputs suffice.

Finally, there is also a broader need to integrate findings from the social sciences and cognitive psychology into AI explanability research (Abdul, Vermeulen, Wang, Lim, & Kankanhalli, 2018).

CONCLUSION

As AI systems increasingly make decisions that have substantial impact on people's lives, the issue of user acceptance of those decisions has gained prominence. To inform the issue of user acceptance, the authors reviewed the concerns arising from AI decisions of consequence, and studies of user preferences for explanations from recommender systems. Based on these reviews, the authors propose a set of principles and corresponding requirements that AI decisions should respect to better satisfy users. Specifically, given a body of decisions, composed of individual decisions, each of which results from an input sent through a decision-making process:

- To conform to the principle of *respect for user preferences*, AIDMSs should provide:
  - The inputs that are influential in making a specific decision about a specific individual.
  - A rationale for why those inputs are relevant to that decision.

- To conform to the principle of *fairness*,
  - AIDMSs should:
    - Not process discriminatory inputs or proxies for such inputs.
    - Provide the influential inputs over the whole body of decisions.
    - Provide descriptions of the decision-making processes.
  - Organizations that rely on AI decision-making should provide sufficient data to verify the absence of biases.
- To conform to the principle of decision *contestability*, AI systems and the organizations that use them should:
  - Respect user preference and ensure fairness.
  - Provide a description of the decision-making process for a specific decision.
- To conform to the principle of AI decision-making *competence*, the organization using the AIDMS should provide:
  - Evidence of decision-making accuracy and/or
  - The input and decision data sets, so that accuracy can be verified by a third party.

A brief examination of common AIDMSs reveals that DTs are more transparent than linear regression, while NNs are the least transparent. Nonetheless, DTs do not provide a rationale for why a specific input is relevant to a decision. As with nearly all modern-day AIDMSs, DTs are based on statistical relationships between inputs and decisions, so the rationale is always limited to the input being statistically related to a corresponding decision. This may be insufficient to satisfy users in some contexts.

Research on how to make AI systems provide better explanations should (and will) continue. However, researchers should not neglect the improvement of user interfaces for interactive exploration of AI decisions and AI system performance. In addition, there should be more research on what features of explanations support user acceptability of AI decisions.

ACKNOWLEDGMENT

The authors are grateful to Danielle Vinson for her assistance with the figures and to Janice Singer for her input.

This research was funded by the Human-Computer Interaction team at the Digital Technologies Research Centre, National Research Council, Canada.

REFERENCES

Abdul, A., Vermeulen, J., Wang, D., Lim, B. Y., & Kankanhalli, M. (2018). Trends and trajectories for explainable, accountable and intelligible systems: An HCI research agenda. In *Proceedings of the 2018 CHI Conference on Human Factors in Computing Systems - CHI '18* (pp. 1–18). ACM. 10.1145/3173574.3174156

Al-Taie, M. (2013). Explanations In Recommender Systems: Overview And Research Approaches. *The International Arab Conference on Information Technology (ACIT'2013)*.

Alonso, J. M., Castiello, C., & Mencar, C. (2018). A bibliometric analysis of the explainable artificial intelligence research field. In *Information Processing and Management of Uncertainty in Knowledge-Based Systems. Theory and Foundations. IPMU 2018. Communications in Computer and Information Science* (Vol. 853, pp. 3–15). Springer International Publishing. Retrieved from http://link.springer.com/10.1007/978-3-319-91473-2

Baldus, D. C., Pulaski, C., & Woodworth, G. (1983). Comparative review of death sentences: An empirical study of the Georgia experience. *The Journal of Criminal Law & Criminology*, *74*(3), 661–753. doi:10.2307/1143133

Bertrand, M., & Mullainathan, S. (2004). Are Emily and Greg more employable than Lakisha and Jamal? A field experiment on labor market discrimination. *The American Economic Review*, *94*(4), 991–1013. doi:10.1257/0002828042002561

Bilgic, M., & Mooney, R. J. (2005). Explaining Recommendations: Satisfaction vs. Promotion. *Proceedings of Beyond Personalization 2005: A Workshop on the Next Stage of Recommender Systems Research at The 2005 International Conference on Intelligent User Interfaces*, 13–18. 10.1145/1040830.1040839

Brewer, B. (2007). Citizen or customer? Complaints handling in the public sector. *International Review of Administrative Sciences*, *73*(4), 549–556. doi:10.1177/0020852307083457

Butler, J. M., Kline, M. C., & Coble, M. D. (2018). NIST interlaboratory studies involving DNA mixtures (MIX05 and MIX13): Variation observed and lessons learned. *Forensic Science International. Genetics*, *37*(April), 81–94. doi:10.1016/j.fsigen.2018.07.024 PMID:30103146

Campolo, A., Sanfilippo, M., Whittaker, M., & Crawford, K. (2017). AI Now 2017 Report. *AI Now*. Retrieved from https://ainowinstitute.org/AI_Now_2017_Report.pdf

Chen, L., & Pu, P. (2012). Critiquing-based recommenders: Survey and emerging trends. *User Modeling and User-Adapted Interaction*, *22*(1–2), 125–150. doi:10.100711257-011-9108-6

Chouldechova, A. (2017). Fair prediction with disparate impact: A study of bias in recidivism prediction instruments. *Big Data*, *5*(2), 153–163. doi:10.1089/big.2016.0047 PMID:28632438

Dastin, J. (2018, October 9). Amazon scraps secret AI recruiting tool that showed bias against women. *Reuters*. Retrieved from https://www.reuters.com/article/us-amazon-com-jobs-automation-insight/amazon-scraps-secret-ai-recruiting-tool-that-showed-bias-against-women-idUSKCN1MK08G

Davis, F. D. (1989). Perceived usefulness, perceived ease of use, and user acceptance of information technology. *Management Information Systems Quarterly*, *13*(3), 319. doi:10.2307/249008

Edwards, L., & Veale, M. (2017). Slave to the algorithm? Why a "right to an explanation" is probably not the remedy you are looking for. *Duke Law and Technology Review*, *16*(1), 18–84. doi:10.2139srn.2972855

Field, A. P. (2000). *Discovering statistics using SPSS for Windows: Advanced techniques for the beginner*. Sage Publications.

Gedikli, F., Jannach, D., & Ge, M. (2014). How should i explain? A comparison of different explanation types for recommender systems. *International Journal of Human-Computer Studies*, *72*(4), 367–382. doi:10.1016/j.ijhcs.2013.12.007

Goodfellow, I., Bengio, Y., & Courville, A. (2016). *Deep Learning*. MIT Press. Retrieved from https://www.deeplearningbook.org/

Guidotti, R., Monreale, A., Ruggieri, S., Turini, F., Giannotti, F., & Pedreschi, D. (2018). A survey of methods for explaining black box models. *ACM Computing Surveys, 51*(5), 1–42. doi:10.1145/3236009

Hacker, P., & Wiedemann, E. (2017). *A continuous framework for fairness*. Retrieved from http://arxiv.org/abs/1712.07924

Herlocker, J. L., Konstan, J. A., & Riedl, J. (2000). Explaining collaborative filtering recommendations. *Proceedings of the 2000 ACM conference on Computer supported cooperative work - CSCW '00*. 10.1145/358916.358995

Hulten, G. (2018). *Building Intelligent Systems: A Guide to Machine Learning Engineering* (1st ed.). Apress. doi:10.1007/978-1-4842-3432-7

Ingold, D., & Soper, S. (2016, April 21). Amazon doesn't consider the race of its customers. Should it? *Bloomberg*. Retrieved from https://www.bloomberg.com/graphics/2016-amazon-same-day/

Johnson, J. F., Bagdasarov, Z., Connelly, S., Harkrider, L., Devenport, L. D., Mumford, M. D., & Thiel, C. E. (2012). Case-Based Ethics Education: The Impact of Cause Complexity and Outcome Favorability on Ethicality. *Journal of Empirical Research on Human Research Ethics; JERHRE, 7*(3), 63–77. doi:10.1525/jer.2012.7.3.63 PMID:22850144

Junker, M., Hoch, R., & Dengel, A. (1999). On the evaluation of document analysis components by recall, precision, and accuracy. In *Proceedings of the Fifth International Conference on Document Analysis and Recognition. ICDAR '99 (Cat. No.PR00318)* (pp. 713–716). IEEE. 10.1109/ICDAR.1999.791887

Kiritchenko, S., & Mohammad, S. M. (2018). *Examining Gender and Race Bias in Two Hundred Sentiment Analysis Systems*. Retrieved from http://arxiv.org/abs/1805.04508

Kizilcec, R. F. (2016). How much information?: Effects of transparency on trust in an algorithmic interface. *Proceedings of the 2016 CHI Conference on Human Factors in Computing Systems - CHI '16*, 2390–2395. 10.1145/2858036.2858402

Milborrow, S. (n.d.). *An example of a CART classification tree*. Retrieved October 12, 2018, from https://commons.wikimedia.org/wiki/File:CART_tree_titanic_survivors.png

Molnar, P., & Gill, L. (2018). *Bots at the gate: A human hights analysis of automated decision-making in Canada's immigration and refugee system*. Toronto, Canada: The Citizen Lab and Faculty of Law, University of Toronto.

Muhammad, K. I., Lawlor, A., & Smyth, B. (2016). A Live-User Study of Opinionated Explanations for Recommender Systems. *Proceedings of the 21st International Conference on Intelligent User Interfaces - IUI '16*, (1), 256–260. 10.1145/2856767.2856813

Nunes, I., & Jannach, D. (2017). A systematic review and taxonomy of explanations in decision support and recommender systems. *User Modeling and User-Adapted Interaction, 27*(3–5), 393–444. doi:10.100711257-017-9195-0

Pasquale, F. (2015). *The black box society: The secret algorithms that control money and information* (1st ed.). Boston: Harvard University Press. doi:10.4159/harvard.9780674736061

Pu, P., & Chen, L. (2007). Trust-inspiring explanation interfaces for recommender systems. *Knowledge-Based Systems*, *20*(6), 542–556. doi:10.1016/j.knosys.2007.04.004

Rumelhart, D. E., Hinton, G. E., & Williams, R. J. (1986). Learining internal representations by error propagation. In *Parallel Distributed Processing: Explorations in the Microstructure of Cognition* (1st ed.). Bradford, MA: MIT Press.

Rumelhart, D. E., & McClelland, J. L. (1986). Parallel distributed processing: Vol. 1. *Foundations* (1st ed.). Bradford, MA: MIT Press.

Russell, S., & Norvig, P. (2003). *Artificial intelligence: A modern approach* (2nd ed.). Prentice Hall. doi:10.1017/S0269888900007724

Tintarev, N., & Masthoff, J. (2007). A survey of explanations in recommender systems. In *2007 IEEE 23rd International Conference on Data Engineering Workshop* (pp. 801–810). IEEE. 10.1109/ICDEW.2007.4401070

Tintarev, N., & Masthoff, J. (2012). Evaluating the effectiveness of explanations for recommender systems. *User Modeling and User-Adapted Interaction*, *22*(4–5), 399–439. doi:10.100711257-011-9117-5

Wachter, S., Mittelstadt, B., & Floridi, L. (2017). Why a right to explanation of automated decision-making does not exist in the General Data Protection Regulation. *International Data Privacy Law*, *7*(2), 76–99. doi:10.1093/idpl/ipx005

Wexler, R. (2018). Life, liberty, and trade secrets: Intellectual property in the criminal justice system. *Stanford Law Review*, *70*(May), 1343–1429.

Wohlin, C. (2014). Guidelines for snowballing in systematic literature studies and a replication in software engineering. In *Proceedings of the 18th International Conference on Evaluation and Assessment in Software Engineering - EASE '14* (pp. 1–10). New York: ACM Press. 10.1145/2601248.2601268

Zanker, M. (2012). The influence of knowledgeable explanations on users' perception of a recommender system. *Proceedings of the Sixth ACM Conference on Recommender Systems - RecSys '12*, 269. 10.1145/2365952.2366011

Zanker, M., & Schoberegger, M. (2014). An empirical study on the persuasiveness of fact-based explanations for recommender systems. *Joint Workshop on Interfaces and Human Decision Making in Recommender Systems*, 33–36.

Zemel, R. S., Wu, Y., Swersky, K., Pitassi, T., & Dwork, C. (2013). Learning fair representations. *Proceedings of the 30th International Conference on Machine Learning, 28*, 325–333. Retrieved from http://jmlr.org/proceedings/papers/v28/zemel13.html

ADDITIONAL READING

Grudin, J. (2009). AI and HCI: Two fields divided by a common focus. *AI Magazine*, *30*(4), 48. doi:10.1609/aimag.v30i4.2271

Molnar, C. (2018). *Interpretable machine learning: A guide for making black box models explainable*. Creative Commons Attribution-Non Commercial-Share Alike 4.0 International License. Retrieved from https://christophm.github.io/interpretable-ml-book/

Pasquale, F. (2015). *The black box society: The secret algorithms that control money and information* (1st ed.). Boston, USA: Harvard University Press. doi:10.4159/harvard.9780674736061

Russell, S., & Norvig, P. (2003). *Artificial intelligence: A modern approach* (2nd ed.). Prentice Hall.

Tintarev, N., & Masthoff, J. (2012). Evaluating the effectiveness of explanations for recommender systems. *User Modeling and User-Adapted Interaction*, *22*(4–5), 399–439. doi:10.100711257-011-9117-5

KEY TERMS AND DEFINITIONS

AI Decision-Making System (AIDMS): An artificial intelligence software system that produces decisions relating to particular inputs.

Artificial Intelligence (AI): The subfield of computer science concerned with the simulation or creation of intelligent behavior in computers.

Automated Linear Regression: A machine-learning technique that learns a model of summed weights to predict outputs from inputs.

Decision Tree (DT): A simple branching structure that organizes a sequence of decisions to reach final decisions. Decision trees can be learned via machine-learning.

Input: Data fed into and processed by an AI decision-making system to generate a corresponding output or decision.

Machine Learning (ML): A set of AI techniques to develop computer systems that learn statistical regularities between inputs and outputs, thereby generating outputs from a set of inputs alone.

Neural Network (NN): In this chapter, it is a layered graph where each layer contains a set of nodes, the nodes of which are fully connected to those in the next layer, the first layer representing inputs and the last representing outputs or decisions. The graph encodes the statistical relationships between the inputs and outputs via machine-learning to generate outputs given only inputs.

Output: A prediction or decision of an AI decision-making system, or other system, that is associated with a particular input.

Random Forest: A collection of decision trees working together to produce decisions.

Recommender System: An AI system that recommends various products, services, articles, or social connections to a user based the user's profile.

User: In this chapter, *user* refers to both the people who use the AI decision-making system to generate decisions as well as the people about whom the decisions are made.

ENDNOTE

[1]   The acceptability of AI decision-making system explanations is complementary to the Technology Acceptance Model (Davis, 1989). It is proposed that users will make use of the AI decision-making systems or comply with their decisions only to the extent users find their explanations acceptable. For example, if a loan applicant were refused a loan without an acceptable explanation, the applicant could well protest by demanding to speak to the manager, or perhaps filing a complaint. Moreover, banks would be reluctant to adopt a system that frequently leads customers to complain.

Section 2
Applications

Chapter 7
Redesign of the Bank Reconciliation Interface of the ContaAzul Software

João Antonio de Menezes Neto
University of the Region of Joinville, Brazil

Victor Rafael Laurenciano Aguiar
University of the Region of Joinville, Brazil

ABSTRACT

This chapter details the redesign process of the bank reconciliation interface of ContaAzul, an online cloud-based financial management software for small businesses in Brazil. The reconciliation is a feature that allows the user to import bank account statements and easily register them into the software, generating automated reports that help companies achieve their financial control. The research problem was motivated by use cases that were not covered in the studied version of this feature, as well as by recent technological advances. Interaction design was chosen as the project approach and Garrett's five planes as the methodology. As the final deliverable, a prototype was composed of static, bitmap screens, elaborated from a participatory design perspective. This research was developed as a course conclusion project in the Master's degree in Design Program of University of the Region of Joinville, Brazil. The first author of this chapter is also a design coordinator at ContaAzul.

INTRODUCTION

This chapter details a Master's Degree in Design course conclusion project that had as a general objective to redesign the ContaAzul software's bank reconciliation interface. The company, that has the same name as the software it develops, has its headquarters in Joinville, Santa Catarina, Brazil, and the first author of this chapter is one of its design coordinators. This chapter follows a professional perspective, detailing the development of the project under the company's context in a case study format.

Bank reconciliation is a feature that is a part of the financial module of the ContaAzul software. Its purpose is to facilitate the registration of the money received, paid or transferred by the user, as presented

DOI: 10.4018/978-1-5225-9069-9.ch007

in his or her bank account statement. By registering this information, it becomes possible to generate automated financial reports, helping the user to control his or her finances (ContaAzul, 2017).

The need for a redesign was primarily motivated by use cases not covered in the previous version of the feature, having as a hypothesis that the redesign could contribute to the satisfaction of the company's customers. As a central research question, the following framing was delimited: how to redesign the ContaAzul software's bank reconciliation interface, considering use cases not covered and the deadline of April 2018, as demanded by the company, considering current users' difficulties and the utmost importance of this interface to the whole software?

Regarding the structure of this chapter, it is divided into three sections. The first one is a contextualization about small businesses and the technological advances of banks in Brazil, along with a brief review about the ContaAzul company and its software, focusing on the current reconciliation interface. The second one introduces the theoretical and methodological basis of the project, listing interaction design as an approach, followed by a comparison to service design, and Garrett's five planes (Garrett, 2010) as the methodology, with adaptations due to the context of the company. The last section details the practical phases of the project, correlating each of Garrett's five planes to a specific objective: strategy, scope, structure, skeleton and surface.

The final deliverable of the project was a static prototype of the redesigned interface, presented with bitmap screens. This prototype was elaborated from a participatory design perspective, that is here considered as an approach in which users co-design solutions and have an active role in the system (Rosa et al., 2012). The prototype was then handed over to the software engineering team of ContaAzul for a technical analysis for further implementation. The chapter ends with a discussion session, that lists the findings of the practice of the case study in a general, design-wide perspective.

BACKGROUND

This section contextualizes the field of activity of the ContaAzul company, discussing a brief profile regarding small businesses and banks in Brazil, which are, respectively, its clients and partners. Other topics covered here are the firm's timeline, the features present in its software and the disposition of its design team.

Small Businesses and Banks in Brazil

According to the Brazilian Small Businesses Support Service (Sebrae, 2017), there are 6.4 million small businesses in Brazil. These companies are responsible for 52% of formal labor contracts in the private sector, equivalent to 16 million workers. The fields of activity of this kind of company are varied, permeating industry, commerce, services and civil construction.

In addition to the formal labor context, there are also 10 million informal workers in Brazil (Papp, Gerbelli, 2016). As there is no requirement for formal qualification in the administrative area to open a business, there are different initiatives in the country, such as Sebrae itself, that provide support and advice to entrepreneurs.

In terms of mortality of small businesses in Brazil, the main causes observed are the inexperience and lack of competence of the entrepreneur, the lack of experience in the field of action and the fluctuation of economic indicators (Chiavenato, 2008). The most critical period for the success of the small business is its first two years, considering that 27% of them close after this stage (Portal Brasil, 2014). The greatest longevity is in industries, followed by commerce and services.

Beyond that, it is also important to recognize banks as stakeholders of influence in relation to financial management. In the Brazilian scenario, the first institution officially established was *Banco do Brasil*, in 1808 (Banco do Brasil, 2017b). As platforms evolved, another bank, *Bradesco*, was the first one in the country to allow online transactions through personal computers, in 1996 (Bradesco, 2017).

It should be noted that the development of national banking services is intrinsic to the changes in the perception of Brazilians regarding their money. Gala (2017), for example, highlights three phenomena in the last century that allowed the growth of gross domestic product (GDP) and stimulated consumption: 1) the shift from the axis of agriculture to the post-crisis industry of 1929; 2) institutional reforms between 1960 and 1980 and 3) the stabilization of inflation during *Plano Real* (Real currency Plan, in direct translation), in the early 2000s.

Another relevant characteristic in this context is the expansion of access to the internet in the country. In the domestic environment, internet access is available in 49% of households (Brasil, 2016). In the business environment, the biennial *TIC Empresas* survey, developed by the Brazilian Internet Governance Committee (CGI), indicates the universalization of internet access among small, medium and large companies. By the historical series, in 2011, 98% of companies with ten or more employees had access to the internet. The most common activities are: send emails (99%), search for information (94%) and do banking transactions (88%) (CGI, 2016).

In the same survey, 80% of the respondents said that the implementation of software solutions provided improvements to the company's processes, as well as helped to make decisions and integrate communication between different departments.

More recently, in 2017, *Banco do Brasil* was the first national institution to use APIs of open banking, making transactions possible through third-party platforms, in a secure and stable manner (Banco do Brasil, 2017a). In the future, these APIs will allow software similar to ContaAzul to serve as white label platforms for financial services (Computerworld, 2017). The API is open to the community and can be used by technology companies that plan to develop integrated solutions.

The ContaAzul Company

Initially called Ágil ERP, the ContaAzul company began its operation in 2007, in the city of Joinville, Santa Catarina, Brazil. In 2011, already using the new nomenclature of ContaAzul, the first round of foreign investments was obtained, and its founders participated of intensive capacitation courses in California, the United States (ContaAzul, 2017). ContaAzul has had more than 800,000 users testing its platform, issuing more than one million invoices (ContaAzul, 2017).

Currently, in 2018, after updating its market positioning, the ContaAzul software is presented as a platform of connections for business management. In relation to its operation, the software runs in internet browsers, that is, without the need to install applications. Its main modules are:

- Sales: Area to register customers and record sales made on a daily basis. For companies that sell products, it has integration with inventory. Allows the issuance of invoices;
- Purchases: Area for the registration of suppliers and carriers. It allows to register purchases of raw material, finished products for resale or generic purchases. Has integration with inventory;

- Financial: Area to register entries of bank and non-bank financial accounts. Has integration with the sales and purchases modules. It also allows the registration of generic expenses, without the need to assign the customer or supplier information. It is in this module that the banking reconciliation feature is present;
- Reports: Through the registrations made in the other modules, this area allows the user to monitor sales performance, cash flow, profit or loss, inventory items, among other indicators;
- Integration with accountant: Allows the user to export his or her financial statements, invoices, payments and receipts for accounting purposes.

The mentioned modules have their navigation performed through a top menu, as shown in Figure 1, which illustrates the initial screen of the platform.

In relation to its design team, the ContaAzul company allocates its professionals in the Research & Development (R&D) department, having as responsibilities to assist in the identification of opportunities and strategies, validate hypotheses with users, prototype interfaces and monitor the development of features, among other activities (Zanini, 2018). Each designer pairs with product managers, business analysts and software engineers, and has independence to delimit his or her design methods, as long as they favor the interoperation of teams in an agile development environment. This modality aims to reduce the bureaucracy present in traditional software development environments, decreasing the documentation required, since the software source code is seen as a document in itself (Fowler, 2017).

ContaAzul's R&D team practices Cagan's (2018) guidelines to technological products development. The author highlights the important of the product manager, the designer and the engineers as catalysts to innovation and customer-centered solutions. These three professionals tend to have different backgrounds, which becomes a key aspect to a healthy creative conflict during ideation. The name given by

Figure 1. ContaAzul's initial screen
Source: Author's archive

the author to the activities done in this phase of projects is "Discovery" (Cagan, 2018), which resembles the contemporary discussions of design itself.

The author of this chapter is the design coordinator of the financial module team and co-responsible for the user experience of the bank reconciliation interface. This fact highlights the relevance of this research, as it might positively contribute to the strategies of the company, especially in relation to user satisfaction.

Bank Reconciliation Interface

The current ContaAzul software's bank reconciliation interface consists of two columns: on the left, the imported information from the bank statement is displayed; and on the right, there are input fields to register the information as a new transaction. The central button, *Reconcile*, is only enabled after typing all of the mandatory information (description, category, date and value). If desired, the user can add supplementary information, such as department, and attach digital receipts. The software also suggests an automatic reconciliation when it identifies a description, value or date similar to transactions previously registered as provisions.

From a technical perspective, the ContaAzul software's bank reconciliation is managed by a complex set of business rules based on use cases and their accounting counterparts. Although the interface is simple, with a few graphical elements (Figure 2), its ideal logic must comprise a wide range of financial events, adapting itself to fit the user's necessity.

As the first activity in this research, the authors examined five competing software with ContaAzul, demonstrating that there were use cases not covered by the current version of ContaAzul's reconciliation feature. These cases were: 1) allow the user to search for transactions and create ones at the same time; 2) permit the user to search for and reconcile mixed-type transactions, such as money received (inbound) and its incurring taxes (outbound); 3) make it possible for the user to create transactions and reconcile mixed-type ones simultaneously. From that standpoint, it has been hypothesized that amplifying the use cases covered may enable users to interact with the ContaAzul software in a more precise way, having the information registered in it as a truthful reflection of the financial events of his or her company, inducing a higher level of satisfaction.

Considering these aspects, the central research question was then framed: how to redesign the ContaAzul software's bank reconciliation interface, considering use cases not covered and the deadline of

Figure 2. Current reconciliation interface
Source: Author's archive

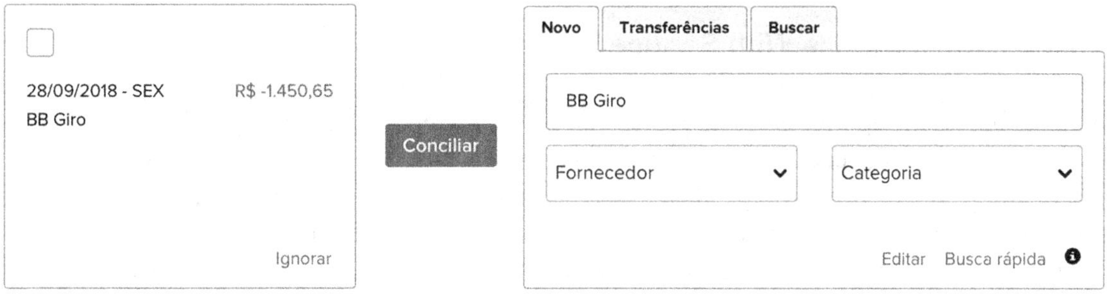

April 2018, as demanded by the company, taking into account current users' difficulties and the utmost importance of this interface to the whole software?

THEORETICAL AND METHODOLOGICAL BASIS

This section reviews references and concepts that contributed to the practical development of the project. It is important to emphasize that this section has the function of providing the theoretical and methodological basis for the project, but adaptations were necessary due to different variables, especially considering the deadline stipulated by the company. There is also a comparison of interaction design and service design, with the objective to identify the most appropriate applicability to projects similar to the case study detailed here.

Interaction Design as a Project Approach

Interaction design is a contemporary design approach that has gained momentum with the popularization and development of personal computers. According to Preece et al. (2013), in order to plan interactions, identifying human needs and consequently conceptualizing solutions are essential activities, and these solutions may be radical or incremental products and services.

In the interaction design field, it is important to consider some usability and user experience best practices. Usability, for instance, is closely related to ergonomics. When applied to the context of interfaces, usability aims to adapt and recognize elements in order to guarantee the correct fulfillment of the user's tasks (Preece et al., 2013). User experience, on the other hand, is fundamentally subjective, being a complimentary perspective to usability, as it goes beyond the graphical layers of an interface. Strategies that adhere to the target audience of a solution, for example, can also provide satisfaction, since user experience is associated with the behavior of products and services in the real world (Garrett, 2010). For Kalbach (2017), one of the ways of mapping the user experience is to consider it as something holistic, personal and situational, i.e., directly dependent on a context.

In addition, for Preece et al. (2013), the evaluation of interfaces is important to balance the different stipulated user needs. Some methods of evaluation rely only on the researcher, and other ones have participation and collaboration of more people.

The approaches suggested by Preece et al. (2013) are "quick-and-dirty" (based on informal feedback from users), usability testing (using camcorders, eye tracking software, among others), field study (performed in real use environment), predictive assessment (experts in user groups) and heuristic evaluation (recommendations validated by specialists).

Points of Convergence With Service Design

The literature review reported so far shows that an in-depth view of the theme-problem can contribute to the increase of assertiveness of a project. It is necessary, then, to evaluate points of convergence of interaction design with other design approaches, providing a comparison. With that in mind, service design was chosen as the complimentary theme to study in this chapter, due to the Master's Degree in Design Program lines of study, which are focused on sustainability and service development.

The correlation between the two approaches is even more latent when considering that websites are services handled through a digital product, even if this is not perceived by users (Roda, Krucken, 2004). Service design intends to discuss the relationship of people to services and their avatars, resulting in varied formats of expression. Organizational structures and operations support processes are two examples (Stickdorn, Schneider, 2012), but one can also design physical elements that are a part of a service. Services can have linear or non-linear trajectories, requiring the flexibility of the designer as a facilitator in the production of these systems.

Nonetheless, taking into account that the problem presented in this chapter is intrinsically linked to a graphical user interface, since its object of study is a software, interaction design still shows itself to be the most appropriate project approach. It is important to note that this does not invalidate the applicability of service design in this type of project but leaves gaps in technical issues or causes the need to opt for isolated methods to meet some research requirements.

With those concepts in mind, interaction design was chosen as the project approach for this initiative, as it is directly compatible with the general objective, especially due to its deep correlation to interfaces, usability and user experience.

After this discussion, the following section describes the methodology of Garrett's five plans (2010), which guided the practical part of the project.

Garrett's Five Planes Methodology

Garrett's five planes methodology, or "the elements of user experience" (Garrett, 2010), uses a layered metaphor, separating the stages of the project into sequential phases. The level of abstraction or concreteness of each step is defined from the hierarchy of these layers. The author considers a vertical division in the planes, dividing them into software interface and hypertext system.

According to Garrett (2010), in an ideal scenario, the next phase must only start when the previous one is complete. The five planes are, from the most abstract to the most objective one: strategy (concentrating commercial and communication goals), scope (defining the elements of the strategy that will be used), structure (mapping user flow of interaction), skeleton (focused on blueprints or wireframes), and surface (elaborating the visible, graphic layer of the interface).

The choice of this method occurred mainly due to the presence of the strategy and structure delimitation stages, which causes the design practice to develop a holistic view before performing the graphical expression of the solution.

The next section details the methods applied in each plane, describing the adaptations conducted in order to reflect the context of the project and the ContaAzul company's *modus operandi*, that prioritizes the participatory design perspective in its initiatives.

PROJECT DEVELOPMENT

The development of the practical part of the project began after the approval in the qualifying examination in the Master's Degree in Design Program, in December 2017, having as a mandatory deadline April 2018. Some of the data considered during the project was collected in previous opportunities, arising from the first author's daily experiences as a ContaAzul company employee. In addition, this whole research was reviewed and approved by the Local Ethics Committee of the University of the Region of Joinville.

As commented in the previous section, different methods were connected to each of Garrett's planes, that served as specific objectives of the research. The methods are presented in the following sections, detailing their application, as well as the results obtained in each phase.

Strategy Plane

The strategy plane, in short, delimits the reach of action of the project (Garrett, 2010). In order to achieve it, it is necessary to parallelize the requirements of the company, the tendencies of the market and the general profile of the target audience of the solution. After obtaining data sources that represent the verbalization of users, either directly or indirectly, it is possible to mitigate research and design biases.

Based on this, it was decided to apply three methods in this phase: a review of ideas submitted by ContaAzul customers, a review of support tickets and a questionnaire.

From the first analysis, 98 clients' suggestions connected to the bank reconciliation thematic were curated, from 2,479 ideas registered in the ContaAzul company's database, all of them read in full. The ten most voted ideas were:

1. Display all pending reconciliations, instead of displaying them month by month;
2. Perform automatic integration with other banks and companies;
3. Improve batch information changes (multiple items);
4. Introduce advanced date filters, with the ability to choose any period of time;
5. Improve the reconciliation of bills and their incident interest rates;
6. Improve the reconciliation of chargebacks;
7. Automate the reconciliation of recurring bills, month by month;
8. Prevent errors arising from duplicate statements;
9. Improve the registration of cost centers;
10. Facilitate the registration of partial payments and receipts.

Then, as a complementary method, 250 support tickets from customers were also read. These tickets were related to usability issues in the current reconciliation interface. Lastly, an anonymous online questionnaire was sent to customers, partners and customer service employees of the company.

Regarding the questionnaire, its main objective was to identify the frequency of use of the bank reconciliation feature, the incidence of usage difficulties and the recurrence of these difficulties. The responses occurred between March 16, 2018 and March 23, 2018. Thirty-seven answers were received, and all respondents indicated that they had had difficulties in ContaAzul's bank reconciliation feature. The most recurring ones cited were:

1. ContaAzul's balance is not equal to the bank balance;
2. Difficulty in registering interest, fine, discount or fee;
3. Difficulty in reconciling a bank statement with mixed entries in ContaAzul (i.e., receipt, payment and transfer at the same time);
4. Difficulty in registering bills paid in cash;
5. Difficulty in searching for entries previously registered in the software and reconciling them;
6. Difficulty in creating new registrations while doing the reconciliation.

From these insights, the team responsible for the bank reconciliation feature wrote a list of strategic objectives, in a session moderated by the first author of this chapter.

As company requirements, the team suggested three aspects: 1) to assist its customers and partners to input financial information with reliability; 2) to highlight the market positioning of the ContaAzul company as a complete platform; 3) to enhance user experience in order to retain current customers and expand to new customer niches.

In reference to market tendencies, the team summarized as follow-up actions: 1) to consider the changes and fluctuation of the Brazilians' perception in relation to the money they earn and spend; 2) to take advantage of the technological advances, such as APIs, that remove friction in the user experience; 3) to keep the team up-to-date with improvements and innovations released by similar software companies.

At last, in a user's perspective, the strategies of consensus were: 1) to be aware that opening a small business is sometimes a latent life necessity, and that it does not require technical training; 2) to equalize language, voice and tone of the interface, communicating the use cases in a clear and simple interface; 3) to offer flexibility to the user to input information as a reflection of the real events occurred in his or her business, avoiding forced adaptations or imprecisions.

Scope Plane

For Garrett (2010), the strategy plane can be interpreted as a "vision", while the scope plane, detailed in this section, is an "agreement". The main purpose of the scope plane is to change the question from "why are we designing this software?" to "what are we actually going to develop?". Based on this approach, the team wrote "user stories", that represent the translation of use cases into practical situations experienced by the person using a platform (Ventura, 2017). Along with this, a technical evaluation of complexity was done by the software engineering team.

The user stories were divided into three parts–user need, qualifying factor, and expected result–, written considering the information obtained in the previous phase, as well as prior projects conducted by the same team. These stories are presented in Table 1. It is a characteristic of this method to use first-person sentences, alluding to a hypothetical verbalization of the user him or herself.

After the exercise of user stories was complete, the engineers of the team evaluated the complexity of implementation of each of them. The participation of engineers early on was important, because, as advocated by Preece et al. (2013), bringing people with different backgrounds and contexts together can boost the amount of ideas and the originality of the solutions. This step was also relevant as the reconciliation feature already exists, so there were limitations in relation to database, programming (Java) and other similar aspects.

Structure Plane

In order to map an interaction flow that considers the requirements defined in the strategy and scope planes, the spatial user journey map method was chosen. For Kalbach (2017), the referred instrument considers the tasks to be performed by a person using direction and navigation metaphors, reminiscent of a "compass", having a correlation to the navigability present in graphic interfaces.

With this in mind, the authors of this chapter created and divided the map into three chronological layers, considering the user's perspective: 1) generator fact (e.g., the act of selling or buying a product

Table 1. User stories

N	User need	Qualifying factor	Expected result
1	I wish to register a payment or receipt...	... that I have not previously provisioned...	... to be able to keep up with my expenses or earnings
2	I wish to indicate the payment or receipt of a bill...	... paid in its entirety...	... to monitor my debts
3	I wish to indicate the payment or receipt of a bill...	... provisioned with a value other than the actual one...	...to adjust it to the correct value
4	I wish to indicate the payment or receipt of a bill with incidence of interest or fine...	... that had not been provisioned with interest or fine...	... to keep up with the reality of my cash flow
5	I wish to indicate the payment or receipt of a discount...	... which had not been provisioned as a discount...	... to visualize my expenses or actual gains
6	I wish to indicate the payment or partial receipt of a bill...	... that had been provisioned in its entirety...	... to follow its lifecycle until its total settlement
7	I wish to indicate a transfer between accounts...	... both of my own ownership...	... without influencing earnings or spending
8	I wish to provision a transfer between accounts…	... whether they are my own or not...	... to keep up with my future cash flow
9	I wish to indicate the payment or receipt of two or more unprovisioned invoices...	... that are presented as a single entry in my bank statement...	... so that it reflects my real financial status
10	I wish to indicate the payment or receipt of two or more invoices previously provisioned...	... that are presented as a single entry in my bank statement…	... so that it reflects my real financial status
11	I want to indicate transactions made via bank and via cash...	... considering that both were used to pay or receive a single bill or invoice…	... so that I can manage my money accurately
12	I wish to indicate the payment of bank tariffs...	... from diverse methods of payment…	... so that I can control my gains and expenses

Source: Author's archive

or service at a small business); 2) accounting evidence (e.g., the act of receiving or paying money for that previous product or service); 3) reporting (e.g., the act of analyzing the result, as of profit or loss).

The map, detailed in Table 2, was developed in a collaborative session, pondering the multiple views of the team responsible for the reconciliation interface. Similar to the user stories, this method utilizes a first-person wording in allusion to the user's verbalization.

Having completed the structure plane, the authors started the studies of the skeleton plane.

Skeleton Plane

The skeleton plane, by definition, is characterized by the development of blueprints or wireframes (Garrett, 2010). Considering the relevance given by the ContaAzul company to participatory design, this phase had a diverse set of methods and stakeholders involved. The activities developed involved a co-creation session, sketches, interface layout in editorial software, generation of alternatives, participatory interface evaluation, and usability testing.

Table 2. User journey map

Chronology	User action	Locations and click sequences
Generator Fact	I, as a user, have a sale or purchase...	1. I access ContaAzul; 2. I click on the menu "Sales" or "Purchases"; 3. I click the "New" button; 4. I register the information of the new sale or purchase, filling the customer or supplier, items, installments, discounts and final value; 5. Then, ContaAzul automatically generates financial provisioning;
Accounting evidence	... after that, I wish to indicate that the sale or purchase was received or paid...	1. I click on the menu in "Finances" and then in "Bank accounts". After that, I select my bank account in the displayed listing; 2. ContaAzul obtains my bank statement automatically through its bank integration feature, displaying my pending reconciliations; 3. On that screen, I check item by item;
	... and during the reconciliation I need to search for an existing sale or purchase...	1. In the same screen, I click "Search" 2. ContaAzul displays an overlapped window with the listing of previously provisioned registration; 3. I look in the list, based on the description, the value, the date, the customer or the supplier; 4. I find the registration I'm looking for and select it; 5. If I wish, I can create as many complementary inputs as I need, no matter if they are receipts, payments or transfers, to indicate for example the incidence of interest, fine or tariff. This is done by clicking the "Create and Add New" button; 6. After selecting and/or creating the correct registration for each item of the bank statement, I click "Reconcile";
Reporting	... since that will tell me how much I have received or spent and my profit and loss.	1. I click on the menu in "Reports"; 2. To see my earnings and expenses, I access the "Cash Flow" report; 3. To see my client's payment status, I access the "Aging" report; 4. To see my profit or loss, I access the "Results" report.

Source: Author's archive

In relation to the co-creation session, the original plan was to recruit ContaAzul's customers and accountants. However, due to timing and personal scheduling, the invited participants could not be present in the originally booked date. As it was impossible to call the session off due to the project's deadline, an adaptation was necessary. With that in mind, five ContaAzul company employees, from different departments, that had not had contact with the research until that moment, were invited to join the session. The participants were:

1. An accountant;
2. A financial analyst, that uses the ContaAzul software's reconciliation interface on a daily basis;
3. An implementation analyst, in charge of the software's customer consulting and onboarding;
4. A support analyst, responsible for telephone, e-mail and chat support to customers;
5. A front-end software engineer from a different team.

It is important to notice that even though the participants were employees of the company, an aspect that was not originally planned, all of them have had wide experience with customers and were aware of pain points in the user experience of the ContaAzul software.

The first author of this chapter acted as a moderator of the session, projecting on a monitor the user stories and difficulties found in the research until that moment. The group discussed each topic:

- "Balance between bank account and ContaAzul did not match": It was the most cited difficulty. The reasons why it happens, according to the participants, vary, since the difficulty of understanding that there are two distinct columns in the interface, e.g., the bank statement on the left and the items to register on the right, causes mismatches to inattentive users;
- "Users cannot reconcile a bank entry with mixed items in ContaAzul (input, output and transfer at the same time)": This was cited as a key factor that prevents the tracking of fees in cash flow when customers receive sales via credit or debit card. As these means of payment have an incidence of tariff to each transaction, the ideal method is to have them as separate items: one for the receipt and another for the tariff. In the studied version of the reconciliation interface, the user could only link a tariff to an existing receipt or payment;
- "Users have difficulty finding previously registered items in the software and reconciling them": During the session, the group commented that for the advanced-level client this aspect was not a problem because this kind of user usually knows the provisions of all of his or her accounts. For the initial-level customer, however, there is a conceptual challenge in understanding the importance of registering receipts and payments beforehand. In a generic way, and in the opinion of the group, this kind of user tends to interpret that the reconciliation is the only way to input information, sometimes unaware of the advantages of registering sales and purchases previously;
- "Users have difficulty to register interest, fine, discount or fee": The group came to the consensus that the ideal way to register this information is as a separate item, so that it is displayed properly in the cash flow report;
- "Users have difficulty to create new items while reconciling": The group commented that the ContaAzul software allows the creation of an item during the reconciliation, but it is not possible to create more than one, to represent times when transfers or multiple payment methods were used;
- "Users have difficulty to register accounts paid in cash": A less commented point, focusing only on the beginner profile user. The solution, in the opinion of the group, is easy: the user should create an account in ContaAzul called "Cash" and do the registration manually.

As soon as the debate was over, the second phase of the session started. It focused on ideation, giving opportunity for the participants to suggest solutions to the difficulties, relating them to graphic interfaces or not. The participants were invited to speak out loud all the ideas they had for each topic. The author served as a graphic facilitator, drawing sketches on sheets of paper as the ideas were exposed. As a result, these drafts ranged from "buttons" and "boxes", in a reference to graphic interfaces, to intangible, generic ideas, such as "teach the users". The main insights were:

- Improve error prevention by allowing the registration of reconciled items to be easily undone;
- Visually differentiate automatic suggestions made by the ContaAzul software;
- Allow the reconciliation of mixed-type items;
- Improve the way in which payments or partial receipts are registered via reconciliation;
- Display an alert on the screen when the bank balance and ContaAzul's balance are divergent;
- Allow the insertion of entries in the bank column;
- Remove the friction present in the day by day usage of the software, stimulating the use of automatic integration, as it prevents the user from forgetting tasks in the software;

- Encourage the accountant to be the focal point of support for the client, with a view and technical knowledge regarding financial management.

As the session finished and the participants were dismissed, the author started wireframing, in paper, interface layouts based on the suggestions of the group. These suggestions were later refined and transposed to an editorial software. The alternatives, in the total of six, were then shared with the team of the ContaAzul reconciliation feature and with the participants of the session. The alternatives were:

1. Integrated multiple registration: promoting lesser change compared to the current interface, this alternative aimed to add the use case of mixed type registration directly in the right column;
2. Facilitation of access: by means of a link, this alternative aimed to facilitate the opening of the superimposed window of the financial input, which tends to facilitate the registration of receipts or partial payments;
3. Mixed search overlapped window: Unlike previous alternatives, this one was intended to allow the case of use of mixed registration and creation of new items by means of an overlapped window;
4. Overlapped window for multiple-item reconciliation: Similar to the first alternative, however, proposing that user actions are performed in an overlapped window instead of on the page;
5. Table integrated to the list: it was intended to occupy the entire width of the page for creating and searching for items, by means of a table;
6. Integrated list and integrated table: similar to the previous alternative, but visually delimiting the belonging to the bank's statement by means of a box with borders.

All participants were invited to evaluate the potential of each alternative to reduce the difficulties previously pointed out. After the evaluation was over, the group agreed as a consensus to choose one of the alternatives. The screen flow was then prototyped, as well as the alternative for an initial round of usability testing was prepared.

The tests were conducted remotely, via videoconference and screen sharing, with nine ContaAzul software's users, recruited considering a diverse set–service, commerce, industry; and entrepreneurs and accountants–, following the standard protocols of the company, that has a structured list of processes for usability testing. The results of the tests allowed iterative improvements to the screen flow, until, as a consensus, the team decided to move forward with one of the alternatives. The test script was:

1. Rapport: Presentation of the researcher and objective of the test;
2. Scenario description: "Imagine that you have a bank statement called "Receipt of a sale" and you want to create two separate items in ContaAzul, as one of them is an interest receipt"
3. Task to perform: "Click on the buttons displayed on the screen and register the entries you need";
4. After-test questions: "What is your opinion about this solution?", "what did you understand and not understand?" and "does this version meet your needs?".

In general, when interacting with alternative 4, which displays a search overlapped window, users lost the referential on the action being performed. The fact that the window covers the contents of the parent page caused conceptual confusion, breaking the interaction flow. There were also doubts about the registration of interest and fines, whether they should be registered as complimentary information to an existing entry or as a separate entry.

But then, during the tests with alternatives 5 and 6, which propose to solve most of the interactions on the page itself, performance in the execution of the task was higher. The number displaying the missing value to allow the reconciliation to happen was a positive point verbalized by the users, as it helped them understand the registration correctly.

The negative factor in these alternatives was the verb "Add", which generated confusion in relation to create new items or search for existing ones. The users did not immediately recognize that it was now possible to perform both actions simultaneously, demonstrating the necessity to improve the instructions on the screen.

Based on the results achieved in the usability tests and in the consensus of the group during the co-creation session, alternative 6 was chosen for further studies.

Surface Plane

The surface plane, according to Garrett (2010), comprises the creation and application of a graphic layer over the wireframes. However, considering that ContaAzul has a preestablished interface elements library, called "design system", this phase was quick to produce, giving efficiency to the process.

As commented before, as soon as alternative 6 was chosen, there was a new round of refinements and usability testing, especially because by this phase of the project all of the screen variations, that respond to the new use cases, were complete. This time, four users participated in the tests. The results were satisfactory, as the users were able to complete the tasks required during the test, with the sensibility to connect it to their own reality and market characteristics. The new and final interface is presented in Figure 3.

Figure 3. New reconciliation interface
Source: Author's archive

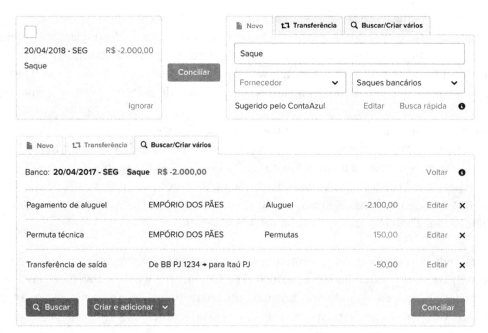

With the concept validated, the final prototype, in static, bitmap screens, with all the variations, was produced and handed over to the software engineering team, accompanied by business rules and design direction documentation. This deliverable concludes the scope of this research, which had the prototype as a final milestone.

As of the next steps, considering the agile development approach, which is used by ContaAzul, the engineering team followed the product roadmap and release plan, dividing the deliveries into different stages. By the time of the writing of this chapter, dated of October 2018, all clients of ContaAzul have had access to the new interface. The team is now evaluating the results, especially customer satisfaction indicators, in order to analyze and internalize the learnings so far.

FUTURE RESEARCH DIRECTIONS

Considering the evolution of human-computer interfaces, this research helps to emphasize the importance of context of use, culture immersion and adaptability in order to provide efficient solutions to people. Facing the complexity of expanding networks of interconnected information, the practice of design has the challenge to make project decisions that connect to a plurality of scenarios, expectations and mental models. This research is focused on the Brazilian market and how people in this country interpret entrepreneurship, money and business administration. Further research might study the expansion of these topics to other cultures, aiming to highlight similarities or discrepancies of the same concept. There has also been valuable learning during the phase of implementation and roll out of the new interface, that might be reported by the authors in future papers, focusing on the transdisciplinary of design and software engineering.

DISCUSSION REGARDING THE FINDINGS AND THEIR GENERAL APPLICABILITY

On a general perspective, the experience obtained in the development of the case study presented in this chapter, has applicability to other similar projects. Although service design is a state-of-the-art approach in the field, its bibliographical references lack specificities to the context of digital interfaces. Interaction design, on the other hand, presented methods directly connected to the area. Both approaches might be used together, but interaction design was proven to be more adequate.

Another general finding is that co-creative sessions can also be applied to the design of user interfaces, even if the group is not technical. It demands, however, the flexibility of the moderator in order to customize the exercises, so that the participants are able to express their intentions clearly.

Regarding the partnership necessary among designers and engineers, the experience obtained shows that engineers should participate in all layers of the project, both on a propositional and evaluative perspectives. Bringing their participation to the beginning of the studies fosters their buy-in and sensitization regarding the theme and context of the user experience in focus.

CONCLUSION

Revisiting the original objective, which was to redesign the ContaAzul software's reconciliation interface considering the use cases not covered, it is possible to affirm that a valid result was achieved, but its real efficiency can only be evaluated by the users themselves. The new interface, that was a collective work of people from different disciplines, from inside and outside the company, will allow, as far as the evidences raised to the present moment go, more precise financial events in the software.

In relation to the specific objectives, which were directly connected to Garrett's five planes, the partial results obtained were also satisfactory. Although the co-creation session had to be adapted at a very short notice, due to scheduling conflicts of the invited participants, it contributed to the studies of the usage difficulties and the alternatives to mitigate them. Direct sources of user information, such as suggestions and support tickets, were also important, even though they might generate biased interpretation if not analyzed correctly. The fact that some adaptations were necessary to Garrett's five planes, a methodology that dates back to 2010, also shows changes in the design practice in the contemporary context, as, for instance, the existence of a preestablished library of interface components.

In addition, ContaAzul utilizes agile development concepts, which is a positive catalyst for user experience, since the incremental deliveries will make it possible to correct any necessary routes with the new reconciliation interface, in this phase of roll out and learning.

Considering the ContaAzul company's mission and vision–help small businesses and accounting firms in Brazil to reach success–, it is possible to affirm that the results of this research tend to help in relation to financial information maturity, as the software will be more robust and complete. As commented earlier, small businesses are very representative in the Brazilian society, making the results of this research even more relevant to its local context.

On a personal level, the experience of working in the technology industry and being able to report that as a central Master's Degree in Design project was flattering. It was an opportunity to connect academia and industry, with an immediate impact to the community–both by the process detailed and the results achieved.

ACKNOWLEDGMENT

The authors would like to thank ContaAzul, with special acknowledgements to Vinicius Roveda Gonçalves, Joaquim Torres, Anderson Borges, José Carlos Sardagna, Thiago Godoy, Laudifer Sfreddo de Castro, Victor Zanini, João Paulo Villa Mello, the Financial Module Engineering Team "Spartans", the Design Team "Lumos", the Customer Experience Team "CX", the Administrative Team "Wall Street", and all the participants of the project, as well as the faculty and students of the Master's Degree in Design (PPGDesign) of the University of the Region of Joinville (Univille), along with our families and friends.

REFERENCES

Banco do Brasil. (2017b). *Nossa história*. Available at: http://www.bb.com.br/pbb/pagina-inicial/sobre-nos/nossa-historia#/

Banco do Brasil. (2017a). *Banco do Brasil lança plataforma de Open Banking*. Available at: http://www.bb.com.br/pbb/pagina-inicial/imprensa/n/55574/Banco%20do%20Brasil%20lança%20plataforma%20de%20Open%20Banking#

Bradesco. (2017). *Nossa história*. Available at: https://banco.bradesco/html/exclusive/sobre/nossa-historia.shtm

Brasil. (2016). *Pesquisa brasileira de mídia*. Available at: http://www.secom.gov.br/atuacao/pesquisa/lista-de-pesquisas-quantitativas-e-qualitativas-de-contratos-atuais/pesquisa-brasileira-de-midia-pbm-2016.pdf/view

Cagan, M. (2018). *Inspired: how to create tech products customers love*. Hoboken, NJ: Wiley.

CGI. (2016). *Cresce a proporção de empresas brasileiras que utilizam conexões à internet mais velozes, aponta Cetic.br*. Available at: http://cetic.br/noticia/cresce-a-proporcao-de-empresas-brasileiras-que-utilizam-conexoes-a-internet-mais-velozes-aponta-cetic- br/

Chiavenato, I. (2008). *Recursos humanos: o capital humano nas organizações*. São Paulo, Brazil: Atlas.

Computerworld. (2017). *ContaAzul conclui integração de sua plataforma com o Banco do Brasil*. Available at: http://computerworld.com.br/contaazul-conclui-integracao-de-sua-plataforma-com-o-banco-do-brasil

ContaAzul. (2017). *Sobre a empresa*. Available at: https://contaazul.com/sobre/

Fowler, M. (2017). *A nova metodologia*. Available at: https://medium.com/desenvolvimento-agil/a-nova-metodologia-69b8f8a379c7

Gala, P. (2017). *100 anos de PIB no Brasil*. Available at: https://www.paulogala.com.br/100-anos-de-pib-no-brasil/

Garrett, J. J. (2010). *The elements of user experience*. New York: New Riders.

Kalbach, J. (2017). *Mapeamento de experiências: um guia para criar valor por meio de jornadas, blueprints e diagramas*. Rio de Janeiro, Brazil: Alta Books.

Papp, A. C., & Gerbelli, L. G. (2016). *Trabalhadores informais chegam a 10 milhões no país*. Available at: http://economia.estadao.com.br/noticias/geral,trabalhadores-informais-chegam-a-10-milhoes-no-pais,10000071200

Portal Brasil. (2014). *Sobrevivência e mortalidade*. Available at: http://www.brasil.gov.br/economia-e-emprego/2012/02/sobrevivencia-e-mortalidade

Preece, J. (2013). *Design de interação: além da interação homem-computador*. Porto Alegre, Brazil: Bookman.

Roda, R., & Krucken, L. (2004). Gestão do design aplicada ao modelo atual das organizações: agregando valor a serviços. In *Congresso Brasileiro de Pesquisa e Desenvolvimento em Design* (Vol. 6). São Paulo, Brazil: FAAP.

Rosa, J. G. S. (2012). *Design participativo*. Rio de Janeiro, Brazil: Riobooks.

Sebrae. (2017). *Pequenos negócios em números*. Available at: https://www.sebrae.com.br/sites/Portal-Sebrae/ufs/sp/sebraeaz/pequenos-negocios-em-numeros,12e8794363447510VgnVCM1000004c0021 0aRCRD

Ventura, P. (2017). *Entendendo definitivamente o que é um caso de uso*. Available at: http://www.ateo-momento.com.br/o-que-e-caso-de-uso/

Zanini, V. (2018). *How we built our user experience team (UX) at ContaAzul, Brazil*. Available at: https://medium.com/design-contaazul/how-we-built-our-user-experience-team-ux-at-contaazul-brazil-93ef648472f7

ADDITIONAL READING

Frei, F., & Morriss, A. (2013). *Feitas para servir: como lucrar colocando o cliente no centro do seu negócio*. São Paulo, Brazil: HSM Editora.

Goodwin, K. (2009). *Designing for the digital age: how to create human-centered products and services*. Indianapolis, USA: Wiley Publishing.

Memória, F. (2005). *Design para a Internet: Projetando a experiência perfeita*. Rio de Janeiro, Brazil: Elsevier.

Perez, C. (2004). *Signos da marca: expressividade e sensorialidade*. São Paulo, Brazil: Thomson.

Pinheiro, T., & Alt, L. (2011). *Design Thinking Brasil: empatia, colaboração e experimentação para pessoas, negócios e sociedade*. Rio de Janeiro, Brazil: Elsevier.

Ries, E. (2011). *The Lean Startup: How Today's Entrepreneurs Use Continuous Innovation to Create Radically Successful Businesses*. New York, USA: Crown Business.

Shneiderman, B. (1998). *Designing the User Interface: Strategies for Effective Human-Computer Interaction*. Reading, USA: Addison-Wesley.

KEY TERMS AND DEFINITIONS

Bank Reconciliation: The task to relate the information present in a bank statement to the information registered in an enterprise resource planning software or similar solution, in order to facilitate the analysis of cash flow and business results.

Bank Statement: A document supplied by a bank that informs all of the transactions done in an account.

Bill: A document that lists a purchase.

Bitmap: A graphic representation designed with aid of computer software.

Cash Flow: A financial report that shows the input and output of money of a company.

Internet Banking: An online interface offered by a bank that allows its client to consult and do transactions.

Invoice: A document that lists a sale.

Open Banking: A concept that comprises the use of APIs—application programming interfaces—that allow the user to own his or her own bank account information, connecting it to third-party applications to obtain products and services not usually offered by the bank.

Product Manager: The person responsible for go-to-market initiatives and general indicators and vision of a product, being it tangible or intangible (software).

Prototype: A mockup of a product or service, that helps with the evaluation of efficiency of a concept.

Chapter 8

Development of Interface for Assisting Energy–Saving Utilizing Information From Network Home Appliances

Takumi Shida
Kanagawa Institute of Technology, Japan

Hiroshi Sugimura
Kanagawa Institute of Technology, Japan

Moe Hamamoto
Kanagawa Institute of Technology, Japan

Masao Isshiki
Kanagawa Institute of Technology, Japan

ABSTRACT

The authors propose an interface for home energy management system (HEMS). This interface is aimed at raising the energy-saving consciousness of users who have little knowledge of energy saving. A possible reason for the low level of consciousness of such users is that HEMS does not provide information which helps users in energy-saving planning. To help users who have insufficient knowledge of energy saving, the interface visualizes power consumption and operational information obtained from network home appliances. In order to show which appliances have potential for significant energy-saving effects, the interface uses icons that visually represent high-power appliances whose power consumption exceeds 400 W, along with their operation periods. By viewing the screen, users can easily recognize how to operate appliances for energy-saving planning as well as which appliances have high energy-saving effects. The authors have developed a tool with a built-in interface and have evaluated it by questionnaire.

DOI: 10.4018/978-1-5225-9069-9.ch008

INTRODUCTION

Electric power occupies almost 50% of the amount of household energy consumption. In view of this, the use of home energy management systems (HEMS) for household energy management has been promoted. The HEMS has two major functions: visualization of power consumption and remote control of home appliances. By utilizing this technique, an energy-saving effect of 3 to 12% can be achieved (Kato, 2011). The visualization of power consumption by the HEMS is aimed at promoting the energy-saving awareness by presenting the state of use of electric power so that users can find better energy-saving methods and realize how effective those methods are. The remote control of home appliances is aimed at assisting users' energy-saving actions by offering the function of remotely controlling home appliances through a single terminal device. However, (Yoshie et al., 2014) have revealed that users with a high level of awareness of energy saving tend to frequently use HEMS, whereas users with a low level of awareness of energy saving use it rather infrequently. Additionally, a practical experiment demonstrated (Osaka City, 2013) that the energy-saving effect by a HEMS system was as high as 22% immediately after the introduction of the system, but decreased to 11% over a period of three months. A probable cause of this decrease in the energy-saving effect is a decrease in the usage rate of the system. We considered that such a decrease in the usage rate occurred due to cumbersome tasks for the energy-saving. Accordingly, studies for assisting energy-saving actions without requiring cumbersome tasks have been made.

Accordingly, methods for assisting users with little knowledge of energy saving have been studied. (Hidenori et al., 2014) and (Yusuke et al., 2010) have proposed a system which provides general advice concerning energy-saving based on power consumption and peak time. This system has an advice list and selects a piece of advice which is likely to produce the highest energy-saving effect for the user based on that list. However, this advice is not optimized for the use condition for each individual user, so the energy-saving action may be burdensome for the user. (Morimoto, 2016) and (Takekazu et al., 2013) have proposed energy-saving methods by an automatic control of home appliance products. Their ideas do not take into account external factors, such as seasonal variations, weather, and time of day.

The use of a system which proposes energy-saving methods or automatically controls home appliances as in conventional studies is likely to cause users to feel the energy-saving tasks burdensome and tend to infrequently use the system. We believe it is necessary to develop a HEMS which can motivate users to voluntarily act on energy saving without feeling reluctance for such actions. To this end, the so-called nudge theory will be useful, which is a technique for appealing to direct reaction and inducing individuals to change their behavior, sometimes involuntarily (Thaler et al., 2008). We consider the induction of the behavioral change according to the nudge theory to be important. So, we will include the idea into our proposed method to develop a HEMS capable of managing energy-saving actions in an intuitive form without requiring users to do cumbersome tasks.

Managing the energy-saving actions requires understanding the contents of energy saving. We analyzed the contents of energy saving and classified them into the four phases of the PDCA cycle, which is a generally used management scheme: energy-saving planning (Plan), energy-saving action (Do), plan analysis (Check) and plan improvement (Action). The visualization in the HEMS can be considered as a function for assisting the energy-saving analysis by the Check element. We have already pointed out that existing visualization methods are insufficient in terms of the energy-saving analysis. For example, a simple form of visualization is insufficient for the energy-saving analysis, because it does not provide useful information concerning the correlation between user operations on home appliances and changes in power consumption. Without such information, users cannot easily determine or improve their energy-saving method. In this study, we propose a tool which provides a comprehensive view in which the visualization of the power consumption is associated with operation information of each home appliance so that users can intuitively understand what method is effective for energy saving.

SUMMARY OF THE SYSTEM

Figure 1 shows visualization screens of conventional HEMS products, including FEMINITY (by TOSHIBA), AiSEG2 (by Panasonic) and ENEDIA (by Mitsubishi Electric). FEMINITY allows for the comparison of the power consumption of the day with those of previous days, as well as the display of the state of power in each room and the power consumption in the entire house. This system can be considered helpful in identifying an appliance which causes a significant waste of power.

AiSEG2 has the function of graphically showing highly power-consuming appliances in descending order of power consumption, as well as the function of displaying how much energy saving has been achieved as compared to an energy-saving target. AiSEG2 assists energy saving by helping users locate appliances which are consuming high amounts of electric power.

ENEDIA displays a comparison of the power consumption of the day with those of previous days as well as the ON/OFF state of each appliance. ENEDIA assists users by displaying the currently operating appliances and the power consumption information so that users can easily locate highly power-consuming appliances. In any of the three products, the visualization function is aimed at helping users easily locate appliances which are consuming high amounts of electric power. Users need to consider which appliance has considerable potential for energy saving and what kind of operation will produce such an effect.

The usability of the interface can be considered as one factor that affects the cumbersomeness of the energy saving. (Steve, 2005) says that making users free from unnecessary thinking improves usability. Krug says that having links, buttons or similar elements whose response to the clicking is unknown to users lowers the level of usability. (Jacob, 1993) claims that usability is composed of five elements: learnability, efficiency, memorability, errors and satisfaction. Applying these insights to the conventional HEMS products reveals the following problems concerning their usability: The conventional HEMS products have various functions integrated together, such as the amount of saved money, visualization, and remote control. Due to the presence of too many links or buttons, those products lack usability in terms of learnability and memorability. (Ben, 2017) claims, as one of his eight golden rules of interface design, that the user interface should be designed to reduce inter-window motions since the human short-term memory is limited. Based on this principle, the proposed technique adopts the design in which the operation information is integrally presented on the visualization window, rather than on a separate window, in order to make the user-interface operation less cumbersome. Annotations are used to display both the operation information and the visualization on the same window. An annotation showing information concerning the operation of an appliance is presented at the point of the operation on the time axis of the visualization. Icons are also used to show appliances which are consuming high amounts of electric power. The icons help intuitive understanding of the appliances which have considerable potential for energy saving. A simple look at the interface allows users to naturally understand the correlation between an operation of an appliance and a change in power consumption, and utilize the correlation for energy-saving analysis. Such a system will enable the energy-saving analysis without requiring cumbersome tasks for the energy saving.

Figure 1. Visualization screens of conventional HEMS products

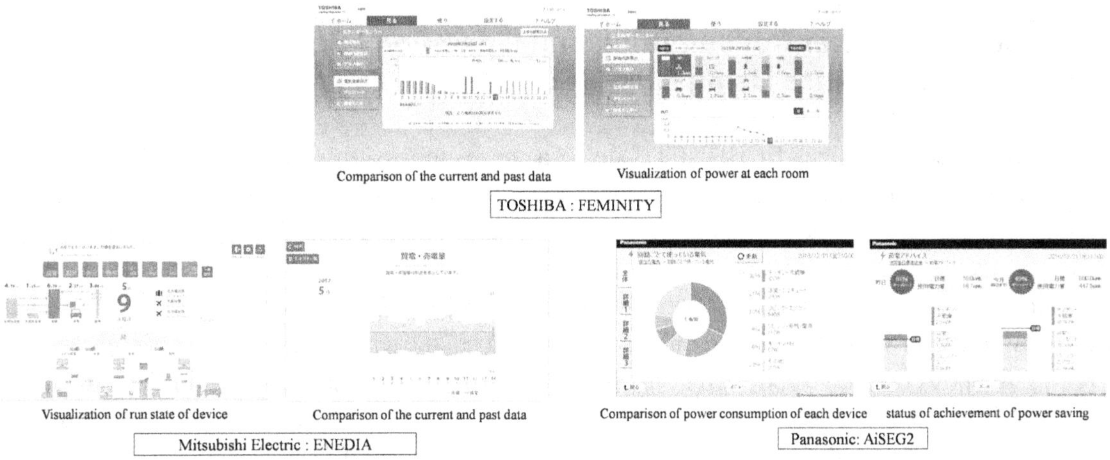

Comparison of the current and past data · Visualization of power at each room

TOSHIBA : FEMINITY

Visualization of run state of device · Comparison of the current and past data

Mitsubishi Electric : ENEDIA

Comparison of power consumption of each device · status of achievement of power saving

Panasonic: AiSEG2

Figure 2 is an overall view of the tool. The annotations are presented by using icons. The graph is divided into upper and lower areas. The information presented by each icon changes depending on the area. Each icon within the upper area represents a home appliance (A) whose power consumption has exceeded 400 W. This icon visualizes the operation period by its horizontal size. Each icon within the lower area represents a home appliance (B) at the point in time when the appliance was operated. The graph (C) visualizes power consumption, using the data acquired on the day and the previous day. This graph also shows the upper limit of the maximum rated current of the switchboard. Visually displaying the maximum rated current helps users easily recognize what percentage of power has been consumed.

Figure 2. General design of the tool

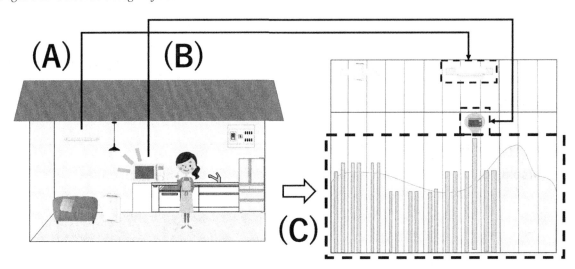

IMPLEMENTATION

1. Acquisition of Power Consumption and Operation Information of Each Home Appliance Using ECHONET Lite

The proposed method utilizes ECHONET Lite to acquire information from home appliances. This enables the construction of a system that is applicable in normal household environments. ECHONET Lite is an OSI-based network communication protocol (ISO / IEC 14543-4-3) standardized for home automation. Its specifications are open to the public. We used an ECHONET-Lite compliant switchboard (Panasonic 84122J) to acquire the power consumption of each home appliance. This switchboard has a built-in power sensor in the master circuit breaker as well as in each of the 32 branch circuit breakers. Therefore, the power, voltage and current in each appliance can be acquired from this switchboard by ECHONET Lite, without using any special sensor. The operation information of each home appliance is acquired from the individual home appliances which are ECHONET Lite-compliant.

2. Presentation of Operation Information by Icons

Figure 3 shows icons showing information regarding an air conditioner. Each home appliance has a unique icon color assigned to it. Icons have two shapes: circular and rectangular. Circular icons indicate the ON/OFF state of the home appliance. A gray icon means "OFF". Other colors mean "ON". Rectangular icons show a change in the operation of the home appliance. The illustration inside this icon allows users to understand what operation was performed.

3. System Implementation

Figure 4 shows the entire system. The entire power consumption is obtained by integrating the power measured in the master circuit breaker. The power consumption of each individual home appliance is obtained by connecting one branch circuit breaker with one wall socket to which one home appliance is connected, and integrating the power measured in the branch circuit breaker. An originally developed script program running on the server acquires information from each home appliance and the switchboard at intervals of 3 minutes through ECHONET Lite communications. The data to be acquired are hexadeci-

Figure 3. Icons used for annotations

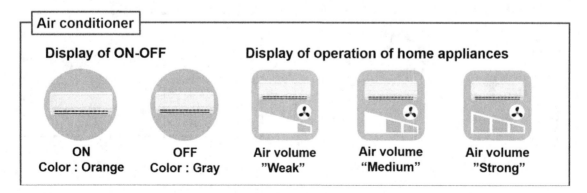

Figure 4. The entire system

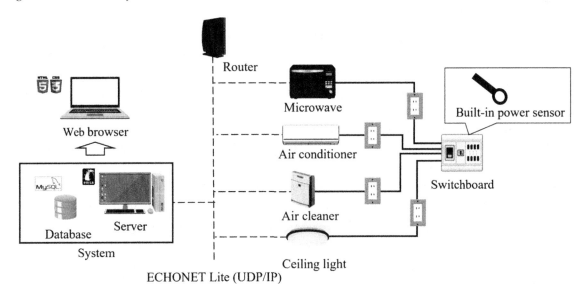

mal packet data. The script program compiles those data into a specified format and stores them in the database. The database has five columns: IP address of the appliance, name of the appliance, acquired content, acquired state, and acquisition time. The interface is implemented as a Web application (Ruby on Rails) and displays information on the Web browser using HTML5. Javascript and jQuery are used to implement the dynamic processing for displaying the annotations. The Highcharts library is used to display the graph.

Table 1 shows the specifications of the ECHONET Lite appliances and the items of information obtained from each appliance. The experimental system obtains operation information from six types of appliances. The items of information concerning user operations which are likely to affect the power consumption are obtained from each appliance. For example, the information to be obtained for an air conditioner includes the ON/OFF switching, operation mode, temperature setting and air volume. Only the ON/OFF state is obtained for the ceiling light and other appliances with low power consumption.

Table 1. Specifications of ECHONET Lite appliances and information to be obtained

Appliance Name	Maker/Model Number	Information to Be Obtained
Air conditioner	TOSHIBA/RAS-221GDRH	Air volume, Temperature, ON/OFF, Operation mode
Air cleaner	SHARP/KJEX100-N	ON/OFF, Operation mode
Ceiling light	TOSHIBA/LEDH81718XLC-LT3	ON/OFF
Microwave	SHARP/AX-XW400	ON/OFF, Output setting
Refrigerator	TOSHIBA/GR-H460FV	Temperature in each compartment, open/close state of each door
Switchboard	Panasonic/BHN87202S2	Integral power

4. User Interface

Figure 5 shows a screen of the tool. The graph indicates current consumption. The yellow barchart shows the current consumption on the day, while the blue line chart shows the current consumption on the previous day. A blue vertical line is drawn at the current time of day to help users quickly locate the latest current consumption from among the variety of data displayed on the graph. The red dashed line indicates the permissible current of the switchboard. The annotations in the upper area of the graph show home appliances whose power consumption exceeds 400 W, as well as their operation periods, while those in the lower area show information on the operation and state of the home appliances. Each annotation in the lower area is represented by an icon with the arrow indicating the operation time on the time axis. In order to avoid the situation in which too many annotations are displayed and overlap each other, the tool has the function of turning on/off the display of each individual annotation within the lower area. With this function, users can select the annotations of the home appliances which they want to display. This interface is intended for indoor use, and therefore, is implemented for use on a tablet or personal computer with a 10-inch or larger screen.

EVALUATION OF THE SYSTEM

We have evaluated the effectiveness of the developed tool by a questionnaire. A total of 11 participants answered the questionnaire, including 9 males and 2 females. We asked them whether they were conscious of energy saving on a routine basis, and whether they thought the tool would be effective for raising the consciousness of energy saving. Figure 6 shows the totalized results divided into two groups, with

Figure 5. Interface of the tool

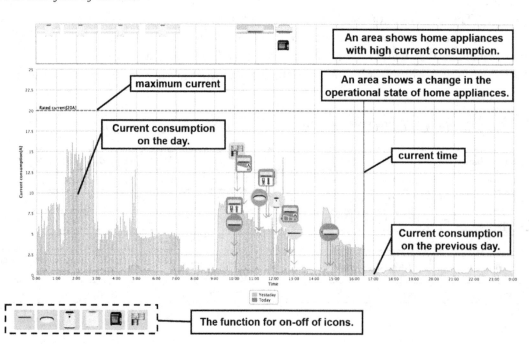

Figure 6. Results of the questionnaire about the effect of the tool on the consciousness of energy saving

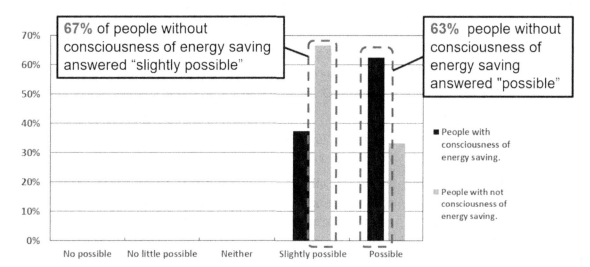

one group including those who were conscious of energy saving on a routine basis and the other group including those who were not.

Questionnaire Items

1. Personal data of respondent (gender, age and number of family members)
2. Four-point-scale evaluation on his/her awareness of energy saving in everyday life
3. Five-point-scale evaluation on whether this tool can improve the awareness of energy saving.
4. Free description

Based on the answer to Question 2 concerning the awareness of energy saving, we classified the respondents into two groups: The respondents who selected 3 or 4 were classified as respondents with a high level of awareness of energy saving, while those who selected 1 or 2 were classified as respondents with a low level of awareness of energy saving. Whether each respondent understood the meaning of the term "awareness" was not tested in the evaluation experiment conducted this time. The result demonstrates that 63% of the respondents who were highly conscious of energy saving said it would be "possible" to raise the consciousness of energy saving by using the tool, and 67% of those whose were less conscious found it "slightly possible". The results were generally favorable, so we believe the tool will help raise the consciousness of energy saving. A possible reason for the high evaluation by the respondents who are highly aware of energy saving is because the correlation between power consumption and operation information of each appliance enabled them to analyze which appliances are suitable for energy saving and clearly recognize necessary actions for energy saving based on their own experience in energy saving. The use of the correlation between power consumption and operation information for assisting the energy-saving analysis also seems to have been effective for the respondents who are less aware of energy saving. The reason for the lower evaluation by the latter group as compared to the former group is probably because the latter users with little experience in energy saving must have felt it difficult to decide what action should be taken for energy saving.

CONCLUSION

In this study, we proposed and implemented a tool corresponding to the "Check" element in the HEMS having the PDCA elements by establishing the correlation between power consumption and operation information. The implemented tool was evaluated by a questionnaire. The result demonstrated that the tool can eliminate cumbersome tasks for energy-saving analysis.

FUTURE RESEARCH

Future studies should additionally deal with the utilization of the competition principle for energy-saving assistance by incorporating the competition principle of gamification and social network communication into our tool. Adapting the system for smartphones or tablet terminals will make the system more useful by allowing its use not only indoors but also outdoors. To this end, a responsive design should be adopted in the designing of the interface screen to make the system more versatile. The evaluation in this study relied only on the questionnaire. It will be necessary for us to additionally refer to various statistical techniques and other related studies when we consider evaluation contents for the system after all functions including the PDCA elements have been proposed and implemented.

REFERENCES

Ben, S. (2017). *Designing the user interface: strategies for effective human-computer interaction*. London: Person Education.

Echonet Consortium. (2018) *ECHONET Lite Overview*. Retrieved form https://echonet.jp/english/

Hidenori, K., Ken-ichiro, N., Toshihiro, M., & Yasushi, S. (2014). Automatic Generating System for Reports on Energy Conservation Tips Based on Electricity Demand Data. *IEEJ Transactions on Electronics Information Systems*, *134*(9), 1394–1405.

Highcharts Overview. (2018). Retrieved from https://www.highcharts.com

Jacob, N. (1993). *Usability Engineering*. San Diego, CA: Academic Press.

Keisuke, T., Shinsuke, M., & Masahide, N. (2013). Towards Personalization of Home Electricity Peak Shaving Application, The Institute of Electronics, Information and Communication Engineers. *Technical Report of Icicle*, *112*(458), 1–6. (in Japanese)

Mitsubishi Electric. (2018). *ENEDIA Overview*. Retrieved from http://www.mitsubishielectric.co.jp/home/enedia/

Morimoto, N. (2016). Energy-on-Demand System Based on Combinatorial Optimization of Appliance Power Consumptions. *Journal of Information Processing*, *25*(1), 268–276.

Osaka City, Japan. (2013). *Results of questionnaire of before and after use of "visualizing equipment"*. Retrieved from http://warp.da.ndl.go.jp/info:ndljp/pid/10189884/www.city.osaka.lg.jp/kankyo/page/0000148884.html

Panasonic. (2018). *AiSEG2 Overview*. Retrieved from http:// https://www2.panasonic.biz/es/densetsu/aiseg/aiseg2/index.html

Rikiya, K. (2011). *Issues of the penetration of Home Energy Management System-Summarizing issues by the investigation of past demonstration projects. Central Research Institute of Electric Power Industry Research Report Y 12011.* (in Japanese)

Steve, K. (2005). *Don't Make Me Think: A Common Sense Approach to Web Usability* (2nd ed.). New York: New Riders.

Takekazu, K., Kenji, Y., & Takashi, M. (2013). Energy On Demand. *Information Processing Society of Japan, 54*(3), 1185–1198.

Thaler, R. H., & Sunstain, C. R. (2008). *Nudge: Improving Decisions About Health, Wealth, and Happiness*. New Haven, CT: Yale University Press.

Toshiba. (2018). *Feminity Overview*. Retrieved from http://feminity.toshiba.co.jp/feminity/feminity_eng/

Yoshie, Y., Yumiko, I., & Yasuhiko, H. (2014). HEMS Browsing Behaviors and the Communication Effects. *Journal of Japan Society of Energy and Resources, 35*(4), 50–58.

Yusuke, N., Kotaro, S., & Akimitsu, N. (2010). Development of the Environment and Energy Information System in Residential House. *AIJ Journal of Technology and Design, 16*(34), 1069–1074. (in Japanese)

Chapter 9
Applied Alternative Tools and Methods in the Replacement of the Game Design Document

Pedro Henrique Roscoe Lage de Oliveira
Minas Gerais State University, Brazil

Carlos Alberto Silva de Miranda
Minas Gerais State University, Brazil

Joao Victor Boechat Gomide
Universidade FUMEC, Brazil

ABSTRACT

This chapter proposes and experiments alternatives to replace or optimize the use of the game design document (GDD). The creation and development of a game is accomplished by relying on the GDD, which contains all the information, such as the script, mechanics, and relevant details, so the team can use as a guide. There is no exact formula for creating a GDD, and several formats are proposed and used nowadays. Information misinterpreted or misunderstood at different levels of responsibility can create irreparable problems after the start of production. This chapter proposes the use of analog prototyping associated with benchmarking techniques and agile development as efficient alternatives to GDD, which are tested in the development of the game Forsaken Dungeons, created by one of the authors.

INTRODUCTION

This chapter analyses a set of methods used as efficient and economic alternatives to GDD topics and digital prototyping, to increase the team efficiency, organization and communication. The game design goals and topics are commented on (CRAWFORD: 1982, 49-50): 'A game must have clearly defined goal. This goal must be expressed in terms of the effects that it will have on player. It is not enough to declare that a game will be enjoyable, fun, exciting or good; the goal must establish the fantasies that the game will support and the types of emotions it will engender in its audience. (…)Once you have settled on your goal, you must select a topic. The topic is the means of expressing the goal (…)'

DOI: 10.4018/978-1-5225-9069-9.ch009

To achieve the goal of developing a game based on the efficiency and economically principles it is assumed that a coordinated set of development techniques and documents are valuable among which we mention benchmarking; analog and paper prototyping; user retention and monetization documents. In addition, it is important to apply agile and vertical improvement techniques during the project development.

The game designer can be defined as the professional who determines the gameplay basic guidelines of the product and the development methods that will be used to produce the final product by the development team (ROUSE: 2001, 18) states that 'at its most elementary level, game design consists of inventing and documenting the elements of a game.'

Jesse Schell shows that the game designer must cultivate many skills, ranging from knowledge in technical writing to mathematics (Schell, 2008: 2-4). The designer will use every skill he has to communicate the ideas and to reach the conclusion of the project with minimum expenses and maximum result.

The first phase of a game development starts before programming, art, marketing or any other subject related to game development. The game designer is responsible for planning the product development strategies, goals and topics, before even involving other professionals. (CRAWFORD. 2016, pg. 51) says that 'during this phase it is critical that you commit little to paper and above all, write no code! (…) You will generate during this phase a great variety of specific implementation ideas for your game. They will not all fit together neatly (…). Indulge yourself in creating implementation ideas, but be prepared to winnow the ruthlessly during design.'

To Ernest Adams, 'a game is designed by creating a concept and identifying an audience in the concept stage, fleshing out the details and turning abstract ideas into concrete plans in the elaboration stage, and adjusting the fine points in the tuning stage (…).' (ADAMS: 2009, 62). Rouse points that 'in many ways, developing a game is all about understanding your limitations and then turning those limitations into advantages.' (ROUSE: 2001, 47-54)

The construction of a digital game depends on the teamwork of a diverse crew with a wide range of technical skills. One of the most delicate parts of development is the efficient and cost-effective use of each member effort. The team must seek a scenario where the professionals work with functional independence and their performances are not limited by product scope, harmonizing each personal set of skills in order to create a coherent product. As observes Rouse, the development team must be organized to divide the product in parts and build the game incrementally. 'Instead of working a little bit on all the different components of the game, you should try to complete one system before moving on to the next. Work on the most basic and essential systems first, and then build the systems that depend on that system. This allows you to implement a system, test it out, see if it 'feels' right, and only then move on to the next system.' (ROUSE: 2001, 254)

Tracy Fullerton (2008: 188) points out 'if you try to design the entire game at once, you might become confused and overwhelmed. There are so many elements in a typical game that it is difficult to know where and how to start. What we recommend is that you isolate the core gameplay mechanics and built out from there.'

The development of game design tools boost the team effectiveness, since the game designer will be able to perform typical gameplay design tasks independently (ROUSE: 2001, 378) notes that 'in order to create superior content, the design team will need to be equipped with well-designed, robust game creation tools. Therefore, one can conclude that designing a good game is about designing good game creation tools'.

In this chapter, analog prototyping, benchmarking and agile development processes are presented as processes for the game designer, which can replace some GDD topics in many productions. Those resources are poorly approached in the literature, never analyzed together, and rarely used by development teams.

GAME DESIGN DOCUMENT

Game development is a multidisciplinary creative process aimed to fulfil the human desire to play and have fun. To develop games it is important that the designer seeks to learn constantly about the most varied subjects. The inspiration for building games come from the most varied academic fields and the ability to listen and learn from your own mistakes.

The game development process is complex, and in practice there will always be scope changes, feature additions and rework. Even in large and consolidated teams these are inevitable constants; however, investing in planning techniques reduces the likelihood of such changes being counterproductive. Good planning generates documents that accurately determine how many arts; songs; animations; levels and how many systems will be needed to achieve the least viable product, which keeps the development team highly producible.

During the development, the design process follows phases of the product creation, starting with the overall planning, designation of responsibilities and set of the tools that will be developed and/or used by the team. The final stage is dedicated to polishing, which involve a large number of iterations with individuals inside and outside the development group.

Writing a GDD is considered a relevant part of the process. It is assumed, in general, that the lack of a GDD guiding the project culminates in failure. There is no perfect formula for a GDD production, along with huge controversies on how to build it. As Adams notes, 'As part of their job, game designers produce a series of documents to tell others about their game design. Exactly what documents they produce and what the documents are for vary from designer to designer and project to project (ADAMS: 2009, 54)

The document has the function of recording decisions and agreements that have been made orally or making explicit the ideas that have been ventilated and approved by the developers. Although there is no standard for composing a GDD, there are proposed structures and recommendations.Those who support the use of GDD as the backbone of game development understand that this document should include several sessions. However, as noted by Rouse, 'different companies may have different standards for what documentation pieces they create in order to assist and guide a game´s development.' (ROUSE. 2001, 302)

The documents that usually are part of the GDD are listed in Adams (ADAMS: 2009, 56-58):High Concept Document, which defines the central concept of the game; Game Treatment Document: the most detailed game description document, considered an extended version of the High Concept Document; Character Design, World Design, Narrative Design and Level Design Documents: those are specifically directed to specific parts of the game; Game Script document: according to Adams, this document cover the stories and mechanics that shape the game core.

Tracy Fullerton (2008: 396) understands that 'You should think of your design document as a living document. You will likely have to make a dozen steps before it is complete, and then you will need to constantly update it to reflect changes that are made during the development process. Because of this, it is important to organize your document on a modular way. If you organize your document carefully from the beginning, it will be easier to update and manage as it grows in size and complexity'.

Some practical issues brought by writing all these documents within the game creation process are justifying the time and effort needed to write them, along with the effectiveness of these documents while producing the game. It is well known that many game developing professionals only read these documents superficially. Others prefer a more informal and intuitive approach, as seen in many productions. The game designer has to be a good communicator to make the others understand the GDD and must track the work of the other professionals, as points (Schell: 2008, 3). Richard Rouse (2001: 292) points out that 'the necessity of game development documentation is a side effect of the increasing size of game development teams. In the early days of game development, when a development team consisted of one multi-talented individual, documenting the functionality of the game was less important. If that one person was able to establish and implement a vision for the project's gameplay, it did not especially matter if she wrote it down or not.'

In recent years, the intensifying of competition and the increasing complexity that has been attributed to products and services have required the developers to adapt their processes with a view to improving quality and reducing time. These adaptations involve management techniques and methods of design, analysis, simulation and optimization. The use of prototypes become an essential condition to increase the company's abilities to identify customer needs as a matter of priority and to provide important subsidies to improve communication among those involved in the process, as well as reduce the chances of failure and increase the chances of success of the enterprise. In addition, prototyping provides the possibility of evaluating the perceptual and sensory experience that will occur in the process of use, in relation to shape, external appearance, color and texture.

In this context, it becomes evident the importance of the prototypes in the development process, considering that these can be used to realize tests that allow the verification of possible problems, besides the opportunities of the optimization of the game functions. Prototyping helps not only to speed up but to make a more secure development, as well as making the investments in subsequent stages more assertive as Medeiros Filho says, 'It does not matter how much experience or talent the professional has in game design, an idea may in practice become quite different from what has been planned, in addition, a number of other elements, previously unseen, may surface, altering the form and scope of the project.'

It is assumed that, in the case of games in genres suitable for analog prototyping, game design documentation coupled with prototyping processes are the most economic and effective way for the development of the product and that the more detailed the prototypes are, the less documentation will be required for the game. A game that can be in its predominance represented by analog and paper prototypes is consequently a game that can have much of its documentation represented by the prototypes, and therefore, communication and the understanding of the game by the team can be made commencing by these prototypes.

ANALOG AND PAPER PROTOTYPING

Prototyping is an essential part of the development since it allows the analysis of its form and functionality before the investments in tooling or definitive platforms. Historically, these representations of products (or simply, prototypes) have been used since the evolution of production processes, evolving from manual representations (sketches, drawings, mockups and physical models, for example) to virtual representations, from the years 80, with the evolution of CAD (computer aided design), and, more recently, with rapid prototypes as comments VOLPATO (2007, p).

In recent years, the intensification of competition and the increasing complexity of the products and services have demanded the companies to adapt their product development processes in order to improve quality and reduce time. The use of prototypes becomes an essential condition to increase the company's abilities to identify customer needs as a matter of priority and to provide important subsidies to improve communication among individuals in the process, as well as reduce the chances of failure of the endeavor. In addition, prototyping provides the possibility of evaluating the perceptual and sensory experience that will occur in the process of use, in relation to shape, external appearance, color and texture, as seen in H. Tai. (TAI, 2017. Pg. 71-86).

Paper prototyping allows designers to quickly test the fluidity of their interface screens by simply using paper and pen so that important creative decisions can be made in the planning phase. Fox notes: 'You are choosing the most important places where you need to spend time and effort.' (FOX, 2005, p.

It is assumed that the materialization of interfaces from paper prototyping will allow them to be approved before the creation of the definitive arts. A well-planned paper prototype will allow all project members to sanction the fluidity of the interfaces presented or, if they believe there is a better way to achieve the desired result, to express their ideas.

Prototyping is an important process for creating a product. The quickness, inexpensiveness and clarity are characteristics of the prototyping process that can be divided into two categories, high fidelity and low fidelity, according to the proximity they have from the final material. Jesse Schell (2008: 86-87) understands that 'every prototype must be created to answer a question and sometimes more than one. (…) Your goal is to loop as usefully and as frequently as possible. So if you can manage it, why not just get the software out of the way? If you are clever, you can prototype your fancy game idea as a simple board game, or what we sometimes call a paper prototype. This lets you spot problems sooner.'

Tracy Fullerton (2008: 176) notes that 'physical prototyping also allows for non-technical team members to participate at a very high level in the design process. No one needs specialized knowledge or expertise in a programming language to give their input, which will allow for a wider variety of perspectives in the design process. Physical prototyping will also allow for a broader and deeper experimentation process simply because it can be done without major cost or use of resources.'

On the subject Kay et al (2003, 6) states that the prototype points out and serves to communicate information and show tangible ideas to the development team, internal management and external clients. Testing and refining the interactions of a game in the prototyping phase means that all other individuals involved in the development are less likely to rebuild parts of the product due to problems identified in later phases.

Digital and analog games have differences, notably the interactions with physical pieces on the first ones and the graphical interface interactions in the second. In addition, there are differences in how they deal with the mechanics and complexity. Digital games have the game system as a final referee for rules. In the other hand, if a rule is contradictory in an analog game, players may discuss and decide what is the best way to apply it. The analog game system is adaptable, while the digital game system is rigid. Moreover, the complexity in digital games can be hidden in the feedback system, which allows the game to remove certain tasks from the player operations, for example, operations that can be made instantly by the computer. On the subject Fullerton (2008: 132) understands that 'when we use the word 'feedback' in general conversation, we often are just referring to the information we get back during an interaction, not what we do with it. But in system terms, feedback implies a direct relationship between the output of an interaction and a change to another system element. Feedback can be positive or negative, and it can promote divergence or balance in the system.'

It is possible to state that a set of systems present in a board game can represent a significant fraction of the systems presented by digital games. As an example, T*he Dark Souls* board game captures the fundamentals of the *Dark Souls* digital game, absorbing its mechanics and translating them into a turn-based combat system.

It is important to note, however, that analog prototyping will be more efficient in developing games with typical board mechanics and are in some cases not recommended (when, for example, the mechanics of a game are based only on combat or running). There are certain game genres that best fit analog prototyping like games with strategy, puzzle, card games, and resource management mechanics.

Tracy Fullerton (2008: 178) understands that: 'Physical prototypes are critical for designing both board games and sophisticated electronic games. Many famous electronic games are based on paper games. The system for digital role-playing games such as Diablo II, Baldur's Gate, EverQuest, Asheron's Call and World of Warcraft are derived from the paper-based system of Dungeons & Dragons.'

Analog prototyping can be used as a key resource in development since it is a quick tool to validate the iteration possibilities of a digital product. Also, the developer must consider that the financial and human expenses implicated in the making of an analog prototype are objectively lower than that of a digital prototype. This method gives the designer superior implementation effectiveness; mechanics can be created and tested without the need to translate them with code, placeholders or art implementation. Furthermore, understanding a game using an analog prototype is easier than reading a GDD, making the game experience perception more fluid to the team since they will actually play the game, being able to perform all critical balancing and mechanics modification before the digital development begins.

Tracy Fullerton (2008: 207) concludes that 'Creating a physical prototype is a critical step in the design of your original game concept. It will save your team tremendous amounts of time because everyone will have a clear understanding of the game you are making. In addition, a physical prototype will enable you to focus your creative energy on the game mechanics without becoming distracted by the production and programming process. And most importantly, making a prototype gives you the freedom to experiment and through experimentation comes innovation.'

(SNYDER: 2003, 12) describes the advantages of paper prototyping for interface prototyping, which she says are good to provide feedback early in the development process, encouraging creativity, promoting rapid iterative development, facilitating communication with the team and customers by enabling a multidisciplinary team to work together since it does not require any technical skills.

BENCHMARKING

Benchmarking techniques can be utilized in the game design process aiming to analyze and applying the best principles in the game development. Benchmarking, according to Elmuti and Kathawala (1997: 229) 'is the process of identifying the highest standards of excellence for products, services, or processes, and then making the improvements necessary to reach those standards, commonly called ´best practices´. The justification lies partly in the question: ´Why reinvent the wheel if I can learn from someone who has already done it?'

Through benchmarking, the game designer can set each goal and topic of his game based on examples of solutions he found in other games, facilitating the set-up of the project and guiding the work of team members. Watson (2007: 3) remembers that benchmarking is a process of comparing in order to learn how to improve. Motivation for a benchmarking study is the desire to improve and become more competitive.'

Elmuti and Kathawala (1997: 229) states that 'the process of benchmarking is more than just a means of gathering data on how well a company performs against others (…). It is also a method of identifying new ideas and new ways of improving processes and, therefore, being better able to meet the expectations of customers.' The benchmarking used in the early phases of development intent to support the team organization. Watson (2007: 8) points out that '(…) benchmarking will provide productivity improvement by concentrating on specific activities that will improve the effectiveness, efficiency, or economy of routine business operations.'

Some tools like Game Analytics can be used for benchmarking the game over time, helping the developer to notice and troubleshoot user retention and other design issues. This tool allows the developer to compare the performance of the game with others in the tool network, helping the developer to make informed decisions with the understanding of the markets the game aim and its individual performance.

By looking outside and researching other games, the designer can identify best practices, qualities and flaws within other games in the same genre typically have, along with ways to fix it. With the use of benchmarking, the game designer can light better ways to reach a high-quality ultimate product. As an example of benchmarking use, there is the game Forsaken Dungeons, created by JetDragon Studios.

The game used as a main reference for the creation of the universe was Battlechasers. Dofus and Dark Quest 2 were the benchmark for scenery, while base gameplay was benchmarked by the board game Gloomhaven and other turn-based tactical games. The Level Design Document was replaced by a Level Editor tool, while the Game Script document was replaced by the analog prototype.

AGILE DEVELOPMENT IN GAME DEVELOPMENT

Analog prototyping and benchmarking are put together in their maximum effectiveness when used inside agile development processes, as opposed to traditional cascade development. The fundamental problem of the cascade development is that game creation is a constant process of learning and iteration. Agile development techniques increase the speed of the development by establishing a workflow capable of allowing the materialization of the project instead of exhaustive documentation, as observed by Clinton Keith (2010: 13): 'We are uncovering better ways of developing software by doing it and helping others do it. Through this work we have come to value: 1.Individuals and interactions over processes and tools; 2.Working software over comprehensive documentation; 3.Customer collaboration over contract negotiation; 4. Responding to change over following a plan.'

Agile development represents a modular structure that makes every effort to build a development progression that is more adaptive and focused on the developers instead of detailed documentation about the game, giving priority to team communication and iterations. Using agile in game development increase the team ability to identify and solve game development problems with efficiency and economy.

On agile development Medeiros Filho comments: 'In the process of game development, different agile production methodologies are adopted by each company. Among them is the SCRUM methodology, an agile production methodology that has become very popular in the gaming industry, where the production focus is characterized by small iteration cycles. The goal is not to define all content at the beginning but to explore possibilities during the process, where teams can even modify the project mindset based on iterations and changes over the course of the cycles. In this sense it is always good or desirable to have some playable prototype. '(MEDEIROS, 2013: page 313).

The creation of a game using agile development is divided into pre-defined time intervals called sprints. Each sprint's objective is to fulfil a specific functionality required by the customer, referred as 'user story'. Each sprint is only completed after development and testing of the corresponding user story features. The next sprint will be planned by prioritizing which features are the most important, and so on, until all the development goals are met. This mindset saves time and removes obstacles that will invariably arise during development.

Analog prototyping and benchmarking work as guides, to define the initial sprints and the first short-term goals, in the agile development process. If the entire team had the opportunity to iterate with the analog product and the benchmark games, the definition of the project scope will be clearer to the developers and much rework will be avoided as the iterations have been already made, ensuring the effectiveness of the game mechanics and the fun of the product-player interactions.

The most commonly methodology used to apply agile development methods and practices is called Scrum. It names three main roles: Product Owner, Scrum Master and Development Team. The Product Owner (usually the game designer) has the final say in the game concepts, while the Scrum Master enables the interaction between all involved parts, removing any obstacles arisen during the development, and the Development Team carries on the technical development of the product.

Game development projects can end up generating unrewarded effort. Usually, among the reasons that cause this problem we can identify: overoptimistic schedules; lack of technical team capacity and feature creep. C. Keith (2010: 17) understands that feature creep is the term given to resources being added to a project inflating the original game scope and impairing the development. The author understands that there are two main reasons for the feature creep, and those are the stakeholder demands and the poor result of implemented features. The feature creep impacts negatively in the game development since it represents the exacerbation of changes widening the project scope. However, it's important to emphasize that the game creation is a practice based on incremental progress and new features and improvements are welcome during the product creation process whenever they don't impact in the development time.

Erik Bethke (2003: 288) says 'Feature creep actually starts during the earliest parts of the Project: requirements gathering and game design. Here it is quite easy to lose track of the core game you are making (because it is still so fresh and new) and start sprawling a bit and tossing in ill-considered, distracting features.'

The game development success comes from the effectiveness of the methodologies applied to detect problems and find solutions during the game creation process. To achieve team-efficiency, the communication between the members is of paramount importance to allow features of the product to be effectively delivered. Furthermore, it is important to integrate potential consumers in the iteration process to ensure the optimal user experience. To achieve these objectives, the use of analog prototyping, benchmarking and agile development techniques can result in the improvement of the team communication and workflow, as well as aiding on solving emergent problems that will during the project evolution.

CASE STUDY

The case study procedures used in this research were divided into stages, they were: definition, planning, execution, data gathering, data analysis and conclusion. Inserted in the case study of this work was made the game development procedure, from its basic concept to the final product following the scheme below: Concept; benchmarking and brainstorming; definition of monetization scheme; definition of user retention mechanics; paper and analog prototyping; mechanical balancing; digital prototyping of interfaces; digital prototyping of basic mechanics and developer tools; agile roadmap; sprint backlogs.

Coming up with ideas is important, but it is just the tip of the iceberg. An idea starts to make sense and be engaging in stages, first the game designer must immerse in the topic he wish to explore (maybe a game about medieval monsters raiding dungeons, or a game about solving murder mysteries in a steampunk setting for example). After preparing the idea the designer will go through an incubation process, this means he will let the idea develop inside the inner of his mind. Then the insight happens, the moment the designer can feel his idea is worth pursuing. Ideas can also be derived from existing games and activities, that's why it is important to research and play many games as possible during this process. Using techniques like benchmarking the developer can understand the 'hot spots' from the games he is analyzing and by doing so he can save himself from a lot of hard work that has been done previously by someone else.

The project definition occurred in the first stage of the research. The game genre chosen was a strategy turn-based game that can have its mechanics easily simulated with the use of analog prototyping.

Game development is a collaborative work. After the basic project definition it's important to make a brainstorming session with the whole team. Working with all the members in that phase not only generates innovative ideas but engage all the crew members in the game creation process. When the project has the basic structures already defined its easier for other members to talk about their own experiences and ideas. Here the designer must exercise one of the most important skills he can have, listen to his team ideas with attention, no criticism or intolerance.

During the brainstorming phase is important to write down the generated insights. During the development of Forsaken Dungeons we made an 'idea deck'. All the ideas we had were transformed into cards with phrases containing them. Then we started picking the ideas one by one and the whole team gave two grades to each card ranging from 1 to 10. The first grade is the appeal of the idea, the 'how cool this idea is metric' (the higher the better) and the second grade is about the complexity and expensiveness of the idea implementation (the lower the better). That does not mean we discarded any idea, we kept all of them in a box, but the idea cards with the appeal and complexity grades would serve as guidelines to the designer during the execution phase.

In the planning phase, the benchmarking process was also done; the basic mechanics of the game were defined; the monetization tactics and the retention techniques that would be applied in the development were established and also brainstormed with the team.

With the benchmarking process is important to study the market opportunities of the game. The benchmarking can heavily persuade the designer to choose a specific monetization model or commonly used retention techniques; these constraints may demand amendments in the overall gameplay.

It is also important to consider during that phase the cost of the game idea. Ideas that are too ambitious should be carefully inspected and most likely scaled down.

In the execution phase, the paper and analog prototypes of the product were made following the ideas gathered with the brainstorming and benchmarking; the pool of ideas were refined and evaluated during the prototyping processes. From the prototypes, screen fluidity tests were performed (using the paper prototypes), and tests were done with the analog prototype (to define mechanics). From the analog prototype all balancing can be done ensuring that the product, at the digital development phase would not need any fundamental changes in its composition.

Forsaken Dungeons mechanics system is composed by a set of modular subsystems. Each unit card have 6 main characteristics, those are:

- Card Base Health Points
- Card Active Skill 1
- Card Active Skill 2
- Card Active Skill 3
- Card Passive Skill 1
- Card Passive Skill 2

To balance the units of the game, each passive and active skill were created and represented by a card in the analog prototype. Each base unit with health point was also represented by a card. By mixing the skill cards with the base unit cards each unit could be balanced and thematically adapted. This unit balancing generated insights regarding the aesthetics of each character; the overall 'average power level' of each unit and also the value of each skill in 'gameplay impact'. During this process it was also possible to define the skill level required to play with each assembled character; each character received grades varying from 1 (very easy to use) to 10 (very hard to use). It's important to highlight that analog prototyping the ideas make the process focus on gameplay rather than technology. Analog prototypes are easier to modify and discard and also allows all the team members independent of their expertises to participate in the iteration process.

With the definition of what the final product will be, a number of user experience tests were done with people inside and outside the development team. Digital development started with the prototyping of the game screens in Photoshop. The paper prototypes provided the basis for their implementation. In addition, from the analog prototypes it was also possible to begin the development of the fundamental mechanics of the game.

It's important to emphasize that digital prototypes are not the finished game, those can be made with bought or free assets, minimal art and sound. The reason to make a digital prototype is to investigate, identify and solve issues related to the game aesthetics, control responsiveness, technology and mechanics. The prototypes may serve as a starting point in the creation of the final product, but its primary function isn't to speed up the development with the reuse of what have been made, but to prevent the project from being delayed due to problems identified too late.

During the digital prototyping was established which developer tools would be important. The need for a level editor; a monsters editor; a skills editor and a player character editor were identified.All these developer tools were subdivided into sprints of 14 days each and in 04 months of development a digital product already existed with a reasonable amount of mechanics implemented; animations; feedback and music. The game progression was meticulously analyzed with a group of 33 individuals who used the product and provided feedback lists to aid development.

During the benchmarking, made in the planning phase, games like Dark Quest 2 (for aesthetics) and Super Mario Maker (for the level builder importance in the game system) were used as conceptual starting points. It was also defined, during this phase, the definitive name of the game, that is, 'Forsaken Dungeons'. Forsaken Dungeons is a dungeon exploration and turn-based strategy game with aspects of RPG, level management and building.

A small document was created, titled 'Base Guidelines' and in it was outlined the shallow concept of the game and also the main mechanics. This document is a summary of the first topics that are usually part of a GDD. In this document the following concept was determined: 'The definitive turn-based strategy game with management and RPG aspects comes to mobile devices powered by a powerful level editor and intense customization of characters within reach of the player's fingers. Explore dungeons, kill monsters, build your city and give birth to true heroes! In Forsaken Dungeons you are the manager of the Brotherhood, a team of atypical adventurers struggling to purge the evil of the world.' This document also specified key product parameters, among which the monetization scheme and retention techniques used.

For monetization the freemium strategy was defined, i.e. the game will be distributed free of charge and players will be able to buy aesthetic products and advantages in an in-game store.

In relation to retention techniques, the following parameters were defined: 'The game will present the following retention techniques in order to keep its users active and engaged in the experience: 1. Progression; 2.Scarcity; 3.Daily Login; 4.Social Reciprocity; 5. Customization.

In terms of Progression and Customization one system do both, i.e., players can customize the skills of their characters; every 30 levels (progression) a new ability is released to the character (customization). The player can choose which ability to attach by modifying the gameplay and adjusting his character to his style of play. In relation to Social Reciprocity, a system was built to connect the game to social networks and the player can ask life potion for his social media friends. The system of Daily login is aimed at the 'Skill Runes'. Every time the player comes into play in a 24 hour period, he will receive a rune that can be used through a crafting system to build a skill (a skill is mounted through 5 runes).

After the 'Base-Guidelines' document, the analog prototype and paper prototypes could be materialized. Mechanics and interface changes were decided with the entire team and with the participation of individuals outside the development team from brainstorming done after iteration experiences with the game. There were 30 days of weekly testing done with punctual changes to the product mechanics to improve gameplay. Individuals outside the development team filled in feedback sheets leaving their opinions on what could be improved in the game. There were nine sessions of controlled playtest (with the developers guiding the gameplay) and four sessions of blindtests (where no developer can guide the gameplay and the users must receive a manual/video with the rules).

Tracy Fullerton (2008: 249) understands that: 'a continual iterative process of play-testing, evaluating and revising is the way to keep the game from straying during that long arduous process of development. Of course, you cannot keep changing the basic game design – after all, the goal is to release the product eventually.'

The product screens were prototyped in Photoshop, based on the paper prototypes, and sought to get as close to the intended end result as possible. The creation of the developer tools also started, which were planned in a brainstorming session marked after the last play-test of the analog prototype made in the execution phase. Sprints were made that lasted 2 months and both the tools and the screens are ready in their entirety. In the 4th month of development it was established that MVP levels would be made using the level editor and also the fundamental screens for the game would be implemented.

Starting from the MVP it is possible to send the product to publishers, which will also require a 'Project Presentation Document', where the proposal is illustrated for potential investors. Illustrations are used in this document through high fidelity prototypes, analog prototypes and other tools to clearly illustrate design, such as a game manual. This document is not a GDD since its purpose is not to present technical aspects of the game and subsystems to the developers. There were two 15-day sprints for completing the MVP; by the 5th month it was done and sent to 33 individuals, including publisher evaluators. Of these submissions, 20 responses were received, which gave shape to a feedbacks list. Questions were included in the feedback document as shown below:

- What is your game first impression
- Can you identify and describe any specially satisfying or frustrating gameplay experience?
- The game duration is good or you feel it could be shorter or longer?
- Did you find the rules easy to understand?
- How the game control feel?
- Is the game looks and music appealing to you?
- You have any ideas for improving the game?

The feedbacks collected were implemented to the game following the priorities and thus continuing with the incremental development of the design sprints.

The methodology applied in the development of Forsaken Dungeons and presented in this work proved to be efficient in the development of digital turn-based strategy products. It got clear that card games and other typically analog games can use this methodology with no problems. The game development process presented in this work can be represented by the graph presented in figure 1.

The advantages of using the methodology proposed in this work are as the diagram in figure 2.

CONCLUSION

This article demonstrates that there are alternative processes to the exclusive use of the game design document, to create and develop a game. Analog prototyping, associated with benchmarking, can replace parts of the GDD depending on the game genre and mechanics, and those methods can be integrated in agile development processes for maximum efficiency. The capability to detect problems and create high-quality communication between the game designer and the rest of the development team and customers makes analog prototyping, benchmarking and agile techniques powerful techniques for creating and iterating with the features of the game.

Figure 1. The game development process presented in this work

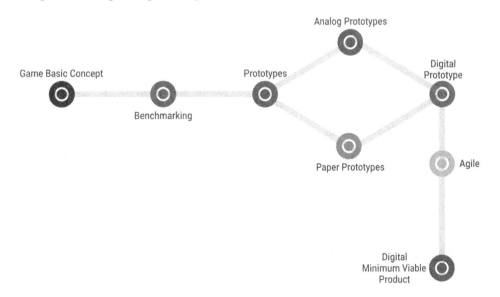

Figure 2. Advantages of using the proposed methodology

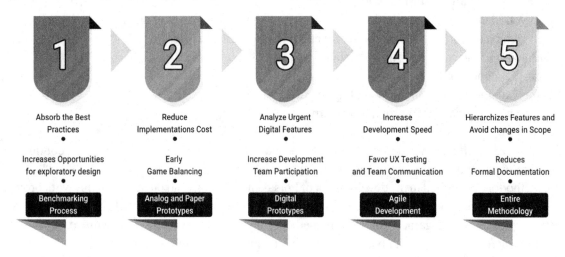

The game design document is in many cases vital for the game development but this use should be analyzed to a greater or lesser extent on a case-by-case basis. Despite being the most used instrument in game development this documentation presents limitations associated with the lack of synergy between the records put on paper and the development stages of a game. There is no single way to work with game design. The alternatives presented in this chapter, although much less used in the mainstream production, have great results when applied especially in genres related to management, strategy and card games. Those methods, when used correctly give as outcome an improvement in the use of human and financial resources, as well as easy and timely identification of flaws during the project, enabling their solution.

ACKNOWLEDGMENT

The authors are grateful to CNPq, FAPEMIG and CoPIC/FUMEC, Brazilian research funding agencies, for the financial support to this work.

REFERENCES

Adams, E. (2009). *Fundamentals of Game Design (2nd ed.). Academic Press.*

Bethke, E. (2003). *Game Development and Production.* Wordware Publishing, Inc.

Buxton, B. (2007). *Sketching User Experiences – Getting the Design right and the Right Design.* Morgan Kaufmann.

Chua, C. K., Leong, K. F., & Lim, C. S. (2003). Rapid Prototyping (2nd ed.). World Scientific. doi:10.1142/5064

Crawford, C. (1982). The Art of Computer Game Design. Vancouver, Canada: Academic Press.

Elmuti, D., & Kathawala, Y. (1997). *An Overview of Benchmarking Process: a tool for continuous improvement and competitive advantage*. Lumpkin College of Business And Applied Sciences.

Fullerton, T. (2008). *Game Design Workshop: a Playcentric Approach to Creating Innovative Games* (2nd ed.). Morgan Kaufmann Publishers.

Keith, C. (2010). *Agile Game Development with Scrum*. Boston: Addison-Wesley.

Medeiros Filho, M., Benicio, I., Campos, F., & Neves, A. (2013). The importance of prototyping in game design. *Proceedings of Brazilian Symposium on Computer Games and Digital Entertainment: Art & Design Track*.

Rouse, R. (2001). *Game Design – Theory & Practice*. Wordware Publishing.

Schell, J. (2008). *The Art of Game Design – A Book of Lenses*. Morgan Kaufmann. doi:10.1201/9780080919171

Snyder, C. (2003). *Paper Prototyping – The Fast and Easy Way to Design and Refine User Interfaces*. San Francisco, CA: Morgan Kaufmann.

Stapenhurst, T. (2009). *The Benchmarking Book – A How-To-Guide to best practice for managers and practitioners*. Oxford, UK: Butterworth-Heinemann.

TAI. (2017). *Hsuan-an. Design: conceitos e métodos*. São Paulo: Blucher.

Watson, G. H. (2007). *Strategic Benchmarking Reloaded with Six Sigma – Improve Your Company's Performance Using Global Best Practice*. John Wiley & Sons.

Chapter 10
Using Augmented–Reality to Aid in Lego Construction:
A Mobile Application

Conrado Ruiz Jr.
De La Salle University, Philippines

Juan Lorenzo Simeon
De La Salle University, Philippines

Kingston Anthony Koa
De La Salle University, Philippines

John Israel Domingo Caingles
De La Salle University, Philippines

Anne Marielle Bagamaspad
De La Salle University, Philippines

ABSTRACT

LEGO structures are generally constructed by following an instruction manual in paper or digital form, which shows the LEGO model at different stages of assembly. Some instructions can be very complicated and difficult to illustrate on paper. Augmented reality (AR) is a technology that superimposes 3D models onto the physical world. This chapter explores the use of AR for assembly through a mobile application for Android devices that serves as an assembly guide for LEGO structures. The system can recognize the current step of the LEGO assembly using data captured via Microsoft Kinect while providing visual feedback through a mobile application. To identify the current step, the system obtains the color and depth data from the Kinect camera and converts the data into a point cloud, which is compared to stored LEGO model data. The system was evaluated based on the accuracy of the recognition, latency of the feedback and the assembly time of the user.

DOI: 10.4018/978-1-5225-9069-9.ch010

INTRODUCTION

LEGO is a toy construction system manufactured by a Danish production company, the LEGO Group. It generally refers to interlocking plastic bricks that can be used to create physical models. Its construction is relatively easy and could be used for prototyping. Building more complicated models however, requires instruction manuals that usually come in printed or digital forms. They guide the user through descriptive, sequential instructions and photos of steps or figures of the model being assembled. However, there are some cases where the model being built is complex, or when the instructions are unclear and it is difficult for the user to follow to correctly assemble the structure. An alternative to these instruction manuals is the use of Augmented Reality (AR) guided assembly.

Augmented reality (AR) is a technology in which information is added or modified into the real physical world, usually through devices like head-mounted displays or mobile devices (Craig, 2013). The effectiveness of this medium to aid in LEGO assembly guidance was confirmed by experiments conducted at Curtin University. It was revealed that an animated AR system yielded shorter task completion times, less assembly errors, and lower total task loads. When the participants relied on their memory and an instruction manual to complete an assembly, they were more prone to making errors (Hou et al., 2015). One of the most recent applications for LEGO assembly is an application that shows an animated partial wireframe of the next step overlaid on the real-world Lego model (Khoung, et al., 2014). Alternatively, the next step can also be shown side-by-side with the actual Lego model. Other similar studies include an application that shows the animated parts while showing their connections (Tang et al., 2003), and an application that shows on-screen the next step in real-time (Gupta, Fox, Curless & Cohen, 2012).

These studies all use either a head-mounted display or a computer monitor to show visual feedback. There is still no context-aware augmented reality mobile phone application that guides the user to build a LEGO structure. Context-aware approaches are systems which take into consideration the current state of the physical model, checking for errors and showing the next state. Augmented reality applications running on mobile devices have a potential of leveraging a large user base, together with their devices (Shmalstieg and Wagner, 2008).

This paper focuses on the development of ARGO, a system that uses augmented reality to show visual feedback to guide users to build LEGO models and is able to recognize when users complete a certain step and move on to the next step automatically. The mobile application guides the user using AR elements by processing color and depth data from Microsoft Kinect camera to recognize the current LEGO model being built. The mobile application communicates and continuously requests data on the current state from the server which interacts with the Kinect camera directly. To compare the physical model to stored steps, the Viewpoint Feature Histogram (VHF) is used (Rusu et al., 2010).

The effectiveness of the system was evaluated based on several factors. First, the accuracy of the recognition of the real-world constructed LEGO to the stored virtual step in the database was measured. The latency of the feedback and the assembly time of the user to construct the LEGO structure were also considered.

BACKGROUND

Augmented Reality (AR) has found applications in numerous areas and has received significant attention from the research community. Hou et al. (2015) found out that the use of AR can cognitively help in manual assembly. They conducted experiments to compare the inclusion and exclusion of AR as a substitute for paper-based manuals. Their conclusion was that using an animated AR system has a positive effect in the cognitive facilitation. Specifically, the learning curve of trainees significantly improved, and fewer errors were made.

AR-based manuals provide immediate feedback and visual instructions. Showing the visualization of the current state of the object reduces the search time in assembly. In addition, AR would lessen the effort of the user in reading textual information. The amount of attention switching is also minimized and, as such, increases productivity. Furthermore, AR could possibly resolve ambiguities through indicators that shows the proper location of a certain component (Khoung et al., 2014).

In order to save time and resources on conducting trainings, the number of tools that help guide manual assembly continue to increase since studies prove it improves the efficiency of manual assembly (Wang, Ong & Nee, 2016). Nasihara and Okamoto (2015) implemented an augmented reality system that guides users in assembly tasks using image processing techniques to recognize the pieces and guide the piece placement with graphic signs. The system of Pathomaree and Charoenseang (2015) was designed to be a guiding tool that helped users assemble objects and structures. Its implementation involved using a camera and augmented reality concepts to detect the interaction and hand gestures made by the user, which represented specific types of commands on navigating through the steps of the assembly of the object.

There are different types of setups for specifically LEGO assembly guidance using AR. They used either an external camera or head-mounted display to view or input the physical model being built by the user. The AR elements or the output are then shown in a separate monitor, visual display or head-mounted display. None of the past studies have yet to consider the use of a mobile phone to display the feedback (Tang et al., 2003).

Context-aware systems like Gupta et al., (2012) developed a real-time guidance program that checks the correct color and position of a LEGO block. Their program then gives feedback to the user. It automatically moves to the next step if the block is correct and informs the user if there is an error so that the user may fix the mistake. Khoung et al. (2014) developed and tested the effectiveness of an AR-based context-aware assembly support system. They stated that context-related visualization of information helps to reduce search time in assembly. They created two AR context-aware visualization modes for their study. One displayed guidance information directly overlaid on the physical model and another featured a virtual model adjacent to the real model. The result was that the visualization mode that rendered guidance information separate from the physical model was preferable over the overlaying visualization mode.

MOBILE AUGMENTED-REALITY APPLICATION FOR LEGO

ARGO is a LEGO assembly guidance mobile application that uses augmented reality to show the bricks that the user must place onto the model that he is building. The system is able to recognize the current stage of assembly and shows the next step. ARGO is also able to detect errors during the assembly phase and notifies the user accordingly. It makes use of a client-server architecture (Figure 1). The client is a mobile application and the server is a desktop where data from a Kinect sensor is processed to track and determine the next step of the model.

Figure 1. Server-client architecture of the mobile AR application for LEGO construction

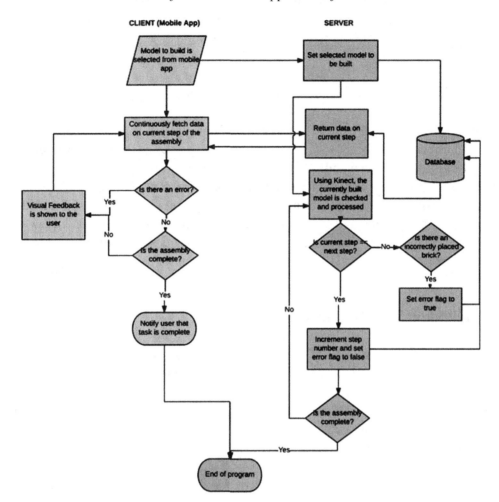

Server-Client Architecture

The task of the mobile application is to provide visual feedback for the user based on the information processed by the server. It accomplishes this through the use of AR elements, specifically showing the next brick or a misplaced brick. The only information being processed on the side of the mobile application is the location on where to display the AR LEGO bricks based on the information sent by the server.

The server, implemented on a desktop computer connected to a Kinect camera, accomplishes the task of processing the current state of the model. This point cloud is compared to the preloaded next step of the model which is being built using the Viewpoint Feature Histogram (Rusu et al., 2010).

Figure 1 shows a summary of the system process flow and how the two components communicate with each other during the assembly process. As the user chooses a model to build from the mobile application, the mobile application communicates this choice to the server while requesting for the next step. The server-side of the system will then take input using the depth sensor of the model. After processing the input, the server then determines the current state of the model as well as the next step using information from the database for the stored LEGO model. As the mobile application obtains this information, it then displays the appropriate visual feedback. The server then waits for any updates in the configuration and then processes the updates accordingly. If it is a correct addition, it moves to the next step; otherwise, it shows an error message. This information is then relayed to the mobile application that displays it to the user.

Physical Set-Up

The physical setup is shown in Figure 2. The system requires the use of an augmented reality marker board, on which the model is being built. The marker board serves as the location where the virtual model would be displayed in the mobile application. The Microsoft Kinect depth camera is placed at a fixed distance, 45.72 cm away from the marker board, 55.88 cm above the table surface, and tilted 30 degrees, overseeing the assembly area. During the assembly process itself, the physical model must be in range of the Kinect and there must be no other objects that may block the Kinect's view or that may be detected as part of the model. The model must also be on a flat tabletop surface using an augmented reality marker board. The area must also be brightly lit for the sensor to recognize the colors in the area accurately.

Mobile Application Implementation

The researchers used the software LeoCAD to virtually represent the LEGO bricks. LeoCAD uses models from the LDraw's Parts Library. It is also used to generate the .ldr files of the virtually built models. This file contains the brick type, step number and coordinates of each brick in the building instructions (Bliss, 2012). The .ldr file is parsed by the mobile app, which acts as the instruction manual and a reference for the phone to know what to show next and guide the user in the building process, The 3D mesh in .3ds format were also generated by this software used to represent the different types of LEGO bricks for the AR of the application.

Using the .ldr files and .3ds files produced by LeoCAD, ARGO can accurately augment the virtual LEGO bricks along with their realistic dimensions and correct positions in 3D space through the smartphone's camera (Figure 3, left) based on the current step of the assembly fetched from the server. This is implemented using ARToolkit. It also notifies the user of a misplaced brick (Figure 3, middle). The user

Figure 2. Physical setup of ARGO, as viewed from different perspectives, top view (left), eye level view (right); seen in the picture is the placement of the marker board, mobile device and the Kinect camera

Figure 3. Visual feedback elements in ARGO. ARGO showing the next step through an animated AR LEGO brick (left). The next block to be placed is animated using an up and down motion to instruct the user of his next move.

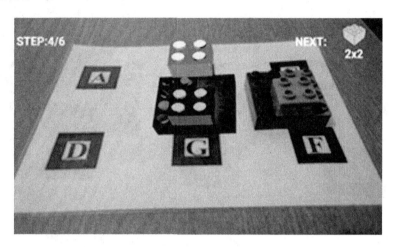

can also go back to a previous step or move forward to the next step by double tapping the corresponding section of the mobile screen as seen in (Figure 3, right).

The server is accessed by the mobile application to obtain data on the current step. The server is implemented using the Django web framework and the database using MySQL. The main purpose of the server's database is to store the list of models that could be built using ARGO. As the user selects a model to assemble on the mobile app, the server receives this and acts as a mediator for the mobile app and the Kinect data processing part of the system.

Mobile Application Interface

The application starts by asking the user to choose from one of the pre-loaded models. The user can swipe left or right to view the selection of LEGO models that can be built (Figure 4). Once the user has chosen a model, he clicks *Build* and is brought to the AR screen.

The application then shows the augmented reality screen superimposing the 3D rendered LEGO model onto the real-world view captured by the camera (Figure 5). The screen shows the current step

Figure 4. The AR mobile application model selection menu

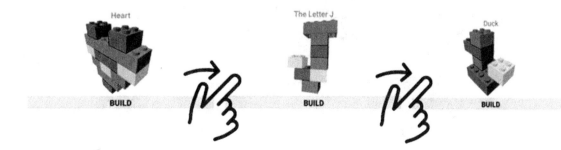

Figure 5. The AR mobile application screen

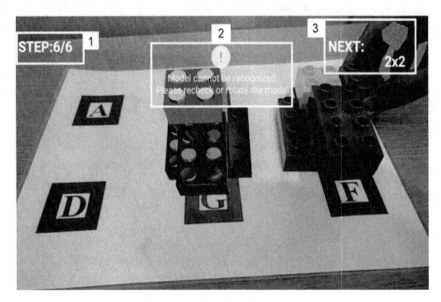

and the number of steps to finish the design on the upper left portion of the screen. The next LEGO block to be placed is shown on the upper right portion of the screen. The middle portion of the screen shows the error messages of the application. The current LEGO block to be placed is animated by an up and down motion.

If the user double taps the left side of the screen, the application shows the previous step/stage of the LEGO assembly. If the double taps the right side of the screen the application shows the next step. A long press of the middle section of the screen toggles the context-based rotation of the model to change the view (Figure 6).

Figure 6. The AR mobile application user interaction using double taps and long press

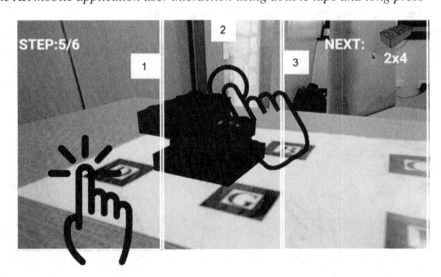

The application automatically detects if the current LEGO assembly step has been completed and automtically moves to the next step. A wrong placement or wrong block will raise an error. Once the system has detected that the user has accomplished the last step of the LEGO Assembly, Figure 7 is shown and then user restart the process and he can choose to try the other models .

Kinect Data Processing

In order to detect the LEGO model constructed by the user in the real world, the Kinect 3D depth data has to be processed and analyzed. The application was implemented in C++ and makes use of the Point Cloud Library, which is a large-scale open project for point cloud processing (Rusu and Cousins, 2011).

Segmentation

The first step is to separate the data points of the LEGO blocks from the points of the desktop and other objects in the environment (e.g. the hands of the user). The depth and RGB data from the Kinect camera are represented as 3D colored point clouds. The table or plane surface of the assembly area is detected using RANSAC. The largest plane in the physical scene's point cloud was assumed to be the plane that is being built upon. The color of the point cloud is then normalized to reduce the effect of lighting changes on the point cloud. The formula used to normalize the RGB color space of a give point f is:

$$f(x, y, z) = (R, G, B)$$
$$total = R + B + G$$

$$R' = \frac{R}{total} x255$$

Figure 7. The AR mobile application final screen when the user finished the construction of the LEGO model

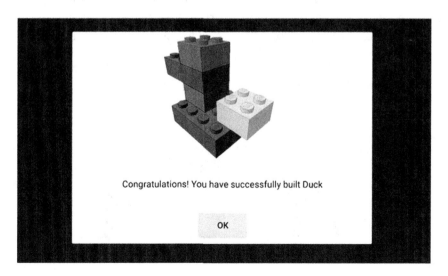

Congratulations! You have successfully built Duck

OK

$$G' = \frac{G}{total} \, x255$$

$$B' = \frac{B}{total} \, x255$$

$$f(x,y,z) = (R', G', B')$$

The points which contain colors of the LEGO bricks (red, green, blue, and yellow only) are isolated by using a color filter on the RGB color space, refer to Figure 8. This leaves only the physical LEGO model, removing points of the hands, table and marker board. After, outliers are removed. These are the points which are farther from the other points based on a distance threshold. This is to account for the presence of some noise in the Kinect camera data, as well as the presence of other colors similar to LEGO bricks, which were detected but not part of the physical model.

Feature Estimation Using Viewpoint Feature Histogram

After segmentation, we need to compare the physical scene to the templates of the point clouds at different steps. The Viewpoint Feature Histogram (VFH) is used as a descriptor for point clouds. Both the geometry and the viewpoint of the point cloud is encoded into this descriptor. The descriptor has been successfully used to differentiate objects with similar shapes, which is the case when considering the consequent steps in LEGO assembly, where configurations only have small differences with each other. VFH uses purely the 3D features of the point cloud and does not take into account the color or 2D features (Junemann 2012; Ruso and Cousins, 2011).

Training

For the physical model's histogram to be compared to the next step, the application must be trained with templates of the point clouds at different steps. ARGO was trained with all the steps in the assembly, each with different poses to account for rotation invariance. A step went through the previous stages, segmentation and feature estimation, and was then saved to a local file for later use. It was then rotated

Figure 8. Output point cloud from the segmentation phase removing the background

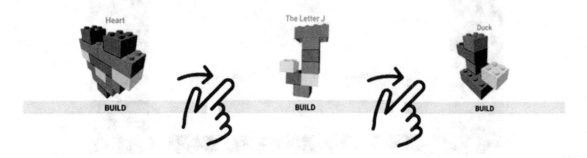

by 20 degrees and then underwent the processing and saved. This was repeated until the physical model was completely rotated. This meant that each step was composed of 18 point clouds, each representing a pose 20 degrees apart.

Feature Matching Using Chi-Square Distance

The application was trained with models and their steps including poses. During runtime, the physical model undergoes the same segmentation and VFH estimation. The physical model's histogram is then matched with the stored histograms of the current step and the next step which were obtained during the training of the system. As each histogram can be measured as a feature vector composed of floating-point values, a distance metric can be calculated. The chi-square distance normalizes each bin of the histograms and is computed by:

$$d_{Chi}(\vec{a}, \vec{b}) = \sqrt{\sum_{i=1}^{m} \frac{(a_i - b_i)^2}{a_i + b_i}}$$

where a and b are vectors composed of floating point values $(a_1, a_2, \ldots a_m)$ and values $(b_1, b_2, \ldots b_m)$ respectively.

Evaluating When to Move to the Next Step

The Kinect camera's data is usually noisy, as such, the results of the chi-square distance computation per frame were inconsistent. Instead of using the results of a single frame, the system takes the moving average for each potential pose and take the one with the least average distance at the end of the number of frames/iterations. From preliminary experiments, 30 iterations/frames were found to be a good balance between accuracy and time. After this, the best candidate would then be checked if it was less than the distance threshold, which was set as 45 from preliminary experiments. The distance threshold is also increased to 60, at lower point cloud sizes. The second-best candidate is also recorded as if the system is about to update the step, and the first and second candidates differ in step, the second best is checked if it was within 5 units of the first, and if it is, the system would not update the step. To lower the number of false positives/negatives, the distance (result of the chi-Square distance) was increased or decreased whether they met the following criteria: point cloud size and perceived number of brick clusters segmented by color.

The size of the point cloud of the candidates of the recognition was compared to the size of the physical model. This is to make it less prone to accept configurations of an earlier step. The perceived number of brick clusters segmented by color was found by using a similar technique as done in the segmentation process, which was segmenting the model to its red, green, blue and yellow components. After which the point cloud data was clustered by distance, leaving several point clouds. Assuming that there are no adjacent colored bricks, this may give an accurate number of the bricks present in the scene. However, this is still reliant on the orientation of the physical model with respect to the Kinect camera and may be prone to errors due to occlusions. The justification for using this feature is the fact that the number of brick clusters between the best candidate in the training data and the physical model must be similar.

RESULTS

The system was evaluated by building 3 models, namely "Duck," "Letter J," and "Heart," composed of 6 bricks, 8 bricks and 12 bricks respectively, seen in Figure 9. The threshold used for the chi-squared distance was empirically obtained and was set to 45. The devices used in testing the system were: a Microsoft Kinect 2.0 (sensor), Google Nexus 6P with a Qualcomm Snapdragon 810 processor and 3GB of RAM (client), and a Dell XPS 15 9560 with a 2.8GHz Intel Core i7-7700HQ processor and 8GB of RAM (server).

Accuracy

The accuracy was evaluated by measuring the difference in the angle as recognized by the system to the actual angle physically. The testing was performed by completing the models 3 times each and measuring the angle difference for each step. The results are shown in Table 1.

After the evaluation using all 3 models, the system could recognize each step and estimate its orientation differing an average angle of 48.27. From the tables above, both the letter J and heart models have

Figure 9. The models that were used to evaluate the system: Duck (left), Letter J (right), Heart (bottom)

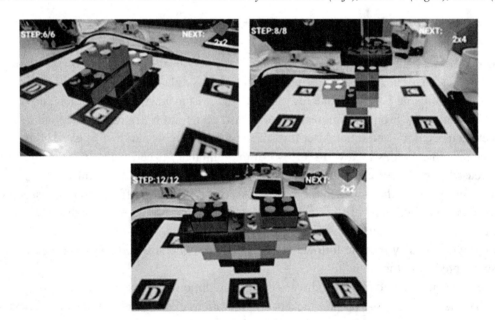

Table 1. Average angle difference of recognized pose to actual pose

Model	Average Angle Difference (degrees)
Duck	38.89
Letter J	53.33
Heart	52.50
Average	48.27

a larger and similar average angle difference compared to the duck model, 53.33 and 52.50 respectively. This is possibly due to how the models are structured, as they are more 2-dimensional as opposed to the duck model. As the system is unable to differentiate bricks misplaced over a small distance, it may have mistaken some steps to be the inverse of themselves. Another difference is that the side view of the letter J and heart is only 1 brick wide, which means that at certain angles, there are less points and therefore less features for the system to use to describe the point cloud, which leads to an inaccurate recognition of the pose.

Latency

Aside from accuracy, the latency of the system was also measured. The speed influenced by the number of iterations/frames it must average data from to arrive at a decision. The number of iterations based on previous experiments was set to 30. The average number of seconds per recognition cycle or per 30 frames for each model is shown in the Table 2. The testing was performed by completing the models 3 times each and measuring how many seconds it took for each cycle. As seen in the table, the latency is shown to be higher for the model with more steps, possibly due to the higher point cloud size. The average number of seconds for all 3 models is 3.96 or almost 4 seconds, which after testing, is still an acceptable amount for assembling a model.

Error Detection

The system could detect incorrect steps or configurations. The study has identified three main classes of errors: wrong brick, wrong orientation and wrong position (Figure 10), which may be identified to be as near (1-2 bricks from supposed location) or far (more than 3 bricks from supposed location). Each step

Table 2. Average number of seconds per cycle per model

Model	Average Seconds per Cycle
Duck	3.66
Letter J	3.70
Heart	4.51
Average	3.96

Figure 10. Errors that can be detected by the system. (a) Correct step, (b) incorrect block, (c) and (d) misplaced block

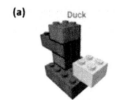   

was then tested for these different classes of error. From these, the application could reject these errors in most cases and prevent them from moving to the next step, except for some wrong position type errors. This can be attributed to the low resolution of the Kinect camera which is unable to determine the small distances from small objects.

Assembly Time

The assembly time of the user through the application is dependent on the number of frames/iterations that are considered by the system before it can decide on the step (Table 3). On the other hand, the latency from the recognition from the desktop application to the phone was found to be bottlenecked by a 2-second delay between fetches from the phone to the server. This delay was issued to deal with conflicts caused by the fetching and sending data of the mobile phone to and from the server.

Since the Full Setup trial was also done to account for human error as well, another factor to consider in Argo's full setup is the time it would take for the user to choose and attach the bricks to their current physical model. There is a noticeable difference in the recognition time when the user relies on the visual feedback solely through the mobile phone.

FUTURE RESEARCH DIRECTIONS

Occlusions are one of the major challenges faced by the system. Occlusions create problematic poses for the physical LEGO model that can lead to false positives and false negatives during step recognition. To solve this, other methods may be explored such as 3D reconstruction of the model before recognition or using concave hulls. Another option would be to take advantage of the image obtained from the mobile phone to aid in the recognition as well, instead of only using the mobile phone for visual feedback. This would help in addressing the problem of occlusions by trying to recognize the current step through reconstructing the model from different viewpoints using 3D registration of features from both the Kinect and mobile phone images.

In today's advancing technology, there are companies that have released smartphones that already have a built-in depth camera, making the development of AR-based apps more feasible in the near future. Given that one of this study's main objectives is to develop a LEGO assembly guidance system through

Table 3. Assembly time to build the LEGO model using the system

Step Number	Server Only (Seconds)	Full Set-up (Seconds)
1	32.96	3.63
2	8.88	11.60
3	18.54	12.58
4	4.39	24.25
5	14.23	48.89
6	5.18	35.18
Total Time	84.18	136.12

an AR-based mobile application, another recommendation would be for future researchers to explore these types of technology and eliminate the need for a separate depth sensor like the Kinect camera. The potential of the system to be a collaborative assembly system with many concurrent users may be also explored, as the current implementation already allows this using the client-server architecture.

CONCLUSION

This paper presented an alternative to paper-based LEGO assembly manuals in the form of an Android mobile application. The application makes use of augmented reality and an AR marker board to visually guide the user by showing a moving brick which is the virtual representation of a LEGO model in each step of the assembly process. To check whether the assembler has correctly followed a step, the server compares data obtained from the Kinect camera and data which was preloaded with the different poses of the steps of the models. This is done by computing a Viewpoint Feature Histogram (VFH) for the physical model and the templates and obtaining their using chi-square distance. The next step is recognized by searching for the template with the nearest average distance for 30 iterations. Using this approach has been shown to yield short assembly time in terms of LEGO construction.

REFERENCES

Bliss, Pobursky, & Howard. (2012). *LDraw.org Standards: File Format 1.0.2*. Available at: www.ldraw.org/

Craig, A. (2013). Chapter 1 - What is augmented reality? In Understanding Augmented Reality. Morgan Kaufmann.

Gupta, A., Fox, D., Curless, B., & Cohen, M. (2012). Duplotrack: a realtime system for authoring and guiding duplo model assembly. In *Proceedings of the 25th Annual ACM Symposium Adjunct on User Interface Software and Technology*. ACM.

Hou, L., Xiangyu, W., Leonhard, B., & Love, P. (2015). *Using animated augmented reality to cognitively guide assembly* (Master's thesis). Curtin University of Technology, Bentley, Australia.

Junemann, M. (2012). *Object detection and recognition with Microsoft Kinect* (B.S. Thesis). Freie Universitat Berlin, Germany.

Khuong, B., Kiyokawa, K., Miller, A., La Viola, J.J., Mashita, T. and Takemura, H. (2014). The effectiveness of an ar-based context-aware assembly support system in object assembly. *Proc. of 2014 IEEE Virtual Reality (VR)*, 57–62.

Pathomaree, N., & Charoenseang, S. (2015). Augmented reality for skill transfer in assembly task. *RO-MAN 2005. IEEE Int'l Workshop on Robot and Human Interactive Communication*, 500–504.

Rusu, R., & Cousins, S. (2011). 3D is here: point cloud library (pcl). *Proceedings of IEEE International Conference on Robotics and Automation (ICRA)*. 10.1109/ICRA.2011.5980567

Rusu, R. B., Bradski, G., Thibaux, R., & Hsu, J. (2010). Fast 3D recognition and pose using the view-point feature histogram. *Proceedings of 2010 IEEE/RSJ International Conference on Intelligent Robots and Systems*, 2155–2162. doi:10.1109/IROS.2010.5651280

Schmalstieg, D., & Wagner, D. (2018). *Mobile Phones as a Platform for Augmented Reality*. Graz University of Technology. Available at: https://data.icg.tugraz.at/~dieter/publications/Schmalstieg_135.pdf

Tang, A., Owen, C., Biocca, F., & Mou, W. (2003). Comparative effectiveness of augmented reality in object assembly. In *Proceedings of the SIGCHI Conference on Human Factors in Computing Systems (CHI '03)*. ACM. 10.1145/642611.642626

Wang, X., Ong, S. K., & Nee, A. Y. C. (2016). Multi-modal augmented-reality assembly guidance based on bare-hand interface. *Advanced Engineering Informatics*, *30*(3), 406–421. doi:10.1016/j.aei.2016.05.004

KEY TERMS AND DEFINITIONS

3D Mesh: A collection of vertices, edges, and faces that represents a 3D object in computer graphics or solid modeling.

Augment Reality: A technology that superimposes a computer-generated images or 3D models to the user's view of the real world.

Depth Camera: A special camera capable of determining the depth information of objects which can be used for 3D reconstruction.

LEGO: A brand of plastic construction toys that are manufactured by a private Danish company, The LEGO Group.

Mobile Devices: A portable computing device like smartphones or tablets.

Point Cloud: A set of data points in 2D or 3D space that are obtained from 3D scanners or depth cameras.

Chapter 11
An ARM Framework for F2P Mobile Games

Marisardo Bezerra de Medeiros Filho
Universidade Federal de Pernambuco, Brazil

Farley Fernandes
ⓘ https://orcid.org/0000-0002-8573-8877
UNIDCOM IADE, Portugal & Universidade da Beira Interior, Portugal

Felipe Matheus Calado
Universidade Católica de Pernambuco, Brazil

André Menezes Marques Neves
Universidade Federal de Pernambuco, Brazil

ABSTRACT

This chapter presents an ARM (acquisition, retention, and monetization) framework for F2P (free-to-play) mobile games to be used as to support game design practice and research. ARM strategies are dispersed throughout various sources such as websites, papers, and books, hampering the work of researchers and practitioners in this field. The aim of this framework is to list and organize these strategies into a single source. A literature research about ARM strategies in F2P mobile games was conducted to identify and select elements. Based on surveys with game development professionals, some of these elements were polished, merged, or removed. Finally, these elements were organized into a single framework, consisting of 3 main categories (acquisition, retention, and monetization), 8 subcategories, and 59 specific elements.

INTRODUCTION

To make profitable Free-to-Play (F2P) games, there are some elements used to promote new players acquisition, retain them playing and drive them to monetize the game. Acquisition - Retention - Monetization (ARM) strategies are an important tool to help game developers to understand elements and relations between such stages, increasing the chances to make more profitable F2P games (Fields and

DOI: 10.4018/978-1-5225-9069-9.ch011

Cotton, 2012; Lovell, 2013; Luton, 2013; Thibault, 2013). However, these ARM strategies are dispersed throughout various sources such as websites, academic works and books. During this research the authors did not find any source that listed or tried to organize, formally, a set of ARM F2P game elements. Such listing can be important for knowledge development about free-to-play mobile game design and help game development professionals and researchers to formally identify possibilities and opportunities related to such games.

The general objective of this work is to organize common ARM F2P game strategies in an unique framework, describing and organizing the content of ARM related elements and strategies. It can be used by to design acquisition, retention and monetization features on F2P games and also be used as a foundation to further academic researches on the subject. The specific objectives of this research are:

- Review the academic and professional literature regarding Acquisition, Retention, Monetization, and ARM Funnel, applied to F2P mobile games, this being the aim of this paper;
- Propose the elements and an architecture to organize an ARM framework for F2P mobile games;
- Evaluate the proposed ARM framework with F2P mobile games experienced professionals;
- Based on the evaluation conducted, make the adjustments needed for the final version of the framework.

This paper is organized with the following structure: The next chapter covers the main aspects about ARM in F2P mobile games; the third chapter lists and presents the main elements regarding user acquisition, retention and monetization; the fourth chapter presents the development and version 1.0 of the framework; and the fifth chapter presents the conclusions and discussions of this work.

ARM IN F2P MOBILE GAMES

The term ARM refers to an analytic framework, often used to describe a business model, in mobile game industry. As an acronym, it means Acquisition, Retention, and Monetization. It could be useful as an aid to understand the business models used by F2P mobile games, and also as a guide for developers when applying the concepts at their own games. Acquisition strategies are used to attract new users to the game; Retention strategies aims to keep them playing and lastly, Monetization strategies are used to make users generate revenue for the game (Kuusisto, 2014; Tao, 2014). However, games that are not F2P use a different framework, named B2P (buy-to-play), where its users first buy the game (Monetization), then discover the gameplay (Acquisition), and finally can repeat the experience (Retention) (Davidovici-Nora, 2014). In this context, the retention is at the end of the process and does not have a direct connection with monetization. On the other hand, F2P games business model architecture is way more complex and can generate multiple interactions among stages and not only a one-to-one relationship.

In F2P games, the monetization stage is pushed to the end of the process as payment is optional to a certain extent. Games with F2P business model put emphasis on experience before monetizing it, in order to accumulate a huge user base and make them engaged. Considering that the price to acquire a F2P game is zero, acquisition stage seems to be an easy and automatic stage in such model when compared with B2P ones (Davidovici-Nora, 2014). Figure 1 shows the ARM funnel initially proposed by Kontagent (2011).

Figure 1. Illustration of ARM funnel for video games (THIBAULT, 2013, p.21)

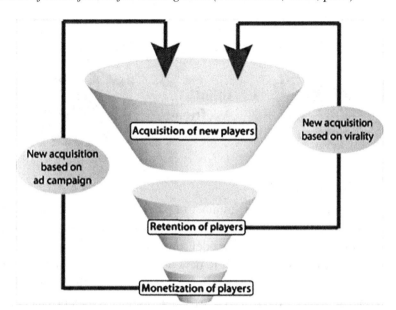

These three stages are strictly linear and act more like a recurring cycle within the overall framework, it can be explained as (Fields & Cotton, 2012): First, the game acquires a large player base (acquisition); Then it should retain some of these players (retention), keeping enough of them coming back so that they will like the game enough to invest their money into it (monetization); Some of the retained players will spread the word about the game and make it viral. They will raise the brand awareness of the game and attract new players (acquisition); Game's profits from monetization can be invested into acquiring more users (advertising campaign). The cycle repeats.

Katkoff (2012a) explained an example that helps understanding how these stages are connected, as can be seen on figure 2. In his example, the player starts building a house, but in order to finish it, he needs some specific items. At this point, the player knows that getting these items require several play sessions and a lot of grinding (retention). The player can skip grinding simply by asking friends to gift these items (something that generates new players acquisition), or, as a third option, just paying to proceed (monetization).

The next chapter of this paper will explain separately every element of the ARM framework applied to F2P mobile games, considering the specific aspects of each one and relations among them.

ARM STRATEGIES

This chapter presents elements used to acquiring, retaining and monetizing through players in F2P games.

Acquisition

In F2P games, player acquisition is the first one to take place, since it is not necessary to buy the game to have it. F2P games have to convince users to spend money after they have already made the acquisition

Figure 2. Most common virality formula (KATKOFF, 2012a)

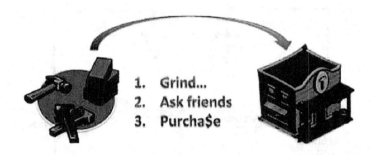

decision. Then, it is usually necessary a large number of players in order to make this model profitable (Alha, Koskinen, Paavilainen, Hamari, & Kinnunen, 2014; Davidovici-Nora, 2014; Nguyen, 2014).

Askelöf (2013) explains that, in the ARM model, user acquisition sources are classified as being either viral or non-viral. Viral user sources refer to new players which have been generated by existing users. Whereas non-viral sources are those that are not generated by existing users, such as: advertising, cross-promotion and offer walls. Based on this research, it was selected a proposal of elements, indicated by professionals and academic researchers as directly related with acquisition in F2P games. Based on Askelöf (2013) explanation, acquisition was divided in two main subcategories: Viral and Non-Viral. The selected categories and subcategories are not excluding among themselves, then an element could also represent, sometimes, more than one of these categories. The selected subcategories are organized below:

Viral Strategies

The Viral strategies are:

- Invitation Mechanics: There are a lot of mechanics to encourage users to invite their friends to try the game, where the player will usually be rewarded with some gifts for every invited person that installs the game (sometimes it is not necessary to install it). This is a way to reward users for sharing the game with some form of free content. This technique is often used by game designers as an incentive for users to invite their friends, increasing the virality. Also, there are some mechanics that encourage players to ask for help to quickly reach some objective, which could attract new players and help their retention as well. Some common examples of invitation rewards are: Boosts, power-ups and gacha tickets (Askelöf, 2013; Katkoff, 2012a; Morel, 2012; Paavilainen, Alha, & Korhonen, 2017);
- Timeline Social Features Sharing: Social features like leaderboards and achievements that players can share on their timeline. It can also increase user base retention and growth (Askelöf, 2013; Maiberg, 2013; Paavilainen, Alha, & Korhonen, 2017);
- Word of Mouth: Natural invitations by players without using actions on the game. If a game is engaging and brings a good experience, it should make more players tell their friends about it (Askelöf, 2013; Kuusisto, 2014; Narinen, 2014; Williams, 2012);
- Chart Position in Market Places: Better chart position in marketplaces will provide more visibility, then it would help a game to gain more installs (Kuusisto, 2014);

Non-Viral Strategies

The Non-viral strategies are:

- Natural Organic Installs: The authors have decided to use this term to represent organic installs that do not take influence by consume of previous players or cross-promotions, like the pure store exposure - without considering charts - or trending news when an updated version of a game is in the store (Kaniel, 2012). Some authors present all organic installs as viral (Khalil, 2016; Williams, 2012), but in the definition used in this research viral is always about players bringing more players;
- Cross-promotions (within other games or Apps): Some companies provide the ability to cross-promote a game with others in their network, allowing reach large audiences at a relatively inexpensive cost basis by mutually advertising. Another example of cross-promotion is to redirect players between other games of the same company. This way, all of the company´s games can get a better chance of exposure (Askelöf, 2013; Luton, 2013; Morel, 2012; Williams, 2012);
- Offer Walls: Through Offer Walls, players can earn in-game currency by performing certain tasks. Examples of such tasks are installing an app or game. However, since the player is often only interested in getting the reward and not in using the offer they signed up for, players obtained through this method tend to quickly abandon. Offer Walls are a common method for monetizing users, but can also be used for player acquisition, by giving offers to players of competitor games (Askelöf, 2013; Morel, 2012);
- Off Game/App Advertising: The authors are considering, in this element, advertising that not occurs through other games or apps. This includes advertisements on websites or on social networks, banners on online stores, or e-mail campaigns (Askelöf, 2013; Kaniel, 2012; Khalil, 2016; Morel, 2012; Nguyen, 2014);

Retention

The second level of the ARM funnel is known as retention. For Thibault (2013), this category is about how to keep players involved into the game and what should be done to retain them on a mid and long-term basis. Retention is a measure of how many players keep playing the game after their initial play session. Since resources have been spent to acquire players, it is important to make them engaged. Then, it is directly linked to player engagement (Narinen, 2014). In a similar way, Luton (2013) explains, as related to retention, that the number of players who are retained over a given time period in a game, indicating how sticky the game is, or how effective it is at keeping players playing.

Askelöf (2013) presents three categories of game mechanics and dynamics used to make a player engage in Social Network Games (SNGs):

- Progress Systems: It is about the common mechanics used in SNGs to manage progress, and how this progress is communicated to the player;
- Social Aspects: These are mechanics that support social interactions;
- Time-Based Limitations: A set of techniques used in SNG to control the length of game sessions.

Then, a set of elements was selected, indicated by professionals and academic researchers, as directly related to retention in F2P games. The elements were divided into three subcategories, as the division proposed by Askelöf (2013) for SNGs. The authors have decided to use the following subcategories since they are self-explanatory and fit better with the selected elements. The name of the subcategory Time-Based Limitations was also changed to Space and Time-Based Limitations, to bear the Location Triggers element. The selected categories and subcategories are not mutually excluding, then an element can represent, sometimes, more than one of these subcategories.

Progress Systems Strategies

The Progress System strategies are:

- Achievements: Often referred to as badges, achievements provide the feeling to reach something, rewarding players who fulfill some required conditions (Askelöf, 2013; Katkoff, 2012b; Lovell, 2013; Maiberg, 2013; Thibault, 2013);
- Points: Players can collect them to reach some task, challenge, better competition position, in-game richness, or more. The following divisions were found in the literature: experience points; redeemable points (or game coins); skill points; karma points; reputation points; progress points (or levelling up) (Askelöf, 2013; Kuusisto, 2014; Lovell, 2013);
- Leaderboards: A leaderboard, sometimes called scoreboard, is a competitive return trigger and its purpose is to make comparisons among players (Askelöf, 2013; Lovell, 2013; Luton, 2013; Nguyen, 2014). In the framework, this element is part of progress system subcategory, as well as social aspects subcategory, because it is about how the player is progressing in relation to others;
- Levels: It is an indication of how far has the player progressed in a game. It is not just about challenge progression, but also about new places and challenges to explore (Askelöf, 2013; Davidovici-Nora, 2014; Luton, 2013; Narinen, 2014);
- Tutorial: Sometimes called onboarding, it is the act of guiding players during specific moments of the game when they need to do something new (Askelöf, 2013; Luton, 2013; Narinen, 2014);
- Objective: An objective is a task, mission, quest or challenge that the player can reach in the game. By giving the player an objective, depth and meaning can be added to the game, creating variety to gameplay and adding constant rewards (Askelöf, 2013; Kuusisto, 2014; Salen and Zimmerman, 2004).

Social Aspects Strategies

The Social Aspects strategies are:

- Leaderboards: Leaderboards are an important social element to keep players competing against each other, while exposing their individual ranking position. Leaderboards can also help monetization when players willing to overcome others pay to do that easier and faster (Askelöf, 2013; Lovell, 2013; Luton, 2013; Nguyen, 2014). As explained before, this element is also part of progress system subcategory and social aspects subcategory as well;

- Achievements sharing: It is a social aspect tool that allows competitive and exposure interactions (Askelöf, 2013; Katkoff, 2012b; Maiberg, 2013; Thibault, 2013);
- Socializing: Also known as goal change, this element refers to a player's willing to play with other friends or teammates, making their goal socialized (Fukada, 2011, apud Askelöf, 2013; Nguyen, 2014);
- Help request: Using invitation mechanics to complete some task or goal in a game, the player can ask for help from their friends. This system encourages players to bring new players in (acquisition) and existing players come back to the game. (Askelöf, 2013; Katkoff, 2012a; Luton, 2013; Morel, 2012; Paavilainen, Alha, & Korhonen, 2017);
- Gifting: That is the possibility to spontaneously give gifts to other players, who are notified and encouraged to join (acquisition) or to come back to the game to return the favor. Reciprocity strengthens the social ties between the players, reminding them to keep playing (Luton, 2013; Paavilainen, Alha, & Korhonen, 2017; Radoff, 2011);
- Challenges: players can invite others to compete with them (Luton, 2013);
- Competition sense: It is about any other kind of situation players competing against the machine, against oneself and against others (Radoff, 2011; Salen and Zimmerman, 2004);
- Cooperation sense: It is about any other kind of situation players interact with each other in a noncompetitive way. Like social commitment, based on the sense that makes players return to complete some waiting action for another player, or helping their guild with some of their specific abilities. The willing to cooperate is the basis of this element (Luton, 2013; Radoff, 2011; Salen And Zimmerman, 2004).

Space and Time-Based Limitations Strategies

The Space and Time-Based Limitations strategies are:

- Energy System: These are common techniques used to limit the length of players' sessions. Each action the players performs consumes energy and, as their energy drains to zero, they need to wait until their energy bar is restored before it is possible to continue (Askelöf, 2013; Katkoff, 2012b; Luton, 2013);
- Time to Complete: Also known as construction time, it is about the time taken to build some object, learn a new ability or complete any other waiting bar that allows new resources in the game, forcing the player to wait or spend money to avoid it (Askelöf, 2013; Narinen, 2014; Luton, 2013);
- Cooldown: It is a time limit on how often certain actions can be used in game. (Askelöf, 2013);
- Reward for Replaying: Also known as incentivize appointment, or reward retention, reward for playing are mechanisms that reward player for returning to the game (Askelöf, 2013; Luton, 2013; Narinen, 2014; Nguyen, 2014);
- Punishment for Absence: It is, in some way, opposite of the reward for replay element. The player receives some penalty for not returning to the game for some specific period of time (Askelöf, 2013);
- Limited-Time Events: Also known as limited time campaigns, these are seasonal events that offer something special for a short period (Askelöf, 2013; Luton, 2013);

- Come Back Message: Also known as nudge triggers, that is appointed as one of the weakest return triggers. These are messages that remember the players about the game when they have not played the game for some time (Luton, 2013; Nguyen, 2014);
- Location Triggers: It is about when the game provides rewards for players playing in some specific places (Luton, 2013).

Monetization

Narinen (2014) explains that, in F2P games, monetization is the act of selling optional services and virtual resources to players within the game. The player can buy these resources with real money, which usually include things like cosmetic changes, virtual items and virtual currencies. Morel (2012) argue it is necessary be prepared to invest money to acquire users, since 2-6% of F2P players pay for something. Regarding free social mobile games, Nguyen (2014) says that two of the most notable ways to monetize them are selling advertisement and virtual items. F2P model lets players play the game without paying up-front, but incentives are constantly given to the user to invest some money in order to further improve their gaming experience. By spending money in the game, a player can boost its abilities, advance quicker and overcome time limitations. About this issue, selling virtual items is consider the main method for monetization in F2P games. Then, instead of requiring players to pay in order to keep playing a game, a F2P one prefers to rely on specific game mechanics to incentivize players to naturally spend money in it (Askelöf, 2013). Appel, Libai, Muller, & Shachar (2017), explain that such products rely on revenues from two sources: paying consumers, and paying advertisers. For Luton (2013) the ways to monetize F2P games are:

- In-app Purchases (IAP): Also known as microtransactions, they are purchases made by a player to acquire virtual goods or virtual currencies, items or usable resources in a game;
- Advertising: Ads provided by third-party suppliers that pay publishers on the number of impressions made in-game (interactions or exhibitions);
- Product placement: It is the practice to insert a real product in a game and reinforce the product estimate among its players by their association. It can be also considered a subtler way of advertising;
- Merchandise: The act of selling of physical goods associated with the game;
- Store Cards: These are physical cards with a code that can be redeemed for credits to be spent in the game. This item can be seen as an alternative to IAPs.

Based on this research, a set of elements was selected, indicated by professionals and academic researchers, as directly related to monetization in F2P games. They were also divided into three subcategories, following the division proposed by Luton (2013), with some adaptations. Store cards were inserted into IPA subcategory since it is another way to monetize by in-app purchases. Furthermore, product placement was inserted into advertising subcategory, because it is just a subtler way of advertising. The selected categories and subcategories are not mutually excluding, then an element can represent, sometimes, more than one of these categories. The subcategories are following bellow.

In-App Purchase Strategies

The In-App Purchase Strategies are:

- Virtual Currencies: These are virtual money that allow players buy things in the game. There are basically two types of them: hard currency and soft currency. Hard currency is rewarded on a finite number of or low frequency of actions and it is commonly purchased, whereas a soft currency is infinitely rewarded through a core loop and commonly earned in large quantities. Hard currencies usually are more used for premium functions (Askelöf, 2013; Kuusisto, 2014; Luton, 2013);
- Content: It consists of more content to explore within the game, such as: maps, levels, new abilities, characters or similar that give players more things to do (Luton, 2013; Radoff, 2011);
- Play Accelerators: Also known as convenience, it consists of the purchase of anything that allows players skips ahead, providing them with something that would usually need time and dedication to reach it (Luton, 2013; Radoff, 2011);
- Competitive Advantage: Stands as anything that provides players with any competitive advantage against the game or other players (Luton, 2013; Radoff, 2011);
- Customization: It is how the game lets players customize their avatar or the game's world, making changes just for vanity or expressive reasons, or changes that could also make difference in gameplay (Askelöf, 2013; Davidovici-Nora, 2014; Kuusisto, 2014; Luton, 2013; Nguyen, 2014; Radoff, 2011);
- Collectibles: These items belong to a set of items that exists only to be collected (Radoff, 2011);
- Gifts: They can help player-to-player interaction, but sometimes also can be acquired by hard currency (Luton, 2013; Paavilainen, Alha, & Korhonen., 2017; Radoff, 2011);
- Store Cards: Physical cards with codes that can be redeemed for credits to be spent in the game.

Advertising Strategies

The Advertising strategies are:

- Banner Ads: It is a thin strip that usually is shown at a top or bottom of the screen (Luton, 2013);
- Interstitial Ads: These are ads that appear between the transitions of two screens and usually are presented full screen. They monetize better than banner ads (Luton, 2013);
- Video Ads: Video ads are one of the most effective ads, but often the most intrusive (Luton, 2013);
- Offer Walls: As a monetize method, offer walls make money through actions that players need to do, as installing another game or signing up for a service. This method is a common way for monetizing users, rewarding players with some limited in-game resources and publishers with monetization (Askelöf, 2013; Luton, 2013; Morel, 2012);
- Affiliate Linking: It is a link to a store, which tracks the player and pays out a percentage of any sales made. For example, the ad takes the players from the game to a store, and if they make some purchase in that store, it monetizes for the publisher (Luton, 2013);
- Product Placement: As explained, it is the use of real products within the game as a way to advertise;
- Merchandise: As explained, it is the act to sell physical goods associated with the game.

THE ARM FRAMEWORK FOR F2P MOBILE GAMES

This chapter presents the development, and the final version, of the ARM Framework for F2P Mobile Games.

The ARM Framework Development

This section explains what approaches were used to define an ARM Framework for F2P Mobile Games, as well any other aspects related to the methodology used to collect the needed data. The development of the *1.0 version* of this framework was made in three main stages. The first was focused on creating a baseline framework.

First Stage: Creating the Baseline Framework

To identify the elements of the baseline framework, an extensive literature review was done, covering authors from the game market and academia, as can be reviewed in chapter 3. A series of elements covered by multiple authors were identified, as well others covered by just one author. The baseline framework elements was selected based on three criteria: What was presented by authors; What is not redundant; What is understood as something that aids the ARM process in F2P Mobile Games.

The subcategories were selected based on what was proposed by the authors and what properly fits all elements founded and selected. Some minor adaptations had to be made to make the framework more intuitive and not redundant, as explained in chapter 3.

Then, forty-five elements and eight subcategories were found and then organized in a cycle graph, to represent the whole first version of the framework, the baseline framework, as presented in figure 3.

Second Stage: Creating a Polished Version

The second step was focused on creating a polished version of the previous one, and on adding new elements, considering feedback from game development professionals. A questionnaire was prepared in order to verify if users could properly identify the meaning of the categories of the ARM framework proposed, just by the label. This was done to minimize the chances of misunderstanding when future interviewees read the next survey, even considering that the label's description will be shown to interviewees on the next survey. In addition, this questionnaire has the goal of evolving the proposed framework, identifying possible problems and opportunities to change.

The survey was conducted through Google Forms, and it was divided into six sections. The first section is called the introduction, where the aim of the study is explained, a necessary basic explanation about ARM and some guidance on the questions; section two is a simple professional profile questionnaire, asking interviewees about subjects such as area of expertise, years of experience, and experience on F2P mobile games; section three presents the baseline ARM framework for F2P mobile games proposed, explaining textually and graphically, how the main categories, subcategories, and elements, are organized; then, sections four, five and six, present the main categories and subcategories with their descriptions, and asks interviewees, based only on their knowledge and perception, to write a short description about how they understand each one of the related elements presented.

Figure 3. Baseline ARM framework for F2P mobile games (the authors)

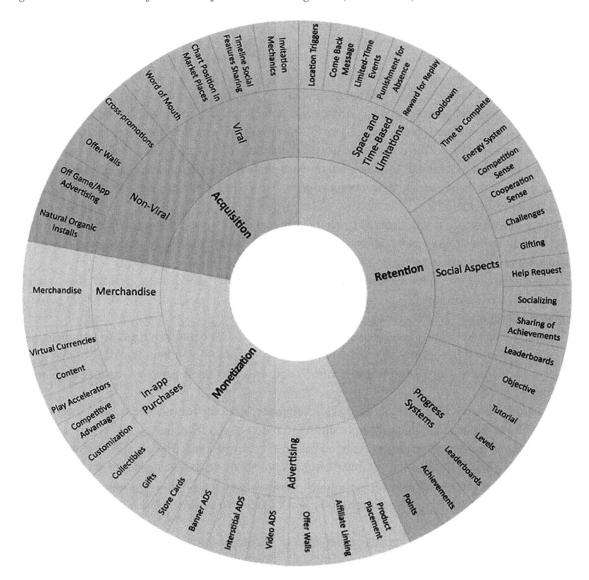

Five game market professionals, with experience in Production, Game Design, Project Management, Game Programming, Game & Data Analysis, Business Development & Marketing, areas, have been part of this survey. All of them have, at least, some experience with game design or production areas, as well as some experience working on mobile F2P games. They work in companies from Germany, Finland, Canada, New Zealand and Sweden.

In this interview the authors presented the framework and explained the meaning of the categories (Acquisition, Retention, and Monetization), and their subcategories as well. The authors did not explain the meaning of the elements inside the subcategories. Then, the interviewees were asked what they understood about each of the elements proposed, considering their categories and subcategories involved. Through this questionnaire, some issues were identified and some adjustments had to be made. The list below presents the analysis and justification for the adjustments:

- Off Game/App Advertising: Although all the interviewees could understand the label, based on an observation made by one interviewee, the authors replaced the term for a more usual one, "Non-Game Media Advertising";
- Objective: The label was changed to "Goals", because it was a more usual term for the interviewees;
- Help Request: This label was changed to "Help Request Mechanics", adding mechanics at the end of the sentence, to make clear that the term refers to some action provided by the game system;
- Gifting: This label was changed to "Gifting Mechanics", adding mechanics at the end of the sentence, to make it clear that the term refers to some action provided by the game system;
- Challenges: Based on three misunderstood labels, the authors perceived that the interviewees understand that as a kind of specific goal or extra challenge, and not a challenge mechanic where the player can invite someone to compete with. To fix this problem, the label was changed to "Challenge Invitation";
- Competition Sense: It was decided to change this label to "Competitive Environment" to make clear that the term does not refer to a specific mechanic, but the whole game environment that involves competitive aspects;
- Cooperative Sense: Like Competitive Sense, the authors decided to change this label to "Cooperative Environment", because it is not about a specific mechanic, but the whole game environment that involves cooperative aspects;
- Time to Complete: Three interviewees understood this as a countdown timer to complete some game challenge. Because of this reductionist interpretation, the authors decided to change this label to "Time to Complete (Waiting Time)" and create a brand new one, called "Countdown Timer";
- Reward for Replay: The authors decided to change this label to "Reward for Return", because two interviewees understood that as the possibility to redo a game challenge;
- Come Back Message: The authors changed this label to "Come Back Message (Push Notification)", just adding "Push Notification" to make clear it's not about a message inside the game;
- Content: The authors perceived it could be confused with any kind of content in the game. Because of that, the label was changed to "Extra Content" to make it more aligned with the original intention;
- Customization: The authors changed this label to "Customization (To Set Up)", because two interviewees understood that the term referred only to cosmetic customizations;
- Collectibles: The authors changed this label to "Collectible Collection", to make clear that the term is not about any kind of item that can be collected;
- Gifts: To make it clearer that ther label refers to a gift the player needs to buy, the authors changed this label to "Purchase Gifts".

The authors also decided to add a new element named "Countdown Timer", which is a time constraint for the player to complete a specific challenge. The element was added because three out of five interviewees identified it, and it is not covered by any other element. This element should be part of the Space and Time-Based Limitations subcategory, inside Retention category. Based on all previous information, the new framework version is represented on figure 4.

Figure 4. Second Version of The ARM Framework for F2P Mobile Games (The Authors)

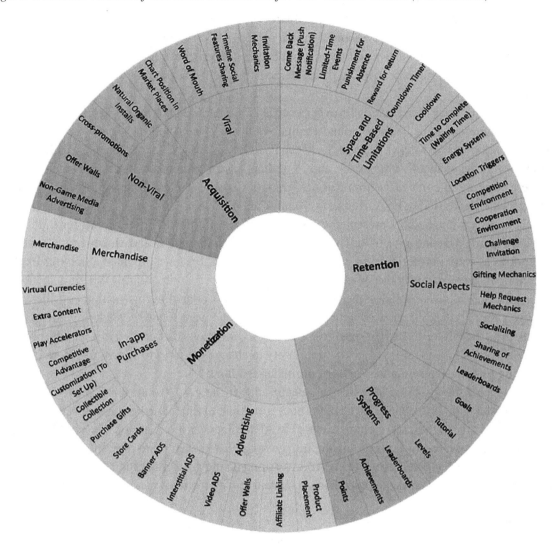

Third Stage: Developing the 1.0 Version

After the second step, the authors prepared a questionnaire of evaluation in order to identify how game market professionals rated the proposed framework, and what they thought should be changed. That was done to maximize the chances the framework will be useful to game market professionals, creating a sense of understanding about the elements, its organization, and possibilities related to ARM. In addition, this questionnaire has the goal of helping evolve the proposed framework, identifying possible problems and opportunities to improve it.

The survey was conducted through Google Forms, and it was divided into three sections. Like the first survey, the first section is called introduction, where the aim of this study is detailed, a necessary basic explanation about ARM, and how to approach and answer the questions is explained; also similar to the first survey, section two is a simple professional profile questionnaire, asking interviewees about subjects related to their professional, mobile, and F2P, experience.

Then, section three presents the Second Version of The ARM Framework for F2P Mobile Games, explaining textually and graphically, how the main categories, subcategories, and elements, are organized, and providing a link with the description of all elements of the framework, as well as their categories and subcategories.

Thirty game market professionals, with experience in Production, Game Design, Project Management, Game Programming, Game Testing, Sound Design, Game & Data Analysis, Academic & Research, Business Development & Marketing areas, have been part of this survey. All of them have, at least, some experience working on mobile F2P games, and 39 of them have experience working as a game designer. They were working in companies from Russia, Finland, Canada, United Kingdom, Brazil, Germany, Australia, Netherlands, India, USA, Romania, Ukraine and Pakistan.

In this interview, the authors presented the second version of the ARM framework for F2P mobile games and explained the meaning of the categories (Acquisition, Retention, and Monetization), and their subcategories as well. Furthermore, as explained before, the authors have provided a link that explains the meaning of the elements in the subcategories.

The authors are also considering the whole group of results related to this section considering the following criteria: At least 2 answers indicating the same issue were found, considering any match of questions; Any kind of feedback that seems to provide good solutions that properly fit into the proposed framework; The authors identified a good opportunity to change the label to something more intuitive, based on suggestions, interpretations or even misunderstandings.

On the second survey, some interviewees identified that there was room for improvement on the framework if the authors keep making changes on it from time to time. Furthermore, it was possible to identify, that new techniques and elements related to ARM practices are continuously being developed, which could make the practice of keeping the framework updated even more relevant.

Therefore, considering the second framework version and the answers of the Likert and open questions of the second survey, these are the changes made to create the third version of the framework:

- Increasing New Elements
  - VIP Subscription / Season Pass: This is an In-App Purchase element, where players pay for exclusive content and advantages. Players that pay for it have temporary access to exclusive content;
  - Up-Sells: This is an In-App Purchase element, that is about the way the game offers better options for buying goods, where the cost savings is proportionally inferior to the quantity purchased. For example, when the game offers a package of 1K gold for 1 dollar and, at the same time, offers 5K gold for 3 dollars;
  - Discounts: It is an In-App Purchase element, where the game offers, for a limited time, an in-game product (or products) cheaper than the normal price;
  - Targeted-Offers: This element is part of the In-App Purchases subcategory. That is an approach where the game offers specific promotions to the players, according to their gameplay style or activity;
  - Gacha: This is another In-App Purchases element. Gacha is a system where players acquire a kind of package, without knowing what comes inside until they open it;

- ○ Annuities: That is an In-App Purchases, as well as a Space and Time-Based Limitations, element. In this technique, the players pay for rewards but need to keep returning at a specific frequency to get them because they are distributed over some period of time. Generally, the game administrator offers better deals when using this technique. It also increases the retention since the players need to keep returning to get the full value for what they have bought;
- ○ Clans: That is a Social Aspects element. Also called guilds, this is an in-game structure that allows players to create or be part of a group that allows them to communicate between themselves, share resources, help each other, chase common goals, or to do other special interactions;
- ○ Visiting Other Players: That is another Social Aspects element. This element is about how the game allows players visit other players' home, and then check how well other players are in the game;
- ○ Community Management: That is a Social Aspects, as well a Viral, element. It is about how the game company deals with the external and internal community of players, through executing events and contests, expanding and maintaining the online community, supporting the community on social media platforms, and more related issues;
- ○ Time Gated Rewards: That is a Space and Time-Based Limitations element. Using this technique, the game limits the amount of rewards the player can acquire in some amount of time. Doing this, the player needs to keep returning to try to acquire new rewards, unlocked over time;
- ○ IP Based: This is a Non-Viral element. It means the game uses established intellectual property (like cartoon or comic book characters), in order to acquire new players. The authors have classified this element as a Non-Viral because it is not something that comes from players, to acquire new players, but something that makes the game more attractive by itself;
- • To be Excluded
  - ○ Socializing, from the Social Aspects subcategory was excluded, because its interpretation could be ambiguous. Also, in some ways, its meaning is covered by the combination of the new Clans element, and other ones, such as Cooperation Environment and Competition Environment;
- • Other Changes
  - ○ The element Collectible Collection, from In-App Purchases subcategory, was added to Progress Systems subcategory, since it was perceived that it could be understood by the player as a long-term goal;
- • Keep Developing
  - ○ Based on some feedback and this work itself, the authors have decided to keep making continuous changes, additions and adaptations to this framework, with the help of the game development community, in the upcoming works;

It is important to note that there were some suggestions proposing elements that are already covered, in some way. Also, there were some suggestions that just do not fit on a framework to design ARM elements on F2P mobile games.

Version 1.0 of The ARM Framework for F2P Mobile Games

Based on all previous feedbacks, the established criteria, and analysis, the new framework version is represented in figure 5, presenting fifty-nine elements. In addition, even though this is the final version of this framework, the authors will keep developing it, based on the feedback of game market professionals, the related literature, and the new trends of the F2P mobile game market.

A brief description, subcategory and category of each element of the third version (version 1.0) framework follows in table 1.

Figure 5. Version 1.0 of the ARM framework for F2P mobile games (the authors)

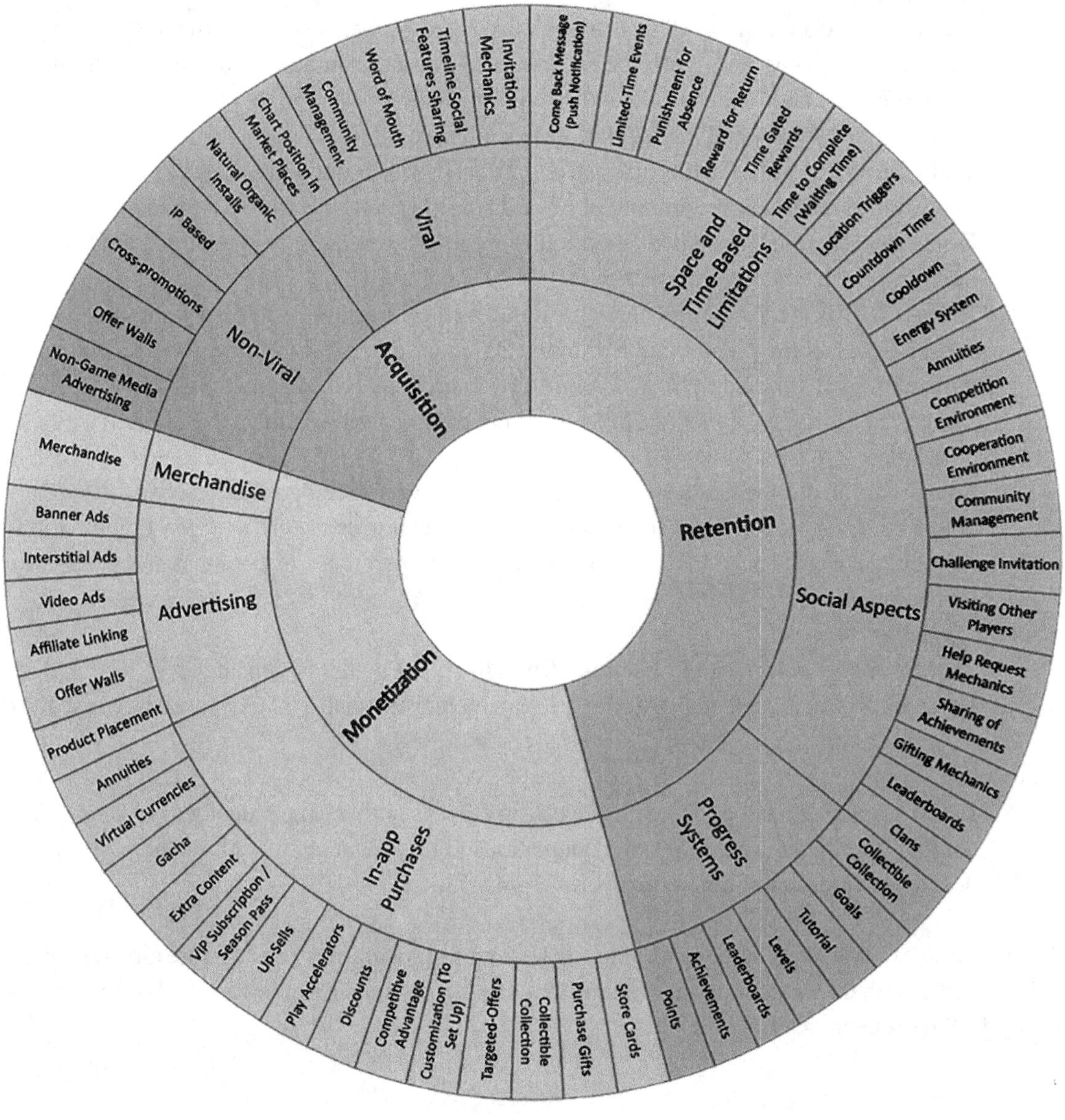

Table 1. Categories, subcategories, elements and descriptions

Category	Subcategory	Element	Description
Retention	Progress Systems	Points	They can be: experience points; redeemable points (or game coins); skill points; karma points; reputation points; progress points (or leveling up)
Retention	Progress Systems	Achievements	Provide the feeling of reaching something, rewarding to players who fulfill the required conditions
Retention	Progress Systems	Collectible Collection	These items belong to a set of items and exist only to be collected.
Retention	Progress Systems	Leaderboards	It is a competitive return trigger, focused on making comparisons between players
Retention	Progress Systems	Levels	It's an indication of how far the player has progressed in the game
Retention	Progress Systems	Tutorial	It is the practice of guiding and teaching players in some moments of the game when they need to do something new
Retention	Progress Systems	Goals	A goal is a task, mission, quest or challenge for the player to clear in the game
Retention	Social Aspects	Leaderboards	Leaderboards are an important social element to keep players competing against each other, while exposing their ranking position
Retention	Social Aspects	Sharing of Achievements	It is a game mechanic that allows players to share what they have achieved
Retention	Social Aspects	Clans	Also called guilds, this is an in-game structure that allows players to create or be part of a group that grants them the ability to perform special interactions between each other
Retention	Social Aspects	Help Request Mechanics	It is a game mechanic where the player can ask for help from their friends
Retention	Social Aspects	Gifting Mechanics	That is the possibility to spontaneously give gifts to other players
Retention	Social Aspects	Visiting Other Players	This element is about how the game allows players to visit other players' homes, and then check how well other players are doing in the game
Retention	Social Aspects	Challenge Invitation	Players can invite others to a challenge
Retention	Social Aspects	Community Management	It is the way the game company deals with the external and internal community of players
Retention	Social Aspects	Cooperation Environment	It's about any other kind of situation players interact with each other to help
Retention	Social Aspects	Competition Environment	It's about any other kind of situation players competing against the machine, against oneself and against others
Retention	Space and Time-Based Limitations	Annuities	In this technique, the player pays for rewards but needs to keep returning at a specific frequency to get them
Retention	Space and Time-Based Limitations	Energy System	This is a system where actions consume energy, and if the players' energy drains to zero, they need to wait until their energy bar is restored to continue
Retention	Space and Time-Based Limitations	Time to Complete (Waiting Time)	That is the time taken to build some object, learn a new ability, or complete any other waiting bar
Retention	Space and Time-Based Limitations	Time Gated Rewards	Using this technique, the game limits the amount of rewards the player can acquire in some amount of time
Retention	Space and Time-Based Limitations	Cooldown	It's a time limit on how often certain actions can be used in game

continued on following page

Table 1. Continued

Category	Subcategory	Element	Description
Retention	Space and Time-Based Limitations	Countdown Timer	That is a time constraint for the player to complete a specific challenge.
Retention	Space and Time-Based Limitations	Reward for Return	These are mechanisms that reward the player for returning to the game
Retention	Space and Time-Based Limitations	Punishment for Absence	The player receives some penalty for not returning for some specific period of time
Retention	Space and Time-Based Limitations	Limited-Time Events	Seasonal events that offer something special for a short period only, like an exclusive quest
Retention	Space and Time-Based Limitations	Come Back Message (Push Notification)	Messages that remind the players about the game when they haven't played the game for some time
Retention	Space and Time-Based Limitations	Location Triggers	Advantages for players playing in some specific places
Acquisition	Viral	Invitation Mechanics	Mechanics to incentivize users to invite their friends to try the game
Acquisition	Viral	Timeline Social Features Sharing	Social features like leaderboards and achievements players can share on their timeline
Acquisition	Viral	Word of Mouth	Things like natural invitations by the players without using actions on the game
Acquisition	Viral	Community Management	It is the way the game company deals with the external and internal community of players
Acquisition	Viral	Chart Position in Market Places	Better chart position in market places will provide more visibility
Acquisition	Non-Viral	Natural Organic Installs	Organic installs that are not influenced by the consumption by previous players or cross-promotions, like the pure store exposure
Acquisition	Non-Viral	IP Based	The game uses established intellectual property, in order to acquire new players.
Acquisition	Non-Viral	Cross-promotions	The ability to cross-promote a game with others
Acquisition	Non-Viral	Offer Walls	Through Offer Walls, the players can earn in-game currency by performing certain tasks
Acquisition	Non-Viral	Non-Game Media Advertising	Advertising that does not occur through other games or apps
Monetization	In-app Purchases	Annuities	In this technique, the player pays for rewards but needs to keep returning at a specific frequency to get them
Monetization	In-app Purchases	Virtual Currencies	Virtual money that allow players buy things in the game
Monetization	In-app Purchases	Extra Content	More content to explore the game, as maps, levels, new abilities, characters, or similar
Monetization	In-app Purchases	VIP Subscription / Season Pass	Players that pay for it, have a kind of temporary access to exclusive content
Monetization	In-app Purchases	Up-Sells	It is when the game offers better options for buying goods, where the cost savings is proportionally inferior to the quantity purchased.
Monetization	In-app Purchases	Play Accelerators	It consists of the purchase of anything that allows players skips ahead, providing them with something that normally would need time and dedication to reach it
Monetization	In-app Purchases	Gacha	It is a system where players acquire a kind of package without knowing what comes inside until they open it

continued on following page

Table 1. Continued

Category	Subcategory	Element	Description
Monetization	In-app Purchases	Discounts	The game offers, for a limited time, an in-game product (or products) cheaper than the normal price
Monetization	In-app Purchases	Competitive Advantage	Anything that provides players with any competitive advantage against the game or other players
Monetization	In-app Purchases	Customization (To Set Up)	How the game lets the players customize the avatar or the game's world
Monetization	In-app Purchases	Targeted-Offers	That is an approach where the game offers specific promotions to the players, according to their gameplay style or activity
Monetization	In-app Purchases	Collectible Collection	These items belong to a set of items and exist only to be collected
Monetization	In-app Purchases	Purchase Gifts	Gifts also can be acquired with hard currency
Monetization	In-app Purchases	Store Cards	Physical cards with codes that can be redeemed for credits to be spent in the game
Monetization	Advertising	Banner Ads	It's a thin strip that is usually shown at the top or bottom of the screen
Monetization	Advertising	Interstitial Ads	Ads that appear between the transition of two screens and are usually full screen
Monetization	Advertising	Video Ads	Video ads are one of the most effective ads
Monetization	Advertising	Offer Walls	Offer walls can monetize through actions that players need to do, such as installing another game or signing up for a service
Monetization	Advertising	Affiliate Linking	It is a link to a store, which tracks the player and pays out a percentage of sales made
Monetization	Advertising	Product Placement	It is the use of real products inside the game to promote advertisement;
Monetization	Merchandise	Merchandise	That is the act of selling physical goods associated with the game.

CONCLUSION

The free mobile game design has specific characteristics that demand an investigation. The proper understanding of these characteristics can allow game professionals to create more profitable and successful mobile games. For example, a set of acquisition, retention, and monetization mobile free-to-play game elements, schematically organized, could be helpful to turns these elements formally accessible to be consciously designed on real games.

In this research the authors have organized a 1.0 version of the framework for F2P mobile games, assembling a set of fifty-nine elements, eight subcategories, and three main categories. These elements were put together through a research focused on professional and academic literature. The authors believe this framework can be very useful for free-to-play game design and game production professionals, as well as researches related to this subject. A formally organized list of applicable elements could turn the selection of F2P solutions more effective, as a checklist of possible options on the game design process. Game designers and producers, while using this framework, can verify if they are forgetting any element or consider alternatives that could help the game to be successful. The authors should also consider the use of the proposed framework as the basis for more research about ARM strategies in games.

Figure 6 illustrates the build process of the ARM framework for F2P mobile games, developed in Study 1. After the literature research, the authors identified a baseline ARM framework with forty-five

Figure 6. The build process of the ARM framework for F2P mobile games (The Author)

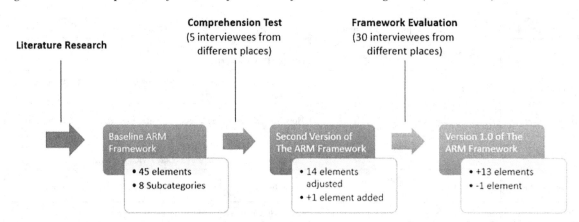

elements. Then, after a comprehension test, the authors created the second version of the ARM framework, with fourteen adjusted elements and one new element. As the final step, after the framework evaluation, the authors finished the version 1.0 of the ARM framework, with thirteen new elements added and one removed.

Furthermore, the developed set of heuristics can provide a structured and well-accepted group of guidelines and best practices to help new and experienced game designers when planning F2P mobile games. In addition, this set can be used as an academic reference, providing a structured way to organize heuristics specifically designed for ARM elements in F2P mobile games, since the authors didn't find anything similar during the research.

It is also necessary to consider that the academic room for contributions, about this specific field, is very large since there is scarce academic literature about it. This work itself is directly contributing to creating the academic basis for ARM in F2P mobile games.

As a future work, the authors are going to keep evolving this framework, validating and modifying its structure and elements, as well its labels. It will be done through continuous surveys with F2P mobile game professionals.

REFERENCES

Alha, K., Koskinen, E., Paavilainen, J., Hamari, J., & Kinnunen, J. (2014). Free-To-Play Games: Professionals' Perspectives. In Proceedings of Nordic Digra (vol. 2014). Visby.

Appel, G., Libai, B., Muller, E., & Shachar, R. (2017). *Retention and The Monetization Of Apps*. Retrieved from: http://www.hitechmarkets.net /files/appellibaimullershachar2017.pdf

Askelöf, P. (2013). *Monetization Of Social Network Games In Japan And The West* (Master's thesis). Lund University, Sweden.

Davidovici-nora, M. (2014). Paid And Free Digital Business Models Innovations In The Video Game Industry. Digiworld Economic Journal, 94, 83.

Fields, T., & Cotton, B. (2012). *Social Gamer Design: Monetization Methods And Mechanics*. Elsevier.

Kaniel, O. (2012). *Events Tracking Technology*. U.S. Patent application n. 13/649,402, 11 out. 2012.

KatkoffM. (2012a). *From Players To Payers*. Retrieved from: https://www.deconstructoroffun.com/blog//2012/05/from-players-to-payers-4-steps-to.html

Katkoff, M. (2012b). *Mid-Core Success Part 2: Retention*. Retrieved from: https://www.deconstructoroffun.com/blog//2013 /10/mid-core-success-part-2-retention.html

Khalil, H. (2016). *Engineering Viral Growth* (Master's thesis). Aalto University, Finland.

Kontagent. (2011). *The Top 7 Metrics Of High Successful Social Companies*. Retrieved from: http://static.kontagent.com /whitepaper/knt_wp_top7metrics_p3_finalx.pdf

Kuusisto, M. (2014). *Evaluating Free-To-Play Monetization Mechanics In Mobile Games: Case: Improvement Proposal To Supersonic-Game* (Bachelor's thesis). Tampere University of Applied Sciences, Finland.

Lovell, N. (2013). *The Pyramid Of Free-To-Play Game Design*. Retrieved from: https://www.gamasutra.com/blogs/ nicholaslovell/20130919/200606/the_pyramid_of_freeto

Luton, W. (2013). Free-To-Play: Making Money From Games You Give Away. New Riders.

Maiberg, E. (2013). *Pearl's Peril Is Wooga's Fastest-Growing Game To Date*. Retrieved from: http://www.adweek.com/ digital/pearls-peril-is-woogas-fastest-growing-game-to-date/

McClure, D. (2007). *Startup Metrics For Pirates: Aarrr! 500 Hats*. Retrieved From: http://500hats.typepad.com/500blogs /2007/09/startup-metrics.html

Morel, R. (2012). *Choosing The Right Business Model For Your Game Or App*. Retrieved from: https://www.adobe.com /devnet/flashplayer/articles/right-business-model.html

Narinen, A. (2014). *How Player Retention Works In Free-To-Play Mobile Games: A Study Of Player Retention Methods* (Bachelor's thesis). Tampere University of Applied Sciences, Finland.

Nguyen, H. (2014). *Monetization For A Free-To-Play Mobile Game* (Bachelor's thesis). Kajaani University of Applied Sciences, Finland.

Paavilainen, J., Alha, K., & Korhonen, H. (2017). A Review Of Social Features In Social Network Games. *Transactions of the Digital Games Research Association*, *3*(2).

Radoff, J. (2011). *Game On: Energize Your Business With Social Media Games*. Indianapolis, IN: Wiley Publishing, Inc.

Salen, K., & Zimmerman, E. (2004). *Rules Of Play: Game Design Fundamentals*. The MIT Press.

Tao, Z., Cheung, M., She, J., & Lam, R. (2014). Item Recommendation Using Collaborative Filtering In Mobile Social Games: A Case Study. *Big Data And Cloud Computing (bdcloud). IEEE Fourth International Conference*, 293-297.

Thibault, C. (2013). *Game Data Analysis–Tools And Methods*. Birmingham, UK: Packt Publishing ltd.

Think Gaming. (2018). *Top grossing all devices-games*. Retrieved from: https://thinkgaming.com

Williams, J. (2012). *Applying Lessons Learned On Facebook To Mobile App Development*. Retrieved from: https://www.gamasutra.com/blogs/joshwilliams/20120117/90918/applying_lessons_learned_on_facebook_to_mobile_app_development.php

KEY TERMS AND DEFINITIONS

Acquisition Strategies: Strategies to attract users to a game.

Free-to-Play Games: Games that the user does not have to pay to download and play.

Game Design: Field of design focused on the creation of games.

Game Development: The act of creating a game, from the conceptual basis to the final, published version.

Mobile Games: Games made to be played on mobile devices (smartphones and tablets).

Monetization Strategies: Strategies to make the user pay and/or generate profits to the game developers.

Retention Strategies: Strategies to keep the users playing a game, once they already played one time.

Chapter 12
Introduction to a Collaborative Mobile Web Platform:
Higher M@t-EduTutor

Isabel Araújo
Instituto Politécnico de Viana do Castelo, Portugal

Pedro Miguel Faria
Instituto Politécnico de Viana do Castelo, Portugal

ABSTRACT

From an early age, young people use mobile devices and are known as a "native digital generation," who constantly access information through mobile devices. Thus, educational practices are not indifferent to this reality. Consequently, several online platforms supporting the teaching-learning process have been developed. Additionally, several higher education institutions have a weekly attendance time, where teachers seek to clarify student's doubts physically in the institution. However, oftentimes, the students do not use that attendance time. In order to seek to improve this issue, a collaborative mobile web platform was developed: Higher M@t-EduTutor. This chapter starts by introducing a theoretical framework and then presents a broad study on collaborative web platforms in order to better relate them with the developed platform. This specific platform, to be used in mobile devices, with the objective of promoting students learning, allows students to clarify doubts with their teachers, collaboratively, in real time and at distance.

INTRODUCTION

Currently, the modern societies live in a knowledge society, strongly signaled by the use of networked technologies (Lucena, 2016). The use of mobile technologies and social digital networks are no exception and put us in constant interaction with (cyber) sociotechnical spaces. The students of the XXI century, known as the native digital generation, are the ones that use those spaces very early, "because they learned from the technologies and the networks, how to interact, to produce and to publish" (Lucena, 2016). They spontaneously access information through these same mobile devices, such as smartphones

DOI: 10.4018/978-1-5225-9069-9.ch012

and tablets. "The mobile phone has reached such an omnipresence that the new generations consider it a product of nature, such as milk or tomato" (Andreoli, 2007: 23).

The increasing access to the Internet through mobile devices (e.g. smartphones, tablets, PCs, game consoles) is remarkable and, inevitably, learning through these devices is a reality in many educational institutions (Attewell et al., 2009; Moura & Carvalho, 2010). It is not possible for education to remain unalterable to this reality. The use of communication technologies in the teaching-learning process is increasing and its relevance has been studied. Computer-based online learning environments are increasingly common in universities (Pulford, 2011), and are fundamental elements of the academic community (Morais, Alves, & Miranda, 2013) and defended by some authors (Bri et al. 2009), as the future in the academic field. Many authors defend the pertinence of educational practices that involve the use of communication technologies (Hernandez, 2017; Noor-UI-Amin, 2013). The evolution of mobile technologies emerges as an innovative tool for teachers and students, which triggered new forms of learning in different contexts (Sharples, 2009; Pachler, 2011). Thus, with the use of wireless mobile technologies in education, a new concept emerged – mobile learning (m-learning) – which simplifies the access to content, anytime and anywhere, facilitating a more flexible organization of learning time. For Ismail et al. (2010) there is a relationship between e-learning and m-learning, due the increasing power and sophistication of mobile devices. Ubiquity and context-aware will always be aspects of mobility that will make m-learning a unique and special approach to education.

The aim of this chapter is to describe a mobile web platform that allows synchronous communication between users, typically teachers and students of higher education institutions, who need to communicate in the context of clarifying doubts regarding the contents taught, particularly in the area of mathematics. In addition to the description of the developed platform (Higher M@t-EduTutor), a comparative analysis is presented, between some mobile web platforms, which allow real-time communication between users through the use of text, free drawing and images.

APPLICATION OF ICT IN LEARNING

Currently, education, namely higher education, has a mission to prepare students for the labor market, increasingly so demanding and competitive. Thus, students face major challenges, in addition to managing a large volume of information. Students build knowledge but also need to develop skills to obtain success in the globally and digitally interconnected world. According to Partnership for 21st Century Skills (Bialik & Fadel, 2015), students' competencies to better address future challenges are: critical thinking, problem solving, communication, collaboration, creativity and innovation.

Employers and society itself require diverse knowledge, skills and attitudes. Thus, it is necessary for students to be able to solve problems, to work with challenges and with diversity, according to the Industry 4.0 paradigm.

Higher education institutions must realize that current students are part of a generation based on Web 2.0 and Web 3.0, since they were born in this technological space and are fully integrated in it. It is not possible to dissociate today's society from ICT. With the growth of ICT, access to information becomes faster and obtained results are more abundant. It should be noted that students already use many of the resources available on the Web, in an almost spontaneous, informal and natural way.

Virtual Learning Environments

The introduction of ICT in various sectors of human activity was involuntary. However, in the case of education, it was imposed for a number of reasons, from allowing access to a greater number of citizens, enabling them to live and to work in a technological society, and to promote an up-to-date education supported in the knowledge society needs (Andrade, 2002). According to this author, the introduction of ICT in schools, allows to provide to them the changes occurring in society, allowing the adoption of new educational practices (Andrade, 2002). Thus, learning experiences in dynamic and flexible environments, using familiar technologies, encourage students to build up their knowledge. On the other hand, learning experiences in dynamic and flexible environments, using technologies with which students are familiar, encourages them to build knowledge. Thus, ICT supported learning environments characterized by further sharing, collaboration, communication and participation have been developed (Ramos, 2007), which may transform the way students acquire, use and build knowledge (Trinder, Guillermo, Margaryn, Littlejohn, & Nicol, 2008). According to some authors (Deaney et al., 2003; Youssef & Dahmani, 2008; Hemmi, et al., 2009), the adoption of technologies provides a better participation, collaboration and interaction among learning scenarios, making them more active, empowering new forms of learning. In this sense, many authors point out a significant improvement in students' performance and attitudes, towards their learning, when digital technology is integrated into the learning process (Kay, 2006; Jimoyiannis & Komis, 2007).

From the point of view of students, according to Ricoy and Couto (2009), ICT can be a source of external motivation in formal educational environments and the use of the Internet fosters educational success. Also for Oliveira and his colleagues (Oliveira, Rego & Villardi, 2007) the internet used as a learning environment, may create a flexible and collaborative virtual space, suitable for building autonomous and meaningful knowledge. Although Moran (2006) recognizes potentialities, regarding the use of the Internet, namely, being a valuable information search tool, to build knowledge, facilitating and motivating learning, the Internet provides interactive environments, which may become dispersive, taking into account the different possible connections. However, despite the possibility of students dispersing, the author acknowledges that ICT plays an important role in the teaching and learning processes, which are motivated by itself. It should also be noticed that not all students are prepared to use these new environments, especially the younger, who are less autonomous. Therefore, the teacher has a crucial role in creating and sustaining conditions for building shared knowledge.

The evolution of the Internet and the ICT has enabled the creation of virtual learning environments (VLE) gradually more sophisticated, based on e-learning platforms. These computer-based online learning environments are increasingly common in universities (Pulford, 2011), and are key elements in the academic community (Morais, Alves & Miranda, 2013) and advocated by some authors (Bri et al, 2009), as the future in the academic field. Such learning environments (VLE), especially if structured according to constructivist perspectives, are considered adequate for higher education (Cardoso, et al, 2008), as they provide the creation of customized environments, allowing the learners to develop their own learning, assigning them an active role in this process (Monteiro, 2012). Thus, as Kanuka and Anderson (1999) argue that constructivist theories constitute a reference paradigm in the development of virtual environments. In this context, Cardoso, Pimenta and Pereira (2008) sought to understand the phenomenon of higher education institutions in adopting e-learning platforms, as a support for learning environments, using ICT, at an undergraduate level. From the study carried out by the authors, there was a broad consensus regarding the need for changes in the teaching activity, associated to the use of ICT as learning technologies. However, paradoxically, it was verified the absence of policies and appropriate decisions in this area, as well the persistence of several difficulties in the implementation of initiatives, which were conditioned by the institutional context, inhibiting innovation in the teaching activity in higher education institutions. Thus, in this same study, the need for a national policy and a program to support the use of ICT in higher education was highlighted.

The VLE can be used both in face-to-face education and in distance education, with mixed models coexisting (Moran, 2002). The e-learning modality, increasingly frequent in the context of higher education (Morais & Cabrita, 2008) allows the student and the teacher to be physically and temporally separated. Information and study material are available on the Internet, and students may access it virtually anytime and anywhere. This modality is quite versatile, since the materials available can be changed, corrected and updated by the author quickly and easily, rewarding access to the latest and most updated information (Cação & Dias, 2003). The b-learning mode (blended learning) is a mixed model that includes online and face-to-face components (id.). The VLE enable the collaborative and cooperative construction of knowledge, provide access to digital educational contents, and greatly enhance the interaction between the subjects, in a synchronous and asynchronous way, promoting different learning modalities. According to Miranda & Torres (2009) the teachers understood that in order to educate the current generation, it is necessary to use the current tools.

Mobile Technologies in Education

In recent decades there has been a significant development of mobile technologies. They stand out for their generalization, and also for the speed with which they have been adopted globally and because they tend to be used with increasing frequency. Mobile technologies stand out among the interactive media, because in addition to promoting interactivity, they have mobility and portability capabilities. Thus, the user has the communication literally in their hands, being able to capture contents and information of the environment where they are (instantaneously) uploading them to the Internet. Spaces become geo-located and communication accessible anywhere, anytime on any machine. Technologies, particularly mobile technologies, have fostered the emergence of new opportunities to improve and guide the teaching and learning process. According to Domenciano and Junior (2017) the use of mobile communication devices, such as smartphones and tablets, have been an alternative to education, with a significant role in the teaching and learning process, capable of strengthening the link between teachers and students. Students acquire a sense of ownership in relation to the learning tasks and technologies used (Scanlon et al, 2005), enhancing motivation and commitment in learning activities.

The emergence and popularization of mobile devices and connection services helped promoting the arising of a new modality of education: the mobile learning, or m-learning. There are many definitions, but in this chapter it is followed the Quinn (2011) definition. He considers that m-learning is any activity that allows an user to be more productive when consuming, interacting or creating information, mediated through a portable compact digital device, small in size, with connectivity and used on a regular basis. Thus, some studies were carried out concerning the use of mobile technologies to support activities in an educational context (Ligi, 2017). However, learning through the use of mobile devices, such as smartphones and tablets, is simply an adjustable part of the educational model, not an autonomous tool in the classroom (Sharples, 2009). These technologies are an adequate support for the development of individual and collaborative learning strategies, suitable for students training.

In a study carried out by Kumar (2011), in which he analyzed the satisfaction of students and teachers concerning the use of m-learning technologies, he observed a decrease in students' face-to-face attendance at the teacher's office. According to the authors, some of the doubts that usually took the students to the teacher's office were clarified through the mobile support service available. In another study, conducted by Mayberry et al. (2012) that involved eight university teachers and their students, the effectiveness of the active learning strategies (developed using iPads they had received) was measured. Those teachers used a video camera to share work experiences, used the YouTube platform to publish the explanation of concepts, and used applications such as blogs for immediate feedback to requests, from students outside the classroom. The author verified that all the teachers involved, and most of the students, adopted a positive attitude in the use of these tools. The studies carried out by Attah (2015), Mwakapina (2016) and Zardini (2015) indicate the relevance of further investigation on using mobile technologies with higher education students. These studies consisted of seeking to understand the advantages and disadvantages of using the WhatsApp application as a teaching tool. Some of the advantages would be the low cost, the ease of use, the availability and simplicity, promoting the dialogue between students and between students and teachers and the possibility of continuing studies outside the classroom. Also, Mwakapina et al. (2016, p.83) believe that WhatsApp, in addition to creating a safe and supportive learning environment, enhances students cooperation and collaboration (e.g. the study of languages goes beyond the classroom) and involves other participants, such as friends and family. Fattah (2015, p. 116) considers that this application brings a freedom of organization inside and outside the school environment. Zardini (2015, p.4) argues that this application allows the construction of new learning communities, support for on-site learning, the formal and informal approach of the student, beyond the continuous learning and communication improvement. However, the authors had also identified some disadvantages. According to Fattah (2015) some of the disadvantages of using WhatsApp are the use of incorrect language and inappropriate content by students, some demonstrate lack of effort to learn, and also the fact that not all students own compatible mobile devices or Internet connections. Mwakapina et al (2016, 83) identify some disadvantages such as the possibility of students to leave the application discussion groups at any time and the difficulty of preventing them to publish their assignments after the deadline established by the teacher. Zardini (2015) highlights as a disadvantage the impossibility to save links and images, since the contents are stored only in the mobile device of the user. Thus, if the group information or conversation is "deleted" the information may be lost.

Thus, mobile technologies have the potential to complement learning practices, in convergence with other methods and other media, allowing the expansion of educational space for society as a whole (Fedoce & Squirra, 2011).

PROBLEM

In Portuguese Higher Education institutions there is a weekly attendance schedule, in which students should be with teachers, in their offices, in order to clarify any doubts related to the subject contents taught in classes. In particular, at the Polytechnic Institute of Viana do Castelo, at the Higher School of Technology and Management, it is established by regulation that teachers must have an attendance schedule of two hours, at least. This attendance schedule is defined by the teachers, at the beginning of each semester. The teachers will be present in their offices to assist any of their students. However, it should be noted that this attendance schedule is not mandatory for students and, unfortunately, in general, they do not use it, even those students with worst results during the semester. The study here presented in this chapter considers the students of a Polytechnic Higher Education Institution of the North of Portugal, attending the Mathematics subject. The students were in the 1st year of Computer Graphics and Multimedia Engineering Degree, and are representative of the problem. This reality has implications in school success. It is believed that if the students having more difficulties, could use the weekly attendance time with the teachers, to clarify their doubts, in a more customized way, they could obtain better results. This would contribute to reduce school failure and, consequently, to reduce the number of students who drop out of school. One of the reasons invoked by students to not use the weekly attendance time is due to the fact of being necessary to be present, physically, in the teacher's office. Thus, analyzing some e-learning platforms (e.g. Moodle, Blackboard) we verify those platforms don't have support to teachers and students be synchronously connected online, for doubts clarification.

PROTOTYPE OF A MOBILE-MEDIATED SOLUTION

Considering the identified problem of students' lack of interest to the weekly attendance schedule, it was sought to identify an alternative that could mitigate the problem. In this sense, taking into account the practices identified in the bibliographic review previously indicated, a possible solution was identified, which involves the use of an online ICT to support the clarification of students' doubts. This led to the idea of developing a technological tool to support students in their studies, more specifically in the clarification of doubts, without the need of a teacher and a student to be physically present in the same space. To achieve this, students could use devices that they usually have at their disposal: the own smartphones, which students informally use in their daily lives. A comprehensive study was carried out, comparing various collaborative mobile web platforms, which exclude the need for students to be physically present in the teachers' offices. The specificities and limitations of some of the studied platforms led to the development of a prototype of a collaborative web platform, to be used with mobile devices, supporting students learning at distance. The prototype intends to simplify the interaction between users (a teacher and a student), in the same shared working area, in real time, in order to help the clarification of doubts. In summary, the main objective was to extend the attendance schedule, beyond the walls of the teacher's office, through a mobile web platform.

MOBILE WEB COLLABORATIVE PLATFORMS

Some mobile devices apps with different functionalities and media support (text, image, audio, video, drawing, among others) have been developed (Arantes et al., 2017). However, not all apps support collaborative work between users, in real-time, an also do not run on browsers. Currently, there are various applications and collaborative platforms available on the internet, many of them having different functionalities, but with the same objective: to allow the access to more than one user, as well as to ensure communication in real time, allowing a collaborative discussion between users, as referred by Palloff and Pratt (2005: 11): "Collaboration enhances learning outcomes and reduces the potential for learner isolation that can occur in the online environment".

In this study it was decided to identify online platforms, classified as whiteboards, which may address the problem stated above. One of the objectives was to identify free-use platforms as well as those with associated licensing plans, in order to identify the features that each one offers. A platform that is not free to use could prevent teachers and students from using it. Thus, it was decided to test three free-use platforms, one platform with the most expensive licensing plan and two platforms with a medium-cost payment plan, when compared with different platforms.

Web Platforms

Google Docs

One of the oldest and most used collaborative platform, which allow document sharing and edition by multiple users, in real time, is Google Docs. In order to be able to do that is sufficient to have a Google account. This platform has similar features to Microsoft Word, concerning text creation and edition. Additionally, it has other functionalities such as "Suggestions Edition", concerning the content edited on the shared document, which can be accepted or rejected by the author, promoting the collaboration between users. Another available feature called "Explore" facilitates the search for text and images, relevant to the content to be produced in the shared document. This collaborative platform allows the communication between users, through a text chat. However, this feature is not available to be down-loadable in mobile devices.

Another collaborative tool from Google is Google Drawings, which allows the free drawing of some graphic primitives. Some of this tool features are partially available in Google Docs. The full version contains a wide variety of graphic shapes that allow the creation of diagrams and graphics, also allow-ing free drawing. This tool, besides the insertion of images, also allows the insertion of video, although this functionality is not directly available in the list of tools (Google Slides is used to do that). Unlike many other Google platforms, Drawings is a web platform that does not support mobile devices such as smartphones and tablets. This tool, although it can be accessed through the browsers of mobile devices, is not properly optimized to that, making it practically impossible to use its features.

AWW

AWW is a collaborative web platform, suitable to work on mobile devices, which has basic drawing/text tools, sharing the drawing area (canvas), "post-it" note creation and chat communication (in the paid plan) through a link share. On this platform the administrator may provide edit or view-only permissions to the invited users, before sharing the workspace. No user registration is required. However, in order to save the online work, it is necessary to register (free of charge). This platform allows the upload of files of several formats, namely images, .pdf and .pptx files. When the contents of these files consist of more than one page, it is spread across multiple work areas, allowing the user to switch between each of them.

GroupBoard

Groupboard requires user registration in order to be used, even with the free plan version. It is a col-laborative whiteboard for online tutoring. The forums creation option is only available for paid version. This platform allows sharing, via a link, with minimal setup time. Groupboard allows users to setup administrator controls, to moderate the whiteboard space, and even ban users or keep the board private. This is especially helpful for any teams that want to keep their collaborative space private, and to prevent unauthorized access to the space. The users can upload images as backgrounds for the board and then use the tools to work in the specific context of the image. This platform has few tools, which simplify the drawings work. It is possible to choose different colors, shapes and pencil sizes.

Realtime Board

Realtime Board is a collaborative platform for work teams. It has some predefined templates that facilitate the process of developing a product or service, within its "infinite canvas", allowing the users to comment and to leave notes, and also use a wide selection of tools. A disadvantage of its free plan is to be limited in terms of features available to the user, such as:

- It allows the creation of only up to 5 working areas;
- The voice and video communication is available only in the paid plan;
- It has a lower administrative capacity, namely in the definition of policies of team members invitations, limit on the number of team members, among others;
- Project export is allowed, but the images have lower quality and are available with a watermark.

For a better workflow and inclusion of new tools and capabilities, this platform allows the installation of some add-ons/plugins (Souza, 2011) and it is a platform used by several companies such as Spotify, Twitter, Netflix and Autodesk.

Web Whiteboard

This platform is a simple and quick alternative to collaboratively draw and/or write on mobile devices. However, the responsiveness of the platform to such devices is not adequate. This platform has only the most basic graphic primitive drawing tools, with only four colors, a rubber and a text tool, with the possibility of inserting notes into "post-its" objects. The Web Whiteboard only requires registration if the user is willing to pay a monthly subscription, from which it becomes possible to save the drawing areas and to manage the permission functionality of the invited users, in order to have, or not, the ability to edit a shared work. However, this platform will only hold free whiteboards for 21 days and thus, after that a paid plan subscription is needed.

WhiteboardFox

Like the previous described platform, this one is also a collaborative, fast-access platform that does not require user registration. In addition to the basic tools like the brush, the eraser and the text tool, this platform already offers a slightly larger selection of available colors, as well as image upload and zoomIn/zoomOut options. Regarding the "eraser" tool, it completely erases an "object" instead of erasing part of the drawing. Thus, the "eraser" tool has a different operating mode when compared with the AWW, Web Whiteboard and Higher M@t-EduTutor platforms. In addition, these workspaces can be saved and used later, being sufficient to save the document link or to download the work as an image.

Specific Platform Features

Considering that it is intended to extend the attendance schedule to a virtual space, in which the student and the teacher can communicate in real time, the platform would has to support some specific features. Considering the technological evolution of mobile devices and the use of these by students, it was decided that the platform to be developed would has to be responsive to mobile devices and to support tactile screens (Feature 1: Responsive, mobile-friendly; Feature 2: Touch support on tactile screens). In order to be able that a student may express his doubts/questions online, it was considered that would be important to have a virtual space, where he could try to clarify those doubts, synchronously connected to a teacher (Feature 9: Real-time text chat). Also is important that the student may graphically present the problem, "drawing" it (e.g. in the context of this study, considering a concrete resolution of a mathematical task) or by uploading a file (e.g. an image) with a possible solution of the proposed exercise, step-by-step. And, then, the teacher, synchronously, be able to "draw" over the image uploaded by the student, solving the problem and commenting it (Feature 5: File import support (e.g. image, .PDF)). Considering that when clarifying doubts, the student and the teacher may need to write/draw on the whiteboard, without any virtual space limitations, it was considered appropriate that the canvas be as large as possible (Feature 3: Flexible drawing area size (canvas)). Moreover, it was considered that the existence of several tools, to support writing and drawing, improves communication between users, namely the possibility of erasing (Feature 4: "Eraser" tool to delete completely or part of an object) and the automatic verification, correction and completion of what the user writes (Feature 8: Spell check and auto-fill). When the students use the attendance schedule, physically in the teacher's office, sometimes they ask the teacher for the sheets in paper format, with the solved exercise and the written notes. Thus, it was considered important that the platform allows to save the working area (Feature 6: Export of drawing canvas as an image). It was also considered the possibility to have audio communication (Feature 7: Audio communication support between users) although it is not essential, as it could act just as a complement to the real-time text chat functionality. Additionally, in the case of students from a public institution, it is deemed advantageous that the platform be open access (Feature 10: Free version of the platform) providing access without any cost, enhancing an increase in the number of platform users, and thus contribute to an inclusive education.

Thus, the features considered in this study are the following:

1. Responsive, mobile-friendly
2. Touch support on tactile screens
3. Flexible drawing area size (canvas)
4. "Eraser" tool to delete completely or part of an object
5. File import support (e.g. image, .PDF)
6. Export of drawing canvas as an image
7. Audio communication support between users
8. Spell check and auto-fill
9. Real-time text chat
10. Free version of the platform

It should be noted that among the 10 features considered in this study, six are essential for the purposes of the platform. Without the availability of the features indicated as 1, 2, 3, 5, 9 and 10, it could not be feasible for all students to indicate their doubts, using their mobile devices, and thus the teacher be able to clarify them in real time, and for that reason it was considered indispensable those six features to be available in a platform, to clarify students doubts, collaboratively and in real time with his teacher. The remain features are useful and complementary but not essential to address the problem identified.

Analysis of the Platforms

The functionalities considered to analysis are presented in Table 1 and for each collaborative platform it is indicated the features available.

From the analyzed platforms, it was verified that all have a free version, although some offer a limited set of features, such as the AWW platform, which for e.g. does not provide the audio communication features for free. The complete free versions are Google Docs, Web Whiteboard and Whiteboard Fox. All platforms support tactile screens and allow exporting the desktop as an image, with the exception of Google Docs. It should be noted that this platform does not have the free drawing features in the mobile application. Although platforms have touch support on tactile screens, the responsiveness of the Web Whiteboard is not suitable for mobile devices, and it is the platform with fewer features, including a very limited canvas. However, this platform has a feature that enhances commenting on the working area, as does AWW and Realtime Board. The only platforms whose canvas is endless are Realtime Board and Whiteboard Fox. Although AWW has a limited canvas, it is the only one that allows the creation of some canvases, allowing to freely switching between them. The analyzed platforms, with the exception of Web Whiteboard, allow importing image files. The AWW and Realtime Board platforms allow also importing .pdf and .ppt files. The import of documents in .pdf and .ppt format differs. While in AWW each imported page creates a new canvas, on Realtime Board the document is imported into the same working area, allowing the user to browse all the pages. With the exception of Google Docs, all platforms allow exporting the desktop as an image.

One of the relevant features on these platforms is the ability to write and draw freely on the working area (canvas), as well as to correct or delete the drawings (in whole or in part). On Whiteboard Fox and Realtime Board the user cannot partially erase a drawing (it is only possible to completely delete the object(s)). However, in AWW, Web Whiteboard and GroupBoard it is possible to delete part of the object. For spell checking and autocomplete, none of the reviewed platforms have this feature.

Table 1. Comparison between different collaborative platforms

	1. Mobile-friendly	2. Touch support	3. Flexible canvas	4. "Eraser" tool	5. Import files	6. Canvas export	7. Audio support	8. Spell check; auto-fill	9. Real-time chat	10. Free version
Google Docs	✓	✓	✗	✗	✓	✗	✗	□	✓	✓
AWW	□	✓	✓	□	✓	✓	✓	✗	✓	□
GroupBoard	✓	✓	✓	□	✓	✓	✗	✗	✓	□
Realtime Board	✓	✓	✓	□	✓	✓	✓	✗	✓	□
Web Whiteboard	✗	✓	✗	□	✗	✓	✗	✗	✗	✓
WhiteboardFox	✓	✓	✓	✓	✓	✓	✗	✗	✗	✓
✗ - does not apply; □ - partially applies; ✓ - applies										

In a collaborative platform, the possibility of communication is fundamental. Therefore, the communication feature via audio or text was analyzed. It has been found that on Google Docs, AWW and Realtime Board platforms text communication is possible, and audio communication is only available on AWW and Realtime Board, but with a paid plan. However, text and audio communication was not implemented on Realtime Board mobile devices versions (browser and app).

Observing the 6 platforms and considering the priority of the features above indicated (1, 2, 3, 5, 9 and 10) and according with Table 1, we verify the following:

- AWW and Web Whiteboard are excluded because they don't support Feature 1;
- Google Docs platform is excluded because it doesn't support Feature 3;
- Whiteboard Fox platform is excluded because it doesn't support Feature 9;
- Groupboard and Realtime Board platforms are excluded due to Feature 10.

Thus, from the comprehensive study made, it was verified the need to develop a prototype of a platform, which may support the six essential functionalities above indicated.

THE HIGHER M@T-EDUTUTOR PLATFORM

Taking into account the initial issue, the target audience (students of the digital generation) and its scope, it was sought to extend the students attendance time, to a virtual environment. In this regard, we considered the development of a technological solution for mobile devices, having a touch screen (e.g. smartphones and tablets), supported on the web, with client-server functionality, and bidirectional communication using technologies such as Node.js and Websockets.

General Purpose

Succinctly, the Higher M@t-EduTutor project can be classified as a prototype of a collaborative, real-time, responsive and mobile-compatible web platform (e.g. smartphones and tablets). One of the main objectives that it is intended to achieve with the development of this platform is to substitute the use of a board like the one that is present in a classroom. This platform has features of an online editor, which includes basic writing and drawing tools, being able to write and draw freely, in real time, with other connected users, having the user at his disposal several tools, among which one text tool, brush, rubber, possibility of loading images, cleaning the drawing area and export the work area as an image.

Structure of the Collaborative Platform

One of the premises of the development of this platform was the availability of collaborative support to several users. The technological solution found for the implementation of the collaborative functionalities includes the implementation of a server, through the use of the node.js framework (Syed, 2014), along with the use of websockets (Wang, 2013). These sockets allow a real-time connection between two applications, capable of transmitting data between them: *"The WebSocket API enables you to establish full-duplex, bidirectional communication over the Web, between your client application and server-side processes"* (Wang, 2013, p.14). The server receives, through sockets, (x and y) coordinates in a 2D area, in result of user interaction with the canvas, by drawing some object. After receiving these messages on the server, the server shares that information with the other connected users, thus allowing real-time collaboration.

Figure 1 represents that internal functional structure of the Higher M@t-EduTutor platform, through the connection of users to a node.js HTTP server, using sockets technology. In order the server may receive information about the work performed by users, it is necessary to send the data of all actions performed in the working area (canvas). The server receives the (x and y) coordinates previously transformed into an object, as well as all the information emitted by the users. In this way, the server transmits all data from one user to the remaining connected users.

Support for Tactile Screens

One of the important features considered in the development of this platform was the possibility of being able to work on mobile devices, having touch support for tactile screens. The development of this functionality is very similar to the implementation of mouse events, being necessary to adapt it to the use of finger touch on the display. To achieve that the detection of 3 events was implemented: *touchStart*, *touchMove* and *touchEnd*, represented in the 3 functions below.

```
function touchStart() {
        getTouchPos();
        onToolTouch();
        sendTouch(touchX, touchY);
        event.preventDefault();
}
function touchMove(e) {
        getTouchPos(e);
```

Figure 1. Functional representation between server and users

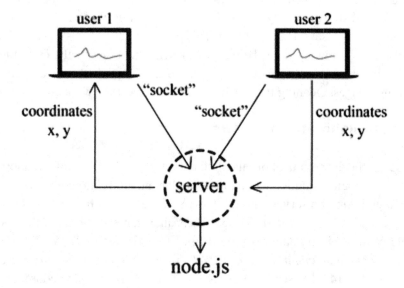

```
        onToolTouch();
        sendTouch(touchX, touchY);
        event.preventDefault();
}
function touchEnd() {
        lastX = -1;
        lastY = -1;
        socket.emit('touchend');
}
```

In *touchStart* and *touchMove* events, the *x* and *y* coordinates are sent through the *sendTouch* function. In the case of the *touchEnd* event it is only intended to inform the server that the user has raised his finger from the display, and thereby to suspend the use of the selected tool.

Front-End

Nowadays, one of the concerns a programmer must pay attention, in the development process of web applications/platforms, is that it must be responsive, in order it can be used on different mobile devices (Shahzad, 2017). In this way, the Higher M@t-EduTutor platform was developed so that it automatically adjusts to different dimensions of the displays in which it is used. When implementing the HTML code and formatting the web page styles, using CSS, it was taken into consideration the purpose of the platform responsiveness.

An HTML element (canvas) was used to create the user's drawing area (Figure 2) in which it is possible to draw text and graphic primitives. The area has a side menu that hides automatically, freeing up space for drawing. This menu consists of various options available to the user.

This drawing functionality results from several x, y points, consecutively represented by the user interaction. Another tool developed similarly to drawing objects is a "rubber". Additionally, the user has the possibility to add text boxes, developed in HTML and using a javascript library (JQuery). In this way, it is possible for the user to write and apply text freely on the working area. Color, font (Arial)

Figure 2. The platform canvas

Figure 3. Example of a platform operation

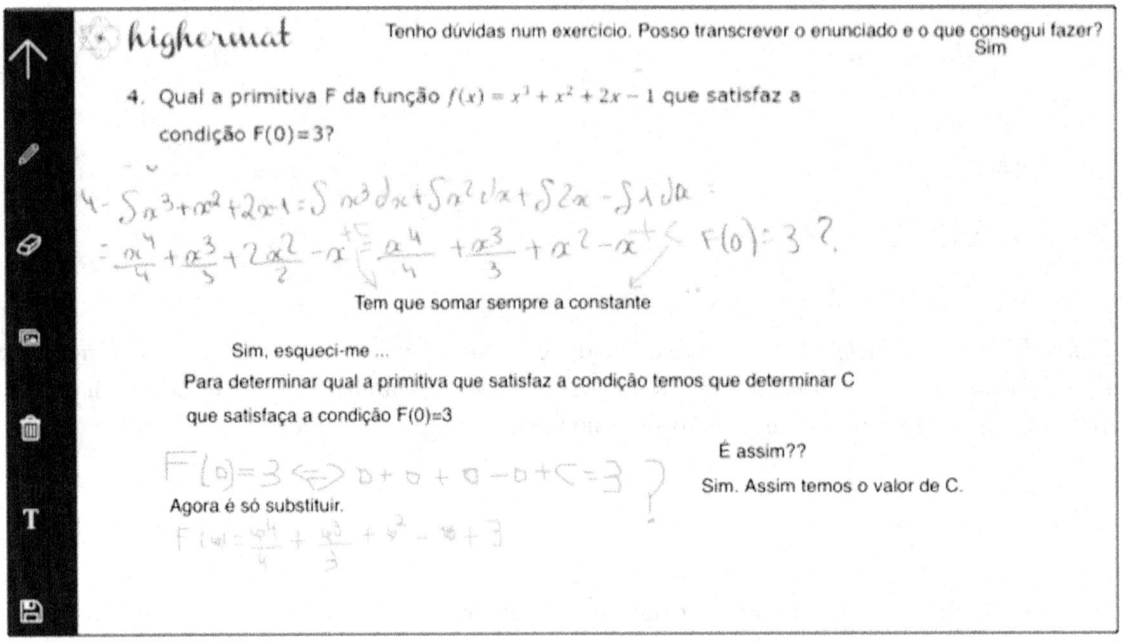

and size were fixed. An import module for image files, locally available, was also developed using the FileReader (W3C, 2017) API. At any time, the user has the possibility to use a "clean/delete" operation of all the content present in the canvas. Another feature available on the prototype allows exporting the canvas as an image file (.jpg) that the user can, for example, save and/or share with someone.

Javascript was chosen to be the programming language, used in the development of several functionalities included in the platform. Some of these developed features allow supporting for user interaction operations with the canvas. This interaction is performed through events (click/pressure and drag/movement) of the pointing system (e.g. the mouse, a pen or the user's finger). The platform continuously collects the 2D x, y coordinates, in result of the pointing system interaction with the canvas, in order to ensure that the drawing is performed in the correct coordinates. Javascript was used also to add support to track events on tactile screens, typically available on mobile devices.

An example of the collaborative use of the Higher M@t-EduTutor platform is shown in Figure 3. Three of the platform features are used, namely free drawing, importing image files and writing text. In this case the figure represents the result of a student who seeks to clarify doubts with a teacher. In this particular example, the student uploaded an image to the canvas, containing a question related with a math exercise. And, using the platform drawing tool, he wrote a mathematical function, in order to simplify the explanation of his doubt to the teacher, who proceeds with the resolution of the exercise. Whenever any user wants, may save on his device a copy of the canvas, as an image. An interesting feature developed in the platform, in order to become easier for users to distinguish between what each one writes/draws on canvas, is the automatic assignment of different objects drawing color, for each user. Thus, a teacher can more easily distinguish what a student writes/draws on the canvas, from what is written/draw by him or vice versa. Another interesting feature available to the users is the possibility to hide the side tool menu, thus obtaining more free space to draw in the canvas area.

Platform Results Analysis

Through the analysis of developed platform, in terms of technical features, considering the features used in the comparative analysis made, it is possible to verify that the Higher M@t-EduTutor free platform is responsive, suitable for mobile devices, has touch support for tactile screens, the size of the canvas is flexible, has a "rubber" tool to erase part of the drawn object, supports the import of files (e.g. images), and it allows to export the drawing canvas as an image. However, it does not support audio communication between users, does not allow for spell checking and automatic text filling, and does not have real-time text chat (known as a typical online text chat), but it possible to the users to simultaneously interact on the same canvas area, supporting communication between users (it is understood in this study that having real-time text chat presupposes the guarantee of written communication between users in real time).

In order to confirm whether the M@t-EduTutor platform fulfills the purpose for which it was designed, and being a prototype, two types of studies were carried out. One was carried out in a first version of the prototype, which consisted of a usability study (Araújo & Faria, 2017). This study was carried out in a teaching context, involving 16 students, who answered to a SUS (System Usability Scale) questionnaire (Brooke, 1986) after using the platform. From that study, all respondents considered that the platform is suitable and useful in an educational context, and an interesting tool to support student learning. Those students considered also that the Higher M@t-EduTutor platform has a high degree of usability and should be applied to other scientific areas.

Another study was made and consisted in requesting two students, who occasionally went to the teacher's office, to use the platform, and in this way it would be possible to investigate the feasibility of clarifying doubts through the M@t-EduTutor platform. Thus, some clarification sessions were held, in which the students imported images to the canvas, containing the exercises and the doubts they had. With the help of the text tool and the drawing tool, doubts were clarified by the teacher. An evidence of one of those sessions is indicated in Figure 3, in which at the blue and orange colors we may identify the teacher and the student interactions, respectively, in the canvas design area. Moreover, it is noteworthy that one of the students considered that this platform had helped him clarifying doubts, so he used it to clarify doubts with the colleagues. According to this student, this platform helped him clarifying doubts, avoiding the need to go to the school, which would involve some time and costs. This student made also a suggestion to improve one of the platform tools, in order the messages written with the text tool could have different colors, according with the users, in a similar way to what happens with the drawing tool. When asked about the relevance of the development of a typical real-time chat (which allows the exchange of written messages instantly and usually it appears in a side window), the student indicated that this might not be so relevant, because when saving/exporting the canvas he had in the same area the questions and the answers, which would be more productive to later study. The other student considered the use of the platform an useful support for the clarification of doubts, being an innovative concept, and he had enjoyed to participate in the experience. He also mentioned that he had been able to clarify his doubts, regarding the contents of the subject. As main advantages he indicated: the possibility to clarify doubts, without the need to go to the school and the possibility to save the canvas area with the teacher clarifications, which in a face-to-face session does not happen. Regarding the disadvantages, this student mentioned as a small difficulty the need to schedule a day and an hour with the teacher and also mentioned as a disadvantage of the platform the lack of audio support, which could complement the clarification session.

CONCLUSION

Throughout the development of this platform we had encountered some difficulties, namely in the inclusion of the tools in a collaborative way and their compatibility with mobile devices with touch screen. However, it was possible to develop a first relatively stable prototype of a web platform, compatible with several browsers, through the implementation of a server using the node.js framework and connections via web sockets, enabling real-time communication. The Higher M@t-EduTutor platform, at the level of the studied features, lacks in communication support via audio between users, spell check and automatic text filling and text chat in real-time (the typical side window), which are not essential. These features are not simultaneously available in any of the analyzed platforms. It should be noted these features, although relevant, could be bridged, by using other parallel platforms specifically for this purpose (e.g. Skype). However, it should be noted that the current version of the platform allows interaction between users, simultaneously on the same canvas, since it is possible to draw and to write using handwritten or the text tool. The student can also present the doubts by uploading image files to the canvas, in order to simplify their description and simultaneously simplify the teacher's explanations. It is possible also to export images of the canvas drawings, among other features. Thus, it was thus possible to create a virtual space where students do not have the need to go to the teacher's office, in order to contact him and clarify their doubts, through the use of their smartphones and a whiteboard-like canvas. The teacher may correct any exercise, explain some content, and do some suggestions about what the student draw, wrote, comment and dialogued through the canvas, enhancing communication between users, becoming this communication easier and more similar with direct and personal contact between teacher and student.

It is considered that the developed Higher M@t-EduTutor platform has the potential to facilitate the interaction between students and teachers, in the clarification of doubts, in a more personalized way, and thus, students would obtain better results, contributing to reduce school failure.

In the future, a number of new features can be implemented, such as allowing users to share their working area through a link, allowing users to collaborate with anyone they want. It would be a plus, the inclusion of text and voice communication among users, since it facilitates the collaboration between them, not having to resort to third-party applications. Another feature to implement will allow users to save their work on the platform itself. This will require the development of a user database support system. In this way, users would be able to access the various interaction sessions, stored through their personal account in the platform, among other features that would enhance the collaborative work between teachers and students.

The technology, including mobile, does not generate better learning but brings other possibilities for building knowledge. Teachers need to understand that the use of these technologies is not restricted to the environment outside the classroom, and reflect on their practices with a more critical thinking to promote more dynamic classes, helping students to solve problems and deal with the challenges they meet.

REFERENCES

Andrade, P., (2002). Aprender por projectos, formar educadores. *Formação de educadores para o uso da informática na escola*. Valente, J.. Núcleo de Informática Aplicada à Educação – Nied.

Andreoli, V. (2007). *O Mundo Digital*. Lisboa: Editorial Presença.

Arantes, F., Freire, F., Breuer, J., Silva, A., Oliveira, R., & Vascon, L. (2017). Towards a Multi-semiotic and Multimodal Editor. *Journal of Computer Science and Technology*, *17*(2), 100–109. doi:10.24215/16666038.17.e14

Araújo, I., & Faria, P. (2017). Higher M@T-EduTutor - A prototype of a platform to support tutoring at distance using mobile devices. *10th annual International Conference of Education, Research and Innovation. ICERI2017 Proceedings*, 6048-6055.

Attewell, J., Savill-Smith, C., & Douch, R. (2009). *The impact of mobile learning examining what it means for teaching and learning*. London: LSN.

Bialik, M., & Fadel, C. (2015). *Skills for the 21st Century: What Should Students Learn?* Center for Curriculum Redesign.

Bri, D., Garcia, M., Coll, H., & Lloret, J. (2009). A study of virtual learning environments. *WSEAS Transactions on Advances in Engineering Education*, *6*(1), 33–43.

Brooke, J. (1986). SUS: a "quick and dirty" usability scale. In *Usability Evaluation in Industry*. London: Taylor and Francis.

Cação, R., & Dias, P. (2003). *Introdução ao e-learning. Sociedade Portuguesa de Inovação*. S. A. 1a Edição.

Cardoso, E., Pimenta, & Pereira, D. (2008). Adopção de Plataformas de e-Learning nas Instituiões de Ensino Superior - modelo do processo. *Revista de Estudos Politécnicos*, *6*(9).

Deaney, R., Ruthven, K., & Hennessy, S. (2003). Pupil perspectives on the contribution of ICT to teaching and learning in the secondary school. *Research Papers in Education*, *18*(2), 141–165. doi:10.1080/0267152032000081913

Domenciano, J., & Junior, R. (2017). Como as tecnologias móveis têm sido utilizadas na educação? Estudo em duas instituições de ensino superior brasileiras. *InFor, Inov. Form., Rev. NEaD-Unesp*, *3*(1), 49-68.

Fattah, S. (2015). The Effectiveness of Using WhatsApp Messenger as one of Mobile Learning Techniques to develop students' writing skills. *Journal of Education and Practice*, *6*(32).

Fedoce, R. & Squirra, S. (2011). The technology and the mobile's communication potential in education. *LOGOS 35 Mediações sonoras*, *18*(2).

Hemmi, A., Bayne, S., & Land, R. (2009). The appropriation and repurposing of social technologies in higher education. *Journal of Assisted Learning*, *25*(Special Issues), 19–30. doi:10.1111/j.1365-2729.2008.00306.x

Hernandez, R. M. (2017). Impacto de las TIC en la educación: Retos y Perspectivas. *Propósitos y Representaciones*, *5*(1), 325–347. doi:10.20511/pyr2017.v5n1.149

Ismail, I., Mohammed Idrus, R. & Mohd Johari, S. (2010). Acceptance on Mobile Learning via SMS: A Rasch Model Analysis. *iJIM - International Journal of Interactive Mobile Technologies*, *4*, 10-16.

Jimoyiannis, A., & Komis, V. (2007). Examinig teacher's beliefs about ICT in education of a teacher preparation programme. *Teacher Development*, *11*(2), 149–173. doi:10.1080/13664530701414779

Kanuka, H., & Anderson, T. (1999). Using constructivism in technology mediated learning: constructing order out of the chaos in the literature. International Journal of Radical Pedagogy, 1(2), 34-46.

Kay, R. (2006). Evaluatting strategies user to incorporate technology into preservice education: A review of the literature. *Journal of Research on Technology in Education, 38*(4), 383. doi:10.1080/15391523. 2006.10782466

Kumar, L. S., Jamatia, B., Aggarwal, A. K., & Kannan, S. (2011). Mobile Device Intervention for Student Support Services in Distance Education Context - FRAME Model Perspective. *European Journal of Open, Distance and E-Learning.*

Ligi, B. & Raja, B. (2017). Mobile learning in higher education. *International Journal of Research Granthaalayah, 5*(4)SE, 1-6.

Lucena, S. (2016). Digital cultures and mobile technologies in education. *Educar em Revista, Curitiba, Brasil, 59,* 277–290. doi:10.1590/0104-4060.43689

Mayberry, J., Hergis, J., Bolles, L., Dugas, A., O'neill, D., Rivera, A., & Meler, M. (2012). Exploring teaching and learning using an iTouch mobile device. *Active Learning in Higher Education, 13*(3), 203–217. doi:10.1177/1469787412452984

Miranda, G. L. (2009). Concepção de conteúdos e cursos Online. Ensino Online e aprendizagem multimédia. *Relógio D'Água,* 81-110.

Miranda, M., & Torres, M. (2009). *La plataforma virtual como estrategia para mejorar el rendimento escolar de los alunos en la I. E. P Coronel José Joaquín Inclán de Piura. Revista Digital Sociedad de la Información, 15.* Edita Crefalea.

Monteiro, A. (2012). O processo de Bolonha e o trabalho pedagógico em plataformas digitais: possíveis implicações. In *Educação online. Pedagogia e aprendizagem em plataformas digitais* (2nd ed.). De facto editores.

Morais, C., Alves, P., & Miranda, L. (2013). Valorização dos ambientes virtuais de aprendizagem por professores do ensino superior. In A. Rocha, L. Reis, M. Cota, M. Painho, & M. Neto (Eds.), Sistemas e Tecnologias de Informação, Atas da 8a Conferência Ibérica de Sistemas e Tecnologias de Informação. 1 (pp. 289-294). Lisboa: Associação Ibérica de Sistemas e Tecnologias de Informação.

Morais, N., & Cabrita, I. (2008). B-Learning: impacto no desenvolvimento de competências no ensino superior politécnico. *Revista de Estudos Politécnicos, 6*(9).

Moran, J. (2002). *O que é o ensino a distância.* Retrieved from http://www.eca.usp.br/prof/moran/dist.htm

Moran, J. (2006). Ensino e aprendizagem inovadores com tecnologias audiovisuais e telemáticas. In Novas Tecnologias e Mediação Pedagógica. São Paulo: Papirus Editora.

Moura, A., & Carvalho, A. (2010). Twitter: A productive and learning tool for the SMS generation. In C.M. Evans (Ed.), Internet Issues: Blogging, the Digital Divide and Digital Libraries. Nova Science Publishers.

Mwakapina, J., Mhandeni, A., & Nyinondi, O. (2016). WhatsApp Mobile Tool in Second Language Learning: Opportunities, potentials and challenges in Higher Education Settings in Tanzania. *International Journal of English Language Education*, 4(2). doi:10.5296/ijele.v4i2.9711

Noor-Ul-Amin, S. (2013). An effective use of ICT for education and learning by drawing on worldwide knowledge, research and experience: ICT as a change agent for education (A Literature review). *Scholarly Journal of Education*, 2(4), 38–45.

Oliveira, E., Rego, M., & Villardi, R. (2007). Aprendizagem mediada por ferramentas de interacção: Análise do discurso de professores em um curso de formação continuada a distância. *Educação & Sociedade. Scielo Brasil*, 28(101), 1413–1434.

Pachler, N., Pimmer, C., & Seipold, J. (2011). *Work-based mobile learning: concepts and cases*. Bern, Switzerland: Peter-Lang. doi:10.3726/978-3-0353-0496-1

Palloff, R., & Pratt, K. (2005). *Learning Together in Community: Collaboration Online*. San Francisco, CA: Jossey-Bass.

Pulford, B. (2011). The influence of advice in a virtual learning environment. *British Journal of Educational Technology*, 42(1), 31–39. doi:10.1111/j.1467-8535.2009.00995.x

Quinn, C. (2011). *Designing mLearning: Tapping into the mobile revolution for organizational performance*. San Francisco: Pfeiffer.

Ramos, F. (2007). Technology: Challenging the Future of Learning. In *Proceedings of eLearning Lisboa 2007*. Lisboa: Portuguese Presidency of the European Union.

Ricoy, M., & Couto, M. (2009). As tecnologias da informação e comunicação como recursos no Ensino Secundário: Um estudo de caso. *Revista Lusófona de Educação*, 14, 145–156.

Scanlon, E., Jones, A., & Waycott, J. (2005). Mobile technologies: Prospects for their use in learning in informal science settings. *Journal of Interactive Media in Education*, 25.

Shahzad, F. (2017). Modern and Responsive Mobile-enabled Web Applications. *Procedia Computer Science*, 110, 410–415. doi:10.1016/j.procs.2017.06.105

Sharples, M., Inmaculada, A. S., Milrad, M. & Vavoula, G. (2009). Mobile Learning. *Technology Enhanced Learning: Principles and Products*. Academic Press.

Souza, M. (2011). *Expert Oracle Application Express Plugins*. Apress.

World Wide Web Consortium - W3C. (2017). *Filereader API*. Retrieved from https://www.w3.org/TR/FileAPI/#dfn-filereader

Youssef, A., & Dahmani, M. (2008). The Impact of ICT on Student Performance in Higher Education: Direct Effects, Indirect Effects and Organisational Change. *Revista de Universidad y Sociedad del Conocimieneto*, 5(1), 45–56.

Zardini, A. (2016). O uso do WhatsApp na sala de aula de Língua Inglesa – relato de experiência em um curso de idiomas. Blucher Design Proceedings, 2(6), 224-235.

ADDITIONAL READING

Araújo, I., & Faria, P. (2017). Higher M@t-EduTutor a prototype of a platform to support tutoring at distance using mobile devices. *ICERI2017 Proceedings 10th annual International Conference of Education, Research and Innovation.*

Araújo, I., Faria, P., Araújo, S., & Oliveira, R. (2016). Adapting the "M@tEducate with Success" Platform to Mobile Learning of Mathematics in Higher Education. *EDULEARN16, Proceedings 8th annual International Conference on Education and New Learning.*

Araújo, I. I., & Cabrita, I. (2015). Motivation for Learning Mathematics in Higher Education Through the "M@tEducate with Success" Platform. In *EDULEARN15 (Proceedings 6th annual International Conference on Education and New Learning Technologies.*

Faria, P. M., Araújo, I., & Moreira, P. M. (2015). MULTISABES: Multimedia Learning by Playing. *ICERI2015 Conference Proceedings.*

Chapter 13

Lesion Boundary Segmentation With Artifacts Removal and Melanoma Detection in Skin Lesion Images

Julie Ann Acebuque Salido
De La Salle University, Philippines & Aklan State University, Philippines

Conrado Ruiz Jr.
De La Salle University, Philippines

Nelson Marcos
De La Salle University, Philippines

ABSTRACT

Melanoma is a severe form of skin cancer characterized by the rapid multiplication of pigment-producing cells. A problem on analysis of these images is interesting because of the existence of artifacts that produces noise such as hair, veins, water residue, illuminations, and light reflections. An important step in the diagnosis of melanoma is the removal and reduction of these artifacts that can inhibit the examination to accurately segment the skin lesion from the surrounding skin area. A simple method for artifacts removal for extracting skin lesion is implemented based on image enhancement and morphological operators. This is used for training together with some augmentation techniques on images for melanoma detection. The experimental results show that artifact removal and lesion segmentation in skin lesion images performed a true detection rate of 95.37% for melanoma skin lesion segmentation, and as high as 92.5% accuracy for melanoma detection using both GoogLeNet and Resnet50.

DOI: 10.4018/978-1-5225-9069-9.ch013

INTRODUCTION

Melanoma is a severe form of skin cancer characterized by the uncontrolled growth of pigment-producing cells. According to the American Cancer Society, there is an estimated 96,480 cases of melanoma of the skin, with about 52,220 in males and 39,260 in females. It is estimated that 7,230 people will die from melanoma in 2019 (Siegel et al., 2019). Melanoma is treatable when detected early, but advanced melanoma can spread to other internal organs, which can result to death. Dermoscopy is used as a non-invasive method (Johr, 2002) that allows an in vivo evaluation of colors and microstructures of the skin specifically the epidermis, dermoepidermal junction, and papillary dermis. Dermoscopy allows examination of the skin and its patterns. Skin cancers in the study of Papamichail et al. (2008) are categorized into two groups, melanoma and nonmelanoma. Melanoma appears as a painless, firm, non-tender, and ulcerated skin lesion. Highly-trained experts and professional equipment are necessary for accurate and early detection of melanoma. Limited access to expert consultation leads to additional challenges in providing adequate levels of care to the population that are at risk with this disease.

There are dermoscopic criteria developed to distinguish melanomas and moles, such as chaos and clues (Rosendahl et al., 2012), 3-point checklist (Soyer et al., 2004), ABCD rule (Stolz et al., 1994), 7-point checklist (Argenziano et al., 2004), Menzies method (Menzies et al., 1996) and CASH (Argenziano et al., 2004). The ABCDE rule based on the works of Argenziano et al. is used for lesion feature identification: asymmetry, border irregularity, color that is not uniform, dermoscopic attributes, and evolving size, shape or color. Dermoscopic attributes or structures of lesions such as, pigment network, negative network, streaks, melia-like cysts, globules and dots among others.

Recent trends in dermoscopy images since 2016 until 2018 (Berseth, 2017) lead to a newest and better technique in classification. This is because of the challenge of skin lesion analysis towards Melanoma Detection in 2017 International Symposium on Biomedical Imaging (ISBI). For the past years, the International Skin Imaging Collaboration (ISIC): Melanoma Project (Gutman et al., 2016), have been doing a skin lesion boundary segmentation task. Skin lesions digital images can be used to educate clinicians, physicians, professionals and the public in melanoma as well as skin cancer recognition. This will directly aid in the diagnosis of melanoma through teledermatology, clinical decision support, and automated diagnosis. At present, the lack of standards for dermatologic imaging undermines the quality and usefulness of skin lesion imaging. ISIC is developing proposed standards to address the technologies, techniques, and terminology used in skin imaging with special attention to the issues of privacy and interoperability.

Recent advances in diagnostic techniques including confocal scanning laser microscopy, MelaFind, Siascopy, noninvasive genomic detections, among others are used in aid in diagnosing melanoma. Some of these technologies cost as much as US$500 per person for examination (Ferris & Harris, 2012). There are several studies that implement traditional telemedicine across the world especially in the developing countries, but the efforts have been characterized with challenges such as the high-cost of sustaining telemedicine solutions and insufficient access to medical expertise when needed. In recent years, there have been high expectations for techniques such as dermoscopy in aiding diagnosis. However, evaluation of pigmented skin lesions is not only expensive to other communities but also complex and highly subjective, thus motivating researches in diagnosis automation. The advances of smartphones and ordinary cameras led to implementation of other applications for skin disease classification.

The most challenging tasks are skin border detection or skin lesion boundary segmentation (Abbas et al., 2011; Argenziano et al., 2003) especially on skin images from ordinary or regular camera. Due to the presence of artifacts that creates noise such as veins, hairs, illuminations, and light reflections, it is difficult to do automatic border detection and image segmentation of lesion on skin images.

Almost all researches on melanoma classification that were in top spot on classification: convolutional neural network (CNN), and some pretrained image model such as AlexNet, GoogLeNet, ResNet, and VGG, with just a slight difference of a micro units in each criterion identified. Analysis of the segmentation results does not reflect the number of images where automated segmentation falls outside the observer's variability. Analysis on the classification of skin images that deep learning approaches performs better when combined with additional augmented data.

In this chapter, a simple method to detect and segment lesion boundary from skin images using image analysis on ordinary skin images is employed for melanoma detection. The lesion segmentation technique is tested on DermIS (Diepgen & Eysenbach, 1998) and DermQuest (Galderma, 2014) datasets. Some examples of regular skin images are shown in Figure 1.

The chapter is organized as follows. In the background, information about the preprocessing techniques that can be applied on the dataset and lesion segmentation and image correction algorithms for digital skin images are presented. In the artifact removal and lesion segmentation section, described are the dataset used in both melanoma and nonmelanoma skin images, artifacts identification, removal and noise reduction, area restoration, and the skin lesion boundary segmentation. Results of the implementation with numerical analysis are presented in the solutions and recommendation section, and last section includes the research future directions and conclusions.

BACKGROUND

The section presents an overview of current methods on lesion boundary segmentation on skin images. It also describes the preprocessing, segmentation, image reconstruction, and lesion segmentation used in the study.

Figure 1. Sample of digital skin images of melanoma and nonmelanoma from DermIS and DermQuest

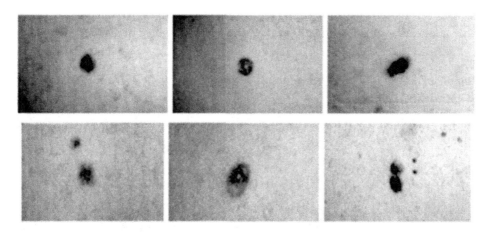

Preprocessing

In pre-processing, color space transformation is an important step in skin images. The skin image colors are in RGB (red, green, blue) values, either directly (in an RGB image) or indirectly (in an indexed image, where the colormap is stored in RGB format). CIELAB color space are identified (Foster, 2008) as the lightness, L*, represents the darkest black at L* = 0, and the brightest white at L* = 100, as maximum luminosity. The color channels, a* and b*, will represent true neutral gray values at a* = 0 and b* = 0. The red/green opponent colors are represented along the a* b* axis, with green at negative a* values and red at positive a* values.

In regular skin images artifacts such as blood vessels, skin lines and illuminations, light reflections and the presence of hairs (see Figure 2) are visible. The direct way to remove these artifacts is to even and smoothen the image using a general-purpose filter such as the Gaussian Filter (GF) (Erkol et al., 2005), median (MF), or anisotropic diffusion filters (ADF) (Abbas et al., 2011). Artifacts in skin images such as luminosity, reflections and different devises lead to different specifications of color spaces for reduction or removal. The presence of these artifacts and noise in skin images could lead to erroneous lesion segmentation of images. Image reconstruction, scene completion or area restoration (Bertalmio et al., 2000; Drori et al.,2003; Shen et al., 2007). The task of restoring a missing part of an image using information from the known part, in this case the skin image minus the hair can be done using image inpainting technique. To repair the removed artifacts information from skin images, a harmonic inpainting method (Chan & Shen, 2001) is used for each color space.

Creating a mask for artifacts and filtering of noise identified are usually done followed by image multiplication. This step will create a new dermoscopy image minus the artifacts and noise identified. Then inpainting or area restoration on the new skin image will be performed. Lesion boundary segmentation will be performed in the new skin image using morphological operators. These will perform skin border detection from skin images. This will enable the system to check for the border and lesion skin structures and attributes identification or classification of the lesion and perform other testing for other attributes of the lesion. Detection of skin features such as color of melanoma can be done at specific boundary identified lesion segmentation.

Lesion Segmentation

Image segmentation is the process of dividing an image into multiple parts. This is used to recognize objects or other applicable information in digital images. The existence of artifacts and noise are a pre-

Figure 2. Example of digital images of melanoma and nonmelanoma from DermIS and DermQuest with artifacts and noise

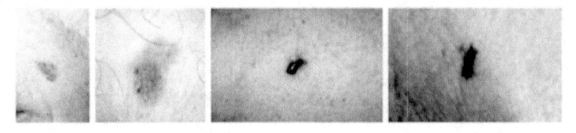

dominant problem in skin images. In this case, if a skin lesion has artifacts and noise, the skin lesion segmentation, pattern analysis and classification tasks will be affected. Thus, an automatic artifacts and noise reduction which preserve the lesion features while keeping the computational cost low for real-time implementation, is a must. The different means to accomplish image segmentation are using thresholding methods, color-based segmentation (Otsu, 1979), edge detection (Canny, 1987), and texture methods (Sonka et al., 2014).

Image Correction Algorithms for Digital Skin Images

The most recent correction algorithms for skin lesion images can only be applied to regular skin images, which already have some filtering due to the advance technology in cameras today. Rather than correcting illumination variation, the goals of these algorithms include color calibration (Haeghen et al., 2000) and normalization for improved lesion classification or contrast enhancement (Celebi et al., 2009) for improved lesion segmentation, that can be improved for use in regular skin images.

Pre-Trained Deep Learning Models

AlexNet

Krizhevsky et al. in 2012, was the first to initiate the use of GPU and parallelization scheme for faster execution of CNN consisting of up to 60M parameters and 650,000 neurons in the paper (Krizhevsky et al., 2012). The model is later named AlexNet. This model was trained to classify around 1.2 million training images of ImageNet (Deng et al., 2009) to 1000 different classes. The architecture has eight hidden layers, comprising of five convolutional and three fully-connected layers. The last fully-connected layer act as the classification layer, ending with a softmax activation function. Moreover, the Rectified Linear Unit (ReLU) non-linearity is applied to the output of every convolutional and fully-connected layer. Dropout that randomly selects nodes and sets their outputs to zero to deactivate the nodes was also used.

GoogLeNet

The GoogLeNet (Szegedy et al., 2015) created by the team led by Szegedy of Google and is the winner of ILSVRC 2014. GoogLeNet has a deeper network, comprising of 22 layers, but employs 12 times fewer parameters than AlexNet. GoogLeNet is based on inception architecture that was grounded on the Hebbian principle and the idea of multi-scale processing. It also makes use of dropout regularization in the fully-connected layer and applies the ReLU activation function in all convolutional layers.

ResNet50

Residual Network, (ResNet) (He et al., 2016) was developed by the Microsoft team led by He and is the winner of the ILSVRC 2015. With increasing depth, ResNet was able to solve the vanishing gradient and degradation problems. The network's depth has many variations including 34, 50, and 101, up to 152 layers. The popular one is ResNet50, containing 33 convolution layers and 1 fully connected layer at the end of the network. ResNet is founded on a traditional feed forward network with a residual connection. The network can be thought of as an ensemble machine of parallel/serial modules operating in blocks of smaller-depth layers. ResNet has no hidden fully connected layers. The network ends with a global average pooling layer and a 1000-way fully-connected layer with softmax activation function.

ARTIFACTS REMOVAL AND LESION SEGMENTATION

This section describes the dataset, preprocessing and artifacts identification, artifact removal and restoration, and lesion boundary segmentation for melanoma and nonmelanoma method from skin images, to lesion segmentation. Figure 3 shows the flow diagram of the lesion segmentation of skin images using image segmentation.

Dataset

The dataset used for lesion segmentation are from DermIS (Dermatology Information System, 2017) and DermQuest (Derm101, 2017). The skin images are of irregular sizes and are taken with different lightings and camera. Skin images are subdivided into melanoma and nonmelanoma from both database with ground truth. Example of skin images with binary ground truth (GT) image are shown in Figure 4. Melanoma skin images are 116 with 42 from DermIS and 74 from DermQuest, and 82 nonmelanoma images of which 24 are from DermIS and 58 from DermQuest. These images have varying illuminations and light reflections, some have veins and hair that overlaps with the lesion, and other parts of the body can be seen.

Image Preprocessing

The existence of hair is a predominant problem in some skin images. If a skin lesion is covered with hair, the skin lesion segmentation tasks will be affected. An automatic hair removal which preserves the lesion features using the technique in the study of (Salido & Ruiz Jr, 2017) is used for hair artifacts. A CEILAB color space also known as CIE L*a*b* is identified for use on skin images in the paper (Zarit et al., 1999), to process the first layer for brightness and illumination. Grayscale and binary images are used as different color space in some part of the new approach. This study converts the skin images to CEILAB to determine the maximum luminosity of the skin image, L* for the lightness, and a* and

Figure 3. Sample images during artifact removal and lesion segmentation for melanoma detection in skin lesion images

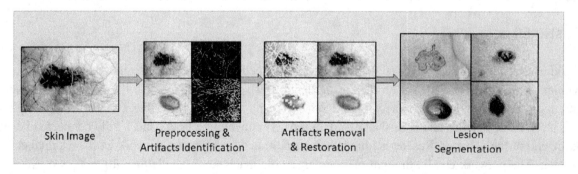

Figure 4. Example of skin images from DermIS and DermQuest with their ground truth

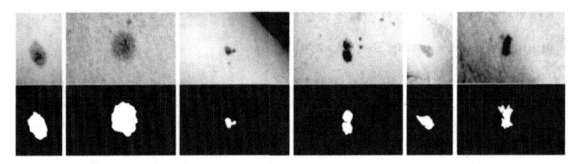

b* for the green–red and blue–yellow color components. We then determine the maximum luminosity using L* and discarded the value of a*b*, that is usually at a range from 0 to 100 and scaled to a range [0, 1] for the intensity of brightness. Then image adjustment is performed that maps the intensity values in grayscale image from the original skin image to new values in the updated skin image. A denoising technique using Gaussian filter is used for image filtering of shadows and unnecessary textures in skin image. Performed histogram matching to a defined image to denoise skin image before edge detection (see Figure 5).

Lesion Segmentation

Edge detection is performed after image enhancement done during image preprocessing to divide a skin images into multiple parts for lesion segmentation. The image segmentation is used to recognize objects or other applicable information in digital images. Edge detection is done using Canny technique with a threshold of 0.3 for all histogram match images from all 3 channels in RGB. Morphological operators such as image dilate using a line function of 0 degree to 90 degree. Image fill is done for all holes, image erosion is done with a disk size of three. The binary perimeter of the lesion is then taken to get the final border for the new segmented lesion. All connected components are then indexed, and the maximum connected components from the list of indexed elements is determined. The mask for the maximum

Figure 5. Sample of skin images during preprocessing, the first column are original images, 2nd column luminosity layer, 3rd column is the output in the Gaussian filter, and is the histogram match skin image

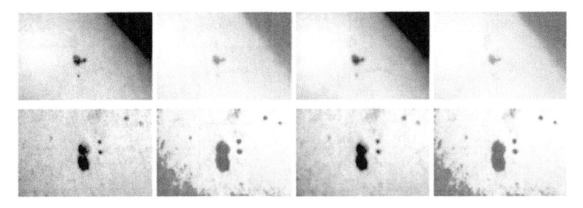

connected components of the skin image is created and added to the original image. The maximum connected components of the image become the new segmented lesion for the automatic border detected.

Melanoma Detection Using Deep Learning

Three deep learning models were implemented as discussed in the pre-trained models. The dataset was randomly divided into 70% training, 20% testing and 10% validation. To build a powerful skin lesion image classifier that avoids the effect of overfitting, given a limited number of images for training, augmentation techniques were used. Augmentation techniques such as rotation, flip, translation of images of 30x30 pixels, artifacts removal, lesion segmentation, and image enhancement technique such as image sharpening, local laplacian filter and image reducing haze are used. These augmentation techniques were able to increase the dataset of melanoma to 2,017 and nonmelanoma to 1,298 for training images only. The last three layers of each pre-trained model were fine-tuned to classify melanoma and nonmelanoma. To speed up learning, the weight and bias learning rate factors of the fully connected layer are both increased to 30. Stochastic gradient descent with momentum optimizer was used, with a mini-batch size of 10. The learning rate is initialized to 0.0001 and the models are trained up of to six epochs. Figure 6 shows the transfer learning workflow as employed in the study.

SOLUTIONS AND RECOMMENDATIONS

There are available lesion segmentation techniques in binary mask, as a reference image or ground truth (GT) with the same size of the original image. The GT in the dataset is used to evaluate the performance of the new approach. The artifact removal and lesion segmentation approaches are implemented in Matlab 9.2. The proposed method took in an average of 3 seconds to segment a skin image. All the computations and implementations were performed on a 2.8 GHz Intel(R) Core (TM) i7-7700HQ CPU

Figure 6. Transfer learning workflow for melanoma detection in skin lesion images

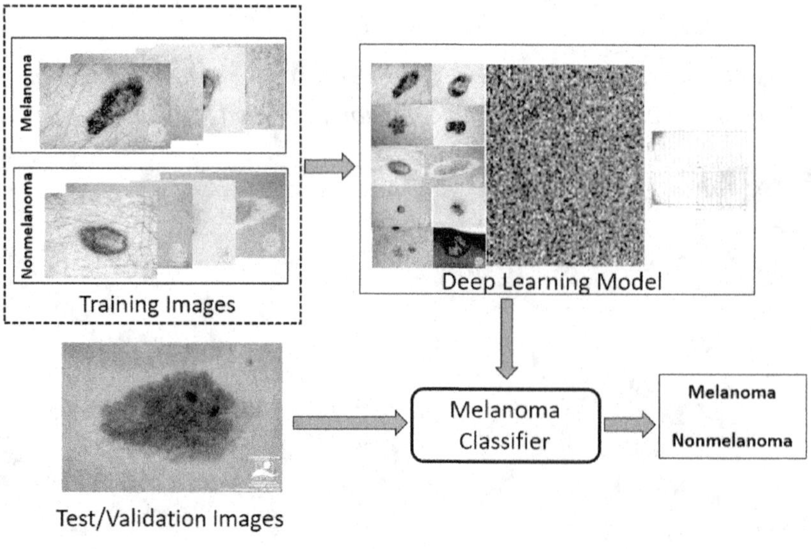

with 64-bit operating system, 20 GB RAM and NVDIA GeForce GTX 1050 video RAM, running on a Windows 10 Home edition. A quantitative evaluation is performed on segmentation by the statistical metrics. The border detection outcomes were compared with the reference images. As shown in Figure 2, one of the factors that complicate the detection of borders in skin images is insufficient detection of contrast between the lesion and the skin. Based on the new approach, it increased the contrast between the lesion and the background skin. This study takes two inputs: an RGB skin image X with n three-component pixels and its GT.

For the preprocessing results, some are shown in Figure 5. The first column shows the original skin image, the second column shows the luminosity layer, and corrected skin image using Gaussian filter, and the last column represents the output of image matching.

Lesion Segmentation

The results of the new method for lesion segmentation are shown in Figure 7. The respective columns of images show the original skin image, the corrected or enhanced skin image denoising and image

Figure 7. Example of results for the new method on lesion segmentation, the first column shows the original image, the second column shows the enhanced image, third column is the border detected, fourth column shows an original image with detected skin border and the fifth column is the skin lesion area considered as mask

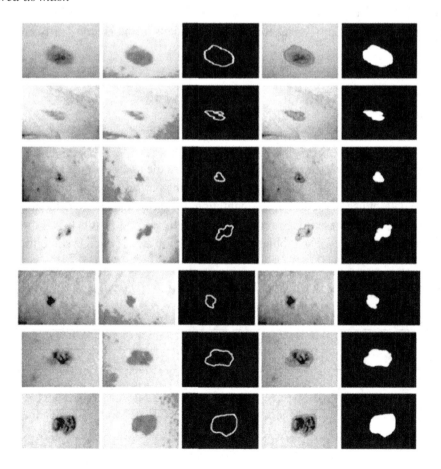

matching, the identified lesion border, the skin image with the lesion border detected, and the area of the identified skin lesion.

For the lesion segmentation analysis, we employed (Celebi et al., 2015). The mean border error (MBE), true detection rate (TDR) and the false detection rate (FDR). In MBE the study calculated the new segmented (NS) lesion disagree with GT using Eq. 1, where NS as new segment lesions and GT as the ground truth. Both the GT and NS are binary image of the lesion detected. The MBE gets mean of the exclusive-OR operation of both the area of the NS and GT.

$$MBE = \frac{area\left(NS\right) \oplus area\left(GT\right)}{area\left(GT\right)} \tag{1}$$

The TDR metric measures the rate of pixels classified by both (NS) lesions and GT using Eq. 2 (Galderma, 2014; Diepgen & Eysenbach, 1998). This solves the number of pixels of intersection of NS and GT to GT.

$$TDR = \frac{\# \left(NS \cap GT\right)}{\# \left(GT\right)} \tag{2}$$

The FDR metric measures the rate of pixels classified by NS and $\overline{GT}$ using Eq. 3 (Galderma, 2014; Diepgen & Eysenbach, 1998). This solves the number of pixels of intersection of NS and not in GT to GT.

$$FDR = \frac{\#\left(NS \cap \overline{GT}\right)}{\#\left(GT\right)} \tag{3}$$

The results of the three metrics are acceptable to measure the skin lesion segmented, with as much as 96.77% TDR and as low as 3.23% FDR. Table 1 shows the performance of the new approach on the skin images in the dataset used. The lesion segmentation difficulty lies on the detection of the different skin types, color, or texture. These image segmentations deliver good results based on the preliminary images using regular skin images. The problem lies on the lesion areas which is sometimes diffused with

Table 1. Results of performance in three metrics using artifact removal and lesion segmentation for melanoma detection in skin lesion images

Metric	Nonmelanoma	Melanoma
TDR (%)	96.77	95.37
FDR (%)	3.23	4.63
MBE	72.43	81.50

the skin and is not well separated from the skin. Because the lesion has two types of segmented regions overlapping each other, only the innermost regions are segmented.

Melanoma Detection Using Deep Learning

Two models obtained excellent performance with above 90% accuracy as shown in Table 2. Of the three, ResNet50 and GoogLeNet have both 92.7% accuracy. As discussed in the previous section, each model is varied with number of hidden layers where AlexNet has 8, GoogLeNet has 22, and 34 for ResNet50. This implies that the depth of the network is a significant factor in classifying skin lesion for melanoma. As shown in Figure 8, Resnet50 and GoogLeNet have converged almost to 100% before the final epoch of 40. For AlexNet, it took only 54 minutes to reach the final epochs with 8,280 iterations, and GoogLeNet with 82 minutes and 50 seconds to reach the final 8,280 iterations. ResNet50 took 371 minutes and 86 seconds to reach the final iterations of 26,520 with 40 epochs.

FUTURE RESEARCH DIRECTIONS

The emerging trends in mobile technology, smartphones and digital cameras make this area of research imperative and important. The current problem of creating a standard in skin images, its quality and interoperability attracts a global concern especially on the clinical diagnosis. In the future, more image segmentation methods for detecting lesion border on skin images may be explored. Possible enhancement on a model for classifying skin may also be useful, especially looking into the problem of varying skin color for different ethnicities. The possibilities of interoperability between regular skin images and dermoscopic images may also be explored.

CONCLUSION

This chapter presented a simple algorithm for lesion segmentation to detect melanoma in skin lesion images. In artifacts removal and noise reduction, the use of morphological operators and inpainting techniques are implemented. This is another approach shown to be as effective as other methods in detecting, removing, and correcting skin images for lesion segmentation. For lesion segmentation, the use of morphological operators, image enhancement, and matching technique were explored. This is an

Table 2. Results of performance in of accuracy during testing of three deep learning techniques for melanoma detection in skin lesion images

Deep Learning Model	Accuracy
AlexNet	78.0%
GoogLeNet	92.5%
ResNet50	92.5%

Figure 8. Performance of the training progress of the three deep learning models from (a) AlexNet, (b) GoogLeNet, and (c) ResNet50

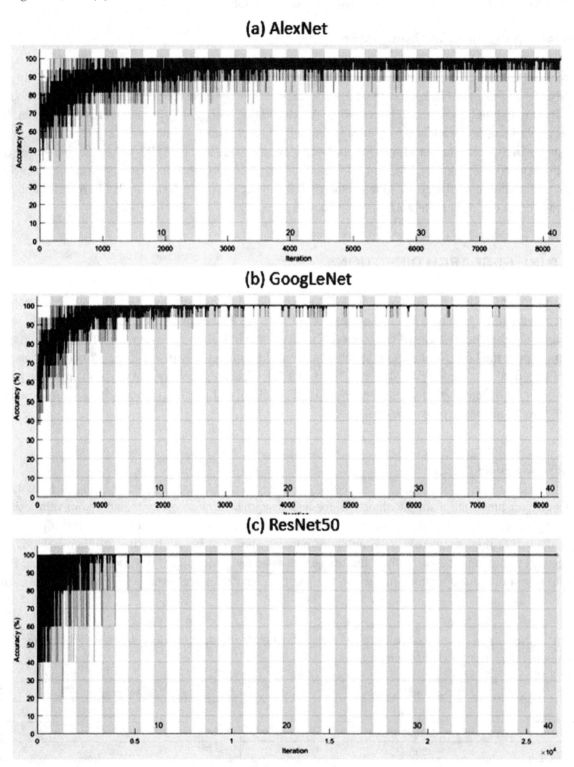

important pre-processing step in the identification and classification of melanomas since this is one of the features for clinical diagnosis. With a true detection rate of 96.77% for nonmelanoma and 95.37% for melanoma lesion segmentation, it indicates satisfactory skin lesion region recognition. ResNet50 and GoogLeNet reached an excellent accuracy performance of 92.5% for both validation and testing. For implementation purposes, GoogLeNet model outperformed ResNet50 in terms of time and space complexity.

REFERENCES

Abbas, Q., Celebi, M. E., & Garcia, I. F. (2011). Hair removal methods: A comparative study for dermoscopy images. *Biomedical Signal Processing and Control*, 6(4), 395–404. doi:10.1016/j.bspc.2011.01.003

Argenziano, G., Soyer, H. P., Chimenti, S., Talamini, R., Corona, R., Sera, F., ... Kopf, A. W. (2003). Dermoscopy of pigmented skin lesions: Results of a consensus meeting via the internet. *Journal of the American Academy of Dermatology*, 48(5), 679–693. doi:10.1067/mjd.2003.281 PMID:12734496

Argenziano, G., Zalaudek, I., Corona, R., Sera, F., Cicale, L., Petrillo, G., ... Soyer, H. P. (2004). Vascular structures in skin tumors: A dermoscopy study. *Archives of Dermatology*, 140(12), 1485–1489. doi:10.1001/archderm.140.12.1485 PMID:15611426

Berseth, M. (2017). *Isic-skin lesion analysis towards melanoma detection*. arXiv preprint arXiv:1703.00523

Bertalmio, M., Sapiro, G., Caselles, V., & Ballester, C. (2000). Image inpainting. In *Proceedings of the 27th annual conference on Computer graphics and interactive techniques* (pp. 417-424). ACM Press/Addison-Wesley Publishing Co.

Canny, J. (1987). A computational approach to edge detection. In *Readings in Computer Vision* (pp. 184–203). Elsevier.

Celebi, M. E., Iyatomi, H., & Schaefer, G. (2009). Contrast enhancement in dermoscopy images by maximizing a histogram bimodality measure. In *Image Processing (ICIP), 2009 16th IEEE International Conference on* (pp. 2601-2604). IEEE. 10.1109/ICIP.2009.5413990

Celebi, M. E., Mendonca, T., & Marques, J. S. (2015). *Dermoscopy image analysis* (Vol. 10). CRC Press. doi:10.1201/b19107

Chan, T. F., & Shen, J. (2001). Nontexture inpainting by curvature-driven diffusions. *Journal of Visual Communication and Image Representation*, 12(4), 436–449. doi:10.1006/jvci.2001.0487

Deng, J., Dong, W., Socher, R., Li, L. J., Li, K., & Fei-Fei, L. (2009, June). ImageNet: A large-scale hierarchical image database. In *Computer Vision and Pattern Recognition, 2009. CVPR 2009. IEEE Conference on* (pp. 248-255). IEEE. 10.1109/CVPR.2009.5206848

Derm101.com. (2017). Retrieved from https://www.derm101.com

Dermatology information system. (2017). Retrieved from https://www.dermis.net/dermisroot/en/home/indexp.htm

Diepgen, T. L., & Eysenbach, G. (1998). Digital images in dermatology and the dermatology online atlas on the World Wide Web. *The Journal of Dermatology*, *25*(12), 782–787. doi:10.1111/j.1346-8138.1998. tb02505.x PMID:9990769

Drori, I., Cohen-Or, D., & Yeshurun, H. (2003). Fragment-based image completion. In ACM Transactions on graphics (TOG) (pp. 303-312). ACM. doi:10.1145/1201775.882267

Erkol, B., Moss, R. H., Joe Stanley, R., Stoecker, W. V., & Hvatum, E. (2005). Automatic lesion boundary detection in dermoscopy images using gradient vector of snakes. *Skin Research and Technology*, *11*(1), 17–26. doi:10.1111/j.1600-0846.2005.00092.x PMID:15691255

Ferris, L. K., & Harris, R. J. (2012). New diagnostic aids for melanoma. *Dermatologic Clinics*, *30*(3), 535–545. doi:10.1016/j.det.2012.04.012 PMID:22800557

Gutman, D., Codella, N. C., Celebi, E., Helba, B., Marchetti, M., Mishra, N., & Halpern, A. (2016). *Skin lesion analysis toward melanoma detection: A challenge at the international symposium on biomedical imaging (ISBI) 2016, hosted by the international skin imaging collaboration (ISIC).* arXiv preprint arXiv:1605.01397

Haeghen, Y. V., Naeyaert, J. M. A. D., Lemahieu, I., & Philips, W. (2000). An imaging system with calibrated color image acquisition for use in dermatology. *IEEE Transactions on Medical Imaging*, *19*(7), 722–730. doi:10.1109/42.875195 PMID:11055787

He, K., Zhang, X., Ren, S., & Sun, J. (2016). Deep residual learning for image recognition. In *Proceedings of the IEEE conference on computer vision and pattern recognition* (pp. 770-778). IEEE.

Johr, R. H. (2002). Dermoscopy: Alternative melanocytic algorithms the ABCD rule of dermatoscopy, Menzies scoring method, and 7-point checklist. *Clinics in Dermatology*, *20*(3), 240–247. doi:10.1016/ S0738-081X(02)00236-5 PMID:12074859

Krizhevsky, A., Sutskever, I., & Hinton, G. E. (2012). ImageNet classification with deep convolutional neural networks. In Advances in neural information processing systems (pp. 1097-1105). Academic Press.

Menzies, S. W., Ingvar, C., Crotty, K. A., & McCarthy, W. H. (1996). Frequency and morphologic characteristics of invasive melanomas lacking specific surface microscopic features. *Archives of Dermatology*, *132*(10), 1178–1182. doi:10.1001/archderm.1996.03890340038007 PMID:8859028

Otsu, N. (1979). A threshold selection method from gray-level histograms. *IEEE Transactions on Systems, Man, and Cybernetics*, *9*(1), 62–66. doi:10.1109/TSMC.1979.4310076

Papamichail, M., Nikolaidis, I., Nikolaidis, N., Glava, C., Lentzas, I., Marmagkiolis, K., & Digalakis, M. (2008). Merkel cell carcinoma of the upper extremity: Case report and an update. *World Journal of Surgical Oncology*, *6*(1), 32. doi:10.1186/1477-7819-6-32 PMID:18328106

Rosendahl, C., Cameron, A., McColl, I., & Wilkinson, D. (2012). Dermatoscopy in routine practice: 'chaos and clues'. *Australian Family Physician*, *41*, 482. PMID:22762066

Salido, J. A. A., & Ruiz, C. Jr. (2017). Using morphological operators and inpainting for hair removal in dermoscopic images. In *Proceedings of the Computer Graphics International Conference* (p. 2). ACM. 10.1145/3095140.3095142

Shen, J., Jin, X., Zhou, C., & Wang, C. C. (2007). Gradient based image completion by solving the Poisson equation. *Computers & Graphics*, *31*(1), 119–126. doi:10.1016/j.cag.2006.10.004

Siegel, R. L., Miller, K. D., & Jemal, A. (2018). Cancer statistics, 2018. *CA: a Cancer Journal for Clinicians*, *68*(1), 7–30. doi:10.3322/caac.21442 PMID:29313949

Sonka, M., Hlavac, V., & Boyle, R. (2014). *Image processing, analysis, and machine vision*. Cengage Learning.

Soyer, H. P., Argenziano, G., Zalaudek, I., Corona, R., Sera, F., Talamini, R., ... Chimenti, S. (2004). Three-point checklist of dermoscopy. *Dermatology (Basel, Switzerland)*, *208*(1), 27–31. doi:10.1159/000075042 PMID:14730233

Stolz, W., Riemann, A., Cognetta, A., Pillet, L., Abmayr, W., Holzel, D., ... Landthaler, M. (1994). Abcd rule of dermatoscopy-a new practical method for early recognition of malignant-melanoma. *European Journal of Dermatology*, *4*, 521–527.

Szegedy, C., Liu, W., Jia, Y., Sermanet, P., Reed, S., Anguelov, D., & Rabinovich, A. (2015). Going deeper with convolutions. In *Proceedings of the IEEE conference on computer vision and pattern recognition* (pp. 1-9). IEEE.

Zarit, B. D., Super, B. J., & Quek, F. K. (1999). Comparison of five color models in skin pixel classification. In *Recognition, Analysis, and Tracking of Faces and Gestures in Real-Time Systems, 1999. Proceedings. International Workshop on* (pp. 58-63). IEEE. 10.1109/RATFG.1999.799224

Section 3
User Experience and Usability Studies

Chapter 14

"Think of the Children!":
The Relationship Between Visual Complexity, Age, Visual Aesthetics, and Learning Motivation With Regard to Children

Hsiu-Feng Wang
National Chiayi University, Taiwan

ABSTRACT

This experiment examined children's visual aesthetics and learning motivation with regard to websites. It applied Berlyne's theory of aesthetic preference to these websites. The experiment explored the relations between visual complexity, visual aesthetics, learning motivation, and children's age, and their effect on websites. A total of 150 children between 10 and 12 years old were involved. The children were asked to rate websites of different levels of perceived visual complexity in terms of visual aesthetic and learning motivation. The results showed that the children preferred websites that displayed a medium level of perceived visual complexity to those that displayed a high or low level of perceived visual complexity. Thus, the results supported Berlyne's theory. However, when aesthetic preference was analyzed with respect to age-related differences, it was found that older children preferred a medium level of perceived visual complexity and younger children preferred a high level of perceived visual complexity.

INTRODUCTION

Recent years have seen an increasing number of children's educational institutions introducing e-learning websites. In order for these websites to be useful they need to be informative; they also need to be usable and attractive. However, while much research has been conducted into the usability of websites (Pee, Jiang, & Klein, 2018; Hasan, 2016; Hart, Chaparro & Halcomb, 2008), little has been carried out into their visual appeal. Research that has been undertaken includes studies into overall impressions (Schenkman & Jönsson, 2000; Tractinsky, Katz & Ikar, 2000), the importance of aesthetics with respect to the layout of the website design (Tuch, Bargas-Avila & Opwis, 2010) and the effect of aesthetics on

DOI: 10.4018/978-1-5225-9069-9.ch014

website (Lopatovska, 2015; Chang, Chih, Liou & Hwang, 2014). Research has also been conducted into users' preferences with regard to perceived visual complexity in websites; however, most of this work has involved adults (see Michailidou, Harper, & Bechhofer, 2008; Pandir & Knight, 2006). As such, little is known of children's appreciation of visual aesthetics with respect to perceived visual complexity in websites and whether varying levels of visual complexity affect their learning motivation. Furthermore, little is known about whether the effect of visual aesthetics with respect to website design changes with age.

Given the various aspects of visual aesthetic influence, the perceptions of websites, and the dearth of research conducted in this area (Tractinsky, 2013), the goal of the current study is to provide a better understanding of the relations between visual complexity, visual aesthetics, learning motivation, and children's age, and their effect on children's websites. In particular, it addresses the following question: what levels of visual complexity (high, medium, and low) and age groups (4th grade and 6th grade) can enhance children's appreciation of visual aesthetics, and their learning motivation on learning websites? The findings are expected to be applicable in a wide range of situations in which researchers, practitioners and children's educators needs to design better websites to motivate children's learning.

BACKGROUND

Visual Complexity and Visual Aesthetics

Aesthetics have been found to play an important role in web design, product design and learning environments. Tractinsky (2013) defined the term "visual aesthetics" as "an artistically beautiful or pleasing appearance on the visual senses". There have been various approaches to the study of aesthetics in HCI and these have resulted in a number of theories (Udsen & Jørgensen, 2005), one of which was Berlyne's theory. Berlyne (1971) published a psychobiological theory of aesthetics which proposed that aesthetic preference is related to the arousal potential of a stimulus and that people prefer medium levels of arousal to low and high levels. Berlyne argued that arousal potential was a function of a number of different "collative variables" (Berlyne, 1971, p.141), one of which was perceived visual complexity.

Since Berlyne formulated his theory, a number of researchers have explored perceived visual complexity in relation to aesthetic preference and websites. In an experiment that involved websites taken from domains such as museums and educational establishments, Wang and Lin (2019) found that children preferred websites that had a medium level of perceived visual complexity to websites that had either a low or high level of visual complexity. Accordingly, their results supported Berlyne's theory. Chassy, Lindell, Jones and Paramei (2015) also conducted an experiment with university students. They were shown 50 images of car fronts and asked to rate them for visual complexity and aesthetic pleasure. The results found that there was a positive relationship between visual complexity and their ratings for aesthetic pleasure. An early experiment conducted by Kaplan, Kaplan and Wendt (1972) obtained comparable results. In their experiment, adult participants were asked to evaluate photographs of landscapes; the researchers found that the participants preferred photographs that had a medium level of perceived complexity to those that did not. Geissler, Zinkhan and Watson (2006) also tested Berlyne's theory. In their study 360 students evaluated home pages that had been specifically created using Netscape Navigator Composer to have different levels of visual complexity. The researchers discovered that the students responded more favourably to the home pages that had been created with a medium level of perceived visual complexity than to those that had been created with a high or low level of perceived complexity. In other words, like Wang and Lin (2019), Chassy, Lindell, Jones and Paramei (2015) and Kaplan, Kaplan and Wendt (1972), the researchers found that Berlyne's theory was supported. However, it should be noted that not all researchers have found that the findings of their experiments support Berlyne's theory. Pandir and Knight (2006) conducted an experiment in which participants ranked paper print-outs of home pages according to their perceived visual complexity, interest and the degree to which they pleased the viewer. The researchers found that while there was strong agreement amongst participants as to which home pages were visually complex and which were not, there was little agreement as to which home pages were pleasing and which were not. As such, Berlyne's theory was not supported. Tuch, Bargas-Avila, Opwis and Wilhelm (2009) also conducted an experiment that involved participants evaluating home pages. Participants were shown a number of home pages of varying levels of perceived visual complexity on a computer screen and, amongst other things, were asked to rate each one for the pleasure it elicited. The researchers found a negative linear relationship between perceived visual complexity and pleasure. Thus, the data did not support Berlyne's theory.

The above paragraphs illustrate that there is a lack of consistency in the literature with respect to results that relate to visual complexity: some experiments support Berlyne's theory while others do not. This suggests that more research is needed in this area. Therefore, we hypothesize that:

Hypothesis One: Different levels of visual complexity in websites will impact on children's appreciation of the visual aesthetics.

Hypothesis Two: Children will be influenced by different factors of visual aesthetic with regard to websites.

Learning Motivation, Aesthetics, and Visual Complexity

Motivation is recognized as being an important component of learning. Pintrich and Schunk (1996) commented that it not only influences why people learn but how they learn. Motivation has been found to help people perform better in instructional environments (Sankaran & Bui, 2001). Pintrich (2003) explains that the word 'motivation' comes from the Latin word 'movere' meaning 'to move'. Hence, motivation can be explained as that which moves (that is, incites) people to behave in a certain way. In psychology, a distinction is made between intrinsic and extrinsic motivation. Intrinsic motivation is that which drives people to do something because it is inherently satisfying; whereas extrinsic motivation is that which drives people to do something because it leads to a separable outcome, such as a work promotion, money or grades (Ryan & Deci, 2000; Williams, Burden & Lanvers, 2002).

Ryan and Deci (2000) stated that intrinsic motivation exists between people and activities. People were intrinsically motivated when the activities were interesting, because they gained the satisfactions from intrinsically motivated task engagement. Thus the reward was in the activity itself. Researchers investigated what task characteristics made an activity interesting. Renninger, Hidi and Krapp (1992) suggested that competence and control, interest and intrinsic motivation were the key ways to motivate students to learn. Research on interestingness has shown that making learning tasks and materials interesting results in higher levels of cognitive engagement and higher levels of achievement (Hidi, 1990; Pintrich & Schunk, 2002). Making learning materials aesthetically appealing was assumed to be one way to make them interesting. Deubel's (2003) study proposed a range of theoretical perspectives for providing interface design guidelines for learning with multimedia. One of the guidelines clearly indicated that a quality user-interface for a learning environment has a strong impact on the learning experience and increases the amount of knowledge retained (Vilamil-Casanova & Molina, 1996). David and Glore (2010) reported that the aesthetics of course materials, such as the layout and the use of graphics, were important in motivating students to learn in a web-based learning environment. More support was provided by an empirical study by Zain, Tey and Goy (2007) which suggested that aesthetics impact upon children's learning motivation; they also found that children are more motivated by web-pages with good aesthetics than web-pages with poor aesthetics. Thus, we hypothesize that:

Hypothesis Three: There is a relationship between children's visual aesthetic appreciation of a website and their learning motivation.

A considerable body of evidence shows that there is a relationship between the visual complexity of an object and an individual's affective aspects such as visual aesthetics (discussed in above section). Among these relations with visual aesthetics are the numbers of elements in art pictures (Osborne & Farley, 1970; Roberts, 2007), the layout of websites (Tuch et al., 2009; Pandir & Knight, 2006; Seckler, Opwis, & Tuch, 2015), and the visual complexity of virtual actors (Kartiko, Kavakli & Cheng, 2010). Thus, following on from the previous discussion, learning materials with appropriate levels of visual complexity are likely to enhance a person's intrinsic learning motivation. Chang, Lin and Lee (2005) provided research evidence to support this idea. They conducted an experiment to explore the different levels of visual complexity and learning motivation in relation to English learning for young children, and their results showed that an image with a higher level of visual complexity enhanced their learning motivation. In a study by Harp and Mayer (1997), students learned about how lightning is formed. Those who learned from many detailed visual images found the learning materials were interesting, but they performed worse than students who learned from simple visual images. Therefore, predicated on the above, it is plausible that different levels of visual complexity are related to learning motivation. Thus, a hypothesis was formed as follows:

Hypothesis Four: Different levels of visual complexity in websites will have an impact upon children's learning motivation.

Age Differences

A number of studies have looked at differences between adults and children with respect to website design (Jo and Han, 2006; Nielsen, 2015). However, in the majority of these studies children are not divided into age groups. It is thus possible that certain age-related issues with regard to the design of websites have been overlooked.

Piaget was the first psychologist to make a systematic study of child cognitive development (Encyclopaedia Britannica, 2013). He claimed that child cognitive development could be divided into four stages and he called the last two stages "the concrete-operational stage" and "the formal operational stage" (Piaget, 1930). Piaget declared that the concrete-operational stage typically started when a child was 7 and lasted for around four years. He maintained that a child in this stage was capable of logical thought and was able to understand physical laws, such as reversibility and transitivity, but was incapable of abstract thought. Piaget argued that it was not until a child reached 11, the formal operational stage, that he/she was able to think scientifically and was capable of constructing abstract theories. Keeping these cognitive differences in mind, it seems conceivable that children of these ages might respond differently to the same websites.

Jolley, Zhi and Thomas (1998) explored how people's focus of interest in illustrations changes with age. Four different age groups were shown a number of illustrations depicting everyday objects and were asked to pair illustrations in "the most important and interesting way" (Jolley, Zhi and Thomas, 1998, p.137). Having done this, the participants were asked why they had paired the illustrations in the way they did. The age groups were: 4-year-olds, 7-year-olds, 10-year-olds and an adult group in which most people were aged between 18 and 25 years. The experiment involved British and Chinese participants. The researchers found that the different age groups tended to focus on different aspects of the illustrations. For example, the 4-year-olds paired illustrations more often by color compared with the other age groups and the 7-year-olds paired illustrations by subject matter more often than the 4-year-olds and the 10-year-olds. In a later study, Lin and Thomas (2002) investigated how people of different ages and educational backgrounds responded to different genres of art. In their experiment, which extended Parsons' (1987) work, the researchers showed 5 sets of postcards to 100 individuals. Each set of postcards showed a different genre of art. The genres shown were: abstract art, fine art, modern art, humorous art and cartoon art. Each participant was assigned to one of five groups according to their age and educational background. The groups were: 4 to 5-year-olds, 8 to 9-year-olds, 12 to 13-year-olds, undergraduate students not studying art and undergraduate students studying art. The researchers found that the differences between the groups with respect to the level of emotional expression they exhibited when shown the postcards (that is, all the genres) were "very large and highly significant" (Lin & Thomas, 2002, p.284). In other words, they found that different aged children (and adults with different educational backgrounds) reacted differently when shown the same images.

Considering that variation has been found in the way different aged children think, react to art, judge illustrations and respond to age related content issues online, it seems reasonable to assume that they might have different preferences when it comes to website aesthetics. The following hypotheses were offered:

Hypothesis Five: Children of different ages will be affected by websites with different levels of visual complexity.

Hypothesis Six: Children of different ages will be motivated by websites with different levels of visual complexity.

Learning Motivation

ARCS is a model that focuses on motivation; it was developed by Keller (1983). The model, which is well-known and widely applied in the field of instructional design (Small, 2000), offers four strategies for boosting and sustaining learner motivation. These strategies are: Attention, Relevance, Confidence and Satisfaction. Attention strategies are those used to arouse students; they include games, the use of humour and the use of storytelling. Relevance strategies are those that help students to recognise the importance of what they are learning; for example, by explaining how the new learning can be used in their lives. Confidence strategies are those that help students believe in themselves; they include giving feedback that contains words of encouragement. Satisfaction strategies are those that offer students a sense of achievement; they include organising real-life opportunities for students in which they can apply their newly acquired knowledge/skills.

In order that instructional materials can be assessed in terms of their motivational characteristics, Keller developed the Instructional Material Motivational Survey (IMMS) (see Keller, 2010). The survey measures students' thoughts about their motivation for studying learning materials. It does this using 36 statements to which students are asked to indicate their level of agreement. The statements relate to the four components of the ARCS model (Attention, Relevance, Confidence and Satisfaction). The survey has been used by a number of researchers (for example, Cook, Beckman, Thomas & Thompson, 2009). However, research by Huang, Huang, Diefes-Dux and Imbrie (2006) indicates that the survey, which was originally created for paper-based learning materials, needs only 20 statements to be effective when applied to computer-based learning materials. Keller's study suggested that the survey statements should be modified to allow for context. We used statements from IMMS to evaluate the learning motivation of children.

Visual Aesthetic

The Visual Aesthetics of Websites Inventory (VisAWI), which was developed by Moshagen and Thielsch (2010), is one of the commonly used multiple-item measures used to assess visual aesthetics in a website. They identified four factors which influenced users' perceived visual appreciation of website aesthetics. First, the simplicity scale measured the orderliness in website design and included unity, clarity and how well structured a website design was. It is closely related to the classical aesthetic which was defined by Lavie and Tractinsky (2004) in a study which discussed visual aesthetics in websites. In their research, they identified two main factors of visual website aesthetics. One is "classical aesthetic", it explored the traditional views of aesthetics, such as well-organized design and good proportions. The other is "expressive aesthetics" which reflected the expression of the designers' creativity and originality. The principle of the "expressive aesthetic" also appears in Moshagen and Thielsch's research as "diversity". This factor is the perception of the designer's creativity in website design and comprises the variety and creativity in a website. The next factor is colorfulness, which refers to the combination of colors used in a website; it includes the selection of color and the attractiveness of color. The last factor is craftsmanship, and it refers to how the website has been designed, relating to coherent integration and design with skill and care.

METHOD

Participants

A total of 150 children participated in the experiment. They all attended the same school in Taichung, Taiwan. Seventy-five were 4th grade students, aged between 10 and 11 years (M=10.46, SD=.45), they were 37 girls and 38 boys. There were seventy-five 6th grade students, aged between 12 and 13 years (M=12.52, SD=.39), 37 girls and 38 boys in the group. All the children used computers regularly both at home and at school. They all had computer lessons at least twice a week, played computer games and used the Internet. After completing the experiment, each participant received a small toy for his/her participation.

Experimental Design

The experiment employed a 3 x 2 between-subject design. The independent variables were visual complexity and age. Visual complexity had three levels: high, medium and low. Age had two levels: young (4th grade elementary students) and older (6th grade elementary students). There were two dependent variables, which were visual aesthetics and learning motivation. Visual aesthetics had four factors: simplicity, diversity, colorfulness and craftsmanship. Learning motivation had three factors: attention, relevance and confidence.

Materials

The experiment involved each child examining a set of three web-pages with the same level of visual complexity, designed by the experimenter. Children were randomly assigned to one of those three levels of visual complexity. In total three sets were created: a set with a high level of visual complexity, a set with a medium level of visual complexity and a set with a low level of visual complexity. In addition to these three sets a further set was created to help the children familiarize themselves with the experimental procedure and their equipment prior to the experiment commencing. In this paper, this familiarization exercise has been called the 'practice trial'. The three sets of web-pages that were used in the experiment were on the topic of nutrition. The words in each set of web-pages were identical and were adapted from a 4th grade text book. While the three web-pages in each set could have been constructed as one long web-page, this was not done as Nielsen (2010) states that children dislike lengthy texts and scrolling. The text contained 792 words (approximately 260-270 words per page) and was written in 14-point. The three different levels of complexity were created with reference to the work of Geissler, Zinkhan and Watson (2006). The researchers found that the more images, visible links and Top Left Corners (TLCs) that a web-page contained, the more visually complex people perceived it to be. Hence, the set that had a high level of visual complexity was created using many of these elements, the set that had a medium level of visual complexity was created using fewer of these elements and the set that had a low level of visual complexity was created using hardly any at all (see Figure 1).

Figure 1. Different levels of visual complexity websites used in the experiment

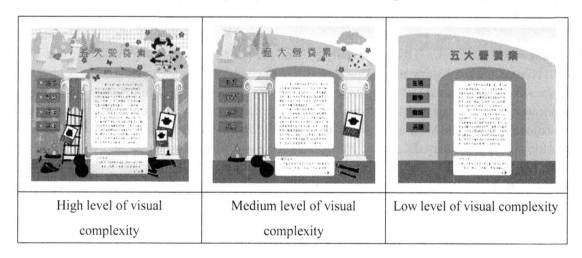

| High level of visual complexity | Medium level of visual complexity | Low level of visual complexity |

The visible links when clicked took the children to The Concise Chinese Dictionary online (http://dict. concised.moe.edu.tw/). It should be noted that Geissler et al. found that the number of words a web-page contained also affected its visual complexity. However, as the experimenter wanted all the children to read the same information, the number of words in each set was the same. Below each web-page was a number of simple multiple choice questions. These were included to ensure that each child read the text.

Procedure

The study was carried out in a computer lab with groups of 15 children in 10 sessions. Each child had his/her own computer and worked alone. Each session lasted no more than 20 minutes and started with the practice trial. The trial involved the children viewing the practice materials and answering multiple-choice questions about them. The questions were straightforward; for example, "What kind of vitamin can keep our bones healthy and strong?" The questions were written on-screen below each web page and required the children to click their mice to answer them. When the author was content that everybody could use his/her equipment satisfactorily, the experiment started. The experiment involved every child viewing the three sets of web pages (i.e. the high visual complexity set, the medium visual complexity set and the low visual complexity set) in a random order and answering the questions below them. The children were told that they could take as long as they wanted to answer the questions and that they could move from one web page to the next using the 'Arrow' button and should click the 'Done' button when finished. Following this, a questionnaire was distributed. Each statement in the questionnaire was explained verbally using simple language to aid understanding. For example, the statement saying, "the colors are appealing" was explained to the children as meaning, "the coolers in the web pages are nice and attractive". The children completed the questionnaire independently. Before leaving the room, each child filled out a short form. The form asked the child for his/her age, gender, reasons for using computers and the amount of time he/she used a computer each week. During the sessions no child showed signs of fatigue.

The Questionnaire

In the experiment a questionnaire was used to collect information from participants. The questionnaire, which was written in Chinese, had three parts. The first part asked children to rate the visual aesthetics of the web-pages they viewed using 7 point Likert scales. The scales ranged from 1 (strongly agree) to 7 (strongly disagree). It used 16 questions (which were modified slightly so the children could understand them more easily) taken from the questionnaire called the Visual Aesthetics of Website Inventory (VisAWI) constructed by Moshagen and Thielsch (2010). The VisAWI was used to assess the perception of visual aesthetics, which had four different factors: simplicity, diversity, colorfulness and craftsmanship. The second part of the questionnaire measured learning motivation based on the Instructional Material Motivational Survey (IMMS), which was developed by Huang et al. (2006) in a study that looked at motivation in computer-based learning. The questionnaire was adapted by Wang, Shih & Ke (2010), for use by Taiwanese children and has been used by other researchers (e.g. Kuo and Wang, 2015; Wang, Bowerman & Yang, 2015). It was this adapted questionnaire that was used in the experiment. It also employed 7- points Likert scales to capture participants' levels of agreement with statements about the web-pages' learning motivation. Four different factors were explored: attention, confidence, relevance and satisfaction. The final part of the questionnaire collected demographic information. It asked children to state their age, gender, reasons for using computers and the amount of time they used a computer each week.

Instrument Validity and Reliability

Principal Component Analysis with varimax rotation is used to examine the construct validity of questionnaires. As a rule of thumb, an item is significant and retained in the questionnaire if its loading coefficient is above 0.6 and without cross loading (Hair, Anderson, Tatham & Black, 1995). In order to ensure construct validity, the items in the visual aesthetic questionnaire (VisAWI) were reduced from the initial 18 items to 16 due to a low loading, one item from the simplicity factors and one item from the craftsman factors. In addition, the learning motivation questionnaire (IMMS) was reduced from the initial 20 items to 14 items. All of the satisfaction factors (six items) were dropped because they exhibited low item loading. The attention factors retained six items, relevance factors retained three items and confidence factors retained five items.

Construct reliability was assessed using Cronbach's α -value for both visual aesthetic and learning motivation questionnaires. After the removal of invalid items, the Cronbach's α for visual aesthetics indicated that the scales used for simplicity scored 0.81, for diversity 0.77, for colorfulness 0.78, and for craftsmanship 0.74. The reliability of learning motivation for attention was 0.86, for relevance 0.81, and for confidence 0.86. Nunnally (1978) recommends that the Cronbach's α reliability of the scale should be greater than 0.7 for items to be used together as a construct. The constructs of both questionnaires passed the construct reliability test in this study.

RESULTS

A two-way ANOVA was carried out to evaluate the effect of visual complexity and participants' age in terms of differences in mean scores, and Scheffé post-hoc comparison was used to test for differences between the various levels of visual complexity. The mean and standard deviation for the rating of visual aesthetic factors and learning motivation were illustrated in Table 1.

Overall Visual Aesthetic

The results showed that there was an interaction between children's age and the different levels of visual complexity had a significant effect on overall visual aesthetic, as illustrated in Figure 2, and a significant main effect for the different levels of perceived visual complexity, $F(2, 144) = 14.452, p=.000, \eta^2=.167$, see Table 2. The overall visual aesthetic ratings for the different levels of visual complexity were the medium level of perceived visual complexity, followed by the high level of perceived visual complexity, and last, the low level of perceived visual complexity. It seems that younger children preferred a high level of visual complexity, followed by a medium level of visual complexity, whereas older children preferred a medium level of visual complexity to a high level of visual complexity.

Table 1. Descriptive statistics for visual aesthetic factors, learning motivation, age and visual complexity

	4th grade		6th grade			4th grade		6th grade	
	M	*SD*	*M*	*SD*		*M*	*SD*	*M*	*SD*
Overall aesthetic					*Overall motivation*				
High	4.31	.49	4.26	.54	High	4.29	.33	4.23	.34
Medium	4.37	.65	4.55	.56	Medium	4.18	.33	4.42	.32
Low	3.93	.56	4.28	.48	Low	4.01	.27	4.00	.25
Simplicity					*Attention*				
High	4.31	.49	4.26	.54	High	4.31	.60	4.27	.41
Medium	4.37	.65	4.55	.56	Medium	4.61	.73	3.94	.46
Low	3.93	.56	4.28	.48	Low	4.05	.73	4.04	.64
Diversity					*Relevance*				
High	4.13	.67	4.43	.78	High	3.95	.55	4.40	.59
Medium	4.09	.62	4.62	.57	Medium	4.29	1.37	4.41	1.03
Low	4.08	.44	3.75	.73	Low	3.87	.67	4.12	.54
Colorful					*Confidence*				
High	4.46	.76	4.11	.55	High	4.51	1.09	4.24	.97
Medium	4.16	.54	4.25	.41	Medium	4.18	1.32	4.45	.71
Low	3.84	.54	3.97	.52	Low	3.96	.61	4.12	.47
Craftsman									
High	4.28	.66	4.11	.61					
Medium	4.11	.70	4.27	.62					
Low	4.17	.44	3.96	.49					

Simplicity

The results showed that a main effect for the different levels of perceived visual complexity was significant, $F (2, 144) = 5.219$, $p = .006$, $\eta^2 = .068$. The simplicity factor ratings for the different levels of visual complexity were the medium level of perceived visual complexity, followed by the high level of perceived visual complexity, and last, the low level of perceived visual complexity. However, no difference was found between the simplicity factor ratings for children's age.

Diversity

The results showed that an interaction between children's age and the different levels of visual complexity had a significant effect on diversity factors, as illustrated in Figure 3, and a significant main effect for the different levels of perceived visual complexity, $F (2, 144) = 6.557$, $p = .002$, $\eta^2 = .083$, see Table 3. The diversity factor ratings for the different levels of visual complexity were the medium level of perceived visual complexity, followed by the high level of perceived visual complexity, and last, the low level of perceived visual complexity. It seems that diversity factor ratings made by older children were affected by the different levels of visual complexity, $F (2, 72) = 10.619$, $p = .000$, $\eta^2 = .228$. In contrast,

Figure 2. Interaction plot. Overall aesthetic ratings for different levels of visual complexity and age

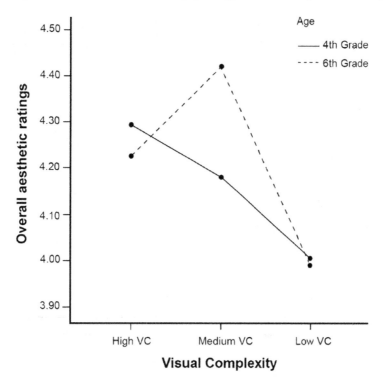

Table 2. Results of ANOVA on overall aesthetics

Sources of variance	df	Mean Square	F value	p value	η^2
Main effects					
Age	1	.102	1.095	.297	.008
Visual complexity	2	1.352	14.452	.000‡	.167
Two-way interactions					
Age x Visual complexity	2	.337	3.603	.030*	.048
Errors	144	.094			

*p<.05. ‡p<.001.

younger children were not affected by the different levels of visual complexity. Older children preferred a medium level of visual complexity, followed by a high level of visual complexity, and last, the low level of perceived visual complexity. In addition, older children evaluated diversity factors higher than younger children.

Colorfulness and Craftsmanship

Analysis of variance showed that the different levels of perceived visual complexity were significant, $F(2, 144) = 6.284$, $p=.002$, $\eta^2=.080$. The colorfulness factor ratings for the different levels of visual com-

Figure 3. Interaction plot: diversity factor ratings for different levels of visual complexity and age

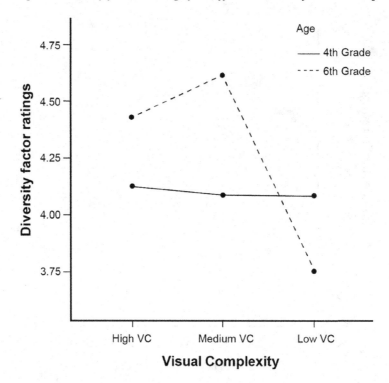

Table 3. Results of ANOVA on diversity factors

Sources of variance	*df*	Mean Square	*F* value	*p* value	η^2
Main effects					
Age	1	1.058	2.541	.113	.017
Visual complexity	2	2.731	6.557	.002*	.083
Two-way interactions					
Age x Visual complexity	2	2.463	5.913	.003*	.076
Errors	144	.417			

*p<.05.

plexity were the high level of perceived visual complexity, followed by the medium level of perceived visual complexity, and last, the low level of perceived visual complexity. However, no difference was found between the colorfulness factor ratings for children's age. No different levels of visual complexity were identified for craftsmanship factors. Additionally, no difference was found between high levels of visual complexity and the participant's age.

Overall Learning Motivation

The results also showed that there was a significant difference between children's learning motivation and three levels of perceived visual complexity $F (2, 144) = 7.089, p=.001, \eta^2=.090$. The overall learning motivation ratings for the different levels of visual complexity were the medium level of perceived visual complexity, followed by the high level of perceived visual complexity, and last, the low level of perceived visual complexity.

Attention

An interaction between children's age and the different levels of visual complexity was found for attention factors, F (2, 144) =4.749, p=.010, η^2=.062. This interaction was illustrated in Figure 4. A significant main effect for the participant's age was also found for attention factors, F (2, 144) =5.989, p=.016, η^2=.040, see Table 4. The attention factor ratings for older children were higher than for younger children. Looking at age separately, for younger children, there was a significant difference between different levels of visual complexity and attention factors, F (2, 144) =4.162, p=.019, η^2=.104. In contrast, older children were not affected by the different levels of visual complexity in relation to attention factors.

Overall Learning Motivation

The results also showed that there was a significant difference between children's learning motivation and three levels of perceived visual complexity F (2, 144) = 7.089, p=.001, η^2=.090. The overall learning motivation ratings for the different levels of visual complexity were the medium level of perceived visual complexity, followed by the high level of perceived visual complexity, and last, the low level of perceived visual complexity.

Figure 4. Interaction plot: attention factor ratings for different levels of visual complexity and age

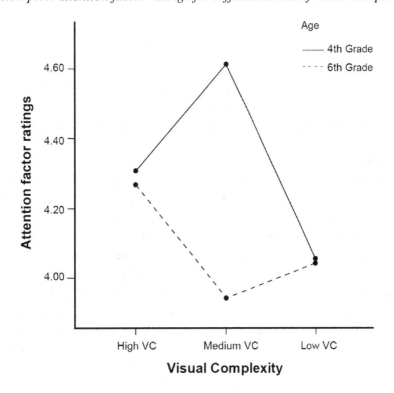

Table 4. Results of ANOVA on attention factors

Sources of variance	df	Mean Square	F value	p value	η^2
Main effects					
Age	1	2.200	5.989	.016*	.040
Visual complexity	2	1.843	2.509	.085	.034
Two-way interactions					
Age x Visual complexity	2	3.489	4.749	.010*	.062
Errors	144	.367			

*p<.05.

Relevance and Confidence

Analyses identified a main effect for relevance factor ratings. Older children rated relevance factor higher than younger children, $F (2, 144) =3.958$, $p=.049$, $\eta^2=.027$. No effect of different levels of visual complexity and participant's age was found for confidence factors.

Correlation Between Visual Aesthetics and Learning Motivation

Pearson's correlation analysis was used to identify the correlation between visual aesthetic ratings and learning motivation. The results showed a positive correlation between visual aesthetic ratings and learning motivation, $r=.217$, $p=.008$. There was also a significant correlation between diversity factors and confidence factors, $r=.211$, $p=.010$.

DISCUSSION

The experiment examined the influence of two variables-visual complexity and children's age-on children's perception of visual aesthetics and learning motivation in relation to children's learning websites. It also tested Berlyne's theory of aesthetic preference: a theory which claims that people prefer a medium level of stimuli to a high or low level of stimuli. A number of interesting results arose from this analysis in relation to children's learning websites. These results are discussed further below.

Some other work has already been done on the question of which visual aesthetics characteristics affect evaluations of website design (Tractinsky & Lavin, 2004). In this study we examined some of those characteristics, and explored the visual aesthetics taking into account four factors: *simplicity, diversity, colorfulness* and *craftsmanship*. In general, the results indicated that different levels of visual complexity had an impact on visual aesthetics (**H1**). Overall, children preferred websites that had a medium level of visual complexity. This finding supported Berlyne's theory and the finding from Wang and Lin (2018) and Wang and Bowerman (2012). A more in depth analysis of the data revealed that children preferred websites that had a medium level of perceived visual complexity with respect to *simplicity* and *diversity* (**H2**). The result reflects the finding that the more attractive websites were associated with these two factors (Tractinsky, Cokhavi, Kirschenbaum & Sharfi, 2006). According to Moshagen and Thielsch (2010), *Simplicity* refers to the traditional interpretation of aesthetic factors, communicating a sense of well organised layout and good proportions, which are highly correlated with usability. The other aesthetic factor was *diversity*, which associated with artistic point of view, and represented creativity, fascination and original design. Clearly, the websites with *diversity* related visual aesthetics interfaces may have produced positive reactions in users, and given the interface a sense of novelty. However, when a website is designed without *simplicity* aesthetic factors in mind (such as unity and clarity), users cannot find information easily, and this leads to basic usability problems. Thus, some general advice can be given. They should balance their websites, incorporating creativity and originality, but at the same time keeping the layout well organized and well proportioned.

The results showed that with respect to *diversity* visual aesthetic ratings, older children preferred the websites that had a medium level of perceived visual complexity, whilst younger children showed no preference for different levels of perceived visual complexity **(H5)**. Thus, in this case, Berlyne's theory was supported only for older children. One possible explanation for why these children perceived diversity visual aesthetics differently is that they were in different stages of cognitive development. When looking at the results relating to age issues, it was noticed that the younger children were 10.5 year-olds in this study, which would place them in Piaget's concrete-operational stage. This would mean that they were capable of understanding physical laws but incapable of abstract thought. On the other hand, the older children in this study were 12.5 year-olds, so in Piaget's formal operational stage, which would mean that they were able to think scientifically and were capable of constructing abstract theories. It is possible that these differences may have occurred because the younger children's abstract thought had not fully developed, so they were unable to judge diversity factors (such as the concepts of creativity and originality) properly. When children reach 11 years old, the formal operational stage, they are able to construct abstract concepts. Thus, they would be able to show their diversity aesthetic judgements with regard to the websites.

There were differences between younger and older children regarding the *relevance* and *attention* motivation factors; older children gave a higher rating than younger children in relation to the *relevance* motivation factor **(H6)**. Instructional designers have used some strategies to encourage students to learn. *Relevance* is one of these, because it can help students to recognize the importance of what they are learning and how it can be used in their lives (Keller, 1983). If students can recognize that the knowledge they are learning is relevant to what they are using, they will be willing to learn. Thus, it is important that students have some previous knowledge of the subject to help them to make the connection to the new knowledge. In general, older children have more computer experience compared with younger children. Thus, due to the degree of that experience, older children gave a higher rating than younger children.

The relationship between a user's appreciation of a website's visual aesthetics and his/her learning motivation was also investigated in this study; the data indicated that visual aesthetics play an important role in learning motivation **(H3)**. The finding that visual aesthetics and learning motivation are correlated provides statistical support for guidelines for learning with multimedia, which were previously based on a theoretical perspective (Deubel, 2003). This result also supported those of an empirical study by Zain, Tey and Goy (2007) which suggested that aesthetic websites can increase children's learning motivation.

The findings also found that the impacts of different levels of visual complexity in websites influenced children's learning motivation with respect to those websites **(H4)**. This finding is similar to that of Chang, Lin and Lee (2005) who, in an experiment which investigated the different levels of visual complexity and learning motivation related to English learning for young children, found that an image with a higher level of visual complexity enhanced their learning motivation.

CONCLUSION

The purpose of the current study is to provide a better understanding of the relations between visual complexity, visual aesthetics, learning motivation and children's age, and their effect on children's websites. The results identified that different levels of visual complexity have a significant impact upon the relationship between children's appreciation of visual aesthetics and children's age. The data showed that children considered that the websites with medium levels of visual complexity were more aesthetically appealing. The results also demonstrated that there were age-related differences with regard to their appreciation of the visual aesthetics and learning motivation of these websites.

This experiment was conducted using three different levels of visual complexity which were developed by the experimenter. Nonetheless, it is highly likely, due to the different levels between the visual complexities used in the testing websites, that the findings of the experiment would be different if the test were repeated. More studies with larger and more varied samples are needed. Moreover, it should be noted that participants' classification of website samples can be prejudiced by their familiarity rather than by visual complexity, as Berlyne's theory suggested that familiarity is another factor which can alter the user's preferences towards websites.

This study contributes to the limited body of work that relates to the designing of websites that enhance children's learning motivation and enrich their appreciation of the visual aesthetic. The findings of this experiment should be useful to practical educators, instructional designers and web designers who wish to create better learning websites for children, especially when they aim to design for different ages.

ACKNOWLEDGMENT

This experiment was kindly supported by a grant from the Ministry of Science and Technology in Taiwan (contract number: MOST107-2410-H-415-031). The author would like to thank Julian Bowerman for his support and comments on the manuscript and Sue Coxhill for her helpful English proof-reading.

REFERENCES

Berlyne, D. E. (1971). *Aesthetics and psychobiology*. New York: Appleton Century Crofts Publishing.

Chang, S. H., Chih, W. H., Liou, D. K., & Hwang, L. R. (2014). The influence of web aesthetics on customers' PAD. *Computers in Human Behavior*, *36*, 168–178. doi:10.1016/j.chb.2014.03.050

Chang, Y.-M., Lin, C.-Y., & Lee, Y.-K. (2005). The preferences of young children for images used in dynamic graphical interfaces in computer-assisted English vocabulary learning. *Displays*, *26*(4-5), 147–152. doi:10.1016/j.displa.2005.06.002

Chassy, P., Lindell, T. A., Jones, J. A., & Paramei, G. V. (2015). A relationship between visual complexity and aesthetic appraisal of car front images: An eye-tracker study. *Perception*, *44*(8-9), 1085–1097. doi:10.1177/0301006615596882 PMID:26562922

Cook, D. A., Beckman, T. J., Thomas, K. G., & Thompson, W. G. (2009). Measuring motivational characteristics of courses: Applying Keller's Instructional Materials Motivation Survey to a web-based course. *Academic Medicine, 84*(11), 1505–1509. doi:10.1097/ACM.0b013e3181baf56d PMID:19858805

David, A., & Glore, P. (2010). *The impact of design and aesthetics on usability, credibility, and learning in an online environment*. Retrieved from http://www.westga.edu/~distance/ojdla/winter134/david_glore134.html

Deubel, P. (2003). An investigation of behaviorist and cognitive approaches to instructional multimedia design. *Journal of Educational Multimedia and Hypermedia, 12*(1), 63–90.

Encyclopaedia Britannica. (2013). Retrieved from http://global.britannica.com/EBchecked/topic/459096/Jean-Piaget

Geissler, G. L., Zinkhan, M. Z., & Watson, R. T. (2006). The influence of home page complexity on consumer attention, attitudes, and purchase intent. *Journal of Advertising, 35*(2), 69–80. doi:10.1080/00913367.2006.10639232

Hair, J. F., Anderson, R. E., Tatham, R. L., & Black, W. C. (1995). *Multivariate data analysis with readings*. Prentice-Hall Press.

Harp, S., & Mayer, R. (1997). The role of internet in learning from scientific text and illustrations: On the distinction between emotional interest and cognitive interest. *Journal of Educational Psychology, 89*(1), 92–102. doi:10.1037/0022-0663.89.1.92

Hart, T. A., Chaparro, B. S., & Halcomb, C. G. (2008). Evaluating websites for older adults: Adherence to 'senior-friendly' guidelines and end-user performance. *Behaviour & Information Technology, 27*(3), 191–199. doi:10.1080/01449290600802031

Hasan, B. (2016). Perceived irritation in online shopping: The impact of website design characteristics. *Computers in Human Behavior, 54*, 224–230. doi:10.1016/j.chb.2015.07.056

Hidi, S. (1990). Interest and its contribution as a mental resource for learning. *Review of Educational Research, 60*(4), 549–571. doi:10.3102/00346543060004549

Huang, W.-H., Huang, W.-Y., Diefes-Dux, H., & Imbrie, P. K. (2006). A preliminary validation of Attention, Relevance, Confidence and Satisfaction model-based Instructional Material Motivational Survey in a computer-based tutorial setting. *British Journal of Educational Technology, 37*(2), 243–259. doi:10.1111/j.1467-8535.2005.00582.x

Jo, M., & Han, J. (2006). Metaphor and Typeface Based on Children's Sensibilities for e-Learning. *International Journal of Information Processing Systems, 2*(3), 178–182. doi:10.3745/JIPS.2006.2.3.178

Jolley, R. P., Zhi, Z., & Thomas, G. V. (1998). How focus of interest in pictures changes with age: A cross-cultural comparison. *International Journal of Behavioral Development, 22*(1), 127–149. doi:10.1080/016502598384540

Kaplan, S., Kaplan, R., & Wendt, S. (1972). Rated preference and complexity for natural and urban visual material. *Perception & Psychophysics, 12*(4), 354–356. doi:10.3758/BF03207221

Kartiko, I., Kavakli, M., & Cheng, K. (2010). Learning science in a virtual reality application: The impacts of animated-virtual actors' visual complexity. *Computers & Education, 55*(2), 881–891. doi:10.1016/j.compedu.2010.03.019

Keller, J. M. (1983). Motivational design of instruction. In C. M. Reigeluth (Ed.), *Instructional design theories and models: an overview of their current status* (pp. 386–434). Hillsdale, NJ: Lawrence Erlbaum Associates.

Keller, J. M. (2010). *Motivational design for learning and performance: The ARCS model approach.* Boston, MA: Springer US. doi:10.1007/978-1-4419-1250-3

Kuo, C. Y., & Wang, L. T. (2015). The study of visual preferences on illustrations in the "Nature and Life Technology" textbook for 3rd and 4th grade elementary school. [in Chinese]. *The Journal of Aesthetics & Visual Arts, 7*, 141–158.

Lavie, T., & Tractinsky, N. (2004). Assessing dimensions of perceived visual aesthetics of web sites. *International Journal of Human-Computer Studies, 60*(3), 269–298. doi:10.1016/j.ijhcs.2003.09.002

Lin, S. F., & Thomas, G. V. (2002). Development of understanding of popular graphic art: A study of everyday aesthetics in children, adolescents, and young adults. *International Journal of Behavioral Development, 26*(3), 278–287.

Lopatovska, I. (2015). Museum website features, aesthetics, and visitors' impressions: A case study of four museums. *Museum Management and Curatorship, 30*(3), 191–207. doi:10.1080/09647775.2015.1042511

Michailidou, E., Harper, S., & Bechhofer, S. (2008). Visual complexity and aesthetic perception of web pages. In *SIGDOC '08: Proceedings of the 26th annual ACM international conference on Design of communication* (pp. 215-224). ACM. 10.1145/1456536.1456581

Moshagen, M., & Thielsch, M. T. (2010). Facets of visual aesthetics. *International Journal of Human-Computer Studies, 68*(10), 689–709. doi:10.1016/j.ijhcs.2010.05.006

Nielsen, J. (2015). *Children (Ages 3-12) on the Web* (3rd ed.). Retrieved from https://www.nngroup.com/reports/children-on-the-web/

Nunnally, J. C. (1978). *Psychometric Theory* (2nd ed.). New York: McGraw Hill.

Osborne, W. J., & Farley, F. H. (1970). The relationship between aesthetic preference and visual complexity in abstract art. *Psychonomic Science, 19*(2), 69–70. doi:10.3758/BF03337424

Pandir, M., & Knight, J. (2006). Homepage aesthetics: The search for preference factors and the challenges of subjectivity. *Interacting with Computers, 18*(6), 1351–1370. doi:10.1016/j.intcom.2006.03.007

Parsons, M. J. (1987). *How we understand art: A cognitive developmental account of aesthetic experience.* Cambridge, UK: Cambridge University Press.

Pee, L. G., Jiang, J., & Klein, G. (2018). Signaling effect of website usability on repurchase intention. *International Journal of Information Management, 39*, 228–241. doi:10.1016/j.ijinfomgt.2017.12.010

Piaget, J. (1930). *The Child's Conception of Physical Causality.* London: Routledge & Kegan Paul.

Pintrich, P. R. (2003). A motivational science perspective on the role of student motivation in learning and teaching contexts. *Journal of Educational Psychology*, *95*(4), 667–686. doi:10.1037/0022-0663.95.4.667

Pintrich, P. R., & Schunk, D. H. (1996). *Motivation in education*. Englewood Cliffs, NJ: Prentice Hall.

Pintrich, P. R., & Schunk, D. H. (2002). *Motivation in education: Theory, research, and applications* (2nd ed.). Upper Saddle River, NJ: Prentice Hall.

Renninger, K. A., Hidi, S., & Krapp, A. (1992). *The role of interest in learning and development*. Hillsdale, NJ: Erlbaum.

Roberts, M. N. (2007). *Complexity and aesthetic preference for diverse visual stimuli* (PhD thesis). Departament de Psicologia, Universitat de les Illes Balears.

Ryan, R. M., & Deci, E. L. (2000). Intrinsic and extrinsic motivations: Classic definitions and new directions. *Contemporary Educational Psychology*, *25*(1), 54–67. doi:10.1006/ceps.1999.1020 PMID:10620381

Sankaran, S. R., & Bui, T. (2001). Impact of learning strategies and motivation on performance: A study in web-based instruction. *Journal of Instructional Psychology*, *28*, 191–198.

Schenkman, B., & Jönsson, F. (2000). Aesthetics and preferences of web pages. *Behaviour & Information Technology*, *19*(5), 367–377. doi:10.1080/014492900750000063

Seckler, M., Opwis, K., & Tuch, A. (2015). Linking objective design factors with subjective aesthetics: An experimental study on how structure and color of websites affect the facets of users' visual aesthetic perception. *Computers in Human Behavior*, *49*, 375–389. doi:10.1016/j.chb.2015.02.056

Small, R. V. (2000). Motivation in instructional design. *Teacher Librarian*, *27*, 29–31.

Tracinsky, N., Cokhavi, A., Kirschenbaum, M., & Sharfi, T. (2006). Evaluating the consistency of immediate aesthetic perceptions of web pages. *International Journal of Human-Computer Studies*, *64*(11), 1071–1083. doi:10.1016/j.ijhcs.2006.06.009

Tractinsky, N. (2013). Visual Aesthetics. In M. Soegaard & R. F. Dam (Eds.), *The Encyclopedia of Human-Computer Interaction* (2nd ed.). Aarhus, Denmark: The Interaction Design Foundation.

Tractinsky, N., Katz, A. S., & Ikar, D. (2000). What is beautiful is usable. *Interacting with Computers*, *13*(2), 127–145. doi:10.1016/S0953-5438(00)00031-X

Tuch, A. N., Bargas-Avila, J. A., & Opwis, K. (2010). Symmetry and aesthetics in website design: It's a man's business. *Computers in Human Behavior*, *26*(6), 1831–1837. doi:10.1016/j.chb.2010.07.016

Tuch, A. N., Bargas-Avila, J. A., Opwis, K., & Wilhelm, F. H. (2009). Visual complexity of websites: Effects on users' experience, physiology, performance, and memory. *International Journal of Human-Computer Studies*, *67*(9), 703–715. doi:10.1016/j.ijhcs.2009.04.002

Udsen, L. E., & Jørgensen, A. H. (2005). The aesthetic turn: Unravelling recent aesthetic approaches to human-computer interaction. *Digital Creativity*, *16*(4), 205–216. doi:10.1080/14626260500476564

Vilamnil-Casanova, J., & Molina, L. (1996). An interactive guide to multimedia. In Que Education and Training (pp. 124-129). Academic Press.

Wang, H. F., & Bowerman, C. J. (2012). The Impact of Perceived Visual Complexity on Children's Websites in Relation to Classical and Expressive Aesthetics. In *IADIS International Conference IADIS Interfaces and Human Computer Interaction 2012* (pp. 269-273). Lisbon: Inderscience Publishers.

Wang, H. F., Bowerman, J., & Yang, F. J. (2015). Do learning websites reflect users' aesthetic preferences? In C. Stroupe (Ed.), *Tenth International Conference on the Arts in Society 2015.* (pp. 1-5). Champaign, IL: The Arts in Society.

Wang, H. F., & Lin, C. H. (2019). An investigation into visual complexity and aesthetic preference to facilitate the creation of more appropriate learning analytics systems for children. *Computers in Human Behavior*, *92*, 706–715. doi:10.1016/j.chb.2018.05.032

Wang, H. F., Shih, L. H., & Ke, Y. H. (2010). A study on the visual appeal of children's website with user performance and perceived visual aesthetic [in Chinese]. *The Journal of Art and Design*, *1*, 21–32.

Williams, M., Burden, R., & Lanvers, U. (2002). 'French is the language of love and stuff': Student perceptions of issues related to motivation in learning a foreign language. *British Educational Research Journal*, *28*(4), 503–528. doi:10.1080/0141192022000005805

Zain, J. M., Tey, M., & Goh, Y. (2007). Does aesthetics of web page interface matters to Mandarin learning? *International Journal of Computer Science and Network Security*, *7*(8), 43–51.

Chapter 15
Instrumental Music Design:
Influence on Task Performance

Brayan Mauricio Rodriguez
Universidad Icesi, Colombia

Carlos Arce-Lopera
Universidad Icesi, Colombia

Ana M. Arboleda
https://orcid.org/0000-0002-7908-5611
Universidad Icesi, Colombia

Javier Diaz-Cely
Universidad Icesi, Colombia

Julian Correa
Musicar SAS, Colombia

Pablo Montoya
Musicar SAS, Colombia

ABSTRACT

The authors describe the importance of music design for background instrumental music and the effect on task performance. Three instrumental music conditions that differ in tempo, articulation, mode, and musical meter were tested using a complex task scenario. The task was performed using a complicated web-interface that required users to focus their attention and perform several specific interactions for successfully finishing the task. All the interactions with the interface were recorded. Moreover, a mixed assessment of the emotional state, perceived task performance, and music perception was asked to participants upon task completion. Experimental results revealed that music design has complex effects on task performance and emotion. Also, the results revealed important trends that can help design music environments to control frustration when confronted to complex and cognitively demanding tasks.

DOI: 10.4018/978-1-5225-9069-9.ch015

INTRODUCTION

The need to understand the effects of music on our behavior and cognitive processing has become increasingly important (Hallam, Price, & Katsarou, 2002). For example, Hallam el al. developed a study in which children aged from 10 to 12 were evaluated in their school under arousing, unpleasant, calming or relaxing background music. The music labeling was the product of a previous categorization effort made by children of the same age range after several listening sessions. In the experiments, they used mood, arousal, pleasure, emotion, and nostalgia as affective variables. They found that calming music had positive effects on math problems, memory, and pro-social behavior. Whilst arousing, aggressive, and unpleasant music had the opposite effect. Also, they found that the music used in school as a tool to improve learning and behavior could also enhance musical knowledge and thinking. These findings suggest that the effects of music on task performance are mediated through its effects on arousal and mood.

Music affects the listener conduct and emotion, but this condition depends on variables of music design. An increased tempo, for example, has mostly a positive impact in customer feelings (arousal) (Michel, Baumann, & Gayer, 2017) and is consistently related with faster actions (Kämpfe, Sedlmeier, & Renkewitz, 2011). Recently, Michel et al. wrote a systematic literature review in which they studied the effects of the presence or absence of in-store music in multiple service settings. They took into account moderating influences (i.e. age, gender, time of day, and service setting), the design of the music (i.e. physical dimension, preferential dimension, and genre), and customer response as characterised by affect (i.e. emotion, perception of time, and evaluation/satisfaction of service) and behavior (i.e. time spent in-store, purchase intention, sales volume, and patronage behavior). They found that, specifically, in the supermarket setting, an increased musical tempo has both positive and negative effects on customer's emotions (arousal) – depending on the moderating variable gender (male or female). Among the various studies compiled in their review, there are some which address customer behavior in relation to in-store music, focusing on four variables: customer's actual time spent in a store, sales volume, customer's purchase intention (expressed by the intention to purchase a good or service in the future), and customer patronage (revisit or loyalty) behavior. They found that an increased musical tempo has mostly a positive impact on customer emotions.

The analysis of the effects of background music on general behavior, cognitive processing and emotion revealed that tempo of background music has a strong impact on behavior: faster tempo consistently correlates with faster behavior (Kämpfe, Sedlmeier, & Renkewitz, 2011). In this respect, background music had a small but positive impact on sports performance. However, apparently, on average, background music slightly impaired memory processes and text understanding; reading tasks might be more disturbed by vocal than by instrumental music. One potential approach used for explaining this impact assumes that an increase in the activation of one brain hemisphere decreases the activation of the other hemisphere.

Also, depending on the setting, volume has a special influence on the customer (Michel et al., 2017) and major and minor modes impact whether customers perceive the music as happy or sad (Peretz, Gagnon, & Bouchard, 1998). Furthermore, genre (or subjective classification as calming or unpleasant) has an influence on cooperative behavior (Hallam et al., 2002; Kniffin, Yan, Wansink, & Schulze, 2017) and school task performance (Hallam et al., 2002; Scott, 1970), reading tasks might be more disturbed by vocal than by instrumental music (Kämpfe et al., 2011), and, in an isolated environment, office workers listening to staccato music significantly decrease their cognitive performance compared to workers listening to legato music (Schlittmeier & Hellbrück, 2009). Finally, the preferential dimension of the music influences the perception of time, for instance, customers spend more time in a department store when they like the in-store music (Michel et al., 2017); however, in the context of task performance, workers are able to differentiate between their personal music preferences and the sound conditions under which they preferred to perform a cognitive task (Schlittmeier & Hellbrück, 2009). Schlittmeier and Hellbrück has shown that apart from the subjective feeling of being disturbed, office noise impairs cognitive performance, especially if it consists of background speech. To prove this, they designed and developed two experiments each one with five sound conditions: silence, office noise only, office noise plus staccato music, office noise plus legato music, office noise plus continuous sound. Instrumental music with prominent staccato passages and even sequences of different tones did not impair verbal short-term memory performance. However, music with prominent legato passages has been shown to affect cognitive performance significantly less than music with prominent staccato passages. Also, they preferred to work with no background sound. But if it had to be present, they preferred legato music. On the other hand, the research results showed that office noise diminished cognitive performance and that its detrimental impact was significantly reduced when superimposed with continuous noise. Moreover, although performance on the serial learning task with office noise plus continuous noise did not differ from performance during silence, office noise plus continuous noise was subjectively rated as clearly more disturbing than silence.

The influence of music on behavior and task performance is mediated through its effects on emotion: arousal and mood (Hallam et al., 2002; Michel et al., 2017). Emotion is significantly associated with recall (Baumann, Hamin, & Chong, 2015) and specifically, arousal level increases task performance up to an optimal level beyond which over-arousal leads to a deterioration in performance (Hallam et al., 2002). Moreover, for simple tasks, an increased level of arousal maintains the concentration yielding a better task performance; but for complex tasks, the level of arousal may become too great and performance may deteriorate (Hallam et al., 2002).

Nevertheless, it remains unclear which attributes of music design can influence positively the task performance when the tasks are complex and require extensive use of cognitive processing. Particularly, sensory marketing solutions aim to improve office workers task performance through instrumental music, but the choice of the specific song is selected by music experts. Here, the authors aim at understanding the effect on emotional state and task performance of 27 instrumental background songs that are used in office settings. The songs differ in tempo, articulation, mode, and musical meter. The task performance was evaluated with a web-based tool simulating a complex and difficult attention-driven interaction.

METHODS

Twenty-seven instrumental songs were subjectively classified in terms of their tempo, articulation, mode, and meter by music experts. Tempo refers to the speed of the song. The articulation was classified in two types: legato and staccato. Legato articulation indicates that musical notes are played smoothly and connected (continuous sound), which produces a relaxing feeling in the listener; and staccato represents a note of shortened duration, separated from the note that may follow by silence, which produces a feeling of motivating or sometimes of tension. In western music, there are two types of modes or triads: minor and major. Musically, the major scale differs from the minor one in three sounds out of seven. Normally, for western listeners, the minor mode suggests a negative emotional tone while the major mode has a more positive connotation (Kastner & Crowder, 1990). Unlike rhythm, metric onsets are not necessarily sounded, but are nevertheless expected by the listener. The triple metre generally imply relaxing music and a comfortable feeling.

The resulting classes were motivating, mid, and relaxing. A difficult to interact web-based tool in which the user had to manipulate the mouse of a personal computer much more than usual, and carefully read the instructions with a non-friendly and confusing graphic interface was used to test differences in emotional state when simultaneously hearing one of the three background instrumental music conditions.

Subjects

Twenty-four volunteers participated in the experiments: 10 females and 14 males. Age range was from 13 to 52 years old (27 years old ± 10) and 15 of them with little or no musical knowledge, which was determined by asking the years in musical education of each participant. Musical knowledge was determined by the years in musical education of each participant. The subjects were recruited in Universidad Icesi. 50% were students, 17% were university staff and 33% were not affiliated with the University.

Materials

Music

The experimental conditions are given by three sets, each set having nine background songs (mot – motivating tempo, mid – mid tempo, rel – relaxing tempo). These songs were evaluated by a group of musicians who carried out a subjective study in order to estimate the stimulus generated. The bpm took a very important role in it but other features such as mode, time signature and articulation were also taken into account. On Figure 1, the tempo from the songs on each group is shown as a density plot.

Figure 1. Density plot with multiple stimulus

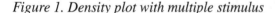
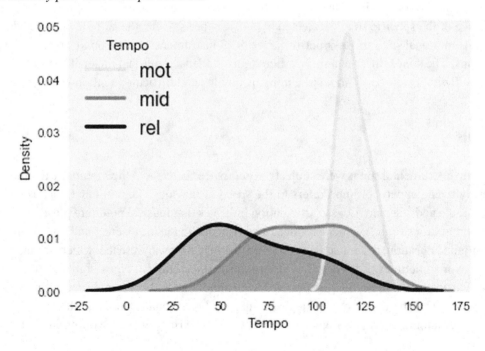

As shown in Figure 2, Figure 3, and Figure 4, the motivating condition mostly has songs in minor mode, staccato articulation, and with an average tempo of 119 bpm in the time signature 4/4. The mid condition is mostly in major mode, legato, and 91 bpm on average with the time signature 4/4. Lastly, the relaxing music is also mostly in major mode and legato, but the bpm is 48 on average with a time signature of 4/4, and in addition has some songs in the time signatures 6/8 and 3/4. As vocal characteristics of music can influence listeners' perceptions (Kämpfe et al., 2011), the selected songs were only instrumental, as follows:

Motivating songs:

- Fuiste Mala by Adolfo & Gustavo Angel
- Polka Caribena by Rey Casas
- Bamboleo by James Last
- Andalucia by Paco Nula
- Lluvia de Primavera by Raul Di Blasio
- Soca Dance by Ray Hamilton & Orchestra
- Buenos Recuerdos by Sergi Vicente
- Gypsy Earrings by Strunz & Farah
- Pop Hits by Tokyo Kosei Wind Orchestra

Mid songs:

- I say little prayer by 20th century Film Orchestra
- I just called to say I love by Acker Bilk
- Beguin The Beguine by Antonio De Lucena
- Killing me softly with his song by Barroker
- Strangers in the Night by Caravelli
- I'll Be There by Romantic Saxophone Quintet
- My Way (Frank Sinatra) by Smooth Groove Masters
- Tears Dry On Their Own by Smooth Jazz All Stars
- Whiter Shade Of Pale by The Bruno Bertone Orchestra

Relaxing songs:

- Summy by Chamin Correa
- The Long And Winding Road by Chris Cozensy
- Once Upon A Time In The West by Francis Goya
- You Needed Me by Gheorghe Zamfir
- Open arms by Javier Ricardo
- Jeux interdits by Nicolas de Angelis
- Tears In Heaven by Sergi Vicente
- Memory by The Bruno Bertone Orchestra
- Love Story by Tokyo Kosei Wind Orchestra

Figure 2. Stacked histogram with modes

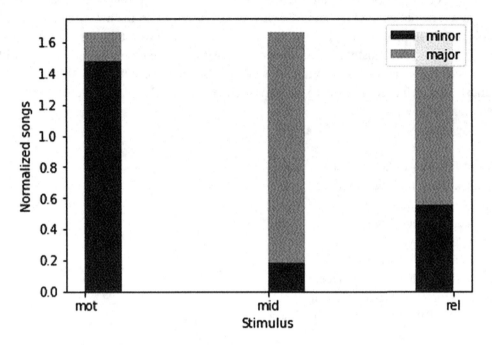

Figure 3. Stacked histogram with articulation

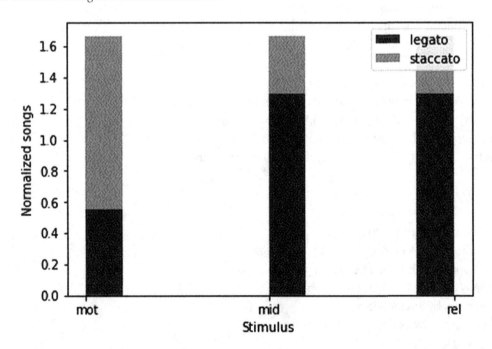

Figure 4. Stacked Histogram with Time Signature

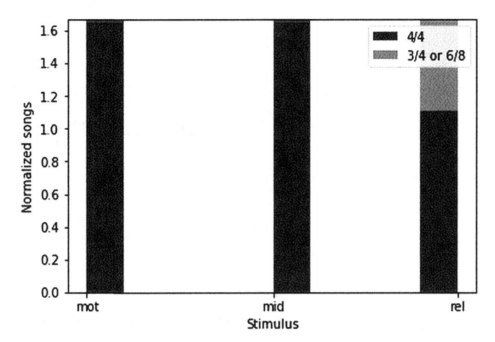

Regarding Music Information Retrieval features, in the Figure 5, entropy means the average rate at which information is produced. This graph shows that the motivating sound condition has more information disorder than the other two conditions.

Figure 6 shows that the amount of high-frequency content in the motivating songs is larger than the content in the relaxing songs.

Figure 5. Relative frequency of entropy feature per sound condition

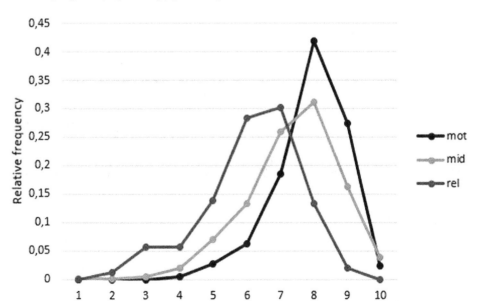

Figure 6. Relative frequency of brightness feature per sound condition

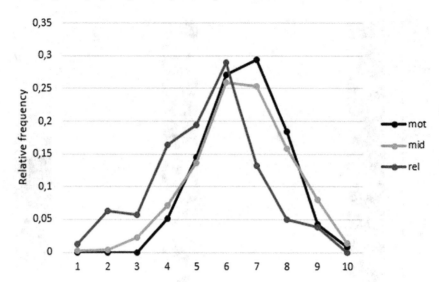

Finally, the Figure 7 shows that the underlying rhythmic can be easily perceived in motivating and mid songs.

Interface

The sound conditions were accompanied by a tedious interface specifically designed so that users encountered difficulties in their interactions with the tool to accomplish the demanded tasks. Hereunder the authors describe the web interface in detail.

Figure 7. Relative frequency of pulse clarity feature per sound condition

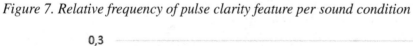

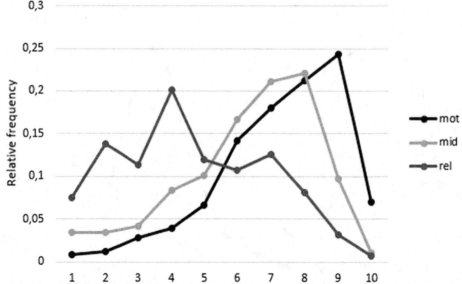

The remaining time and budget are shown at the top of the web page (Figure 8) in order to force the user to scroll up every time she/he wants to know any of the two pieces of information.

The symbols of the amenities (Figure 9) in the hotel are also described at the top of the web page in order to constrain the user to scroll up and down to understand them.

In the screen, 16 hotels are always shown (4 per possible destination city) but only the ones belonging to the selected city are able to be selected as shown in Figure 10. This design also forces the user to scroll up and down and confuses her/him a bit to check the hotels in the selected city.

As shown in Figure 11, the user has to select the number of vacation days in a JavaScript Range Slider that was modified so that its steps change randomly with each movement which made more difficult the selection of the decision taken.

Figure 8. The top of the web interface showing the title of the activity "Vacation Plan", the remaining time, the partial budget, and the remaining budget.

Plan de vacaciones

13:37

Total parcial:
COP$0

Presupuesto restante:
COP$2.000.000

Figure 9. The symbols of the amenities in the hotel. From left to right: smoking allowed, breakfast included, casino, recreationalist, cradle. Disco, kids allowed, children's pool, motorcycle renting, smoking forbidden. Kids forbidden, open bar, free parking, pool party. 24-hours reception, spa, TV in room, and WiFi coverage.

Permitido fumar. Incluye desayuno. Casino. Recreacionista. Cuna.

Discoteca. Permitidos los niños. Piscina para niños. Alquiler de motocicletas. Prohibido fumar.

Prohibido entrada de niños. Barra libre. Estacionamiento gratis. Pool party.

Recepción 24 horas. Spá. Cuarto con televisión. Wifi.

Figure 10. Images from hotels. The top ones are enable and the bottom ones are disabled. Each image contains the name of the hotel and the actual cost per night.

Hotel Makondo
Costo/noche: COP $1.221.910
Hotel Casa Nadia & Sandro
Costo/noche: COP $452.128

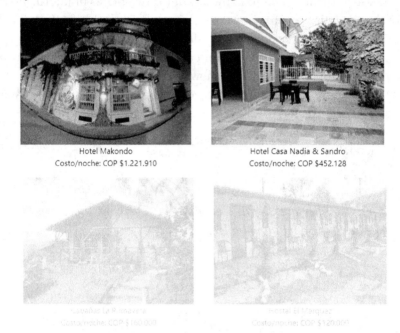

Figure 11. Slider to select the number of vacation days. The recommendation is: "Select the number of days you plan to go on vacation". And at the bottom is the number selected.

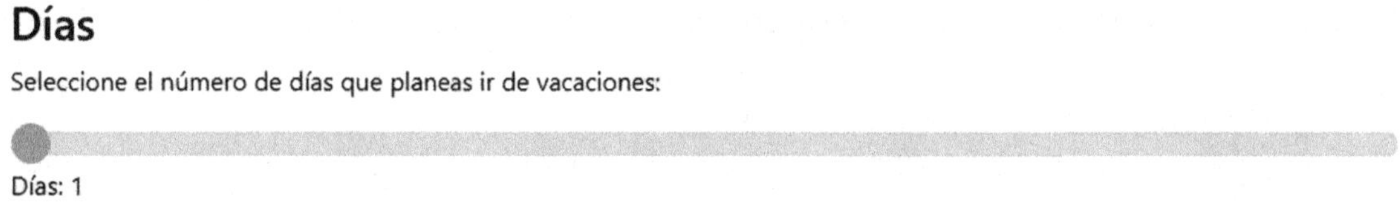
Días
Seleccione el número de días que planeas ir de vacaciones:
Días: 1

The user has to designate the budget for food with a numeric input form element (Figure 12) which has a step of COP $1.000 to make difficult to reach the desired number. Even though, the user is able to write the number with the numeric keyboard.

Subjects were requested to stay in an isolated room with computers in which the activity would be carried out. They were asked to use the same headphones every time to listen the background music in a fixed volume.

Figure 12. Numeric input form to select budget for food during vacation. The recommendation is: "Enter the budget you want to spend in food during this vacation".

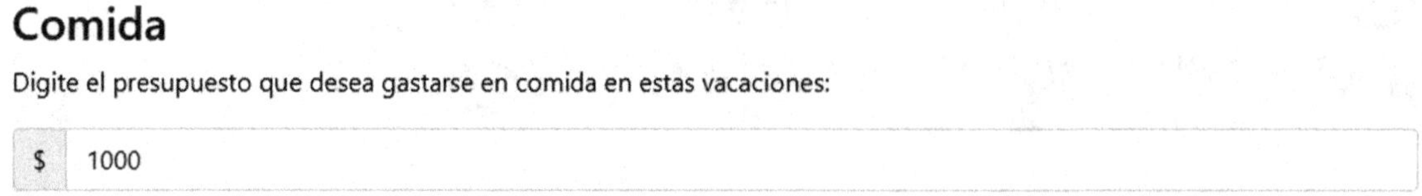
Comida
Digite el presupuesto que desea gastarse en comida en estas vacaciones:
$
1000

Procedure

Subjects were invited to participate in an experience where they were asked to act as travel agents who plan a vacation trip for a particular client with specific demands. The demands were carefully designed with different profiles and required the user to interact intensively with the interface. The purpose of the task was to have participants involved within some decision-making activities. However, this task takes place during annoying conditions.

Participants had to interact with a web page to achieve their objectives. The interactions were not intuitive by design. During the task, participants listened to a song belonging to one of the three music set conditions. The instrumental songs were randomly chosen for each participant and played back cyclically until the participant finished the task. Loudness was identical for each participant.

When he/she click "Play", the screen showed the following written instructions:

"The Best Vacation Plan

Suppose you are a travel agent, you will get to plan a vacation trip for a profile described below. They have a specified amount of money to invest in the trip and you will be able to make decisions regarding the place (considering the transportation costs), hotel (each one with some amenities) the number of vacation days and the budget for food. You may deal with all the money the person has available for the trip or you can recommend him/her to save part of it. What matters is that your decisions take you to the Best Vacation Plan."

The maximum available time to complete the vacation plan was 15 minutes and the maximum budget was COP $2.000.000. Besides, there were three profiles of the person or group of people for whom participants had to plan a vacation. Client profiles were randomly chosen among three predefined stereotypes:

1. A 20 years old party youngster who is looking to enjoy alcohol drinking and cigarette smoking. He hopes for a hotel in which he can enter at any time, a casino, a disco, a whole room for him, adult entertainment, and a pool party every night. Besides, he would like for the hotel to be in the immediacy of the most important discos. Finally, he hopes to spend the least amount of money as he can.

2. A family with a kid and a baby. They hope for a hotel in which smoking is not allowed, with a children pool and play area, parking spaces, and free breakfast. In the room, they would like to encounter a double bed, a sofa-bed, and a cradle. Also, they would like to be able to eat out of the hotel with part of the established budget.

3. A college student on vacation, looking for a quiet place in which kids are not allowed. She hopes to find a TV in the room and wide Wi-Fi coverage. Also, she would like for the hotel to offer relaxation and entertainment facilities, as well as free transportation and free breakfast. Finally, she wants to be able to use part of the established budget exploring the local culinary culture.

Next, the cities are shown together with a picture in order to recognize it and the transportation costs. The city options were:

1. Cartagena (Bolivar): This is a major port city in Colombia's Caribbean coast region. It is the fifth-largest city in Colombia and the second largest in the region, after Barranquilla. In 1984, Cartagena's colonial walled city and fortress were designated a UNESCO World Heritage Site. In the downtown area, you can find mainly a colonial style, but republican and Italian style buildings, such as the

Cathedral's bell tower, can be seen. The city has a warm climate, colonial style, and coasts which have made Cartagena one of the most important touristic cities of Colombia. Cartagena is also famous for the parties. The whole transportation cost is COP $500.000.

2. Pavas (Valle del Cauca): Pavas is a small town of La Cumbre city in the Valle del Cauca department. It is a small village suitable for taking a break from the busy life. Pavas is known for its simplicity, lack of hustle and small-town way of life. There is a large green area and a lot of roads to walk through. The whole transportation cost is COP $20.000.

3. Honda (Tolima): Honda is a town in the Tolima department. Honda is called "the City of Bridges" with more than 40 of them on the rivers. The downtown area is historic and of colonial style. This downtown area is the most important touristic appeal for visitors. The whole transportation cost is COP $100.000.

4. Medellin (Antioquia): Medellin is the second-largest city in Colombia and the capital of the department of Antioquia. The city is promoted internationally as a tourist destination and is considered a global city type "Gamma -" by GaWC. It is well-known by the urbanism and the organization of the city (e.g. the only one Metro in Colombia). Finally, it also has parks to do ecotourism. The whole transportation cost is COP $1.221.910.

As shown in the Figure 13, the hotel is displayed together with a picture, the name and the costs per night. The name of the hotels is real but the amenities are assumed and they were grouped by city as follows:

In Cartagena:

1. Hotel Isla del Pirata: This is a hotel in which there is an open bar, it is not allowed to smoke. The reception desk is available the 24 hours. They organize pool parties every night and the disco is always available. The cost per night is COP $1.221.910.

2. Apartamentos Morros Cartagena: Smoking is allowed and it has open bar, reception and disco available 24 hours. Besides, they organize pool parties every night. The cost per night is COP $ 452.128. As you can note, this is the perfect hotel for the 20 years old party youngster.

3. Hotel Makondo: In this hotel, they offer free breakfast and services such as clown and cradles for babys. Moreover, there is a casino inside of it and it smoking is allowed. The cost per night is COP $1.221.910.

4. Hotel Casa Nadia & Sandro: Although smoking is allowed, kids are also allowed and a service of clowns. Moreover, they offer services such as disco in the hotel and motorcycle lending. The cost per night is COP $452.128.

In Pavas:

1. Cabañas La Primavera: This is a hotel with free Wi-Fi coverage where kids are not allowed. They offer services such as free breakfast, motorcycle lending, and spa. The cost per night is COP $160.000. As you can note, this is the perfect hotel for the college student on vacation.

2. Hostal El Marquez: In this hotel the traveler can find a casino, a disco, a pool party every night, free breakfast, and the kids are not allowed. The cost per night is COP $120.000.

Figure 13. Graphic User Interface showing hotel amenities

Hotel

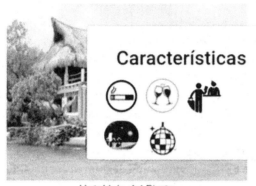

Hotel Isla del Pirata
Costo/noche: COP $1.221.910

Apartamentos Morros Cartagena
Costo/noche: COP $452.128

3.   Hotel Villa Saman: This hotel offers parking spaces for visitors, open bar and reception 24 hours. In the hotel room, the customer is able to enjoy Wi-Fi coverage and TV services. The cost per night is COP $130.000.

4.   Hotel Recito De Los Sueños: This hotel offers parking spaces, reception 24 hours and spa. In this hotel neither kids nor smokers are allowed. The cost per night is COP $ 5.128.

In Honda:

1.   El Virrey Hotel Boutique: In every room of this hotel, visitors are able to enjoy Wi-Fi coverage and TV services. Even though kids are not allowed, they offer a service of clown. Finally, they offer motorcycle lending service. The cost per night is COP $100.555.

2.   Hotel y Parque Acuatico Agua Sol Alegria: In this hotel, kids can enjoy of cradle in the room and a pool specialized for them. In the hotel there is Wi-Fi coverage and smoking is not allowed. The cost per night is COP $100.555.

3.   Hotel la Piragua: In this hotel, the customer is able to get free breakfast, open bar and reception desk 24 hours, and parking spaces. In the room there is TV service. The cost per night is COP $50.000.

4.   Hotel Las Piscinas: In this hotel, customers are able to smoke and enjoy casino and disco services. Moreover, kids are able to enjoy of a pool specialized for them and clown service. The cost per night is COP $125.000.

In Medellin:

1.   Hostal Casa Prado: Here, there is a pool specialized for kids, smoking is not allowed, and children can enjoy a clown service. Furthermore, there is a casino available. The cost per night is COP $25.000.

2. La Campana Hotel Boutique: This hotel counts on an open bar, a spa, and Wi-Fi coverage and TV services in the room. They organize pool parties every night. The cost per night is COP $157.475.

3. The Charlee Lifestyle: The customer is able to get Wi-Fi coverage, reception desk 24 hours, and free breakfast. In the hotel, there is a disco and kids are not allowed. The cost per night is COP $579.223.

4. Hotel Estelar Blue: In this hotel, smoking is not allowed. It offers services such as parking spaces, pool specialized for kids, free breakfast and cradle for babies. The cost per night is COP $226.950.

The amenities are revealed in a tooltip when the mouse pointer is over the hotel; the layout of the web page forces the user to scroll up and down to understand the hotel amenities symbols because the meanings were in the upper section of the page.

Below, the modified JavaScript Range Slider element had to be used to choose the number of vacation days. Finally, the user had to designate the budget for food with a numeric input form element which had a step of COP $1.000 to make difficult to reach the desired number.

If the participant chose another city or hotel, he/she would be compelled to select the number of days and the budget for food again. He/she finished the task by clicking on the "submit decision" button. If a hotel does not match the priorities of the traveler, participants had to keep on looking until finding the right hotel or until the 15 minutes are over.

When the user found the correct decision or the time was up, the application appeared as if it were making some calculations, and the following message is shown on the screen: "please wait while we analyze the selections." 30 seconds later, this message is followed by the final message "Thank you for waiting. Good-bye".

DATA COLLECTION

Interaction Events

All interaction events including scroll changes (one scroll change counts if the user was scrolling down and suddenly began to scroll up), decision changes, final decision, time spent, number of bad submissions, and whether the time is over or not, are collected.

Post Interaction Data

After the submission, a series of surveys concerning the tasks were applied to each subject as follows:

Emotional State

An emotional state measurement is applied with the purpose of determining the point in which a facial emotion changes in a carefully design video (Niedenthal, Brauer, Halberstadt, & Innes-Ker, 2001). This measurement is used to set the level of annoyance with the interface, namely a level greater than 30 out of 60 represents that the participant is feeling pleased. For further details refer to Figure 14.

Figure 14. Two faces that respectively represents two emotions. These are the extreme points of an emotional state measurement video in which the participant has to decide the point in that the emotion changes.

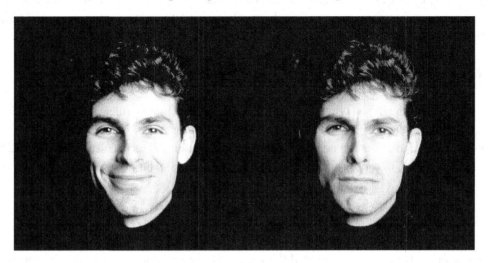

NASA Task Load Index

The NASA Task Load Index (TLX) is applied to determine the perception of mental demand, physical demand, temporal demand, performance, effort, and frustration with the interface (Hart & Staveland, 1988). For this purpose the questions were:

- How mentally demanding was the task? (Mental Demand)
- How physically demanding was the task? (Physical Demand)
- How hurried or rushed was the pace of the task? (Temporal Demand)
- How successful were you in accomplishing what you were asked to do? (Performance)
- How hard did you have to work to accomplish your level of performance? (Effort)
- How insecure, discouraged, irritated, stressed and annoyed were you? (Frustration)

These questions needs to be responded in a ten-point scale regarding the level of the participant perception.

Time and Music Perception

Time and music perception are also evaluated by asking the perception of minutes spent and if the background music was perceived as fast or slow.

Attitudes, Satisfaction, and Attention to Music

Attitudes towards the experience are measured on a four-item seven-point semantic differential scale: very bad/ very good, unfavorable/favorable, not at all likable/ very likable, and unappealing/appealing. Further, an overall satisfaction measurement in the same scale is added, asking if the participants are satisfied with their results.

Attention to the music is evaluated on a seven-point Likert scale, ranging from strongly disagree (1) to strongly agree (7), for the following four items: paid much attention to the music in the interaction, followed the music more than the decisions, had the music in mind while taking decisions, and followed the music in the activity. These measurements are adapted to the experience from (Macinnis & Park, 1991).

Likability and Familiarity of Music

Moreover, likability of the music is assessed through three items (likable, pleasant, and good) on a Likert scale. Familiarity with the music is evaluated through three items (songs sound familiar, songs make me think about my past, and songs are personally relevant to me) in a Likert scale. The Likert scale ranges from totally disagree (1) to totally agree (7) (Macinnis & Park, 1991).

ANALYSIS OF DATA

For each participant, the authors calculated the mean of each variable measured during the interaction and post interaction phases with its standard deviation. In order to examine the relationship between the stimulus manually tagged to each song and each of the variables, a an ANOVA general linear model was fit between the stimulus as the factor variable and the other ones as the response variables and then a Tukey's honest significance test between the stimulus and each response variable in order to check if the means of the subjects tagged with one of the stimulus (according to the song listened) are significantly different from the others in each variable measured. As mentioned above, there are eight subjects per stimulus, then the degrees of freedom are determined by this number.

RESULTS

The time spent interacting with the interface was 9 minutes and 52 seconds on average, with a minimum time of 3 minutes and 26 seconds and a maximum time of 15 minutes, the time limit. There was, on average per participant, 59 scroll changes of direction, 5 errors or bad submissions (up to 21), and 14 decision changes until the correct plan was chosen or the time was up.

Three people (2 on mid music condition and 1 on relaxing music condition) couldn't finish the activity within the allotted time. A striking result is that the participants under the motivating music condition took the best decisions, regarding to the budget for food and number of vacation days, when the traveler profile was the party youngster or the family and, on the other hand, when the traveler was the quiet student, participants under relaxing music took the best decisions. Besides, in the interaction, participants who listened to relaxing songs had more scroll direction changes but fewer bad submissions than the ones who listened mid and motivating songs.

The emotional state measurement had an average of 39 out of 60, indicating that users were inclined to feel pleased and the interface was not very annoying. The perception of the music was fast for the participants on motivating music condition and slow for the mid and relaxing condition. The time perception was from 1 to 18 minutes averaging 9 minutes and 30 seconds and the difference of each participant time perception with the actual time spent was 3 minutes and 2 seconds on average. Regarding the NASA-TLX dimensions, as shown in Figure 15, the lowest scored was the physical demand with

Figure 15. Averages of NASA-TLX dimensions per sound condition

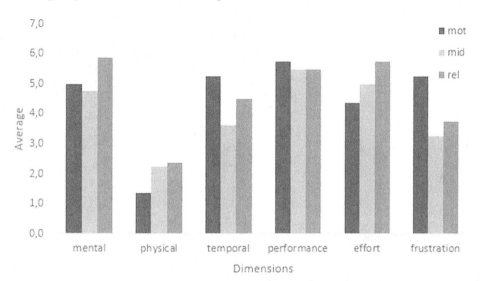

an average of 2 out of 10; the frustration was 4.1/10; the temporal demand, 4.5/10; the effort, 5/10; the mental demand, 5.2/10; and the performance, 5.6/10. It must be noted that for all dimensions, except for the frustration dimension, there were not noteworthy differences between the three sound conditions. The difference found in frustration means that subjects under motivating music felt more frustrated than the ones under the other two music conditions.

Furthermore, on average, attitudes towards the experience was 5.1/7, which means that attitudes were mostly positive. Attention to the music was 3.7/7, indicating that subjects did not significantly perceived the music. Music likability and familiarity was 5.1/7 and 3.9/7 respectively.

According to the music likability measurement (average between likability, pleasant, goodness), as shown in Figure 16, there was a significant difference in the scores under the motivating background music and the mid one (t (8) =-2.57, p=0.045) and, also, compared to subjects under the relaxing one (t (8) =3.82, p=0.003); namely the relaxing and mid music was significantly more liked than the motivating music.

The subjects under the motivating music condition spent less time and perceived less time spent than the other ones. Attention to the music was better scored by participants under relaxing music especially in the music in mind item. However, neither of these differences nor that of frustration (in NASA TLX) are statistically significant.

DISCUSSION

The results regarding the interaction time show that the design of the web page indeed created a complicated interaction that required attention and effort to achieve a desired result. However, the scores in the emotional state measurement, task load index, and attitudes towards the experience reveal that, despite that complicated interaction, the emotion mostly remained positive.

Figure 16. Scores of likability measurement in motivating, mid, and relaxing songs respectively

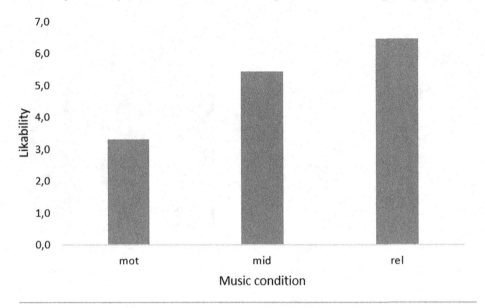

The trends described above reveal that there is a direct correlation between the motivating music and dynamic application contexts and, in this way, the relaxing music directly impacts in quiet and simple contexts. In addition, motivating music also makes people do the activity faster and it seems that relaxing music makes they think and doubt more (scroll and item changes) before submitting the decision.

Despite the stimulus for doing faster the task, the authors found a poor likability and attention of the motivating music which can be related with the results of the perceived frustration, where this music condition was perceived more frustrating. With this in mind, people that carried out the task faster under a motivating condition were driven in a frustrating and unliked ambient. Nevertheless, people under a relaxing song took conscientious and analyzed final decisions driven in the opposite ambient.

It has to be pointed out that most of the differences are not statistically significant (with $\alpha=0.05$) and for that reason the authors must enlarge our sample size and diversify it in order to prove statistically these trends.

CONCLUSION AND FUTURE WORK

The authors designed and implemented a web-based tool in which the users had a difficult interaction when trying to register their decisions. This complex behavior was verified by measurements obtained from the interaction with the interface. Then, the researchers were able to measure the influence of three different sound contexts on their task performance and load.

Most of the experiments in the literature measure the influence of background music on emotions specifically arousal and, by doing so, the effects on listener behavior or task performance. Whereas, this work attempts to evaluate the emotion of the user when confronted with a complex interface and using several measurement tools that can give insight on the complex relation between music and users emotion and performance in the computer. It has to be pointed out that the results and the aim of this project have implications on the understanding of the behavior of users of technological interfaces.

Comparisons between the three music conditions did not reveal significant differences in the participants' emotional state but revealed better decisions regarding the traveler profile and some important trends on task performance and one dimension of the task load.

In order to determine how to improve the task performance through the influence of background instrumental music, first the authors need to determine if the trends illustrated in the results can be significantly different by widening the sample size. Furthermore, in future work, the technology readiness should be considered because this could become decisive, for example, in the time spent in the activity. Finally, the researchers are considering to analyze the relationships between some Music Information Retrieval features and the effects on listener behavior.

REFERENCES

Baumann, C., Hamin, H., & Chong, A. (2015). The role of brand exposure and experience on brand recall—Product durables vis-à-vis FMCG. *Journal of Retailing and Consumer Services*, *23*, 21–31. doi:10.1016/j.jretconser.2014.11.003

Hallam, S., Price, J., & Katsarou, G. (2002). The Effects of Background Music on Primary School Pupils' Task Performance. *Educational Studies*, *28*(2), 111–122. doi:10.1080/03055690220124551

Hart, S. G., & Staveland, L. E. (1988). Development of NASA-TLX (Task Load Index): Results of Empirical and Theoretical Research. *Advances in Psychology*, *52*, 139–183. doi:10.1016/S0166-4115(08)62386-9

Kämpfe, J., Sedlmeier, P., & Renkewitz, F. (2011). The impact of background music on adult listeners: A meta-analysis. *Psychology of Music*, *39*(4), 424–448. doi:10.1177/0305735610376261

Kastner, M., & Crowder, R. (1990). Perception of the Major/Minor Distinction: IV. Emotional Connotations in Young Children. *Music Perception*, *8*(2), 189–201. doi:10.2307/40285496

Kniffin, K. M., Yan, J., Wansink, B., & Schulze, W. D. (2017). The sound of cooperation: Musical influences on cooperative behavior. *Journal of Organizational Behavior*, *38*(3), 372–390. doi:10.1002/job.2128 PMID:28344386

Macinnis, D. J., & Park, C. W. (1991). The Differential Role of Characteristics of Music on High- and Low- Involvement Consumers' Processing of Ads. *The Journal of Consumer Research*, *18*(2), 161. doi:10.1086/209249

Michel, A., Baumann, C., & Gayer, L. (2017). Thank you for the music – or not? The effects of in-store music in service settings. *Journal of Retailing and Consumer Services*, *36*, 21–32. doi:10.1016/j.jretconser.2016.12.008

Niedenthal, P. M., Brauer, M., Halberstadt, J. B., & Innes-Ker, Å. H. (2001). When did her smile drop? Facial mimicry and the influences of emotional state on the detection of change in emotional expression. *Cognition and Emotion*, *15*(6), 853–864. doi:10.1080/02699930143000194

Peretz, I., Gagnon, L., & Bouchard, B. (1998). Music and emotion: Perceptual determinants, immediacy, and isolation after brain damage. *Cognition, 68*(2), 111–141. Retrieved from http://www.ncbi.nlm.nih.gov/pubmed/9818509. doi:10.1016/S0010-0277(98)00043-2 PMID:9818509

Schlittmeier, S. J., & Hellbrück, J. (2009). Background music as noise abatement in open-plan offices: A laboratory study on performance effects and subjective preferences. *Applied Cognitive Psychology, 23*(5), 684–697. doi:10.1002/acp.1498

Scott, T. J. (1970). The use of music to reduce hyperactivity in children. *The American Journal of Orthopsychiatry, 40*(4), 677–680. doi:10.1111/j.1939-0025.1970.tb00725.x PMID:5507301

Chapter 16
Impact of Evaluating the Usability of Assisted Technology Oriented by Protocol

Ana Carolina Oliveira Lima
University of Aveiro, Portugal

Maria de Fatima Queiroz Vieira
 https://orcid.org/0000-0001-7901-4867
Federal University of Campina Grande, Brazil

Ana Isabel Martins
Institute of Electronics and Informatics Engineering of Aveiro, Portugal

Nelson Pacheco Rocha
University of Aveiro, Portugal

Joana Catarina Mendes
Instituto de Telecomunicações Campus Universitário de Santiago, Portugal

Ronaldo da Silva Ferreira
Universidade de Aveiro, Portugal

ABSTRACT

The main objective of this research is to provide a procedure set, oriented by a clear and rigorous protocol that allows the replication of results regarding the accessibility claims of products and systems available for the blind community, thus validating their robustness. The goal during the experiment was to compare user preferences and effectiveness when performing tasks with the voice synthesizers JAWS and DOSVOX and a braille keyboard. The adopted evaluation protocol includes the following methods: usability testing, focus group, and user satisfaction survey. The study developed with the proposed protocol investigates assistive technology adequacy to target users. The tasks performed by 30 users were categorized as activities of entertainment, learning, and social inclusion. It is considered that the main contribution of this chapter is to provide the protocol and methodology, adapted for use in evaluations of accessibility products and devices.

DOI: 10.4018/978-1-5225-9069-9.ch016

INTRODUCTION

Accessibility has become a major concern of computer system developers. However, unlike its counterpart usability, there is no established protocol that can be used to evaluate the quality of products and systems developed for particular users or communities.

For many interactive software systems, a large part of the interaction between user and technology depends on the use of visually presented material (ISO, 2008). In particular, the individuals typically use the keyboard, mouse, or other pointing devices to provide information and various screen types as output devices. On the other hand, blind or visually impaired users employ their auditory and tactile senses as visual sense. In this case, the typical non-visual forms of interface used in interactive software are auditory or tactile (Sodnik, Grega & Tomazic, 2011). Screen readers, the software tool most commonly used by visually impaired users, are based on speech synthesizers that read the contents of the computer screen using synthesized artificial speech (Chen & Raman, 2008).

Although the scientific literature presents several studies evaluating the accessibility and usability of assistive technologies for blind people (e.g. (Sanchez & Hassler, 2017; Pascual, Ribera, Granollers & Coiduras, 2014; Ferreira, Silveira, Capra & Ferreira, 2012)), a general experimental protocol able to be instantiated for the evaluation of different devices and systems is still lacking. Targeting to overcome this issue, the present chapter presents an experimental protocol that provides a script with procedures that is aided by documents that guide the evaluator during experiments planning and conduct.

Successfully designing universally accessible interfaces requires technical and cultural changes and strategic commitment: Usability and accessibility must be an objective of system development (Queirós, Silva, Alvarelhão, Rocha & Teixeira, 2015).

In a general way, there are some examples of how Human Computer Interaction has been shaping the new demands of market, social, economic and user specificities, which is very clear in several studies (Smith-jacksonb & Hartsona, 2009; Jokinen, 2015; Findlater & McGrenere, 2010).

In terms of accessibility: software should be as accessible as possible so that it can be used by as many individuals as possible, including people with physical, mental or sensory disabilities.

Some people cannot see clearly or distinguish certain colors, and some cannot operate a normal keyboard or mouse. Access to sites of the future by people with physical disabilities requires new forms of interaction based on the use of, for example, voice.

Software should be inclusive and universal, so it favors not only the disabled people, as well as all others, whether they have a limitation or not.

The evaluation of usability applied to the universal project brings impacts in different areas, among which are:

- Multicultural interfaces: these are factors to be analyzed in the new conceptions of interfaces. Creating a solution that is usable by people in many different countries and cultures is a great challenge. The reader should be led to understand that creating a version for a specific group of users based on language or location could be important, just as colors and icons have different representations for different cultures (Miah, 2004).
- Multiplatform software: which is a technological challenge for programmers to adapt their software to be used by different software platforms. It is noted that in many cases, the newly developed software needs to run on several platforms and integrate with each one of them. The main problem

with cross-platform software is consistency and lack of interoperability (Dias, Martins, Queirós & Rocha, 2018).

- Multimedia Interfaces: graphics and text are not the only ways to provide information, it is currently possible to use sound and, in some cases, tactile feedback to convey information. The issue of discussion is how use these output devices to produce a good quality user interface in the future (Sangiorg, 2014).

Originally designed to evaluate the interactive products and systems usability, this protocol was adapted to evaluate the usability level of accessibility resources available to the visually impaired, thus evaluating the accessibility level from the utilitarian point of view. Help resources can consist of specific systems and components designed to increase accessibility levels, such as hardware, software, or input / output devices. The protocol was conceived, formalized and adopted over the years in research and products usability evaluation in the Laboratory of Human Machine Interfaces (LIHM) of the Federal University of Campina Grande (UFCG) (Aguiar & Vieira, 2009), (Lima, Vieira & Aguiar, 2010).

The suitability of the adapted protocol to evaluate screen readers accessibility level and Braille keyboard, when used by blind and visually impaired people, was validated. Moreover, factors that can lead to a prediction of the impact a certain assistive technology can have on the target population were also analyzed.

BACKGROUND

Ideally, the usability evaluation should be present at all stages of development, and should be iterative, allowing a continuous evolution of the product quality. The literature describes several methods and tools to ensure the usability of a product or service.

The evaluation can be done in the laboratory, but since the context of use is very important, whenever possible it should be carried out under real conditions of use (Simes-Marques & Nunes, 2012).

Some methods use user data, while others rely on usability experts. There are usability assessment techniques for all phases of design and development, from product definition to the latest changes in the final product (Hanington & Martin, 2012). Many of the methods and techniques are suitable for a specific developmental stage (Simes-Marques & Nunes, 2012).

Usability evaluation methods can be analytical (based on expert analysis of an interactive system and / or potential interactions) or empirical (based on actual user data). Usability evaluation methods are usually specified in a rather incomplete way, which makes it difficult to apply them consistently. For this reason, the usability assessment can be expected to involve a combination of several methods that, together, can contribute to the understanding of potential users (Hanington & Martin, 2012).

The usability assessment methods mainly used are test methods, inquiry and inspection.

Test methods are user-centered methods that involve observation while the user performs tasks with a particular product or service (Nielsen, 1993). Usability testing methods aim at observing and measuring the interaction of the user with the interface and consist of collecting mostly quantitative data (Afonso, Lima, & Cota, 2013). These methods focus on people and their tasks and look for empirical evidence on how to improve the usability of an interface (Hanington & Martin, 2012). Testing usability usually involves systematic observation under controlled conditions to determine how well participants can use the product or service. The focus of usability testing focuses on what the user does, rather than on what the user says, and therefore the focus is on the behavior (Mitchell, 2007). Within the test methods, the most frequently used techniques are: rapid prototyping, performance evaluation, observation, think-aloud, remote usability testing and simulation (Martins, Queirós, Silva & Rocha, 2014).

Moreover, inspection methods involve the participation of experts to evaluate the different aspects of user interaction with a given product or service. The inspection methods are mainly based on heuristic evaluation technique, cognitive walkthrough techniques and task analysis (Martins, Queirós, Silva & Rocha, 2015).

Finally, inquiry methods involve the collection of qualitative user data. Although the data collected is subjective, it provides valuable insight about what users want. The questionnaires are the most frequent of the inquiry methods, followed by the interview focus group and diary study methods (Martins et al., 2015).

To optimize the usability assessment, the use of a combination of methods is a common practice, especially a combination of test and inquiry methods (Martins, Queirós, Silva & Rocha, 2016). Usability evaluation is a complex task even when it comes to assessing the usability of relatively simple systems. Given the complexity of new assistive products and services it is clear that the use of only one method may not be sufficiently comprehensive to thoroughly assess all relevant issues associated with a given product or service.

The combination of methods allows a comprehensive assessment of the various characteristics of a product or service. Hanington & Martin (2012) suggest that the combination of various methods for usability assessment is required because the specifications of the different methods is too incomplete to allow for a consistent and systematic use. In addition, the various methods have different capabilities and limitations, and provide information of different types, so their combination is very important (Hanington & Martin, 2012).

Concerning the evaluation of usability and accessibility features, few studies have been found mentioning the adoption of a protocol during the evaluation of devices usability and of resources for accessibility.

The research cited in (Sanchez & Hassler, 2017) reports an evaluation of speech synthesizers. However, these assessments were qualitative in nature, e.g. based on user opinion and focused exclusively on screen readers and speech synthesizers used to access Internet sites. The evaluation experiments cited did not mention the support of an experimental protocol and were limited to a small number of participants. Samples of users with fewer than ten participants were not significant to support the reported inferences. In addition, the mechanisms used for data collection and analysis were only superficially addressed. In the researched literature, few reports of usability tests applied to evaluate the accessibility of devices for visually impaired users were found. Here follows a brief presentation of the relevant work found on this subject.

Pascual et al., (2014) evaluate the mood of disabled users while interacting with two websites with parallel content, but opposite accessibility characteristics (A-website, an accessible website, and NA-website, a non-accessible website). The authors used a JAWS screen reader to do the survey. The results confirm that the A-website had better results than the NA-website in terms of efficiency, effectiveness and user satisfaction.

The research described in (Ferreira et al., 2012) analyzes two observation methods involving people with totally impaired vision in order to develop a protocol with recommendations that can assist professionals in the identification of characteristics and problems, which can be solved or minimized during the interface's evaluations thus facilitating the process of system access focusing on users with totally impaired vision. The usability test was performed with fifteen participants: four blind, two with low vision, three with learning disabilities, two deaf, two deaf-blind and two without any type of disability. Despite its contribution, this protocol is focused on evaluating a screen reader when accessing the Internet and is not comprehensive enough to be used in the evaluation of other resource types. The need of specific participants during the tests (such as human assistants to act as interpreters) is not mentioned.

In (Sánchez & Hassler, 2017), a protocol to evaluate the usability of AUDIOMUD, a virtual reality software game for blind users, is described. The game goal is to place the player in the human body in order to cure diseases, based on the listed symptoms, changing the conditions to which the body is subjected. The interaction with this virtual environment is based on a text reader (synthesizer) that guides the player along the navigation allowing interactions with other players, through a system of chat.

It is important to note that in most of the cited publications the experiments were designed to evaluate a specific device or help resource designed to improve the accessibility of web browsing activity.

Gahlawat and co-workers (Gahlawat, Malik & Bansal, 2014) discuss an approach to develop a natural sound speech synthesizer. Five parameters (naturalness, intelligibility, usability, localization awareness and expressions) were considered for analysis of the speech synthesizer (Gahlawat et al., 2014).

From the review, it was clear that in rare cases where an experimental protocol is described, this is too shallow to answer the questions raised regarding the conditions under which the tests were performed. In addition, the sample size was too small to support the conclusions drawn. Hence the need to propose an experimental protocol to support the evaluation of usability devices and systems designed to support the accessibility, as well as the accessibility level achieved. Therefore, the authors adopted an experimental protocol was adopted to provide a set of procedures and related documents to guide the evaluator during experiments planning and conduction.

MATERIALS AND METHODS

The experiment consisted in evaluating the usability of three accessibility aid features: a Braille keyboard and two voice synthesizers (DOSVOX and JAWS) for blind users. DOSVOX software was developed for Portuguese language and is available for free for blind people. The software tools evaluated were: text editor, screen reader and e-mail. JAWS is marketed by Freedom Scientific and the features tested were the screen reader and the internet browser. The version chosen for tests was the most recent one at the time of the test preparation (version 4.1), with a platform developed for DOS environment instead of Windows. The JAWS version was 12.0, also the latest available at the time. JAWS and DOSVOX, as well as the Braille keyboard, were chosen because of their popularity amongst users of the Institute for Blind People.

An experimental usability protocol consists of a set of interrelated steps, processes and activities to guide an evaluation team during the phases: planning, conducting, collecting data, analyzing and reporting the results. These steps are presented in (Aguiar & Vieira, 2009). The adapted protocol supported the planning and evaluation phases of usability assessment experiences during which people with visual impairment performed tasks to demonstrate the suitability of specific accessibility features. As the protocol proposed by (Aguiar & Vieira, 2009) has a comprehensive and modular structure, the adaptation required to accommodate the usability assessment of the accessibility of systems and devices resulted in small changes in the steps and processes, without changes in the structure. Its application is to verify that a visual support, under evaluation, conforms to an adequate technical standard of accessibility. The adequacy requirements are presented in (Lima et al., 2010) and (Lima et al., 2018).

Inference of the User's Help Towards Performance and Motivation Levels

The protocol used during the experiment, aimed to investigate the hypothesis that the users' performance and motivation level can be affected by the particular usability tool used to perform a certain task. In order to achieve this goal, the protocol included activities that can be classified in the categories learning, leisure and social inclusion.

Before starting the activities, users were asked to express their preferences by choosing the keyboard type (Braille or conventional keyboard) and the desired media on which they wanted to read the script describing the tasks (Ledor, JAWS or DOSVOX system or printed Braille). Likewise, users had different possibilities to answer the questions at the end of each task: writing in Braille, typing on the keyboard, or having their voice responses recorded. The tasks to be performed consisted of:

- **Task 1 (task category: learning):** The user alone or, when needed, with the help of a team member expert, was asked to read and understand a predefined text using speech synthesizer support. The user had to choose between three texts, in different themes (1- World Cup, 2- Brazilian dance festival and 3- explanations on how to apply for jobs in the public sector). After reading, the user was asked to answer related questions.
- **Task 2 (task category: fun, entertainment):** The user alone or, when needed, with the help of a team member expert, was asked (i) to access a news site, (ii) to elect and read news and (iii) to highlight (orally or in writing) the aspects considered most relevant and interesting.
- **Task 3 (task category: social inclusion):** The user alone or, when needed, with the help of a team member expert, was requested to access a specific financial website (http://www.caixa.gov.br), which is the financial agent from the Brazilian government's program that offers loans to low-income families to buy houses, and to simulate the application for a loan, filling out the necessary forms.

User Group Recruitment

Recruitment of participants (users) was carried out through interviews based on the profile of the individuals and their availability and interest in participating in the research; the selected user group consisted of thirty-two people that perceived the relevance and potential impact the tool to be tested would have on their community. The group of participants consisted of 30 individuals, aged between 18 and 60, both genders, with blindness or acquired blindness, from a generalized background (teachers and students of a school for blind people).

This study focused on participant's computing skills and familiarity with screen readers. According to their abilities they were classified as inexperienced (rarely used computers and had poor screen reader skills), intermediate (were learning to use screen readers) and experienced (highly skilled in using screen readers and computers) users. Ten participants were identified as inexperienced, ten as intermediate and ten as experienced users of JAWS and DOSVOX screen readers; it should be noted that these resources offer similar features.

Group Performance: Testing Criteria

The groups were compared in performance using the ANOVA test with classification criteria and with the Tukey test, to evaluate the conditions of normality and homogeneity necessary for the tests validation. The system used for analysis was Minitab 15 (Minitab - 2012). The ANOVA and Tukey (Box, Hunter & Hunter, 1978; Hoaglin, Mosteller & Tukey, 2009) tests were chosen to compare the averages among the three groups of users, depending on the characteristics in the sampling universe (size and homogeneity) and the significance criterion for the two tests. In order to support this analysis, the following metrics were considered: total number of errors, time spent on the task, number of times help was requested, number of errors due to interpretation of the text, number of times participants reported difficulty understanding audio and number of incorrect actions.

Group Performance Testing

The usability test followed the steps of the experimental protocol, with preparation of materials followed by a pilot test to validate the adequacy of resources and materials directed to the data collection and analysis of variables of interest. The experiments were carried out at the Laboratory of Human Machine Interfaces (LIHM) of the Federal University of Campina Grande (UFCG), and at the Institute of blinds in Campina Grande (Brazil). Users and usability specialists followed the procedures specified in the experimental protocol, duly adapted to the specific context of working with visually impaired people.

As specified in the protocol, participants were invited to sign an agreement stating the purpose of the experiment and the rules of participation, including their right to anonymity. The right to stop participation at any time during the test was highlighted. Conditions accepted, participants were also asked to state otherwise if they agreed to the recording of video images. All participants agreed to video recording. At the beginning of the session, participants received the test script containing a description of each task to be performed. The script was available in Braille printed form and in electronic format, which could be read using a screen reader.

After introducing the participants to the test, they were asked to perform the tasks specified in the script. Inexperienced users were previously given a brief training. The participants were filmed during the test and data were pooled for further analysis.

User Satisfaction

The satisfaction of the 30 participants was evaluated by means of a quiz following the standards adopted by LIHM - WebQuest (Queiroz, 2001); the satisfaction index was calculated from the collected data using the model in (Bailey & Pearson, 1983). The quiz is composed by ten questions associating a three-level relevance indicator to each researched characteristic. The model followed by quiz was adapted from the model proposed in (Bailey & Pearson, 1983) and is described in the following paragraphs:

1. The scale used to measure the participants reactions has three levels (-1, 0 and 1), instead of the seven levels between -3 and 3 adopted by the LIHM.
2. Only one semantic scale was associated with the quiz questions, instead of the four differential semantic scale of the original model.

3. The importance of the items was evaluated using a three point scale with values comprised between 0.1 and 1.0 and a gap of 0.5; on the other side, the original scale has seven points and the values lie between 0.1 and 1.0 with a gap of 0.15.
4. An importance index was associated with each question of the quiz, as suggested by Bailey and Pearson.

The equations of the original model by Bailey and Pearson were modified accordingly to the changes made.

Equation (1) is originally used in a scenario where each factor is characterized with four adjectives; in the current case only one adjective is used. The modified equation used in the current study is the following:

$$R_{ij} = \sum_{j=1}^{n} I_{ijk} \tag{1}$$

where R_{ij} is the reaction of a user and I_{ijk} is a numerical response of the user to the adjective k of the factor j.

Similarly, only one adjective term, instead of four, was used for Equation (2):

$$S_i = \sum_{j=1}^{n} \frac{w_{ij}}{j=1} I_{ijk} \tag{2}$$

where S_i is the survey satisfaction index and w_{ij} is the importance given to factor j by user i.

In Equation (3), the modification consisted of using the value one as the maximum level instead of the value three:

$$NS_i = \frac{S_i}{F_i} \tag{3}$$

where NS_i is the normalized satisfaction index for each user i, and F_i is the number of significant factors.

The three-point scale and the normalized satisfaction levels are depicted in Figure 1; values between 0 and 0.49 are associated with a positive response from the participant, 0.5 reflects a neutral reaction and values between 0.5 and 1 translate a negative reaction from the participant.

Focus Group

The focus group is a qualitative data collection technique involving a small number of participants in an informal discussion group, focused on a specific subject (Bevan & Bruval, 2003). A moderator introduces topics and guides the discussion. The objective is to extract perceptions, feelings, attitudes and ideas

Figure 1. Levels used for the satisfaction index

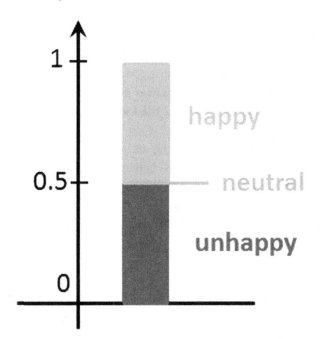

from the participants on a certain subject. This technique is often used in the design and development of new products or services (Wilkinson, 2015).

The usability of a tool, when assessed from the point of view of the user, includes a component that reflects the subjectivity related with the individual differences and goals of the different users. To overcome this issue, it was decided to introduce a focus group evaluation; the users were required to give their opinion about the strong and weak points of the accessibility resources and were encouraged to give suggestions for improvements. The focus group was composed by 16 individuals, 15 of them were blind and 1 was visually impaired. Only 2 out of the 16 individuals of the focus group did not participate in the usability text. The procedure that was followed is described in the following paragraphs.

At the beginning of the session, the moderator presented the goal of the discussion and encouraged the participants to identify themselves in a quick presentation. The moderator guided the discussion and motivated the participants with previously chosen topics of interest; the chosen topics were related with the issues detected during the usability tests and aimed at evaluating the ease of learning and use of the following resources: Braille keyboard and *JAWS* and *DOSVOX* screen readers. The session took place on the Instituto of the Blind in Campina Grande, taking advantage of the familiarity of the participants with the place, and lasted for two hours. The session was divided in three parts dedicated to the three accessibility resources. The discussion was organized around the following topics:

1. General opinion about the resource;
2. General feeling about the resource;
3. Suggestions for the improvements required to facilitate the interaction with a computer;
4. Description of the characteristics of an ideal resource to facilitate the interaction with a computer.

RESULTS

Performance Indicators

In order to calculate the performance indicators, each task was considered to be performed (i) successfully, (ii) with help or (iii) incompletely; in case the task was not successfully concluded, it was considered that the participant (iv) failed to perform the task. Table 1 shows the performance indicators for the three tasks, based on the type of participant.

Only Task 1 was finished by all the participants, and in most cases help from the evaluation team was required. These results reflect the participants' generalized lack of knowledge about the tools. On the other hand, the group of experienced users was able to complete Tasks 1, 2 and 3, although some of them with errors. The participants familiar with JAWS and DOSVOX systems were, as expected, more successful in performing the tasks, irrespectively of their nature.

Parametric Tests

In order to take into account the different backgrounds of the participants, the results of the groups were compared using parametric tests. The performance of the groups was compared using the ANOVA test, with classification criteria and the Tukey test. The normality and homogeneity conditions required for the validation of the tests were accepted. The results of the statistical test are shown in Table 2.

Regarding the number of requests for assistance and incorrect actions, the p-value obtained and used was lower than the criterion of significance adopted for the ANOVA test described in section *Group Performance: Testing Criteria*, which allowed rejection of their respective null hypothesis. Thus, Tukey's test was applied, resulting in statistically significant differences between the averages of the two groups (experienced and intermediate) and (experienced and inexperienced). Therefore, since the value zero does not belong to the confidence interval, it follows that the group of experienced users shows better performance.

Regarding incorrect actions, differences can be found between the average results of experienced and inexperienced participants with inexperienced users exhibiting better performances (section *Group Performance: Testing Criteria*). This result could be explained by considering that inexperienced users were submitted to a brief training (section *Group Performance Testing*) and being less experienced were more careful in performing their tasks, thus reducing the errors incidence.

Thus, with the presented inferences, the previous experience of participant with the resource did not interfere with the performance level of Task 1. The analysis of the usability results based on the nature

Table 1. Performance levels (% of participants) versus nature of tasks

Task name	Task 1 learning			Task 2 fun			Task 3 social inclusion		
	Experienced	Intermediate	Beginner	Experienced	Intermediate	Beginner	Experienced	Intermediate	Beginner
Performed successfully	0	0	13	0	0	19	0	0	40
Performed with help	36	32	0	0	0	0	0	0	0
Incomplete	0	0	0	43	0	0	0	0	0
Failed	0	0	19	9	0	29	0	0	60

Table 2. Results and relevance of ANOVA and Tukey tests for the adopted metrics

Metric	Average			ANOVA (p)	TUKEY
	Experienced	**Intermediate**	**Beginner**		
Total task time	14.6	14.2	14.5	0.98	
Total number of errors	2.4	4.9	3.8	0.9	
Number of help requests	0.01	4.6	4.2	0.0	Group3= Group2 (0,9 a 1,7) Group1 ≠ Group3 (3,1 a 5,8) Group1 ≠ Group2 (2,7 a 5,4)
Text interpretation error	2.9	2.9	2.4	0.08	
Difficulty to understand audio	0.2	0.9	0.9	0.05	
Number of incorrect actions	0.5	0.4	0.0	0.03	Group3= Group2 (0 a 0,8) Group1 = Group3 (0,5 a 0,3) Group1 ≠ Group2 (0,9 a 0,2)

of the task was performed only for the group of participants enabled in the Using the JAWS and DOS-VOX systems, since this was the only group able to perform all tasks, considering the null hypothesis for the ANOVA test.

There were no significant differences between the averages of the groups nor in the total number of errors incurred in performing Tasks 1, 2 and 3. This suggests that the number of errors is reduced when the participant is highly motivated to accomplish the task.

For the ANOVA test, the average of the total number of errors decreased in the following order: the highest was obtained for Task 2 ($T_2 = 7.7$) followed by Task 1 ($T_1 = 2.4$) and finally by Task 3 ($T_3 = 1,2$). The value of the significance criterion p ($p = 0.01$) was lower than the level of significance adopted for the hypothesis test, therefore, the null hypothesis was rejected. The Tukey test suggests that:

- The average of total number of errors incurred during Task 1 and Task 3 is the same, since the confidence interval does not exclude zero (-3.9 to 6.3);
- The average of total number of errors incurred during Task 3 and Task 2 is different, since the confidence interval excludes zero (1.3 to 11.6), meaning that the participants achieved a better performance during Task 3;
- The average of total number of errors identified during Task 1 and Task 2 is different because the confidence interval excludes zero (0.1 to 10.4), meaning that the participants achieved a better performance during Task 3.

The usability of Braille keyboard was evaluated considering the difficulty felt by the participant in locating characters during the evaluation test (Figure 2). As none of the participants had prior experience with the Braille keyboard, the predominant feature during the analysis was the participant's previous knowledge about Braille, rather than previous experiences with the keyboard itself. Among the 30 participants in the test, the clear majority (27 out of 30) opted for Braille.

Regarding Task 1, 45% of the participants did not have any difficulties in using the Braille keyboard; on the other hand, for Task 2, only 13% of the users had difficulties in using the Braille keyboard. During this task, all participants reported some kind of difficulty in using the keyboard. Finally, the majority of

Figure 2. Ability to use the Braille keyboard during the test

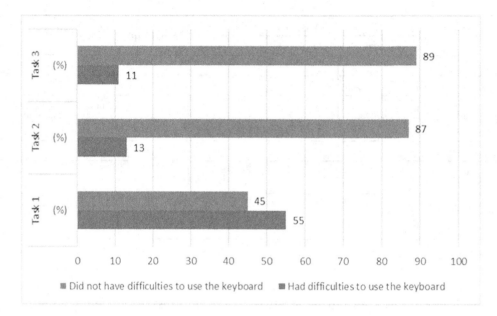

participants were able to perform Task 3; thanks to the familiarity obtained during the execution of the previous tasks, the reported level of difficulty was low.

Group Performance Testing

Given the experimental protocol modularity, the changes that were made in order to adapt it to accessibility assessment consisted of small adjustments in some steps, processes and activities; these consisted mainly in planning the stages of the experiment in order to adapt the test environment to the specific needs of the group of participants.

The protocol described in section *Group Performance Testing* proved to be adequate for the purpose of supporting the usability evaluation of the accessibility resources, promoting an appropriate ethical treatment to the participants of the experiment. Given the metrics: total task time, total number of errors and errors in text interpretation due to the difficulty in understanding the audio produced by the synthesizer, the results obtained from usability point of view, indicate that previous experience with specific help resources does not directly influence the performance of the user. According to the results, it was verified that the inexperienced users, in some tasks, presented better performance than experienced users, which can be explained by the introductory training session, as well as by their behavior: being less confident and therefore less experienced, these participants asked for help more often than experienced participants. This result is evidenced by the fact that only the experienced participants completed Tasks 1 and 2. It is important to mention that, despite the experience of experienced participants with computer systems and accessibility aids, difficulties were observed in the group, which prevented them from performing tasks more efficiently.

On the other hand, without the help of the evaluation team, inexperienced users would not have been able to participate in the experiment. Regarding the Braille keyboard usage, according to results, the difficulties observed in Tasks 1, 2 and 3 were higher among participants who did not know the Braille method. During the last step of the experiment, participants were encouraged to discuss their experience; at this stage the participant's educational background impact on the expectations and opinions on the accessibility aids evaluated was highlighted.

The participants incurred in some errors when performing the different tasks. According to the LIHM experimental protocol, errors can be classified as:

- **Serious:** errors that cause discomfort and seriously compromise the regular action flow, preventing the user from reaching the desired goal;
- **Moderate:** errors that cause some discomfort and force a change in the regular action flow but don't prevent the user from reaching the desired goal;
- **Light:** errors that cause some discomfort and required the user do adapt his/her actions but don't compromise him/her from reaching the desired goal.

Table 3 lists the errors incurred by the participants while performing the different tasks.

User Satisfaction

Table 4 lists the results of DOSVOX and JAWS user satisfaction quiz. The satisfaction indexes attributed by the users are described in Figure 1. The general satisfaction of the DOSVOX users was, for most items of the quiz, quite good. All the satisfaction indexes were higher than 0.51 with the exception of "Browsing simplicity", for which both inexperienced and experienced users revealed a neutral position (index of 0.5).

Table 3. Participant knowledge about Braille versus ability to use the Braille keyboard during the test

Task	Error type	Error name	Error description	# Occurrences
1	Serious	JAWS1	Time-out control mechanisms are missing	26
		JAWS3	Information related with interface elements is missing	28
		JAWS3	Spelling checker is missing	15
	Moderate	JAWS4	Explicit and implicit information related with commands is missing	45
2	Serious	DOSVOX1	Names of interface elements are inappropriate and don't follow the conventions of the platform	20
		DOSVOX2	"Undo" or "confirm" buttons are missing	21
	Moderate	DOSVOX3	Explicit and implicit information related with commands is missing	45
		DOSVOX4	Mechanisms that redirect the user to the error location are missing	40
	Light	DOSVOX5	Mechanisms that allow for the reduction of the number of steps required to perform a task are missing	40
		DOSVOX6	The aesthetic appearance of the interface is not minimalist	21
3	Serious	JAWS5	Alternative access to relevant audio and video tasks is missing	12

Relatively to JAWS system, the satisfaction indexes and the arithmetic average are, for experienced and intermediate users, much higher than 0.51 (0.9 and 0.8, respectively), revealing a generalized satisfaction with the system. However, the arithmetic average of the satisfaction indexes of inexperienced users is 0.5, revealing a neutral position. This happens because the satisfaction indexes of "Ease of use" and "Browsing simplicity" questions is lower than 0.49 (0.3 in both cases); in addition, for the question "Initial learning difficulty" the inexperienced users revealed a neutral position. Relatively to the other questions, the satisfaction of inexperienced users was also high.

Considering the arithmetic average of all the satisfaction indexes for all the users (0.8 for VOSDOX and 0.7 for JAWS), the participants evaluated both systems in a positive way.

Table 5 lists the results of Braille and conventional keyboards user satisfaction quiz. The users revealed a general satisfaction with both keyboards.

Focus Group Results

In order to analyze the data related with the opinions of the users from the institute *Instituto dos Cegos,* they were organized as teachers (T) and student (S) groups. The teachers and students group were composed by 3 and 13 individuals, respectively, of the institute. Like was mentioned in the section ***Erro! A origem da referência não foi encontrada.***, only 2 out of the 16 users had not participated in the usability test.

Table 6 summarizes the opinions (A – agree, D – disagree, and N – neutral opinion) of the participants of the teachers and students' groups regarding the different q that were arisen by each group.

Table 4. Satisfaction indexes for DOSVOX and JAWS systems

Quiz questions	DOSVOX				JAWS			
	Experienced	Intermediate	Beginner	All	Experienced	Intermediate	Beginner	All
Ease of use	1.0	0.9	0.7	0.8	0.9	0.7	0.3	0.6
Required learning time	0.9	0.9	0.7	0.8	1.0	0.7	0.7	0.8
Initial learning difficulty	1.0	0.7	0.7	0.8	0.8	0.9	0.5	0.7
Voice quality	0.6	0.8	0.7	0.7	0.9	0.8	0.6	0.8
Help	0.9	0.9	0.8	0.9	0.9	0.7	0.8	0.7
Browsing simplicity	0.5	0.6	0.5	0.6	0.9	0.8	0.3	0.7
Arithmetic average	0.8	0.8	0.7	0.8	0.9	0.8	0.5	0.7

Table 5. Satisfaction indexes for Braille and conventional keyboards

Quiz questions	Braille keyboard				Conventional keyboard			
	Experienced	Intermediate	Beginner	All	Experienced	Intermediate	Beginner	All
Ease of keyboard use	0.9	1.0	0.6	0.8	0.8	0.9	0.6	0.8

Table 6. System flaws identified by the Focus Group and participants opinion; A – agree; D – disagree; N – neutral opinion

Resource	Question	Source group	A	D	N	A	D	N
DOSVOX	Appropriate for teaching usability resources	Teachers	3	0	0	4	0	9
	Adaptable to web browsing	Teachers	3	0	0	13	0	0
	Facilitates access to text and spreadsheet editors, graphical objects and pdf documents	Teachers	3	0	0	5	1	7
	Difficulties in web browsing	Students	3	0	0	10	0	3
	Improvements in navigation mechanisms required	Students	3	0	0	9	0	4
	Good voice quality	Students	1	2	0	11	0	2
	Accessible tutorial missing	Students	3	0	0	13	0	0
JAWS	Limited screen readers	Students	3	0	0	7	0	6
	Quality of automatic voice is not good	Teachers	3	0	0	13	0	0
	Spelling checker is missing	Teachers	3	0	0	3	0	10
	Screen readers are flexible to use	Students	0	0	3	8	0	5
	Screen readers influence the learning process of formal written language	Teachers	3	0	0	2	8	3
Braille keyboard	Facilitates learning process	Teachers	3	0	0	10	3	0
	Problem with signal standards	Students	3	0	0	5	0	8
	Useful for home and teaching/learning use but not for work environment	Teachers	3	0	0	7	6	0
	Appropriate for users with low vision	Teachers	1	0	2	0	0	13
	Easy to use	Students	3	0	0	9	4	0
	For experienced users the height of the signals is confusing when compared with the height of signals in conventional keyboards	Students	0	1	2	10	3	0

Table 7 presents the total number of users that agreed, disagreed or remained neutral relatively to the questions raised during the meeting. The data show that the opinions of both groups of participants, teachers and students, were quite similar. On the other hand, the vast majority of participants (25, 24 and 21 for DOSVOX, JAWS and Braille keyboard, respectively) that did not emit an opinion belonged to the students group. Regarding the resource DOSVOX, most students and teachers agreed with the

Table 7. Participants opinion regarding the system flaws identified by the focus group

Resource	Total number of opinions	Teachers			Students		
		Agree	Disagree	Neutral	Agree	Disagree	Neutral
DOSVOX	7	19	2	0	65	1	25
JAWS	5	12	0	3	33	8	24
Braille keyboard	6	13	1	4	41	16	21

questions that were arisen (65 and 19, respectively); the opposite opinions totalized 2 and 1 among the teachers and the students, respectively. The tendency observed for the resource JAWS is slightly different: 33 and 12 agreeing opinions among students and teachers, respectively, against 8 opposite opinions among the teachers (no student manifested disagreement relatively to the questions that were arisen).

The general opinions of the participants relatively to the usability of each of the tested resources are summarized in the following paragraphs.

DOSVOX:

5.   **Teaching of accessibility resources in teaching institutions:** The users reported that the first contact they had with screen readers was DOSVOX and that their teaching institutions stimulate the use of DOSVOX.
6.   **Can be adapted for web browsing.**
7.   **Should guarantee access to text and spreadsheet editors, graphical objects and pdf documents.** The users revealed dissatisfaction relatively to the limitations of DOSVOX in the reading of images and graphical objects. The suggestion of upgrading VOSDOX to read also pdf documents was not consensual because some users believed that VOSDOX already reads this type of documents while the other users believed otherwise.
8.   **Difficulties in browsing the internet.** The users suggested that DOSVOX should be used to access the web sites. However, in this case the design of the websites would have to follow the accessibility standards. This, together with the graphical contents of the websites and the help of screen readers, would solve the issues of reading web content.
9.   **Browsing mechanisms need to be improved.**
10. **Good voice quality.** The users consider that DOSVOX is better than JAWS relatively to the audio quality.
11. **Missing accessibility tutorial.** The DOSVOX tutorial is available online, however the Braille or audio versions are missing.

JAWS:

12. **The use of screen readers is limited.**
13. **The quality of the robotized voice is low.**
14. **Spell checkers are missing.**
15. **The screen readers are flexible.**
16. **The use of screen readers has an impact in the learning process of formal written language.**

Braille keyboard:

17. **The use of the Braille keyboard facilitates the learning process.**
18. **Issues with the signal standards.** The users reported that the Braille tags did not match the standard keys map.
19. **Applicability of the keyboard in home, teaching or work environments.** This was another controversial question. Some users affirm that the Braille keyboard is appropriate for home applications, while other users affirm the keyboard is more appropriate for commercial applications.

20. **Appropriate for users with low vision.** The tags are large and this facilitates the use of this resource by people with low vision.
21. **Easy to use.** This was another controversial item. Beginners approve the Braille keyboard, since it facilitates the finding of the keys. Experienced users affirm the Braille keyboard brings no added-value since they had already memorized the position of the keys in the conventional keyboards.
22. **Height of the Braille signals is confusing.** Experienced users affirm the height of the board signs in confusing in comparison with traditional keyboards.

The opinions of teachers and students regarding the discussed items differ in some aspects. However, the analysis of the objects of discrepancy points to four major disagreements relatively to the DOSVOX, JAWS and Braille keyboard resources:

- **Quality of voice:** teachers consider that the voice in DOSVOX and JAWS systems is hard to understand, while the students consider that the understanding comes after some training.
- **Access to contents and help systems:** the students consider the resources are robust, however they refer that some more experience is required before the potential of the applications can be fully exploited.
- **The use of screen readers as an alternative to Braille reading:** the teachers consider that the first may have a detrimental effect in the capacity of using the written language, however the students believe that the adaptation of spell checkers may provide the solution for this issue.
- **Use of Braille keyboard:** the students consider that the location of characters in the Braille keyboard is confusing, while the teachers consider that the Braille keyboard enriches the Braille method and can be a fundamental resource towards the inclusion of the inexperienced user in the learning and work environments.

DISCUSSION

Given the experimental protocol modularity and scope for usability evaluation, the necessary changes to adapt it to the accessibility evaluation consisted in minor adjustments in some steps, processes and activities; mainly in the planning steps of the experiment to adapt the testing environment for the specific needs of the group of participants.

The adapted protocol proved to be adequate for the purpose of supporting the assessment of the usability of accessibility features, promoting an ethical and adequate treatment to participants of the experiment.

A multi-method data collection approach was used, implementing quantitative (performance evaluation and user satisfaction survey) and qualitative data collection methods (focus group). This ensured a more comprehensive and adequate usability evaluation (Martins et al., 2016).

The results obtained, from the usability point of view, indicate that there is no direct influence of previous experience with specific aid resources, on the user's performance, given the metrics: total task time; total number of errors; text interpretation errors due to the difficulty in understanding the audio produced by the synthesizer. According to the results, it was found that inexperienced users, in some tasks, displayed a better performance, which can be explained by an introductory training session, more numerous requests for help from the evaluation team, besides being less confident and therefore more careful than the experienced participants. This result is evidenced by the fact that only the experienced participants completed Tasks 1 and 2; with the latter being completed successfully only by this group. It is important to mention that despite the experience of the experienced participants with computer systems and accessibility aids, difficulties were observed in this group, which prevented them from performing the tasks more efficiently. On the other hand, inexperienced users were only able to use the accessibility aid products with the help of the team, without which would have been unviable the participation in experiment. Given the last step of the experiment, during which the participants were enticed to discuss their experience, it was highlighted the impact of the participant's educational background on the expectations and opinions about the evaluated accessibility aids.

The following steps in this research consist on refining the experiment materials and extending its application to an even bigger sample which allows for more inference between subgroups of participant's profiles. The availability of the protocol should facilitate the planning and performing of the usability tests, hopefully exposing the difficulties faced by the visually impaired community when using accessibility resources, as well as their acceptance levels regarding perception, comprehension and ease of interaction.

Even though the focus of this research was not to evaluate the voice synthesizers JAWS and DOSVOX, the results from the protocol application suggest that there are resources that users can benefit from the redesign of some features related to the usability problems found.

The results of the usability evaluation indicate that navigation failures have a relevant impact on the overall usability of the system. Experienced users generally tend to memorize commands to access the system, having a significant advantage over other user profiles. It is also worth mentioning that errors related to navigation and error prevention mechanisms, such as notification mechanisms and predictable navigation, would prevent experienced and inexperienced users from performing incorrect actions. This finding refers to the results presented in Table 1, in which only the group of experienced users completed tasks 1 and 2, and the latter was successfully completed only by part of this group. In the results presented in Table 2, the help request metric showed a difference between the means of the user groups, with inexperienced users presenting better performance. Although in the incorrect actions item the inexperienced users performed better, this result can be explained by the help that these users had during the accomplishment of the task, besides these users have been restricted to the execution of actions presented during the training.

In this study, the subjective satisfaction of users does not directly reflect the failures usability of the system. Actually, the literature reports that the opinion of the users, collected through the filling of generic self-reported subjective scales, does not fully reflect users' performance (Martins et al., 2016). In fact, the work developed by Bangor and colleagues examined 200 studies that evaluated the usability using the System Usability Scale and found that the results do not follow all performance spectrum (Bangor, Kortum & Miller, 2008).

The confrontation of the data obtained with the satisfaction survey with those obtained from the focus group may also differ due to the context in which the opinions were collected. The focus group is a less formal method and therefore was more favorable to the spontaneity of the users, when issuing their opinions. The focus group reflected both usability failures and suggestions for improvements.

In general, users were satisfied with the JAWS and DOSVOX system, however a difference was identified between inexperienced, intermediate and experienced users. It was noticed that the greater the time and the frequency of use, the more favorable the users' opinions tend to be.

According to the results of the evaluation trial, the reports of difficulties using the Braille keyboard, in performing Tasks 1, 2 and 3, was higher among users who did not know the Braille method.

It has been found that the *DOSVOX* system needs revisions in several aspects that are listed below:

- Provide a graphical interface associated with the audio description of all elements presented on the screen;
- Develop an electronic help system, which allows on-line access to system help information;
- Migrate to a platform that accepts graphic elements, in which it is possible to configure accessibility (Since DOSVOX was developed for the DOS environment);
- Develop of significant notification mechanisms to the user.

Regarding the JAWS system, it is suggested a re-planning of the navigation elements such as menus to access the systems and communication with other applications such as text and image editors.

It is also proposed to extend the evaluation to other accessibility features in order to classify them in terms of suitability to the context: domestic use, work environment and public environments.

Finally, it is proposed to extend the application of the methodology to evaluations of accessibility resources in general, including resources for other types of limitations: motor, cognitive, etc.

The data obtained from the experiment allowed the testing of the assumptions, leading to the conclusion that the adapted methodology and protocol are effective for the comprehensive usability evaluation, as it highlighted which methods are most effective in locating specific categories of usability problems.

CONCLUSION

It is considered that the main contribution of this paper is to provide a protocol with a set of methods and procedures, adapted for use in evaluations of accessibility products and devices, for the blind community.

The future steps of this research include refining the materials of the experiment and extend its application to an even larger sample that allows more inference between subgroups of participant profiles. The availability of the protocol should facilitate planning and usability testing, hopefully exposing the difficulties faced by the visually impaired community when using accessibility features, as well as their levels of acceptance regarding perception, understanding and ease of interaction. Although the focus of this research was not to evaluate the JAWS and DOSVOX speech synthesizers, the protocol application results suggest that resource users may benefit from the redesign of some features related to the usability problems that were found.

REFERENCES

Afonso, A. P., Lima, J. R., & Cota, M. P. (2013, June). Usability assessment of web interfaces: User Testing. In Information Systems and Technologies (CISTI) (pp. 1-7). IEEE.

Aguiar, Y. P. C., & Vieira, M. F. Q. (2009). Proposal of a protocol to support product usability evaluation. *Fourth IASTED International Conference Human-Computer Interaction*, 282-289.

Bailey, J. E., & Pearson, S. W. (1983). Development of a tool for measuring and analyzing computer user satisfaction. *Management Science, 29*(5), 530–545. doi:10.1287/mnsc.29.5.530

Bangor, A., Kortum, P. T., & Miller, J. T. (2008). An empirical evaluation of the system usability scale. Intl. *Journal of Human–Computer Interaction, 24*(6), 574–594. doi:10.1080/10447310802205776

Bevan, N., & Bruval, P. (2003). *Usability net: Tools & methods*. Available: http://www.usabilitynet.org/tools/list.htm

Borges, J. A. S. (2009). Tecnopolicy and the regulation of competition between blind with computer and computer unassisted sighted people in taking exams to get into Brazilian universities. *Society for Social Studies of Leuthold Science Annual Meeting, 2009, Washington. 4S'2009 Annual Meeting, 2009.*

Box, G. E., Hunter, W. G., & Hunter, J. S. (1978). *Statistics for experimenters*. Academic Press.

Dias, A., Martins, A. I., Queirós, A., & da Rocha, N. P. (2018). Interoperability in Pervasive Health: Is It Tackled as a Priority? In HEALTHINF (pp. 57-65). Academic Press.

Ferreira, S. B. L., da Silveira, D. S., Capra, E. P., & Ferreira, A. O. (2012). Protocols for evaluation of site accessibility with the participation of blind users. *Procedia Computer Science*, *14*, 47–55. doi:10.1016/j.procs.2012.10.006

Findlater, L., & McGrenere, J. (2010). Beyond performance: Feature awareness in personalized interfaces. *International Journal of Human-Computer Studies*, *68*(3), 121–137. doi:10.1016/j.ijhcs.2009.10.002

Gahlawat, M., Malik, A., & Bansal, P. (2014). Natural speech synthesizer for blind persons using hybrid approach. *Procedia Computer Science*, *41*, 83–88. doi:10.1016/j.procs.2014.11.088

Hanington, B., & Martin, B. (2012). *Universal methods of design: 100 ways to research complex problems, develop innovative ideas, and design effective solutions*. Rockport Publishers.

Hansen, E. G., Mislevy, R. J., Steinberg, L. S., Lee, M. J., & Forer, D. C. (2005). Accessibility of tests for individuals with disabilities within a validity framework. *System*, *33*(1), 107–133. doi:10.1016/j.system.2004.11.002

Hoaglin, D. C., Mosteller, F., & Tukey, J. W. (Eds.). (2009). *Fundamentals of exploratory analysis of variance* (Vol. 367). John Wiley & Sons.

Howarth, J., Smith-Jacksonb, T., & Hartsona, R. (2009). Supporting novice usability practitioners with usability engineering tools. Int. *J. Human-Computer Studies.*, *67*(6), 533–540. doi:10.1016/j.ijhcs.2009.02.003

ISO 9241-171 (2008). Ergonomics of human-system interaction: Guidance on software accessibility, London, UK. Part 171.

Jokinen, J. P. (2015). Emotional user experience: Traits, events, and states☆. *International Journal of Human-Computer Studies*, *76*, 67–77. doi:10.1016/j.ijhcs.2014.12.006

Lima, M., & Vieira, L. A. (2010). Experimental Protocol for Accessibility. In *IADIS 2010 IADIS International Conference Interfaces and Human Computer Interaction Experimental Protocol for Accessibility*. Freiburg, Germany: IADIS.

Lima, M., Vieira, R. S., Ferreira, Y. P., Aguiar, M. P., & Bastos, S.L. (2018). Evaluating System Accessibility Using An Experimental Protocol Based On Usability. *Computer Graphics, Visualization, Computer Vision And Image Processing 2018.*

Loiacono, E. T., Djamasbi, S., & Kiryazov, T. (2013). Factors that affect visually impaired users' acceptance of audio and music websites. *International Journal of Human-Computer Studies, 71*(3), 321–334. doi:10.1016/j.ijhcs.2012.10.015

Martins, A. I., Queirós, A., Silva, A. G., & Rocha, N. P. (2015). Usability evaluation methods: a systematic review. In Human Factors in Software Development and Design (pp. 250-273). IGI Global. doi:10.4018/978-1-4666-6485-2.ch013

Martins, A. I., Queirós, A., Silva, A. G., & Rocha, N. P. (2016). Usability evaluation of ambient assisted living systems using a multi-method approach. *Proceedings of the 7th International Conference on Software Development and Technologies for Enhancing Accessibility and Fighting Info-exclusion*, 261-268. ACM. 10.1145/3019943.3019981

Martins, A. I., Queirós, A., Silva, A. G., & Rocha, N. P. (2016). ICF based Usability Scale: evaluating usability according to the evaluators' perspective about the users' performance. In *Proceedings of the 7th International Conference on Software Development and Technologies for Enhancing Accessibility and Fighting Info-exclusion* (pp. 378-383). ACM. 10.1145/3019943.3019997

Mesquita, L., Sánchez, J., & Andrade, R. M. (2018, July). Cognitive Impact Evaluation of Multimodal Interfaces for Blind People: Towards a Systematic Review. In *International Conference on Universal Access in Human-Computer Interaction* (pp. 365-384). Springer. 10.1007/978-3-319-92049-8_27

Miah, S. J. (2004). Accessibility improvement of multicultural educational web interface by using the User Centred Design (UCD) approach. In *Proceedings of the 2004 Informing Science and IT Education Joint Conference* (pp. 25-28). Informing Science Institute.

Mitchell, P. P. (2007). *A step-by-step guide to usability testing*. iUniverse, Inc.

Nielsen, J. (1993). *Usability Engeneering. Academic Press Inc*. Boston: Academic Press.

Pascual, A., Ribera, M., Granollers, T., & Coiduras, J. L. (2014). Impact of accessibility barriers on the mood of blind, low-vision and sighted users. *Procedia Computer Science, 27*, 431–440. doi:10.1016/j.procs.2014.02.047

Queirós, A., Silva, A., Alvarelhão, J., Rocha, N. P., & Teixeira, A. (2015). Usability, accessibility and ambient-assisted living: A systematic literature review. *Universal Access in the Information Society, 14*(1), 57–66. doi:10.100710209-013-0328-x

Queiroz, J. E. (2001). *Abordagem Híbrida para a Avaliação da Usabilidade de Interfaces com o Utilizador. Tese (Doutorado em Engenharia Elétrica)*. Campina Grande, Paraíba, Brasil: Universidade Federal da Paraíba.

Raman, V. (2003) Specialized browsers. In WebAccessibility: A Foundation for Research,1st Edition. Springer-Verlag.

Sánchez, J., & Hassler, T. (2007). AudioMUD: A multiuser virtual environment for blind people. *IEEE Transactions on Neural Systems and Rehabilitation Engineering, 15*(1), 16–22. doi:10.1109/TNSRE.2007.891404 PMID:17436871

Sangiorgi, U. B. (2014). Electronic sketching on a multi-platform context: A pilot study with developers. *International Journal of Human-Computer Studies*, *72*(1), 45–52. doi:10.1016/j.ijhcs.2013.08.018

Simões-Marques, M., & Nunes, I. L. (2012). Usability of interfaces. In *Ergonomics-A Systems Approach*. InTech. doi:10.5772/37299

Sodnik, J., Dicke, C., Tomažič, S., & Billinghurst, M. (2008). A user study of auditory versus visual interfaces for use while driving. *International Journal of Human-Computer Studies*, *66*(5), 318–332. doi:10.1016/j.ijhcs.2007.11.001

Vatavu, R. D., Cramariuc, G., & Schipor, D. M. (2015). Touch interaction for children aged 3 to 6 years: Experimental findings and relationship to motor skills. *International Journal of Human-Computer Studies*, *74*, 54–76. doi:10.1016/j.ijhcs.2014.10.007

Wilkinson, S. (Ed.). (2015). *Qualitative psychology: A practical guide to research methods*. Sage.

Chapter 17

The Convergence Between Challenge-Based Learning and Game Design Thinking Methodologies:
Exploring Creativity and Innovation in the Game Development Process

Isabel Cristina Siqueira da Silva
UniRitter, Brazil

ABSTRACT

The process of game development is constantly evolving in order to meet the different demands of players as well as the need to adapt to the employment of new technologies and trends in the gaming market. The game design thinking methodology that adds quality to the game development once is focused on the game design and development based on design thinking, an interactive design process focused on collaboration between developers and users to propose user-centered solutions. The challenge-based learning methodology presents to the learners (and future professionals) a challenge scenario asking them to think about a number of possible solutions using a variety of interactive tools. This chapter proposes to combine both game design thinking and challenge-based learning methodologies into the process of game development in order to assist the game learners and professionals to be able to integrate different aspects necessary to the proposal of a game, considering its multidisciplinary nature and understanding the human needs involved.

INTRODUCTION

The area of game design and development evolves rapidly but still lacks proven methodologies that help the student and the professional in the area to think about the process of the game in the sense of design. This issue involves the constant need for innovation and reinvention in order to meet new audiences, new static and new experiences. Innovation and creativity are characteristics present in the day to day

DOI: 10.4018/978-1-5225-9069-9.ch017

of the game designers besides the use of methodologies aimed at establishing design patterns that aid in the development stages of games.

Game design is related to designing, creating, and coordinating the game that will be created. The professional that develops games must be able to integrate different aspects necessary to the design of a game, which has a multidisciplinary nature involving concepts of art, programming, audio, artificial intelligence, user experience, narrative among others. Therefore, it is the responsibility of the game designer the planning of the interface, interactivity, plot and mechanics of the game that should entertain the player. In other words, it is this professional who should think of ways to make the game fun, engaging and interesting for the public.

Thus, it is interesting for the future professional game designer to study higher education in games design in order to learn the methodologies and tools most used to become a developer. However, the area of games design still requires discussions involving the proposal of effective methodologies for game developing. The methodologies used in the development of software such as the cascade model, scrum among others, are not suitable for the development of games mainly because the teams are disciplinary, and the projects are dynamic.

For the game developing learners, the use of appropriate methodologies can increase the sense of creativity, innovation and inspiration to the different stages of game design. Considering that the minds of students born in the last decades have undergone significant cognitive modifications, it is noted that these modifications impel a new variety of needs and preferences. According to Mendes (2012), a large part of the problem related to the learning of digital natives lies in the fact that it is laborious to train the brain to construct thought from the traditional linearity of reading and writing, once this thought is formed due to the contact with different digital media. Then, innovative education models are needed in order to train more creative and bold professionals who are not afraid to err or exploit new possibilities for games proposes.

According to Gestwicki e McNely (2012), design thinking applied to game design (game design thinking) is adequate for providing immersive, research-based learning, bringing academic objectives closer to business environments. Design thinking is a way to solve problems, develop products and think projects based on the cognitive process that designers use. In addition to immersion, the generation of ideas, the prototyping of possibilities, the selection of solutions and the implementation are characteristics of design thinking that can be adapted to the game developing.

Considering the game designer learning, game design thinking concepts can contribute significantly to the methodology adopted in the classroom, especially in higher education institutions. The game design thinking makes learning more dynamic, persistent and interesting as it assists students in the development of greater autonomy and critical sense on a certain subject. In the same way, for the professional game designer the methodology of game design thinking favors the innovation in the development of games in order to explore opportunities in the market.

However, game design thinking can be combined with another methodology so that students are able to see the creation of a game as a challenge and thus research the area of this challenge in terms of events taking place in the world around them, the connection between what they learn in school and what they perceive outside it. This other methodology is called challenge-based learning and proposes to broaden the classroom environment by requiring access to communication tools and real-world project management to encourage studies beyond the school day. Challenge-based learning uses strategies focused on student autonomy that converge to the solution of the challenge identified and elaborated by the student himself.

Binder et al. (2017) highlight the flexible and open character of the challenge-based learning that generates a need for integration with other methods and techniques in any of its phases. Johnson et a. (2008) highlight that because challenge-based learning takes its ideas from real-world issues that students then must translate into solutions of local applicability. When integrated as a regular part of the curriculum, challenge-based learning practices naturally lead to discovery of relevant subject matter in many areas. This is an important proposal for game designers that looks for the ability to analyze and evaluate real open-ended nature problems, leading to more experiential perspective.

This chapter presents the proposal of to combine both game design thinking and challenge-based learning methodologies in order to investigate the convergence between these concepts and the gains in student engagements and game design results. The main goal is to encourage future game designers to think about the game design process broadly and effectively, to continually reflect on the content and process, and to understand the importance of the user-centric approach. This proposal was applied in undergraduate game classes and the results, obtained from a case study, are analyzed and discussed highlighting insights on the combination of both methodologies challenge-based learning and game design thinking. These results indicate the production of more creative, innovative and robust results.

The text is organized as follows. In addition to this introductory section, the next section presents the main guiding themes: challenge-based learning and game design thinking. In sequence, related work to this proposal are discussed. Then, the proposed methodology and the case study are discussed, and, at the end, the results and the final considerations are presented.

CHALLENGE BASED LEARNING

The challenge-based learning approach emerged as a byproduct of a collaborative initiative that began in 2008, called "Apple Classroom of Tomorrow - Today" (Apple, 2008), whose goal was to identify the key principles for designing educational environments in the 21st century, helping schools come closer to this generation of students in order to increase the engagement of these in the school. According to Nichols et al. (2016), challenge-based learning is a learning framework initiated at Apple, Inc. that empowers learners to address challenges while acquiring content knowledge in diverse fields. Through challenge-based learning, students and teachers proving that learning can be deep, engaging, meaningful, and purposeful.

Challenge Based Learning provides (Nichols et al., 2016):

- A flexible and customizable framework that can be implemented as a guiding pedagogy or integrated with other progressive approaches to learning;
- A scalable model with multiple points of entry and the ability to start small and build big;
- A free and open system with no proprietary ideas, products or subscriptions;
- A process that places all Learners in charge, and responsible for the learning;
- An authentic environment for meeting academic standards and making deeper connections with content;
- A focus on global ideas, meaningful challenges and the development of local and age appropriate solutions;
- An authentic relationship between academic disciplines and real-world experience;
- A framework to develop 21st-century skills;

- Purposeful use of technology for researching, analyzing, organizing, collaborating, networking, communicating, publishing and reflecting;
- The opportunity for Learners to make a difference now;
- A way to document and assesses both the learning process and products;
- An environment for deep reflection on teaching and learning.

While problem-based learning and project-based learning are usually focused on a driving question or problem, in the challenge-based learning the practical activity (the challenge) defines the content that must be studied (Jonassen, 1999) (Baloian et al., 2004) (Johnson et al., 2008) (Robinson, 2013) (Binder et al., 2017). Then, the question or the problem is replaced by a challenge. The challenge-based learning framework is shown in the Figure 1.

The challenge-based learning methodology starts from a general theme, on which essential questions, guiding questions, activities and reflections will be debated. With each basic question raised it is necessary to engage a challenge that can be converted into a practical action by the students. To do this, the general theme must be broad enough to be open to several issues.

In this context, challenge-based learning presents three main steps: (1) engage, (2) investigate, and (3) act. These three steps are interconnected in a process where the student is responsible for his/her learning based in a challenge. Each step prepares the learners to move to the next stage, encouraging them to use technologies of their daily lives to solve real world problems by creating a space where students can direct their own research using critical thinking about how to apply what they learn. Thus, the learning does not follow the passive approach, and the teacher is also a collaborator.

As can be seen in the framework of Figure 1, the engage step is related to three main issues: big idea, essential question, and challenge. An essential questioning allows the learners to contextualize and personalize the big idea (broad concept), moving from this to a concrete and actionable challenge, that is immediate and actionable. The goal is to connect to academic content through identification, development, and ownership related to a compelling challenge. In other words, the big ideas are related to broad concepts that are explored in multiple ways and are relevant to the learners, allowing for the generation of essential questions that reflect personal interests and the needs of the community. The challenge has the role of turning the essential issue into a necessity to learn deeply about it.

In the investigate step, according to Nichols et al. (2016), the learners plan and participate in a journey that builds the foundation for solutions and addresses academic requirements. For this purpose, the survey of guiding questions, guiding activities and resources are carried out. The guiding questions include everything that needs to be learned to develop an informed solution to the challenge being categorized and prioritized in order to create an outline for the learner's journey. At the end, the analysis of the lessons learned through the guiding questions and activities is performed, allowing the identification of solutions. Any resource or activity that helps answer the guiding questions and develop an innovative, insightful, and realistic solution can be used.

The last step of challenge-based learning is the act, where a solution is developed, applied in a real environment, and evaluated. For that, after the solution concept is approved, the learners develop prototypes, experiment and test. This iterative design cycle will raise new guiding questions requiring further research and swing them back into the investigate step. After developing their solutions, students implement, evaluate and reflect on the results, determining their impact on the challenge. Upon completion of the implementation, students can continue to refine the solution or share their work, publish their solutions and results.

Figure 1. Challenge-based learning methodology
(reproduced from Nichols et al., 2016)

GAME DESIGN THINKING

The game design thinking methodology considered in this work was proposed by Silva and Bittencourt (2016) and aims to develop games based on design thinking and lean and agile concepts of project development. The game design thinking is divided into four main stages: team definition, conception, prototyping and validation. These steps are described below and are summarized in the schematic of Figure 2.

The team definition that will work in a game development is a fundamental step to reach the objectives of the game, given the interdisciplinary characteristic involved in the different stages of conception and prototyping. Team members should interact, identify opportunities and come up with creative and innovative solutions to the problems of game development. Game design teams need members who play at least the roles of game designer, programmer, 2D/3D artist, sound producer. For this first stage, two strategies are proposed: influence map and T-Shaped profile (Glushko, 2008).

In T-Shaped profile technique, the participants of a team present the areas in which they have some experience, albeit superficial, and a specific area in which they have deep knowledge. This allows identifying people who can solve complex challenges while at the same time having autonomy to coordinate multidisciplinary teams.

Figure 2. Game design thinking methodology
(adapted from Silva and Bittencourt, 2016)

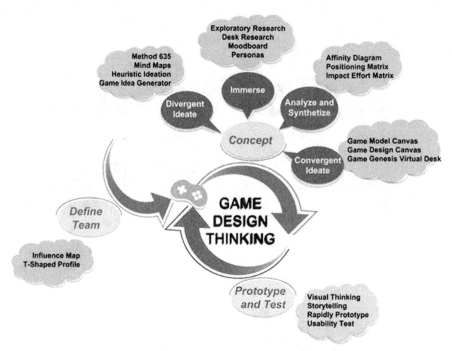

The game conception depends on four phases of conception: divergent ideation, immersion, analysis and synthesis, and convergent ideation. It is noted, therefore, that the conception begins, and ends based on the creative process and its two types of thinking: divergent and convergent.

Divergent ideation seeks to create options, from a significant quantity and diversity of ideas, in order to promote a variety of options for the immersion phase. In order to do that, different brainstorming techniques can be applied, as the method 635 (Rohrbach, 1969), the mental map (Buzan and Buzan, 2006) and the heuristic ideation technique (Gray at al., 2010).

Method 635 is intended to produce a relevant set of ideas and solutions in a short period of time. The denomination of the method originates from: groups of six participants, where each one suggests three ideas for a given problem in five minutes. As soon as the first five minutes have elapsed, each participant sends their written ideas/suggestions to another participant, which complements them with three more ideas. The process of generating ideas ends when all participants suggest three ideas for each initial proposal.

The mind map starts from a central idea linked to ideas that complement it in some way, such as a tree. Mind maps seek to represent, with as much detail as possible, the conceptual relationship between information that is usually fragmented, diffused, and sprayed in a given context.

The heuristic ideation technique consists of combining two attributes arranged in rows and columns of a table. At the intersection of row and column (cell), a combination is placed between the two values which may serve as insight into the production of new ideas.

After divergent ideation, where ideas about the game are raised, the immersion step starts, where the identification of needs and opportunities that will guide the generation of solutions in the next phase of the project are carried out. For the development of a game, four techniques are suggested at this stage: exploratory research, desk research, moodboard and empathy maps or personas (Vianna et al., 2012) (Gray et al., 2010).

The desk research complements the exploratory research, helping to identify the scenario of the game, and consists of a search of information about the theme of the project in diverse sources (websites, books, magazines, blogs, articles, among others). Thus, the identification of market niches, little exploited and with potential for expansion, is carried out. A feasibility study is also conducted, identifying similar games, platforms and categories with higher financial returns. Finally, it focuses on the target audience by surveying the profile of potential users. This whole study can be summarized in insight cards.

Another technique that assists in the immersion during the design of a game is the outline of moodboards, with a collage of texts and/or images in a panel that serve as inspiration for the developers. Empathy maps or personas are another immersion technique to increase developers' knowledge of players:

- *Who is this person?*
- *What does she like?*
- *What are your fears?*
- *What are your dreams?*
- *Who are the people she admires?*

In the analysis and synthesis step, definitions related to the game must make. In addition to considering the data gathered in the exploratory survey and the moodboard panel, cards created in the desk search can be arranged in an affinity diagram to identify similarities and patterns between them. Then, ideas and information are grouped in order to stimulate creativity and facilitate the conception of new ideas, favoring their convergence in the next stage.

The positioning and impact matrices (Gray et al., 2010) constitute further proposals for this phase. The first is the definition of criteria, such as time, complexity, innovation, costs, team members' abilities, motivation, among others. Each criterion is placed in a row and in each column the groupings of ideas are defined. One or two clusters with higher sum values go to the next steps, because they meet the pre-defined criteria best. It is important to emphasize that it does not mean that the other ideas are bad, but in front of the predefined constraints, one chooses the groupings that fit the most.

The impact matrix can be used after the positioning matrix and serves as another analysis technique. The dimensions present the effort to develop such a grouping of ideas and the impact, be it in innovation, in the market, in the receptivity of the public. So, distribute the ideas in this plan and try to identify those that generate greater impact with less effort.

The convergent ideation closes the game design phase and is characterized by making choices based on existing alternatives related to it. In this step, the ideas generated in the previous steps are critically analyze and judge so as to select them based on previously defined criteria, expanding the original ideas. In this stage, the use of two very effective tools for the convergent ideation of the game: the game model canvas (Jiménez, 2013) and game design canvas (Vekony, 2013) is suggested. To help generate new ideas while the canvas is being filled, it may be interesting to use the game genesis virtual deck (Gehling, 2016).

The term game model canvas refers to the creation of a panel with information, usually in the form of a post it, that refers to the business model of the game being developed. This panel allows to relate the information in a systemic, integrated and fast way, providing perceptions about how the development team should act in order to compose the business. It thus helps game developers build, differentiate and innovate processes, improving their business model to win audiences and earn greater profits. The panel consists of information that answers the following questions: What? Who? As? How much?

The game design canvas allows a quick synthesis of the ideas that guide the game to be developed, in order to present an overview of the game design in a single panel. Items such as gameplay, characters, mechanics, game flow, interaction among others are examples of elements covered by this creativity tool.

As an alternative, a single-page game design (design doc one page) (Librande, 2016) can be used, which consists of creating a blueprint, a schematic floor plan of the game level and the main elements surrounding it. Then, the game genesis virtual deck can be applied to make combinations of elements of game styles, reflecting on their different aspects.

During prototype and tests, four major actions should be considered at this stage: rapidly prototype, publicize/publish the game for feedback and evaluation, feedback analyze and make improvements if necessary. However, before proceeding to prototyping itself, is important to align the development process with the team members and two resources can be used: visual thinking and storytelling. These are intended to facilitate understanding of the flow of the game. Once the whole process is clear to team members, one starts off with the implementation of the game itself, choosing technologies that are easily integrated and make it possible to obtain the final product designed.

Finally, one must publish the game in order to obtain feedbacks and evaluation of player users. To this end, we recommend remote and face-to-face usability testing using the likert scale. According to Nielsen (1994), usability comprises five dimensions: learning, memorization, errors, efficiency and satisfaction/acceptance.

RELATED WORKS

Currently, there are few studies addressing game design thinking and/or challenge-based learning as methodology to aid the game design process. However, some relevant work related to this process are listed below.

Related to game design, more than a decade ago, Hunicke et al. (2006) proposed the MDA framework - mechanical, dynamic and aesthetic, a formal approach to understanding the game, bridging the gap between design and development, critique and research on games. In this way, the authors seek to reinforce the iterative processes of game developers, academics and researchers, helping study and design games and artifacts.

In the same year, Gurgel et al. (2006) discussed the importance of assessing the games usability describing the process of developing a serious game focusing on testing the graphical interface and player interaction. The authors point out that the performance of usability tests with specialists should be tested throughout the entire process of developing a game, with special emphasis between the pre-production and production phases.

Gestwicki e McNely (2012) present a case study involving the development of an educational game about curatorial and museum operations. This development was based on Kembel's design thinking model (Kembel, 2009), consisting of 5 steps: empathy, problem definition, ideation, prototyping and testing. The authors point out that immersive learning provides a differential for students as it is combined with regular empathy, which stems from a deep understanding of stakeholders and their needs, and the interactive approach.

Murakami et. al (2016) followed the traditional steps of design thinking for the development of a serious game: immersion, analysis and synthesis, ideation and prototyping. In the proposed methodology, the analysis and synthesis phase start from the compilation of the information obtained in the immersion phase in a game design document, shared via the web with the study participants. Next, in the ideation phase, the authors game design document and gameplay bricks, the concept and other aspects of the game were refined and implemented in the prototyping phase in the following sequence: definition of conceptual art, generation of graphic elements, definition of graphic interface, search for programming solutions and generation of versions of the game.

Bem et al. (2014) discuss the importance of the game design process and affirm that the alternatives for this issue are still in the process once is a recent area of study. The work explores possibilities of methodologies for generating alternatives, creative techniques and tools. The authors do not relate this process to design thinking alternatives, but to generic design methods such as subject research, object research, generation and selection of alternatives, and prototyping.

Jewell (2016) uses the term game design as a synonym for gamification and discusses its use in the development of serious games and applications in higher education and in business. The author argues that the concept of serious games, as well as providing fun and entertainment for players, involves important aspects of different sciences, thus providing great benefits for people who have access to a learning environment and/or training.

Still in relation to gamification, Kristiansen and Rasmussen (2014) point out that the use of Lego blocks aid in training and creative learning. This method is known as Lego serious play (2018) and features similarity to design thinking, combining descriptive, creative and challenging imagination to form strategic imagination. Thus, Lego blocks help participants to apply descriptive imagination, followed by the challenging imagination, where images are formed to interfere in different situation and, finally, the imagination is used creating a new scenario in order to advance the solution of the initial problem.

Related to the challenge-based learning methodology, there are no relevant works related to the application of challenge-based learning to the game development process. However, some interesting works addressing the integration of challenge-based learning with different methodologies, which were also used in the basement of this present study, are discussed below.

Marin et al. (2013) discuss the integration of challenge-based learning and iPad mobile learning technology using design thinking for maximize college English language students' learning. The authors applied the stages of design thinking to redesign the courses to better align them with the strengths of the mobile learning environment. As result, the authors conclude that there was a relative agreement at faculty level about challenge-based learning being more beneficial for student learning than a more traditional approach. The course turned the teacher/researcher into a learning observer and a guide, launching the classroom and allowing students to take responsibility and guide their own learning experiences.

Santos et al. (2013) propose to combine challenge-based learning and scrum framework for mobile application development in order to prepare students for the development market. The authors discuss an empirical study evaluated through a series of post surveys. The obtained results indicate that a teaching and learning environment based combining the challenge-based learning with the scrum framework process is an effective model to promptly teach undergraduates how to be successful mobile application developers.

Gabriel (2014) adopted a modified challenge-based learning design for a biochemistry course to improve student satisfaction and engagement, resulting in increased learning and satisfaction. As a result, students demonstrated greater interest in learning compared to traditional teaching methods.

Silveira (2016) presents a strategy for teaching GoF (for Gang of Four) design patterns through a game development process, under a flipped classroom pedagogical context. The author observes that the methodology employed motivated students in their participation and interest in theoretical discussions about this family of standards. It was realized that, compared to a traditional and expository approach, the students' contact with this abstract subject of patterns would not be converted into meaningful learning.

Binder et al. (2017) propose to apply challenge-based learning for the teaching of software development for mobile devices in order to minimize the difficulties encountered in this type of environment and with traditional teaching and learning methods. The authors evaluated the use of challenge-based learning for one year in four classes of a course with 110 students and the results were analyzed through thematic networks. Although the challenge-based learning helps in understanding problems to be solved through challenges, the authors highlight some negative points as the inadequacy of the method for certain student profiles that present the following characteristics: lack of commitment, lack of theoretical and technical base, as well as resistance to autonomy.

From these presented works, its noticed that the game design still requires specific methodologies, in order to give developers, the understanding of the design process of a complete project. In this sense, the game design thinking methodology seeks new ways for game innovation from a user-centered approach where multidisciplinarity, collaboration and tangibilization of thoughts and processes lead to innovative solutions. Besides, challenge-based learning aims the acquisition of skills by developing a solution to a real problem identified and proposed by the student. Thus, the contents that must be studied arise from the needs of this proposed challenge.

COMBINING CHALLENGE BASED LEARNING AND GAME DESIGN THINKING METHODOLOGIES

This section discusses the proposal of combination between both characteristics of game design thinking (GDT) and challenge-based learning (CBL) in a case study realized in classrooms of an undergraduate games course with sixty students. In order to combine both GDT and CBL approaches, the Table 1 presents the proposal of mapping between concepts.

As presented in the Table 1, this proposal starts with the CBL engage step and the first stage is the GDT team's definition. The definition of the team has a crucial importance because the team components must know each other, focusing on the personality of the members as well as their professional aptitude. It is necessary to give these collaborators autonomy so that they can think creatively, make associations, have the support of professionals from other sectors of the organization in order to allow the team to observe and test activities.

Table 1. Game design thinking and challenge-based learning approaches correspondence

Challenge Based Learning	Game Design Thinking
Engage: Big Idea, Essential Question, Challenge	Team Define; Concept: Divergent Ideate
Investigate: Guiding Questions, Guiding Activities/Resources, Analysis Act: Solution, Implementation, Evaluation Publishing: Student Solutions and Reflections	Concept: Immerse, Analyze and Synthesize Concept: Convergent Ideate; Prototype and Test Publishing: Game

Then, with the teams already formed, the GDT conception phase began with the divergent ideation based on brainstorming involving initial big ideas about the game. Thus, the big idea, the essential question and the challenge, proposed in challenge-based learning methodology, emerge.

The engage step ends with the induction of students to reflect on their game proposal from the following provocative questions:

1. What is the core of the game that sets it apart from the existing ones? Summarize the game story in one line.
2. What are the main inspirations and motivations for the proposal? Cite examples of games, applications, arts (with URL for access) that refer to the motivations mentioned above.
3. What is the genre of the game (e.g. Shooter)? Please, justify your choice.
4. What style of the game (e.g. Spatial)? Please, justify your choice.
5. What is the theme of the game (e.g. Western)? Please, justify your choice.
6. Which platform was chosen? Please, justify your choice.
7. Which audience was defined? Please, justify your choice.
8. Which dimension of the game (2D or 3D)? Please, justify your choice.
9. Single or multiplayer? Please, justify your choice.
10. What is the average duration of the match for this game?
11. What will make a player loyal and want to play it again?
12. What is the number of components in the group? Why is this number needed? List the names and indicate the functions of each component.

After the engage step completed, starts the CBL investigate, whose correspondent stages in the GDT are immerse, analyze and synthesize. Then, once the ideas about the game are raised, GDT immersion starts with the identification of needs and opportunities that will guide the generation of solutions in the next phase of the project. This phase enables the proposition of CBL guiding questions, that point towards the knowledge the learners will need to develop a solution to the challenge, and activities and resources, used to answer the guiding questions.

The CBL investigate step ends with the analysis of the lessons learned through the guiding activities that provides a foundation for the identification of solutions. The possibilities previously raised can be analyzed in order to identify similarities and patterns between them. So, ideas and information are grouped in order to stimulate creativity, facilitating the conception of new ideas and favoring their convergence in the next stage. Many of these groupings can be evaluated considering how much effort will be required to implement them.

The last phase of CBL is the act step, where evidence-based solutions are projected, implemented and evaluated with an authentic audience. In GDT, we have the last stage of concept, with convergent ideate, followed by prototype and tests. It is time to critically analyze and judge the ideas generated in the previous steps so as to select them based on previously defined criteria, expanding the original ideas.

Then, the developing of the prototype is initialized focusing in the tangibilization of the big idea, promoting the passage from the abstract to the physical in order to represent reality and provide validations, considering the optics of the player and the developer. At the end, tests are performed and, according to Nichols et al. (2016), provide the opportunity to assess the effectiveness of the solution, adjust and deepen subject area knowledge.

Finally, students publish their games to obtain feedbacks and evaluation of player users.

CASE STUDY

The proposed methodology was applied to final classrooms of an undergraduate games course, reaching around sixty students. Initially, the students presented their influence maps and T-Shaped profile in order to get to know each other better in terms of personal preferences and professional profile, since they came from different semesters. The size of the teams varied between three and five members. The Figures 3 presents the personal influence map of a student.

The influence map was used, in this context, for the personality mapping of each team participant, in order to identify common patterns and affinities. It was thus sought to identify what causes changes in decision making and wisdom prevailing over time as well as the influence of participants' actions in proposing solutions to problems.

Once the teams are set, the students propose the big idea of the game in the conception phase, from the divergent ideation based on the brainstorming of the initial ideas about the games (entertainment or serious games). Each team was responsible for generating the big idea of their own game, although colleagues from other teams collaborated with the essential questions during the brainstorming.

For this, method 635 was used in this work, where, at the end, the students presented their original ideas, the ideas suggested by the colleagues that would be included in their work and the ideas discarded, justifying the choices. Starting from the big idea, a set of questions that reflect current global problems related to the theme was elaborate. After reflection and dialogue, team members should reduce these issues to only one major issue that is to be resolved and which gives rise to the challenge.

Once the challenge is clear and definite, a set of guiding questions is raised to better understand the problem and what skills are needed to solve it. In order to do that, the immersion in the challenge, the analysis and the synthesis stages start through the two techniques: desk research and moodboard elaboration.

For the desk research, the items surveyed were summarized in insight cards containing title, brief description, source and date of the searched data. In order to analyze and synthesize the information

Figure 3. Influence map

collected during the immersion phase, students constructed affinity diagrams, identifying clusters from the insight cards and complemented them with moodboards, and big pictures (Figure 4). The analysis stage of the process allowed more rational considerations to be made in view of the next steps.

The convergent ideation (solution design) stage synthesized ideas in the form of game model canvas and game design canvas (Figure 5). Thus, both the business model and the game concept could be sketched in an agile way, intensifying details of definition of the scope of the game and its design concepts.

To finish the process, we adopted the visual thinking and the making of a board game, related to the proposed game, in order to visualize the game flow and mechanics. At the end, before the prototype step, the team members were invited to fill a chronogram clearly indicating the roles and responsibili-

Figure 4. Challenges: affinity diagrams and big pictures (one challenge per team)

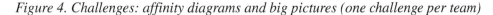

Figure 5. Challenge: game model canvas and game design canvas (one challenge per team)

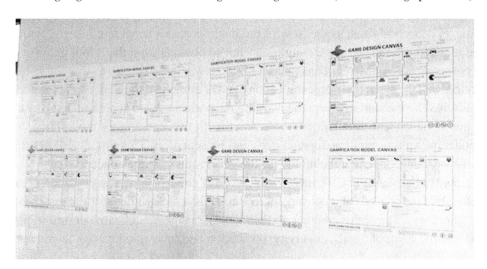

ties of each member. Then, the proposals implementations were started following, in a first moment, the methodology rapidly prototype, where games toys were presented in a video and tested in order to find some concept problems and get initial insights from the target audience. After that, the complete implementation was started.

The tests with the prototypes (toy and complete) was performed by usability tests (face to face and remote), where subjects (target audience) completed a pre-test questionnaire, a questionnaire in a likert scale format, with five assertions: "strongly agree", "agree", "undecided", "disagree" and "strongly disagree", and a post-test questionnaire where they could express suggestions and criticisms. For this study, design cycle was applied, where the students' prototype, test and refine their solution concepts.

DISCUSSION AND CONCLUSION

Nowadays, the game market needs professionals with profiles of game designers who, although they can act in a specific activity like programming, modeling, animation, audio production among others, need to know the entire process of developing a game. In this sense, undergraduate game courses require that their teachers adopt methodologies that assist the student in understanding the process as a whole, encouraging him in the interdisciplinary training that the area in question demands.

This work presents the proposal to combine GDT and CBL methodologies in order to engage the future game designer professional to think the process of a game design in a more innovative, creative and effective way. The main objective with the integration of both methodologies is to complement the GDT with CBL: while the GDT stimulates different mental states through divergent thoughts, essential to arrive at convergent thoughts, the CBL starts from a general theme, on which related essential questions, guiding questions, activities and reflections will be raised. Thus, the concept stage of GDT starts with a basic question raised proposed by CBL, which is tied to a challenge that will be converted into a practical action by the students. In this context, the definition of a challenge and its guiding questions help the student to focus on the proposal and development of the game, facilitating the tasks of analysis and synthesis of GDT.

Through an empirical analysis, it can be observed that the classrooms that applied the methodologies of GDT and CBL allowed the groups of students to work in a "freer" way, without the initial concern with the programming language and the modeling of scenarios and characters for example but focusing on high-level concepts. Thus, as the flow of the methodologies progressed, it was noticed that the students had more creative ideas, connecting points not so obvious from the initial premises, as well as trying to serve segments of different consumers.

It was noticed that the phase of divergent ideation of GDT combined the CBL challenge and their guiding questions raised by the students form the learning route necessary to accomplish the task presented, which will guide the student through the whole process. In order to convey the content, the students employed podcasts, videos, multimedia resources and presentation. This process allows the teams an enriching brainstorming, "opening the mind" for the generation of game concepts.

The alignment of the phases of CBL investigate and GDT concept allows an evolution in the students' original ideas while the analysis and convergent ideation allow the synthesis of the game concept in an agile and efficient way. The teams summarize the models, business, and game design in panels which facilitate the identification of trends, creativity, inspiration and innovation among team members.

During the prototype step, the adoption of visual thinking and/or storytelling allows the entire visualization of the game flow and mechanics, visualizing the narrative of the game as it develops over time. Later, the construction of a game toy based on rapidly prototype promotes the insights about mechanics and interaction before the realization of a complete prototype developing, avoiding the well-known pitfall of cascade methods, where errors can be detected only at a final stage.

Unlike other methodologies (scrum, problem-based learning, project-based learning, etc.), the combination of GDT with CBL allows students to solve challenges creatively, innovatively, and from different perspectives. The student becomes a protagonist in the proposition of challenges and solutions allowing him to reflect on these. In addition, the students direct the course of their learning, involving teachers in a collaborative way.

This case study allowed to conclude that the fact of the student can choose his challenge related to the game design is an additional motivation factor, as it encourages the freedom and, especially, the possible personal projects that many students have when starting and finishing a course. Thus, the future professionals of game area can be better prepared in proposing new products that involve innovation and creativity to achieve their goals and satisfy their target audience.

The continuity of this study will be achieved through the increase in the number of students who will use the combination of both methodologies proposed in this work as well as the follow-up of these students as professionals, after finishing their undergraduate course.

REFERENCES

Apple. (2008). *Apple Classrooms of Tomorrow - Today*. Technical Report. Apple Inc.

Apple. (2012). *Challenge Based Learning: A Classroom Guide*. Technical Report. Apple Inc.

Baloian, N., Breuer, H., Hoeksema, K., Hoppe, U., & Milrad, M. (2004). Implementing the Challenge Based Learning in Classroom Scenarios. In *Proceedings of the Symposium on Advanced Technologies in Education*. Argostoli, GRE.

Bem, R. F. S., Alquete, T., & Martins, V. F. (2014). *Proceedings of XIII Brazilian Symposium on Computer Games and Digital Entertainment (SBGames)*. Porto Alegre, Brazil: Academic Press.

Binder, F. V., Nichols, M., Reinehr, S., & Malucelli, A. 2017. Challenge Based Learning Applied to Mobile Software Development Teaching. *IEEE 30th Conference on Software Engineering Education and Training (CSEE&T)*. 10.1109/CSEET.2017.19

Buzan, T., & Buzan, B. (2006). *The Mind Map Book*. New York: BBC Active.

Gabriel, S. E. (2014). A modified challenge-based learning approach in a capstone course to improve student satisfaction and engagement. *Journal of Microbiology & Biology Education, 15*(2), 316–318.

Gehling, M. (2016). Game Genesis Virtual Deck: uma ferramenta para criar ideias de jogos. *Proceedings of XV Brazilian Symposium on Computer Games and Digital Entertainment (SBGames)*.

Gestwicki, P., & Mcnely, B. (2012). A case study of a five-step design thinking process in educational museum game design. Proceedings of Meaningful Play.

Glushko, R. J. (2008). Designing a Service Science Discipline with Discipline. *IBM Systems Journal*, *47*(1), 15–38. doi:10.1147j.471.0015

Gray, D., Brown, S., & Macanufo, J. (2010). *Gamestorming. A Playbook for Innovators, Rulebreakers, and Changemakers*. O'Reilly Media.

Gurgel, I., Arcoverde, R. L., Almeida, E. W., Sultanum, N. B., & Tedesco, P. A. (2006). A importância de avaliar a usabilidade dos jogos: a experiência do Virtual Team. *Proceedings of V Brazilian Symposium on Computer Games and Digital Entertainment (SBGames)*.

Hunicke, R., Leblanc, M., & Zubek, R. (2004). MDA: A Formal Approach to Game Design and Game Research. In *Proc. AAAI workshop on Challenges in Game*. AAAI Press.

Jewell, D. (2016). *Game-Design Thinking in Education and Beyond*. Available in: http://www.pearsoned.com/education-blog/game-design-thinking-in-education-and-beyond/

Jimenéz, S. (2013). *Gamification Model Canvas*. Available in: http://www.gameonlab.com/canvas/

Johnson, L., Smith, R., Smythe, J., & Varon, R. (2008). *Challenge based learning: An approach for our time*. Austin, TX: The New Media Consortium.

Jonassen, D. H. (1999). Designing Constructivist Learning Environments. In Instructional-Design Theories and Models: A New Paradigm of Instructional Theory. Lawrence Erlbaum Associates.

Kembel, G. (n.d.). *Awakening creativity*. Available in: http://fora.tv/2009/08/14/George_Kembel_Awakening_Creativity

Kristiansen, P., & Rasmussen, R. (2014). Building a Better Business Using the Lego Serious Play Method. John Wiley & Son.

Lego Serious Play. (2018). *The Method*. Available in: https://www.lego.com/en-us/seriousplay/the-method

Librande, S. (n.d.). *One-page designs*. Available in: http://www.gdcvault.com/play/ 1012356/One-Page

Marin, C., Hargis, J., & Cavanaugh, C. (2013). iPad learning ecosystem: Developing challenge-based learning using design thinking. *Turkish Online Journal of Distance Education*, *14*(2), 22–34.

Mendes, T. G. (2012). *Games e educação: diretrizes do projeto para jogos digitais voltados à aprendizagem* (Master's dissertation). Federal University of Rio Grande do Sul, Porto Alegre.

Murakami, L. C., Leite, A. J. M., Jr., Sabino, R. F. S., & Macedo, D. A. (2016). *Design Thinking como metodologia alternativa para o desenvolvimento de jogos sérios*. Nuevas Ideas en Informática Educativa 2014. Memorias del XIX Congresso Internacional Informática Educativa (TISE), Fortaleza, Brasil. Available in: http://www.tise.cl/volumen10/TISE2014/tise2014_submission_200.pdf

Nichols, M., Cator, K., & Torres, M. (2016). *Challenge Based Learner User Guide*. Redwood City, WA: Digital Promise.

Nielsen, J. (1994). *Usability Engineering*. London: Academic Press.

Robinson, J. K. (2013). Project-based learning: Improving student engagement and performance in the laboratory. *Analytical and Bioanalytical Chemistry*, *405*(1), 7–13. doi:10.100700216-012-6473-x PMID:23104311

Rohrbach, B. (1969). Kreativ nach Regeln – Methode 635, eine neue Technik zum Lösen von Problemen [Creative by rules - Method 635, a new technique for solving problems]. *Absatzwirtschaft*, *12*, 73–53.

Santos, A. R., Fernandes, P., Sales, A., & Nichols, M. (2013). Combining Challenge-Based Learning and Scrum Framework for Mobile Application Development. *ACM Conference on Innovation and Technology in Computer Science Education*, 189-194.

Silva, I. C. S., & Bittencourt, J. R. (2016). Proposta de Metodologia para o Ensino e o Desenvolvimento de Jogos Digitais Baseada em Design Thinking. *Proceedings of XII Brazilian Congress on Design Research and Development, Blucher Design Proceedings*, 9(2), 2317-2328. doi:10.5151/despro-ped2016-0198

Silveira, I. (2016). A Game Development-based strategy for Teaching Software Design Patterns through Challenge-Based Learning under a Flipped Classroom Approach. *24º Workshop sobre Educação em Computação (WEI)*.

Vekony, D. (2013). *Game Design Canvas – Seu projeto de jogo em uma página!* Available in: http://www.marketingegames.com.br/game-design-canvas/

Vianna, M., Vianna, Y., Adler, I., Lucena, B., & Russo, B. (2012). *Design Tshinking: inovação em negócios. MJV Press*.

Chapter 18
Mindfulness and HCI

Jacek Sliwinski
University of the Sunshine Coast, Australia

ABSTRACT

Mindfulness is constantly increasing in popularity, having demonstrated benefits for psychological health and cognitive performance. Not only current psychotherapies have integrated mindfulness, but also digital technology for the general public such as mobile apps and games strive to incorporate mindfulness either explicitly (as mindfulness solutions) or implicitly (by training factors associated with mindfulness). The goal of this chapter is to clarify how mindfulness can be used in the context of HCI and provide practical insights for researchers and developers on how to create positive digital experiences. After a brief introduction of the intersection between those two fields, this chapter focuses on the challenge of operationalizing mindfulness and how it can be measured in HCI. Two review studies are presented, along with design recommendations, which are then applied in a case study. Results and implications are discussed.

INTRODUCTION

The benefits of technological ubiquity come with consequences. The availability of technological pastimes (such as social media) increases distraction, hence mindlessness (unawareness) about one's own experiences and surroundings. This often results in stress and decreased physical (Campisi et al., 2012) and psychological wellbeing (Kalpidou, Costin, & Morris, 2011). Studies suggest that media consumption and multi-tasking are associated with lower levels of personal contentment and academic achievement (Rideout, Foehr, & Roberts, 2010), and impair learning and attention, especially for children (Wallis, 2010). Furthermore, multi-tasking in the form of frequent social media interactions decreases productivity (Mark, Iqbal, Czerwinski, & Johns, 2015), and the interruptions caused by sending and receiving emails (from anywhere at any time) causes stress (Barley, Meyerson, & Grodal, 2011). Heavy multi-tasking was also associated with increased susceptibility to distractions (Ophir, Nass, & Wagner, 2009) and thus, reduced mindfulness (i.e. not being in the present moment). More recent studies have included mindfulness as a factor when investigating the effects of social media, finding that mindfulness improves resilience to emotional exhaustion and increases a sense of personal accomplishment, meaning

DOI: 10.4018/978-1-5225-9069-9.ch018

that people with low levels of mindfulness deal worse with stress and emotional challenges, therefor having a greater risk to develop psychological disorders such as burnout (Charoensukmongkol, 2016; Sriwilai & Charoensukmongkol, 2016).

This research acknowledges that modern life is demanding and views technology as a platform for improving mindfulness and gaining its associated benefits. Searching the dominant app stores (iTunes and Google Play) for mindfulness reveals many hits, which reflects the demand for technology-supported solutions in this area (Mani, Kavanagh, Hides, & Stoyanov, 2015; Plaza, Demarzo, Herrera-Mercadal, & García-Campayo, 2013). Mindfulness exercises are often promoted as do-it-yourself techniques for coping with stress, addressing the greatest concern of young people today (Fildes, Robbins, Cave, Perrens, & Wearring, 2014). There is an interest in mindfulness as a way to "keep in touch with our essence" (Williamson, 2003, p.18). Apart from individual benefits (which are discussed below), mindfulness has a broad, social impact by improving interpersonal relationships (Sahdra, Shaver, & Brown, 2010). Realising its value, companies and institutions offer mindfulness courses to their employees (e.g. Google; Shachtman, 2015) to lower stress, increase productivity (Levy, Wobbrock, Kaszniak, & Ostergren, 2012), and improve the moral and emotional standards of their leaders (Waddock, 2001). On a cultural and societal level, it facilitates the development of cultural intelligence (Thomas, 2006) and ethical values (Gilpin, 2008), which can positively influence a world filled with political tensions and social unrest.

The definition of mindfulness (translated from "sati") is: a present-moment awareness that is a transformative process (rather than a state) associated with ethical development towards virtues such as patience, harmlessness, compassion, acceptance, equanimity, generosity, courage, loving kindness, and sympathy (Gilpin, 2008; Grossman, 2015). Developing mindfulness is not considered an end in itself, but a way to liberate oneself from all suffering, which corresponds to full enlightenment (Hart, 2011). According to Buddhist teachings, this can be achieved by overcoming the three root causes of suffering ("dukkha"): attachment (causing craving and greed), aversion (causing hatred and aggression), and delusion of the (egoic) self (causing the misbelief of being separate from other beings (Gethin, 1998). Mindfulness is traditionally developed through the systematic practice of calm abiding meditation (Dalai Lama, 2003). In Western culture, mindfulness is growing in popularity as attention and emotion regulation training and as a subject of scientific research. There is no consensus on the conceptual definition and operationalisation of mindfulness, but the unifying theme of most programs and studies is the open and non-judgemental experience of the present (Singh, 2012).

Practising mindfulness refers to training mental focus with a basic orientation characterised by open, non-judgemental perception. Attention is directed towards inner experiences, increasing sensitivity to one's own perceptions, sensations, and thoughts. Embracing all of these experiences with an accepting and non-judgemental attitude disrupts the process of maladaptive reactivity, which in turn results in improved emotion regulation (Brown et al., 2007; Cahn & Polich, 2006; Kang, Gruber, & Gray, 2013; Leung, Lo, & Lee, 2014; Lutz, Slagter, Dunne, & Davidson, 2008). Mindfulness cultivates an emotion regulation strategy that is characterised by an open (non-avoidant), accepting, and non-judgemental orientation to emotions, which promotes acceptance while diminishing avoidance, suppression, and rumination (Chambers, Gullone, & Allen, 2009). These regulation strategies are trained using an experiential process. In mindfulness meditation, *passive* (i.e. non-reactive) interaction with emotions is exercised by embracing each experience non-avoidantly and without suppression, while carefully examining and accepting one's own state of mind without engaging in rumination. This practice increases the ability to delay or suspend (reflexive and habitual) emotional reactions. By becoming more conscious about one's own state of mind, the ability to respond appropriately to events is improved (Kang et al., 2013).

Mindfulness meditation is the traditional and predominant mindfulness practice (Kabat-Zinn, 1994) and mistakenly both terms (mindfulness and meditation) are sometimes used interchangeably (e.g. Kudesia & Nyima, 2015). Meditation refers to techniques that self-regulate the body and mind (Cahn & Polich, 2006). These techniques often involve a period of conscious sitting, during which the core skills required to systematically deploy attention and non-reactively observe experiences are developed. Though this may sound simple, meditation is difficult to learn and practise for beginners (Lomas, Cartwright, Edginton, & Ridge, 2015). Challenges such as physical discomfort (e.g. back pain), an inability to concentrate, and unpleasant side-effects such as tiredness and boredom (Lomas et al., 2015; Shapiro, 1992) make meditation difficult for most beginners, disrupting regular practice and causing people to cease meditation completely (Lomas et al., 2015). These challenges have a significant impact on motivation and while people might feel they *should* practise, the new habit of meditating often fails to form because of the associated negative experiences.

Mindfulness meditation was developed in the absence of modern technology and there has been little scientific exploration using interactive technologies for mindfulness training to overcome the challenges experienced by beginners (Mani et al., 2015; Plaza et al., 2013). Given the current technological opportunities to solve complex problems, the focus of the current research explores how HCI, in particular digital games, can be used to develop an engaging and motivating mindfulness practice, as well as deriving general design guidelines for mindful digital interactions. Acknowledging the full value of traditional mindfulness meditation, this research proposed, developed, and evaluated a digital game-based mindfulness program to complement and support meditation training for beginners. The overall goal is to make mindfulness practice more accessible to beginners, who experience severe challenges during meditation, and to apply mindfulness into the digital context. *Mindfulising* a modern technological and game-based context fills a significant research gap between mindfulness research and HCI. Moreover, distributing digital mindfulness applications that have positive effects on mindfulness might contribute to individual wellbeing, and stimulate cultural, social, and global change.

The interactive nature of games allows for the development of experiential knowledge, making it comparable to meditation which relies on experiential processes for the cultivation of mindfulness. But in contrast to meditation, which can be perceived as a daunting task (Lomas et al., 2015), digital games are designed to be motivating, engaging, and entertaining and are generally perceived as a fun medium that does not require persuasion for use (Brand & Todhunter, 2016). Games can be sufficiently engaging to make their players forget about time, creating an absorbing interaction (Sherry, 2004). Therefore, gaming has been described as a meditative practice (Gackenbach, 2008). This quality is parallel to that of mindfulness meditation, facilitating deep concentration. Both mindfulness practice and gaming are often described as non-striving, effortless effort or as doing nothing (Kabat-Zinn, 1994; Sweetser & Wyeth, 2005), referring to the ability to lose oneself in the experience, sharing the feature of flow. The state of flow is used to describe the optimal experience, which is characterized by complete control and absorption in an activity, an optimal challenge, and the loss of a sense of time and self-consciousness (Csikszentmihalyi, 1992). Digital games are well suited to facilitate a flow state of consciousness because they strive for an engaging experience by design, and provide defined rules and goals, as well as various levels of difficulty for an optimal challenge (Sherry, 2004; Sweetser & Wyeth, 2005). Mindfulness is also described as closely related to flow, as both states share the similar positive experiential characteristics of full focus and engagement in the present moment (Jackson, 2016).

Although the grey literature repeatedly blames games for many societal problems (e.g. causing real-world violence, obesity, poor social skills, and lower academic achievement (American Academy of

Child and Adolescent Psychiatry, 2011; Bushman, 2013; Russell, 2010), these statements are not based on empirical evidence (or its appropriate interpretation) and cannot be generalised to all games. In fact, research demonstrates that digital games provide beneficial effects if designed appropriately (see Connolly, Boyle, MacArthur, Hainey, and Boyle (2012) for a review on *serious games*). Furthermore, longitudinal studies disprove the commonly believed link between virtual violence and real violence (Ferguson, 2015). In the context of training mindfulness, an interactive application can provide an opportunity to externalise aspects of the mindfulness practice, decreasing a practitioner's cognitive load; this facilitates training by making it less demanding. Furthermore, digital games can provide clear instructions and multisensory feedback, which are essential for guiding users to practise mindfulness independently with opportunities to check and correct their practice.

The feasibility of such an approach is supported by the acceptance of games as a medium of daily use (Brand & Todhunter, 2016) and the general view that games are fun (especially among children and young adults). On average, people use their mobile devices for 3.6 hours per day, spending most of that time engaged with applications (apps), the majority of which are games (Pearson & Hussain, 2015). The game qualities of engagement and immersion support the natural tendency of games towards focus and sustained attention (Boot, Kramer, Simons, Fabiani, & Gratton, 2008), which is a major challenge for beginner meditators (Lomas et al., 2015). Furthermore, casual games are reported to decrease stress and increase mood (Russoniello, O'Brien, & Parks, 2009) and are therefore ideal for fusion with mindfulness. In addition to their training potential, digital games can gather data unobtrusively, which has two main implications. First, the game environment can adapt dynamically and in real-time based on user behaviour, creating individual, optimised training and experiences. Second, it is possible to use the game as a measurement instrument for mindfulness, where player's choices and task performance are used as indicators of mindfulness. This chapter addresses the research gap of conceptualising mindfulness in the context of HCI, reviewing ways of interaction and measurement with interactive technologies and digital games, as well as presenting a case study and discussing implications of applied mindfulness technology.

MEASUREMENT

Mindfulness is a mechanism that is related to introspection and self-reflection and many approaches to measuring mindfulness use self-report measures. Currently, there are at least ten questionnaires which (cl)aim to measure mindfulness (Park, Reilly-spong, & Gross, 2013). The working definition for this study is based on the Comprehensive Inventory of Mindfulness Experiences (CHIME) by Bergomi, Tschacher, and Kupper (2014), which was developed to unify other available questionnaires and provide a comprehensive measure of mindfulness. Nine aspects of mindfulness were identified that are covered by previous operationalisations of mindfulness (2013b; 2014). Those aspects were factor analysed and reduced to eight factors, which are (1) awareness towards inner experiences, (2) awareness towards outer experiences, (3) acting with awareness (being in the present moment), (4) acceptance (accepting, non-judging and (self-)compassionate orientation), (5) decentering (non-identification and non-reactivity), (6) openness to experience (non-avoidance), (7) relativity of thoughts and beliefs, and (8) insightful understanding. Although all factors are interrelated to some degree, each factor accounts for enough exploratory power and internal consistency that it can be measured as an individual mindfulness skill.

Self-report measures are currently the predominant form of assessing mindfulness, which come with many limitations (see e.g. Park et al., 2013). Scholars have been keen to develop new questionnaires, without defining the specific phenomenon that is being measured. Thus, it is not clear whether these questionnaires measure *real* mindfulness, the expression of mindfulness, or an outcome variable resulting from mindfulness training. This section explores alternative mindfulness measures and provides recommendations for adequate and embedded ways to assess mindfulness in HCI applications.

One way to measure mindfulness objectively is through neuroimaging methods. Although this research field is still in its infancy, several key discoveries have been made. Structural and functional neuroimaging studies have revealed that mindfulness impacts the functioning of the insula and amygdala, as well as the medial cortex and associated *default mode network* that is responsible for automatic thoughts and self-referential thinking (Marchand, 2014). Furthermore, many studies have shown that mindfulness triggers changes in the lateral frontal regions and basal ganglia in some cases (Marchand, 2014). The general limitation of the neuroimaging approach is that only physical proxy states can be measured, which are associated with mindfulness; there is no insight into the subjective conscious experiences (i.e. *qualia*). Furthermore, the apparatus that is required to capture a sufficient high-resolution image of the brain is large and expensive. Thus, it is not an accessible or easy-to-use mindfulness intervention for the general population. Although there are several consumer EEGs on the market, they provide only low spatial or temporal resolution, while introducing high variability and adverse artefacts to the data (Maskeliunas, Damasevicius, Martisius, & Vasiljevas, 2016), which makes them less feasible as reliable tools for the objective measurement of mindfulness.

To include more objectivity, mindfulness can be measured indirectly as a consequence of the participant's behaviour. Frewen, Evans, Maraj, Dozois, and Partridge (2008) conducted meditation sessions with students and measured their level of mindfulness by instructing them to raise their left hand (while keeping their eyes closed) when their attention was focused on their breathing and raise their right hand when it was wandering each time a bell was rung (which happened multiple times across the session). As the students focused on their breath more often, they were considered more mindful. The authors named this measure the Meditation Breath Attention Score (MBAS).

To measure the quality of meditation in real-time, the mobile application 'Mindfulness Focus Now' (Marcial Arredondo Rosas, 2013) was developed for use while meditating. Users keep their device on their lap with their index and middle finger holding the device and placed on the left and right half of the screen. During meditation, whenever the users realise that their mind has wandered off, they tap their left finger. The number of taps correspond to the perceived duration of the distraction (one tap means less than ten seconds, two taps mean ten seconds to one minute, three taps mean more than a minute). After that, users tap their right finger to indicate their evaluation of the content of the distraction (zero taps mean neutral, one tap means positive, two taps mean negative, and three taps mean mixed feelings). The Mindfulness Focus Now app requires its users to remember the time and valence coding scales, which requires a significant amount of attention and might alter the quality of the meditation, thus becoming a confounding factor or source of error. Furthermore, both the Mindfulness Focus Now app and the MBAS methods rely on the participants' self-reports and are therefore subject to many of the limitations discussed previously.

To assess the quality of practice, the mobile application 'Breathe Daily' (Mu Studios, 2013) captures procedural data. It instructs the user to exercise breath meditation by holding the finger on the screen when inhaling and releasing when exhaling. Visual feedback is provided by gradually changing the background colour when a finger is touching and releasing the screen. Starting from blue, the background turns yellow and then blue again. The app recommends users wait until the screen turns to its original blue before inhaling again, providing guidance for regular breathing. Furthermore, users are instructed to count their breaths and slide their finger after every tenth inhalation. The background colour then turns green or red, indicating whether they counted correctly and whether their focus was maintained successfully. A report screen at the end of a 5 or 15-minute meditation shows the total number of inhales and the number of focused key breaths. By comparing focused and unfocused breaths, and thus controlling for the correct counting and testing the user's focus, the attentional control of the user during meditation can be observed. While adding feedback is generally useful, the colours for the visual representation of system states must be chosen carefully since colour vision deficiencies are common, especially red-green colour blindness (affecting ca. 8% of European males; Deeb & Motulsky, 2015). Furthermore, the emotional inducing effects of colour and related cultural differences should be considered.

The method of breath counting was evaluated in four independent studies (Levinson, Stoll, Kindy, Merry, & Davidson, 2014). In study one (Levinson et al., 2014), the validity of breath counting was explored by correlating it with various other measures. More than 200 participants were instructed to "be aware… of the movement of breath" and count their breaths from one to nine repeatedly. For breaths one through eight they pressed one button, and on breath nine they pressed another. The correct input on the ninth breath measured counting accuracy. Approximately every 90 seconds (60-120 second range), momentary assessment was conducted on state mind wandering and meta-awareness. Counting accuracy was associated with better moods, decreased mind-wandering, increased meta-awareness, and correlated with trait mindfulness.

Another approach to measuring mindfulness objectively is applying a language-based measure. In a study by Collins et al. (2009), participants in a mindfulness-based relapse prevention program were asked to provide written responses to open-ended questions about their experience. The answers were analysed with a computer program and matched to linguistic categories, which were assumed to reflect different degrees of mindfulness. Participants who expressed themselves in a mindful way (i.e. verb tense, pronoun use, affect, anger, insight, body, and perception) were considered more mindful than those with lower correlates of mindful language. Greater use of mindful language was also correlated with fewer days of alcohol and other drug use during a four-month follow-up period. The main limitation of this instrument is that it requires a high degree of language proficiency from participants. Unsurprisingly, the participant's ethnic background was a mediator of mindful language use (Collins et al., 2009).

To study the attention component of mindfulness, researchers have addressed various specific elements of attention. The clinical model of attention by Sohlberg and Mateer (1989) is an established framework for assessing attention, which is a rational model based on the analysis of task performance, errors, and subjective experience complaints of humans with brain injuries. This model divides attention into five components: (1) focused attention, the ability to respond discretely to stimuli; (2) sustained attention, the maintenance of attention during continuous activity; (3) selective attention, freedom from distractibility; (4) alternating attention, mental flexibility that allows shifting of attentional focus between tasks; and (5) divided attention, the ability to respond to multiple tasks simultaneously. Furthermore, to measure individual factors of attention, cognitive psychologists have developed a series of applications. Attention tests such as the computerised continuous performance task (CPT; Klee & Garfinkel, 1983) measure selective and sustained attention by presenting visual stimuli on a screen and asking participants to react according to specific instructions. By calculating error scores and average reaction times and comparing them to normative scores, the participant's attentional performance can be examined.

Another popular method of psychological experimentation is the Stroop task (Stroop, 1935), which measures selective attention. Participants are presented with the names of colours. These names are either written in the same colour as the word's meaning or a different colour. According to automation of reading, a congruent condition (e.g. blue) results in a significantly lower reaction time for the participant's response than an incongruent condition (e.g. blue). Task performance on the Stroop task yielded mixed results with regard to mindfulness; some studies showed that mindfulness has a significant positive effect (Moore & Malinowski, 2009) and others did not demonstrate an effect of mindfulness on attentional control (Anderson, Lau, Segal, & Bishop, 2007).

A variation of the Stroop test is the Emotional Stroop Test (Williams, Mathews, & MacLeod, 1996). Rather than using words of colours, this test shows words that are either neutral (e.g. clock) or emotional (e.g. death). Participants with underlying clinical conditions have demonstrated attentional bias towards emotionally relevant words. For example, patients with depression show much higher (slower) reaction times for emotional words than neutral words. Drawing on the mechanisms of the Emotional Stroop Test, a similar test could measure the mindfulness component of equanimity (i.e. having an observing, non-reactive, and non-judgemental perspective towards experiences). Using the Emotional Stroop Test, a cross-sectional study with 247 non-clinical adults by Sauer et al. (2011) tested the hypothesis that mindful people are less emotional. *Present* participants reacted to the Emotional Stroop Test significantly faster, made significantly fewer errors, and had significantly more positive (less aversive) word rating scores. These study results provide partial evidence that mindfulness is associated with decreased reactive emotional behaviour (Sauer et al., 2011). Moreover, participants in this study were not instructed to be mindful. Using the paradigm of the Emotional Stroop Task, emotional words or pictures could be used to induce moods in a digital environment. The reaction (expressed as a player's choice) or the reaction time might be used as a dependent variable to measure improvement in mindfulness. Affective stimuli could be displayed either explicitly (e.g. as text) or implicitly (i.e. hidden in the game world as part of the virtual environment, such as bad weather).

In summary, alternative and more objective ways to measure mindfulness include neuroimaging, simple indicators of present moment awareness, and language-based and attention tasks. Additional opportunities to examine mindfulness include the study of actual behaviour (in real and virtual environments), thus treating mindfulness as a performance mediator. This approach, however, should be used cautiously and with comparison to other valid measures because causal relationships are particularly hard to prove with such an approach. When measuring mindfulness, close attention must be paid to the expected target population and the context of use for a mindfulness intervention (Park et al., 2013). The findings of this section acknowledge existing objective methods for measuring mindfulness and their opportunities for complementary use with self-report measures.

For the objective measurement of mindfulness, digital games may provide a unique use case, as they allow for the unobtrusive and automated collection of data. Games enable the creation of complex and engaging scenarios as well as the acquisition of sophisticated user input, which can be used as a process measure. Moreover, games are an accepted, popular, and preferred medium for many people (Brand & Todhunter, 2016). They present an opportunity to develop a mindfulness training method that is entertaining and captures objective data about players' progress and success by measuring interaction patterns and interpreting them in a meaningful way. Furthermore, various biofeedback measures that are shown to correlate with mindfulness can be included (e.g. heart rate variability; (Burg & Wolf, 2012). To date, game-based mindfulness training is largely unevaluated.

DESIGN

The aim of this research is to investigate how interactive technology and digital games can be used for mindfulness training and assessment. To identify relevant HCI applications and their mechanisms of action, two review studies have been conducted, based on which design guidelines were developed and applied in a case study.

In a review study by Sliwinski, Katsikitis, and Jones (2018a), for each mindfulness factor, as defined by (Bergomi et al., 2014), appropriate games and interactive applications were presented together with research evidence showing their efficacy for mindfulness training. Effective software was disaggregated according to their mechanics, dynamics, and aesthetics (Hunicke, LeBlanc, & Zubek, 2004) to provide design recommendations, see Table 1. In a subsequent study (Sliwinski et al., 2018a) two experiments were conducted to validate whether these games can improve mindfulness. Firstly, an expert review was conducted, where domain experts rated the fit of games to their associated mindfulness factor. In the first Study, the games showed a positive fit with their associated mindfulness factors, supporting research evidence. Secondly, a laboratory study tested the effect of three games on mindfulness, for which no research evidence was found linking to games. The three proposed games showed a significant effect on state mindfulness at post-test.

In a second review study (Sliwinski, Katsikitis, & Jones, 2017), a broader definition of mindfulness was applied, namely the self-awareness, self-regulation, and self-transcendence (S-ART) model of mindfulness by Vago and Silbersweig (2012), to address the ethical and spiritual dimensions of mindfulness. The CHIME mindfulness model (Bergomi et al., 2014) and S-ART neurobiological framework (Vago & Silbersweig, 2012) were used to identify the research gap, outlining components of mindfulness that have not been studied in this context. The identified design recommendations to develop interactive digital experiences for mindfulness include the use of personalization, gamification, and social features for Intention and motivation; biofeedback training and narrative for Emotion regulation; moral dilemmas, perspective taking, and cooperative design for Prosociality; and explorative self-reflection, visualization and immersive feedback, and the integration of internal stimuli for Self-transcendence.

Figure 1 elaborates these findings into a framework for the design of games for mindfulness, which provides a way of understanding and organising the key concepts and effective training aspects of mind-

Figure 1. Framework for the design of mindful games

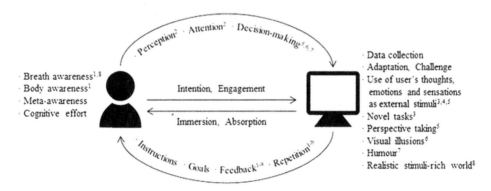

Training of mindfulness skills:
[1]Awareness towards inner experiences, [2]Awareness towards outer experiences, [3]Openness to experience, [4]Decentering, [5]Acceptance, [6]Relativity of thoughts and beliefs, [7]Insightful understanding, [8]Acting with Awareness

Table 1. Mindfulness games and interactive applications with relevant research evidence for each CHIME mindfulness factor

Mindfulness factor	Evaluated programs	Training aspect	Game elements		
			Mechanics	Dynamics	Aesthetics
1 Awareness towards inner experiences, 8 Acting with Awareness	Awareness Online, Breathing training visualizations	Keeping interoceptive attention through ongoing cognitive demand by counting breaths.	Single button input (tap) by user for each inhale/exhale, every 10th time different button has to be pushed.	Warm-up block (tutorial) provided, key breaths (10th) used to calculate accuracy score.	Awareness Online: Visual feedback on tap (in warm-up). Breathe Daily app only: Visual feedback (fading colours) indicate inhale/exhale. Breathing training: Animated wave form design.
2 Awareness towards outer experiences	Action/Shooter games	Training multisensory perception through stimuli rich virtual environments.	Players have a weapon with which they shoot enemies. Limited health and ammo.	Aiming is challenging, constant movement is required to not get shot. Sensory challenge through vast amount of stimuli, requiring fast information-processing and reactions.	Very detailed (realistic) representation of the world.
3 Openness to experience	Positive Activity Jackpot (modified)	Encouraging users to perform novel tasks for interoceptive awareness.	User pulls the lever, slot machine starts spinning, activity (task to increase interoceptive awareness) gets drawn. Users confirm activity and schedule it in calendar.	Spinning slot machine creates sense of excitement and luck.	Spinning animation is accompanied by authentic sound and vibration pattern of the phone. Users can choose to swipe instead of tap the lever (natural behaviour).
4 Decentering	AEON	Watching a visualized thought or emotion fading out.	User enters text, text is displayed, text disappears by swiping.	Disappearing of text is gradual to total length of swipe, sound (water ripple on touch).	Calm backgrounds (e.g. sand), animated water surface, disappearing of text by gradual black to transparent fade.
5 Acceptance	Compassion game	Training Acceptance through cognitive bias modification.	User is presented with a 4x4 matrix of faces of which one has a compassionate expression while all others are critical. User is instructed to click on the compassionate face as quickly as possible.	After user input, next matrix of faces is presented. Challenge is created by a sense of time pressure.	All faces are monochrome.
5 Acceptance	VR self-compassion game	Training Acceptance by using a digital embodied version of the two-chair method.	Dedicated roles between crying child and soothing adult.	The roles switch mid-game, letting the player experience a reflectional self.	The player's virtual character has an identical appearance as the player.
6 Relativity of thoughts and beliefs	The Bridge	Demonstrating volatility of thoughts and beliefs through visual-illusionary experiences.	Player navigates through an ambiguous 2D world. Player is allowed to rotate the world.	Sensory challenge through ambiguous interpretation of architecture.	Monochrome cartoonish world.
7 Insightful understanding	Octodad: Dadliest Catch	Making the player see life with ease and humour.	Player impersonates an octopus with tentacles with which everyday tasks (e.g. walking) have to be executed.	Challenging controls cause unintended results (damage), system is forgiving.	Presentation of narrative and gameplay is humorous.
8 Acting with Awareness	Action/Shooter games	Training sustained and focused attention through the presentation of context-relevant stimuli in virtual worlds.	The system provides many clear objects of interest whose focus upon is vital for the player.	Game objects are not static but moving (and shooting).	Detailed (realistic) representation of the world.

Note: Effective training aspects disaggregated accordingly to the MDA framework. See Sliwinski et al. (2015)+2018 for a detailed discussion about the selection of games.

fulness games. It is aimed to inform and offer guidance for the design and development of interactive mindfulness technology such as digital games. The framework is divided into two entities, which stand in mutual relationship with one another, the user or player (left) and the software or game (right). In the first process, along the top, the player forms an intention and engages (i.e. becomes cognitively involved) with the software, using their perception (seeing/hearing/feeling what is on the screen or own mind and body if instructed), deliberately focusing and sustaining attention on the content (e.g. tracking a virtual bird or the own breath), and making decisions (e.g. controlling the virtual avatar or directing awareness into a different part of the body).

This in turn provides the player a sense of immersion and presence (i.e. perception of being enveloped by and part of the experience (Witmer & Singer, 1998)) that results in an absorbing interaction (along the bottom) ideally causing the user to forget about time and space. The game provides instructions and clear goals on what to do and gives the user feedback about their current state and progress. Through repetition, beneficial game elements that improve attention and emotion regulation skills are used to condition the player's mind to be more mindful. Furthermore, the game has the technical capability to collect data about the play style and progress, allowing it to adapt the game environment and the general level of challenge continuously to optimise the game experience and improve the player's motivation in further interacting with the game.

Based on prior research findings (see Table 1), mechanics, dynamics, and aesthetics of effective games for each individual mindfulness factor were identified, which can be used as design inspirations. To improve *awareness towards inner experiences* (breath awareness, body awareness), it is recommended to use the player's internal stimuli instead of external stimuli in the virtual world. Breath counting and focusing on the sensations produced by breathing were found to be effective for this factor (Levinson et al., 2014). Directing the player's attention to different parts of the body with novel tasks can improve *openness to experience* (stage 2), and integrating the player's thoughts in the game in order to defuse them improves *decentering* (Chittaro & Vianello, 2014). Emotions such as compassion and *acceptance* can be trained by using narrative scenarios in conjunction with different perspectives, for example mirroring the player's acts of compassion from a 3rd person perspective (Falconer et al., 2014). A realistic game world that is cognitively demanding stimulates the player's senses and improve their perception and *awareness towards outer experiences* (Bavelier & Davidson, 2013; Boot, Kramer, Simons, Fabiani, & Gratton, 2008; Donohue, Woldorff, & Mitroff, 2010; Green & Bavelier, 2003, 2006; Green & Bavelier, 2012; Trick, Jaspers-Fayer, & Sethi, 2005), as well as sharpens their focus and concentration, which improve the mindfulness factor *acting with awareness* (Chisholm, Hickey, Theeuwes, & Kingstone, 2010; Dye, Green, & Bavelier, 2009; Gackenbach & Bown, 2011; Mishra, Zinni, Bavelier, & Hillyard, 2011). Visual illusions can be used to create ambiguous situations that are open for interpretation and demonstrate *relativity of thoughts and beliefs*. Narrative design and humour in particular could be vital ways for the cultivation of wisdom and *insightful understanding*, and can additionally enrich the game experience by providing context and explanations about mindfulness. The proposed design recommendations are evidence-based, but there might be many more ways to improve mindfulness with digital games (Sliwinski, Katsikitis, & Jones, 2015). This framework is a starting point for understanding how to create a more mindful digital landscape, and invites fellow researchers and designers to consider its application and iteration.

As a case study, a research-based mindfulness game was developed following user-centred design principles, including persona development, heuristic analysis and requirements engineering, as well as integrating knowledge acquired about designing effective game elements to train mindfulness. The

Interactive Mindfulness Program and Virtual Evaluation (IMProVE) game is an HTML5 based game in the infinite runner genre, designed as a casual game, which uses embedded game metrics to analyse the player's mindfulness state. IMProVE is themed with a water setting, and the player has the role of a mindfulness student, stranded on the sea with their kayak and a mission to navigate through the water and reach the mainland. Movement is linked to the mindfulness mechanic of conscious breathing, i.e. using the metaphor of alternate paddle strokes for inhaling and exhaling. Based on the design framework, which targets individual mindfulness factors, practical game elements were integrated to benefit each factor.

IMProVE was tested for its efficacy on state mindfulness and user experience with 94 participants (Sliwinski, Katsikitis, & Jones, 2018b). A significant learning effect was demonstrated on state mindfulness, which confirms the game's suitability for mindfulness training. To examining mindfulness comprehensively, all eight CHIME aspects were measured by means of a self-developed visual-analog scale. A significant positive effect was found for the Decentering factor, confirming the successful implementation of its game design element as proposed by the AEON app (Chittaro & Vianello, 2014). A significant positive effect was measured for the factor Acting with Awareness, which suggests a beneficial effect and successful implementation of breath counting as the core game mechanic (Levinson et al., 2014). All qualitative aspects, as identified by the user experience questionnaire, were positive, which implies a successful execution of the applied user-centred design approach in the development of IMProVE. Especially its most salient features of being friendly, easy to learn, and slow, support its compatibility with tailoring it for mindfulness practice.

IMPLICATIONS

The implications of this research are diverse and relate to distinct areas. IMProVE poses one of few evidence-based serious games for mindfulness (Mani et al., 2015; Plaza et al., 2013), and is the only that targets mindfulness comprehensively. Its underlying design framework and effective mechanics, dynamics, and aesthetics, are applicable to other digital games and interactive approaches, facilitating the tailored development of mindfulness experiences. Since contemporary psychotherapies (e.g. ACT, DBT) have integrated elements of mindfulness, this research can facilitate their digital evolution by providing guidance on how to design effective training elements for known aspects of mindfulness. Internet-based digital therapies (e.g. Lappalainen et al., 2014) and mindfulness interventions (e.g. Boettcher et al., 2014) are recognised, effective, and cost-efficient training methods for improving psychological health. The addition of interactive game-based elements would benefit established approaches not only regarding efficacy, but also by improving (i.e. decreasing) their attrition rate through increased fun and engagement.

Recent developments in HCI and mindfulness have yielded new studies, which are relevant to this research. A study by Ahmed, Silpasuwanchai, Niksirat, and Ren (2017) explored the role of multi-modal feedback (i.e. touch, vision, and audio) in relation to focus and relaxation for interactive meditation. IMProVE and its underlying design framework relies heavily on the visual representation of game elements to train associated mindfulness aspects. While in the study by Ahmed et al. (2017), vision was tested with a neutral non-interactive animation (i.e. floating bubbles), the findings of this research suggest a more nuanced approach to account for the possibility of rich and meaningful visual content. Although the authors found that vision is particularly beneficial for focus compared to the other two modalities, the results of IMProVE's evaluation (Sliwinski et al., 2018b) show that this can be equally (and simultaneously) true for relaxation. Furthermore, the breath tracking mechanic was generally perceived as improving concentration, and the slow tempo and calm graphics were perceived as relaxing. Participant comments about confirmed that the audio was most beneficial for inducing relaxation. This research proposes that audio can also be used to improve focus, as Sas and Chopra (2015) found that the application of binaural beats deepens meditation (Sas & Chopra, 2015). Touch, as a feasible way to facilitate focus (Ahmed et al., 2017), poses an opportunity for a future smartphone-based version of IMProVE.

A recent study by Zhu, Hedman, and Li (2017) proposed a scheme for the classification of mindfulness technology, which is supported by the findings of this research. It presents four levels of digital mindfulness experiences. The first level is called *digitalized mindfulness* and it describes text, audio, and video guidance in digital form (Zhu et al., 2017). The second level of the scheme is named *personalized mindfulness* and refers to digital mindfulness training, which is tailored to the user's gender, age, or context (Zhu et al., 2017). An example of a mindfulness application on this level is a guided audio meditation that specifies the type of audio played based on the user's current location (e.g. on the bus). The third level of mindfulness technology is *quantified mindfulness*, which differentiates innovative interactive approaches that sense the user's performance and provide adaptive feedback (Zhu et al., 2017). The fourth and highest level in the scheme is called *presence-in and presence-with*, which is different from the other three levels that are summarized as *presence-through* (Zhu et al., 2017). While the first three levels describe instrumental, goal-driven practices, the fourth level approaches the cultivation of mindfulness as a transcendental experience (Zhu et al., 2017).

The design framework of this research did not employ a rigid classification because, although some platforms come with inherent merits, effective mindfulness training relies on the successful integration of its content (i.e. suitable elements to train aspects of mindfulness). This research distinguished between two categories of mindfulness technology: interactive and non-interactive. The first two levels from Zhu et al. (2017) relate to non-interactive presentations of mindfulness training and were deliberately excluded from the literature and software reviews conducted within the scope of this research. Although these types of applications can teach mindfulness techniques, they do not tap into the potential to build experiential knowledge through interactivity, which is a focus of this thesis. Interactive mindfulness technology was further categorised according to CHIME or S-ART for a more detailed analysis and to derive more specific design recommendations.

Zhu et al. (2017) developed a hierarchy of mindfulness experiences, where *presence-in and presence-with* is at the top. In contrast, this thesis advocates for a non-judgemental categorisation, where no single aspect of mindfulness is rated as superior. *Presence-in and presence-with* (Zhu et al., 2017) and its associated qualities are most comparable to the mindfulness component *self-transcendence*, as examined in Sliwinski et al. (2017). Since this quality corresponds to one aspect of mindfulness, its practice does not necessarily need to fulfil the proposed features of not being instrumental or goal-driven. On the contrary, a goal-driven game-like experience (e.g. RelaWorld; (Kosunen et al., 2016); see Sliwinski et al. (2017) for a review) was found to enhance states of *self-transcendence*.

To achieve *self-transcendence* or *presence-in and presence-with*, Zhu et al. (2017) recommended fostering three concrete design qualities. The first is *bare attention to the present moment*, which is similar to the concept of meta-awareness or the two CHIME factors of awareness towards inner and outer experience. The second design quality is *integration with daily life* (Zhu et al., 2017), which is a general recommendation for a user-centred method and adaptation. For IMProVE, this is reflected in its pattern of use as a casual game through multiple, natural, quick play sessions during the day, which has become an established behaviour for modern smartphone users (Brand & Todhunter, 2016).

The third design quality is termed *aesthetics for non-judgmental acceptance*, which recommends the presentation of stimuli in a manner that fosters self-reflection (Zhu et al., 2017). An example of this quality is the artistic installation Mind Pool (Long & Vines, 2013). Participants sit in front of a bowl with magnetic fluid that reacts to their brainwaves. The provided feedback is deliberately ambiguous to motivate participants to interact with the system and stimulate them to draw their own interpretations of their mental states. The design framework of this research addresses this aspect with the CHIME factor *relativity of thoughts and beliefs*, which can be accomplished through visual illusions. Given the ubiquity of smartphones and wearable sensors in the form of smartwatches and fitness bands, data about the user's internal states can be leveraged and integrated into the respective game elements. In the future, playful mindfulness practices could be developed as ambient features of modern, connected, smart-home environments (e.g. using interactive wallpapers to create an embodied contemplative experience that transcends qualities of mindfulness).

In summary, the classification of mindfulness technology by Zhu et al. (2017) and its recommendations for achieving mindfulness experiences address existing mindfulness factors which have been explored in this research. Practical insights from this thesis, however, provide a greater level of detail, covering all CHIME factors and providing guidance through specific mechanics, dynamics, and aesthetics. Zhu et al. (2017) suggest that digital games have the potential to fulfil all design qualities that are required for the fourth level of mindfulness experience, but the experience is contingent upon the correct intention of the user, which is out of the designer's control. While this last point is valid, the careful briefing (i.e. game tutorial) and ongoing guidance of the digital experience might alleviate this concern. In Sliwinski et al. (2017), intention was explored as part of the S-ART framework (Vago & Silbersweig, 2012), identifying personalisation, gamification, and social features as valuable methods for its correct adjustment.

CONCLUSION

Interest in mindfulness is growing rapidly and it has become widely integrated in contemporary psychotherapies as a do-it-yourself practice for improving psychological wellbeing. However, its definition and operationalisation are still debated, which presents challenges for its successful training. This research used comprehensive models of mindfulness to explore how mindfulness can be promoted by means of interactive technology and digital games, which are an engaging medium with potential to overcome the challenges of mindfulness practice. Research discussed in this chapter clarified how games and interactive media can be designed to achieve benefits for mindfulness. It was investigated how challenges in measurement can be addressed with embedded metrics of HCI applications. The development of IM-ProVE, a novel mindfulness game, presents a use case for the application of the knowledge and insight from this research. Its evaluation, demonstrated the game's potential and opportunities to use digital games in the context of mindfulness training and assessment. Research deliverables from this chapter constitute novel and original contributions to the field of HCI by informing and guiding future research about the design, development, and measurement of mindful, positive, and playful digital experiences. Developers of creative digital technology and games are invited to adopt the research insights from this chapter to create mindful experiences that have a positive impact on people's wellbeing. Moreover, the adaptation of mindfulness elements in the digital landscape and games market might spread individual wellbeing and stimulate social change on a global scale.

REFERENCES

Ahmed, M. M. H., Silpasuwanchai, C., Niksirat, K. S., & Ren, X. (2017). Understanding the Role of Human Senses in Interactive Meditation. In *Proceedings of the 2017 CHI Conference on Human Factors in Computing Systems* (pp. 4960-4965). ACM. 10.1145/3025453.3026000

American Academy of Child and Adolescent Psychiatry. (2011). Children and Video Games: Playing with Violence. *Facts for Families.* Retrieved from http://www.aacap.org/AACAP/Families_and_Youth/ Facts_for_Families/Facts_for_Families_Pages/Children_and_Video_Games_Playing_with_Violence_91. aspx

Analayo, V. (2003). *Satipatthana: The direct path to realization.* Cambridge: Windhorse.

Anderson, N. D., Lau, M. A., Segal, Z. V., & Bishop, S. R. (2007). Mindfulness-based stress reduction and attentional control. *Clinical Psychology & Psychotherapy*, *14*(6), 449–463. doi:10.1002/cpp.544

Barley, S. R., Meyerson, D. E., & Grodal, S. (2011). E-mail as a source and symbol of stress. *Organization Science*, *22*(4), 887–906. doi:10.1287/orsc.1100.0573

Bergomi, C., Tschacher, W., & Kupper, Z. (2014). Construction and first validation of the Comprehensive Inventory of Mindfulness Experiences. *Diagnostica*, *60*(3), 111–125. doi:10.1026/0012-1924/a000109

Boettcher, J., Åström, V., Påhlsson, D., Schenström, O., Andersson, G., & Carlbring, P. (2014). Internet-based mindfulness treatment for anxiety disorders: A randomized controlled trial. *Behavior Therapy*, *45*(2), 241–253. doi:10.1016/j.beth.2013.11.003 PMID:24491199

Boot, W. R., Kramer, A. F., Simons, D. J., Fabiani, M., & Gratton, G. (2008). The effects of video game playing on attention, memory, and executive control. *Acta Psychologica*, *129*(3), 387–398. doi:10.1016/j. actpsy.2008.09.005 PMID:18929349

Brand, J. E., & Todhunter, S. (2016). *Digital Australia 2016.* Eveleigh: IGEA.

Brown, K. W., Ryan, R. M., & Creswell, J. D. (2007). Mindfulness: Theoretical foundations and evidence for its salutary effects. *Psychological Inquiry*, *18*(4), 211–237. doi:10.1080/10478400701598298

Buddhaghosa, B. (1976). *Vissuddhimagga [The Path of Purification]* (C. O. Boulder, Trans.). Seattle, WA: Shambala.

Burg, J. M., & Wolf, O. T. (2012). Mindfulness as self-regulated attention. *Swiss Journal of Psychology*, *71*(3), 135–139. doi:10.1024/1421-0185/a000080

Bushman, B. (2013). Video games can spark aggression. *New York Daily News.* Retrieved from http:// www.nydailynews.com/opinion/video-games-spark-aggression-article-1.1293112

Cahn, B. R., & Polich, J. (2006). Meditation states and traits: EEG, ERP, and neuroimaging studies. *Psychological Bulletin*, *132*(2), 180–211. doi:10.1037/0033-2909.132.2.180 PMID:16536641

Campisi, J., Bynog, P., McGehee, H., Oakland, J. C., Quirk, S., Taga, C., & Taylor, M. (2012). Facebook, Stress, and Incidence of Upper Respiratory Infection in Undergraduate College Students. *Cyberpsychology, Behavior, and Social Networking*, *15*(12), 675–681. doi:10.1089/cyber.2012.0156 PMID:23020744

Chambers, R., Gullone, E., & Allen, N. B. (2009). Mindful emotion regulation: An integrative review. *Clinical Psychology Review*, *29*(6), 560–572. doi:10.1016/j.cpr.2009.06.005 PMID:19632752

Chisholm, J. D., Hickey, C., Theeuwes, J., & Kingstone, A. (2010). Reduced attentional capture in action video game players. *Attention, Perception & Psychophysics*, *72*(3), 667–671. doi:10.3758/APP.72.3.667 PMID:20348573

Chittaro, L., & Vianello, A. (2014). Computer-supported mindfulness: Evaluation of a mobile thought distancing application on naive meditators. *International Journal of Human-Computer Studies*, *72*(3), 337–348. doi:10.1016/j.ijhcs.2013.11.001

Collins, S. E., Chawla, N., Hsu, S. H., Grow, J., Otto, J. M., & Marlatt, G. A. (2009). Language-based measures of mindfulness: Initial validity and clinical utility. *Psychology of Addictive Behaviors*, *23*(4), 743–749. doi:10.1037/a0017579 PMID:20025383

Connolly, T. M., Boyle, E. A., MacArthur, E., Hainey, T., & Boyle, J. M. (2012). A systematic literature review of empirical evidence on computer games and serious games. *Computers & Education*, *59*(2), 661–686. doi:10.1016/j.compedu.2012.03.004

Csikszentmihalyi, I. S. (1992). *Optimal experience: Psychological studies of flow in consciousness*. Cambridge, UK: Cambridge University Press.

Dalai Lama. (2003). *Stages of meditation: Training the mind for wisdom*. London: Penguin Random House.

Deeb, S. S., & Motulsky, A. (2015). Red-green color vision defects. In GeneReviews®. Seattle, WA: University of Washington.

Dye, M. W., Green, C. S., & Bavelier, D. (2009). Increasing speed of processing with action video games. *Current Directions in Psychological Science*, *18*(6), 321–326. doi:10.1111/j.1467-8721.2009.01660.x PMID:20485453

Falconer, C. J., Slater, M., Rovira, A., King, J. A., Gilbert, P., Antley, A., & Brewin, C. R. (2014). Embodying Compassion: A Virtual Reality Paradigm for Overcoming Excessive Self-Criticism. *PLoS One*, *9*(11), e111933. doi:10.1371/journal.pone.0111933 PMID:25389766

Ferguson, C. J. (2015). Does Media Violence Predict Societal Violence? It Depends on What You Look at and When. *Journal of Communication*, *65*(1), 1–22. doi:10.1111/jcom.12129

Fildes, J., Robbins, A., Cave, L., Perrens, B., & Wearring, A. (2014). *Mission Australia's 2014 Youth Survey Report*. Sydney: Mission Australia.

Frewen, P. A., Evans, E. M., Maraj, N., Dozois, D. J., & Partridge, K. (2008). Letting go: Mindfulness and negative automatic thinking. *Cognitive Therapy and Research*, *32*(6), 758–774. doi:10.100710608-007-9142-1

Gackenbach, J. (2008). Video game play and consciousness development: A transpersonal perspective. *Journal of Transpersonal Psychology*, *40*(1), 60–87.

Gackenbach, J., & Bown, J. (2011). Mindfulness and video game play: A preliminary inquiry. *Mindfulness*, *2*(2), 114–122. doi:10.100712671-011-0049-2

Gethin, R. (1998). *The foundations of Buddhism*. Oxford, UK: Oxford University Press.

Gilpin, R. (2008). The use of Theravāda Buddhist practices and perspectives in mindfulness-based cognitive therapy. *Contemporary Buddhism*, *9*(2), 227–251. doi:10.1080/14639940802556560

Grossman, P. (2015). Mindfulness: Awareness Informed by an Embodied Ethic. *Mindfulness*, *6*(1), 17–22. doi:10.100712671-014-0372-5

Hart, W. (2011). *The art of living: Vipassana meditation: As taught by SN Goenka*. Onalaska: Pariyatti.

Hunicke, R., LeBlanc, M., & Zubek, R. (2004). MDA: A Formal Approach to Game Design and Game Research. *Proceedings of the AAAI Workshop on Challenges in Game AI*.

Jackson, S. (2016). Flowing with mindfulness. In I. Ivtzan & T. Lomas (Eds.), *Mindfulness in positive psychology: The science of meditation and wellbeing*. Abingdon, UK: Routledge.

Kabat-Zinn, J. (1994). *Wherever you go, there you are: Mindfulness meditation in everyday life*. New York: Hyperion.

Kalpidou, M., Costin, D., & Morris, J. (2011). The relationship between Facebook and the well-being of undergraduate college students. *Cyberpsychology, Behavior, and Social Networking*, *14*(4), 183–189. doi:10.1089/cyber.2010.0061 PMID:21192765

Kang, Y., Gruber, J., & Gray, J. R. (2013). Mindfulness and De-Automatization. *Emotion Review*, *5*(2), 192–201. doi:10.1177/1754073912451629

Kiyota, M. (1978). *Mahayana Buddhist Meditation. Theory and Practice*. Hawaii University Press.

Klee, S. H., & Garfinkel, B. D. (1983). The computerized continuous performance task: A new measure of inattention. *Journal of Abnormal Child Psychology*, *11*(4), 487–495. doi:10.1007/BF00917077 PMID:6689172

Kosunen, I., Salminen, M., Järvelä, S., Ruonala, A., Ravaja, N., & Jacucci, G. (2016). RelaWorld: Neuroadaptive and Immersive Virtual Reality Meditation System. In *Proceedings of the 21st International Conference on Intelligent User Interfaces* (pp. 208-217): ACM. 10.1145/2856767.2856796

Kudesia, R. S., & Nyima, V. T. (2015). Mindfulness Contextualized: An Integration of Buddhist and Neuropsychological Approaches to Cognition. *Mindfulness*, *6*(4), 910–925. doi:10.100712671-014-0337-8

Lappalainen, P., Granlund, A., Siltanen, S., Ahonen, S., Vitikainen, M., Tolvanen, A., & Lappalainen, R. (2014). ACT Internet-based vs face-to-face? A randomized controlled trial of two ways to deliver Acceptance and Commitment Therapy for depressive symptoms: An 18-month follow-up. *Behaviour Research and Therapy*, *61*, 43–54. doi:10.1016/j.brat.2014.07.006 PMID:25127179

Leung, N. T. Y., Lo, M. M., & Lee, T. M. C. (2014). Potential Therapeutic Effects of Meditation for Treating Affective Dysregulation. *Evidence-Based Complementary and Alternative Medicine*, *2014*, 1–7. doi:10.1155/2014/402718 PMID:25197309

Levinson, D. B., Stoll, E. L., Kindy, S. D., Merry, H. L., & Davidson, R. J. (2014). A mind you can count on: Validating breath counting as a behavioral measure of mindfulness. *Frontiers in Psychology*, *5*(1202). doi:10.3389/fpsyg.2014.01202 PMID:25386148

Levy, D. M., Wobbrock, J. O., Kaszniak, A. W., & Ostergren, M. (2012). The effects of mindfulness meditation training on multitasking in a high-stress information environment. *Proceedings of Graphics Interface, 2012*, 45–52.

Lomas, T., Cartwright, T., Edginton, T., & Ridge, D. (2015). A Qualitative Analysis of Experiential Challenges Associated with Meditation Practice. *Mindfulness, 6*(5), 848–860. doi:10.100712671-014-0329-8

Long, K., & Vines, J. (2013). *Mind pool: Encouraging self-reflection through ambiguous bio-feedback. In CHI'13 Extended Abstracts on Human Factors in Computing Systems* (pp. 2975–2978). ACM. doi:10.1145/2468356.2479588

Lutz, A., Slagter, H. A., Dunne, J. D., & Davidson, R. J. (2008). Attention regulation and monitoring in meditation. *Trends in Cognitive Sciences, 12*(4), 163–169. doi:10.1016/j.tics.2008.01.005 PMID:18329323

Malinowski, P. (2008). Mindfulness as psychological dimension: Concepts and applications. *The Irish Journal of Psychology, 29*(1-2), 155–166. doi:10.1080/03033910.2008.10446281

Mani, M., Kavanagh, D. J., Hides, L., & Stoyanov, S. R. (2015). Review and Evaluation of Mindfulness-Based iPhone Apps. *JMIR mHealth and uHealth, 3*(3), e82. doi:10.2196/mhealth.4328 PMID:26290327

Marchand, W. R. (2014). Neural mechanisms of mindfulness and meditation: Evidence from neuroimaging studies. *World Journal of Radiology, 6*(7), 471. doi:10.4329/wjr.v6.i7.471 PMID:25071887

Marcial Arredondo Rosas. (2013). *Mindfulness Focus Now* [Mobile app]. Retrieved from https://play.google.com/store/apps/details?id=com.identitat.mindfulness

Mark, G., Iqbal, S., Czerwinski, M., & Johns, P. (2015). Focused, Aroused, but so Distractible: Temporal Perspectives on Multitasking and Communications. *Proceedings of the 18th ACM Conference on Computer Supported Cooperative Work & Social Computing*, 903-916. 10.1145/2675133.2675221

Mishra, J., Zinni, M., Bavelier, D., & Hillyard, S. A. (2011). Neural basis of superior performance of action videogame players in an attention-demanding task. *The Journal of Neuroscience, 31*(3), 992–998. doi:10.1523/JNEUROSCI.4834-10.2011 PMID:21248123

Moore, A., & Malinowski, P. (2009). Meditation, mindfulness and cognitive flexibility. *Consciousness and Cognition, 18*(1), 176–186. doi:10.1016/j.concog.2008.12.008 PMID:19181542

Mu Studios. (2013). *Breathe Daily* [Mobile app]. Retrieved from https://itunes.apple.com/us/app/id659230503

Ophir, E., Nass, C., & Wagner, A. D. (2009). Cognitive control in media multitaskers. *Proceedings of the National Academy of Sciences of the United States of America, 106*(37), 15583–15587. doi:10.1073/pnas.0903620106 PMID:19706386

Park, T., Reilly-spong, M., & Gross, C. R. (2013). Mindfulness: A systematic review of instruments to measure an emergent patient-reported outcome (PRO). *Quality of Life Research: An International Journal of Quality of Life Aspects of Treatment, Care and Rehabilitation, 22*(10), 2639–2659. doi:10.100711136-013-0395-8 PMID:23539467

Pearson, C., & Hussain, Z. (2015). Smartphone Use, Addiction, Narcissism, and Personality: A Mixed Methods Investigation. *International Journal of Cyber Behavior, Psychology and Learning*, *5*(1), 17–32. doi:10.4018/ijcbpl.2015010102

Plaza, I., Demarzo, M. M. P., Herrera-Mercadal, P., & García-Campayo, J. (2013). Mindfulness-Based Mobile Applications: Literature Review and Analysis of Current Features. *JMIR mHealth and uHealth*, *1*(2), e24. doi:10.2196/mhealth.2733 PMID:25099314

Rideout, V. J., Foehr, U. G., & Roberts, D. F. (2010). *Generation M [superscript 2]: Media in the Lives of 8-to 18-Year-Olds*. Menlo Park, CA: Henry J. Kaiser Family Foundation.

Russell, A. S. (2010). Negative Potential of Video Games. *Educational Media Corporation.* Retrieved from http://www.education.com/reference/article/negative-potential-video-games/

Russoniello, C., O'Brien, K., & Parks, J. M. (2009). The effectiveness of casual video games in improving mood and decreasing stress. *Journal of Cyber Therapy and Rehabilitation*, *2*(1), 53–66.

Sahdra, B. K., Shaver, P. R., & Brown, K. W. (2010). A scale to measure nonattachment: A Buddhist complement to Western research on attachment and adaptive functioning. *Journal of Personality Assessment*, *92*(2), 116–127. doi:10.1080/00223890903425960 PMID:20155561

Sas, C., & Chopra, R. (2015). MeditAid: A wearable adaptive neurofeedback-based system for training mindfulness state. *Personal and Ubiquitous Computing*, *19*(7), 1169–1182. doi:10.100700779-015-0870-z

Sauer, S., Walach, H., Schmidt, S., Hinterberger, T., Horan, M., & Kohls, N. (2011). Implicit and explicit emotional behavior and mindfulness. *Consciousness and Cognition*, *20*(4), 1558–1569. doi:10.1016/j.concog.2011.08.002 PMID:21885296

Shachtman, N. (2015). In Silicon Valley, Meditation Is No Fad. It Could Make Your Career. *Wired.* Retrieved from http://www.wired.com/2013/06/meditation-mindfulness-silicon-valley/

Shapiro, D. H. (1992). Adverse effects of meditation: A preliminary investigation of long-term meditators. *International Journal of Psychosomatics*, *39*(1-4), 62–67. PMID:1428622

Sherry, J. L. (2004). Flow and media enjoyment. *Communication Theory*, *14*(4), 328–347. doi:10.1111/j.1468-2885.2004.tb00318.x

Singh, A. (2012). Use of mindfulness-based therapies in psychiatry. *Progress in Neurology and Psychiatry*, *16*(6), 7–11. doi:10.1002/pnp.254

Sliwinski, J., Katsikitis, M., & Jones, C. M. (2015). Mindful Gaming: How Digital Games Can Improve Mindfulness. *Human-Computer Interaction–INTERACT*, *2015*, 167–184.

Sliwinski, J., Katsikitis, M., & Jones, C. M. (2017). A review of interactive technologies as support tools for the cultivation of mindfulness. *Mindfulness*, *8*(5), 1150–1159. doi:10.100712671-017-0698-x

Sliwinski, J., Katsikitis, M., & Jones, C. M. (2018a). Design and Evaluation of Smartphone-based Training for Mindfulness and Openness to Experience. In *Proceedings of the 11th International Conference on Game and Entertainment Technologies* (pp. 177-184). IADIS.

Sliwinski, J., Katsikitis, M., & Jones, C. M. (2018b). Design and Evaluation of the Interactive Mindfulness Program and Virtual Evaluation (IMProVE) Game. *Journal of Cognitive Enhancement*. doi:10.100741465-018-0092-1

Sohlberg, M. M., & Mateer, C. A. (1989). *Introduction to cognitive rehabilitation: Theory and practice*. New York: Guilford Press.

Stroop, J. R. (1935). Studies of interference in serial verbal reactions. *Journal of Experimental Psychology*, *18*(6), 643–662. doi:10.1037/h0054651

Sweetser, P., & Wyeth, P. (2005). GameFlow: A model for evaluating player enjoyment in games. *Computers in Entertainment*, *3*(3), 1–24. doi:10.1145/1077246.1077253

Thomas, D. C. (2006). Domain and Development of Cultural Intelligence The Importance of Mindfulness. *Group & Organization Management*, *31*(1), 78–99. doi:10.1177/1059601105275266

Vago, D. R., & Silbersweig, D. A. (2012). Self-awareness, self-regulation, and self-transcendence (S-ART): A framework for understanding the neurobiological mechanisms of mindfulness. *Frontiers in Human Neuroscience*, *6*(296), 1–30. doi:10.3389/fnhum.2012.00296 PMID:23112770

Waddock, S. (2001). Integrity and mindfulness. *Journal of Corporate Citizenship*, *2001*(1), 25–37. doi:10.9774/GLEAF.4700.2001.sp.00006

Wallis, C. (2010). The impacts of media multitasking on children's learning and development: Report from a research seminar. In *The Joan Ganz Cooney Center at Sesame Workshop*. New York: The Joan Ganz Cooney Center and Stanford University.

Williams, J. M. G., Mathews, A., & MacLeod, C. (1996). The emotional Stroop task and psychopathology. *Psychological Bulletin*, *120*(1), 3–24. doi:10.1037/0033-2909.120.1.3 PMID:8711015

Williamson, P. R. (2003). Commentary: Mindfulness in medicine, mindfulness in life. *Families, Systems & Health*, *21*(1), 18–20. doi:10.1037/h0089496

Witmer, B. G., & Singer, M. J. (1998). Measuring presence in virtual environments: A presence questionnaire. *Presence (Cambridge, Mass.)*, *7*(3), 225–240. doi:10.1162/105474698565686

Zhu, B., Hedman, A., & Li, H. (2017). Designing Digital Mindfulness: Presence-In and Presence-With versus Presence-Through. In *Proceedings of the 2017 CHI Conference on Human Factors in Computing Systems* (pp. 2685-2695). ACM. 10.1145/3025453.3025590

Chapter 19

Proposal of a User's Cognitive Load-Centric Methodology for HCI-Based Control Panel Design

Naveen Kumar
Indian Institute of Technology Delhi, India

Jyoti Kumar
Indian Institute of Technology Delhi, India

ABSTRACT

Cyber-physical production system (CPPS) is being envisioned as the fourth major paradigm shift in the way industrial production happens. This chapter argues that though information technology-enabled automation will be used in CPPS, human intervention for production supervision would be required especially in critical scenario and human cognitive load would continue to affect the industry efficiency. The complexity of HCI-based control panel design would increase in CPPS due to task complexities and type of information presented through HCI systems. Also, the design methodologies for HCI systems have remained mostly technology centric and have not been able to include the cognitive load measurement caused by the design as a necessary consideration in the design process. Therefore, this chapter proposes user's cognitive load centric methodology for HCI based control panel design in context of CPPS. Cognitive load measurement should become a pivot for the HCI design process. In support of that, this chapter presents a case study using proposed UCLCD4 methodology.

INTRODUCTION

Human beings were not satisfied with the nature given tools for achieving their purpose hence they started creating their own tools. As the man-made tools evolved and became more sophisticated they started demanding greater learning, attention and expertise. New age tools demand more training beforehand and more effort during their usage. Simple tools evolved into complicated computing machines with time. Several continuous and disruptive changes in manufacturing industry have marked the history of these man-made tools (Astrom, 1985). As the complications of tools have increased with each change, tools have become more demanding to human beings at cognitive level (Wittenberg, C., 2015).

DOI: 10.4018/978-1-5225-9069-9.ch019

Advent of Information and Communication Technology (ICT) in manufacturing industry influences the working profile of the factory operators (MacDougall, 2014). With increase in use of ICT, workload of the factory operator will increasingly have shifted from physical to cognitive. Manufacturing industry is about to undergo a cyber-revolution which will further consume more of human's cognitive power than their physical power during industrial operations (MacDougall, 2014). Such a shift will be happened due to the use of digitally networked computing machines which manage the robots to help reduce manufacturing time, increases the quality and improve productivity (Lee, Bagheri, & Kao, 2014). Increase in cognitive load due to task complexity has caused increase in human errors, time on task, attention & stress (Cain, 2007; Wittenberg C., 2015).

Authors posit here that as the cognitive load caused by decision making tasks using new computing systems are increasing. Therefore, there is a need for greater precision in measurement of the cognitive load as the information complexity and criticality of tasks are increasing. The human interface design process for the control panels will now have to focus on objective measurements of cognitive loads in order to ensure cognitive efficiency in new control panel designs for 'smart factories'.

Therefore, there is a need of user cognitive load centric methodology for control panel design especially in context of fourth industrial revolution (Industry 4.0). This chapter argues for a new methodology and proposes a User Centred Design (UCD) focus on Cognitive Load (CL) measurement called as *User's Cognitive Load Centric Design for Industry 4.0 (UCLCD4)*.

BACKGROUND

Evolution of Industry and Shift in Paradigm of Control Panel Design

Industry 1.0 began with mechanical looms led by invention of steam engines. The first industrial revolution facilitated production units with small capacities where manual production processes were converted to mechanical machines (Deane, 1965). Use of human powered mechanical tools were still prevalent during the production process. Even during the use of steam engine operated production units, mostly physical power of human beings was used (Streans, 2013). This was the era where industries caused more physical work load on workers rather than cognitive load.

Segregation of various departments was yet not prevalent. Various departments of the manufacturing industry were located simultaneously and indistinguishably, both physically and tactically, in a small place (Deane, 1965). This increased complexity of physical workplace and often created unsafe working environments for workers. Shop floor tasks were often not well documented. Large number of workers were required in the manufacturing units to manage the production operations (Deane, 1965). Workers worked to own the production process together and specializations within workforce were not prevalent as a practice. Dedicated operators were not required to monitor the production processes. As there were no dedicated roles of operators within factories and no special attention was given to understand the operator's needs during the factory design process. Machine display units in production systems were few and simple to operate. Isolated dials of process parameters were in practice. Often isolated large size dials were used to represent a process parameter attached with functioning module. Extensive education or training was not required to learn the reading of simple dials and operate thereon.

Industry 2.0 started with intervention of heavy electrical machines and large production units with detailed workflow management of specialized workforces. Use of electro-mechanical dials, knobs and switches had started to monitor and control the process operations in manufacturing industry (Astrom, 1985). Though practice of isolated control rooms were not common, dedicated small display panels were often attached with machines and supervision of process operations with a few dedicated operators had started. In comparison to Industry 1.0, physical work load had slightly reduced and small shift towards mental workload for machine operators had begun.

Industry 3.0 started with introduction of computing devices to automate production processes (Greenwood, 1997). Specialized production and planning departments were set up to manage the product development process. Introduction of high-end instrumentation, automation systems such as Distributed Control Systems (DCS), Programmable Logic Controllers (PLC) and Supervisory Control and Data Acquisition systems (SCADA) had started in industry. Due to advent of technologies like DCS, PLC, SCADA etc, dedicated and isolated control rooms became possible. Process information started being presented in a Human Machine Interface (HMI) system for plant supervision. HMIs presented information of process operations to the factory operators and supervisors. Often information in HMIs were presented in graphic format using GUI (Graphical User Interface). The GUI was also connected to Programmable Logic Controller (PLC) for controlling sensors of the shop floor (Bailey, D., & Wright, E., 2003). Operators managed the production units remotely. Operators monitored the whole production processes through PID (Process Instrumentation Diagrams) and gathered real time information from sensor at machines. Specialization among operators had started and operators were trained in specific computer-based control systems (Beniger, 2009). Operators planned and executed production workflows and hence role of operators became key to production efficiency of manufacturing units. An individual operator engaged with multiple tasks within short time frames to complete demanding tasks. During task fulfilment, operators interacted with complex display systems which increased mental workload. Use of ergonomic principles to reduce control panel complexity and thereby increase production efficiency became prevalent (Bridger, 1995). The shift from physical to mental workload got further accelerated during industry 3.0.

Industry 4.0 is the fourth industrial revolution which is likely to introduce combination of Information Technology (IT) and automation in manufacturing units. Physical systems (sensors & actuators) in the manufacturing unit will be identified, controlled and managed through remote locations with help of authorised internet protocols (Zuehike, 2010) (Gorecky, Schmitt, Loskyll, & Zühlke, 2014). This fusion of internet protocols with physical things is known as Internet of Things (IoT) (Li Da, X., He. W., & Li. S., 2014). With IoT, supervision of process operations will become possible from anywhere and anytime. Present control rooms may shrink in size and may become limited to tasks like onsite maintenance, quality check and trouble shooting. While increased cyber flexibility in supervision of process operations is likely to increase the visibility and ubiquity of supervisory tasks, it may come at the cost of increased mental demand from operators (Meixner, Petersen & Koessling, 2010). Operators of smart factories will be required to be more computing competent and will need more training to deal with complex human machine interfaces. Operators may have to use multiple sensory channels to interact with machines, like visual signal processing, hand gesture (Gope, 2011), pressure sensitive touch (Hinckley & Sinclair, 1999) and voice commands (Kwang & Roger, 2006) etc. User Interfaces will become more complex in terms of information representation (Gorecky et al., 2014). A variety of tangible and intangible user interfaces will further increase the cognitive load on information processing abilities of human operators.

The overload of display information in control panels in decision making conditions are likely to increase the cognitive demand in operators (Wittenberg, C.,2015). In this new context of increased cognitive load in control panel usage, new method for control panel design will be required. Following section discusses role of HCI and CPPS in industry 4.0 context and proposes a new methodology for control panel design.

HCI and CPPS in Industry 4.0

Cyber Physical Production Systems (CPPS) is forecasted backbone of the Industry 4.0 (Lee, J., Bagheri, B., & Kao., 2014). CPPS is characterized by sharing production operation information over the internet with multiple systems in the smart factory. Also, machines will be able to communicate production data with each other using embedded network systems known as Machine to Machine (M2M) communication. Technologies like smart machines, network cloud computing, Wireless Network Systems (WNS), Internet of Things (IoT) (Li Da et al., 2014), smart transportation and smart grid (Gungor, Sachine, & kocak, 2011) etc. is likely to be key technological ingredients of CPPS and industry 4.0 subsequently. CPPS will facilitate operators to identify, manage and control physical machines over the internet (Zuehike, 2010).

CPPS users are likely to use touch-based Human-Computer Interactions (HCI) modules in industry 4.0 environment which will simultaneously monitor more than one shop floor production information. Handheld computing devices may provide for majority of operators where HCI will be used for managing status of the production process information like sensor information, operational information, maintenance data, managerial data etc. HCI modules will have dynamic screens with multiple functionality (Meixner et al., 2010). Process operation information will be sent and received from one factory to another factory using IoT technology. CPPS tasks are likely to be done using HCI systems with small display screens, dynamic user interfaces (UI), dynamic UI layouts, multimodal interactions, ubiquitous access etc. Multiple HCI systems mays be used in different types of situations and places.

Prevalent Control Panel Design Methods

While control panels have been designed since the first Industrial revolution in some form or the other, methods of design have primarily remained technology centric. Often, advent of a new technology (e.g. HMI) has led to new designs of control panels. Cognitive load to the user has not been prime focus of the design methodologies. This section presents a study on the exiting design approaches and then establishes the need for a new methodology in changed context.

Literature is replete with methods for design of control panels. Most of these reports have focussed on design of specific elements of control panel like alarm systems, numeric keypads, knob controls, push buttons etc. These reports have provided guidelines and methods to measure 'good design'. Most of the proposed measures of control panel designs have been subjective measurement by designers or researchers. Few objective measures like Fitt's law, Hicks Hyman Law etc. have also been suggested in control panel design process. Table 1 summarises some of the prominent literature available on control panel designs and design evaluations. Some attempts to objectively measure efficiency of control panel design have been made in past, for example, operator response time and operator error rate were used to measure efficiency of alarm systems for the control panels (Stanton, Booth, & Stammers, 1992). Error detection and time on task of the user were calculated for designing alphanumeric, digital and graphical display system followed by verbal analysis to validate the control panel design (Coury & Pietras, 1989).

Table 1. Existing control panel design evaluation methods

Author & Year	Control panel components	Methods	Measure
(Coury, & Pietras, 1989)	Alphanumeric, digital and graphical display	Subjective rating, error analysis and task time	Failure detection in display system, Task time and performance
(Wang, Liu, & Pan, 1991)	Push button, toggle switch, lever & pedal type control, knob control and thumbwheel control	Subjective rating: Likert scale, questionnaire scores	Number of controls, size, number of functional groupings, length-to-width ratio of panel and grid size
(Stanton & Booth, 1992)	Alarm indication, acceptance, massages, reset, investigate	Theoretical modelling of alarm handling	Alarm handling aspects of the tasks presented a model of alarm handling
(Hoffmann, 1994)	Knob control and numeric keypads, control panel layout	Fit's law: Movement Time (MT), Index of Difficulty (ID)	Finger width, control element diameter
(Jung, Park, & Chang, 1995)	Hand wheel control, knob control, push button, toggle switch, lever type control	Subjective rating, ergonomic principles and design constraints	Spatial compatibility, frequency to use control, functional grouping and sequence of components.
(Burt, Bartolome, & Burdette, 1995)	Three different auditory warning signals	Subjective rating, reaction time and EEG spectral power and ERP	Tracking tasks, attention and arousal measures
(K. MacMillan, Beach, Cheng, & Eberts, 1999)	Push button, keypads	Human factors guidelines	Anthropometric data collection from operators
(Stanton & Edworthy, 1999)	Auditory warning signals design for panels	Subjective rating on Likert scale	Recognition test, appropriateness ranking test, confusion test, operational test
(Francis, 2000)	Multifunction display buttons & mouse click buttons	Mathematical modelling, search time and movement time	Interval distance between controls, size of button
(Holman, Carnahan, & Bulfin, 2003)	Numeric keypad, directional control keypad, joystick and push button	Linear programming optimization using anthropometric data	Frequency of use, interval of controls, pre-defined position constraints
(Han, Kim, Rhie, & Choi, 2015)	LED indication, push button, key control and continuous rotary control	Subjective study: 7-point Likert scale	Frequency to use, grouping, sequence and importance of control components

Measurement of finger width, control element diameter has been measured through movement time and index of difficulty using Fits law was used by Hoffmann (Hoffmann, 1994).

Systematic multi-criteria method for designing control panel layout was proposed and used to measure the algorithmic approach of layout design which showed average performance of 95.2% in comparison to the ideal layout (Wang, Liu, & Pan, 1991). Constraint Satisfaction Problem (CSP) technique to measure parameters such as frequency of use of control panel elements (hand wheel control, knobs, push button and toggle switch), functional grouping and sequence of components through subjective rating and ergonomic design principles has been proposed (Jung, Park, & Chang, 1995). Types and efficiency of auditory warning signals for control panel designs using psycho-physiological markers have also been reported (Burt, Bartolome, & Burdette, 1995). While several authors have reported use only subjective measures for cognitive load and a few (Burt et al., 1995) have used both subjective and physiological measures as well, there is a lack of systematic step by step control panel design process for the overall design from cognitive load perspective. Further, there have been reported measures of the mental work-load in literature (Ryu & Myung, 2005) (Millera, Rietschel, McDonald, & Hatfield, 2011). Ergonomic design for human centered system has been proposed in ISO 9241-210.2010 in order to make system more efficient and usable (DIS, I., 2009) but there have been very few attempts to apply them in context of control panel design process. Next section discusses a new methodology for control panel design which is centred on user's cognitive load.

PROPOSAL OF A NEW METHODOLOGY

User Centred Design (UCD) as a design methodology which focuses on identifying user need, specify context of use and develop design solutions with focus on user needs (Norman & Draper, 1986). The steps under UCD was shown in Figure 1. UCD emphasizes on iterative involvement of user's during design process. UCD involves gathering of user information, both of proactive type (verbalized needs) and reactive type (response to a design), during the entire design process (Norman, 2013). UCD methodology have not been used from cognitive load perspective. The iteration of design was based on design principles. As information complexity has increased in HCI designs therefore there is a need for specific methodology for HCI designs which focuses on user's cognitive load. Thus, a new methodology for HCI design from cognitive perspective is proposes in this chapter.

This chapter proposes to employ User's Cognitive Load Centric Design methodology (UCLCD4) in four steps (figure 2), namely, user research, task analysis, design and validation. In user research step, first persona is proposed to be created. Persona creation will be followed by scenario narration. Task analysis will involve characterization, prioritization and sequencing of tasks in different scenario. In design step, control panel design synthesis will be through iterations of designs using cognitive load heuristics, sketching, prototyping etc. Fourth step in UCLCD4 is validation, which will include control panel design validation through subjective and objective measurement of cognitive load. These steps have been discussed in detail in below sections user research, task analysis, design and validation.

Figure 1. User Centred Design (UCD) methodology by (Norman & Draper, 1986)

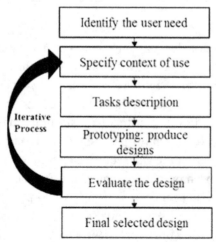

Figure 2. UCLCD4 methodology for control panel design

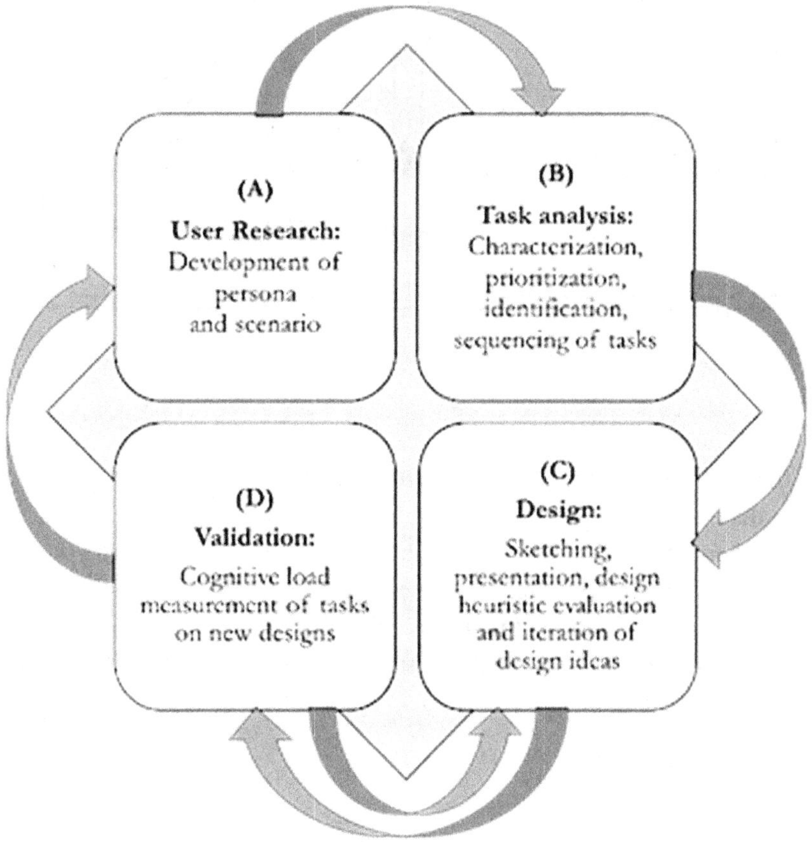

User Research

User research step in the UCLCD4 for control panel design will focus on understanding user needs, factors for efficient performance, causes of errors, motivation for completing tasks etc. As understanding user needs, motivations and experiences is not possible with a single technique, it is proposed that user research for industry 4.0 be done using multiple methods. For instance, 'contextual inquiry' be used to understand complexities of user's in tasks and a given scenario, 'qualitative interviews' be used to understand deep motivations behind tasks, 'focus group discussion' be used to get consensus on priority of tasks (Gill, Stewart, & Chadwick, 2008) etc.

In order to identify user related issues, it is recommended that before user research starts, first persona of the user's be created (Pruitt & Adlin, 2010) (Nielson,1994) and secondly a detailed scenario (Rogger, Sharp, & Preece, 2011) of use situation be built (Figure 3). Persona creation to understand need and motivation of user's of cyber physical production system from demographic and psychographic information. Scenario may focus on the device used, environment of use, user aims and task fulfilment conditions (Rogger, Sharp, & Preece, 2011). Persona and scenario for operators in Industry 4.0 can be built through user observations, contextual enquiry, surveys, expert interviews etc.

Figure 3. User research process for control panel design

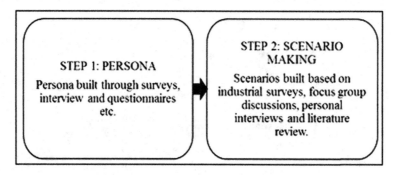

Task Analysis

Once persona of the user's and scenario of the control panel operations are identified, next step is to create list of tasks that users must perform through control panels. To start with, existing user's of production units and their control panel tasks can be formed. Before redesigning the control panel, it is recommended that tasks be analysed for inconsistencies and redundancies. Task analysis can be divided into four steps, namely, characterization of tasks, prioritization of tasks, identification of group of tasks within critical usage scenarios and sequencing of tasks by creation of task flow diagrams to identify alternative paths for reducing cognitive load.

Characterization of Tasks

In order to prioritize design activity and identify cognitive load created by various tasks, it is proposed that a list of tasks against type of user's be created to start with. The list can be created either from an existing document or fresh data collected from stakeholders of industry being studied. Once the list of tasks is ready, it is proposed that respective cognitive loads be mapped against each task. This can be done by either using physiological measures while users are conducting tasks or by personal reports of users or with help of experts. Here, an expert evaluation has been conducted for example to identify cognitive loads caused by various tasks.

A study using Delphi method was conducted to create a generic characterization of tasks in Industry 4.0 for UCLCD4 methodology. This study was conducted to understand task characterization process and to generate an example for use by others. This study can be further refined or used as it is in a control panel design process. However, the list tabulated here is very generic and presents an overview of broad tasks rather than tasks specific to an industry type.

The qualitative study using Delphi method was done with three manufacturing domain experts. One of the three experts were an academician in an Indian management school with research interest in Industry 4.0 and had multiple publications in Industry 4.0 domain. The other expert was from industrial domain with experience of 10 years in a machine tool manufacturing company in Germany. The third expert was an engineering professional who had 7 years of experience in automobile manufacturing company in Japan and he was well versed with Industry 4.0 manufacturing environment.

Study with experts was carried out in two phases. In phase 1, Industry 4.0 and CPPS was discussed with experts and opinion of experts about user's and their tasks for industry 4.0 was gathered. First, experts were asked about likely types of user's of control panels. Research publication by WB Rouse was used in the discussion as a starting point (Rouse, 1988). All three experts agreed on the common user types as 'operators', 'maintenance' and 'management' as suggested. However, one of the experts added another user type named 'designer', but the expert discussed that the usage of control panel by 'designers' was less frequent, hence it was decided to drop this user type for this study. The other two experts suggested that 'helpers', 'assemblers' and 'technicians' may also be likely user's of control panels. Upon discussion it was agreed that the prior three user types, 'operators', 'maintenance' and 'management', covered all these user types as well, in a broad sense of the term, hence it was decided that only three user types will be kept for the phase 2 of study (shown in grey cells in first row of table 2).

After agreement on types of users, experts were asked to write down the list of tasks which can be perform by CPPS user's in general in Industry 4.0 control panels as per their experience and expertise in domain. All the three experts mentioned two broad types of tasks, which are possible on control panels, online and offline tasks. A list of tasks based on the discussion, like, control, monitor, share sensor information, schedule/ reschedule, alarming, error detection, troubleshooting, response on warning signals, sensor information selection, report generation and explanation etc. were commonly iterated by the experts. Sometimes, different names for the same task were used by experts, like 'feedback' for

Table 2. Example of list of user's and tasks in CPPS

USER'S	Operator	Maintenance	Management
LIST OF TASKS	Rating on 9-point scale: task cognitive demand	Rating on 9-point scale: task cognitive demand	Rating on 9-point scale: task cognitive demand
ONLINE TASKS	Experts (1,2,3)	Experts (1,2,3)	Experts (1,2,3)
Monitoring	6,7,5	7,6,6	6,2,2
Controlling	7,6,6	7,5,5	7,1,1
Sharing sensors Information	6,6,7	5,5,6	5,2,2
Schedule/ Reschedule	7,7,8	8,8,8	7,1,1
Alarm detection	6,7,6	4,5,4	6,1,1
Error troubleshooting	7,8,8	7,7,8	7,0,1
Respond on warning signals	8,7,7	4,5,5	7,0,3
Fault detection	6,6,5	8,7,7	1,1,1
OFFLINE TASKS			
Production report generation	5,4,4	3,4,3	7,7,9
Report evaluation	2,1,2	4,4,5	7,7,8
Sensor data analysis	3,2,3	3,2,3	7,7,8
Production planning	2,1,1	2,3,2	7,7,8
Explanation of production conditions	1,1,1	2,2,1	7,7,6
Design information seeking	0,1,0	2,3,3	7,7,6
Implementation	1,1,1	5,4,4	7,8,8
Design products	0,0,0	0,1,0	0,1,1

'response', 'alarm'; 'communication with management' for 'share information' etc. were used, which were eliminated and finally a list of common tasks against commonly agreed user's was created (shown in grey cells in first column of table 2).

Reliability analysis of the gathered rating given by the three experts for different CPPS user's have been analysed through Cronbach's alpha. Internal reliability (Cronbach's alpha) of task rating by all the three experts for all three users namely, operator ($\alpha = 0.747$), maintenance engineer ($\alpha = 0.922$) and management executive ($\alpha = 0.826$) against the whole list of online tasks was found to be significant ($0.7 \leq \alpha \leq 0.99$). Further, internal reliability (Cronbach's alpha) of task rating by all the three experts for all three user's namely, operator ($\alpha = 0.966$), maintenance engineer ($\alpha = 0.944$) and management executive ($\alpha = 0.975$) against the whole list of offline tasks was also found to be significant ($0.7 \leq \alpha \leq 0.99$). This meant that the experts mutually agreed on the cognitive loads caused by both online and offline tasks for CPPS users. Table 2 summarizes the findings form the Delphi study with experts. Overall, mean and standard deviation of cognitive demand for three types of users was tabulated (table 3).

From above table 3, it is observed that all the three user types are likely to undergo significant cognitive load as per expert opinion. However, operators have been rated highest for cognitive demand in comparison to other two users. Design teams of control panels in Industry 4.0 may do industry specific physiological studies to further verify the operators cognitive load caused by the tasks. Here, in this research, this exercise was done as an example.

Prioritization of Tasks

Further, role of operators in context of usage of control panels is critical because all the functions of the industry are continuously monitored and managed by operators. Therefore, for this study, operators' tasks were further taken for a more in-depth analysis. In next step, task frequency for each operator task was added (table 4). The task frequency was added by experts based on their personal understanding.

Based on table 4, a prioritization chart was created (figure 4). The chart was used to categorize the different tasks based on cognitive demand level in Y-axis and frequency on X-axis. In order to design a control panel, identification of tasks which are of high frequency and high cognitive load will help prioritize the design activities.

First quadrant (High, High) has highest level of cognitive demand due to tasks and task frequency which shows highest priority for control panel design, whereas third quadrant has lowest priority for design see figure 4. As depicted in table 4, tasks such as monitoring, controlling and sharing information lie in first quadrant, whereas 'alarm detection', 'error detection' and 'respond on warning signals' lie in second quadrant. Tasks in these two quadrants are most critical for improving cognitive load through redesign activity because these tasks include high cognitive demand during task fulfilment.

Table 3. Cognitive demand between users: Mean and SD

USER'S	Mean	SD
Operator	6.7	0.7
Maintenance	6.2	1.4
Management	1.4	0.5

Table 4. Operators tasks cognitive demand with task frequency

USER'S	Operator	Tasks frequency
LIST OF TASKS	Rating on 9-point scale: task cognitive demand level	Rating on 9-point scale
ONLINE TASKS	Experts (1,2,3), Mean values	Experts (1,2,3)
Monitoring	6.0	7,7,7
Controlling	6.3	5,6,5
Sharing sensors Information	6.3	5,4,6
Schedule/ Reschedule	8.0	2,2,3
Alarm detection	6.3	1,1,2
Error troubleshooting	7.6	2,1,1
Respond on warning signals	8.0	2,1,2
Fault detection	5.6	1,2,1
OFFLINE TASKS		
Production report generation	4.3	1,1,2
Report evaluation	1.6	0,0,1
Sensor data analysis	2.6	1,0,0
Production planning	1.3	0,0,0
Explanation of production conditions	1.0	2,1,0
Design information seeking	0.3	0,0,0
Implementation	1.0	0,1,0
Design products	0.0	0,0,0

Identification

Identification is a creation of group of tasks within critical usage scenarios.

Once the task characterization is done and a prioritization chart is made, the next step proposed is to identify critical tasks in critical scenarios. At a time, one of the quadrants from figure 4 can be isolated and usage scenarios will be documented which will involve the tasks of the quadrant. Figure 5 illustrates first quadrant tasks with different critical scenarios which can be prioritised for design. Similar mapping can be done with other quadrants to form group of tasks.

Suppose that quadrant system of figure 4 represents nine tasks in control panel. These nine tasks are not sequentially performed in order to operate control panel but under some scenario these tasks form a group. For example, five tasks which are sequentially performed within one scenario of usage (Group 1) has selected and two tasks from group 1 in scenario 1 are identified as (high task frequency, high cognitive demand level) first quadrant tasks.

Such different combinations of tasks within the quadrant task group are possible according to the scenario of usage. Scenario identification for a task usage gives a realistic picture for redesign activity aimed at decreasing the cognitive load. Hence, this step of binding tasks within scenarios becomes an important step. As a case, single scenario will be used here to understand the no. of tasks involved in the scenario. As depicted in figure 5, one scenario may involve with five tasks out of which two tasks

Figure 4. Task cognitive demand level vs. Task frequency

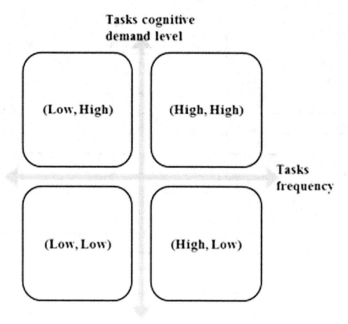

Figure 5. Task and scenario mapping for first quadrant

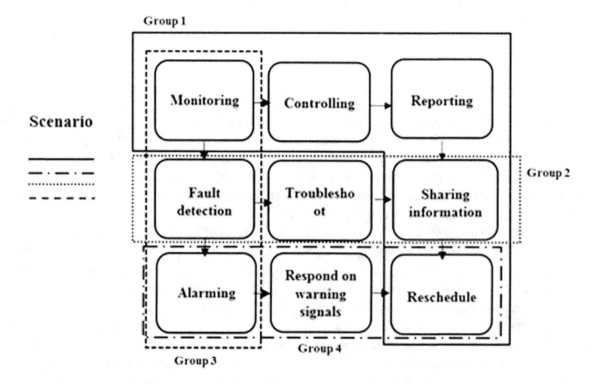

are from first quadrant of figure 4 involving 'high criticality and high frequency'. These tasks have high cognitive demand and high task frequency. For example, one of the imaginary critical scenarios may be-

During night shift in a pharmaceutical factory, control panel operator is alone in the control room. An unstable condition of the plant gets reported at 12:05 AM due to rise of reaction time of one of the reagents used for the product. The operator starts **monitoring** *of display dials. Suddenly, the temperature dial starts beeping as the temperature reaches beyond production process stable range. Immediately, he rotates some knobs and sliders to* **control** *the flow of different raw materials into the reaction chamber to make the system stable. After that he notes down all the readings and* **prepares report** *to* **share** *the occurrence with the operations manager. Operations manager gives instruction to operator to* **reschedule** *the machine with other stable set points.*

This scenario was created, and it involve specific group of tasks which can be used both for design purpose as well as in testing situations. During design phase the designer will deliberate upon the scenario and tasks to create alternative designs while in testing phase this scenario will be narrated to the participants and asked them to perform tasks.

Sequencing

Sequencing is a creation of task flow diagram to identify alternative paths for reducing cognitive load.

Task flow diagram provides the no. of steps involved in completion of groups of the tasks in a given scenario. Task flow diagram gives a very detailed view of the actual use of behaviours involved in completion of the tasks. For example, in the scenario narrated earlier (task analysis section- identification), task flow diagram for group of tasks can be illustrated as figure 6. Task flow diagrams are suggested to be created to depict no of steps and their details in a set of tasks required in a given scenario. The flow diagrams depict the usual start, processes and decision boxes.

For example, a task flow diagram based on one of the scenarios in figure 6 as narrated in above section has been created. Tasks of control panels like 'monitoring', 'controlling', 'reporting', 'sharing information' and 'reschedule' were identified from the scenario narrated in the above section.

Steps involved in a given group of tasks are as follows:

Step 1: Start the machine by pressing the button 'ON'.
Step 2: Look at the current sensor readings in the dial of the control panel
Step 3: Compare the current value with the unstable range of the sensor value (critical value). (Details provided by process planning executives).
Step 4: Interpret the sensors value continuously.
Step 5. If current sensor value start going beyond the critical value of the sensor readings. If not then go back to step 2. If yes, then go to step 6.
Step 6: Take control action- manage sensor values through controlling knobs to some extent to make current sensor value into the stable range.
Step 7: Create report to share sensor information with the operations manager.
Step 8: Reschedule the machine with new set points.
Step 9: Stop the machine by pressing the button 'OFF'.

Figure 6. Task flow diagram

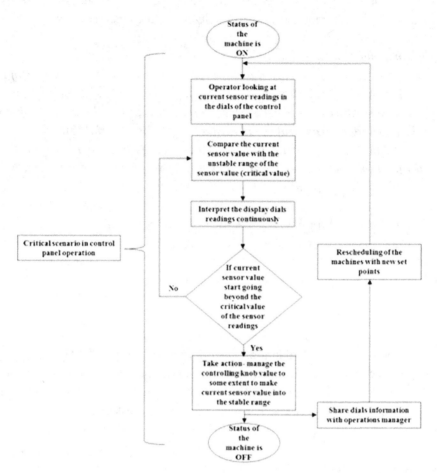

This technique will be helpful to identify the task steps and task duration in control panel operation. Through calculation of time taken to perform the given tasks, operator performance can be calculated. Further, this flow diagram also gives clues for reasons of increased cognitive loads in tasks, in a given scenario. It also provides opportunities to think through alternative paths that a user may take and accordingly new designs with lesser cognitive loads can be created.

Design

During the design process, apart from the information gathered from user research and task analysis steps, some basic cognitive science literature will be useful for the design team while ideating the control panel design for industry 4.0 context. The *design* step of UCLCD4 is further broken into four sub-steps: (i) introduction of cognitive load heuristics (ii) concept sketching (iii) evaluation and iteration (iv) prototyping shown in figure 7.

In design process, cognitive load heuristics will aid designers to streamline their creative thinking in CL measurement terms and further the heuristics can aid them in quick iterative evaluations of the design

Figure 7. Process for designing control panels

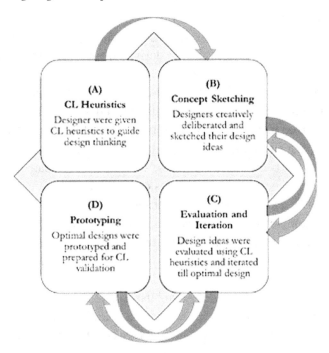

options that they ideate. Concept sketching will involve quick hand drawn or digital sketches where designers will create various design options. Third step is evaluation and iteration of design options using CL heuristics scores. Designers iterate the designs till reached to optimum CL. Fourth step is prototyping. Final prototype of optimum designs can be prepared for testing and validation. The interactive prototypes can be validated through physiological and subjective CL measures in the next step of UCLCD4. These four design steps are proposed to be performed iteratively to achieve optimal CL designs.

CL Heuristic

Heuristics in design have been used in past to aid HCI designers. For example, design heuristics pertaining to usability focus in design has been suggested by Jacob Nielsen (Nielsen, 1994). Similarly, UI design heuristics have been suggested by Ben Shneiderman (Shneiderman, 2000). While absolute laws for design thinking are difficult to formulate as by definition design is the activity of 'ill-defined problem solving' (Simon, 1978), heuristics provide some guidance to otherwise fuzzy intra-mental creative design thinking (Nagai & Noguchi, 2003). Designers opportunistically expand boundaries of design problem space and iteratively seek mapping of problem and solution spaces (Nagai & Noguchi, 2003). The proposed CL heuristics will be useful to HCI designers working to manage CL in high information design contexts by provide them initial guidance in solution finding as well as to help them in quick evaluation of their design concepts.

In this section, proposed design heuristics to minimise the CL for users have been tabulated in tables 5 to 8. Three CL heuristic tables based on each of the three types of cognitive load has been described in tables 5 to 7, namely ICL, ECL and GCL heuristic principles. A brief description of each principle has also been given in the tables. By definition, Intrinsic Cognitive Load (ICL) is caused due to 'inherent level of difficulty in tasks' (Sweller, 1988). ICL is concerned with the way tasks are designed in the control panel. If the task complexity could be decreased by design, then the ICL will be lower for the design option. Three heuristic principles have been derived from this definition as tabulated in table 5 to help the designer think through while designing new interfaces.

By definition, Extraneous Cognitive Load (ECL) is caused due to 'presentation of irrelevant information in the task' (Sweller, 1988). ECL is concerned with layout design, content design and visual design of the control panel. If a given piece of information in not required to complete the task, it should be removed from the screens that a user has to go through. The ECL can be lowered for the design option. Three heuristic principles have been derived from this definition as tabulated in table 6.

By definition, Germane Cognitive Load (GCL) is caused due to 'adding new relevant information in task' (Sweller, 1988). New relevant information causes the user to form new 'mental models' (Laird, 1983) and hence it is a cognitive cost of the new design to the user. If new information is reduced or kept closest to the previous 'mental model' or old established designs are used as it is, then GCL can be lowered. Three heuristic principles have been derived from this definition as tabulated in table 7.

The above heuristics can be used for evaluation of design concepts generated by HCI designers (table 8). Above CL evaluation heuristics can be used within the design team, by designer himself/herself or by other team members. The objective of using above heuristics for design evaluation is to generate quick assessment of designed concepts without involving real users. This process will save effort in getting the actual users and getting tasks done. Heuristic evaluations of initial conceptual designs can be used to iterate the designs till an optimal and satisfactory design solution is arrived at.

Table 5. CL heuristics for intrinsic cognitive load

S. No.	Heuristic Principle	Description
1.	Reduce *no. of tasks and no. of steps* in each task.	Design the interface of HCI system such that it reduces the no. of steps in the task and the no. of tasks to minimum possible to achieve the same goal.
2.	Reduce the *amount of information* required to be processed by user.	Design the interface of HCI system such that it reduces the amount of information to be processed by the user in order to complete the task.
3.	Reduce *frequency of task* by task allocation	Design the interface of HCI system such that it reduces repetitive tasks and allocates non-decision tasks to system rather than human user.

Table 6. CL heuristic for extraneous cognitive load

S. No.	Heuristic Principle	Description
1.	Remove unnecessary decoration and *irrelevant information* in task at visual, auditory and kinaesthetic levels in design.	Design the interface of HCI system such that visual information (in terms of colours, text, images, videos etc.) is minimum and layouts look clean and organised.
2.	Increase the *legibility and readability* of the information (text, graphics, numerals etc.)	Design the information presentation on screen in such a way that information can be easily identified and read.
3.	Create clear *visual hierarchy* of the information and create a *sense of place* on each screen.	Design the interface of HCI system such that the users can easily understand the information on screen without the need to look for the context.

Table 7. CL heuristic for germane cognitive load

S. No.	Heuristic Principle	Description
1.	Reduce unnecessary **novelty of the display designs.**	Design the HCI based control panel displays such that users can use their existing mental models to understand them.
2.	Reduce the **novelty of interaction.**	User's surprises during the interaction should be minimised through design to avoid extra mental load.
3.	Reduce **novelty in tasks**	Novel ways to perform a traditional industry task leads to extra learning efforts. If new technology forces development of new methods in task, then the designer should keep the new design as close to old as possible.

Table 8. CL evaluation heuristics

Confidently 'Yes'		Weakly 'Yes'	Not sure	Weakly 'No'	Confidently 'No'	
(1)		(2)	(3)	(4)	(5)	
S. No.	Type	Heuristic Principle			Ratings on 5-point scale	Total CL
1.		Has the design option ensured that the no. of tasks and no. of steps in each task is optimally reduced?				
2.	ICL Measures	Is the amount of information that user must process for completion of each task been optimally reduced?				
3.		Have the frequent and non-decision tasks allocated to system?				
4.		Has the design reduced the irrelevant information to minimum?				
5.	ECL Measures	Is the relevant information legible and readable?				
6.		Has the visual hierarchy and sense of place been ensured?				
7.		Is the unnecessary novelty in displays removed?				
8.	GCL Measures	Is the interaction designed close to users' expectations?				
9.		Is the task design close to the existing mental models of users?				

Concept Sketching

A design workshop with designers were conducted. Total of 16 designers participated in the workshop and they came up with 16 different design options for a given persona and scenario. These 16 designers were in their final year of Master of Design degree at Industrial Design program and had done prior interface design based projects.

All the 16 participants were seated simultaneously in a large room where they were first given a broad overview of design process (figure 7). The context of Industry 4.0 technologies was introduced to the participants. Then the workshop participants were given the persona and scenario on a printed A4 sheet. The task list of users was also given to participants. After the participants assimilated the persona and scenario information, cognitive load heuristic principles were given to participants for consideration during design ideation. The participants were encouraged to sketch design concepts on plain sheets of paper using colour pencils and sketch pens (figure 8) while keeping the cognitive load heuristic principles in mind (table 5 to table 7). Each participant was asked to identify any one of the designs that they felt was

Figure 8. Concept sketching

suitable for the persona, scenario and tasks. Then participants were encouraged to create a high-fidelity digital mock-up of the selected design option. The digital mock ups of the concepts were then evaluated using cognitive load heuristics in group. While most of the design concepts were found to have a clear difference cognitive load heuristic score (table 9), other designs seemed similar in scores (table 10).

Evaluation and Iteration

Photoshop and Invision software were used to create the digital mock-ups of the selected design options. Then participants mutually rated cognitive load for each design using CL heuristic evaluation scores provided. It was encouraged that more than one person rated each design and then with mutual consensus the final ratings be arrived. In the process of rating, the designer of the concept explained the details of design as and when required for a clarification. Researcher took notes of salient discussion points that happened during the rating. Table 9 lists some of the designs obtained from the workshop, their ratings by participants and the salient discussions that occurred during ratings.

During the workshop, different and creative approaches to designing the same HCI based control panel for the same persona, scenario and tasks were observed from different participants. UCLCD4 had facilitated creative freedom while providing broad suggestions for designing to minimize cognitive load. It was also observed that many designs had used similar display options and control options.

Design outcomes of workshop gave a glimpse of how touch based handheld and mobile HCI devices for Industry 4.0 will allow creative explosion of ways in which the control panels will be designed. Further, it was also observed that among the many different design possibilities, it will be difficult to choose the least cognitively demanding designs by mere speculation and rigorous validation methods will be required.

From the workshop outcomes, it was also observed that some of the participants had created designs which proposed to use analog, digital or combination of analog and digital display for HCI based control panels. The present CL heuristics did not cover any differentiation in cognitive load based on different display types and hence one was not sure which display type will be cognitively less demanding.

For example, table 10 has shown three different display designs which had reported similar CL heuristic ratings. These three options were not differentiable and have almost similar cognitive load. The designer was encouraged to then create similar look and feel for all the three design options which

Table 9. Design concepts of control panels and their CL heuristic evaluations

Design Concept	Heuristic Evaluation Scores	Discussions for Score Value
	CL heuristic scores: ICL Score = 7 ECL Score = 8 GCL Score = 14 Total CL score = 29	ICL is low: no. of steps in task was less, amount of information required to be processed in task was relevant and less, non-decision making tasks was allocated to the system. ECL is low: use of irrelevant information in task was less, Legible and readable of information was good. Sense of placement of dials and indicators are appropriate. However, too many colors were used in dials. GCL is high: unnecessary novelty in information presentation and use of novel dial design. Without knobs, interaction became difficult.
	CL heuristic scores: ICL = 11 ECL = 13 GCL = 14 Total CL = 38	ICL is high: use of single knob operation for all the dials makes controlling task difficult, amount of information required to be processed in a task is high and many non-decision making tasks were allocated to users. ECL is high: shows irrelevant information in task (for e.g.-needle pointed on red and LED blink was green). Too many colors were used in dials. GCL is high: unnecessary novelty in design was not removed. Dials designs were not close to the user's mental model. However, use of colors in dials were not adding any novelty.
	CL heuristic scores: ICL = 7 ECL = 15 GCL = 7 Total CL = 29	ICL is low: steps in task was less, amount of information required to be processed in task was less and non-decision making tasks were allocated to the systems. ECL is high: use of irrelevant information in task is more (for example-operator image shown in left top of the screen and pop up massage of machine suggestions covers dial information). Too many colors were used in indication. Color indication in tasks was irrelevant. GCL is low: new type of information display added in design which is close to the user's mental model (for example-use of color indication in "analog display and "graphical display" dials). No novel interaction mode used in design.

are depicted in Table 10. As in table 10, 'design 1' has 'analog display', 'design 2' has 'digital display' and 'design 3' has a 'hybrid display' combination of the two display types. These three designs were then rated on CL heuristics by mutual consensus in group. The CL heuristic scores were observed to be nearly similar for all the three designs (17, 19, and 16 respectively). It was not much clear from the heuristic evaluations which of the design options would be highly cognitively more demanding for the users and which design give lowest cognitive load. It was subjectively clear that digital design was high

Table 10 Heuristic evaluation of three design concepts having similar scores

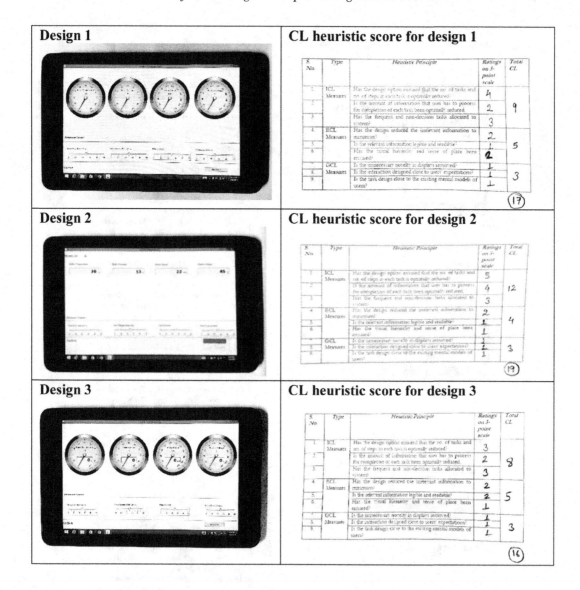

in cognitive load compared to other two designs but quantitatively it was not clear. Therefore, it was decided that these designs (table 10) will be taken up for validation using physiological method in order to explore whether physiological methods would further differentiate them on the basis of CL. It was also decided that cognitive load caused due to three control panel design types will be measured using EEG (objective CL measurement) and NASA Task Load Index (subjective CL measurement).

Prototyping

In order to do physiological validation, an interactive prototype was required so that tasks could be performed realistically by participants on the prototypes while physiological data would be collected. It was then decided to convert the digital mock-ups into interactive prototypes were thus developed using JAVA programming (figure 9). Necessary coding to make the interface interactive and give a feel of realistic control panel was done.

Validation

Combination of subjective and objective (physiological) measures of 'cognitive load' have been proposed for validation. Benefit of combining verbally reported subjective cognitive load assessment by participants and physiologically measured objective mental load is to ensure that the mental load *felt* by the participant and mental load recorded by the physiological measurement instrument are congruent and true assessments. As the phenomena being observed is cognitive load, which is subtle and not easily observable and has a *felt* component, it is proposed here that the combined method would yield better validation of the designs. Real participants who are representative users are expected to participate in the validation test. It is proposed that EEG be used for the physiological measurement of cognitive load data and NASA TLX be used for the self-reported subjective measurement of cognitive load data from the participants.

Designers participated in the workshop has ideated various design options of HCI based control panels (refer design section). Designers have created three types of display dials which were common in various control panel design options namely, **analog, digital and hybrid** and their CL heuristic ratings were also almost same. This was the reason here that authors have been selected these three control panels which have purely analog, digital and hybrid control panel designs. In order to check the difference between the display types, authors decided to validate the designs from cognitive load perspective using physiological and NASA TLX measure. Authors have hypothesized that which display type causes less cognitive load?

Two tasks were given to the participants namely, *'monitoring' & 'controlling'* and scenario were explained. Monitoring and controlling tasks were categorised as 'frequent & highly cognitively demanded' (Refer task analysis section). Control panel design were based on hypothetical pharmaceutical company in context of Industry 4.0.

Each design was subjected to validation process using EEG and NASA Task Load Index, with *15 participants* who were engineers by profession and their age is between 20 to 30 years, Mean (25.6 years) and Standard Deviation (2.06 years). Three designs are namely, 'ANALOG', 'DIGITAL' and 'HYBRID'

Figure 9. Three interactive prototypes with three different display types

modalities for display of 'temperature', 'pressure', 'motor speed' and 'station voltage'. The participants were given these designs on a touch-based tablet of 8 inches size. Participant sat on a comfortable chair holding tablet in their hands in a closed room (figure 10).

There was no disturbance in the room. EEG headset were placed on the head of the participant during experimentation. EEG of six electrode data was recorded during the tasks. EEG electrode were placed on the frontal region of the brain. As several researchers reported in literature that higher beta band power across frontal region is associated with higher cognitive load (Antonenko, Paas, Grabner, & Gog, 2010) (Kumar & Kumar, 2016). Analysis of EEG data and NASA Task Load Index is discussed and presented separately as follows.

In the NASA TLX scale, participants were asked to rate the three display designs on a 10-point scale *'frustrations'*, *'mental effort'*, *'task performance'*, *'temporal demand'*, *'physical demand'* and *'mental demand'* at the end of the task completion. ANOVA between all three display designs for six NASA TLX parameters were calculated. Out of six NASA TLX parameters, four parameters *'frustration'*, *'mental effort'*, *'performance'* and *'mental demand'* have found significant difference in three designs i.e., (F=5.62, p<0.05), (F=5.21, P<0.05), (F=3.18, P<0.05) and (F=4.23, P<0.05) respectively. Other two NASA TLX parameters, *'temporal demand'* (F=0.56, P>0.05) and *'physical demand'* (F=0.01, P>0.05) parameters were not found to have significant difference. This concludes that participants did not felt time pressure caused due to task. Also, physical demand in the task was very low due to tablet based interaction design.

From the mean values, the differences in all the NASA TLX parameters, digital display design was found to be worse than the hybrid and analog designs in critical condition. As depicted in figure 11, hybrid design was reported to be less in frustration, less in mental effort, high in performance, low in temporal demand, low in physical demand and low in mental demand across all the 15 participants. Analog display design was moderate in majority of the parameters whereas, digital design was high in frustration, high in mental effort, lowest in performance, highest in mental demand.

In EEG analysis, frontal region namely AF3, AF4, F3, F4, F7 and F8 EEG data were recorded and pre-processed. From recorded and processed EEG channels, beta band power was calculated. In this case study authors have been used beta band power for cognitive load measurement to validate the control panel design. It is reported in literature that beta band power has been used for cognitive load measure-

Figure 10. Experimental setup

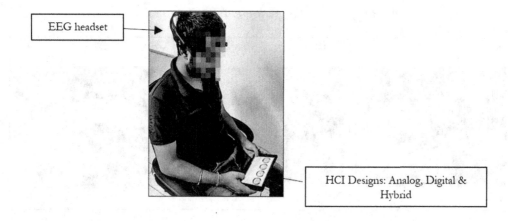

Figure 11. Rating on NASA TLX parameters for different display designs on 10-point scale

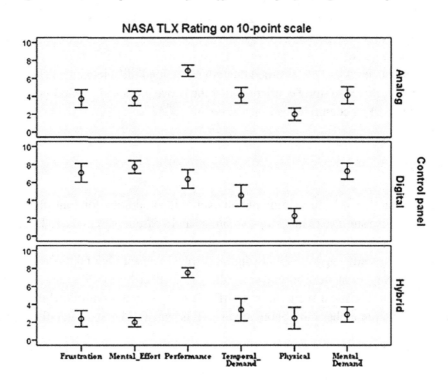

ment and beta band power (freq. range 13-30Hz) increases due to increase in task difficulty (Brookings, Wilson, & Swain, 1996) (Knoll et. al., 2011) (Zarjam, Epps, & Chen, 2011). In this case study authors have been used beta band power for cognitive load measurement to validate the control panel design.

Beta band power of all the frontal region channels has been statistically presented in table 5. ANOVA between all three display types (*analog, digital and hybrid*) in monitoring and controlling tasks for *15 participants* showed significant difference in each EEG frontal channels (see Table 11).

It is evident from table 11 that there was significant difference ($p < 0.05$) in cognitive load caused by the three types of display designs. Mean of beta band power across frontal region electrodes (AF3, AF4, F3, F4, F7, F8) was found to be higher in digital display design in comparison to analog and hybrid

Table 11. F values at P<0.05 for Beta band power using ANOVA between different designs

Analog vs Digital		Digital vs Hybrid		Hybrid vs Analog	
AF3	F= 9.05, P=0.045	AF3	F= 22.5, P=0.000	AF3	F= 10.5, P=0.040
AF4	F= 11.7, P=0.035	AF4	F= 25.2, P=0.000	AF4	F= 4.1, P=0.065
F3	F= 20.3, P=0.010	F3	F= 24.3, P=0.000	F3	F= 11.8, P=0.040
F4	F= 16.1, P=0.020	F4	F= 19.7, P=0.010	F4	F= 9.2, P=0.045
F7	F= 14.8, P=0.025	F7	F= 27.2, P=0.000	F7	F= 10.2, P=0.040
F8	F= 14.5, P=0.025	F8	F= 21.3, P=0.010	F8	F= 12.3, P=0.030

which indicates higher mental activity and higher cognitive load (refer figure 12). The mean of beta band power across frontal region electrodes was found to be lowest in hybrid display design for monitoring and controlling task.

Results of beta band power across frontal region, AF3, AF4, F3, F4, F7 and F8 channels and parameters of NASA TLX data both have determined the 'cognitive load' difference in different control panel display designs. Hence, this case study confirmed that the above proposed methodology can be used for design validation focused on cognitive load measurement.

CONCLUSION

The novelty of this chapter has been to bring out an overall methodology for control panel design from cognitive load perspective suitable to Industry 4.0 context and a case study conducted using the proposed UCLCD4 methodology.

Findings of the case study suggested that 'digital display' caused high cognitive load compared to analog and hybrid display for monitoring and controlling tasks in critical CPPS scenario. Digital display acquires more attention in critical scenario and difficult in operating controls while threshold values for the parameters must remember throughout the task. It is suggested that digital display should not be

Figure 12. Mean value [Power ($10log*10(\mu V^2)$)] of beta band power across frontal region for different control panel designs

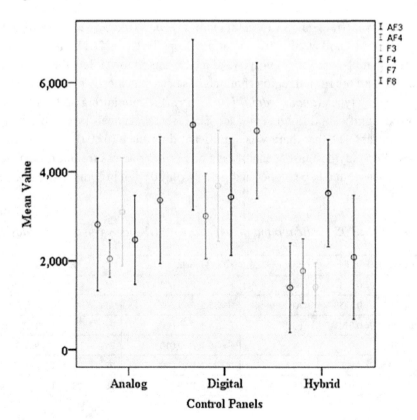

use in control panel design where task complexity and task frequency is high. This study paves ways for much needed cognitive load consideration in HCI based control panel designs and provides useful information for interface designers.

Authors proposed three evaluation methods which is further compared to understand the benefit of the multi-method use. First was CL heuristic method, second was physiological method and third was NASA task load index method. Results were congruent across these data. CL heuristic rating for hybrid display was rated as lowest (16) and digital display was rated highest (19). Similarly, NASA TLX rated highest mental demand (F=4.23, P<0.05) for digital display and lowest for hybrid display design. Also, EEG beta band power across frontal region of the human brain was found highest values for digital display design and lowest for hybrid display design. It is concluded that all the three methods can be used for design evaluation.

From this chapter, it is also concluded that, designers evaluate designs based on CL heuristic principle (CL ratings) was not measure cognitive load quantitatively but discusses score values which provide helpful information for designers to rate the level of cognitive load of their designs and understand the need of quantitative measurement of cognitive load. CL heuristic provide effective results in less time. Even designer would not require any expensive tool for evaluating their designs. CL heuristic method would give better qualitative measure compared to NASA task load index. As NASA TLX gives only rating on specific parameters (*mental demand, physical demand, temporal demand, mental effort, frustration, performance*) which was not very useful for identifying specific redesigning elements of the control panels. Therefore, it is suggested that NASA TLX method for CL measurement was not much useful for designers to evaluate their designs and not much helpful for control panel redesigning process.

From the above two methods, physiological method for cognitive load was more reliable and provide quantitative analysis of CL caused due to different designs. Drawbacks of physiological method are use of expensive EEG tool, requires huge time for EEG data analysis and require EEG data interpretation expertise. Overall, it is suggested that for quick evaluation of control panel designs using CL heuristics will be a better method compared to other two methods. Whereas, for rigorous evaluation of complex control panels designs and redesigning based on task complexity, physiological method along with CL heuristic rating will be best.

REFERENCES

Antonenko, P., Paas, F., Grabner, R., & Gog, T. V. (2010). Using Electroencephalography to measure cognitive load. *Educational Psychology*, 22(4), 425–438.

Astrom, K. (1985). Process control--Past, present and future. *IEEE Control Systems Magazine*, 5(3), 3–10. doi:10.1109/MCS.1985.1104958

Bailey, D., & Wright, E. (2003). *Practical SCADA for industry*. Burlington, MA: Elsevier.

Beniger. (2009). *The control revolution: Technological and economic origins of the information society.* Cambridge, MA: Harvard University Press.

Bridger, R. S. (1995). *Introduction to ergonomics*. London, UK: Taylor and Francis Group. doi:10.4324/9780203426135

Brookings, J. B., Wilson, G. F., & Swain, C. R. (1996). Psychophysiological responses to changes in workload during simulated air traffic control. *Biological Psychology*, *42*(3), 361–377. doi:10.1016/0301-0511(95)05167-8 PMID:8652753

Burt, J. L., Bartolome, D. S., Burdette, D. W., & Comstock, J. R. Jr. (2007). A psychophysiological evaluation of the perceived urgency of auditory warning signals. *Ergonomics*, *38*(11), 2327–2340. doi:10.1080/00140139508925271 PMID:7498191

Cain, B. (2007). A review of the mental workload literature. Toronto, Canada: Defence Research and Development, NATO RTO Report.

Coury, B., & Pietras, C. (1989). Alphanumeric and graphic displays for dynamic process monitoring and control. *Ergonomics*, *32*(11), 1373–1389. doi:10.1080/00140138908966912 PMID:28080931

Li Da, X., He, W., & Li, S. (2014). Internet of Things in Industries: A Survey. *IEEE Transaction on Industrial Informatics, 10*(4), 2233-2243.

Deane, P. (1965). *The first industrial revolution*. Cambridge, UK: Cambridge University Press.

DIS. (2009). 9241-210: 2010. Ergonomics of human system interaction-Part 210: Human-centred design for interactive systems. International Standardization Organization (ISO).

Francis, G. (2000). Designing multifunction displays: An optimization approach. *International Journal of Cognitive Ergonomics*, *4*(2), 107–124. doi:10.1207/S15327566IJCE0402_2

Gill, P., Stewart, K., Treasure, E., & Chadwick, B. (2008). Methods of data collection in qualitative research: Interviews and focus groups. *British Dental Journal*, *204*(6), 291–295. doi:10.1038/bdj.2008.192 PMID:18356873

Gope, D. (2011). Hand gesture interaction with human computer. *Global Journal of Computer Science and Technology*, *11*(23), 1–11.

Gorecky, D., Schmitt, M., Loskyll, M., & Zühlke, D. (2014). Human machine interaction in Industry 4.0 era. In *12th IEEE International Conference on industrial informatics* (pp. 289-294). Porto Alegre, Brazil: IEEE. 10.1109/INDIN.2014.6945523

Greenwood. (1997). *The third industrial revolution: technology, productivity, and income inequality*. Washington, DC: American Enterprise Institute.

Gungor, V., Sachine, D., & Kocak, T. (2011). Smart grid technologies: communication technologies and standards. *IEEE Transaction of Industrial Informatic, 7*(4), 529-539.

Han, J., Kim, Y., Rhie, Y., & Choi, H. (2015). Design optimization of control layout for naval MFC (multifunction console) using a modified layout analysis method. In *Proceeding of the human factor and ergonomics society 59th annual meeting* (pp. 1351-1355). SAGE Publications.

Hart, S. G., & Staveland, L. E. (1988). Development of NASA-TLX (Task Load Index): Results of empirical and theoretical research. *Advances in Psychology*, *52*, 139–183. doi:10.1016/S0166-4115(08)62386-9

Hinckley, K., & Sinclair, M. (1999). Touch-sensing input devices. In *CHI '99 Proceedings of the SIGCHI Conference on Human Factors in Computing Systems* (pp. 223-230). ACM.

Hoffmann, E. (1994). Optimum layout of an array of controls. *International Journal of Industrial Ergonomics*, *14*(3), 251–261. doi:10.1016/0169-8141(94)90101-5

Holman, G., Carnahan, B., & Bulfin, R. (2003). Using linear programming to optimize control panel design from an ergonomics perspective. In *Proceedings of the human factors and ergonomics society annual meeting* (Vol. 47, issue 10, pp. 1317-1321). Los Angeles, CA: SAGE Publication.

Jung, E., Park, S., & Chang, S. (1995). A CSP technique based interactive control panel layout. *Journal of Economics*, *38*(9), 1884–1893.

Knoll, A., Wang, Y., Chen, F., Xu, J., Ruiz, N., Epps, J., & Zarjam, P. (2011). Measuring cognitive workload with low-cost electroencephalograph. In P. Campos, N. Graham, J. Jorge, N. Nunes, P. Palanque, & M. Winckler (Eds.), Lecture Notes in Computer Science: Vol. 6949. *Human-Computer Interaction – INTERACT 2011*. Berlin: Springer. doi:10.1007/978-3-642-23768-3_84

Kumar, N., & Kumar, J. (2016). Measurement of Cognitive Load in HCI Systems Using EEG Power Spectrum: An Experimental Study. *Procedia Computer Science*, *84*, 70–78. doi:10.1016/j.procs.2016.04.068

Laird, P. (1983). *Mental models: towards a cognitive science of language, inference, and consciousness.* Cambridge, MA: Harvard University Press.

Lee, J., Bagheri, B., & Kao, H.-A. (2014). A Cyber physical systems achitechture for Industry4.0- based manufacturing systems. *Manufacturing Letters*, *3*, 18–23. doi:10.1016/j.mfglet.2014.12.001

MacDougall, W. (2014). *Industry 4.0: Smart manufacturing for the future*. Berlin, Germany: GTAI.

MacMillan, K. G., Beach, J., Cheng, K.-C., & Eberts, R. E. (1999). operator interface. In G. Millan (Eds.), Process industrial instrument and control handbook (pp. 8.1-8.25). TMH Press.

Meixner, G., Petersen, N., & Koessling, H. (2010). User interaction evolution in the SmartFactoryKL. In *Proceedings of the 24th BCS Interaction Specialist Group Conference* pp. (211–220). Dundee, UK. British Computer Society.

Millera, M. W., Rietschel, J. C., McDonald, C. G., & Hatfield, B. D. (2011). A novel approach to the physiological measurement of mental workload. *International Journal of Psychophysiology*, *80*(1), 75–78. doi:10.1016/j.ijpsycho.2011.02.003 PMID:21320552

Nagai, Y., & Noguchi, H. (2003). An experimental study on the design thinking process started from difficult keywords: Modelling the thinking process of creative design. *Journal of Engineering Design*, *14*(4), 429–437. doi:10.1080/09544820310001606911

Nielson, J. (1994). *Usability engineering*. AP Professional.

Norman, D. (2013). *The design of everyday things*. New York: Basic Book Group.

Norman, D. A., & Draper, S. W. (1986). *User centered system design: New perspectives on human-computer interaction*. CRC Press. doi:10.1201/b15703

Pruitt, J., & Adlin, T. (2006). *The Persona Lifecycle: Keeping people in mind throughout product design*. San Francisco, CA: Elsevier.

Rogger, Y., Sharp, H., & Preece, J. (2011). *Interaction design: Beyond human - computer interaction.* West Sussex, UK: John Wiley & Sons.

Rouse, W. (1988). The human role in advanced manufacturing system. In W. D. Compton (Ed.), *Design and analysis of integrated manufacturing systems* (pp. 148–166). Washington, DC: National Academy Press.

Ryu, K., & Myung, R. (2005). Evaluation of mental workload with a combined measure based on physiological indices during a dual task of tracking and a mental arithmetic. *International Journal of Industrial Ergonomics, 35*(11), 991–1009. doi:10.1016/j.ergon.2005.04.005

Shneiderman, B. (2000). Universal usability. *Communications of the ACM, 43*(5), 84–91. doi:10.1145/332833.332843

Simon, H. A. (1978). Information-processing theory of human problem solving. In H. A. Simon (Ed.), *Handbook of learning and cognitive processes* (pp. 271–295). New York: Psychology Press.

Stanton, N. A., Booth, R., & Stammers, R. B. (1992). Alarms in human supervisory control: A human factors perspective. *International Journal of Computer Integrated Manufacturing, 5*(2), 81–93. doi:10.1080/09511929208944518

Stanton, N. A., & Edworthy, J. (1999). *Human factors in auditory warnings.* New York: Ashgate Publications.

Streans, P. N. (2013). *The Industrial Revolution in World History.* New York: Taylor & Francis.

Sweller, J. (1988). Cognitive Load During Problem Solving: Effects on Learning. *Cognitive Science, 12*(2), 257–285. doi:10.120715516709cog1202_4

Wang, M., Liu, C., & Pan, Y. (1991). Computer aided panel layout using a multi-criteria heuristic algorithm. *International Journal of Production Research, 29*(6), 1215–1233. doi:10.1080/00207549108930129

Wittenberg, C. (2015). Cause the Trend Industry 4.0 in the Automated Industry to New Requirements on User Interfaces? In M. Kurosu (Ed.), Lecture Notes in Computer Science: Vol. 9171. *Human-Computer Interaction: Users and Contexts. HCI 2015* (pp. 238–245). Los Angeles, CA: Springer, Cham.

Zarjam, P., Epps, J., & Chen, F. (2011). Spectral EEG features for evaluating cognitive load. *33rd Annual International Conference of the IEEE EMBS* (pp. 3841-3844). Boston: IEEE.

Zuehike, D. (2010). SmartFactory - Towards a factory-of-things. *Annual Reviews in Control, 34*(1), 129–138. doi:10.1016/j.arcontrol.2010.02.008

Chapter 20
Groupwise Non-Rigid Image Alignment Using Few Parameters:
Registration of Facial and Medical Images

Ahmad Hashim Aal-Yhia
Aberystwyth University, UK & University of Baghdad, Iraq

Bernard Tiddeman
Aberystwyth University, UK

Paul Malcolm
Norfolk Norwich University Hospital, UK

Reyer Zwiggelaar
Aberystwyth University, UK

ABSTRACT

Groupwise non-rigid image alignment is a difficult non-linear optimization problem involving many parameters and often large datasets. Previous methods have explored various metrics and optimization strategies. Good results have been previously achieved with simple metrics, requiring complex optimization, often with many unintuitive parameters that require careful tuning for each dataset. In this chapter, the problem is restructured to use a simpler, iterative optimization algorithm, with very few free parameters. The warps are refined using an iterative Levenberg-Marquardt minimization to the mean, based on updating the locations of a small number of points and incorporating a stiffness constraint. This optimization approach is efficient, has very few free parameters to tune, and the authors show how to tune the few remaining parameters. Results show that the method reliably aligns various datasets including two facial datasets and two medical datasets of prostate and brain MRI images and demonstrates efficiency in terms of performance and a reduction of the computational cost.

DOI: 10.4018/978-1-5225-9069-9.ch020

INTRODUCTION

The process of image registration is to extract and combine significant information from a group of two or more images (Fischer & Modersitzki, 2008) by estimating the optimal transformations which allow them to be matched and their features aligned well (Sidorov K., 2010).

Non-rigid image registration is an important step in many image analysis problems. It involves geometrically distorting the images to align common features. Manual annotation of features is time consuming and prone to errors, and so can form a bottle neck in processes involving human-computer interactions such as image-based animation, image analysis and medical diagnosis and research. As a result, considerable research effort has been applied to developing fully automatic processes to align the images. One approach to image registration that is extensively used, is to select one image from the image set to act as a reference or template and then repeatedly align each image of the set to that reference by using a pairwise registration algorithm (Zitova & Flusser, 2003), (Cootes T., Twining, Petrovic, Schestowitz, & Taylor, 2005),(Cootes, Twining, & Taylor, 2004), (Rueckert, Frangi, & Schnabel, 2001) so as to find deformation fields between the reference and each image in the set.

If the images are very consistent, or the selected target image happens to be particularly well chosen, this approach might work well. However, using this approach gives us a biased representation to the reference image (Polfliet, et al., 2018), consequently there are likely to be some errors in the final alignment. If the selection of the reference image is not suitable and missing important features, the registration process will give sub-optimal results (Sidorov, Richmond, & Marshall, 2009), (Marsland, Twining, & Taylor, 2008). Also, the resulting information from the pairwise registration of two images, which does not include all the features of the images in the set, will lead to inaccurate results (Polfliet, et al., 2018).

Groupwise registration algorithms have been developed recently to avoid the problems of pairwise registration described above (Cootes T., Twining, Petrovic, Babalola, & Taylor, 2010), (Sidorov, Richmond, & Marshall, 2009), (Cootes T., Twining, Petrovic, Schestowitz, & Taylor, 2005), (Cootes, Marsland, Twining, & Smith, 2004), (Cristinacce & Cootes, 2008), (Davies, Twining, & Taylor, 2008), (Twining, et al., 2005). Groupwise methods use the information in all the images in the set in the registration process simultaneously. Therefore, this total information is used at each iteration instead of using only the information from two images (Sidorov, Richmond, & Marshall, 2009). So, the deformation fields, which are obtained during groupwise registration, are optimised simultaneously (Polfliet, et al., 2018), for performing the alignment efficiently (Sidorov, Richmond, & Marshall, 2009).

The algorithms of groupwise alignment have been experimentally demonstrated to be better than pairwise algorithms by computing the dense correspondences across a group of the estimated shapes (Sidorov, Richmond, & Marshall, 2009), (Cootes T., Twining, Petrovic, Schestowitz, & Taylor, 2005), which has not been exploited in the literature (Cootes T., Twining, Petrovic, Babalola, & Taylor, 2010), (Baker, Matthews, & Schneider, 2004), (Cootes T., Twining, Petrovic, Schestowitz, & Taylor, 2005).

Active Appearance Models (AAMs) (Cootes, Edwards, & Taylor, 2001), (Matthews & Baker, 2004) present efficient ways to optimize shape and appearance models (usually based on PCA derived models) to an image. The fitting of the AAM model is achieved by minimising an objective function to find the model shape update parameters δp, which comes from a Taylor series approximation. The AAM style optimisation is not suitable for a large number of parameters, as it requires inverting an N^2 matrix for minimising N parameters. Nevertheless, if a way can be found to reduce the number of parameters involved in the minimisation, AAM style optimisation represents an efficient alignment strategy, with very few parameters to tune.

In this chapter, we expand on the algorithmic details of the proposed method described in our earlier paper (Aal-Yhia, Malcolm, Zwiggelaar, & Tiddeman, 2018). In addition, we use an additional brain MRI images medical dataset, and an additional evaluation method (Dice overlap) for the prostate and brain datasets. The algorithm aims to reduce the requirements for careful tuning of many parameters required in many optimisation procedures. The remaining parameters are fairly intuitive (such as the number of control points used each iteration), except for one "stiffness" parameter that controls the relative contribution of the image pixel error and the stiffness. Later in section (Estimation of the Stiffness Parameter) we describe a simulation approach for tuning this remaining parameter.

In the proposed optimisation method, we use some advantages of the previous techniques mentioned in the background section and avoid some of their disadvantages. The use of a small set of feature points to build up a complex warp allows an AAM style optimization, which can be further optimized by only updating the derivative images of the matrix A and dot product of the matrix A^TA once per iteration over the set of images. Leave-one-out optimization and alignment to the mean have been proved effective and efficient in previous works mentioned in the background section, and we use them in the proposed method in this chapter. The use of the Levenberg-Marquardt algorithm provides stability and automatic tuning of the damping term. The key to the power in the proposed method in this chapter is that we developed a novel iterative linear optimisation approach for doing groupwise alignment with no complex parameter tuning required as is the case using some optimisation algorithms such as the simultaneous perturbation stochastic approximation (SPSA) algorithm. Intuitive parameters such as grid size, step size, and resolution parameter are known, δp is computed within the proposed algorithm and the only remaining free parameter is the stiffness parameter that controls the relative contribution of the image pixel error and the stiffness. In this chapter we also presented an elastic constraint that can be included in the groupwise algorithm and propose a novel simulation method that can be used for estimating the stiffness parameter for the elastic constraint.

BACKGROUND

Applications of groupwise image registration have multiple areas such as: face alignment (Zhang, Smith, Dessein, Pears, & Dai, 2016), characters recognition (Mac Parthalain & Strange, 2013), modelling of medical images, for example multispectral imaging of the retina and choroid (Lin, et al., 2016).

The groupwise non-rigid image alignment methods have been developed recently (Aal-Yhia, Malcolm, Zwiggelaar, & Tiddeman, 2018), (Polfliet, et al., 2018), (Wu, et al., 2016), (Zhang, Smith, Dessein, Pears, & Dai, 2016) (Aal-Yhia, Malcolm, Akanyeti, Zwiggelaa, & Tiddeman, 2018) to avoid the problems of pairwise registration.

The groupwise image registration is to warp a set of images into a common reference (Tang, Jiang, & Fan, 2013) by using an effective way to estimate the deformation fields of these images simultaneously (Wu, et al., 2012) Therefore, the obtained deformation fields are used to find the correspondence across the set of images by using that common reference (Zheng, Li, & Szekely, 2017). Wu et al (Wu, et al., 2016) have developed a graph shrinkage approach, which uses pairwise demons registration to calculate the "warp velocity" direction between each image and a local graph mean. The method shows promising results, but at high computational cost. Recently, groupwise registration methods have been used to build a statistical model automatically across a set of images for computing the deformation fields (Aal-Yhia, Malcolm, Zwiggelaar, & Tiddeman, 2018), (Cootes T., Twining, Petrovic, Babalola, & Taylor, 2010).

Non-rigid alignment of a group of images is required for many applications such as analysis of face images (Cootes T., Twining, Petrovic, Schestowitz, & Taylor, 2005) and constructing anatomical atlases from medical images (Twining, Marsland, & Taylor, 2004). Analysing the structure of the alignment across groups of images can be used for building statistical models of appearance and shape, such as AAMs (Cootes, Edwards, & Taylor, 2001) (Matthews & Baker, 2004) which can then be used for interpreting those and other images. When building such models from large databases, automation is essential for avoiding using manual annotation that is time consuming and prone to error. Using the statistical model in training with a set of images provides a set of deformation fields across this group without manual intervention (Cootes T., Twining, Petrovic, Schestowitz, & Taylor, 2005).

Previous methods have integrated three main components: representation of the deformation fields between images, an objective function, and a suitable optimisation algorithm (Cootes T., Twining, Petrovic, Babalola, & Taylor, 2010). For the deformation field, there are three common ways of representing the deformation fields. A composition of simple warps (Cootes, Marsland, Twining, & Smith, 2004), (Lötjönen & Mäkelä, 2001), dense fields representing the movement of each pixel (Jones & Poggio, 1998) or a sparse set of control points that control a set of splines (Twining, Marsland, & Taylor, 2004) or the nodes of a triangulated mesh (Cootes T., Twining, Petrovic, Schestowitz, & Taylor, 2005).

Optimisation of dense warp fields, or high resolution meshes is computationally expensive. Multi-resolution meshes, going from low resolution to high can help reduce the computational complexity in the early stages, but optimisation over many parameters is still required in the later stages where detail is required. Sidorov et al. (Sidorov, Richmond, & Marshall, 2009) showed that complex warps can be built from a set of simpler warps, reducing the need for high dimensional optimisation, which is exploited in the proposed method in this chapter.

Optimisation of the alignment requires the selection of a suitable error metric. The Minimum Description Length (MDL) metric was proposed by (Davies, Cootes, & Taylor, 2001) to align similar 2D shapes and has been extended to image and surface alignment (Twining, Marsland, & Taylor, 2004), (Davies, Twining, & Taylor, 2008). MDL is mathematically well motivated, but can be very expensive in terms of computations for image alignment, as it requires repeatedly rebuilding principal component analysis (PCA) models (Twining, Marsland, & Taylor, 2004). Other work has demonstrated that good results can be achieved on image sets with much simpler metrics, such as minimisation of the sum of squared errors from the current estimate of the mean (Cootes T., Twining, Petrovic, Babalola, & Taylor, 2010), (Sidorov, Richmond, & Marshall, 2009).

The final element of the algorithm is the selection of a suitable optimisation strategy. Previous work has used gradient descent, line minimisation or SPSA. Gradient descent is known to be expensive and requires the selection of a suitable step size. Line minimisation can also be slow and expensive, only optimising along a single direction in the high dimensional space. SPSA requires as many steps as gradient descent, but each step is cheaper as it requires fewer function evaluations. These and other optimisation algorithms require selecting good parameters for getting efficient and accurate performance (Yang, Deb, Loomes, & Karamanoglu, 2013) which is well known to be a difficult problem (Ridge, 2007), (Yang, Deb, Loomes, & Karamanoglu, 2013). Therefore, the performance of the optimisation algorithm relies on solving the problem of parameter tuning for the optimisation algorithm (Ridge, 2007).

METHODS

This section describes the algorithmic details of the proposed methods that consist of two phases. The first phase is for initialisation of the groupwise non-rigid alignment. The second phase uses the resulting images with their warps fields and a stiffness parameter to achieve a groupwise non-rigid alignment algorithm, updating the warps for each image of the set. Each of these phases is described in more detail in the following sections.

Inverse Average of Warps-Based Initialisation

In this algorithm (Aal-Yhia, Malcolm, Zwiggelaar, & Tiddeman, 2018), an image is selected at random to use as an initial reference. Pairwise registration is performed between all training images with the initial reference (Cootes, Twining, & Taylor, 2004) by using demons registration (Kroon & Slump, 2009) for getting the warp fields to each image. An average of the resulting warp fields is computed and then it is inverted. The inverse average of the warp fields is concatenated (Tiddeman, Duffy, & Rabey, 2001) with the warp field of each training image, which provides the initial warps for all the training images to the initial estimate of the average shape. The original training images are warped with their new warp fields in order to obtain the initial aligned training images and mean image. Figure 1 shows the steps of the initialisation procedure.

Figure 1. Shows steps of the inverse average of warps-based initialisation

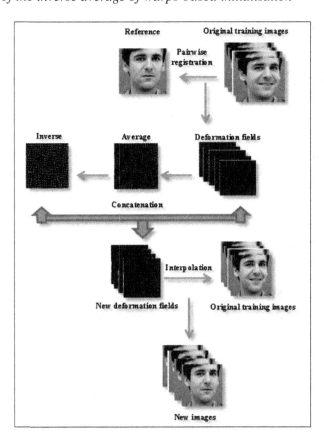

Groupwise Registration Approach

In the second phase, the resulting images, their warp fields and a stiffness parameter specified for each dataset are then used as inputs to the groupwise alignment algorithm (Aal-Yhia, Malcolm, Zwiggelaar, & Tiddeman, 2018). We need to estimate the stiffness parameter β to be used with the elastic constraint that can be included in the proposed groupwise approach. Our experiments use the control points on two different datasets of face images and two datasets of medical images and each of them varies in terms of brightness and contrast, and so requires a different value for β. Later in section (Estimation of the Stiffness Parameter) we describe in details the simulation approach for tuning this stiffness parameter. We do the whole process in a multi-resolution way so that an image starts blurry and gradually gets sharper as shown in Figure 2. We used multi-resolution meshes because going from low resolution to high can help reduce the computational complexity in the early stages. Values of the resolution parameter are Gaussian blurring with widths 8, 4, 2 and 1, respectively.

An average of all the images is computed to get an average image, which is recomputed over iterations. So, the new average image is computed using all images and current warps as shown in Figure 3.

In each iteration we aim to minimise an objective function by updating the location of the control points on the target image. The objective function used is given in vector form by equation 1:

$$x^2 = \beta \big(K(w\big(p + \delta p\big)) + c\big)^2 + \big(S + A\delta p - T\big)^2 \tag{1}$$

where β is the stiffness parameter, K is the stiffness matrix that calculates the vector difference between each control point's movement and the average of its neighbours, S is the average image, T is the target image, $w(p+\delta p)$ is the vector of warped control points, δp is the vector of control point location updates, p is the current estimate of their movement, c is the offset vector which is computed using $-K*w(p)$ in the first iteration, and we have used a first order Taylor series approximation for $S(p+\delta p)$ using the matrix of derivative images A. Figure 4 shows the structure of the stiffness matrix, K.

The stiffness parameter is required to avoid large distortions that may not reduce the error much, particularly in featureless parts of the image. The basis of the stiffness is how differently a point moves compared to its neighbours. The point should move together with its neighbours. If the point moves in a different way to its neighbours, it increases the "stretch" which needs to be minimised. Figure 5 shows the idea of the stiffness model used.

Figure 2. An image starts blurry and gradually gets sharper, values of resolution parameter are from the left 8, 4, 2 and 1, respectively

Figure 3. All images and current warps are used to get an average image per iteration

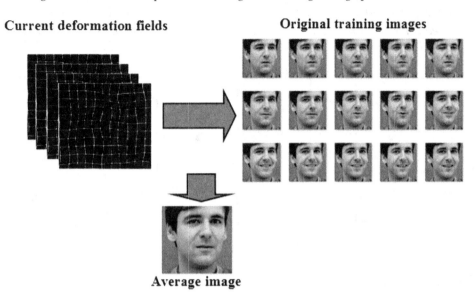

Figure 4. K is the stiffness matrix that calculates the vector difference between each control point's movement and the average of its neighbours

$$
\begin{bmatrix}
1 & 0 & -1/3 & 0 & 0 & \cdots & -1/3 & 0 & -1/3 & \cdots & 0 & 0 \\
0 & 1 & 0 & -1/3 & 0 & & & & & & & \\
-1/5 & 0 & 1 & 0 & -1/5 & & & & & & & \\
0 & -1/5 & 0 & 1 & 0 & & & & & & & \\
& & & & & & & & & & & \\
& & & & & & & & & & & \\
& & & & & & & & & & 0 & -1/5 \\
& & & & & & & & & & 1 & 0 \\
0 & 0 & 0 & 0 & 0 & \cdots & & & & & 0 & 1 \\
\end{bmatrix}
$$

We approximate $w(p+\delta p)$ by its first order Taylor series per control point and derivatives only need to be evaluated at that point. The error function can then be approximated by equation 2:

$$x^2 = \beta(K\left(w\left(p\right) + D\delta p\right) + c\big)^2 + \left(S + A\delta p - T\right)^2 \tag{2}$$

where D is a block diagonal matrix, with each block a *2x2* matrix of the derivatives of the warp from the previous iteration at the corresponding point. Figure 6 shows the structure of the D matrix.

Figure 5. Each point has a number of neighbours. The average of these neighbours is computed and the difference from this point, plus a small offset, is minimised. We include a small offset because the points are placed randomly rather than on a regular grid, so the point does not start at the mean of its neighbours.

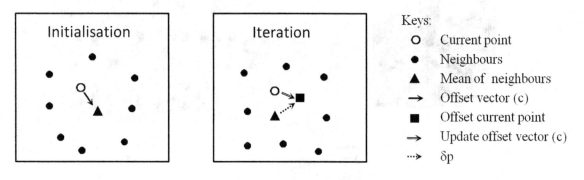

Figure 6. If the warp is w(p) = (U(x1,y1), V(x1,y1)) and Ux is the x derivative of U, etc. then D would have the structure shown

$$\begin{bmatrix} Ux(x1,y1) & Uy(x1,y1) & 0 & 0 & \ldots & 0 \\ Vx(x1,y1) & Vy(x1,y1) & 0 & 0 & \ldots & 0 \\ 0 & 0 & Ux(x2,y2) & Uy(x2,y2) & \ldots & 0 \\ 0 & 0 & Vx(x2,y2) & Vy(x2,y2) & \ldots & 0 \\ \cdot & \cdot & \cdot & \cdot & & \cdot \\ \cdot & \cdot & \cdot & \cdot & & \cdot \\ 0 & 0 & 0 & \ldots & Ux(xN,yN) & Uy(xN,yN) \\ 0 & 0 & 0 & \ldots & Vx(xN,yN) & Vy(xN,yN) \end{bmatrix}$$

Taking the derivative of equation 2 with respect to the update parameters and setting the result to zero gives the update equation 3:

$$2\beta D^T K^T \left(KD\left(w\left(p\right)+\delta p\right)+c\right) + 2A^T\left(S+A\delta p - T\right) = 0 \tag{3}$$

Rearranging gives equation 4:

$$\left(\beta\left(D^T K^T KD\right)+A^T A\right)\delta p = -\beta D^T K^T\left(Kw\left(p\right)+c\right)-A^T\left(S-T\right) \tag{4}$$

in line with the usual Levenberg-Marquardt procedure, we modify the equation 4 to vary smoothly between the Gauss-Newton version (above) and the gradient descent method, via the inclusion of a damping term by equation 5:

$$\left(B + \lambda diag\left\{B\right\}\right)\delta p = -\beta D^T K^T \left(Kw\left(p\right) + c\right) - A^T \left(S - T\right) \tag{5}$$

where $B = (\beta(D^T K^T KD) + A^T A)$ and λ is the damping term. In each iteration across the set, the (random) control points are fixed, as is the average and its derivatives, and so we only need to update the matrix according to the damping parameter and invert a small matrix. The damping term λ is initialized with the value 10 and decreased by a factor of 10 for steps that improve the error. For steps where the error worsens, the damping factor is increased by a factor of 10 and the step is discarded. The proposed groupwise registration method proceeds as shown in Algorithm 1.

Computational Complexity Analysis

The algorithm described here iterates over the N images, at 4 resolutions, of P pixels each k times. The algorithm is linear in terms of the number of images i.e. $O(N)$, but more iterations (k) may be needed for more complex image sets. If we assume that larger images require additional resolutions for efficient convergence, the algorithm is logarithmic in the number of pixels i.e. it is $O(\log(P))$. We have taken some of the more complex steps, such as calculating the image derivatives and the Hessian approximation matrix, out of the inner loop, so these are computed only once per iteration over the image set, considerably improving the efficiency.

Algorithm 1. Groupwise registration algorithm overview (Aal-Yhia, Malcolm, Zwiggelaar, & Tiddeman, 2018)

```
inputs: Pairwise registered images, initial warp functions, and stiffness pa-
rameter for every dataset
outputs: Updated warps for each image
for each resolution from lowest to highest do
    for k iterations do
        Compute average image;
        Calculate new random control points;
        Calculate derivatives of average image (A);
        Calculate AᵀA+βDᵀKᵀKD
        for each image do
            Warp the current image using the current warp;
            Set up the control points on the average image and warped image;
            Find update to the control points using Levenberg-Mardquart algo-
rithm;
            Warp using new control points;
            Concatenate the previous and new warps;
        end
    end
end
```

Initialising the Grid of Control Points

The deformation fields are represented by a set of control points that parameterize Thin Plate Splines (TPS) (Bookstein, 1989). The grid of control points consists of 25 points. The height and width of an image are partitioned to five parts in order to get five locations for every row and column. So, the locations of the control points are changed in random order within the 25 areas for the current and average image per iteration across the set as shown in Figure 7.

Calculation of Derivatives

The partial derivatives of the average with respect to the movement of each control point are calculated using a finite difference approximation. For every control point on the average image, the x or y value is modified by δp. For example, for the first point, the value of the step size is added to the x value of the control point for calculating $\dfrac{\partial S}{\partial p_x^0}$ or to the y value for calculating $\dfrac{\partial S}{\partial p_y^0}$ and the values of all the other control points are fixed. The control points without change and the control points with one point changed in x or y are input to a TPS function to create a warp for the image. As a result, the derivative images will be obtained by subtracting the warped image from the average image as shown in Figure 8. The resulting image is divided by δp.

Figure 7. Locations of the control points are changed in random order within 25 areas

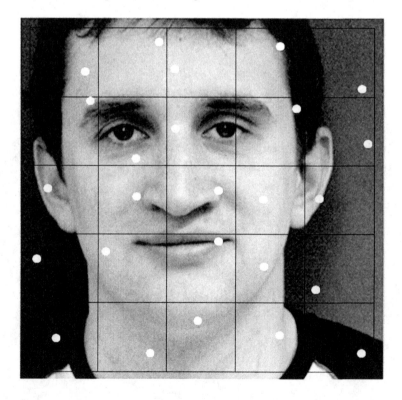

Figure 8. Subtracting a warped image from an original image for getting a derivative image (Aal-Yhia, Malcolm, Zwiggelaar, & Tiddeman, 2018)

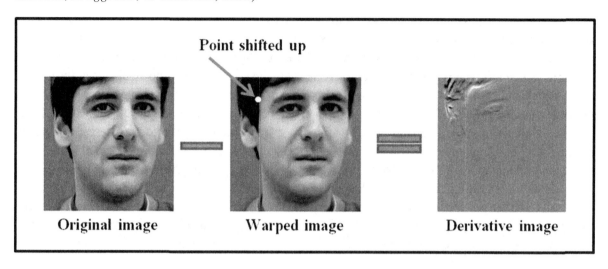

The Objective Function

It is difficult to minimise an objective function by searching the space of all deformation fields of images (Sidorov, Richmond, & Marshall, 2009). In several studies, e.g. (Cootes T., Twining, Petrovic, Babalola, & Taylor, 2010) and (Sidorov, Richmond, & Marshall, 2009), the deformation fields are found by performing an optimisation of control points to minimise the objective function. Previous studies (Cootes, Marsland, Twining, & Smith, 2004), (Sidorov, Richmond, & Marshall, 2009), (Cootes T., Twining, Petrovic, Babalola, & Taylor, 2010), (Davies, Twining, Cootes, Waterton, & Taylor, 2002), (Cootes T., Twining, Petrovic, Schestowitz, & Taylor, 2005) found that optimisation of the deformation fields for one image at a time is sufficient. In (Cootes T., Twining, Petrovic, Babalola, & Taylor, 2010) the number of control points used was large (320 points), in fixed initial locations, and the results indicated that performance is poor when using a small number of them. However (Sidorov, Richmond, & Marshall, 2009) used a small number of control points in randomised locations per iteration and achieved good alignment. Some studies (Cootes, Marsland, Twining, & Smith, 2004), (Cootes T., Twining, Petrovic, Babalola, & Taylor, 2010), (Davies, Twining, & Taylor, 2008) used non-linear optimisation, but they are often expensive in computations and slow in performance.

In our objective function, we used the derivative images $(\delta S^0, \delta S^1, \delta S^2, ..., \delta S^N)$ that are saved as a matrix A. Then, a matrix $A^T A$ is computed by applying the dot product operator between all pairs of derivatives contained in matrix A. The step size δp is varied with the resolution, going from *4, 3, 2* and *1* from lowest to highest, respectively.

The resolution parameter (r) controls a Gaussian blurring and its values are selected according to values of the step size (s) by using the formula $r = 2^{s-1}$. So, values of the resolution parameter are with widths 8, 4, 2 and 1, respectively. The objective function is formed from a stiffness term and an intensity error term as shown in equation 2. The stiffness term is $(K(w(p)+D\delta p)+c)$ and the intensity error term is $(S+A\delta p-T)$. The stiffness term penalises control points that move differently to their neighbours, whilst the intensity error term penalises pixels with different intensity. We use the first order Taylor series approximation for $w(p+\delta p)$ and $S(p+\delta p)$.

Estimation of the Stiffness Parameter

This section presents a simulation method (Aal-Yhia, Malcolm, Zwiggelaar, & Tiddeman, 2018) that can be used to tune the stiffness parameter β. Our experiments are carried out on four different datasets of facial and medical images and each of them varies in terms of brightness and contrast, and so requires a different value for β. This method proposes to create synthetic images with a known update as the ground truth, which can be used to calculate an optimal value for β. In theory, this approach could be used to estimate a unique value for each image pair, but for efficiency we estimate a single value for each dataset.

The synthetic training data is created by applying a small random warp to each target image, according to a set of random control points placed in the same way as for the main update algorithm. To make the problem more closely match the real data, we also apply a histogram equalisation step, based on matching the histogram of the warped target image to another image in the set, selected at random.

We assume the previous warp to be the identity *(I)*, so only a small update is needed, hence *D=I*. So, the first term of equation 3 is replaced by $2\beta(K^T K(\delta p))$ and the stiffness parameter is estimated from this equation, solved for β in the least-squares sense over a set of synthetic example training images i.e. the following equation 6 is minimised.

$$x^2 = \sum_{i \in \Omega} \left(\beta a_i - b_i \right)^2 \tag{6}$$

where $a_i = (K^T K(\delta p_i))$ is the stiffness vector term given by the stiffness matrix and known required update for the ith example, and $b_i = (A_i)^T (S_i + A_i \delta p_i - T_i)$ is the vector corresponding to the image error and derivatives from the ith example. The solution is given by the following equation 7:

$$\beta = \frac{\sum_{i \in \Omega} a_i \cdot b_i}{\sum_{i \in \Omega} a_i \cdot a_i} \tag{7}$$

We select just five images from each dataset at random and estimate a different value of β for each image set. The random offset of each control point is limited to twice the step size for that resolution. Figure 9 shows the steps used for estimating the stiffness parameter and some example synthetic images are shown in Figure 10.

Measuring Model Quality

This section describes the datasets used in the experiments. These are the FGNET, IMM, prostate T2-MRI and brain LPBA40 datasets. This section also explains different methods used to evaluate the results such as: specificity, pixels' intensity error, feature points error and Dice overlap. In addition, this section states statistical analysis used to compare the results.

Figure 9. Steps involved in estimating the stiffness parameter

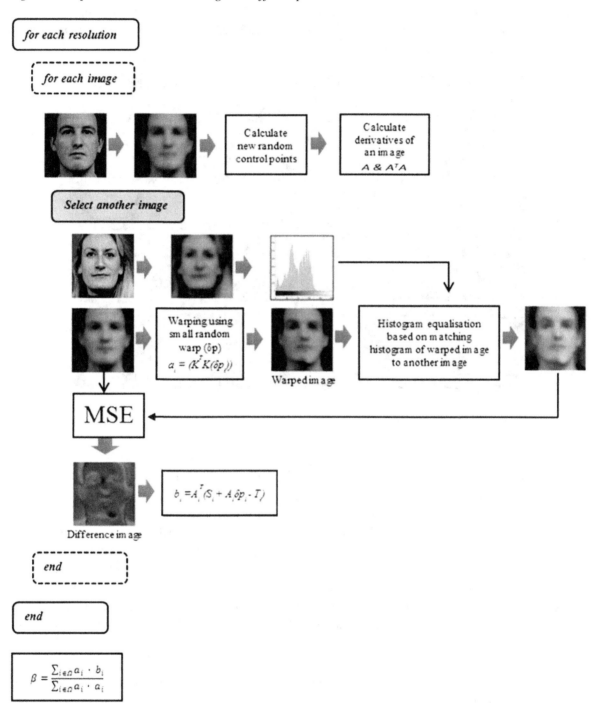

Figure 10. Examples of the original FGNET, IMM, prostate T2-MRI, and brain LPBA40 images with example synthetic images created using a random warp and offset of each control point. From left to right, the original target image, synthetic images at 4 different scales, with their histograms mapped to a target image, the target image used to provide the histogram.

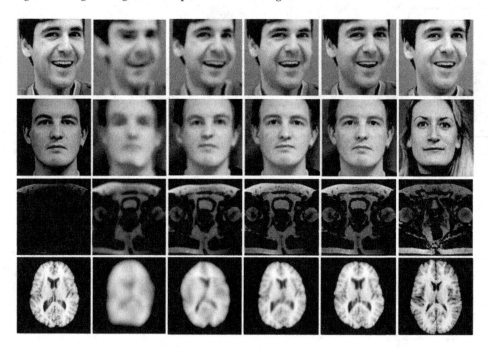

Datasets

We tested the method on a number of sets of faces and medical images. The first set is 100 face frames (every 10th frame) from the FGNET "franck" dataset (FGNET, 2004). Figure 11 shows the example images which are used in our experiments (note that we first converted the images to greyscale for all our experiments). The second set is 37 front-facing faces from the IMM database (Nordstrøm, Larsen, Sierakowski, & Stegmann, 2004). Figure 12 shows some example images which were used in our experiments (note that we first converted the images to greyscale for all our experiments). The third set is our dataset which comprises 38 prostate T2-Weighted MRI images from different patients, where every image represents a slice from a patient. Figure 13 shows the example images which are used in our experiments. The fourth set is the LONI Probabilistic Brain Atlas (LPBA40) (Shattuck, et al., 2008). The

Figure 11. Example images from the FGNET dataset that are used of our experiments (after converting to greyscale) (FGNET, 2004)

Figure 12. Example images from the IMM dataset that are used of our experiments (after converting to greyscale) (Nordstrøm, Larsen, Sierakowski, & Stegmann, 2004)

Figure 13. Example images from the prostate T2-MRI dataset that are used of our experiments

brain MRI images are taken from 40 healthy volunteers. Every image used in the experiments represents a slice taken from a set of the slices for a volunteer. The ages of the volunteers were between 16 and 40 and the number of males and females is equal. Figure 14 shows some examples of the images which are used in our experiments.

Specificity

We use the specificity measure as described in (Cootes T., Twining, Petrovic, Schestowitz, & Taylor, 2005) to assess our model. By using the aligned images and warps obtained from the groupwise approach, we have used the PCA method to build appearance and shape models. The affine part is removed from the aligned warps before building the shape model. The appearance and shape model distributions are used to construct a set of random images - 1000 images were generated for each dataset. We apply the estimate of the affine transformation obtained from the aligned warps to the original training images to produce the affine registered images. We use the random images and the affine registered images for computing the specificity measure. Figure 15 shows the steps used for computing the specificity measure.

Pixel Intensity Errors

We have calculated the error of the pixels' intensity for evaluating the performance of our model. The errors of the pixel intensities are calculated for the four datasets by computing the error between the average image and a groupwise registered image.

Figure 14. Example images from the brain LPBA40 dataset that are used of our experiments (Shattuck, et al., 2008)

Figure 15. The steps used for computing the specificity measure for each dataset

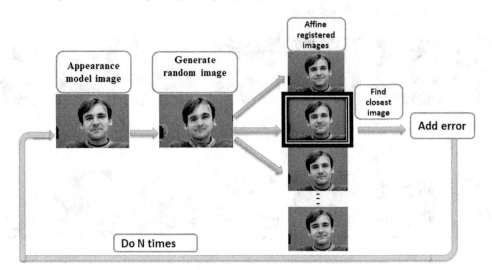

Feature Point Errors

We have calculated the error of feature shapes (either point locations or segmented areas) for evaluating the performance of the model. The error on feature points is performed for FGNET and IMM datasets by using the manual ground truth points which are available publicly (FGNET, 2004), (Nordstrøm, Larsen, Sierakowski, & Stegmann, 2004). The evaluation metric of the errors on feature points used in this chapter is similar to that described by (Cootes T., Twining, Petrovic, Babalola, & Taylor, 2010). The feature points used for each image are twenty points as shown in Figure 16. The warp fields of the groupwise registered images are used for computing a mean location for each point for all images on the final average image to estimate the true position of the feature points. Then the warp fields are used to project those mean reference points back to each groupwise registered image for comparing them with the actual positions of the ground truth points.

Dice Overlap Errors

For the prostate and brain MRI images, we have the location of the prostate and details of the brain annotated by a clinical expert as a region segmentation rather than as feature points. Figure 16 shows an example of labelled images from the prostate and brain datasets. It is important to note that the prostate region is lacking in clear intensity variations, and so is a particularly challenging region for automatic alignment. We used the Dice overlap to evaluate the results of the prostate and brain images as described in (Cootes T., Twining, Petrovic, Babalola, & Taylor, 2010). The deformation fields of the groupwise registered images are used to warp each segmented prostate or brain image (label image). The resulting warped label images are averaged and thresholded at 0.5, and this average is considered as the ground truth segmentation of the average. This ground truth is used with each warped label image, which is also thresholded at 0.5, to compute the Dice overlap for a particular image. Then the values of the mean Dice overlap of all prostate images in the T2-MRI dataset and all brain images in the LPBA40 dataset are computed.

Figure 16. Left to right: example ground truth points used for evaluation of the FGNET dataset, ground truth points used for evaluation of the IMM dataset (Aal-Yhia, Malcolm, Zwiggelaar, & Tiddeman, 2018), ground truth region segmentation of the prostate used to evaluate the T2-MRI dataset and ground truth region segmentation of the brain used to evaluate the LPBA40 dataset (Shattuck, et al., 2008)

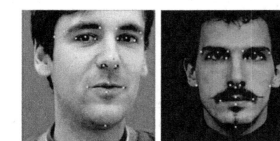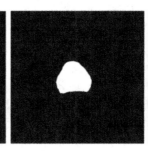

RESULTS

Specificity

The results of the specificity are 0.028, 0.084, 0.098 and 0.051 for FGNET, IMM, T2-MRI and LPBA40 datasets respectively. These results indicate a good performance of the proposed method. The results of the FGNET and LPBA40 datasets have low specificity value while the results of the IMM and T2-MRI datasets have higher specificity value. Also, these results are better than the results in (Tiddeman & Hunter, 2011) for IMM dataset that it was ranged (0.157 - 0.196). The results for the four datasets are shown in Figure 17.

Figure 17. Results of specificity for four datasets FGNET, IMM, T2-MRI and LPBA40

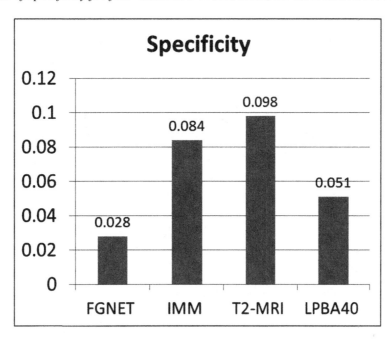

Pixel Intensity Errors

The results of the mean and standard deviation of the intensity error are as follow: FGNET dataset is 0.0286 (0.0072), IMM dataset is 0.0658 (0.0122), T2-MRI dataset is 0.0935 (0.0228) and LPBA40 dataset is 0.0566 (0.0087). The results of the mean and standard deviation of the intensity error for the four datasets are shown in Figure 18.

Feature Point Errors

The results of the mean and standard deviation of the feature point error are as follow: FGNET dataset is 0.1028 (0.087) and IMM dataset is 0.3121 (0.2155), The results of the mean and standard deviation of the feature point error for the FGNET and IMM datasets are shown in Figure 19.

Dice Overlap Errors

The results of the error of feature shapes (segmented areas) of the mean are as follow: T2-MRI dataset is 0.479 and LPBA40 dataset is 0.3794 as shown in Table 1.

Figure 20 shows the evolution of the mean of the FGNET, IMM, T2-MRI and LPBA40 datasets using the proposed model.

Figure 18. Shows normalised error of the pixels' intensity for FGNET, IMM, T2-MRI and LPBA40 datasets. Grey filled circles indicate individual values obtained from pairwise image comparisons. Black filled circles and error bar point to the mean and standard deviation, respectively.

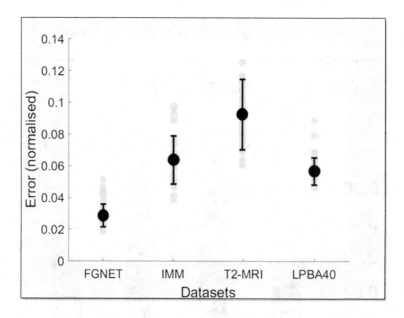

Figure 19. Shows normalised error from points manually placed on two datasets FGNET and IMM. Grey filled circles indicate individual values obtained from comparisons of the used method. Black filled circles and error bar point to the mean and standard deviation, respectively.

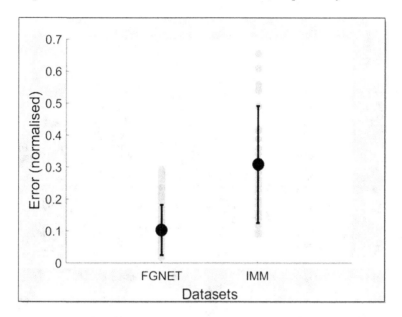

Table 1. The results of the mean Dice overlap for the T2-MRI prostate and the LPBA40 brain datasets

Dataset	Mean of Dice overlap
Prostate T2-MRI	47.9%
Brain LPBA40	37.9%

FUTURE RESEARCH DIRECTIONS

Future work will be to extend the proposed method to 3D images and explore its performance with additional and more complex medical images. In addition, we intend to use a different initialisation step with the proposed method in order to deal with images lying on more complex manifolds, for example, rotated faces.

CONCLUSION

In this chapter, we have developed an iterative linear optimisation approach for doing groupwise alignment with no complex parameter tuning required. The elastic constraint has been presented to be included in the proposed groupwise method. Also, we have proposed a simulation method for estimating

Figure 20. Evolution of the mean for the four datasets FGNET, IMM, T2-MRI, and LPBA40. Left to right: the Values of the resolution parameter of the mean for each dataset are Gaussian blurring with widths 8, 4, 2 and 1, respectively.

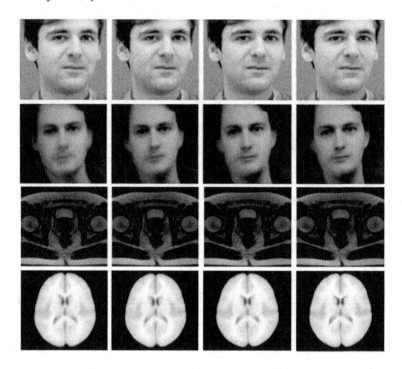

the stiffness parameter for the elastic constraint. The model of the proposed method has been tested on two different datasets of the facial images and two different datasets of the medical images (prostate and brain MRI images). These tests indicate good results and demonstrate the efficiency of the performance and reduction of the computational requirements.

ACKNOWLEDGMENT

Ahmad Aal-Yhia thanks Iraqi Ministry of Higher Education and Scientific Research for funding his PhD.

REFERENCES

Aal-Yhia, A., Malcolm, P., Akanyeti, O., Zwiggelaa, R., & Tiddeman, B. (2018). *Groupwise non-rigid image alignment with graph-based initialisation. In Computer Graphics and Visual Computing (CGVC)* (pp. 15–21). The Eurographics Association.

Aal-Yhia, A., Malcolm, P., Zwiggelaar, R., & Tiddeman, B. (2018). Towards parameter free groupwise non-rigid image alignment. In CGVCVIP (pp. 245-252). Madrid, Spain: IADIS.

Baker, S., Matthews, I., & Schneider, J. (2004). Automatic construction of active appearance models as an image coding problem. *IEEE Transactions on Pattern Analysis and Machine Intelligence, 26*(10), 1380–1384. doi:10.1109/TPAMI.2004.77 PMID:15641725

Bookstein, F. L. (1989). Principal warps: Thin-plate splines and the decomposition of deformations. *IEEE Transactions on Pattern Analysis and Machine Intelligence, 11*(6), 567–585. doi:10.1109/34.24792

Cootes, T., Marsland, S., Twining, C., & Smith, K. (2004). Groupwise diffeomorphic non-rigid registration for automatic model building. In *European conference on computer vision* (pp. 316–327). Springer. 10.1007/978-3-540-24673-2_26

Cootes, T., Twining, C., Petrovic, V., Babalola, K., & Taylor, C. (2010, November). Computing Accurate Correspondences across Groups of Images. *IEEE Transactions on Pattern Analysis and Machine Intelligence, 32*(11), 1994–2005. doi:10.1109/TPAMI.2009.193 PMID:20847389

Cootes, T., Twining, C., Petrovic, V., Schestowitz, R., & Taylor, C. (2005). Groupwise Construction of Appearance Models using Piece-wise Affine Deformations. *Proceedings of 16th British Machine Vision Conference (BMVC)*, 5, pp. 879-888. 10.5244/C.19.88

Cootes, T., Twining, C., & Taylor, C. (2004). Diffeomorphic statistical shape models. *15th British Machine Vision Conference*, 1, pp. 447–456.

Cootes, T. F., Edwards, G. J., & Taylor, C. J. (2001). Active appearance models. *IEEE Transactions on Pattern Analysis and Machine Intelligence, 23*(6), 681–685. doi:10.1109/34.927467

Cristinacce, D., & Cootes, T. (2008). Facial motion analysis using clustered shortest path tree registration. *The 1st International Workshop on Machine Learning for Vision-based Motion Analysis.*

Davies, R., Cootes, T., & Taylor, C. (2001). A minimum description length approach to statistical shape modelling. In *Biennial International Conference on Information Processing in Medical Imaging* (pp. 50-63). Springer. 10.1007/3-540-45729-1_5

Davies, R., Twining, C., Cootes, T., Waterton, J., & Taylor, C. (2002). A minimum description length approach to statistical shape modelling. *IEEE Transactions on Medical Imaging, 21*(5), 525–537. doi:10.1109/TMI.2002.1009388 PMID:12071623

Davies, R., Twining, C., & Taylor, C. (2008). Groupwise surface correspondence by optimization: Representation and regularization. *Medical Image Analysis, 12*(6), 787–796. doi:10.1016/j.media.2008.03.009 PMID:18511333

FGNET. (2004). *Face and gesture network: talking face dataset*. Retrieved from http://www-prima.inrialpes.fr/FGnet/data/01-TalkingFace/talking_face.html

Fischer, B., & Modersitzki, J. (2008). Ill-posed medicine—an introduction to image registration. *Inverse Problems*, 1–16.

Jones, M. J., & Poggio, T. (1998). Multidimensional morphable models. In *Sixth International Conference on Computer Vision* (pp. 683–688). IEEE. 10.1109/ICCV.1998.710791

Kroon, D. J., & Slump, C. H. (2009). MRI modalitiy transformation in demon registration. In *IEEE International Symposium on Biomedical Imaging: From Nano to Macro*, (pp. 963-966). Boston: IEEE.

Lin, J., Zheng, Y., Jiao, W., Zhao, B., Zhang, S., Gee, J., & Xiao, R. (2016). Groupwise registration of sequential images from multispectral imaging (MSI) of the retina and choroid. *Optics Express*, *24*(22), 25277–25290. doi:10.1364/OE.24.025277 PMID:27828466

Lötjönen, J., & Mäkelä, T. (2001). Elastic matching using a deformation sphere. In *International Conference on Medical Image Computing and Computer-Assisted Intervention* (pp. 541–548). Springer.

Mac Parthalain, N., & Strange, H. (2013). Fuzzy-entropy based image congealing. In *2013 IEEE International Conference on Fuzzy Systems (FUZZ)* (pp. 1-8). IEEE.

Marsland, S., Twining, C., & Taylor, C. (2008). A minimum description length objective function for groupwise non-rigid image registration. *Image and Vision Computing*, *26*(3), 333–346. doi:10.1016/j.imavis.2006.12.009

Matthews, I., & Baker, S. (2004). Active Appearance Models Revisited. *International Journal of Computer Vision*, *60*(2), 135–164. doi:10.1023/B:VISI.0000029666.37597.d3

Nordstrøm, M., Larsen, M., Sierakowski, J., & Stegmann, M. (2004). *The IMM face database - an annotated dataset of 240 face images. Technical report, Informatics and Mathematical Modelling*. Technical University of Denmark.

Polfliet, M., Klein, S., Huizinga, W., Paulides, M., Niessen, W., & Vandemeulebroucke, J. (2018). Intrasubject multimodal groupwise registration with the conditional template entropy. *Medical Image Analysis*, *46*, 15–25. doi:10.1016/j.media.2018.02.003 PMID:29502030

Ridge, E. (2007). *Design of Experiments for the Tuning of Optimisation Algorithms*. York, UK: Department of Computer Science, The University of York.

Rueckert, D., Frangi, A., & Schnabel, J. (2001). Automatic construction of 3D statistical deformation models using non-rigid registration. In *International Conference on Medical Image Computing and Computer-Assisted Intervention* (pp. 77-84). Springer. 10.1007/3-540-45468-3_10

Shattuck, D., Mirza, M., Adisetiyo, V., Hojatkashani, C., Salamon, G., Narr, K., ... Toga, A. (2008). Construction of a 3D probabilistic atlas of human cortical structures. *NeuroImage*, *39*(3), 1064–1080. doi:10.1016/j.neuroimage.2007.09.031 PMID:18037310

Sidorov, K. (2010). *Groupwise non-rigid registration for automatic construction of appearance models of the human craniofacial complex for analysis, synthesis and simulation*. Cardiff University.

Sidorov, K. A., Richmond, S., & Marshall, A. D. (2009). An Efficient Stochastic Approach to Groupwise Non-rigid Image Registration. In *IEEE Conference on Computer Vision and Pattern Recognition (CVPR 2009)*, (pp. 2208-2213). Miami Beach, FL: IEEE. 10.1109/CVPR.2009.5206516

Tang, Z., Jiang, D., & Fan, Y. (2013). Image registration based on dynamic directed graphs with groupwise image similarity. In *IEEE 10th International Symposium on Biomedical Imaging*, (pp. 488-491). San Francisco, CA: IEEE.

Tiddeman, B., Duffy, N., & Rabey, G. (2001). A general method for overlap control in image warping. *Computers & Graphics*, *25*(1), 59–66. doi:10.1016/S0097-8493(00)00107-2

Tiddeman, B., & Hunter, D. (2011). Groupwise Non-rigid Image Alignment-Results of a Multiscale Iterative Best Edge Algorithm. In *International Conference on Computer Vision Theory and Applications* (pp. 22-29). VISAPP.

Twining, C., Cootes, T., Marsland, S., Petrovic, V., Schestowitz, R., & Taylor, C. (2005). A unified information-theoretic approach to groupwise non-rigid registration and model building. In *Biennial International Conference on Information Processing in Medical Imaging* (pp. 1-14). Springer. 10.1007/11505730_1

Twining, C., Marsland, S., & Taylor, C. (2004). Groupwise nonrigid registration of medical images: The minimum description length approach. Medical Image Analysis and Understanding (MIAU 04).

Wu, G., Jia, H., Wang, Q., Shi, F., Yap, P.-T., & Shen, D. (2012). Emergence of groupwise registration in MR brain study. *Biosignal Processing: Principles and Practices*.

Wu, G., Peng, X., Ying, S., Wang, Q., Yap, P.-T., Shen, D., & Shen, D. (2016). eHUGS: Enhanced hierarchical unbiased graph shrinkage for efficient groupwise registration. *PLoS One*, *11*(1), 1–21. doi:10.1371/journal.pone.0146870 PMID:26800361

Yang, X., Deb, S., Loomes, M., & Karamanoglu, M. A. (2013). A framework for self-tuning optimization algorithm. *Neural Computing & Applications*, *23*(7-8), 2051–2057. doi:10.100700521-013-1498-4

Zhang, C., Smith, W., Dessein, A., Pears, N., & Dai, H. (2016). Functional faces: Groupwise dense correspondence using functional maps. In *Proceedings of the IEEE Conference on Computer Vision and Pattern Recognition* (pp. 5033-5041). IEEE. 10.1109/CVPR.2016.544

Zheng, G., Li, S., & Szekely, G. (2017). *Statistical Shape and Deformation Analysis: Methods, Implementation and Applications*. Academic Press.

Zitova, B., & Flusser, J. (2003). Image registration methods: A survey. *Image and Vision Computing*, *21*(11), 977–1000. doi:10.1016/S0262-8856(03)00137-9

ADDITIONAL READING

Davies, R. twining, c., & Taylor, C. (2008). Statistical Models of Shape: Optimisation and Evaluation. London: Springer Science + Business Media.

Gavin, H. (2019). The Levenberg-Marquardt method for nonlinear least squares curve-fitting problems. *Department of Civil and Environmental Engineering, Duke University*, 1-19. Retrieved from http://people.duke.edu/~hpgavin/ce281/lm.pdf. (Accessed 10 Jan 2019)

Goshtasby, A. (2012). *Image registration: Principles, tools and methods*. Springer Science + Business Media.

Goshtasby, A. (2017). *Theory and applications of image registration*. John Wiley & Sons. doi:10.1002/9781119171744

Holden, M. (2008). A review of geometric transformations for nonrigid body registration. *IEEE Transactions on Medical Imaging*, 27(1), 111–128. doi:10.1109/TMI.2007.904691 PMID:18270067

Liu, Q., & Wang, Q. (2014). Groupwise registration of brain magnetic resonance images: A review. *Journal of Shanghai Jiaotong University (Science)*, 19(6), 755–762. doi:10.100712204-014-1576-5

Markelj, P., Tomaževič, D., Likar, B., & Pernuš, F. (2012). A review of 3D/2D registration methods for image-guided interventions. *Medical Image Analysis*, 16(3), 642–661. doi:10.1016/j.media.2010.03.005 PMID:20452269

Modersitzki, J. (2004). *Numerical methods for image registration*. Oxford University Press on Demand.

Rueckert, D., & Aljabar, P. (2010). Nonrigid registration of medical images: Theory, methods, and applications [applications corner]. *IEEE Signal Processing Magazine*, 27(4), 113–119. doi:10.1109/MSP.2010.936850

Sidorov, K., Marshall, D., & Richmond, S. (2010). Nonrigid image registration using groupwise methods. In C. Kau, & S. Richmond, Three-dimensional imaging for orthodontics and maxillofacial surgery (pp. 290-304). Blackwell Publishing Ltd. doi:10.1002/9781118786642.ch18

KEY TERMS AND DEFINITIONS

Error Function: The formula that defines the quantity that we wish to optimize. In our case, it is based on the intensity error and a stiffness constraint.

Groupwise Image Alignment: The simultaneous alignment of a group of images to a common reference frame by applying non-rigid alignments to each image.

Intensity Error: A measure of the similarity of greyscale values between the warped images and the average.

Optimization Algorithm: The routine used to find the parameters that minimize the error function. We minimize the objective function by taking the derivative w.r.t. δp and incorporate it into a Levenberg-Marquardt procedure, which automatically varies between gradient descent with a small step size to faster Gauss-Newton using a damping term.

Shape Error: A measure of how well landmarks or areas labelled on the face, prostate, or brain images are aligned by the warps.

Specificity: An error measure that identifies how the alignments help us represent the image set compactly.

Stiffness Constraint: A term in the optimization that simulates a resistance to shape changes. The basis of our stiffness constraint is how differently a point moves compared to its neighbors. To estimate a good value for our stiffness parameter we generate synthetic images with a known optimal update, and find the stiffness that produces the closest match to the optimal update in a least-squares sense.

Chapter 21
Evaluating an E-Learning Application to Protect Vulnerable Users From Cyberbullying

Marian McDonnell
Dun Laoghaire Institute of Art Design and Technology, Ireland

Hannah O'Sheehan
Dun Laoghaire Institute of Art Design and Technology, Ireland

Irene Connolly
Dun Laoghaire Institute of Art Design and Technology, Ireland

ABSTRACT

This research project evaluates Let's Be Safe, an e-learning application. This application aims to educate young adults with intellectual disability about cyberbullying—an issue prevalent among this population—and cybersafety. Twenty-two individuals with mild to moderate intellectual disability took part in the research. The study employed a mixed-methods design including observational and inquiry methods of usability evaluation as well as focus groups. The evaluation investigated the relationships between perceived aesthetics, emotional response, and usability for the application. The focus group gathered information from the participants regarding their knowledge and experience of cyberbullying and cybersafety. The analyses found no significant relationships between aesthetics, emotional response, and usability for this user group. However, the research gathered data, which will contribute to the development of Let's Be Safe. The findings of the focus group revealed that cyberbullying is an issue among this population.

DOI: 10.4018/978-1-5225-9069-9.ch021

INTRODUCTION

Overview

Despite the abundance of literature in the area of human-computer interaction (HCI), there is limited HCI research about users with intellectual disability (ID). This chapter evaluates *Let's Be Safe*, an eLearning application which aims to educate young adults with intellectual disability about cyberbullying - an issue prevalent among this population - and cybersafety. Twenty-two individuals with mild to moderate intellectual disability took part in the research. The study employed a mixed-methods design including observational and inquiry methods of usability evaluation. The evaluation investigated the relationships between perceived aesthetics, emotional response and usability for the application. The analyses found no significant relationships between aesthetics, emotional response and usability for this user group. However, the research gathered data, which will contribute to the development of *Let's Be Safe*. Users wanted the developers to include more games and video modelling in the future iterations of the application. More emoticons, appropriate cartoons and age appropriate photographic images will be incorporated into the next version of *Let's Be Safe*. The findings also highlight the significance of further research in the area of HCI for users with ID and the importance of research into the area of cyberbullying among this same population. The research also aims to explore the lived experiences of individuals within this population, in relation to cyberbullying and cybersafety. The findings aim to contribute to the development of the *Let's Be Safe* eLearning application. Additionally, this research will add to the existing literature within the area of instructional and educational technologies, as well as cybersafety and cyberbullying, for the ID population

Intellectual Disability

Intellectual disability (ID) is a neurodevelopmental disorder involving impaired intellectual and adaptive functioning. ID is characterised by deficits in three domains; conceptual, social and practical (American Psychiatric Association, 2013). Individuals with ID experience deficits in areas of problem solving, abstract thinking, judgement and learning. Deficits in adaptive functioning result in failing to reach developmental and sociocultural standards for independence and social responsibility. This can limit a person's ability to function in daily life (Toth, Lacy & King, 2016). At one-time, ID was referred to as a person-centred trait or deficit. Today, it is understood that ID is not an absolute trait (Schalock, Luckasson, & Shogren, 2007). Instead, ID is an ever-changing interaction between the individual's intellectual and adaptive abilities, participation in activities, interactions with others, social roles, and health (Schalock, Luckasson, & Shogren, 2007). These factors are then considered in the context of the individual's immediate and cultural environment in determining supports. Interventions are required to support and encourage an individual to live their life to the fullest capacity, independently. The ID construct supports and recognises what the disability identity of the individual to include "self-worth, subjective well-being, pride, common cause, policy alternatives, and engagement in political action" (Shalock, Luckasson, & Shogren, 2007, p.117).

People with ID are increasingly being recognised for their own unique strengths (Shogren, et al., as cited in American Psychological Association, 2018). An intellectual disability (ID) as defined by the American Association on Intellectual and Developmental Disabilities (AIDD), is a significant limitation of adaptive behaviour and intellectual functioning, originating before the age of 18 and is "expressed in conceptual, social and practical adaptive skills" (Schalock, Luckasson, & Shogren, 2007, p. 118). Adaptive behaviour is a term that encompasses the impairments of ID in maturation, learning and social adjustment, as compared to peers (Heber, 1961). ID has replaced the term "mental retardation" frequently used in literature. The AIDD, the International Association have acknowledged ID as a term more appropriate in representing the construct of ID for the Scientific Study of Intellectual Disabilities, and the President's Committee for People with Intellectual Disabilities (Schalock, Luckasson, & Shogren, 2007). ID focuses on the interaction of the person with the environment, i.e. the ecological dimension (Schalock, Luckasson, & Shogren, 2007). The American Psychological Association (APA) guidelines require that the behaviour of an individual be assessed within context, to address the ecological approach (American Psychological Association, 2018). An ecological approach requires assessment of an individual by observation within natural settings, without intrusion and avoids interpretations based on norms (American Psychological Association, 2018). ID as a construct recognises "that the systematic application of individualized supports can enhance human functioning" (Schalock, Luckasson, & Shogren, 2007, p. 117). Recognising and enhancing individual strengths has a positive impact on self-image and the ability to deal with life (Dunn & Dougherty; Dykes, as cited in American Psychological Association, 2018). Interventions are required to support and encourage an individual to live their life to the fullest capacity, independently. The ID construct supports and recognises what is called the disability identity of the individual to include "self-worth, subjective well-being, pride, common cause, policy alternatives, and engagement in political action" (AIDD; WHO, as cited in Schalock, Luckasson, & Shogren, 2007, p.117). People with ID are increasingly being recognised for their own unique strengths (Shogren, et al., as cited in American Psychological Association, 2018). Designing an appropriate intervention for individuals with ID will not always take the form of the most explicit needs. Needs of an individual must be addressed without assuming treatment based purely on the diagnosed disability (Butz et al, as cited in American Psychological Association, 2018). Interventions must be delivered within an established and secure working relationship. It must be based on an individual's life and disability related experiences. Educational psychology is required to consider the strengths along with the identified limitations of an individual with ID, assessing an individual within a context (Luckasson et al., 2007). Reframing identified difficulties is possible using a social paradigm to encourage a more collaborative relationship between the marginalised community of people with disabilities and the psychologist (Gill, Kewman, & Brannon, 2003).

Social Restrictions for People With Intellectual Disability

Individuals with ID are often isolated from social interactions as a precautionary measure to protect them. Being classified as a vulnerable person prompts safe guarding concerns for the people involved with their daily care. Efficient habilitation has been suggested as a reason for service providers taking control of decision making for people with developmental disabilities (Bannerman, Sheldon, Sherman, & Harchik, 1990). Habilitation is the instruction given to develop skills to lead as independent a life as possible (Bannerman et al., 1990). Valuable as this is, the opportunity to develop choice is often lost in the scheduling required to develop these skills. An individual's need to interact and socialise is often overshadowed by their disability. Within the construct of disability, an individual is limited by impairment in body, structure, or activity (Schalock, Luckasson, & Shogren, 2007). Individuals with ID often lack in development of social skills, possibly due to the restriction of the natural interaction allowed for the general population (Anderson, Sherman, Sheldon, & McAdam, 1997). Restricted social participation creates disadvantages personally and within the environment (Schalock, Luckasson, & Shogren, 2007).

Designing Interventions for People With ID

Designing an appropriate intervention for individuals with ID will not always take the form of the most explicit needs. Needs of an individual must be addressed without assuming treatment based purely on the diagnosed disability (American Psychological Association, 2018). Interventions must be delivered within an established and secure working relationship and based on an individual's life and disability related experiences (American Psychological Association, 2018).Educational psychology is required to consider the strengths along with the identified limitations of an individual with ID, assessing an individual within a context. Reframing identified difficulties is possible using a social paradigm to encourage a more collaborative relationship between the marginalised community of people with disabilities and the psychologist (Gill, Kewman, & Brannon, 2003). Interventions that encourage individuals in advocating for their own social and personal relationships may assist in the development of a greater sense of empowerment and wellbeing for individuals with ID (American Psychological Association, 2018). Involvement in developing interventions and educational planning builds self-determination (Bannerman et al.; Gill et al., as cited in American Psychological Association, 2018).

Intellectual Disability, Technology, and Design

Technology holds much potential for aiding individuals with disabilities within many aspects of their everyday lives (Vicente & López, 2010). The use of information and communication technologies (ICT) can be empowering for individuals with disabilities. It has been suggested that the use of technology has the capability to improve quality of life for those with ID. This is especially true in the case of assistive and support technologies (Tanis et al., 2012). Despite the many benefits, research shows that technology is underutilised by individuals with intellectual disability (Tanis et al., 2012; Vicente & López, 2010). Technology is a beneficial platform, which supports innovative ways to teach and learn. The use of technology for educational content increases the user's interest in learning and their attention (Fernández-López, Rodríguez-Fórtiz, Rodríguez-Almendros & Martínez-Segura, 2013). eLearning is learning conducted through technology (Mayes & de Freitas, 2007). The use of eLearning among individuals with ID can expand their opportunities for learning. It also has the potential to reduce the impact of the digital divide amongst this population (Arachchi, Sitbon & Zhang, 2017). Despite the advances in technologies, accessibility remains an issue for many individuals with disabilities. It is often hindered due to factors such as inadequate skills and training. Additionally, the design of technology can be an obstacle for users with ID (Tanis et al., 2012). In order to design technologies that are accessible for such individuals there are certain requirements. As the need to better integrate this population in society is becoming increasingly recognised, these requirements have become an important goal (Persson, Åhman, Yngling & Gulliksen, 2015). In the area of design, approaches such as Universal Design, Inclusive Design and Design for All have been promoted as ways to increase accessibility of ICT. Such approaches encourage developers to consider the needs of the user throughout the design process (Persson et al., 2015).

Aesthetics, Emotion, and Usability

Hassenzahl (2008) defines aesthetics as "a predominantly affect-driven evaluative response to the visual Gestalt of an object". It is the visual appeal of an interface or product (Hassenzahl, 2008). Users' perceptions of aesthetics comprise of two dimensions: classical and expressive aesthetics. Classical aesthetics represents the extent to which a design is clean and balanced; while expressive aesthetics is reflected by the creativity and originality of design (Lavie & Tractinsky, 2004). Despite being an essential component of user experience, it is only in recent years that emotion in human-computer interaction (HCI) has gained attention in research. During an interaction with an interface, users experience an emotional response (Agarwal & Meyer, 2009). This emotional response, in conjunction with the thoughts and perceptions evoked during the interaction, can be defined as user experience (Tullis & Albert, 2013). The International Organization for Standardization (1998) define usability as "extent to which a product can be used by specified users to achieve specified goals with effectiveness, efficiency and satisfaction in a specified context of use." In the case of eLearning, usability is considered a crucial element in educational effectiveness. Usability problems can distract users from the educational goals of applications. The better the usability of the application, the greater the benefit for users (Virvou & Katsionis, 2008).

Relationship Between Aesthetics: Emotion and Usability

Research suggests that a user's perception of usability can be influenced by the interface aesthetics. It has been found that designs deemed more aesthetically pleasing were also perceived as more usable (Hartmann, Sutcliffe & De Angeli, 2007; Sonderegger & Sauer, 2010; Thüring & Mahlke, 2007). A relationship between aesthetics and emotion has been recognised within HCI research (Sonderegger & Sauer, 2010; Thüring & Mahlke, 2007). The emotion of an individual can be positively influenced by the aesthetic design of an interface (Sonderegger, Zbinden, Uebelbacher & Sauer, 2012). Subsequently, this improves the user's experience with, judgement of and attitudes towards the technology (Hartmann et al., 2007). The usability of a system is likely to influence the emotional response of the user (Agarwal & Meyer, 2009). Good usability, leading to a more fluid human-computer interaction, is suggested to increase levels of pleasure (Porat & Tractinsky, 2012). Individuals with ID can have a desire to please those perceived as authority figures, which can lead to inaccurate responses. During usability testing carried out with individuals with Down Syndrome, the most common cause of ID, Cáliz, Martínez, & Cáliz (2017) found that participants are likely to provide "friendly" answers to usability questionnaires in spite of the individual's experience. Subsequently, usability reported by this user group can differ significantly from the observed usability. Although these elements have been the concentration of much research within the area of HCI, there is a paucity of research focusing specifically on users with ID.

Cyberbullying and Intellectual Disability

With the advancement of technology, cyberbullying has become increasingly pervasive. Cyberbullying is characterised by deliberate and repeated harm towards an individual carried out in an electronic context. As the popularity of social networking rises, it is likely such forms of communication will emerge as platforms for victimisation (Heiman & Olenik-Shemesh, 2015). Research shows students with learning difficulties were more likely to be cyberbullied and to carry out cyber bullying (Heiman, et. al., 2015).

In this study, participants consisted of 149 students with learning disabilities and 242 atypical students. All completed a self-reporting questionnaire.

There is evidence to suggest a high prevalence of victimisation and bullying behaviour among individuals with ID (Kowalski, Morgan, Drake-Lavelle & Allison, 2016). Bullying, both traditional and cyber, occurs between individuals among whom there is an imbalance of power. This imbalance can be associated with physical, social, relational or psychological factors (Kowalski, Giumetti, Schroeder & Lattanner, 2014; Olweus, 2013). This suggests that individuals within vulnerable populations, such as those with intellectual disability, may be at increased risk of becoming a victim of bullying. A longitudinal study on bullying compared 46 teenagers with ID and 91 typically developing teenagers. The study aimed to investigate the development of behavioural issues and social competence. Most (94.9%) of the participants took part in the study were from age 3 until 13. The others began the study at age 13. In some cases, only mothers of the participants were interviewed and sometimes both the mothers and teenagers were interviewed. Sixty-two percent with ID reported being victims of bullying compared to 41% in typically developing teenagers. This may be due to slower development of social skills in teenagers with ID. There was no difference in the change of bullying rates over the time period between the two groups (Christensen, Fraynt, Neece & Baker, 2012).There is heightened concern for young adults with ID and their safety online as they are viewed as more naïve than neurotypical peers (Sorbring, Molin & Löfgren-Mårtenson, 2017). The high prevalence of cyberbullying among individuals with ID suggests the necessity for coping, intervention and prevention strategies (McGrath, Jones & Hastings, 2009). A study in the Netherlands with 114 participants, aged 12-19 years with ID and the ability to read, investigated cyberbullying. Results found that 16% had cyberbullied through the internet at least once a month and four percent once a week. Twenty-six percent of victims reported being cyberbullied once a month and nine percent once a week. The results also showed a strong relationship between cyberbullying and IQ, computer usage frequency and self-esteem and depressive feelings (Didden, et al., 2009). Educational initiatives teaching about cybersafety are pivotal to ensure the safety of individuals with ID online. The implementation of awareness-raising and teaching skills to enable individuals to recognise and report bullying in service environments is vital (McGrath et al., 2009).

Present Study

Slonje, Smith and Frisén (2013) suggest the use of technologies as mediums for interventions for cyberbullying. *Let's Be Safe* is an eLearning application in development designed specifically for the use of individuals with ID. This application intends to educate young adults with ID about cyberbullying and cybersafety through video, audio, reading activities and games. There is limited research within the area of instructional and educational technologies for individuals with ID. It is becoming increasingly recognised that attention to research in this area is crucial. Furthermore, there is a lack of involvement of people with ID in usability studies, an essential element in the process of designing for users with ID (Caton & Chapman, 2016). The present study intends to investigate the relationship between aesthetics, emotion and usability in an eLearning application for users with ID. The research also aims to explore the lived experiences of individuals within this population, in relation to cyberbullying and cybersafety. The findings aim to contribute to the development of the *Let's Be Safe* eLearning application. Additionally, this research will add to the existing literature within the area of instructional and educational technologies, as well as cybersafety and cyberbullying, for the ID population.

Research Questions

1. Is there a relationship between perceived aesthetics and reported usability for this user group?
2. Is there a relationship between observed usability and reported usability for this user group?
3. Is there a relationship between observed emotional response and observed usability for this user group?
4. Is there a common theme in preferred images for individuals within this user group?
5. Do the lived experiences of this user group suggest the need for prevention and intervention strategies?

METHOD

Design

This study employed a mixed-methods design, using observational and inquiry methods of usability evaluation and focus groups. Correlational design was used to analyse the relationships between aesthetics, emotion and usability, reported and observed. Qualitative methods were applied to gather rich data related to the usability of the application, the emotional response of the user during the interaction as well as the lived experience of the user group. Qualitative thematic analyses were conducted to examine data collected during the focus group and the observational evaluations.

Participants

Purposive sampling was used to recruit participants with mild to moderate intellectual disability. This method of sampling was considered suitable as it gathers participants who can provide valuable information regarding the research topic (Palinkas et al., 2013). A total of twenty-two participants took part. The individuals recruited were nominated by care staff at Carmona House Services, Glenageary, Co. Dublin. Participants ranged in communication, literacy, cognitive and ICT skills. All participants met the following inclusion criteria:

1. Adults (18 years of age or above) with intellectual disability,
2. Sufficient verbal communication skills to express thoughts and experience of the interaction.

Participants involved were representative of the target user group for the *Let's Be Safe* application.

Materials and Accessibility

The format of materials must be considered when designing for participants with ID. Simplifying the language used in the materials and the use of shorter sentence structures can alleviate comprehension problems experienced by participants with ID (Jen-Yi, Krishnasamy & Der-Thanq, 2015). Additionally, graphics can support the understanding of the information for this user group (Cáliz et al., 2017). As the prevalence of vision impairments is high among individuals with ID, font style and size should be carefully considered (Owens, Kerker, Zigler & Horwitz, 2006). All materials to be used by the participants were adapted to provide an accessible and comprehensive format. These documents were in an easy-to-read format, using simple language and clear font, and included images to aid understanding. An information sheet explained the purpose of the study. An expression of interest form was distributed to individuals interested in taking part in the study. It gave potential participants the opportunity to confirm their interest in participating in the focus group and study. Consent forms were provided. A demographic form collected basic information about participants including gender, age and experience with technology. A debrief form thanked participants and restated the purpose of the study. Contact information of the primary researcher was also provided on the debrief form. A list of questions was compiled and used to guide the focus group. The focus group questions involved questions about individuals' experiences online, online safety, bullying and cyerberbullying. Coded observation sheets, extracted from the adapted DEVAN method, were developed to measure usability and emotional response. This method was used successfully in usability tests and observations carried out with children with Down Syndrome (Macedo, Trevisan, Vasconcelos & Clua, 2015). The System Usability Scale (SUS) was adapted for individuals with ID and is considered a suitable satisfaction questionnaire for this user group (Cáliz et al., 2017). This was used to gather opinions from participants of their experience using *Let's Be Safe*. It incorporated Smileyometers used to record participants' opinions on the usability and aesthetics of the eLearning application. The Smileyometers were based on a 4-point Likert scale.

Apparatus

A desktop computer was set up for each participant in order to conduct the usability testing. All computers were equipped with standard mice and headphones. The *Let's Be Safe* prototype was running on all computers. TechSmith Camtasia screen recording software captured participants' interaction with the application, recording screen activity such as the users' navigation of the interface and errors.

Procedure

Overview

Prior to recruitment of participants and commencement of the study, ethical approval was granted from the Saint John of Gods Ethics Committee and the Department of Technology and Psychology Ethics Committee. Participants attended one of three sessions at the Institute of Art, Design and Technology, Dun Laoghaire, Co Dublin. Care staff with whom they were familiar accompanied them. The care staff were available to assist individuals with forms and instructions, as well as to provide support. Each session took place in a computer laboratory and was two hours in length. On the day of each session, the participants were greeted and shown to the computer laboratory where the study took place. They were each assigned a number with which they would be identified throughout the study. They were introduced to the researchers and seated at a table with their identifying number in front of them. The study was explained and the process was clearly communicated. Participants were reminded they can stop at any stage during the study and were free to withdraw. The demographic form was distributed and completed by each participant. Care staff were present to assist any individuals requiring help.

Focus Group

Focus groups have proven to be effective in researching among populations with ID. They are particularly suitable within this population as literacy skills are not required of participants in order to contribute (Doyle, 2007). A question led focus group was conducted at the beginning of each session. The discussion was guided by one researcher while the other researchers took notes. This focus group gathered information from participants about their knowledge and experience of bullying, cyberbullying and cybersafety.

Usability Testing

Usability testing is the most frequently used method for evaluating the usability of a product or system. This method involves testing a prototype with the intended user group by simulating the interaction under controlled conditions (Dumas & Redish, 1999; Sonderegger & Sauer, 2010). Providing specific tasks for the users to perform while using the system allows the functionality and usability to be explored. The performance of these tasks will suggest the extent to which the system can support the proposed functions (Ruben & Chisnell, 2008). Participants sat individually at a desktop computer on which the *Let's Be Safe* prototype was running. Each participant was given a task sheet and instructed to follow the steps provided to perform the set tasks. The tasks included watching videos, reading information, listening to audio and playing games.

Simple games were designed with a concise layout and avoided the use of any unnecessary text. The games consisted of pictures and buttons with little other distractions on the page, creating a clean environment. The buttons were simple and clear. The navigational buttons were visible and comprehendible with little room for error. There are specific features which must be taken into consideration when designing interfaces for individuals with intellectual disabilities. In order to implement an accessible game interface, these features were explored and implemented within the prototype as it was developed. Kennedy, Evans & Thomas (2010) identified a number of factors which would aid the development of an accessible interface for those with intellectual disabilities. These factors include the incorporation of pictures, the use of sounds and other interactive elements, the implementation of simple and clear navigation, as well as limiting the amount of text used. Problematic eyesight is common among individuals with intellectual disabilities sans serif fonts were used to provide clear text.

Thirty minutes was assigned to complete the usability test. Researchers were able to assist any participants that encountered difficulties during the interaction. The care workers were present to support participants if they became frustrated while experiencing difficulty using the application.

Observation

The observational method of usability evaluation collects data by observing the users' experience of interacting with the system (Cáliz et al., 2017). Participants were observed as they performed the tasks during their interaction with the application. This observation focused primarily on usability and emotional response. The frequency of behaviours and actions observed were noted on the observation sheets. The context of the observed behaviour/action was also recorded. Researchers observing the interactions recorded any relevant free-form notes. Participants were each observed for ten-minute periods. An assistant researcher timed the observations. After the usability testing, the participants were provided with the adapted SUS to complete. Care staff and researchers were present to assist any individuals that required help. The individuals were thanked for their participation and debriefed before leaving the computer laboratory.

RESULTS

Overview

The present study investigated the relationship between aesthetics, emotion and usability for users with ID. A Spearman's correlation was performed to examine these relationships. Observational analysis was conducted to investigate these relationships further. Thematic analysis examined the lived experience of this user group.

Descriptive Statistics

Participants were males and females ranging from 19 to 34 years (M = 22.23 years, SD = 3.72). Participants took part in one of three sessions. Eight individuals participated in session one, nine in session two and five in session three. The demographic form collected data from participants relating to their ICT habits. All participants had experience using technology. Almost two-thirds of participants use technology daily. The Adapted SUS included a Smileyometer measuring the opinions of participants in relation to the aesthetics and usability of *Let's Be Safe*. The majority of participants reported that they found *Let's Be Safe* very aesthetically pleasing. Half of the participant responses reported that *Let's Be Safe* was very easy to use.

Inferential Statistics

A Spearman's correlation was conducted to determine the relationship between self-reported factors and observed factors. The correlation between reported aesthetics and reported usability was found to be not significant ($r_s (20) = .014$, $p = .954$). The correlation between reported usability and observed usability was found to be not significant ($r_s (20) = .310$, $p = .171$). The correlation between observed usability and observed emotional response was also found to be not significant ($r_s (20) = .071, p = .754$).

Analysis Procedure

Thematic, Focus Group, and Observational Analysis

Thematic analysis is a flexible qualitative analytic research tool. This process is used to examine data and identify, analyse and report themes within. There are two methods of identifying themes within data; the inductive or deductive approach. The inductive approach involves the identification of themes from the data themselves. The structure of the analysis is derived from the data. The deductive approach involves using a framework while analysing the data. This method is used when collecting data relative to a specific research question (Braun & Clarke, 2006).

This research involved evaluating the experiences of this user group in regard to bullying, cyberbullying and cybersafety. Focus groups were conducted to gather such information from the participants. Focus groups are an appropriate method of data collection for capturing the lived experience (Barrett & Kirk, 2000; Braun & Clarke, 2013). Analysis of the data collected during the focus group used the inductive approach. Inductive analysis was considered a suitable approach as there is limited research within this area. The themes identified were established without the use of a pre-established framework. Hand-written notes recorded by the researchers during the focus group were copied into typed documents using Microsoft Word. The data were examined and coded. From the coded data, key themes were identified. Analysis of the identified themes revealed additional sub-themes.

A combination of both inductive and deductive approaches of thematic analysis is used in this research study. The advantage of this approach is the integration of themes derived from literature with themes that emerge from the data examined (Anderton & Ronald, 2017). The observational method of usability evaluation used in the present research focused on usability and emotional response of users during the interaction. Thematic analysis was conducted on the data collected during the observations. Deductive thematic analysis was applied, using a coding frame from the literature. Prior to the data collection process, ten primary themes were identified. Five themes corresponded to usability and five were representative of the emotional response of users. The inductive approach was utilised when analysing the data collected to identify sub-themes.

Findings

The present study aimed to explore the relationship between aesthetics, emotional response and usability for users with intellectual disability interacting with the application, *Let's Be Safe*. Additionally, this study examined the lived experiences of this user group to investigate their understanding, knowledge and experience of cyberbullying and cybersafety.

Focus Group

The thematic analysis of the data collected during the focus group identified four major themes; Safety Online, Experiences, Emotional Impact and Coping Strategies. These key themes and their accompanying sub-themes are illustrated in Table 1.

Table 1. Major themes and sub-themes identified in analysis of focus group

Major themes	Sub-themes
Online Safety	· Recognising strangers · Ignore strangers
Experiences	· Bullying · Cyberbullying
Emotional Impact	· Hurt
Coping Strategies	· Talk to someone · Ignore the bully · Walk away · Stand up for yourself

The feedback from the focus group supports the research suggesting the need for this population to be informed and educated about cyberbullying and cybersafety. The majority of participants had seen cases of bullying or cyberbullying while some disclosed having personally experienced victimisation.

Observation

The observation applied a coding framework from the literature. This framework identified ten major themes: five responding to usability and five to emotional response. The data collected from the observation were analysed and sub-themes were identified.

Usability

Theme 1. *Errors* (Sub-theme: *Inconsistent layout*): The errors made during the interaction with the prototype were predominantly because of inconsistency in the layout of the interface. The majority of screens placed menu items at the centre of the interface. Errors occurred when menu items were arranged at the top of the interface and users clicked elements at the centre of the screen. Theme 2. *Assistance Required* (Sub-themes: *Reading difficulties*): The majority of the users required at least minor assistance during the interaction due to difficulties encountered. Some participants were illiterate while others struggled with reading. Subsequently, these individuals required assistance throughout the usability testing. Assistance was also required if an error was made and the user was confused. Theme 3. *Confusion* (Sub-themes: *Inconsistency*): Following on from errors due to inconsistent layout, several participants showed confusion with inconsistent layout and design. Users struggled to find menu items arranged at the top of the interface as the majority of menus were arranged at the centre of the screen. Theme 4. *Physical/Motor Problems:* There were no physical or motor problems observed. Theme 5. *Perception Problems:* There were no perception problems observed.

Emotional Response

The themes relating to emotional response captured engagement and enjoyment. These emotional responses create the overall user experience. Theme 6. *Task Completion:* The majority of participants completed all given tasks. Theme 7. *Interest/Boredom:* Most participants showed clear interest throughout the interaction. The videos and games were observed to be the most engaging elements. A number of participants were disengaged during the listening activity, looking around them or facial expression suggesting boredom. Participants with reading difficulties were unable, or struggled, to engage with the reading activity. Theme 8. *Like/Dislike:* Some participants showed a particular liking towards the game elements of the module. Observed dislike was mostly in response to the topic as opposed to elements of the prototype. Theme 9. *Vocalisation – Positive and Negative* (Sub-themes: *Cheer, Sigh, Frustration*): There was very little vocalisation from participants during the observation. A number of users cheered when answering questions within the game correctly. Some users with reading difficulties let out a sigh when struggling with reading modules. One user expressed frustration when unable to locate the Stories module. Theme 10. *Behaviour – Positive and Negative* (Sub-themes: *Smile, Frown, Upset*): A number of participants showed a positive emotional response when answering questions within the game correctly. Negative behaviours expressed were mostly in response to the topic rather than the elements of the prototype. One participant became upset because of experiencing difficulties using the application.

Image Preferences

The adapted SUS recorded participants' favourite and least favourite image within *Let's Be Safe*. Twenty participants responded to the question recording their preferred image. Overall, the majority of individuals within this user group prefer graphics such as emoticons and cartoons. This is in line with research carried out by McDonnell and Verdes (2016).

DISCUSSION

Discussion of Present Findings

The aims of the present study were to investigate the relationship between perceived aesthetics, emotional response and usability for young adults with mild to moderate intellectual disability during their interaction with the eLearning application, *Let's Be Safe*. Previous research carried out among neurotypical users found significant relationships between perceived aesthetics of an interface, emotional response and usability during human-computer interaction (Porat & Tractinsky, 2012; Sonderegger & Sauer, 2010; Sonderegger et al., 2012). However, the analyses of the data found no significant relationships between perceived aesthetics, emotional response and usability. These factors have been the focus of much research within the area of HCI while the scarcity of research with a focus on users with ID is evident. The findings of this present research are contradictory to the expectations. Additionally, this research aimed to explore the lived experiences of individuals with ID with respect to cyberbullying and cybersafety. The focus group conducted revealed that cyberbullying is a problem among this population, in accordance with the literature in this field (Heiman & Olenik-Shemaesh, 2015; Kowalski et al., 2016).

Aesthetics, Emotional Response, and Usability

Aesthetics received the highest rating on the self-report measures with the majority of users reporting to like the aesthetic design of the interface a lot. The observation suggested that participants found it difficult to navigate through the interface, yet the interface of *Let's Be Safe* was perceived as very aesthetically pleasing. This is inconsistent with previous research, which has found that impaired usability can impact negatively on perceived aesthetics (Hartmann et al., 2007). Research shows that the usability of a system can influence the emotional response of the user (Thüring & Mahlke, 2007; Sonderegger et al., 2012). Participants who experienced major usability issues were observed showing signs of frustration and upset. However, the analysis found no significant relationship between observed emotional response and observed usability. The findings of the self-reported usability collected in the SUS suggest that users found the application very easy to use. However, the data collected during the usability observation suggest that the majority of users had difficulty using the prototype independently. This contradiction is in line with expectations and consistent with the research, which suggests participants in this user group are likely to provide "desired" responses to usability questionnaires contrary to the individual's experience during the interaction (Cáliz et al., 2017).

Image Preferences

The *Let's Be Safe* application is designed for use by individuals with ID. The interface consists of many images to aid understanding and promote familiarity (Arachchi et al. 2017). The majority of participants reported the graphic images - emoticons and cartoons - as their preferred image. Images of real people were the second favoured style of image. Participants were reluctant to report images they did not like. This may be explained by the pleasing nature of individuals in this population (Cáliz et al., 2017).

Lived Experiences

The majority of information gathered during the focus group is consistent with literature within this field of research; however, there was one prominent contradiction. Previous research has shown that technology is underutilised by individuals with intellectual disability (Tanis et al., 2012; Vicente & López, 2010). Conversely, this research found high ICT usage among the participating users; smartphones, tablets and computers. The findings of this research found that cyberbullying is problematic among the young adults with ID in this user group. This is in accordance with the current literature (Heiman & Olenik-Shemaesh, 2015; Kowalski et al., 2016). A number of participants in this user group had personally experienced cyberbullying while others had seen instances of cyberbullying. Participants expressed having experienced negative implications resulting from victimisation. The majority of participants stated they are uneducated about methods to keep themselves safe online. These findings support previous research which suggest the need for the implementation of prevention and intervention strategies regarding cyberbullying among the ID population (McGrath et al., 2009). Future research within this area is vital in order to minimise the abuse of new technologies and ensure the safety of individuals with ID online.

Theoretical and Practical Implications

The current research contributes to the copious amount of literature within the area of human-computer interaction while adding originality through the involvement of users with intellectual disability, a population often disregarded in this research area. The observational analyses have provided rich information regarding the nature of usability difficulties and sources of users' emotional response. The results of this research will be the foundation for recommendations made to the developers of *Let's Be Safe* in order to increase the accessibility of the application for the target users. The current study also contributes to research in cyberbullying and cybersafety for young adults with ID. There is a paucity of literature within this area of research, particularly in relation to prevention and intervention strategies. The findings of this study show evidence that the development and implementation of such initiatives is of critical importance. These findings may be beneficial for staff and teachers within service environments.

Strengths and Limitations of the Present Study

A major strength is the involvement of individuals with ID in the development process of a system targeting this user group. The quality of data collected during the user testing suggests the importance of involving the target user group in the development process as well as the need for further research with this user group (Caton & Chapman, 2016). Another strength of this study is the large number of participants involved in comparison to previous qualitative research within both the population and research topic (Slonje et al., 2013). A limitation of this research is that the validity of responses is uncertain as it is unknown whether the responses reflect the actual thoughts and experiences of the individuals. Responses collected may be inaccurate due to the tendency of this population to please perceived authority figures (Cáliz et al., 2017).

Future Research

Future research may want to consider the teaching methods applied in the activity-based learning modes. Activity scheduling has been shown to be successful in encouraging self-initiated engagement in social activities of people with limited mental capacity (Anderson, et al., 1997). Where there are skills that need to be developed, instructional designers could use photographic visual scheduling within the application modules, to represent a sequence of activities. This type activity scheduling has been used with people with limited receptive ability to teach skills for independence .Accompanying scripts to fit the context could be used to match or identify the context and what is appropriate. Introducing levels to the application would allow for age appropriate or stage appropriate skill development to support independence and social interaction (Blum-Dimaya, et al., 2010).

While engagement in the focus group conversations offer insights stimulated by the questions and offer a starting point for research (Coolican, 2004), a lived experience can come forward in smaller groups (Barrett & Kirk, 2000). Interviews could provide a richer understanding of the experiences of people with ID that are directly related to bullying and cyberbullying. A semi-structured interview is guided but still informal and can provide "more realistic information on the interviewee's own terms" (Coolican, 2004 p. 155). Audio recording would capture the "exact terms and richness of the interview" (Coolican, 2004 p. 160). Video recording of observation sessions would provide a record of non-verbal communication (Coolican, 2004) and further analysis of responses to the application that are missed through researcher note taking.

Future studies may benefit from the use of facial recording software during the user testing. Due to ethical constraints, permission to use facial recording software during the interaction with the prototype was not granted due to ethical constraints. The use of such devices would capture supplementary material, which would support and contribute to the data collected during observation.

CONCLUSION

Utilising the insight into the lived experience of people with ID will allow movement towards a more empowering approach, by involving these individuals in the decision-making process and understanding their needs rather than assuming needs based on their diagnosis (American Psychological Association, 2018). Interventions that facilitate the independence and decision-making ability for people with ID lead to a better quality of life (Anderson, et al., 1997). This provides an opportunity to develop social skills that may be lacking in the structured living of people with ID to lead a full and satisfying life (Bannerman et al., 1990). As educational psychology is required to consider the strengths of people with ID ((American Psychological Association, 2018), the focus group contributions remind us of what these strengths are. We see the difference between the literature and the voices of this group, what they are capable of, with self-determination and choice, avoiding interpretations based on norms (Shogren, et al., as cited in American Psychological Association, 2018). With users as the driving force in development, an application can be well-designed based on identified skills and judgements (Preece, Sharp, & Rogers, 2015). Understanding identified needs and challenges will inform the process of development to create an appropriate instructional resource intervention with educational value for the user with ID, engaging them, to build empowerment (Schalock, Luckasson, & Shogren, 2007) and stay safe from traditional bullying and to mitigate against the negative consequences and victimisation of cyberbullying.

Although the relationships between aesthetics, emotional response and usability has been extensively researched within the field of HCI, the current study was diverse as its focus was on a population often overlooked; users with intellectual disability. Contrary to expectations, this research did not achieve significant results in examining the relationship between aesthetics, emotional response and usability for this user group. However, the research gathered rich data, which will contribute to the improvement and development of the *Let's Be Safe* eLearning application. Users wanted the developers to include more games and video modelling in the future iterations of the application. More emoticons, appropriate cartoons and age appropriate photographic images will be incorporated in the next version of *Let's be Safe*. The findings also highlight the significance of further research in the area of HCI for users with ID and the importance of research into the area of cyberbullying among this same population.

REFERENCES

Agarwal, A., & Meyer, A. (2009). Beyond usability: evaluating emotional response as an integral part of the user experience. In *CHI'09 Extended Abstracts on Human Factors in Computing Systems* (pp. 2919–2930). New York, NY: ACM Press. doi:10.1145/1520340.1520420

American Psychiatric Association. (2013). *Diagnostic and Statistical Manual of Mental Disorders* (5th ed.). Arlington, VA: American Psychiatric Publishing.

Anderson, M. D., Sherman, J. A., Sheldon, J. B., & McAdam, D. (1997). Picture activity schedules and engagement of adults with mental retardation in a group home. *Research in Developmental Disabilities*, *18*(4), 231–250. doi:10.1016/S0891-4222(97)00006-1 PMID:9216024

Anderton, B. N., & Ronald, P. C. (2017). Hybrid thematic analysis reveals themes for assessing student understanding of biotechnology. *Journal of Biological Education*, *1*, 1–12.

Arachchi, T. K., Sitbon, L., & Zhang, J. (2017). Enhancing Access to eLearning for People with Intellectual Disability: Integrating Usability with Learning. In *IFIP Conference on Human-Computer Interaction* (pp. 13-32). Cham, Switzerland: Springer. 10.1007/978-3-319-67684-5_2

Bannerman, D. J., Sheldon, J. B., Sherman, J. A., & Harchik, A. E. (1990). Balancing the right to habilitation with the right to personal liberties: The rights of people with developmental disabilities to eat too many doughnuts and take a nap. *Journal of Applied Behavior Analysis*, *23*(1), 79–89. doi:10.1901/jaba.1990.23-79 PMID:2186017

Barrett, J., & Kirk, S. (2000). Running focus groups with elderly and disabled elderly participants. *Applied Ergonomics*, *31*(6), 621–629. doi:10.1016/S0003-6870(00)00031-4 PMID:11132046

Blum-Dimaya, A., Reeve, S. A., Reeve, K. F., & Hoch, H. (2010). Teaching children with autism to play a video game using activity schedules and game-embedded simultaneous video modelling. *Education & Treatment of Children, 33*(3).

Braun, V., & Clarke, V. (2006). Using thematic analysis in psychology. *Qualitative Research in Psychology, 3*(2), 77–101. doi:10.1191/1478088706qp063oa

Braun, V., & Clarke, V. (2013). *Successful qualitative research: A practical guide for beginners.* London: Sage.

Butz, M. R., Bowling, J. B., & Bliss, C. A. (2000). Psychotherapy with the mentally retarded: A review of the literature and the implications. *Professional Psychology, Research and Practice, 31*(1), 42–47. doi:10.1037/0735-7028.31.1.42

Cáliz, D., Martínez, L., & Cáliz, R. (2017). Helping people with down syndrome through a usability testing guide proposal for mobile applications. *International Journal of Computer Science Engineering and Information Technology, 7*(2), 1–19.

Caton, S., & Chapman, M. (2016). The use of social media and people with intellectual disability:A systematic review and thematic analysis. *Journal of Intellectual & Developmental Disability, 41*(2), 1–15. doi:10.3109/13668250.2016.1153052

Christensen, L. L., Fraynt, R. J., Neece, L. C., & Baker, B. L. (2012). Bullying Adolescents With Intellectual Disability. *Journal of Mental Health Research in Intellectual Disabilities, 5*(1), 49–65. doi:10.1080/19315864.2011.637660

Coolican, H. (2004). *Research methods and statistics in psychology.* Hodder and Stoughton.

Didden, R., Scholte, R. H., Korzilius, H., De Moor, J. M., Vermeulen, A., O'Reilly, M., & Lancioni, G. E. (2009). Cyberbullying among students with intellectual and developmental disability in special education settings. *Developmental Neurorehabilitation, 12*(3), 146–151. doi:10.1080/17518420902971356 PMID:19466622

Doyle, J. (2009). *Using focus groups as a research method in intellectual disability research: A practical guide.* The National Federation of Voluntary Bodies Providing Services to People with Intellectual Disabilities. Retrieved from http://www.fedvol.ie/_fileupload/ Research/focus 20groups20a20practical-20guide.pdf

Dumas, J. S., & Redish, J. (1999). *A practical guide to usability testing.* Portland, OR: Intellect Books.

Fernández-López, Á., Rodríguez-Fórtiz, M. J., Rodríguez-Almendros, M. L., & Martínez-Segura, M. J. (2013). Mobile learning technology based on iOS devices to support students with special education needs. *Computers & Education, 61*, 77–90. doi:10.1016/j.compedu.2012.09.014

Gill, C. J., Kewman, D. G., & Brannon, R. W. (2003). Transforming psychological practice and society: Policies that reflect the new paradigm. *The American Psychologist, 58*(4), 305–312. doi:10.1037/0003-066X.58.4.305 PMID:12866397

Hartmann, J., Sutcliffe, A., & De Angeli, A. (2007). Investigating attractiveness in web user interfaces. In *Proceedings of the SIGCHI conference on Human Factors in Computing Systems* (pp. 387-396). New York, NY: ACM Press. 10.1145/1240624.1240687

Hassenzahl, M. (2008). Aesthetics in interactive products: Correlates and consequences of beauty. In H. N. J. Schifferstein & P. Hekkert (Eds.), *Product experience* (pp. 287–302). San Diego, CA: Elsevier. doi:10.1016/B978-008045089-6.50014-9

Heber, R. (1961). *A manual on terminology and classification on mental retardation* (Rev. ed.). Washington, DC: American Association on Mental Deficiency.

Heiman, T., & Olenik-Shemesh, D. (2015). Cyberbullying experience and gender differences among adolescents in different educational settings. *Journal of Learning Disabilities*, *48*(2), 146–155. doi:10.1177/0022219413492855 PMID:23784784

Jen-Yi, L., Krishnasamy, M., & Der-Thanq, C. (2015). Research with persons with intellectual disabilities: An inclusive adaptation of Tourangeau's model. *ALTER-European Journal of Disability Research/ Revue Européenne de Recherche sur le Handicap, 9*(4), 304-316.

Kennedy, H., Evans, S., & Thomas, S. (2010). Can the web be made accessible for people with intellectual disabilities? *The Information Society*, *27*(1), 29–39. doi:10.1080/01972243.2011.534365

Kowalski, R. M., Giumetti, G. W., Schroeder, A. N., & Lattanner, M. R. (2014). Bullying in the digital age: A critical review and meta-analysis of cyberbullying research among youth. *Psychological Bulletin*, *140*(4), 1073–1137. doi:10.1037/a0035618 PMID:24512111

Kowalski, R. M., Morgan, C. A., Drake-Lavelle, K., & Allison, B. (2016). Cyberbullying among college students with disabilities. *Computers in Human Behavior*, *57*, 416–427. doi:10.1016/j.chb.2015.12.044

Macedo, I., & Trevisan, D. G. (2013, July). A method to evaluate disabled user interaction: A case study with down syndrome children. In *International Conference on Universal Access in Human-Computer Interaction* (pp. 50-58). Berlin: Springer. 10.1007/978-3-642-39188-0_6

Mahlke, S., & Thüring, M. (2007, April). Studying antecedents of emotional experiences in interactive contexts. In *Proceedings of the SIGCHI Conference on Human Factors in Computing Systems* (pp. 915-918). New York, NY: ACM Press. 10.1145/1240624.1240762

Mayes, T., & de Freitas, S. (2007). Learning and e-learning: The role of theory. In H. Beetham & R. Sharpe (Eds.), *Rethinking pedagogy for a digital age: Designing and delivering e-learning* (pp. 13–25). London, UK: Routledge.

McDonnell, M., & Verdes, C. (2016), Designing for Intellectual Disability users to teach Independent Life Skills. *Proceedings of the 10th International Conference on Interfaces and Human Computer Interaction*, 264-269.

McGrath, L., Jones, R. S. P., & Hastings, R. P. (2009). Outcomes of anti-bullying intervention for adults with intellectual disabilities. *Research in Developmental Disabilities*, *31*(2), 376–380. doi:10.1016/j.ridd.2009.10.006 PMID:19897338

Olweus, D. (2013). School bullying: Development and some important challenges. *Annual Review of Clinical Psychology, 9*(1), 751–780. doi:10.1146/annurev-clinpsy-050212-185516 PMID:23297789

Owens, P. L., Kerker, B. D., Zigler, E., & Horwitz, S. M. (2006). Vision and oral health needs of individuals with intellectual disability. *Developmental Disabilities Research Reviews, 12*(1), 28–40. doi:10.1002/mrdd.20096 PMID:16435325

Palinkas, L. A., Horwitz, S. M., Green, C. A., Wisdom, J. P., Duan, N., & Hoagwood, K. (2015). Purposeful sampling for qualitative data collection and analysis in mixed method implementation research. *Administration and Policy in Mental Health, 42*(5), 533–544. doi:10.100710488-013-0528-y PMID:24193818

Persson, H., Åhman, H., Yngling, A. A., & Gulliksen, J. (2015). Universal design, inclusive design, accessible design, design for all: Different concepts —one goal? On the concept of accessibility — historical, methodological and philosophical aspects. *Universal Access in the Information Society, 14*(4), 505–526. doi:10.100710209-014-0358-z

Porat, T., & Tractinsky, N. (2012). It's a pleasure buying here: The effects of web-store design on consumers' emotions and attitudes. *Human-Computer Interaction, 27*(3), 235–276.

Preece, J., Sharp, H., & Rogers, Y. (2015). Experimental design. *Interaction Design: Beyond Human-Computer Interaction*, 486.

Rubin, J., & Chisnell, D. (2008). *Handbook of usability testing: How to plan, design, and conduct effective tests*. Indianapolis, IN: Wiley Publishing, Inc.

Schalock, R. L., Luckasson, R. A., & Shogren, K. A. (2007). The renaming of mental retardation: Understanding the change to the term intellectual disability. *Intellectual and Developmental Disabilities, 45*(2), 116–124. doi:10.1352/1934-9556(2007)45[116:TROMRU]2.0.CO;2 PMID:17428134

Shogren, K. A., Wehmeyer, M. L., Reese, R. M., & O'Hara, D. (2006). Promoting self-determination in health and medical care: A critical component of addressing health disparities in people with intellectual disabilities. *Journal of Policy and Practice in Intellectual Disabilities, 3*(2), 105–113. doi:10.1111/j.1741-1130.2006.00061.x

Sonderegger, A., & Sauer, J. (2010). The influence of design aesthetics in usability testing: Effects on user performance and perceived usability. *Applied Ergonomics, 41*(3), 403–410. doi:10.1016/j.apergo.2009.09.002 PMID:19892317

Sonderegger, A., Zbinden, G., Uebelbacher, A., & Sauer, J. (2012). The influence of product aesthetics and usability over the course of time: A longitudinal field experiment. *Ergonomics, 55*(7), 713–730. doi:10.1080/00140139.2012.672658 PMID:22506866

Sorbring, E., Molin, M., & Löfgren-Mårtenson, L. (2017). "I'm a mother, but I'm also a facilitator in her every-day life": Parents' voices about barriers and support for internet participation among young people with intellectual disabilities. *Cyberpsychology (Brno), 11*(1), 43–60. doi:10.5817/CP2017-1-3

Tanis, E. S., Palmer, S., Wehmeyer, M., Davies, D. K., Stock, S. E., Lobb, K., & Bishop, B. (2012). Self-report computer-based survey of technology use by people with intellectual and developmental disabilities. *Intellectual and Developmental Disabilities, 50*(1), 53–68. doi:10.1352/1934-9556-50.1.53 PMID:22316226

Thüring, M., & Mahlke, S. (2007). Usability, aesthetics and emotions in human–technology interaction. *International Journal of Psychology, 42*(4), 253–264. doi:10.1080/00207590701396674

Toth, K., de Lacy, N., & King, B. H. (2016). Intellectual disability. In M. K. Dulcan (Ed.), *Dulcan's textbook of child and adolescent psychiatry* (2nd ed.; pp. 105–134). Arlington, VA: American Psychiatric Publishing. doi:10.1176/appi.books.9781615370306.md07

Tullis, T., & Albert, W. (2013). *Measuring the user experience: collecting, analyzing, and presenting usability metrics* (2nd ed.). Waltham, MA: Morgan Kaufmann.

Vicente, M. R., & López, A. J. (2010). A multidimensional analysis of the disability digital divide: Some evidence for Internet use. *The Information Society, 26*(1), 48–64. doi:10.1080/01615440903423245

Virvou, M., & Katsionis, G. (2008). On the usability and likeability of virtual reality games for education: The case of VR-ENGAGE. *Computers & Education, 50*(1), 154–178. doi:10.1016/j.compedu.2006.04.004

Chapter 22
BlueEyes:
A Pilot Project and a New Way to See the World

Ana Rita Teixeira
Polytechnic of Coimbra, Portugal

Anabela Gomes
Polytechnic of Coimbra, Portugal

Joao Gilberto Orvalho
ⓘ https://orcid.org/0000-0002-9185-4479
Polytechnic of Coimbra, Portugal

ABSTRACT

As reported by the World Health Organization, an estimated 253 million live with visual impairment that cannot be corrected with glasses or contact lenses. It's necessary to bring awareness and understanding of the challenges blind people face and help to motivate research into new technology to answer those questions. This chapter starts to identify the challenges people with visual disabilities face in their life. The problem of navigation and orientation as well as the different possibilities to deal with the loco-motion situation is also addressed. It describes the traditional navigational solutions as well as other which involves more sophisticated technological devices and their multimodal interfaces. The chapter ends with the description of the BlueEyes project, consisting in a solution using beacons to help blind people moving in a city. The phases of the project are described, and the actual research situations is also slightly explained.

1. INTRODUCTION

The challenges of being blind are in everyday activities like reading, cooking, shopping, going outside, using the internet, withdrawing money from an ATM, determining how much of a liquid is in a glass, handling cash, among others (Andress, 2015). According to the research, "eighty to eighty five percent of our perception learning cognition and activities are mediated through vision" (Politzer, 2015). So, all

DOI: 10.4018/978-1-5225-9069-9.ch022

the corresponding activities represents a challenge for a person with vision disability and the difficulty to overcome it, can lead to isolation, loneliness and bring along emotional, social and financial impacts on her/his life. Within these varied challenges, it is possible to group them in two lifelong challenges: accessing the world of information and navigating through space. Society has done a far better job of opening the world of information but it has just started to identify and analyse the serious navigational limitations the blind travellers normally face. Unfortunately, these limitations are the ones that have a severe and bigger negative impact on their life development (Baldwin, 2015).

Currently, technology is a way to support some of their needs and has the potential of improving in a certain extent their life. In fact, it can be stated that today's infrastructure technology is accessible to facilitate blind people to join school, jobs and in leisure activities on a par with sighted peers. On the other hand, there is no such progress concerning blind navigation and therefore, management of mobility and orientation represents still a big and important challenge which needs to be addressed and supported by technology (Baldwin, 2015). Reduced visual capacity challenges people's spatial problem solving every day and, in many ways, e.g. how to obtain, recognise, understand, and process information needed in the environment. Indeed, wayfinding can be very stressful and can cause anxiety and become a strong reason not to leave home if it is necessary to visit unfamiliar or complex places, such as shopping malls, train, metro and bus stations, among others (Saarela, 2015). It is vital that public places and community settings will be designed to be secure, as inclusive as possible and accessible for all. It is in this context that the BlueEyes project arises, enabling an easy navigation with the help of objects that already integrate people's daily lives, such as smartphones, allowing a navigation as intuitive and natural as possible. The use of beacons and the associated research foreseen in this project will be of great use not only in the BlueEyes project but certainly in other future projects linked to internet of things.

This chapter is divided into five main sections. First, the introduction of the problem is done, second some theorical information and framework related to current tools and projects to assist blind people in navigation (section 2) and related to multimodal interaction design (section3) are presented and discussed based on literature. In section 4, the BlueEyes project is considered, the main tasks were descripted and the beacons technology is introduced. In the last section, some conclusions and further work is done.

2. CURRENT TOOLS AND PROJECTS TO ASSIST BLIND PEOPLE IN NAVIGATION

As mentioned before, one big challenge blind people face in everyday life, is mobility and orientation. Orientation refers to the "ability of understanding the spatial properties of an environment and being aware of one's position and his/her relationship with the surroundings"; on the other hand, mobility indicates the "capability of efficiently and safely moving in an environment (e. g. in a city by using public transport) (Giudice and Legge, 2008). As a result, visually impaired people usually are dependent on other sensory information in order to avoid obstacles and to navigate. There are many ways for a visually impaired person to move in the environment. Here are the 5 methods which they used most: (1) Unaidel Travel Techniques, (2) Human-guides Techniques, (3) Cane Techniques, (4) Dog-guides Techniques and (5) Sensory Guidance Devices. In order to get an overview of the current tools which helps blind people in their navigation, these five methods are grouped/ divided in two general categories (Baldwin, 2015): Traditional Systems and Assistive Technology.

2.1 Traditional Systems

Currently established navigational strategies which includes independent travel, using human sensory abilities with no other technological aids (Baldwin, 2015). In this context, there are some important intrinsic aspects, such as auditory and tactile sense. The movement of dynamic hurdle produces noise allowing blind people to decide the approximate/rough location using their auditory senses. The additional use of tactile senses is required for precise obstacle position. For this purpose, a white cane is usually used by visually impaired, which has two disadvantages. It is comparatively short and the detection occurs only by making contact with the obstacle which could sometimes may be harmful, not providing information about the aerial obstacles (head and waist height obstacles. Another popular navigation tool for blind people is a service dog-guides technique. These are the simplest and the most inexpensive navigations and available tools (guide dog and the white cane) (Baldwin, 2003). Even though these tools are very widespread, they cannot offer the blind all information and structures for safe mobility, which are accessible to people with eyesight (Shah et al., 2006).

2.1.1 White Cane and Guide Dogs

White canes are principally used to scan user's environment for obstacles or orientation landmarks, but they are also useful for other people to identify the user as blind and take the necessary precautions. The latter is the reason for the cane's famous white colour, which in many jurisdictions is mandatory. Used in combination with normal sensory monitoring (and often with a sighted guide), the long cane allows for travel in both familiar and unfamiliar areas. It is cheap, light, portable, needs little maintenance, and it is easy to use (Baldwin, 2015). There are three types of white canes, depending on a person's visual impairment, age, height and specific needs: Identification Canes, White Support Canes and Long Canes. Identification Canes: lightweight, can collapse to fit in a pocket or briefcase are used by the person to indicate to others that they are blind or visually impaired; they can be used to assist with depth perception on stairs or curbs. White Support Canes: collapsible, or rigid are designed to support a person's weight and to help him or her walk. Long Canes are used as bumpers and probes, mainly for independent travel in the home or unfamiliar places requiring specialized training from an orientation and mobility instructor (FFB, 2018). The main disadvantage of the white cane is its incomplete resolution. It is a near space tool and it does not recognize spatial position or objects. It doesn´t bring blind travellers closer to the abilities obtainable by sight (Baldwin, 2015). The guide dog is also a "mobility aid" that can assist blind people so they can travel safely. They can guide people around obstacles and through crowds, stop at curbs and stairs, and sometimes even be trained to find a limited number of objects that are within sight when given orders. The guide dog user can also train the dog to find frequently used landmarks, such as a bus stop pole or a mailbox (Noriega, 2018). But it is necessary to be aware that guide dogs are expensive as well as their maintenance and care. Also, people misinterpret their use: the person who is blind or has low vision directs the dog; the function and purpose of the dog is to merely guide the person around obstacles and indicate the location of steps and curbs. Studies relating different mobility aids (Whitmarsh, 2001) highpoint the diverse purposes, advantages and disadvantages of guide dogs and other aids, such as long canes. For example, guide dog's mobility are more likely to be considered more relaxing than long cane mobility, since the previous implicates obstacle prevention and the latter obstacle detection. A guide dog also offers more advantages than long canes in unfamiliar surroundings or in unknown routes. On the other hand, long canes do not need the care and domestic space of a guide dog (Miner, 2001). Still, the cane and guide dog have similar limitations. "They are most effective for detection of proximal cues, are limited in detecting overhanging or non-ground-level obstructions and do not provide much in the way of orientation information about the user's position (Giudice, 2008).

2.2 Assistive Technology

All the systems, services, devices and appliances that are used by disabled people to help in their daily lives, make their activities easier, and provide a safe mobility are designated as assistive technology.

Since 1960s evolving technology helped, many researchers built electronic navigational aids which includes many portable/wearable technological devices developed to improving locomotion for people with visual impairments. Many obstacle detection and avoidance systems have been introduced during the last decade to assist visual impaired to navigate in known or unknown, indoor and outdoor environments. The assistive technology can mainly be divided into three categories (Dakopoulos & Bourbakis, 2010; Thakare, Shubham, Ankit, Ajinkya, & Om, 2017), (Peterson, Wolffsohn, Rubinstein, & Lowe, 2003): i) Vision Replacement, ii) Vision Enhancement, and iii) Vision Substitution. The Vision Replacement category is more complex than the other two categories. Vision Replacement systems involves displaying the information directly to the visual cortex of the human brain or via the optic nerve. Vision Substitution and Vision Enhancement systems have almost same working principles with respect to environment detection process, however, each provides the environmental information differently. Vision Enhancement involves input from a camera, process the information, and output on a visual display (Peterson et al., 2003). In its simplest form it may be a miniature head-mounted camera with the output on a head-mounted visual display (as used in some virtual reality systems). In Vision Substitution the output being nonvisual, typically tactual or auditory or some combination of the two and since the senses of touch and hearing have a much lower information capacity than vision.

The Classification of electronic devices for visually-impaired people is summarized in Figure 1. Each one of the three categories try to enhance the blind people's mobility with slight differences. The

Figure 1. Classification tools for blind people

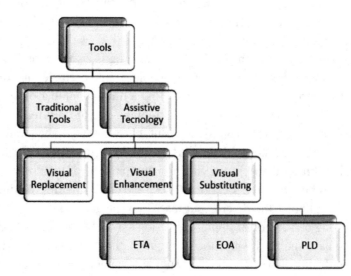

main focus in this literature survey is the vision substitution category including its three subcategories; Electronic Travel Aids (ETA), Electronic Orientation Aids (EOA), and Position Locator Devices (PLD).

Note that the navigational technologies are classified according to their sensor characteristics: sonar-based devices (using sonic sensors), vision-based (using cameras or lasers), infrared (IR) or GPS devices (Nicholas, 2008). Sonar-based devices detect and localize objects in order to offer those people a sense of the external environment using sensors. The sensors also aid the user with the mobility task based on the determination of dimensions, range and height of the objects. Camera or laser-based devices use a technology that converts images from a camera into patterns of vibrations delivered through an array of vibrotactile stimulators on the tongue. Infrared signage are systems consisting of infrared transmitters and a handheld IR receiver. Usually the transmitters are placed in strategic locations in the environment. Each sign sends short audio messages, via a constantly emitted IR beam, which can be decoded and spoken when picked up by the receiver. GPS devices enables the user to know his/her position when navigating outdoors, due to the location's information provided by satellite.

However, these systems present some drawbacks. Sonar-based devices have some limitations. They are not very effective in crowded environments because the signal is prone to reflection errors and the technology is also expensive. Camera-based devices need a high bandwidth. Even though GPS technology has made tremendous advances on outdoor navigating systems, methods for tracking position and orientation in indoor environments are still not reliable. Next, some considerations on the technology currently accepted and used by blind population is made.

In the next three sections, the three categories associated with the substitution of vision will be described in detail along with the presentation of some projects and studies described in the literature.

2.2.1 Electronic Travel Aids (ETA)

Electronic travel aids are devices that transform information about the environment that would normally be relayed through vision into a form that can be conveyed through another sensory modality. Literature shows that efforts in ETAs research aimed mainly at obstacle detection and avoidance, but in (Loomis, Klatzky, & Golledge, 2001) it is indicated that these devices have failed in contributing to the accomplishment of a more efficient navigation. The main reason is that providing a way of improving the navigation of blind people depends on information that is beyond the reach of these devices. Many studies are insufficient to determine the real needs of blind people when navigating in familiar and unfamiliar environments. One of the problems of current ETAs is the lack of usability assessments to validate the design of interfaces being used by blind people. For example, some devices use a set of headphones that affect the auditory perception of blind individuals and on which they base most of their navigation. Other devices require users to use both hands to operate them, thus preventing the blind from using cane or self-protection techniques.

The National Research Council's guidelines for ETAs are (Sánchez & Elías, 2007):

1. Detection obstacles in the travel path from ground level to head height for the full body width.
2. Travel surface information including textures and discontinuities.
3. Detection of objects bordering the travel path for shore lining and projection.
4. Distant object and cardinal direction information for projection of a straight line.
5. Landmark location and identification information.
6. Information enabling self-familiarization and mental mapping of an environment.

7. In addition: ergonomic, operate with minimal interface with natural sensory channels, single unit, reliable, user choice of auditory or tactile modalities, durable, easily repairable, robust, low power and cosmetically accepted.

2.2.2 Electronic Orientation Aids (EOA)

Electronic Orientation Aids (EOAs) are devices that provide pedestrians with directions in unfamiliar places (Kammoun, J-M Macé, Oriola, & Jouffrais, 2011), and support on finding out the route for the best path, providing mobility instructions and path signs to guide the user and develop her/his brain about the environment. It means it aids the blind in finding their way in an unknown environment. EOA systems usually need much environmental information to analyze the scope of unknown environment. A combination of a camera and other multiple sensors is usually used to get more information to draw the shapes of passageway and obstacles (Huang, Hsieh, & Yeh, 2015), (Hoang et al., 2017). EOA is only for occasional use in unknown environments or for very difficult routes that are not used frequently. The drawback of EOAs is that they need more complex computing to hardly be realized as a real-time and lightweight guiding device.

The guidelines of EOAs are given in (Kammoun et al., 2011):

1. Defining the route to select the best path;
2. Tracing the path to approximately calculate the location of the user;
3. Providing mobility instructions and path signs to guide the user and develop her/his brain about the environment.

As mentioned, blind people encounter several difficulties when walking and crossing roads, especially in big cities where traffic jams are more intense. APS (Accessible Pedestrian Signals) support blind pedestrians by using a device that communicates information about pedestrian timing in non-visual format such as audible tones, verbal messages, and/or vibrating surfaces. There are different types of APS´s within different countries which provide different information (audible and vibrotactile signals). It can be about the existence and location of the push button that activates a "Walk" signal; the beginning of the walk interval; the direction of the crosswalk and the location of the destination curb; intersection street names in braille, raised print, or speech messages, intersection signalization with a speech message, and intersection geometry through tactile maps and diagrams or through speech messages (Harkey, 2011).

2.2.3 Position Locator Devices (PLD)

Position Locator Devices (PLD) - these are devices that define the exact position of its holder such as devices that use GPS technology (Spinsante et al., 2017).

As within APSs the orientation on crossing streets is very helpful for blind pedestrians, but still they are not aware of the street name or their position in order to reach a certain destination. With the support of a global positioning system (GPS), the user is able to know his position when navigating outdoors, due to the location's information provided by satellite. This information is displayed on various smartphone applications, for instance Google Maps or dedicated GPS devices (Ruffa et al., 2015) "GPS-based navigation systems are a true orientation aid, as the satellites constantly provide updated position information whether or not the pedestrian is moving" (Giudice & Legge, 2008).

There are several GPS-based navigation systems available on the market which use visual display (and some that even provide coarse speech output for in-car route navigation), but they cannot be used fully by blind navigators. Examples of available GPS devices for blind people are the Wayfinder system (Kowalik & Kwasniewski, 2004), the Trekker system and the Navigator system (Kowalik & Kwasniewski, 2004).

The last one "Navigator" was designed to specific parameters to reflect the special needs of the user. Those include:

1. Blind people specific functions that the GPS is capable of sustaining,
2. The use of the functions bringing into focus the simplicity of use,
3. Identifying ways to transmit the results of the functions without too much intrusion.

The information provided by a GPS is "expected to greatly improve blind orientation performance and increase user confidence in promoting safe and independent travel. No other technology can provide the range of orientation information that GPS-based systems make available"(Giudice & Legge, 2008) .There are nevertheless certain limitations on this technology: although the accessible software is not expensive, the indispensable software is quite costly. Additionally, the user needs to periodically buy new maps and databases of commercial posts of interest. But the most significant disadvantage of GPS is that it cannot be used indoors and it is also unable to tell a user about the presence of drop-offs, obstacles, or moving objects in the environment, such as cars or other pedestrians (Hersh, Farcy, Leroux, & Jucha, 2006).

2.3 Important Projects

Literature survey shows that different researches are done in the field of blind stick using navigation system. Most electronic aids that provide services for visually-impaired people depend on the data collected from the surrounding environment (via either laser scanner, cameras sensors, or sonar) and transmitted to the user either via tactile, audio format or both. Different opinions on which one is a better feedback type are discussed, and this is still an open topic.

As mentioned above, all devices gather information about the surrounding environment and transfer it to the user through sensor cameras, sonar, or laser scanners. The main objective is to help the blind people to avoid obstacles. There are numerous projects and devices described in the literature.

Several studies have applied available technology to mobility assistive devices, with most effort devoted to assistive technology for avoiding obstacle, namely improve the efficiency of the white canes.

To overcome the disadvantages of the white canes and improve the independence and safety of the blinds during navigation some studies are presented and discussed in the literature with different ways. In (Kumar et al., 2014) it is presented a study that discusses about the development of a cane with ultrasonic distance sensors as the navigational aid. The proposed device used 3 pairs of ultrasonic trans-receivers such that the obstacles (both grounded and aerial) can be efficiently detected. In (Garcia Ramirez et al., n.d.) a new cane was proposed. It has ergonomic design and embedded electronics inside the grip to improve spatial and tactile perception. Observations, surveys, and interviews were conducted to evaluate barrier detection and mobility. The results indicate the feasibility of the electronic long cane project. The study also shows that the prototype is fully capable of being used as an assistive technology product. In (Dhall, Sharma, Thakur, Agarwal, & Rastogi, n.d.) the authors focuses on designing a device for visually impaired people that help them to travelling independently and also it must be comfortable to use. The proposed device is used for guiding individuals who are blind or partially sighted. Moreover, it provides the voice alert to avoid obstacles based on ultrasonic sensors.

In (Bhatlawande et al., 2014) a wearable assistive system is proposed to improve mobility of visually impaired people (subjects). This system has been implemented in the shape of a bracelet and waist-belt in order to increase its wearable convenience and cosmetic acceptability. A camera and an ultrasonic sensor are attached to a customized waist-belt and bracelet, respectively. The proposed modular system will act as a complementary aid along with a white cane. Its vision-enabled waist-belt module detects the path and distribution of obstacles on the path. In (Wada, Sugimura, Ienaga, & Kimuro, n.d.) it is proposed a guidance system to the blind based on several sensors mounted on special shoes.

In (Hoffmann, Spagnol, Kristjánsson, & Unnthorsson, 2018) it is proposed a system based on Sound of Vision (SoV). The goal was to evaluate the efficiency of the Sound of Vision system for mobility, compare it with the white cane, and quantify training effects. There are in the literature others studies, projects and prototypes developed, such as Range-It (Zeng et al., 2017), NavBelt (Shoval, Ulrich, & Borenstein, 2003), CyARM (Akita, komatsu, Ito, Ono, & Okamoto, 2009) amongst others.

In (Rastogi et al., 2017) a project is presented to provide an acoustic assistance to the blind people and also to deal with the problems faced by them to walk like the normal human beings. Thus, the project aims to develop a device that would serve as a guiding assistance to them. The paper focuses on designing a device for visual impaired (or blind) people that would help them to travel independently and also with more ease. The project consists of the smart shoes and the smart cane (stick) that alerts visually-impaired people over obstacles coming between their ways and could help them in walking with less collision. The main aim of this paper is to address a reliable solution encompassing of a cane and a shoe that could communicate with the users through voice alert and pre-recorded message. In (Scheggi, Talarico, & Prattichizzo, 2014) it is presented a remote guidance system which provides the visually impaired with haptic directional cues, useful for navigating in unknown environments. The blind user is equipped with a pair of camera glasses, two vibrotactile bracelets and a cane which is used to avoid potential obstacles. The video captured by the camera glasses is streamed to a remote operator who can properly navigate the impaired person by activating the vibrotactile stimulations.

Considering systems based on GPS, many prototypes and systems have been developed, such as, NavCog (Ahmetovic, Gleason, Kitani, Takagi, & Asakawa, 2016), URNA (Bohonos, Lee, Malik, Thai, & Manduchi, 2007), Drishti (Helal, Moore, & Ramachandran, n.d.). The last one is a wireless pedestrian navigation system. It integrates several technologies including wearable computers, voice recognition and synthesis, wireless networks, Geographic Information System (GIS) and Global positioning system (GPS).

3. MULTIMODAL INTERACTION DESIGN

When it comes to building interfaces for blind people, it is necessary to explore multimodal interfaces. How is it to navigate without seeing? Finding such Human Computer Interface (HCI) concepts from augmentative and alternative communication can serve designers, engineers or educators in various ways in order to reduce social disability.

Multimodal human-computer interaction refers to "interaction with the virtual and physical environment through natural modes of communication" (Bourguet, 2003). Multimodal systems can offer a flexible, efficient and usable environment allowing users to interact through input modalities, such as speech, vibration or hand gesture, and to receive information from the system through output modalities, such as speech synthesis, smart graphics and other modalities, opportunely combined. Multimodal interfaces can increase task efficiency. In (Sánchez, Darin, & Andrade, 2015) a summary of approaches and technologies currently in use for the development of mental maps, cognitive spatial structures, and navigation skills in learners who are blind by using multimodal videogames is presented. This work shows some trends in interface characterization and interaction style that worth to be read. One aspect is that all of the 21 applications used at least one aural interface element, although most of the cases combined two or more aural elements. The prevailing combination was between iconic and spatialized sound in 3D environments. Iconic sounds were the most common type of sonorous feedback (16 applications), followed by spatialized sounds (11 applications). The spoken audio (11 applications) was more prevalent than speech synthesis (7 applications), even though 5 applications combine the two types. Stereo sound was also used in 5 applications. Only one application used music/tones to represent different objects. Another aspect worth to be mentioned was the fact that 20 applications presented a graphic interface in addition to the aural elements and there were not applications with sound-only interfaces.

Then we will make an analysis into the literature through different modes of interaction starting with audio. A number of virtual environments have been developed for blind people based on different type of audio, from simple sounds to 3-D audio. We can highlight, for instance, AudioMUD (Sanchez & Hassler, 2007) using spoken text to describe the environment, navigation, and interaction. It also includes some collaborative features into the interaction between blind users and includes a simulated virtual environment inside the human body. Several other systems use Spoken text (Orly Lahav & Mioduser, 2008), (Sánchez & Aguayo, 2008), (Torrente et al., n.d.). Several systems using Spatialized sound were also already proposed (Sánchez, Sáenz, & Ripoll, 2009), (Lumbreras & Sánchez, 1999) and (Sánchez & Aguayo, 2008).

During the last years different techniques of the use of sounds to represent visual scenes, especially for blind people were proposed. The sonification processes varied from the parameters used to acoustically describe an image, as well as the number of channels and the dimensional complexity of the sonification produced. The purpose of audio-based applications is to improve knowledge, spatial representation and localization, orientation and mobility, contextual and associative memory and to enhance the ability to perform problem-solving tasks. Another tendency in sonification consists in mapping arbitrary information such as the distance to an obstacle or changes in temperature into sound. It consists in the systematic representation of data using sounds, such as text-to-speech, colour readers, Geiger counters, acoustic radars, and MIDI synthesizers. Sanz and colleagues (Sanz & et al, 2014) survey existing sonification systems and suggest a taxonomy of algorithms and devices. Another issue is the representation of Non-verbal sound, cues that can be used to convey different kinds of information and are often used for both simple and more complex types of feedback in computer games. Non-verbal sound cues can be divided into two different categories; auditory icons, that are sounds that represent real world events, and earcons and morphocons, that are abstract synthetic or musical sounds. In contrast to earcons (the audio analog of icons), which map a unique sound to a particular meaning, morphocons are short audio units that are used to construct a sonic grammar based on temporal-frequency patterns, rather than fixed sound samples. Although there are many systems using iconic sounds (Espinoza, Sánchez, & de Borba Campos, 2014); (Sánchez et al., 2009); (Sánchez & Mascaró, 2011); (Sánchez & Sáenz, 2010); (Sánchez, 2012); (O. Lahav & Mioduser, 2008)) only one was found with the use of abstract icons (Espinoza et al., 2014).

Concerning verbal sound, voice message is a speech channel used either through an input or output modality generally considered self-sufficient, carrying most of the informational content in a multimodal interface. There are significant advantages such as:

- Creates a time-efficient interaction. Just as we try to limit the number of clicks a user must make to complete an action, limit the amount of voice interaction needed.
- Keeps messages short and allows interruptions. Don't force a user to listen to long messages or lists of choices without a way to continue forward.
- Let users control the speech rate. "Many blind users of screen readers can listen to text as exceedingly fast speeds." Designers should recognize this enhanced skill and design accordingly.
- Makes it discoverable. Consider how the ability to speak with a device is conveyed. If it is expected that a user speaks to a device, make sure that user knows it exists and can open a dialog" (Bo Campbell, 2017).

Unfortunately, speech input typically uses a limited vocabulary, forcing the user to recall a particular command syntax. Ambiguities can appear as a result of recognition errors as well as erroneous language constructs (Bo Campbell, 2017). We can point several systems of spoken audio using sentences pre-recorded in a human voice, to describe relevant information about the actions and objects.

Voice Vision substitution is similar to vision enhancement, yet the result constitutes non-visual display, which can be vibration, auditory or both, based on the hearing and touch senses that can be easily controlled and felt by the blind user. For example, a smart cane uses a special vibrator glove which has a specific vibration for each finger, and each one has a specific meaning (Bourguet, 2003). Another example is the "Path Force Feedback belt" to help blind people navigate outside. It uses three components: "the main unit (the process) with two dual video cameras, power supply which is packed into a pocket and the belt to be worn around the user's waist. The belt has a number of cells that gives feedback to the user" (Oliveira, 2013). The corresponding cells will vibrate around the belt and show the user the right path. The system is designed such that each feature has its own signature use of the vibration pattern. So, each vibration frequency differentiates a specific feature or obstacle, e.g., the sidewalk's border marked in some way.

Another interesting idea found consisted in a system that can help the blind for handling currency. They used image processing techniques to scan the currency (an IPR sensor is used instead of a camera for sensing the object), remove the noise, mark the region of interest and convert the image into text and then to sound which can be heard by the blind (Kamesh, Nazma, Sastry, & Venkateswarlu, 2016).

In the field of sound other approaches consist in Text-to-speech synthesizers, applications that convert text into spoken word. This conversion is made by analysing and processing the text using Natural Language Processing (NLP) and subsequently using Digital Signal Processing (DSP) technology to convert this processed text into synthesized speech representation of the text. The idea of this artificial production of human speech (Suendermann, Höge, & Black, 2010), (Espinoza et al., 2014) stays as closely as possible, a native speaker of the language reading that text. A computer system used for this purpose is called a speech synthesizer and can be implemented in software or hardware. A synthesizer can incorporate a model of the vocal tract and other human voice characteristics to create a completely "synthetic" voice output (Rubin, Baer, & Mermelstein, 1981). A speech synthesizer of good quality can produce human voice in a way that is well understood, particularly to blind people. As examples of speech synthesizers we can cite NVDA (Sampurna Guha, n.d.), JAWS (Kapperman, Koster, & Burman, n.d.), Windows-Eyes (Windows_Eyes, 2018), SAToGo or VoiceOver (Apple, n.d.). Text-to-speech (TTS) systems have evolved significantly over the years from the earlier Homer Dudley vocoder (Dudley, 1940) passing by several other systems and methods (Allen, Hunnicutt, Klatt, Armstrong, & Pisoni, 1987), (Boeffard et al., 1993), (Dutoit & Leich, 1993), (Möller, Hinterleitner, Falk, & Polzehl, 2010),

(Wang, Ling, & Dai, 2016), (Morise, Yokomori, & Ozawa, 2016) to today' systems, such as char2wav (Sotelo et al., 2017), Deep voice2 (Arik et al., 2017), or Google's wavenet (Van Den Oord et al., n.d.). Although the existence of so many text-to-speech systems there are also systems for synthesizing and manipulating natural-sounding vocalizations (nonverbal vocalizations) we can mention, for instance, Soundgen (Anikin, 2018).

Other assistive technologies that blind are used are screen readers assisting them to access and use applications (Ferreira, Nunes, & da Silveira, 2012), (Erdem, 2017) even though most of them don't completely satisfy the blind user's needs (Schinazi, Thrash, & Chebat, 2016), (Shinohara & Kristen, 2006). Usually the majority of applications are not prepared for such tools to communicate the content of an image or describing the layout of an interface.

Another interaction trend respects to gesture-based interactions (Karam & schraefel, n.d.). In (Rekimoto & Jun, 1996) Rekimoto had already proposed a system using a device tilt as a 3D (3-dimentional) motion gesture. Through this mechanism he presented interaction techniques for several functions ranging from menus and scrollbars to more complicated functions such as map browsing. Kane and colleagues presented a gesture study (Kane, Wobbrock, & Ladner, 2011) where touch screen gestures performed by blind and sighted people were compared. This study, reporting design guidelines for accessible touch screen interfaces, found that blind people have different gesture preferences from sighted people. The authors of a study (Dim & Ren, 2014) based on another study (Ruiz, Li, & Lank, 2011) identified the differences between gestures performed by two user groups through gesture taxonomy and user-defined gesture sets.

Another aspect that we are interested in is the exploration in the interaction with mobile devices. Mobile phones are the most commonly carried devices by blind people in their daily lives (Kane, Jayant, Wobbrock, & Ladner, 2009). Smartphones are nowadays integrated with sophisticated motion sensors, such as accelerometers and gyroscopes, to detect 3D movements suitable for motion gesture interactions especially useful for blind people.

The idea of gestures interaction is that blind users don't have to memorize things (buttons localization) but to interact in a natural way. For the implementation of a set of gestures appropriate to the blind population, it would be desirable to make direct observations and interviews in order to perceive the gestures actually used by them. However, since it was not possible to carry out these studies, the literature was searched in order to find similar studies that could give real support to this need. We found a study (Dim & Ren, 2014) where the authors investigated the most usable gestures for blind people in order to find the best practices to design the usable motion gestures for them. For this, the authors conducted a user-defined study where the participants were asked to define their own gestures to invoke some common tasks in a smartphone, and to mention the rationale and heuristics for the gestures they performed. Findings from the study indicated that motion gesture interfaces are more efficient than traditional button interfaces. The study results also gave us important orientations for the designing of the interface and interactions of our smartphone applications, described next:

- Designing relative gestures for "Application Pause", "Program Close", "Power Off", "Cancel", and "Resume" can make the interfaces more learnable because they are more logical to the blind.
- Blind people are sometimes not aware of the visual-based actions that sighted people perform (for example, a gesture for hanging up the call). Designers should avoid gestures including these kinds of actions.
- The gestures tend to include more translations and rotations than simple single motions.

- Wherever possible, symbolic gestures and the direct depiction of visual objects should also be avoided.
- Regarding the physical characteristics of gestures, they found that the participants used large movements to generate gestures, therefore the demand for motion accuracy should be reduced.
- Designers should pay specific care not to include gestures that are unexpected by these users.
- Gesture customization is a very acceptable and beneficial interface option for blind users.
- Feedback should be provided to every gesture the participant made. Vibration feedback or speech feedback to each gesture input is advisable. Vibration feedback should be provided to every action that had no speech output.

Hand gesture was also extensively studied as an efficient input modality. Gesture languages with different levels of complexity (starting from grasp-release commands to Sign Language) were proposed for various applications (Popescu, Burdea, & Trefftz, n.d.). In addition to input modalities, emerging technologies such as indirect sensing of neural activity (e.g., brain–computer interfaces) may become practical components of multimodal interaction systems in the near future (Turk, 2013).

Another tendency is haptic feedback and it can happen in different ways. Force feedback devices allow the haptic feedback measuring the positions and contact forces of the user's hand or fingers, displaying contact forces and positions to the user. This type of interaction allows manual interactions with the multimedia environment through touch. The tactile feedback provides the sensations of vibration, pressure, touch and texture. Touch sensation could be represented in Braille or through different tactile sensations, stimulating the skin surface, such as texture, heat or cold (Hinckley & Sinclair, 1999). As this interaction mode is related to the motor skills it reduces the cognitive mind load of the user (Hinckley & Sinclair, 1999) what is an important aspect as the brain structure of a blind person highly relates to touch stimuli (M. Bates, 2012) acting as a substitution for the loss of vision (Murphy et al., 2016).

We can conclude that there are several modes through what a blind user can interact, providing input to the application, determining the style of interaction available. It will also influence the type of feedback that the application provides to an interaction. We are now designing the mock-ups of the application, combining several interaction approaches having in mind the previous analysis for the types of interactions.

4. PROJECT: BLUEEYES

The aim of this project (Orvalho, 2016) is to help the blind to be aware of the environment in which they live, where navigation and way finding is crucial to guarantee their mobility and to improve their quality of life. We also know that people with visual disabilities in new environments usually feel totally disoriented and isolated. It is not easy for blind people to move independently, therefore it is urgent to ensure easy mobility for them. Therefore, the aim is to improve the social inclusion of these citizens, with novel mobility solution to assist the visually impaired in their daily journey, using a smartphone, without the need for any special hardware, and Bluetooth Low Energy (BLE) technology. Thus, a practical scientific research is proposed supported by three Beacon's Living Labs, in Coimbra, Caldas da Rainha and Tábua.

Another aim is to determine a good architectural model for context-aware mobile apps that leverage Beacons and determine their strengths and limitations for context-awareness for real-world settings. These applications will act like a city guide with accurate tracking and micro-location context-aware on a mobile device with BLE. Each Living Lab network contains iBeacons (Apple) and Eddystone Beacons (Google).

In the city of Coimbra, the living lab will be at SMTUC (a Portuguese acronym for Municipal Transport Services of Coimbra) line 5 (25 bus stops and 5 buses) to support the mobility of blind citizens in the city of Coimbra. The system will assist the visually impaired to the proximity of a stop and inform the number of buses and their route. Additionally, it can calculate the best route for their destination. In the event of routine changes, customers will be informed. Blind customers can interact and determine decisions of SMTUC services, especially those that are intended to function. Inside the bus, the blind may have access to more usable audio information from these stops, the current stop, as well as additional information to support route and route changes in order to move to the desired destination.

In the city of Caldas da Rainha, the living lab will be at the Bordaliana Route, to support the mobility of blind citizens. This is a cultural route dedicated to Rafael Bordallo Pinheiro, with his giant works of art to integrate an urban street art project. Designed for walking, Bordaliana Route offers a longer route, which approximately takes two hours to be completed, to see unique toponymic parts, human scale and read about episodes of Rafael Bordallo Pinheiro's life and a bit of history of the city.

In the city of Tábua the living lab will be at the centre of the town, to help the pedestrian movement of visually impaired people to access services at public buildings.

The first phase of the project is ready: the survey for an exact number of beacons for each Living Lab network with beacons, the study of the points of their placement and the acquisition of beacons from different manufacturers was already made. Its facilities, tests and validation are already in working mode. Also underway is the creation of a public web site with georeferenced information of the location of each beacon and technical information inherent in the operation and the maintenance plan.

Understanding our Users and their HCI needs is a crucial aspect of BueEyes project. Our primary users are blind people. UX projects typically consist of three main phases, a research phase, a design phase and a further research phase, designed to test and validate the designs, including the prototypes. The target audience will be distributed in the 3 aforementioned cities. In the next subsections the tasks and methodology used in this project is presented and is shortly described.

4.1 Tasks and Methodology

This project is divided into six main tasks, as shown in next diagram, Figure 2.

Figure 2. Description of main tasks - project BlueEyes

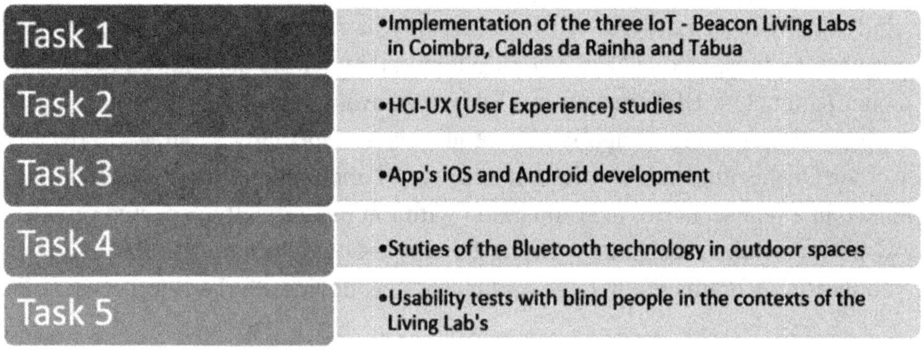

Task 1	• Implementation of the three IoT - Beacon Living Labs in Coimbra, Caldas da Rainha and Tábua
Task 2	• HCI-UX (User Experience) studies
Task 3	• App's iOS and Android development
Task 4	• Stuties of the Bluetooth technology in outdoor spaces
Task 5	• Usability tests with blind people in the contexts of the Living Lab's

4.1.1 Task 1: Implementation of the Three IOT: Beacon Living Labs in Coimbra, Caldas, Da Rainha, and Tábua

This task consists in the survey for exact number of beacons for each Living Lab network with iBeacons and Eddystone Beacons. The study of the points of their placement; the acquisition of beacons from different manufacturers (there is an interesting amount of industry to produce beacons); the installation, tests and validation of the acquired beacons; the creation of a Content Management System (CMS); the creation of a public web site with georeferenced information on the location of each beacon and technical information inherent in the operation and maintenance plan are also subtasks of this task.

4.1.2 Task 2: HCI-UX (User Experience) Studies

This task involves in understanding of our Users and their usability and accessibility needs: our primary users are visually-impaired people. UX projects typically consist of three main phases, a research phase, a design phase and a further research phase, designed to test and validate the designs, included prototypes. The target audience - visually-impaired people - will be distributed by 3 cities. UX studies will be developed in the context of usability lab IPC (a Portuguese acronym for Instituto Politécnico de Coimbra). All case studies, creation of personas, wireframes and prototypes will involve the blind citizens of the towns of living labs. It will take many interventions in the physical space of the living labs in factual situations with blind people.

4.1.3 Task 3: App's iOS and Android Development

In this task it will be developed the iOS and Android applications, according to the specifications of each of the 3 Living Labs: Coimbra - circulation SMTUC municipal transport; Caldas da Rainha - interaction with street art pieces of Bordaliana Route; Tábua - pedestrian movement in the city center with access services public buildings by visually impaired citizens. It will take many interactions in living labs and in fact situations, requiring many trips in order to fully test the developed applications.

4.1.4 Task 4: Studies of the Bluetooth Technology in Outdoor Spaces

An issue where there isn't so much related research information it's about BLE technology in outdoor spaces with huge factors conditioning and a vast different manufacturer. Therefore, at this stage we propose the study, in 3 Living Labs, on "BLE technology in outdoor spaces and its trade-off between energy consumption, latency, piconet size, and throughput that mainly depends on the connInterval and connSlaveLatency parameters. BLE iBeacon and Eddystone evaluation results show how these parameters can be tuned wisely in order to meet application requirements, specially accuracy in the case of pieces closes to each other. On the other hand, we have noted several implementation constraints that may reduce BLE performance in a real scenario, in comparison with the theoretically expected one. BLE emerges as a strong low-power wireless technology strong for single-hop communication use cases, which may contribute to connecting a dramatically large number of new devices to the Internet of Things (IoT).

4.1.5 Task 5: Usability Tests With Blind People in the Contexts of the Living Lab's

In the framework of the IPC' Usability Laboratory it will be designed, developed and applied usability tests with blind people in the context of the three already mentioned Living Labs. Usability tests will also be carried out in the spaces of the living labs in cities with blind citizens. It will take many trips: evaluators and volunteer participants, blind and visually impaired.

4.1 Beacons Technology

As stated before, indoor navigation technology still needs further development. There are several devices for specific daily needs, but it is missing a stable accepted technology that provides information about the user's immediate surroundings. This can be in a shopping-mall, a grocery store, airport, train station etc. So, the path of technology development on mobility and orientation tools for visual disabled people should be towards the enhancement of the potential for smarter interaction and accessibility, by adding multisensory features into environments, and by developing multisensory way-finding solutions.

iBeacon can be used as a possible solution, because it is a technology which its potential can be exploited for multisensory and mobility in order to facilitate the tracking, routing and mapping solutions. An iBeacon is a small-scale network transmitter that instead of using latitude and longitude to define the location uses a Bluetooth low energy signal, which iOS devices detect (Gilchrist, 2014). In other words, it's a tiny device with low power consumption that can be placed in a wall or another part of a building. It transmits constantly an identification number via Bluetooth to enable devices which are around to use the corresponding application. BLE beacons-based indoor navigation apps can help visually-impaired and blind people understand the surrounding world in a similar way as GPS technology already does. BLE Beacons (also called Bluetooth Smart or Version 4.0+ of the Bluetooth specification) is the power and application-friendly version of Bluetooth that was built for the Internet of Things (IoT) (Apple, 2018).

One example of a project that builds up a smart environment was developed in Helsinki in a Shopping Mall. The environment was tagged with iBeacons that communicated with blind people's smartphone and BlindSquare App. iBeacons were set on locations that had landmark recognized by blind or visually impaired people (Saarela, 2015). Another project from Indoo.rs whose target was to develop a solution for Terminal 2 at Los Angeles Airport and designed as a mobile app with a voice assistant that helps visually-challenged travellers find their way to any location at the terminal. Another project is an indoor navigation solution for the London tube called Wayfindr. It has been designed by the ustwo studio in close collaboration with the Royal London Society for Blind People. The developers successfully tested the new system in the Pimlico station in the spring of 2015. They launched Wayfindr as the first open navigation standard for blind people in October 2015" (Suddia, 2018).

For successful navigation, users need at least a "smartphone with BLE (Bluetooth Low Energy) onboard (iOS 7, Android 4.3 or later) and a pre-installed app. The app contains maps of the facility and it guides people via voice directions. This might not be comfortable for other people so the users need bone-conduct earbuds or Google Glass. This will make the directions inaudible for others, but the app's users will still hear what is going on outside. Another option is a smart watch which receives directions from a smartphone application and transmits them as tactile signals" (Suddia, 2018).

Therefore, we hope that the Beacons technology will be of great advantage not only for BlueEyes project but also a world of possibilities concerning the internet of things.

4.2 Emotions Analysis

Another important aspect relates to the emotional issues that visually impaired people experience when navigating. We consider that navigation does not only include practical and physical issues but are also part of mental and emotional aspects. It is important to remember that the brain of visual sight people store lots of experiences in pictures usually associated with emotions. Emotions consist of several elements (Wolff, Stiglmayr, Bretz, Lammers, & Auckenthaler, 2007): somatic responses; Behavioral components; cognitive processes; motivational components and subjective components. However, the visually impaired people have some limitations corresponding to some of them, for instance, it is impossible to analyze visual clues such as facial expressions, body gestures and other social non-verbal interactions. This has a debilitating effect on their social interaction, while sighted people could infer several emotions.

Our idea is, on one hand, to work with social assistive aids to improve and help blind people to recognize universal emotions. On the other hand, try to understand what types of interactions most fulfil the blind emotionally, and consequently how to trigger good emotions in individuals who have this handicap.

For that, in this study we want to analyze various forms of interaction, in addition to the classical ones. Some considered interaction modalities are haptic, auditory, and based on physiological signals. We are not only particularly interested in determining the modality that triggers the best emotions but the set of modalities or multimodal interactions that provide them. Multiple sensory channels jointly can activate several emotional experiences however the deficiency in one channel may alter the experience and change the whole emotion and, perhaps can affect physiological responses and brain processes. The idea of multimodal interaction, concerning blind people, is not only to overcome the deficiencies in the visual channel and study the best channel combinations to compensate and complement it but also to discover the best emotional stimulus. Some studies suggest that emotional stimuli themselves attract attention more robustly and are more readily detected than are non-emotional stimuli (Ohman, Flykt, Esteves, & Institute, 2001), (Anderson, 2005), (Vuilleumier & Huang, 2009).

We plan to analyze all of the above not only to obtain what users say that trigger their emotions but also to use equipment that captures, in an undeceivable way, emotionally relevant cues in order to call the user's attention and selectively enhance perception (Vuilleumier, 2005), (Pourtois, Schettino, & Vuilleumier, 2013). For that the use of Brain Computer Interaction (BCI) is envisioned. BCIs are direct functional interactions between a human brain and an external device (Dietrich, Lang, Bruckner, Fodor, & Muller, 2010). A BCI measures a user's brain activity to identify the pattern of a particular thought or action, in our case using EEG. Brain activity is measured by the detection of small voltage changes in specific areas of the brain. For that we are planning a set of experiments using the Mindwave device.

5. CONCLUSION AND FURTHER WORK

In this chapter we described the idea underlying the BlueEyes project, consisting in a useful system for the orientation and navigation of blind people. The project is being implemented in 3 Portuguese cities with different needs and realities. This document provides information related to problems blind people are facing, starting from the challenges that are beyond their daily life and then emphasizes one of the most complex and important challenge that is navigation and orientation in indoor and outdoor environments. Specially, mobility challenges in large complex buildings concerns almost everyone. It is critical that public places and community settings will be designed to be safe, as inclusive as possible and accessible for all. There are several technologies in development with multimodal human-computer interaction that can turn these indoor locations into smart environments. The future of new solutions brings us to the world of the artificial intelligence and intelligent machines through smaller and cheaper solutions. These navigational tools will be personalized, prescribed appliances, designed to satisfy individual tastes as well as needs. These tools will be part of clothing, unseen, but probably not unheard. The device will be linked to the internet, to a powerful server computer specifically tailored to the blind traveller. In the age of technology, people with disabilities have certainly new hope coming in wave's year after year, like never before in history.

ACKNOWLEDGMENT

Cofinanciado por:

REFERENCES

Ahmetovic, D., Gleason, C., Kitani, K. M., Takagi, H., & Asakawa, C. (2016). NavCog. In *Proceedings of the 13th Web for All Conference on - W4A '16* (pp. 1–2). New York: ACM Press. doi:10.1145/2899475.2899509

Akita, J., komatsu, T., Ito, K., Ono, T., & Okamoto, M. (2009). CyARM: Haptic Sensing Device for Spatial Localization on Basis of Exploration by Arms. *Advances in Human-Computer Interaction, 2009*, 1–6. doi:10.1155/2009/901707

Allen, J., Hunnicutt, M. S., Klatt, D. H., Armstrong, R. C., & Pisoni, D. B. (1987). *From text to speech : the MITalk system*. Cambridge University Press. Retrieved from https://dl.acm.org/citation.cfm?id=28587

Anderson, A. K. (2005). Affective Influences on the Attentional Dynamics Supporting Awareness. *Journal of Experimental Psychology. General, 134*(2), 258–281. doi:10.1037/0096-3445.134.2.258 PMID:15869349

Anikin, A. (2018). Soundgen: An open-source tool for synthesizing nonverbal vocalizations. *Behavior Research Methods*, 1–15. doi:10.375813428-018-1095-7 PMID:30054898

Apple. (n.d.). *Vision Accessibility - Mac - Apple*. Retrieved October 25, 2018, from https://www.apple.com/accessibility/mac/vision/

Arik, S., Diamos, G., Gibiansky, A., Miller, J., Peng, K., Ping, W., … Zhou, Y. (2017). *Deep Voice 2: Multi-Speaker Neural Text-to-Speech*. Retrieved from https://arxiv.org/abs/1705.08947v1

Basak Bjayanta, J., Sudarshan, A., Trivedi, D., & Santhanam Santh, M. S. (2004). Weather Data Mining Using Independent Component Analysis. *Journal of Machine Learning Research*, 5, 239–253.

Bates, M. (2012). Super Powers for the Blind and Deaf. *Scientific American*, 1–5. Retrieved from https://www.scientificamerican.com/article/superpowers-for-the-blind-and-deaf/

Bhatlawande, S., Sunkari, A., Mahadevappa, M., Mukhopadhyay, J., Biswas, M., Das, D., & Gupta, S. (2014). Electronic Bracelet and Vision-Enabled Waist-Belt for Mobility of Visually Impaired People. *Assistive Technology*, *26*(4), 186–195. doi:10.1080/10400435.2014.915896 PMID:25771603

Bo Campbell. (2017). *Tips for Designing Accessibility in Voice User Interfaces*. Retrieved October 25, 2018, from https://uxdesign.cc/tips-for-accessibility-in-conversational-interfaces-8e11c58b31f6

Boeffard, O., Cherbonnel, B., Emerard, F., Larreur, D., Le Saint-Milon, J. L., Métayer, I., … White, S. (1993). *ICASSP-93 : 1993 IEEE International Conference on Acoustics, Speech, and Signal Processing, April 27-30, 1993, Minneapolis Convention Center, Minneapolis, Minnesota. Proceedings of the 1993 IEEE international conference on Acoustics, speech, and signal processing: speech processing - Volume II*. Institute of Electrical and Electronics Engineers. Retrieved from https://dl.acm.org/citation.cfm?id=1946943.1946996

Bohonos, S., Lee, A., Malik, A., Thai, C., & Manduchi, R. (2007). Universal real-time navigational assistance (URNA). In *Proceedings of the 1st ACM SIGMOBILE international workshop on Systems and networking support for healthcare and assisted living environments - HealthNet '07* (p. 83). New York: ACM Press. 10.1145/1248054.1248080

Bourguet, M.-L. (2003). Designing and Prototyping Multimodal Commands. In *INTERACT'03* (pp. 717–720). Retrieved from http://citeseerx.ist.psu.edu/viewdoc/download?doi=10.1.1.98.1958&rep=rep1&type=pdf

Dakopoulos, D., & Bourbakis, N. G. (2010). Wearable Obstacle Avoidance Electronic Travel Aids for Blind: A Survey. *IEEE Transactions on Systems, Man and Cybernetics. Part C, Applications and Reviews*, *40*(1), 25–35. doi:10.1109/TSMCC.2009.2021255

Dhall, P., Sharma, P., Thakur, S., Agarwal, R., & Rastogi, S. (n.d.). *A review paper on assitive shoes: cane for visually impaired people*. Retrieved from http://www.ijsrms.com

Dietrich, D., Lang, R., Bruckner, D., Fodor, G., & Muller, B. (2010). Limitations, possibilities and implications of Brain-Computer Interfaces. In *3rd International Conference on Human System Interaction* (pp. 722–726). IEEE. 10.1109/HSI.2010.5514488

Dim, N. K., & Ren, X. (2014). Designing Motion Gesture Interfaces in Mobile Phones for Blind People. *Journal of Computer Science and Technology*, *29*(5), 812–824. doi:10.100711390-014-1470-5

Dudley, H. (1940). The Vocoder—Electrical Re-Creation of Speech&lt!--<xref reftype="other" rid="fn1-10.5594_J10096">*</xref>--&gt. *Journal of the Society of Motion Picture Engineers*, *34*(3), 272–278. doi:10.5594/J10096

Dutoit, T., & Leich, H. (1993). *MBR-PSOLA: Text-To-Speech synthesis re-synthesis of the segments database. Speech Communication* (Vol. 13). Retrieved from https://ac.els-cdn.com/016763939390042J/1-s2.0-016763939390042J-main.pdf?_tid=bdb55144-ecb2-4952-bf4c-20ac4a65beb9&acdnat=1540464083_c90c34a2b4096715a3cbeb108795639c

Erdem, R. (2017). Students with Special Educational Needs and Assistive Technologies: A Literature Review. *TOJET: The Turkish Online Journal of Educational Technology*, *16*. Retrieved from http://link.springer.com

Espinoza, M., Sánchez, J., & de Borba Campos, M. (2014). *Videogaming Interaction for Mental Model Construction in Learners Who Are Blind*. Cham: Springer. doi:10.1007/978-3-319-07440-5_48

Ferreira, S. B. L., Nunes, R. R., & da Silveira, D. S. (2012). Aligning Usability Requirements with the Accessibility Guidelines Focusing on the Visually-Impaired. *Procedia Computer Science*, *14*, 263–273. doi:10.1016/j.procs.2012.10.030

Garcia Ramirez, A. R., Fonseca, R., Da Silva, L., Cinelli, M. J., Durán, A., & De Albornoz, C. (n.d.). Evaluation of Electronic Haptic Device for Blind and Visually Impaired People: A Case Study. *Journal of Medical and Biological Engineering, 32*(6), 423–428. doi:10.5405/jmbe.925

Giudice, N. A., & Legge, G. E. (2008). Blind Navigation and the Role of Technology. In *The Engineering Handbook of Smart Technology for Aging, Disability, and Independence* (pp. 479–500). Hoboken, NJ: John Wiley & Sons, Inc. doi:10.1002/9780470379424.ch25

Harkey, E. (2011). Accessible Pedestrian Signals: A Guide to Best Practices (Workshop Edition 2010). Washington, DC: Transportation Research Board. doi:10.17226/22902

Helal, A., Moore, S. E., & Ramachandran, B. (n.d.). Drishti: an integrated navigation system for visually impaired and disabled. In *Proceedings Fifth International Symposium on Wearable Computers* (pp. 149–156). IEEE Comput. Soc. 10.1109/ISWC.2001.962119

Hersh, M. A., Farcy, R., Leroux, R., & Jucha, A. (2006). Electronic Travel Aids and Electronic Orientation Aids for blind people: technical, rehabilitation and everyday life points of view. *CVHI 2006: Conference on Assistive Tecnology for Vision and Hearing Impairment*. Retrieved from http://citeseerx.ist.psu.edu/viewdoc/summary?doi=10.1.1.112.8880

Hinckley, K., & Sinclair, M. (1999). Touch-sensing input devices. In *Proceedings of the SIGCHI conference on Human factors in computing systems the CHI is the limit - CHI '99* (pp. 223–230). New York: ACM Press. 10.1145/302979.303045

Hoang, V.-N., Nguyen, T.-H., Le, T.-L., Tran, T.-H., Vuong, T.-P., & Vuillerme, N. (2017). Obstacle detection and warning system for visually impaired people based on electrode matrix and mobile Kinect. *Vietnam Journal of Computer Science*, *4*(2), 71–83. doi:10.100740595-016-0075-z

Hoffmann, R., Spagnol, S., Kristjánsson, Á., & Unnthorsson, R. (2018). Evaluation of an Audio-haptic Sensory Substitution Device for Enhancing Spatial Awareness for the Visually Impaired. *Optometry and Vision Science*, *95*(9), 757–765. doi:10.1097/OPX.0000000000001284 PMID:30153241

Huang, H.-C., Hsieh, C.-T., & Yeh, C.-H. (2015). An Indoor Obstacle Detection System Using Depth Information and Region Growth. *Sensors (Basel)*, *15*(10), 27116–27141. doi:10.3390151027116 PMID:26512674

Kamesh, D. B. K., Nazma, S., Sastry, J. K. R., & Venkateswarlu, S. (2016). Camera based Text to Speech Conversion, Obstacle and Currency Detection for Blind Persons. *Indian Journal of Science and Technology*, *9*(30). doi:10.17485/ijst/2016/v9i30/98716

Kammoun, S., Macé, J.-M. M., Oriola, B., & Jouffrais, C. (2011). *LNCS 6949 - Toward a Better Guidance in Wearable Electronic Orientation Aids.* Retrieved from https://www.irit.fr/~Marc.Mace/pdfs/kammoun_s_11_624.pdf

Kane, S. K., Jayant, C., Wobbrock, J. O., & Ladner, R. E. (2009). Freedom to roam. In *Proceeding of the eleventh international ACM SIGACCESS conference on Computers and accessibility - ASSETS '09* (p. 115). New York: ACM Press. 10.1145/1639642.1639663

Kane, S. K., Wobbrock, J. O., & Ladner, R. E. (2011). Usable gestures for blind people. In *Proceedings of the 2011 annual conference on Human factors in computing systems - CHI '11* (p. 413). New York: ACM Press. 10.1145/1978942.1979001

Kapperman, G., Koster, E., & Burman, R. (n.d.). *The Study of Foreign Languages by Students Who Are Blind Using the JAWS Screen Reader and a Refreshable Braille Display.* Retrieved from https://files.eric.ed.gov/fulltext/EJ1182385.pdf

Karam, M., & Schraefel, M. C. (n.d.). *A taxonomy of Gestures in Human Computer Interaction.* Retrieved from https://eprints.soton.ac.uk/261149/1/GestureTaxonomyJuly21.pdf

Kowalik, R., & Kwasniewski, S. (2004). *Navigator – A Talking GPS Receiver for the Blind.* Berlin: Springer; doi:10.1007/978-3-540-27817-7_65

Kumar, K., Champaty, B., Uvanesh, K., Chachan, R., Pal, K., & Anis, A. (2014). Development of an ultrasonic cane as a navigation aid for the blind people. In *2014 International Conference on Control, Instrumentation, Communication and Computational Technologies (ICCICCT)* (pp. 475–479). IEEE. 10.1109/ICCICCT.2014.6993009

Lahav, O., & Mioduser, D. (2008). Construction of cognitive maps of unknown spaces using a multi-sensory virtual environment for people who are blind. *Computers in Human Behavior*, *24*(3), 1139–1155. doi:10.1016/j.chb.2007.04.003

Lahav, O., & Mioduser, D. (2008). Haptic-feedback support for cognitive mapping of unknown spaces by people who are blind. *International Journal of Human-Computer Studies*, *66*(1), 23–35. doi:10.1016/j.ijhcs.2007.08.001

Loomis, J. M., Klatzky, R. L., & Golledge, R. G. (2001). Navigating without vision: basic and applied research. *Optometry and Vision Science : Official Publication of the American Academy of Optometry*, *78*(5), 282–289. Retrieved from http://www.ncbi.nlm.nih.gov/pubmed/11384005

Lumbreras, M., & Sánchez, J. (1999). Interactive 3D sound hyperstories for blind children. In *Proceedings of the SIGCHI conference on Human factors in computing systems the CHI is the limit - CHI '99* (pp. 318–325). New York: ACM Press. 10.1145/302979.303101

Möller, S., Hinterleitner, F., Falk, T. H., & Polzehl, T. (2010). *Comparison of Approaches for Instrumentally Predicting the Quality of Text-To-Speech Systems.* INTERSPEECH. Retrieved from https://pdfs.semanticscholar.org/b39b/05dbfff7d21d8e9e50385c9786e6f7a9a007.pdf

Morise, M., Yokomori, F., & Ozawa, K. (2016). WORLD: A Vocoder-Based High-Quality Speech Synthesis System for Real-Time Applications. *IEICE Transactions on Information and Systems, E99.D*(7), 1877–1884. doi:10.1587/transinf.2015EDP7457

Murphy, M. C., Nau, A. C., Fisher, C., Kim, S.-G., Schuman, J. S., & Chan, K. C. (2016). Top-down influence on the visual cortex of the blind during sensory substitution. *NeuroImage, 125*, 932–940. doi:10.1016/j.neuroimage.2015.11.021 PMID:26584776

Ohman, A., Flykt, A., Esteves, F., & Institute, K. (2001). Emotion Drives Attention: Detecting the Snake in the Grass. *Journal of Experimental Psychology. General, 130*(3), 466–478. doi:10.1037/0096-3445.130.3.466 PMID:11561921

Oliveira, J. F. (2013). The path force feedback belt. In *2013 8th International Conference on Information Technology in Asia (CITA)* (pp. 1–6). IEEE. 10.1109/CITA.2013.6637564

Peterson, R. C., Wolffsohn, J. S., Rubinstein, M., & Lowe, J. (2003). Benefits of electronic vision enhancement systems (EVES) for the visually impaired. *American Journal of Ophthalmology, 136*(6), 1129–1135. doi:10.1016/S0002-9394(03)00567-1 PMID:14644225

Popescu, V., Burdea, G., & Trefftz, H. (n.d.). *Chapter 25: Multimodal interaction modeling.* Retrieved from https://pdfs.semanticscholar.org/68b0/fa1297635ba133e7d76489884fbc55023ec3.pdf

Pourtois, G., Schettino, A., & Vuilleumier, P. (2013). Brain mechanisms for emotional influences on perception and attention: What is magic and what is not. *Biological Psychology, 92*(3), 492–512. doi:10.1016/j.biopsycho.2012.02.007 PMID:22373657

Rastogi, S., Sharma, P., Dhall, P., Agarwal, R., Thakur, S., & Scholar, U. G. (2017). Smart assistive shoes and cane: solemates for the blind people. *International Journal of Advanced Research in Electronics and Communication Engineering, 6.* Retrieved from http://ijarece.org/wp-content/uploads/2017/04/IJARECE-VOL-6-ISSUE-4-334-345.pdf

Rekimoto, J., & Jun. (1996). Tilting operations for small screen interfaces. In *Proceedings of the 9th annual ACM symposium on User interface software and technology - UIST '96* (pp. 167–168). New York: ACM Press. 10.1145/237091.237115

Rubin, P., Baer, T., & Mermelstein, P. (1981). An articulatory synthesizer for perceptual research. *The Journal of the Acoustical Society of America, 70*(2), 321–328. doi:10.1121/1.386780

Ruffa, A. J., Stevens, A., Woodward, N., Zonfrelli, T., Belz, M., Hou, Z., … Blindesamfund, D. (2015). *Assessing iBeacons as an Assistive Tool for Blind People in Denmark An Interactive Qualifying Project Denmark Project Center*. Retrieved from http://www.wpi.edu/academics/ugradstudies/project-learning.html

Ruiz, J., Li, Y., & Lank, E. (2011). User-defined motion gestures for mobile interaction. In *Proceedings of the 2011 annual conference on Human factors in computing systems - CHI '11* (p. 197). New York: ACM Press. 10.1145/1978942.1978971

Sampurna Guha, M. (n.d.). *Effect of Assistive Devices on Educational Efficiency for Persons with Visual Impairment*. Retrieved from http://www.jodys.info/journal/march_2017/02_jodys_march_2017.pdf

Sánchez, J. (2012). Development of Navigation Skills Through Audio Haptic Videogaming in Learners Who are Blind. *Procedia Computer Science*, *14*, 102–110. doi:10.1016/j.procs.2012.10.012

Sánchez, J., & Aguayo, F. (2008). AudioGene: Mobile Learning Genetics through Audio by Blind Learners. In Learning to Live in the Knowledge Society (pp. 79–86). Boston, MA: Springer US. doi:10.1007/978-0-387-09729-9_10

Sánchez, J., Darin, T., & Andrade, R. (2015). *Multimodal Videogames for the Cognition of People Who Are Blind: Trends and Issues*. Springer International Publishing. doi:10.1007/978-3-319-20684-4_52

Sánchez, J., & Elías, M. (2007). *LNCS 4662 - Guidelines for Designing Mobility and Orientation Software for Blind Children*. Retrieved from https://link.springer.com/content/pdf/10.1007%2F978-3-540-74796-3_35.pdf

Sanchez, J., & Hassler, T. (2007). AudioMUD: A Multiuser Virtual Environment for Blind People. *IEEE Transactions on Neural Systems and Rehabilitation Engineering*, *15*(1), 16–22. doi:10.1109/TNSRE.2007.891404 PMID:17436871

Sánchez, J., & Mascaró, J. (2011). *Audiopolis, Navigation through a Virtual City Using Audio and Haptic Interfaces for People Who Are Blind*. Berlin: Springer. doi:10.1007/978-3-642-21663-3_39

Sánchez, J., & Sáenz, M. (2010). Metro navigation for the blind. *Computers & Education*, *55*(3), 970–981. doi:10.1016/j.compedu.2010.04.008

Sánchez, J., Sáenz, M., & Ripoll, M. (2009). Usability of a multimodal videogame to improve navigation skills for blind children. In *Proceeding of the eleventh international ACM SIGACCESS conference on Computers and accessibility - ASSETS '09* (p. 35). New York: ACM Press. 10.1145/1639642.1639651

Sanz, P., & et al. (2014). Scenes and Images into Sounds: A Taxonomy of Image Sonification Methods for Mobility Applications. *Journal of the Audio Engineering Society*, *62*(3), 161–171. doi:10.17743/jaes.2014.0009

Scheggi, S., Talarico, A., & Prattichizzo, D. (2014). A remote guidance system for blind and visually impaired people via vibrotactile haptic feedback. In *22nd Mediterranean Conference on Control and Automation* (pp. 20–23). IEEE. 10.1109/MED.2014.6961320

Schinazi, V. R., Thrash, T., & Chebat, D.-R. (2016). Spatial navigation by congenitally blind individuals. *Wiley Interdisciplinary Reviews: Cognitive Science, 7*(1), 37–58. doi:10.1002/wcs.1375 PMID:26683114

Shinohara, K., & Kristen. (2006). Designing assistive technology for blind users. In *Proceedings of the 8th international ACM SIGACCESS conference on Computers and accessibility - Assets '06* (p. 293). New York: ACM Press. 10.1145/1168987.1169062

Shoval, S., Ulrich, I., & Borenstein, J. (2003). Robotics-based obstacle-avoidance systems for the blind and visually impaired - Navbelt and the guidecane. *IEEE Robotics & Automation Magazine, 10*(1), 9–20. doi:10.1109/MRA.2003.1191706

Sotelo, J., Mehri, S., Kumar, K., Santos, J. F., Kastner, K., Courville, A., & Bengio, Y. (2017). Char-2wav: end-to-end speech synthesis. In *Workshop track - ICLR 2017*. Retrieved from http://josesotelo.com/speechsynthesis

Spinsante, S., Montanini, L., Gambi, E., Lambrinos, L., Pereira, F., Pombo, N., & Garcia, N. (2017). *Smartphones as Multipurpose Intelligent Objects for AAL: Two Case Studies*. Academic Press. doi:10.1007/978-3-319-61949-1_14

Suendermann, D., Höge, H., & Black, A. (2010). Challenges in Speech Synthesis. In *Speech Technology* (pp. 19–32). Boston, MA: Springer US. doi:10.1007/978-0-387-73819-2_2

Thakare, P. U., Shubham, K., Ankit, P., Ajinkya, R., & Om, S. (2017). Smart Assistance System for the Visually Impaired. *International Journal of Scientific and Research Publications, 7*(12), 378. Retrieved from www.ijsrp.org

Torrente, J., Del Blanco, Á., Serrano-Laguna, Á., Ángel Vallejo-Pinto, J., Moreno-Ger, P., & Fernández-Manjón, B. (n.d.). Towards a Low Cost Adaptation of Educational Games for People with Disabilities. *Computer Science and Information Systems, 11*(1), 369–391. doi:10.2298/CSIS121209013T

Turk, M. (2013). Multimodal interaction: A review. *Pattern Recognition Letters*. doi:10.1016/j.patrec.2013.07.003

Van Den Oord, A., Dieleman, S., Zen, H., Simonyan, K., Vinyals, O., Graves, A., … Kavukcuoglu, K. (n.d.). *Wavenet: A generative model for raw audio*. Retrieved from https://arxiv.org/pdf/1609.03499.pdf

Vuilleumier, P. (2005). How brains beware: Neural mechanisms of emotional attention. *Trends in Cognitive Sciences, 9*(12), 585–594. doi:10.1016/j.tics.2005.10.011 PMID:16289871

Vuilleumier, P., & Huang, Y.-M. (2009). Emotional Attention. *Current Directions in Psychological Science, 18*(3), 148–152. doi:10.1111/j.1467-8721.2009.01626.x

Wada, C., Sugimura, Y., Ienaga, T., & Kimuro, Y. (n.d.). Basic Research on the Method of Presenting Distance Information to the Blind by Means of Gait Measurement. *Journal of Medical and Biological Engineering, 31*(4), 283–287. doi:10.5405/jmbe.793

Wang, X., Ling, Z.-H., & Dai, L.-R. (2016). Concept-to-Speech generation with knowledge sharing for acoustic modelling and utterance filtering. *Computer Speech & Language, 38*(C), 46–67. doi:10.1016/j.csl.2015.12.003

Windows_Eyes. (2018). *Window-Eyes - Offer for Users of Microsoft Office*. Retrieved October 25, 2018, from http://www.windoweyesforoffice.com/

Wolff, S., Stiglmayr, C., Bretz, H. J., Lammers, C.-H., & Auckenthaler, A. (2007). Emotion identification and tension in female patients with borderline personality disorder. *British Journal of Clinical Psychology*, *46*(3), 347–360. doi:10.1348/014466507X173736 PMID:17535527

Zeng, L., Weber, G., Simros, M., Conradie, P., Saldien, J., & Ravyse, I., … Mioch, T. (2017). Range-IT. In *Proceedings of the 19th International Conference on Human-Computer Interaction with Mobile Devices and Services - MobileHCI '17* (pp. 1–6). New York: ACM Press. 10.1145/3098279.3125442

Compilation of References

Aal-Yhia, A., Malcolm, P., Zwiggelaar, R., & Tiddeman, B. (2018). Towards parameter free groupwise non-rigid image alignment. In CGVCVIP (pp. 245-252). Madrid, Spain: IADIS.

Aal-Yhia, A., Malcolm, P., Akanyeti, O., Zwiggelaa, R., & Tiddeman, B. (2018). *Groupwise non-rigid image alignment with graph-based initialisation. In Computer Graphics and Visual Computing (CGVC)* (pp. 15–21). The Eurographics Association.

Abbas, Q., Celebi, M. E., & Garcia, I. F. (2011). Hair removal methods: A comparative study for dermoscopy images. *Biomedical Signal Processing and Control*, 6(4), 395–404. doi:10.1016/j.bspc.2011.01.003

Abdul, A., Vermeulen, J., Wang, D., Lim, B. Y., & Kankanhalli, M. (2018). Trends and trajectories for explainable, accountable and intelligible systems: An HCI research agenda. In *Proceedings of the 2018 CHI Conference on Human Factors in Computing Systems - CHI '18* (pp. 1–18). ACM. 10.1145/3173574.3174156

Adams, E. (2009). *Fundamentals of Game Design (2nd ed.). Academic Press.*

Afonso, A. P., Lima, J. R., & Cota, M. P. (2013, June). Usability assessment of web interfaces: User Testing. In Information Systems and Technologies (CISTI) (pp. 1-7). IEEE.

Agarwal, A., & Meyer, A. (2009). Beyond usability: evaluating emotional response as an integral part of the user experience. In *CHI'09 Extended Abstracts on Human Factors in Computing Systems* (pp. 2919–2930). New York, NY: ACM Press. doi:10.1145/1520340.1520420

AGID-Project. (2018). *About the Project*. Retrieved February 18, 2019, from http://agid-project.eu/index.php/en/project/about-the-project

Aguiar, Y. P. C., & Vieira, M. F. Q. (2009). Proposal of a protocol to support product usability evaluation. *Fourth IASTED International Conference Human-Computer Interaction*, 282-289.

Ahmed, M. M. H., Silpasuwanchai, C., Niksirat, K. S., & Ren, X. (2017). Understanding the Role of Human Senses in Interactive Meditation. In *Proceedings of the 2017 CHI Conference on Human Factors in Computing Systems* (pp. 4960-4965). ACM. 10.1145/3025453.3026000

Ahmed, S., Wallace, K. M., & Blessing, L. T. (2003). *Understanding the differences between how novice and experienced designers approach design tasks*. Research in Engineering. doi:10.100700163-002-0023-z

Ahmetovic, D., Gleason, C., Kitani, K. M., Takagi, H., & Asakawa, C. (2016). NavCog. In *Proceedings of the 13th Web for All Conference on - W4A '16* (pp. 1–2). New York: ACM Press. doi:10.1145/2899475.2899509

Akita, J., komatsu, T., Ito, K., Ono, T., & Okamoto, M. (2009). CyARM: Haptic Sensing Device for Spatial Localization on Basis of Exploration by Arms. *Advances in Human-Computer Interaction*, 2009, 1–6. doi:10.1155/2009/901707

Alha, K., Koskinen, E., Paavilainen, J., Hamari, J., & Kinnunen, J. (2014). Free-To-Play Games: Professionals' Perspectives. In Proceedings of Nordic Digra (vol. 2014). Visby.

Allen, C. (2014, July 22). *The Proficiency Ladder. Life With Alacrity.* Retrieved July 22, 2014, from http://www.Life-WithAlacrity.com

Allen, J., Hunnicutt, M. S., Klatt, D. H., Armstrong, R. C., & Pisoni, D. B. (1987). *From text to speech : the MITalk system.* Cambridge University Press. Retrieved from https://dl.acm.org/citation.cfm?id=28587

Alonso, J. M., Castiello, C., & Mencar, C. (2018). A bibliometric analysis of the explainable artificial intelligence research field. In *Information Processing and Management of Uncertainty in Knowledge-Based Systems. Theory and Foundations. IPMU 2018. Communications in Computer and Information Science* (Vol. 853, pp. 3–15). Springer International Publishing. Retrieved from http://link.springer.com/10.1007/978-3-319-91473-2

Al-Taie, M. (2013). Explanations In Recommender Systems: Overview And Research Approaches. *The International Arab Conference on Information Technology (ACIT'2013).*

American Academy of Child and Adolescent Psychiatry. (2011). Children and Video Games: Playing with Violence. *Facts for Families.* Retrieved from http://www.aacap.org/AACAP/Families_and_Youth/Facts_for_Families/Facts_for_Families_Pages/Children_and_Video_Games_Playing_with_Violence_91.aspx

American Psychiatric Association. (2013). *Diagnostic and Statistical Manual of Mental Disorders* (5th ed.). Arlington, VA: American Psychiatric Publishing.

Analayo, V. (2003). *Satipatthana: The direct path to realization.* Cambridge: Windhorse.

Anderson, A. K. (2005). Affective Influences on the Attentional Dynamics Supporting Awareness. *Journal of Experimental Psychology. General, 134*(2), 258–281. doi:10.1037/0096-3445.134.2.258 PMID:15869349

Anderson, L. W. (2001). *A taxonomy for learning, teaching, and assessing: A revision of Bloom's taxonomy of educational objectives, abridged edition.* White Plains, NY: Longman.

Anderson, M. D., Sherman, J. A., Sheldon, J. B., & McAdam, D. (1997). Picture activity schedules and engagement of adults with mental retardation in a group home. *Research in Developmental Disabilities, 18*(4), 231–250. doi:10.1016/S0891-4222(97)00006-1 PMID:9216024

Anderson, N. D., Lau, M. A., Segal, Z. V., & Bishop, S. R. (2007). Mindfulness-based stress reduction and attentional control. *Clinical Psychology & Psychotherapy, 14*(6), 449–463. doi:10.1002/cpp.544

Anderton, B. N., & Ronald, P. C. (2017). Hybrid thematic analysis reveals themes for assessing student understanding of biotechnology. *Journal of Biological Education, 1,* 1–12.

Andrade, P., (2002). Aprender por projectos, formar educadores. *Formação de educadores para o uso da informática na escola.* Valente, J.. Núcleo de Informática Aplicada à Educação – Nied.

Andreoli, V. (2007). *O Mundo Digital.* Lisboa: Editorial Presença.

Anikin, A. (2018). Soundgen: An open-source tool for synthesizing nonverbal vocalizations. *Behavior Research Methods,* 1–15. doi:10.375813428-018-1095-7 PMID:30054898

Antonenko, P., Paas, F., Grabner, R., & Gog, T. V. (2010). Using Electroencephalography to measure cognitive load. *Educational Psychology, 22*(4), 425–438.

Appel, G., Libai, B., Muller, E., & Shachar, R. (2017). *Retention and The Monetization Of Apps.* Retrieved from: http://www.hitechmarkets.net /files/appellibaimullershachar2017.pdf

Apple. (2008). *Apple Classrooms of Tomorrow - Today.* Technical Report. Apple Inc.

Apple. (2012). *Challenge Based Learning: A Classroom Guide.* Technical Report. Apple Inc.

Apple. (n.d.). *Vision Accessibility - Mac - Apple.* Retrieved October 25, 2018, from https://www.apple.com/accessibility/mac/vision/

Arachchi, T. K., Sitbon, L., & Zhang, J. (2017). Enhancing Access to eLearning for People with Intellectual Disability: Integrating Usability with Learning. In *IFIP Conference on Human-Computer Interaction* (pp. 13-32). Cham, Switzerland: Springer. 10.1007/978-3-319-67684-5_2

Arantes, F., Freire, F., Breuer, J., Silva, A., Oliveira, R., & Vascon, L. (2017). Towards a Multisemiotic and Multimodal Editor. *Journal of Computer Science and Technology, 17*(2), 100–109. doi:10.24215/16666038.17.e14

Araújo, I., & Faria, P. (2017). Higher M@T-EduTutor - A prototype of a platform to support tutoring at distance using mobile devices. *10th annual International Conference of Education, Research and Innovation. ICERI2017 Proceedings,* 6048-6055.

Argenziano, G., Soyer, H. P., Chimenti, S., Talamini, R., Corona, R., Sera, F., ... Kopf, A. W. (2003). Dermoscopy of pigmented skin lesions: Results of a consensus meeting via the internet. *Journal of the American Academy of Dermatology, 48*(5), 679–693. doi:10.1067/mjd.2003.281 PMID:12734496

Argenziano, G., Zalaudek, I., Corona, R., Sera, F., Cicale, L., Petrillo, G., ... Soyer, H. P. (2004). Vascular structures in skin tumors: A dermoscopy study. *Archives of Dermatology, 140*(12), 1485–1489. doi:10.1001/archderm.140.12.1485 PMID:15611426

Arik, S., Diamos, G., Gibiansky, A., Miller, J., Peng, K., Ping, W., ... Zhou, Y. (2017). *Deep Voice 2: Multi-Speaker Neural Text-to-Speech.* Retrieved from https://arxiv.org/abs/1705.08947v1

Askelöf, P. (2013). *Monetization Of Social Network Games In Japan And The West* (Master's thesis). Lund University, Sweden.

Astrom, K. (1985). Process control--Past, present and future. *IEEE Control Systems Magazine, 5*(3), 3–10. doi:10.1109/MCS.1985.1104958

Atman, C., Chimka, J., Bursic, K., & Nachtmann, H. (1999). A comparison of freshman and senior engineering design processes. *Design Studies, 20*(2), 131–152. doi:10.1016/S0142-694X(98)00031-3

Atorf, D., Hensler, L., & Kannegieser, E. (2016). Towards a concept on measuring the flow state during gameplay of serious games. In *European conference on games based learning (ecgbl)* (pp. 955–959). Paisley, UK: ECGBL. Retrieved from http://publica.fraunhofer.de/documents/N-438328.html

Attewell, J., Savill-Smith, C., & Douch, R. (2009). *The impact of mobile learning examining what it means for teaching and learning.* London: LSN.

Bach, D. R., Friston, K. J., & Dolan, R. J. (2010). Analytic measures for quantification of arousal from spontaneous skin conductance fluctuations. *International Journal of Psychophysiology, 76*(1), 52–57. doi:10.1016/j.ijpsycho.2010.01.011 PMID:20144665

Bachrach, Y., Graepel, T., Kohli, P., Kosinski, M., & Stillwell, D. (2014). Your digital image: factors behind demographic and psychometric predictions from social network profiles. In *Proceedings of the 2014 international conference on Autonomous agents and multi-agent systems.* International Foundation for Autonomous Agents and Multiagent Systems.

Bailey, D., & Wright, E. (2003). *Practical SCADA for industry.* Burlington, MA: Elsevier.

Bailey, J. E., & Pearson, S. W. (1983). Development of a tool for measuring and analyzing computer user satisfaction. *Management Science*, *29*(5), 530–545. doi:10.1287/mnsc.29.5.530

Baker, S., Matthews, I., & Schneider, J. (2004). Automatic construction of active appearance models as an image coding problem. *IEEE Transactions on Pattern Analysis and Machine Intelligence*, *26*(10), 1380–1384. doi:10.1109/TPAMI.2004.77 PMID:15641725

Baldus, D. C., Pulaski, C., & Woodworth, G. (1983). Comparative review of death sentences: An empirical study of the Georgia experience. *The Journal of Criminal Law & Criminology*, *74*(3), 661–753. doi:10.2307/1143133

Balharová, K., Motschnig, R., Struhár, J., & Hagelkruys, D. (2013). A Case Study of Applying Card- sorting as an Initial Step in the Design of the LITERACY – Portal for People with Dyslexia. In *Proceedings of the Conference Universal Learning Design*. Brno: Masaryk University.

Baloian, N., Breuer, H., Hoeksema, K., Hoppe, U., & Milrad, M. (2004). Implementing the Challenge Based Learning in Classroom Scenarios. In *Proceedings of the Symposium on Advanced Technologies in Education*. Argostoli, GRE.

Banco do Brasil. (2017a). *Banco do Brasil lança plataforma de Open Banking*. Available at: http://www.bb.com.br/pbb/pagina-inicial/imprensa/n/55574/Banco%20do%20Brasil%20lança%20plataforma%20de%20Open%20Banking#

Banco do Brasil. (2017b). *Nossa história*. Available at: http://www.bb.com.br/pbb/pagina-inicial/sobre-nos/nossa-historia#/

Bangor, A., Kortum, P. T., & Miller, J. T. (2008). An empirical evaluation of the system usability scale. Intl. *Journal of Human–Computer Interaction*, *24*(6), 574–594. doi:10.1080/10447310802205776

Bannerman, D. J., Sheldon, J. B., Sherman, J. A., & Harchik, A. E. (1990). Balancing the right to habilitation with the right to personal liberties: The rights of people with developmental disabilities to eat too many doughnuts and take a nap. *Journal of Applied Behavior Analysis*, *23*(1), 79–89. doi:10.1901/jaba.1990.23-79 PMID:2186017

Barley, S. R., Meyerson, D. E., & Grodal, S. (2011). E-mail as a source and symbol of stress. *Organization Science*, *22*(4), 887–906. doi:10.1287/orsc.1100.0573

Barret, F. J., & Fry, R. E. (2005). *Appreciative inquiry: a positive approach to building cooperative capacity*. Chagrin Falls, OH: Academic Press.

Barrett, J., & Kirk, S. (2000). Running focus groups with elderly and disabled elderly participants. *Applied Ergonomics*, *31*(6), 621–629. doi:10.1016/S0003-6870(00)00031-4 PMID:11132046

Basak Bjayanta, J., Sudarshan, A., Trivedi, D., & Santhanam Santh, M. S. (2004). Weather Data Mining Using Independent Component Analysis. *Journal of Machine Learning Research*, *5*, 239–253.

Bates, M. (2012). Super Powers for the Blind and Deaf. *Scientific American*, 1–5. Retrieved from https://www.scientificamerican.com/article/superpowers-for-the-blind-and-deaf/

Battarbee, K., & Koskinen, I. (2005). Co-experience: User experience as interaction. *CoDesign*, *1*(1), 5–18. doi:10.1080/15710880412331289917

Baumann, C., Hamin, H., & Chong, A. (2015). The role of brand exposure and experience on brand recall—Product durables vis-à-vis FMCG. *Journal of Retailing and Consumer Services*, *23*, 21–31. doi:10.1016/j.jretconser.2014.11.003

Bell, L. (2009). *Web Accessibility: Designing for Dyslexia*. Retrieved October 15, 2013, from http://lindseybell.com/documents/bell_dyslexia.pdf

Bem, R. F. S., Alquete, T., & Martins, V. F. (2014). *Proceedings of XIII Brazilian Symposium on Computer Games and Digital Entertainment (SBGames)*. Porto Alegre, Brazil: Academic Press.

Beniger. (2009). *The control revolution: Technological and economic origins of the information society.* Cambridge, MA: Harvard University Press.

Ben, S. (2017). *Designing the user interface: strategies for effective human-computer interaction.* London: Person Education.

Bergomi, C., Tschacher, W., & Kupper, Z. (2014). Construction and first validation of the Comprehensive Inventory of Mindfulness Experiences. *Diagnostica, 60*(3), 111–125. doi:10.1026/0012-1924/a000109

Berlyne, D. E. (1971). *Aesthetics and psychobiology.* New York: Appleton Century Crofts Publishing.

Berseth, M. (2017). *Isic-skin lesion analysis towards melanoma detection.* arXiv preprint arXiv:1703.00523

Bertalmio, M., Sapiro, G., Caselles, V., & Ballester, C. (2000). Image inpainting. In *Proceedings of the 27th annual conference on Computer graphics and interactive techniques* (pp. 417-424). ACM Press/Addison-Wesley Publishing Co.

Bertrand, M., & Mullainathan, S. (2004). Are Emily and Greg more employable than Lakisha and Jamal? A field experiment on labor market discrimination. *The American Economic Review, 94*(4), 991–1013. doi:10.1257/0002828042002561

Bethke, E. (2003). *Game Development and Production.* Wordware Publishing, Inc.

Bevan, N., & Bruval, P. (2003). *Usability net: Tools & methods.* Available: http://www.usabilitynet.org/tools/list.htm

Bhatlawande, S., Sunkari, A., Mahadevappa, M., Mukhopadhyay, J., Biswas, M., Das, D., & Gupta, S. (2014). Electronic Bracelet and Vision-Enabled Waist-Belt for Mobility of Visually Impaired People. *Assistive Technology, 26*(4), 186–195. doi:10.1080/10400435.2014.915896 PMID:25771603

Bialik, M., & Fadel, C. (2015). *Skills for the 21st Century: What Should Students Learn?* Center for Curriculum Redesign.

Bilgic, M., & Mooney, R. J. (2005). Explaining Recommendations: Satisfaction vs. Promotion. *Proceedings of Beyond Personalization 2005: A Workshop on the Next Stage of Recommender Systems Research at The 2005 International Conference on Intelligent User Interfaces,* 13–18. 10.1145/1040830.1040839

Binder, F. V., Nichols, M., Reinehr, S., & Malucelli, A. 2017. Challenge Based Learning Applied to Mobile Software Development Teaching. *IEEE 30th Conference on Software Engineering Education and Training (CSEE&T).* 10.1109/CSEET.2017.19

Bliss, Pobursky, & Howard. (2012). *LDraw.org Standards: File Format 1.0.2.* Available at: www.ldraw.org/

Blum-Dimaya, A., Reeve, S. A., Reeve, K. F., & Hoch, H. (2010). Teaching children with autism to play a video game using activity schedules and game-embedded simultaneous video modelling. *Education & Treatment of Children, 33*(3).

Bo Campbell. (2017). *Tips for Designing Accessibility in Voice User Interfaces.* Retrieved October 25, 2018, from https://uxdesign.cc/tips-for-accessibility-in-conversational-interfaces-8e11c58b31f6

Boeffard, O., Cherbonnel, B., Emerard, F., Larreur, D., Le Saint-Milon, J. L., Métayer, I., … White, S. (1993). *ICASSP-93 : 1993 IEEE International Conference on Acoustics, Speech, and Signal Processing, April 27-30, 1993, Minneapolis Convention Center, Minneapolis, Minnesota. Proceedings of the 1993 IEEE international conference on Acoustics, speech, and signal processing: speech processing - Volume II.* Institute of Electrical and Electronics Engineers. Retrieved from https://dl.acm.org/citation.cfm?id=1946943.1946996

Boettcher, J., Åström, V., Påhlsson, D., Schenström, O., Andersson, G., & Carlbring, P. (2014). Internet-based mindfulness treatment for anxiety disorders: A randomized controlled trial. *Behavior Therapy, 45*(2), 241–253. doi:10.1016/j.beth.2013.11.003 PMID:24491199

Bohonos, S., Lee, A., Malik, A., Thai, C., & Manduchi, R. (2007). Universal real-time navigational assistance (URNA). In *Proceedings of the 1st ACM SIGMOBILE international workshop on Systems and networking support for healthcare and assisted living environments - HealthNet '07* (p. 83). New York: ACM Press. 10.1145/1248054.1248080

Bonnardel, N. (2000). Towards understanding and supporting creativity in design: Analogies in a constrained cognitive environment. *Knowledge-Based Systems, 13*(7–8).

Bookstein, F. L. (1989). Principal warps: Thin-plate splines and the decomposition of deformations. *IEEE Transactions on Pattern Analysis and Machine Intelligence, 11*(6), 567–585. doi:10.1109/34.24792

Boot, W. R., Kramer, A. F., Simons, D. J., Fabiani, M., & Gratton, G. (2008). The effects of video game playing on attention, memory, and executive control. *Acta Psychologica, 129*(3), 387–398. doi:10.1016/j.actpsy.2008.09.005 PMID:18929349

Borges, J. A. S. (2009). Tecnopolicy and the regulation of competition between blind with computer and computer unassisted sighted people in taking exams to get into Brazilian universities. *Society for Social Studies of Leuthold Science Annual Meeting, 2009, Washington. 4S'2009 Annual Meeting, 2009.*

Bourguet, M.-L. (2003). Designing and Prototyping Multimodal Commands. In *INTERACT'03* (pp. 717–720). Retrieved from http://citeseerx.ist.psu.edu/viewdoc/download?doi=10.1.1.98.1958&rep=rep1&type=pdf

Box, G. E., Hunter, W. G., & Hunter, J. S. (1978). *Statistics for experimenters.* Academic Press.

Bradesco. (2017). *Nossa história.* Available at: https://banco.bradesco/html/exclusive/sobre/nossa-historia.shtm

Brand, J. E., & Todhunter, S. (2016). *Digital Australia 2016.* Eveleigh: IGEA.

Brasil. (2016). *Pesquisa brasileira de mídia.* Available at: http://www.secom.gov.br/atuacao/pesquisa/lista-de-pesquisas-quantitativas-e-qualitativas-de-contratos-atuais/pesquisa-brasileira-de-midia-pbm-2016.pdf/view

Braun, V., & Clarke, V. (2006). Using thematic analysis in psychology. *Qualitative Research in Psychology, 3*(2), 77–101. doi:10.1191/1478088706qp063oa

Braun, V., & Clarke, V. (2013). *Successful qualitative research: A practical guide for beginners.* London: Sage.

Brewer, B. (2007). Citizen or customer? Complaints handling in the public sector. *International Review of Administrative Sciences, 73*(4), 549–556. doi:10.1177/0020852307083457

Bri, D., Garcia, M., Coll, H., & Lloret, J. (2009). A study of virtual learning environments. *WSEAS Transactions on Advances in Engineering Education, 6*(1), 33–43.

Bridger, R. S. (1995). *Introduction to ergonomics.* London, UK: Taylor and Francis Group. doi:10.4324/9780203426135

British Dyslexia Association. (2016). *Dyslexia Friendly Style Guide.* Retrieved February 17, 2019, from http://www.bdadyslexia.org.uk/common/ckeditor/filemanager/userfiles/About_Us/policies/Dyslexia_Style_Guide.pdf

British Dyslexia Association. (2019). *Dyslexia Research Information.* Retrieved February 20, 2019, from http://www.bdadyslexia.org.uk/about-dyslexia/further-information/dyslexia-research-information-.html

Brooke, J. (1986). SUS: a "quick and dirty" usability scale. In *Usability Evaluation in Industry.* London: Taylor and Francis.

Brookings, J. B., Wilson, G. F., & Swain, C. R. (1996). Psychophysiological responses to changes in workload during simulated air traffic control. *Biological Psychology, 42*(3), 361–377. doi:10.1016/0301-0511(95)05167-8 PMID:8652753

Brown, K. W., Ryan, R. M., & Creswell, J. D. (2007). Mindfulness: Theoretical foundations and evidence for its salutary effects. *Psychological Inquiry, 18*(4), 211–237. doi:10.1080/10478400701598298

Buchanan, R. (1992). Wicked problems in design thinking. *Design Issues*, *8*(2), 5–21. doi:10.2307/1511637

Buchenau, M., & Suri, J. F. (2000, August). Experience prototyping. In *Proceedings of the 3rd conference on Designing interactive systems: processes, practices, methods, and techniques* (pp. 424-433). ACM. 10.1145/347642.347802

Buddhaghosa, B. (1976). *Vissuddhimagga [The Path of Purification]* (C. O. Boulder, Trans.). Seattle, WA: Shambala.

Burg, J. M., & Wolf, O. T. (2012). Mindfulness as self-regulated attention. *Swiss Journal of Psychology*, *71*(3), 135–139. doi:10.1024/1421-0185/a000080

Burt, J. L., Bartolome, D. S., Burdette, D. W., & Comstock, J. R. Jr. (2007). A psychophysiological evaluation of the perceived urgency of auditory warning signals. *Ergonomics*, *38*(11), 2327–2340. doi:10.1080/00140139508925271 PMID:7498191

Bushman, B. (2013). Video games can spark aggression. *New York Daily News*. Retrieved from http://www.nydailynews.com/opinion/video-games-spark-aggression-article-1.1293112

Butler, J. M., Kline, M. C., & Coble, M. D. (2018). NIST interlaboratory studies involving DNA mixtures (MIX05 and MIX13): Variation observed and lessons learned. *Forensic Science International. Genetics*, *37*(April), 81–94. doi:10.1016/j.fsigen.2018.07.024 PMID:30103146

Butz, M. R., Bowling, J. B., & Bliss, C. A. (2000). Psychotherapy with the mentally retarded: A review of the literature and the implications. *Professional Psychology, Research and Practice*, *31*(1), 42–47. doi:10.1037/0735-7028.31.1.42

Buxton, B. (2007). *Sketching User Experiences – Getting the Design right and the Right Design*. Morgan Kaufmann.

Buzan, T., & Buzan, B. (2006). *The Mind Map Book*. New York: BBC Active.

Caballero, L., Moreno, A. M., & Seffah, A. (2014). Persona as a Tool to Involving Human in Agile Methods: Contributions from HCI and Marketing. In Human-Centered Software Engineering (pp. 283–290). Springer Berlin Heidelberg.

Cação, R., & Dias, P. (2003). *Introdução ao e-learning. Sociedade Portuguesa de Inovação*. S. A. 1a Edição.

Cagan, M. (2018). *Inspired: how to create tech products customers love*. Hoboken, NJ: Wiley.

Cahn, B. R., & Polich, J. (2006). Meditation states and traits: EEG, ERP, and neuroimaging studies. *Psychological Bulletin*, *132*(2), 180–211. doi:10.1037/0033-2909.132.2.180 PMID:16536641

Cain, B. (2007). A review of the mental workload literature. Toronto, Canada: Defence Research and Development, NATO RTO Report.

Cairns, P., Cox, A., Berthouze, N., Jennett, C., & Dhoparee, S. (2006). Quantifying the experience of immersion in games. Cognitive Science of Games and Gameplay workshop at Cognitive Science.

Calde, S., Goodwin, K., & Reimann, R. (2002). SHS Orcas: the first integrated information system for long-term healthcare facility management. In Case studies of the CHI2002|AIGA Experience Design FORUM on - CHI '02 (pp. 2–16). AIGA. doi:10.1145/507752.507753

Cáliz, D., Martínez, L., & Cáliz, R. (2017). Helping people with down syndrome through a usability testing guide proposal for mobile applications. *International Journal of Computer Science Engineering and Information Technology*, *7*(2), 1–19.

Campisi, J., Bynog, P., McGehee, H., Oakland, J. C., Quirk, S., Taga, C., & Taylor, M. (2012). Facebook, Stress, and Incidence of Upper Respiratory Infection in Undergraduate College Students. *Cyberpsychology, Behavior, and Social Networking*, *15*(12), 675–681. doi:10.1089/cyber.2012.0156 PMID:23020744

Campolo, A., Sanfilippo, M., Whittaker, M., & Crawford, K. (2017). AI Now 2017 Report. *AI Now*. Retrieved from https://ainowinstitute.org/AI_Now_2017_Report.pdf

Canny, J. (1987). A computational approach to edge detection. In *Readings in Computer Vision* (pp. 184–203). Elsevier.

Cardoso, E., Pimenta, & Pereira, D. (2008). Adopção de Plataformas de e-Learning nas Instituiões de Ensino Superior - modelo do processo. *Revista de Estudos Politécnicos*, *6*(9).

Cardoso, C., & Badke-Schaub, P. (2011). The Influence of Different Pictorial Representations During Idea Generation. *The Journal of Creative Behavior*, *45*(2), 130–146. doi:10.1002/j.2162-6057.2011.tb01092.x

Carroll, J. M. (2003). *HCI models, theories, and frameworks: Toward a multidisciplinary science*. Morgan Kaufmann.

Caton, S., & Chapman, M. (2016). The use of social media and people with intellectual disability:A systematic review and thematic analysis. *Journal of Intellectual & Developmental Disability*, *41*(2), 1–15. doi:10.3109/13668250.2016.1153052

Celebi, M. E., Iyatomi, H., & Schaefer, G. (2009). Contrast enhancement in dermoscopy images by maximizing a histogram bimodality measure. In *Image Processing (ICIP), 2009 16th IEEE International Conference on* (pp. 2601-2604). IEEE. 10.1109/ICIP.2009.5413990

Celebi, M. E., Mendonca, T., & Marques, J. S. (2015). *Dermoscopy image analysis* (Vol. 10). CRC Press. doi:10.1201/b19107

CGI. (2016). *Cresce a proporção de empresas brasileiras que utilizam conexões à internet mais velozes, aponta Cetic. br.* Available at: http://cetic.br/noticia/cresce-a-proporcao-de-empresas-brasileiras-que-utilizam-conexoes-a-internet-mais-velozes-aponta-cetic- br/

Chamberlin, B., Trespalacios, J., & Gallagher, R. (2012). The learning games design model: Immersion, collaboration, and outcomes-driven development. *International Journal of Game-Based Learning*, *2*(3), 87–110. doi:10.4018/ijgbl.2012070106

Chambers, R., Gullone, E., & Allen, N. B. (2009). Mindful emotion regulation: An integrative review. *Clinical Psychology Review*, *29*(6), 560–572. doi:10.1016/j.cpr.2009.06.005 PMID:19632752

Chang, S. H., Chih, W. H., Liou, D. K., & Hwang, L. R. (2014). The influence of web aesthetics on customers' PAD. *Computers in Human Behavior*, *36*, 168–178. doi:10.1016/j.chb.2014.03.050

Chang, Y.-M., Lin, C.-Y., & Lee, Y.-K. (2005). The preferences of young children for images used in dynamic graphical interfaces in computer-assisted English vocabulary learning. *Displays*, *26*(4-5), 147–152. doi:10.1016/j.displa.2005.06.002

Chan, T. F., & Shen, J. (2001). Nontexture inpainting by curvature-driven diffusions. *Journal of Visual Communication and Image Representation*, *12*(4), 436–449. doi:10.1006/jvci.2001.0487

Chassy, P., Lindell, T. A., Jones, J. A., & Paramei, G. V. (2015). A relationship between visual complexity and aesthetic appraisal of car front images: An eye-tracker study. *Perception*, *44*(8-9), 1085–1097. doi:10.1177/0301006615596882 PMID:26562922

Cheng, M.-T., She, H.-C., & Annetta, L. (2015). Game immersion experience: Its hierarchical structure and impact on game-based science learning. *Journal of Computer Assisted Learning*, *31*(3), 232–253. doi:10.1111/jcal.12066

Chen, L., & Pu, P. (2012). Critiquing-based recommenders: Survey and emerging trends. *User Modeling and User-Adapted Interaction*, *22*(1–2), 125–150. doi:10.100711257-011-9108-6

Cheong, P. H. (2010). Faith Tweets: Ambient Religious Communication and Microblogging Rituals. M/C Journal, 13(2).

Chiavenato, I. (2008). *Recursos humanos: o capital humano nas organizações.* São Paulo, Brazil: Atlas.

Chisholm, J. D., Hickey, C., Theeuwes, J., & Kingstone, A. (2010). Reduced attentional capture in action video game players. *Attention, Perception & Psychophysics, 72*(3), 667–671. doi:10.3758/APP.72.3.667 PMID:20348573

Chittaro, L., & Vianello, A. (2014). Computer-supported mindfulness: Evaluation of a mobile thought distancing application on naive meditators. *International Journal of Human-Computer Studies, 72*(3), 337–348. doi:10.1016/j.ijhcs.2013.11.001

Chouldechova, A. (2017). Fair prediction with disparate impact: A study of bias in recidivism prediction instruments. *Big Data, 5*(2), 153–163. doi:10.1089/big.2016.0047 PMID:28632438

Christensen, L. L., Fraynt, R. J., Neece, L. C., & Baker, B. L. (2012). Bullying Adolescents With Intellectual Disability. *Journal of Mental Health Research in Intellectual Disabilities, 5*(1), 49–65. doi:10.1080/19315864.2011.637660

Chua, C. K., Leong, K. F., & Lim, C. S. (2003). Rapid Prototyping (2nd ed.). World Scientific. doi:10.1142/5064

Collins, S. E., Chawla, N., Hsu, S. H., Grow, J., Otto, J. M., & Marlatt, G. A. (2009). Language-based measures of mindfulness: Initial validity and clinical utility. *Psychology of Addictive Behaviors, 23*(4), 743–749. doi:10.1037/a0017579 PMID:20025383

Computerworld. (2017). *ContaAzul conclui integração de sua plataforma com o Banco do Brasil.* Available at: http://computerworld.com.br/contaazul-conclui-integracao-de-sua-plataforma-com-o-banco-do-brasil

Connolly, T. M., Boyle, E. A., MacArthur, E., Hainey, T., & Boyle, J. M. (2012). A systematic literature review of empirical evidence on computer games and serious games. *Computers & Education, 59*(2), 661–686. doi:10.1016/j.compedu.2012.03.004

ContaAzul. (2017). *Sobre a empresa.* Available at: https://contaazul.com/sobre/

Cook, D. A., Beckman, T. J., Thomas, K. G., & Thompson, W. G. (2009). Measuring motivational characteristics of courses: Applying Keller's Instructional Materials Motivation Survey to a web-based course. *Academic Medicine, 84*(11), 1505–1509. doi:10.1097/ACM.0b013e3181baf56d PMID:19858805

Coolican, H. (2004). *Research methods and statistics in psychology.* Hodder and Stoughton.

Cooper, A. (1999). *The Inmates Are Running the Asylum: Why High-Tech Products Drive Us Crazy and How to Restore the Sanity.* Sams Publishing.

Cootes, T. F., Edwards, G. J., & Taylor, C. J. (2001). Active appearance models. *IEEE Transactions on Pattern Analysis and Machine Intelligence, 23*(6), 681–685. doi:10.1109/34.927467

Cootes, T., Marsland, S., Twining, C., & Smith, K. (2004). Groupwise diffeomorphic non-rigid registration for automatic model building. In *European conference on computer vision* (pp. 316–327). Springer. 10.1007/978-3-540-24673-2_26

Cootes, T., Twining, C., Petrovic, V., Babalola, K., & Taylor, C. (2010, November). Computing Accurate Correspondences across Groups of Images. *IEEE Transactions on Pattern Analysis and Machine Intelligence, 32*(11), 1994–2005. doi:10.1109/TPAMI.2009.193 PMID:20847389

Cootes, T., Twining, C., Petrovic, V., Schestowitz, R., & Taylor, C. (2005). Groupwise Construction of Appearance Models using Piece-wise Affine Deformations. *Proceedings of 16th British Machine Vision Conference (BMVC), 5,* pp. 879-888. 10.5244/C.19.88

Cootes, T., Twining, C., & Taylor, C. (2004). Diffeomorphic statistical shape models. *15th British Machine Vision Conference, 1,* pp. 447–456.

Corry, M. D., Frick, T. W., & Hansen, L. (1997). User-centered design and usability testing of a web site: An illustrative case study. *Educational Technology Research and Development, 45*(4), 65–76. doi:10.1007/BF02299683

Courage, C., & Baxter, K. (2005). *Understanding Your Users: A Practical Guide to User Requirements Methods, Tools, and Techniques.* San Francisco, CA: Morgan Kaufmann Publishers.

Coury, B., & Pietras, C. (1989). Alphanumeric and graphic displays for dynamic process monitoring and control. *Ergonomics, 32*(11), 1373–1389. doi:10.1080/00140138908966912 PMID:28080931

Craig, A. (2013). Chapter 1 - What is augmented reality? In Understanding Augmented Reality. Morgan Kaufmann.

Crawford, C. (1982). The Art of Computer Game Design. Vancouver, Canada: Academic Press.

Cristinacce, D., & Cootes, T. (2008). Facial motion analysis using clustered shortest path tree registration. *The 1st International Workshop on Machine Learning for Vision-based Motion Analysis.*

Cross, N. (2001). Design Cognition. In Design Knowing and Learning: Cognition in Design Education (pp. 79–103). Academic Press. doi:10.1016/B978-008043868-9/50005-X

Csikszentmihalyi, M. (1996). *Flow: Creativity and the psychology of discovery and invention.* Academic Press.

Csikszentmihalyi, I. S. (1992). *Optimal experience: Psychological studies of flow in consciousness.* Cambridge, UK: Cambridge University Press.

Csikszentmihalyi, M. (1991). *Flow: The psychology of optimal experience.* New York, NY: Harper Perennial. Retrieved from http://www.amazon.com/gp/product/0060920432/ref=si3_rdr_bb _product/104-4616565-4570345

Culén, A. L., & Karpova, A. (2014). Designing with Vulnerable Children: A Researcher's Perspective. In P. Isaías & K. Blashki (Eds.), *Human-Computer Interfaces and Interactivity: Emergent Research and Applications* (pp. 118–136). Hershey, PA: IGI Global. doi:10.4018/978-1-4666-6228-5.ch007

Dahiya, A., & Kumar, J. (2018a). Do Design Outcomes Get Influenced by Type of User Data? An Experimental Study with Primary and Secondary User Research Data. In *International Conference on Human Systems Engineering and Design: Future Trends and Applications* (pp. 191-197). Springer.

Dahiya, A., & Kumar, J. (2018b). How empathizing with persona helps in design thinking: An experimental study with novice designers. *12th International Conference on Interfaces and Human Computer Interaction.*

Dakopoulos, D., & Bourbakis, N. G. (2010). Wearable Obstacle Avoidance Electronic Travel Aids for Blind: A Survey. *IEEE Transactions on Systems, Man and Cybernetics. Part C, Applications and Reviews, 40*(1), 25–35. doi:10.1109/TSMCC.2009.2021255

Dalai Lama. (2003). *Stages of meditation: Training the mind for wisdom.* London: Penguin Random House.

Dastin, J. (2018, October 9). Amazon scraps secret AI recruiting tool that showed bias against women. *Reuters.* Retrieved from https://www.reuters.com/article/us-amazon-com-jobs-automation-insight/amazon-scraps-secret-ai-recruiting-tool-that-showed-bias-against-women-idUSKCN1MK08G

David, A., & Glore, P. (2010). *The impact of design and aesthetics on usability, credibility, and learning in an online environment.* Retrieved from http://www.westga.edu/~distance/ojdla/winter134/david_glore134.html

Davidovici-nora, M. (2014). Paid And Free Digital Business Models Innovations In The Video Game Industry. Digiworld Economic Journal, 94, 83.

Davidson, D. (Ed.). (2009). Well Played 1.0: video games, value and meaning. Lulu.com.

Davies, R., Cootes, T., & Taylor, C. (2001). A minimum description length approach to statistical shape modelling. In *Biennial International Conference on Information Processing in Medical Imaging* (pp. 50-63). Springer. 10.1007/3-540-45729-1_5

Davies, R., Twining, C., Cootes, T., Waterton, J., & Taylor, C. (2002). A minimum description length approach to statistical shape modelling. *IEEE Transactions on Medical Imaging, 21*(5), 525–537. doi:10.1109/TMI.2002.1009388 PMID:12071623

Davies, R., Twining, C., & Taylor, C. (2008). Groupwise surface correspondence by optimization: Representation and regularization. *Medical Image Analysis, 12*(6), 787–796. doi:10.1016/j.media.2008.03.009 PMID:18511333

Davis, F. D. (1989). Perceived usefulness, perceived ease of use, and user acceptance of information technology. *Management Information Systems Quarterly, 13*(3), 319. doi:10.2307/249008

De Freitas, S., & Neumann, T. (2009). The use of 'exploratory learning' for supporting immersive learning in virtual environments. *Computers & Education, 52*(2), 343–352. doi:10.1016/j.compedu.2008.09.010

De Freitas, S., & Oliver, M. (2006). How can exploratory learning with games and simulations within the curriculum be most effectively evaluated? *Computers & Education, 46*(3), 249–264. doi:10.1016/j.compedu.2005.11.007

De Freitas, S., & Routledge, H. (2013). Designing leadership and soft skills in educational games: The e-leadership and soft skills educational games design model (ELESS). *British Journal of Educational Technology, 44*(6), 951–968. doi:10.1111/bjet.12034

de Sepibus, G. (1678). *Romani collegii Societatis Jesu musaeum celeberrimum.* Amsterdam: Janssonius van Waesberge.

Deane, P. (1965). *The first industrial revolution.* Cambridge, UK: Cambridge University Press.

Deaney, R., Ruthven, K., & Hennessy, S. (2003). Pupil perspectives on the contribution of ICT to teaching and learning in the secondary school. *Research Papers in Education, 18*(2), 141–165. doi:10.1080/0267152032000081913

Deci, E., & Ryan, R. (1985). *Intrinsic motivation and self-determination in human behavior.* Academic Press.

Deeb, S. S., & Motulsky, A. (2015). Red-green color vision defects. In GeneReviews®. Seattle, WA: University of Washington.

Deng, J., Dong, W., Socher, R., Li, L. J., Li, K., & Fei-Fei, L. (2009, June). ImageNet: A large-scale hierarchical image database. In *Computer Vision and Pattern Recognition, 2009. CVPR 2009. IEEE Conference on* (pp. 248-255). IEEE. 10.1109/CVPR.2009.5206848

Derm101.com. (2017). Retrieved from https://www.derm101.com

Dermatology information system. (2017). Retrieved from https://www.dermis.net/dermisroot/en/home/indexp.htm

Deubel, P. (2003). An investigation of behaviorist and cognitive approaches to instructional multimedia design. *Journal of Educational Multimedia and Hypermedia, 12*(1), 63–90.

Dhall, P., Sharma, P., Thakur, S., Agarwal, R., & Rastogi, S. (n.d.). *A review paper on assitive shoes: cane for visually impaired people.* Retrieved from http://www.ijsrms.com

Dias, A., Martins, A. I., Queirós, A., & da Rocha, N. P. (2018). Interoperability in Pervasive Health: Is It Tackled as a Priority? In HEALTHINF (pp. 57-65). Academic Press.

Didden, R., Scholte, R. H., Korzilius, H., De Moor, J. M., Vermeulen, A., O'Reilly, M., & Lancioni, G. E. (2009). Cyberbullying among students with intellectual and developmental disability in special education settings. *Developmental Neurorehabilitation, 12*(3), 146–151. doi:10.1080/17518420902971356 PMID:19466622

Diepgen, T. L., & Eysenbach, G. (1998). Digital images in dermatology and the dermatology online atlas on the World Wide Web. *The Journal of Dermatology, 25*(12), 782–787. doi:10.1111/j.1346-8138.1998.tb02505.x PMID:9990769

Dietrich, D., Lang, R., Bruckner, D., Fodor, G., & Muller, B. (2010). Limitations, possibilities and implications of Brain-Computer Interfaces. In *3rd International Conference on Human System Interaction* (pp. 722–726). IEEE. 10.1109/HSI.2010.5514488

Dim, N. K., & Ren, X. (2014). Designing Motion Gesture Interfaces in Mobile Phones for Blind People. *Journal of Computer Science and Technology, 29*(5), 812–824. doi:10.100711390-014-1470-5

DIS. (2009). 9241-210: 2010. Ergonomics of human system interaction-Part 210: Human-centred design for interactive systems. International Standardization Organization (ISO).

Domenciano, J., & Junior, R. (2017). Como as tecnologias móveis têm sido utilizadas na educação? Estudo em duas instituições de ensino superior brasileiras. *InFor, Inov. Form., Rev. NEaD-Unesp, 3*(1), 49-68.

Dominowski, R. L., & Dallob, P. (1995). Insight and Problem Solving. In R. Sternberg & J. Davidson (Eds.), *The nature of insight* (pp. 33–62). Cambridge, MA: MIT Press.

Donovan, M. S., Bransford, J. D., & Pellegrino, J. W. (1999). How people learn. Academic Press.

Dormann, C., & Biddle, R. (2008), November. Understanding game design for affective learning. In *Proceedings of the 2008 Conference on Future Play: Research, Play, Share* (pp. 41-48). ACM.

Doyle, J. (2009). *Using focus groups as a research method in intellectual disability research: A practical guide.* The National Federation of Voluntary Bodies Providing Services to People with Intellectual Disabilities. Retrieved from http://www.fedvol.ie/_fileupload/ Research/focus 20groups20a20practical20guide.pdf

Drori, I., Cohen-Or, D., & Yeshurun, H. (2003). Fragment-based image completion. In ACM Transactions on graphics (TOG) (pp. 303-312). ACM. doi:10.1145/1201775.882267

Dudley, H. (1940). The Vocoder—Electrical Re-Creation of Speech&lt!--<xref ref-type="other" rid="fn1-10.5594_J10096">*</xref>--&gt. *Journal of the Society of Motion Picture Engineers, 34*(3), 272–278. doi:10.5594/J10096

Dumas, J. S., & Redish, J. (1999). *A practical guide to usability testing.* Portland, OR: Intellect Books.

Dutoit, T., & Leich, H. (1993). *MBR-PSOLA: Text-To-Speech synthesis re-synthesis of the segments database. Speech Communication* (Vol. 13). Retrieved from https://ac.els-cdn.com/016763939390042J/1-s2.0-016763939390042J-main.pdf?_tid=bdb55144-ecb2-4952-bf4c-20ac4a65beb9&acdnat=1540464083_c90c34a2b4096715a3cbeb108795639c

Dye, M. W., Green, C. S., & Bavelier, D. (2009). Increasing speed of processing with action video games. *Current Directions in Psychological Science, 18*(6), 321–326. doi:10.1111/j.1467-8721.2009.01660.x PMID:20485453

Dyslexia International. (2014). *Duke Report.* Retrieved February 18, 2019, from https://www.dyslexia-international.org/wp-content/uploads/2016/04/DI-Duke-Report-final-4-29-14.pdf

Echonet Consortium. (2018) *ECHONET Lite Overview.* Retrieved form https://echonet.jp/english/

Edelson, D. C. (2001). Learning-for-use: A framework for the design of technology-supported inquiry activities. *Journal of Research in Science Teaching, 38*(3), 355–385. doi:10.1002/1098-2736(200103)38:3<355::AID-TEA1010>3.0.CO;2-M

Edwards, L., & Veale, M. (2017). Slave to the algorithm? Why a "right to an explanation" is probably not the remedy you are looking for. *Duke Law and Technology Review, 16*(1), 18–84. doi:10.2139srn.2972855

Elmuti, D., & Kathawala, Y. (1997). *An Overview of Benchmarking Process: a tool for continuous improvement and competitive advantage.* Lumpkin College of Business And Applied Sciences.

Encyclopaedia Britannica. (2013). Retrieved from http://global.britannica.com/EBchecked/topic/459096/Jean-Piaget

Erdem, R. (2017). Students with Special Educational Needs and Assistive Technologies: A Literature Review. *TOJET: The Turkish Online Journal of Educational Technology, 16.* Retrieved from http://link.springer.com

Erkol, B., Moss, R. H., Joe Stanley, R., Stoecker, W. V., & Hvatum, E. (2005). Automatic lesion boundary detection in dermoscopy images using gradient vector of snakes. *Skin Research and Technology, 11*(1), 17–26. doi:10.1111/j.1600-0846.2005.00092.x PMID:15691255

Ermi, L., & Mäyrä, F. (2005). *Fundamental components of the gameplay experience: Analysing immersion.* Academic Press.

Espinoza, M., Sánchez, J., & de Borba Campos, M. (2014). *Videogaming Interaction for Mental Model Construction in Learners Who Are Blind.* Cham: Springer. doi:10.1007/978-3-319-07440-5_48

Ess, C. M. (2004). *Critical Thinking and the Bible in the Age of New Media.* Lanham, MD: University Press of America.

European Dyslexia Association. (2014). *Dyslexia in Europe.* Retrieved February 18, 2019, from https://www.eda-info.eu/dyslexia-in-europe

Eyal, N. (2013). The App of God. *The Atlantic.* Retrieved from http://www.theatlantic.com/technology/archive/2013/07/the-app-of-god/278006/

Ezzeldin A. Bashir, M., Gyu Lee, D., Akasha, M., Yi, G., Jong Cha, E., Bae, J.-W., . . . Ryu, K. (2010). *Highlighting the current issues with pride suggestions for improving the performance of real time cardiac health monitoring.* Academic Press.

Falconer, C. J., Slater, M., Rovira, A., King, J. A., Gilbert, P., Antley, A., & Brewin, C. R. (2014). Embodying Compassion: A Virtual Reality Paradigm for Overcoming Excessive Self-Criticism. *PLoS One, 9*(11), e111933. doi:10.1371/journal.pone.0111933 PMID:25389766

Fattah, S. (2015). The Effectiveness of Using WhatsApp Messenger as one of Mobile Learning Techniques to develop students' writing skills. *Journal of Education and Practice, 6*(32).

Fedoce, R. & Squirra, S. (2011). The technology and the mobile's communication potential in education. *LOGOS 35 Mediações sonoras, 18*(2).

Ferguson, C. J. (2015). Does Media Violence Predict Societal Violence? It Depends on What You Look at and When. *Journal of Communication, 65*(1), 1–22. doi:10.1111/jcom.12129

Fernández-López, Á., Rodríguez-Fórtiz, M. J., Rodríguez-Almendros, M. L., & Martínez-Segura, M. J. (2013). Mobile learning technology based on iOS devices to support students with special education needs. *Computers & Education, 61*, 77–90. doi:10.1016/j.compedu.2012.09.014

Ferreira, S. B. L., da Silveira, D. S., Capra, E. P., & Ferreira, A. O. (2012). Protocols for evaluation of site accessibility with the participation of blind users. *Procedia Computer Science, 14*, 47–55. doi:10.1016/j.procs.2012.10.006

Ferreira, S. B. L., Nunes, R. R., & da Silveira, D. S. (2012). Aligning Usability Requirements with the Accessibility Guidelines Focusing on the Visually-Impaired. *Procedia Computer Science, 14*, 263–273. doi:10.1016/j.procs.2012.10.030

Ferris, L. K., & Harris, R. J. (2012). New diagnostic aids for melanoma. *Dermatologic Clinics*, *30*(3), 535–545. doi:10.1016/j.det.2012.04.012 PMID:22800557

FGNET. (2004). *Face and gesture network: talking face dataset*. Retrieved from http://www-prima.inrialpes.fr/FGnet/data/01-TalkingFace/talking_face.html

Field, A. P. (2000). *Discovering statistics using SPSS for Windows: Advanced techniques for the beginner*. Sage Publications.

Fields, T., & Cotton, B. (2012). *Social Gamer Design: Monetization Methods And Mechanics*. Elsevier.

Fildes, J., Robbins, A., Cave, L., Perrens, B., & Wearring, A. (2014). *Mission Australia's 2014 Youth Survey Report*. Sydney: Mission Australia.

Findlater, L., & McGrenere, J. (2010). Beyond performance: Feature awareness in personalized interfaces. *International Journal of Human-Computer Studies*, *68*(3), 121–137. doi:10.1016/j.ijhcs.2009.10.002

Finkelde, J., & Finkelde, F. (2016). *Grow a healthy church*. Retrieved from https://www.growahealthychurch.com/7-reasons-why-churches-stop-growing-and-decline-into-impotence/

Fischer, B., & Modersitzki, J. (2008). Ill-posed medicine—an introduction to image registration. *Inverse Problems*, 1–16.

Fowler, M. (2017). *A nova metodologia*. Available at: https://medium.com/desenvolvimento-agil/a-nova-metodologia-69b8f8a379c7

Francis, G. (2000). Designing multifunction displays: An optimization approach. *International Journal of Cognitive Ergonomics*, *4*(2), 107–124. doi:10.1207/S15327566IJCE0402_2

Frewen, P. A., Evans, E. M., Maraj, N., Dozois, D. J., & Partridge, K. (2008). Letting go: Mindfulness and negative automatic thinking. *Cognitive Therapy and Research*, *32*(6), 758–774. doi:10.100710608-007-9142-1

Fu, F.-L., Su, R.-C., & Yu, S.-C. (2009). Egameflow: A scale to measure learners' enjoyment of e-learning games. *Computers & Education*, *52*(1), 101–112. doi:10.1016/j.compedu.2008.07.004

Fullerton, T. (2008). *Game Design Workshop: a Playcentric Approach to Creating Innovative Games* (2nd ed.). Morgan Kaufmann Publishers.

Gabriel, S. E. (2014). A modified challenge-based learning approach in a capstone course to improve student satisfaction and engagement. *Journal of Microbiology & Biology Education*, *15*(2), 316–318.

Gackenbach, J. (2008). Video game play and consciousness development: A transpersonal perspective. *Journal of Transpersonal Psychology*, *40*(1), 60–87.

Gackenbach, J., & Bown, J. (2011). Mindfulness and video game play: A preliminary inquiry. *Mindfulness*, *2*(2), 114–122. doi:10.100712671-011-0049-2

Gahlawat, M., Malik, A., & Bansal, P. (2014). Natural speech synthesizer for blind persons using hybrid approach. *Procedia Computer Science*, *41*, 83–88. doi:10.1016/j.procs.2014.11.088

Gala, P. (2017). *100 anos de PIB no Brasil*. Available at: https://www.paulogala.com.br/100-anos-de-pib-no-brasil/

Garcia Ramirez, A. R., Fonseca, R., Da Silva, L., Cinelli, M. J., Durán, A., & De Albornoz, C. (n.d.). Evaluation of Electronic Haptic Device for Blind and Visually Impaired People: A Case Study. *Journal of Medical and Biological Engineering*, *32*(6), 423–428. doi:10.5405/jmbe.925

Garrett, J. J. (2010). *The elements of user experience*. New York: New Riders.

Gasparini, A. (2015). Perspective and use of empathy in design thinking. In *The Eight International Conference on Advances in Computer-Human Interactions* (pp. 49-54). ACHI.

Gaver, B. (2011). Prayer Companion 2010, Interaction Design Studio, Goldsmith, University of London. In Talk to Me: Design and Communication between People and Objects. New York: The Museum of Modern Art.

Gedikli, F., Jannach, D., & Ge, M. (2014). How should i explain? A comparison of different explanation types for recommender systems. *International Journal of Human-Computer Studies*, 72(4), 367–382. doi:10.1016/j.ijhcs.2013.12.007

Gee, J. P. (2003). What video games have to teach us about learning and literacy. *Computers in Entertainment*, 1(1), 20–20. doi:10.1145/950566.950595

Gehling, M. (2016). Game Genesis Virtual Deck: uma ferramenta para criar ideias de jogos. *Proceedings of XV Brazilian Symposium on Computer Games and Digital Entertainment (SBGames)*.

Geissler, G. L., Zinkhan, M. Z., & Watson, R. T. (2006). The influence of home page complexity on consumer attention, attitudes, and purchase intent. *Journal of Advertising*, 35(2), 69–80. doi:10.1080/00913367.2006.10639232

Georgiou, Y., & Kyza, E. A. (2017). The development and validation of the ari questionnaire. *International Journal of Human-Computer Studies*, 98(100), 24–37. doi:10.1016/j.ijhcs.2016.09.014

Gestwicki, P., & Mcnely, B. (2012). A case study of a five-step design thinking process in educational museum game design. Proceedings of Meaningful Play.

Gethin, R. (1998). *The foundations of Buddhism*. Oxford, UK: Oxford University Press.

Gibbs, S. (2017, August 23). The future of funerals? Robot priest launched to undercut human-led rites. *The Guardian*.

Gill, C. J., Kewman, D. G., & Brannon, R. W. (2003). Transforming psychological practice and society: Policies that reflect the new paradigm. *The American Psychologist*, 58(4), 305–312. doi:10.1037/0003-066X.58.4.305 PMID:12866397

Gill, P., Stewart, K., Treasure, E., & Chadwick, B. (2008). Methods of data collection in qualitative research: Interviews and focus groups. *British Dental Journal*, 204(6), 291–295. doi:10.1038/bdj.2008.192 PMID:18356873

Gilpin, R. (2008). The use of Theravāda Buddhist practices and perspectives in mindfulness-based cognitive therapy. *Contemporary Buddhism*, 9(2), 227–251. doi:10.1080/14639940802556560

Giudice, N. A., & Legge, G. E. (2008). Blind Navigation and the Role of Technology. In *The Engineering Handbook of Smart Technology for Aging, Disability, and Independence* (pp. 479–500). Hoboken, NJ: John Wiley & Sons, Inc. doi:10.1002/9780470379424.ch25

Glushko, R. J. (2008). Designing a Service Science Discipline with Discipline. *IBM Systems Journal*, 47(1), 15–38. doi:10.1147j.471.0015

Goel, V., & Pirolli, P. (1992). The structure of design problem spaces. *Cognitive Science*, 16(3), 395–429. doi:10.120715516709cog1603_3

Goldschmidt, G. (1990). Linkography: assessing design productivity. In R. Trappl (Ed.), *Cyberbetics and System '90* (pp. 291–298). Singapore: World Scientific.

Gonzalez, J. J. (2013). My Journey With Inquiry-Based Learning. *Journal on Excellence in College Teaching*, 24(2).

Goodfellow, I., Bengio, Y., & Courville, A. (2016). *Deep Learning*. MIT Press. Retrieved from https://www.deeplearningbook.org/

Gope, D. (2011). Hand gesture interaction with human computer. *Global Journal of Computer Science and Technology*, *11*(23), 1–11.

Gorecky, D., Schmitt, M., Loskyll, M., & Zühlke, D. (2014). Human machine interaction in Industry 4.0 era. In *12th IEEE International Conference on industrial informatics* (pp. 289-294). Porto Alegre, Brazil: IEEE. 10.1109/INDIN.2014.6945523

Gorman, C. R. (2009). *Religion on demand: Faith-based design. Design and Culture, 1(1),* 9–22.

Gravenhorst, F., Muaremi, A., Tröster, G., Arnrich, B., & Grünerbl, A. (2013). *Towards a mobile galvanic skin response measurement system for mentally disordered patients.* Academic Press.

Gray, D., Brown, S., & Macanufo, J. (2010). *Gamestorming. A Playbook for Innovators, Rulebreakers, and Changemakers.* O'Reilly Media.

Greeno, J. G., Collins, A. M., & Resnick, L. B. (1996). Cognition and learning. Handbook of Educational Psychology, 77, 15-46.

Greenwood. (1997). *The third industrial revolution: technology, productivity, and income inequality.* Washington, DC: American Enterprise Institute.

Groff, J., Clarke-Midura, J., Owen, V. E., Rosenheck, L., Beall, M. (2015). *Better learning in games: A balanced design lens for a new generation of learning games.* Academic Press.

Grossman, P. (2015). Mindfulness: Awareness Informed by an Embodied Ethic. *Mindfulness, 6*(1), 17–22. doi:10.100712671-014-0372-5

Grudin, J. (2006). Why personas work: The psychological evidence. *The Persona Lifecycle*, 642-663.

Guidotti, R., Monreale, A., Ruggieri, S., Turini, F., Giannotti, F., & Pedreschi, D. (2018). A survey of methods for explaining black box models. *ACM Computing Surveys*, *51*(5), 1–42. doi:10.1145/3236009

Gungor, V., Sachine, D., & Kocak, T. (2011). Smart grid technologies: communication technologies and standards. *IEEE Transaction of Industrial Informatic, 7*(4), 529-539.

Gunter, G. A., Kenny, R. F., & Vick, E. H. (2008). Taking educational games seriously: Using the RETAIN model to design endogenous fantasy into standalone educational games. *Educational Technology Research and Development*, *56*(5-6), 511–537. doi:10.100711423-007-9073-2

Gupta, A., Fox, D., Curless, B., & Cohen, M. (2012). Duplotrack: a realtime system for authoring and guiding duplo model assembly. In *Proceedings of the 25th Annual ACM Symposium Adjunct on User Interface Software and Technology.* ACM.

Gurgel, I., Arcoverde, R. L., Almeida, E. W., Sultanum, N. B., & Tedesco, P. A. (2006). A importância de avaliar a usabilidade dos jogos: a experiência do Virtual Team. *Proceedings of V Brazilian Symposium on Computer Games and Digital Entertainment (SBGames).*

Gutman, D., Codella, N. C., Celebi, E., Helba, B., Marchetti, M., Mishra, N., & Halpern, A. (2016). *Skin lesion analysis toward melanoma detection: A challenge at the international symposium on biomedical imaging (ISBI) 2016, hosted by the international skin imaging collaboration (ISIC).* arXiv preprint arXiv:1605.01397

Hacker, P., & Wiedemann, E. (2017). *A continuous framework for fairness.* Retrieved from http://arxiv.org/abs/1712.07924

Haeghen, Y. V., Naeyaert, J. M. A. D., Lemahieu, I., & Philips, W. (2000). An imaging system with calibrated color image acquisition for use in dermatology. *IEEE Transactions on Medical Imaging, 19*(7), 722–730. doi:10.1109/42.875195 PMID:11055787

Hagemann, T. (2017). Digitalisierung und technische Assistenz im Sozial- und Gesundheitswesen. In *Gestaltung des Sozial- und Gesundheitswesens im Zeitalter von Digitalisierung und technischer Assistenz* (pp. 9–18). Baden-Baden, Germany: Nomos Verlag. doi:10.5771/9783845279435-9

Hair, J. F., Anderson, R. E., Tatham, R. L., & Black, W. C. (1995). *Multivariate data analysis with readings*. Prentice-Hall Press.

Hallam, S., Price, J., & Katsarou, G. (2002). The Effects of Background Music on Primary School Pupils' Task Performance. *Educational Studies*, *28*(2), 111–122. doi:10.1080/03055690220124551

Hanington, B., & Martin, B. (2012). *Universal methods of design: 100 ways to research complex problems, develop innovative ideas, and design effective solutions*. Rockport Publishers.

Han, J., Kim, Y., Rhie, Y., & Choi, H. (2015). Design optimization of control layout for naval MFC (multifunction console) using a modified layout analysis method. In *Proceeding of the human factor and ergonomics society 59th annual meeting* (pp. 1351-1355). SAGE Publications.

Hansen, E. G., Mislevy, R. J., Steinberg, L. S., Lee, M. J., & Forer, D. C. (2005). Accessibility of tests for individuals with disabilities within a validity framework. *System*, *33*(1), 107–133. doi:10.1016/j.system.2004.11.002

Harkey, E. (2011). Accessible Pedestrian Signals: A Guide to Best Practices (Workshop Edition 2010). Washington, DC: Transportation Research Board. doi:10.17226/22902

Harp, S., & Mayer, R. (1997). The role of internet in learning from scientific text and illustrations: On the distinction between emotional interest and cognitive interest. *Journal of Educational Psychology*, *89*(1), 92–102. doi:10.1037/0022-0663.89.1.92

Hart, W. (2011). *The art of living: Vipassana meditation: As taught by SN Goenka*. Onalaska: Pariyatti.

Hartmann, J., Sutcliffe, A., & De Angeli, A. (2007). Investigating attractiveness in web user interfaces. In *Proceedings of the SIGCHI conference on Human Factors in Computing Systems* (pp. 387-396). New York, NY: ACM Press. 10.1145/1240624.1240687

Hart, S. G., & Staveland, L. E. (1988). Development of NASA-TLX (Task Load Index): Results of Empirical and Theoretical Research. *Advances in Psychology*, *52*, 139–183. doi:10.1016/S0166-4115(08)62386-9

Hart, T. A., Chaparro, B. S., & Halcomb, C. G. (2008). Evaluating websites for older adults: Adherence to 'senior-friendly' guidelines and end-user performance. *Behaviour & Information Technology*, *27*(3), 191–199. doi:10.1080/01449290600802031

Hasan, B. (2016). Perceived irritation in online shopping: The impact of website design characteristics. *Computers in Human Behavior*, *54*, 224–230. doi:10.1016/j.chb.2015.07.056

Hassenzahl, M. (2008). Aesthetics in interactive products: Correlates and consequences of beauty. In H. N. J. Schifferstein & P. Hekkert (Eds.), *Product experience* (pp. 287–302). San Diego, CA: Elsevier. doi:10.1016/B978-008045089-6.50014-9

Heber, R. (1961). *A manual on terminology and classification on mental retardation* (Rev. ed.). Washington, DC: American Association on Mental Deficiency.

Heiman, T., & Olenik-Shemesh, D. (2015). Cyberbullying experience and gender differences among adolescents in different educational settings. *Journal of Learning Disabilities*, *48*(2), 146–155. doi:10.1177/0022219413492855 PMID:23784784

He, K., Zhang, X., Ren, S., & Sun, J. (2016). Deep residual learning for image recognition. In *Proceedings of the IEEE conference on computer vision and pattern recognition* (pp. 770-778). IEEE.

Helal, A., Moore, S. E., & Ramachandran, B. (n.d.). Drishti: an integrated navigation system for visually impaired and disabled. In *Proceedings Fifth International Symposium on Wearable Computers* (pp. 149–156). IEEE Comput. Soc. 10.1109/ISWC.2001.962119

Hemmi, A., Bayne, S., & Land, R. (2009). The appropriation and repurposing of social technologies in higher education. *Journal of Assisted Learning, 25*(Special Issues), 19–30. doi:10.1111/j.1365-2729.2008.00306.x

Henke, N. (2017). Dieser enorm gruselige Roboter-Priester segnet dich – und verfolgt dich bis in deine Träume. *Gallileo TV*. Retrieved from https://www.galileo.tv/tech-trends/dieser-enorm-gruselige-roboter-priester-segnet-dich-und-verfolgt-dich-bis-in-deine-traeume/

Herlocker, J. L., Konstan, J. A., & Riedl, J. (2000). Explaining collaborative filtering recommendations. *Proceedings of the 2000 ACM conference on Computer supported cooperative work - CSCW '00.* 10.1145/358916.358995

Hernandez, R. M. (2017). Impacto de las TIC en la educación: Retos y Perspectivas. *Propósitos y Representaciones, 5*(1), 325–347. doi:10.20511/pyr2017.v5n1.149

Hersh, M. A., Farcy, R., Leroux, R., & Jucha, A. (2006). Electronic Travel Aids and Electronic Orientation Aids for blind people: technical, rehabilitation and everyday life points of view. *CVHI 2006: Conference on Assistive Tecnology for Vision and Hearing Impairment.* Retrieved from http://citeseerx.ist.psu.edu/viewdoc/summary?doi=10.1.1.112.8880

Hevner, A. R., March, S. T., Park, J., & Ram, S. (2004). *Design science in information systems research. MIS Quarterly, 28(1),* 75–105.

Hidenori, K., Ken-ichiro, N., Toshihiro, M., & Yasushi, S. (2014). Automatic Generating System for Reports on Energy Conservation Tips Based on Electricity Demand Data. *IEEJ Transactions on Electronics Information Systems, 134*(9), 1394–1405.

Hidi, S. (1990). Interest and its contribution as a mental resource for learning. *Review of Educational Research, 60*(4), 549–571. doi:10.3102/00346543060004549

Highcharts Overview . (2018). Retrieved from https://www.highcharts.com

Hinckley, K., & Sinclair, M. (1999). Touch-sensing input devices. In *CHI '99 Proceedings of the SIGCHI Conference on Human Factors in Computing Systems* (pp. 223-230). ACM.

Hinckley, K., & Sinclair, M. (1999). Touch-sensing input devices. In *Proceedings of the SIGCHI conference on Human factors in computing systems the CHI is the limit - CHI '99* (pp. 223–230). New York: ACM Press. 10.1145/302979.303045

Hjarvard, S. (2008). The mediatization of religion: A theory of the media as agents of religious change. *Northern Lights, 6*(1), 9–26. doi:10.1386/nl.6.1.9_1

Hoaglin, D. C., Mosteller, F., & Tukey, J. W. (Eds.). (2009). *Fundamentals of exploratory analysis of variance* (Vol. 367). John Wiley & Sons.

Hoang, V.-N., Nguyen, T.-H., Le, T.-L., Tran, T.-H., Vuong, T.-P., & Vuillerme, N. (2017). Obstacle detection and warning system for visually impaired people based on electrode matrix and mobile Kinect. *Vietnam Journal of Computer Science, 4*(2), 71–83. doi:10.100740595-016-0075-z

Hoffmann, E. (1994). Optimum layout of an array of controls. *International Journal of Industrial Ergonomics, 14*(3), 251–261. doi:10.1016/0169-8141(94)90101-5

Hoffmann, R., Spagnol, S., Kristjánsson, Á., & Unnthorsson, R. (2018). Evaluation of an Audio-haptic Sensory Substitution Device for Enhancing Spatial Awareness for the Visually Impaired. *Optometry and Vision Science*, *95*(9), 757–765. doi:10.1097/OPX.0000000000001284 PMID:30153241

Holman, G., Carnahan, B., & Bulfin, R. (2003). Using linear programming to optimize control panel design from an ergonomics perspective. In *Proceedings of the human factors and ergonomics society annual meeting* (Vol. 47, issue 10, pp. 1317-1321). Los Angeles, CA: SAGE Publication.

Hong, S. M. (2009). User Research and User Centered Design; Designing, Developing, and Commercializing Widget Service on Mobile Handset. In Human Centered Design (pp. 854–861). Academic Press.

Hope, C. (2012). *Volunteer Duty Psychology Testing*. Retrieved from https://www.flickr.com/photos/tim_uk/8135755109/

Hou, L., Xiangyu, W., Leonhard, B., & Love, P. (2015). *Using animated augmented reality to cognitively guide assembly* (Master's thesis). Curtin University of Technology, Bentley, Australia.

Howarth, J., Smith-Jacksonb, T., & Hartsona, R. (2009). Supporting novice usability practitioners with usability engineering tools.Int. *J. Human-Computer Studies.*, *67*(6), 533–540. doi:10.1016/j.ijhcs.2009.02.003

Huang, H.-C., Hsieh, C.-T., & Yeh, C.-H. (2015). An Indoor Obstacle Detection System Using Depth Information and Region Growth. *Sensors (Basel)*, *15*(10), 27116–27141. doi:10.3390151027116 PMID:26512674

Huang, W.-H., Huang, W.-Y., Diefes-Dux, H., & Imbrie, P. K. (2006). A preliminary validation of Attention, Relevance, Confidence and Satisfaction model-based Instructional Material Motivational Survey in a computer-based tutorial setting. *British Journal of Educational Technology*, *37*(2), 243–259. doi:10.1111/j.1467-8535.2005.00582.x

Hulten, G. (2018). *Building Intelligent Systems: A Guide to Machine Learning Engineering* (1st ed.). Apress. doi:10.1007/978-1-4842-3432-7

Hunicke, R., Leblanc, M., & Zubek, R. (2004). MDA: A Formal Approach to Game Design and Game Research. In *Proc. AAAI workshop on Challenges in Game*. AAAI Press.

Hunicke, R., LeBlanc, M., & Zubek, R. (2004). MDA: A Formal Approach to Game Design and Game Research. *Proceedings of the AAAI Workshop on Challenges in Game AI*.

Hutchings, T. (2014). *Now the Bible is an app: digital media and changing patterns of religious authority. In Religion, Media, and Social Change* (pp. 151–169). Oxford, UK: Routledge.

Ickes, W. J. (Ed.). (1997). *Empathic accuracy*. Guilford Press.

IDEO. (2015). *The field guide to human-centered design*. San Francisco: IDEO.org / Design Kit. Retrieved February 18, 2019, from https://www.ideo.com/post/design-kit

IJsselsteijn, W. A., de Kort, Y. A. W., & Poels, K. (2013). *The Game Experience Questionnaire*. Eindhoven: Technische Universiteit Eindhoven.

Ingold, D., & Soper, S. (2016, April 21). Amazon doesn't consider the race of its customers. Should it? *Bloomberg*. Retrieved from https://www.bloomberg.com/graphics/2016-amazon-same-day/

Ismail, I., Mohammed Idrus, R. & Mohd Johari, S. (2010). Acceptance on Mobile Learning via SMS: A Rasch Model Analysis. *iJIM - International Journal of Interactive Mobile Technologies*, *4*, 10-16.

ISO 9241 (2010). Ergonomics of human-system interaction – Part 210: Human-centered design for interactive systems.

ISO 9241-171 (2008). Ergonomics of human-system interaction: Guidance on software accessibility, London, UK. Part 171.

Jackson, S. (2016). Flowing with mindfulness. In I. Ivtzan & T. Lomas (Eds.), *Mindfulness in positive psychology: The science of meditation and wellbeing.* Abingdon, UK: Routledge.

Jacob, N. (1993). *Usability Engineering.* San Diego, CA: Academic Press.

Jenkins, J. (2017). The (holy) ghost in the machine: Catholic thinkers tackle the ethics of artificial intelligence. *Religion News Service.* Retrieved from https://religionnews.com/2018/05/22/the-holy-ghost-in-the-machine-catholic-thinkers-tackle-the-ethics-of-artificial-intelligence/

Jennett, C., Cox, A. L., Cairns, P., Dhoparee, S., Epps, A., Tijs, T., & Walton, A. (2008). Measuring and defining the experience of immersion in games. *International Journal of Human-Computer Studies, 66*(9), 641–661. doi:10.1016/j.ijhcs.2008.04.004

Jen-Yi, L., Krishnasamy, M., & Der-Thanq, C. (2015). Research with persons with intellectual disabilities: An inclusive adaptation of Tourangeau's model. *ALTER-European Journal of Disability Research/Revue Européenne de Recherche sur le Handicap, 9*(4), 304-316.

Jewell, D. (2016). *Game-Design Thinking in Education and Beyond.* Available in: http://www.pearsoned.com/education-blog/game-design-thinking-in-education-and-beyond/

Jimenéz, S. (2013). *Gamification Model Canvas.* Available in: http://www.gameonlab.com/canvas/

Jimoyiannis, A., & Komis, V. (2007). Examinig teacher's beliefs about ICT in education of a teacher preparation programme. *Teacher Development, 11*(2), 149–173. doi:10.1080/13664530701414779

Johnson, J. F., Bagdasarov, Z., Connelly, S., Harkrider, L., Devenport, L. D., Mumford, M. D., & Thiel, C. E. (2012). Case-Based Ethics Education: The Impact of Cause Complexity and Outcome Favorability on Ethicality. *Journal of Empirical Research on Human Research Ethics; JERHRE, 7*(3), 63–77. doi:10.1525/jer.2012.7.3.63 PMID:22850144

Johnson, L., Smith, R., Smythe, J., & Varon, R. (2008). *Challenge based learning: An approach for our time.* Austin, TX: The New Media Consortium.

Johr, R. H. (2002). Dermoscopy: Alternative melanocytic algorithms the ABCD rule of dermatoscopy, Menzies scoring method, and 7-point checklist. *Clinics in Dermatology, 20*(3), 240–247. doi:10.1016/S0738-081X(02)00236-5 PMID:12074859

Jokinen, J. P. (2015). Emotional user experience: Traits, events, and states☆. *International Journal of Human-Computer Studies, 76,* 67–77. doi:10.1016/j.ijhcs.2014.12.006

Jolley, R. P., Zhi, Z., & Thomas, G. V. (1998). How focus of interest in pictures changes with age: A cross-cultural comparison. *International Journal of Behavioral Development, 22*(1), 127–149. doi:10.1080/016502598384540

Jo, M., & Han, J. (2006). Metaphor and Typeface Based on Children's Sensibilities for e-Learning. *International Journal of Information Processing Systems, 2*(3), 178–182. doi:10.3745/JIPS.2006.2.3.178

Jonassen, D. H. (1999). Designing Constructivist Learning Environments. In Instructional-Design Theories and Models: A New Paradigm of Instructional Theory. Lawrence Erlbaum Associates.

Jones, M. J., & Poggio, T. (1998). Multidimensional morphable models. In *Sixth International Conference on Computer Vision* (pp. 683–688). IEEE. 10.1109/ICCV.1998.710791

Junemann, M. (2012). *Object detection and recognition with Microsoft Kinect* (B.S. Thesis). Freie Universitat Berlin, Germany.

Jung, E., Park, S., & Chang, S. (1995). A CSP technique based interactive control panel layout. *Journal of Economics, 38*(9), 1884–1893.

Junker, M., Hoch, R., & Dengel, A. (1999). On the evaluation of document analysis components by recall, precision, and accuracy. In *Proceedings of the Fifth International Conference on Document Analysis and Recognition. ICDAR '99 (Cat. No.PR00318)* (pp. 713–716). IEEE. 10.1109/ICDAR.1999.791887

Kabat-Zinn, J. (1994). *Wherever you go, there you are: Mindfulness meditation in everyday life.* New York: Hyperion.

Kalbach, J. (2017). *Mapeamento de experiências: um guia para criar valor por meio de jornadas, blueprints e diagramas.* Rio de Janeiro, Brazil: Alta Books.

Kalpidou, M., Costin, D., & Morris, J. (2011). The relationship between Facebook and the well-being of undergraduate college students. *Cyberpsychology, Behavior, and Social Networking, 14*(4), 183–189. doi:10.1089/cyber.2010.0061 PMID:21192765

Kamesh, D. B. K., Nazma, S., Sastry, J. K. R., & Venkateswarlu, S. (2016). Camera based Text to Speech Conversion, Obstacle and Currency Detection for Blind Persons. *Indian Journal of Science and Technology, 9*(30). doi:10.17485/ijst/2016/v9i30/98716

Kammoun, S., Macé, J.-M. M., Oriola, B., & Jouffrais, C. (2011). *LNCS 6949 - Toward a Better Guidance in Wearable Electronic Orientation Aids.* Retrieved from https://www.irit.fr/~Marc.Mace/pdfs/kammoun_s_11_624.pdf

Kämpfe, J., Sedlmeier, P., & Renkewitz, F. (2011). The impact of background music on adult listeners: A meta-analysis. *Psychology of Music, 39*(4), 424–448. doi:10.1177/0305735610376261

Kane, S. K., Jayant, C., Wobbrock, J. O., & Ladner, R. E. (2009). Freedom to roam. In *Proceeding of the eleventh international ACM SIGACCESS conference on Computers and accessibility - ASSETS '09* (p. 115). New York: ACM Press. 10.1145/1639642.1639663

Kane, S. K., Wobbrock, J. O., & Ladner, R. E. (2011). Usable gestures for blind people. In *Proceedings of the 2011 annual conference on Human factors in computing systems - CHI '11* (p. 413). New York: ACM Press. 10.1145/1978942.1979001

Kang, Y., Gruber, J., & Gray, J. R. (2013). Mindfulness and De-Automatization. *Emotion Review, 5*(2), 192–201. doi:10.1177/1754073912451629

Kaniel, O. (2012). *Events Tracking Technology.* U.S. Patent application n. 13/649,402, 11 out. 2012.

Kanuka, H., & Anderson, T. (1999). Using constructivism in technology mediated learning: constructing order out of the chaos in the literature. International Journal of Radical Pedagogy, 1(2), 34-46.

Kaplan, S., Kaplan, R., & Wendt, S. (1972). Rated preference and complexity for natural and urban visual material. *Perception & Psychophysics, 12*(4), 354–356. doi:10.3758/BF03207221

Kapperman, G., Koster, E., & Burman, R. (n.d.). *The Study of Foreign Languages by Students Who Are Blind Using the JAWS Screen Reader and a Refreshable Braille Display.* Retrieved from https://files.eric.ed.gov/fulltext/EJ1182385.pdf

Karam, M., & Schraefel, M. C. (n.d.). *A taxonomy of Gestures in Human Computer Interaction.* Retrieved from https://eprints.soton.ac.uk/261149/1/GestureTaxonomyJuly21.pdf

Kartiko, I., Kavakli, M., & Cheng, K. (2010). Learning science in a virtual reality application: The impacts of animated-virtual actors' visual complexity. *Computers & Education, 55*(2), 881–891. doi:10.1016/j.compedu.2010.03.019

Kastner, M., & Crowder, R. (1990). Perception of the Major/Minor Distinction: IV. Emotional Connotations in Young Children. *Music Perception, 8*(2), 189–201. doi:10.2307/40285496

Kath.net. (2013). *Originell: Weltweit erster Automat für Rosenkränze*. Retrieved from http://www.kath.net/news/41705

Katkoff, M. (2012b). *Mid-Core Success Part 2: Retention*. Retrieved from: https://www.deconstructoroffun.com/blog//2013/10/mid-core-success-part-2-retention.html

KatkoffM. (2012a). *From Players To Payers*. Retrieved from: https://www.deconstructoroffun.com/blog//2012/05/from-players-to-payers-4-steps-to.html

Kavakli, M., & Gero, J. (2001). The Structure of concurrent cognitive actions: A case study of novice and expert designers. *Design Studies*.

Kay, R. (2006). Evaluatting strategies user to incorporate technology into preservice education: A review of the literature. *Journal of Research on Technology in Education, 38*(4), 383. doi:10.1080/15391523.2006.10782466

Keisuke, T., Shinsuke, M., & Masahide, N. (2013). Towards Personalization of Home Electricity Peak Shaving Application, The Institute of Electronics, Information and Communication Engineers. *Technical Report of Icicle, 112*(458), 1–6. (in Japanese)

Keith, C. (2010). *Agile Game Development with Scrum*. Boston: Addison-Wesley.

Keller, J. M. (1983). Motivational design of instruction. In C. M. Reigeluth (Ed.), *Instructional design theories and models: an overview of their current status* (pp. 386–434). Hillsdale, NJ: Lawrence Erlbaum Associates.

Keller, J. M. (2010). *Motivational design for learning and performance: The ARCS model approach*. Boston, MA: Springer US. doi:10.1007/978-1-4419-1250-3

Kembel, G. (n.d.). *Awakening creativity*. Available in: http://fora.tv/2009/08/14/George_Kembel_Awakening_Creativity

Kennedy, H., Evans, S., & Thomas, S. (2010). Can the web be made accessible for people with intellectual disabilities? *The Information Society, 27*(1), 29–39. doi:10.1080/01972243.2011.534365

Khalil, H. (2016). *Engineering Viral Growth* (Master's thesis). Aalto University, Finland.

Khuong, B., Kiyokawa, K., Miller, A., La Viola, J.J., Mashita, T. and Takemura, H. (2014). The effectiveness of an ar-based context-aware assembly support system in object assembly. *Proc. of 2014 IEEE Virtual Reality (VR)*, 57–62.

Kiili, K., De Freitas, S., Arnab, S., & Lainema, T. (2012). The design principles for flow experience in educational games. *Procedia Computer Science, 15*, 78–91. doi:10.1016/j.procs.2012.10.060

Kim, J. Y., Chien, T. Y., Liao, S., & York, D. (2011). The Messenger. 2010. In Talk to Me: Design and Communication between People and Objects. New York: The Museum of Modern Art.

Kim, E., & Kim, K. (2015). Cognitive styles in design problem solving: Insights from network-based cognitive maps. *Design Studies*, 40.

King, E. (2002). Clockwork Prayer: A Sixteenth-Century Mechanical Monk. Blackbird. *An Online Journal of Literature and the Arts, 1*(1), 1–29.

Kircher, A. (1646). *Ars magna lucis et umbrae in decem libros digesta: Quibus admirandae lucis et umbrae in mundo, atque adeò universa natura, vires effectus[que] uti nova, ita varia novorum reconditiorum[que] speciminum exhibitione, ad varios mortalium usus, panduntur*. Roma: Scheus.

Kiritchenko, S., & Mohammad, S. M. (2018). *Examining Gender and Race Bias in Two Hundred Sentiment Analysis Systems*. Retrieved from http://arxiv.org/abs/1805.04508

Kison, M. (2007). *Ticker Cross, European Media Art Festival, Osnabrueck, Germany.* Retrieved from http://www.markuskison.de/

Kiyota, M. (1978). *Mahayana Buddhist Meditation. Theory and Practice.* Hawaii University Press.

Kizilcec, R. F. (2016). How much information?: Effects of transparency on trust in an algorithmic interface. *Proceedings of the 2016 CHI Conference on Human Factors in Computing Systems - CHI '16*, 2390–2395. 10.1145/2858036.2858402

Klee, S. H., & Garfinkel, B. D. (1983). The computerized continuous performance task: A new measure of inattention. *Journal of Abnormal Child Psychology*, *11*(4), 487–495. doi:10.1007/BF00917077 PMID:6689172

Kniffin, K. M., Yan, J., Wansink, B., & Schulze, W. D. (2017). The sound of cooperation: Musical influences on cooperative behavior. *Journal of Organizational Behavior*, *38*(3), 372–390. doi:10.1002/job.2128 PMID:28344386

Knoll, A., Wang, Y., Chen, F., Xu, J., Ruiz, N., Epps, J., & Zarjam, P. (2011). Measuring cognitive workload with low-cost electroencephalograph. In P. Campos, N. Graham, J. Jorge, N. Nunes, P. Palanque, & M. Winckler (Eds.), Lecture Notes in Computer Science: Vol. 6949. *Human-Computer Interaction – INTERACT 2011*. Berlin: Springer. doi:10.1007/978-3-642-23768-3_84

Kontagent. (2011). *The Top 7 Metrics Of High Successful Social Companies.* Retrieved from: http://static.kontagent.com/whitepaper/knt_wp_top7metrics_p3_finalx.pdf

Köppen, E., & Meinel, C. (2015). Empathy via design thinking: creation of sense and knowledge. In *Design thinking research* (pp. 15–28). Cham: Springer.

Koskinen, I., Battarbee, K., & Mattelmäki, T. (2003). *Empathic design: User experience in product design.* IT Press.

Kosunen, I., Salminen, M., Järvelä, S., Ruonala, A., Ravaja, N., & Jacucci, G. (2016). RelaWorld: Neuroadaptive and Immersive Virtual Reality Meditation System. In *Proceedings of the 21st International Conference on Intelligent User Interfaces* (pp. 208-217): ACM. 10.1145/2856767.2856796

Kouprie, M., & Visser, F. S. (2009). A framework for empathy in design: Stepping into and out of the user's life. *Journal of Engineering Design*, *20*(5), 437–448. doi:10.1080/09544820902875033

Kowalik, R., & Kwasniewski, S. (2004). *Navigator – A Talking GPS Receiver for the Blind.* Berlin: Springer; doi:10.1007/978-3-540-27817-7_65

Kowalski, R. M., Giumetti, G. W., Schroeder, A. N., & Lattanner, M. R. (2014). Bullying in the digital age: A critical review and meta-analysis of cyberbullying research among youth. *Psychological Bulletin*, *140*(4), 1073–1137. doi:10.1037/a0035618 PMID:24512111

Kowalski, R. M., Morgan, C. A., Drake-Lavelle, K., & Allison, B. (2016). Cyberbullying among college students with disabilities. *Computers in Human Behavior*, *57*, 416–427. doi:10.1016/j.chb.2015.12.044

Krapp, A., Schiefele, U., & Schreyer, I. (2009). *Metaanalyse des Zusammenhangs von Interesse und schulischer Leistung. postprint.* Institut für Philosophie.

Kristiansen, P., & Rasmussen, R. (2014). Building a Better Business Using the Lego Serious Play Method. John Wiley & Son.

Krizhevsky, A., Sutskever, I., & Hinton, G. E. (2012). ImageNet classification with deep convolutional neural networks. In Advances in neural information processing systems (pp. 1097-1105). Academic Press.

Kroon, D. J., & Slump, C. H. (2009). MRI modalitiy transformation in demon registration. In *IEEE International Symposium on Biomedical Imaging: From Nano to Macro*, (pp. 963-966). Boston: IEEE.

Kudesia, R. S., & Nyima, V. T. (2015). Mindfulness Contextualized: An Integration of Buddhist and Neuropsychological Approaches to Cognition. *Mindfulness*, *6*(4), 910–925. doi:10.100712671-014-0337-8

Kumar, L. S., Jamatia, B., Aggarwal, A. K., & Kannan, S. (2011). Mobile Device Intervention for Student Support Services in Distance Education Context - FRAME Model Perspective. *European Journal of Open, Distance and E-Learning*.

Kumar, K., Champaty, B., Uvanesh, K., Chachan, R., Pal, K., & Anis, A. (2014). Development of an ultrasonic cane as a navigation aid for the blind people. In *2014 International Conference on Control, Instrumentation, Communication and Computational Technologies (ICCICCT)* (pp. 475–479). IEEE. 10.1109/ICCICCT.2014.6993009

Kumar, N., & Kumar, J. (2016). Measurement of Cognitive Load in HCI Systems Using EEG Power Spectrum: An Experimental Study. *Procedia Computer Science*, *84*, 70–78. doi:10.1016/j.procs.2016.04.068

Kuo, C. Y., & Wang, L. T. (2015). The study of visual preferences on illustrations in the "Nature and Life Technology" textbook for 3rd and 4th grade elementary school. [in Chinese]. *The Journal of Aesthetics & Visual Arts*, *7*, 141–158.

Kuusisto, M. (2014). *Evaluating Free-To-Play Monetization Mechanics In Mobile Games: Case: Improvement Proposal To Supersonic-Game* (Bachelor's thesis). Tampere University of Applied Sciences, Finland.

Lahav, O., & Mioduser, D. (2008). Construction of cognitive maps of unknown spaces using a multi-sensory virtual environment for people who are blind. *Computers in Human Behavior*, *24*(3), 1139–1155. doi:10.1016/j.chb.2007.04.003

Lahav, O., & Mioduser, D. (2008). Haptic-feedback support for cognitive mapping of unknown spaces by people who are blind. *International Journal of Human-Computer Studies*, *66*(1), 23–35. doi:10.1016/j.ijhcs.2007.08.001

Laird, P. (1983). *Mental models: towards a cognitive science of language, inference, and consciousness*. Cambridge, MA: Harvard University Press.

Landauer, T. K. (1988). Research Methods in Human-Computer Interaction. In Handbook of Human-Computer Interaction (pp. 905–928). Elsevier. doi:10.1016/B978-0-444-70536-5.50047-6

Lányi, C. S. (2009). Multimedia Software Interface Design for Special-Needs Users. In M. Khosrow-Pour (Ed.), *Encyclopedia of Information Science and Technology* (2nd ed.; pp. 2761–2766). doi:10.4018/978-1-60566-026-4.ch440

Lappalainen, P., Granlund, A., Siltanen, S., Ahonen, S., Vitikainen, M., Tolvanen, A., & Lappalainen, R. (2014). ACT Internet-based vs face-to-face? A randomized controlled trial of two ways to deliver Acceptance and Commitment Therapy for depressive symptoms: An 18-month follow-up. *Behaviour Research and Therapy*, *61*, 43–54. doi:10.1016/j.brat.2014.07.006 PMID:25127179

Lavie, T., & Tractinsky, N. (2004). Assessing dimensions of perceived visual aesthetics of web sites. *International Journal of Human-Computer Studies*, *60*(3), 269–298. doi:10.1016/j.ijhcs.2003.09.002

Lee, J., Bagheri, B., & Kao, H.-A. (2014). A Cyber physical systems achitechture for Industry4.0- based manufacturing systems. *Manufacturing Letters*, *3*, 18–23. doi:10.1016/j.mfglet.2014.12.001

Lee, Y. (2008). Designing with users, how? In *Investigate users involvement tactics for effective inclusive design processes. Design Thinking: New Challenges for Designers, Managers and Organizations*. Cergy-Pointoise.

Lego Serious Play. (2018). *The Method*. Available in: https://www.lego.com/en-us/seriousplay/the-method

Leonard, D., & Rayport, J. F. (1997). Spark innovation through empathic design. *Harvard Business Review*, *75*, 102–115. PMID:10174792

Leung, N. T. Y., Lo, M. M., & Lee, T. M. C. (2014). Potential Therapeutic Effects of Meditation for Treating Affective Dysregulation. *Evidence-Based Complementary and Alternative Medicine, 2014*, 1–7. doi:10.1155/2014/402718 PMID:25197309

Levinson, D. B., Stoll, E. L., Kindy, S. D., Merry, H. L., & Davidson, R. J. (2014). A mind you can count on: Validating breath counting as a behavioral measure of mindfulness. *Frontiers in Psychology, 5*(1202). doi:10.3389/fpsyg.2014.01202 PMID:25386148

Levy, D. M., Wobbrock, J. O., Kaszniak, A. W., & Ostergren, M. (2012). The effects of mindfulness meditation training on multitasking in a high-stress information environment. *Proceedings of Graphics Interface, 2012*, 45–52.

Li Da, X., He, W., & Li, S. (2014). Internet of Things in Industries: A Survey. *IEEE Transaction on Industrial Informatics, 10*(4), 2233-2243.

Librande, S. (n.d.). *One-page designs.* Available in: http://www.gdcvault.com/play/ 1012356/One-Page

Ligi, B. & Raja, B. (2017). Mobile learning in higher education. *International Journal of Research Granthaalayah, 5*(4)SE, 1-6.

Liimatainen, J., Häkkinen, M., Nousiainen, T., Kankaanranta, M., & Neittaanmäki, P. (2012). A mobile application concept to encourage independent mobility for blind and visually impaired students. In *ICCHP'12 Proceedings of the 13th international conference on Computers Helping People with Special Needs* (vol. 2, pp. 552-559). Berlin: Springer Verlag. 10.1007/978-3-642-31534-3_81

Lima, M., & Vieira, L. A. (2010). Experimental Protocol for Accessibility. In *IADIS 2010 IADIS International Conference Interfaces and Human Computer Interaction Experimental Protocol for Accessibility.* Freiburg, Germany: IADIS.

Lima, M., Vieira, R. S., Ferreira, Y. P., Aguiar, M. P., & Bastos, S.L. (2018). Evaluating System Accessibility Using An Experimental Protocol Based On Usability. *Computer Graphics, Visualization, Computer Vision And Image Processing 2018.*

Lin, J., Zheng, Y., Jiao, W., Zhao, B., Zhang, S., Gee, J., & Xiao, R. (2016). Groupwise registration of sequential images from multispectral imaging (MSI) of the retina and choroid. *Optics Express, 24*(22), 25277–25290. doi:10.1364/OE.24.025277 PMID:27828466

Lin, S. F., & Thomas, G. V. (2002). Development of understanding of popular graphic art: A study of everyday aesthetics in children, adolescents, and young adults. *International Journal of Behavioral Development, 26*(3), 278–287.

LITERACY Project. (2018). *About LITERACY.* Retrieved February 18, 2019, from http://www.literacyportal.eu/en/info/about-literacy.html

Loiacono, E. T., Djamasbi, S., & Kiryazov, T. (2013). Factors that affect visually impaired users' acceptance of audio and music websites. *International Journal of Human-Computer Studies, 71*(3), 321–334. doi:10.1016/j.ijhcs.2012.10.015

Lomas, T., Cartwright, T., Edginton, T., & Ridge, D. (2015). A Qualitative Analysis of Experiential Challenges Associated with Meditation Practice. *Mindfulness, 6*(5), 848–860. doi:10.100712671-014-0329-8

Long, F. (2009). Real or imaginary: The effectiveness of using personas in product design. In *Proceedings of the Irish Ergonomics Society Annual Conference* (vol. 14). Irish Ergonomics Society.

Long, K., & Vines, J. (2013). *Mind pool: Encouraging self-reflection through ambiguous bio-feedback. In CHI'13 Extended Abstracts on Human Factors in Computing Systems* (pp. 2975–2978). ACM. doi:10.1145/2468356.2479588

Loomis, J. M., Klatzky, R. L., & Golledge, R. G. (2001). Navigating without vision: basic and applied research. *Optometry and Vision Science : Official Publication of the American Academy of Optometry, 78*(5), 282–289. Retrieved from http://www.ncbi.nlm.nih.gov/pubmed/11384005

Lopatovska, I. (2015). Museum website features, aesthetics, and visitors' impressions: A case study of four museums. *Museum Management and Curatorship, 30*(3), 191–207. doi:10.1080/09647775.2015.1042511

Lötjönen, J., & Mäkelä, T. (2001). Elastic matching using a deformation sphere. In *International Conference on Medical Image Computing and Computer-Assisted Intervention* (pp. 541–548). Springer.

Lovell, N. (2013). *The Pyramid Of Free-To-Play Game Design.* Retrieved from: https://www.gamasutra.com/blogs/nicholaslovell/20130919/200606/the_pyramid_of_freeto

Lubart, T. I. (2001). Models of the creative process: Past, present and future. *Creativity Research Journal, 13*(3-4), 295–308. doi:10.1207/S15326934CRJ1334_07

Lucena, S. (2016). Digital cultures and mobile technologies in education. *Educar em Revista, Curitiba, Brasil, 59,* 277–290. doi:10.1590/0104-4060.43689

Lucero, A., Karapanos, E., Arrasvuori, J., & Korhonen, H. (2014). Playful or gameful?: creating delightful user experiences. *Interactions, 21*(3), 34-39.

Lumbreras, M., & Sánchez, J. (1999). Interactive 3D sound hyperstories for blind children. In *Proceedings of the SIGCHI conference on Human factors in computing systems the CHI is the limit - CHI '99* (pp. 318–325). New York: ACM Press. 10.1145/302979.303101

Luton, W. (2013). Free-To-Play: Making Money From Games You Give Away. New Riders.

Lutz, A., Slagter, H. A., Dunne, J. D., & Davidson, R. J. (2008). Attention regulation and monitoring in meditation. *Trends in Cognitive Sciences, 12*(4), 163–169. doi:10.1016/j.tics.2008.01.005 PMID:18329323

Mac Parthalain, N., & Strange, H. (2013). Fuzzy-entropy based image congealing. In *2013 IEEE International Conference on Fuzzy Systems (FUZZ)* (pp. 1-8). IEEE.

MacDougall, W. (2014). *Industry 4.0: Smart manufacturing for the future.* Berlin, Germany: GTAI.

Macedo, I., & Trevisan, D. G. (2013, July). A method to evaluate disabled user interaction: A case study with down syndrome children. In *International Conference on Universal Access in Human-Computer Interaction* (pp. 50-58). Berlin: Springer. 10.1007/978-3-642-39188-0_6

Macinnis, D. J., & Park, C. W. (1991). The Differential Role of Characteristics of Music on High- and Low- Involvement Consumers' Processing of Ads. *The Journal of Consumer Research, 18*(2), 161. doi:10.1086/209249

MacMillan, K. G., Beach, J., Cheng, K.-C., & Eberts, R. E. (1999). operator interface. In G. Millan (Eds.), Process industrial instrument and control handbook (pp. 8.1-8.25). TMH Press.

Mahlke, S., & Thüring, M. (2007, April). Studying antecedents of emotional experiences in interactive contexts. In *Proceedings of the SIGCHI Conference on Human Factors in Computing Systems* (pp. 915-918). New York, NY: ACM Press. 10.1145/1240624.1240762

Maiberg, E. (2013). *Pearl's Peril Is Wooga's Fastest-Growing Game To Date.* Retrieved from: http://www.adweek.com/digital/pearls-peril-is-woogas-fastest-growing-game-to-date/

Malinowski, P. (2008). Mindfulness as psychological dimension: Concepts and applications. *The Irish Journal of Psychology, 29*(1-2), 155–166. doi:10.1080/03033910.2008.10446281

Malone, T. W. (1981). Toward a theory of intrinsically motivating instruction. *Cognitive Science*, *5*(4), 333–369. doi:10.120715516709cog0504_2

Manaugh, G. (2016). Why Catholics Built Secret Astronomical Features into Churches to Help Save Souls. *Atlas Obscura*. Retrieved from https://www.atlasobscura.com/

Mani, M., Kavanagh, D. J., Hides, L., & Stoyanov, S. R. (2015). Review and Evaluation of Mindfulness-Based iPhone Apps. *JMIR mHealth and uHealth*, *3*(3), e82. doi:10.2196/mhealth.4328 PMID:26290327

Manning, H., Temkin, B., & Belanger, N. (2003). The power of design personas. *Forrester Research*. Retrieved from http://www.forrester.com/ER/Research/Report/0,1338,33033,00.html

Mäntylä, M., Adams, B., Destefanis, G., Graziotin, D., & Ortu, M. (2016). Mining valence, arousal, and dominance: Possibilities for detecting burnout and productivity? In *Proceedings of the 13th international conference on mining software repositories* (pp. 247–258). MSR '16. doi:10.1145/2901739.2901752

Marchand, W. R. (2014). Neural mechanisms of mindfulness and meditation: Evidence from neuroimaging studies. *World Journal of Radiology*, *6*(7), 471. doi:10.4329/wjr.v6.i7.471 PMID:25071887

Marcial Arredondo Rosas. (2013). *Mindfulness Focus Now* [Mobile app]. Retrieved from https://play.google.com/store/apps/details?id=com.identitat.mindfulness

Marin, C., Hargis, J., & Cavanaugh, C. (2013). iPad learning ecosystem: Developing challenge-based learning using design thinking. *Turkish Online Journal of Distance Education*, *14*(2), 22–34.

Mark, G., Iqbal, S., Czerwinski, M., & Johns, P. (2015). Focused, Aroused, but so Distractible: Temporal Perspectives on Multitasking and Communications. *Proceedings of the 18th ACM Conference on Computer Supported Cooperative Work & Social Computing*, 903-916. 10.1145/2675133.2675221

Marsland, S., Twining, C., & Taylor, C. (2008). A minimum description length objective function for groupwise non-rigid image registration. *Image and Vision Computing*, *26*(3), 333–346. doi:10.1016/j.imavis.2006.12.009

Martín-Roldán Pérez, S., & Ehrman, B. (2012). D1.2 Report on the mapping the planned functional Portal. Deliverable of the LITERACY-Project, Madrid.

Martins, A. I., Queirós, A., Silva, A. G., & Rocha, N. P. (2015). Usability evaluation methods: a systematic review. In Human Factors in Software Development and Design (pp. 250-273). IGI Global. doi:10.4018/978-1-4666-6485-2.ch013

Martins, A. I., Queirós, A., Silva, A. G., & Rocha, N. P. (2016). ICF based Usability Scale: evaluating usability according to the evaluators' perspective about the users' performance. In *Proceedings of the 7th International Conference on Software Development and Technologies for Enhancing Accessibility and Fighting Info-exclusion* (pp. 378-383). ACM. 10.1145/3019943.3019997

Martins, A. I., Queirós, A., Silva, A. G., & Rocha, N. P. (2016). Usability evaluation of ambient assisted living systems using a multi-method approach. *Proceedings of the 7th International Conference on Software Development and Technologies for Enhancing Accessibility and Fighting Info-exclusion*, 261-268. ACM. 10.1145/3019943.3019981

Masiero, A. A., Carvalho Destro, R., Curioni, O. A., & Aquino, P. T. Junior. (2013). Expanding Personas: How to Improve Knowledge About Users. In *Proceedings of the IADIS International Conferences Interfaces and Human Computer Interaction and Game and Entertainment Technologies* (pp. 103-109). Praga: IADIS.

Matthews, I., & Baker, S. (2004). Active Appearance Models Revisited. *International Journal of Computer Vision*, *60*(2), 135–164. doi:10.1023/B:VISI.0000029666.37597.d3

Matthews, T., Judge, T., & Whittaker, S. (2012). How do designers and user experience professionals actually perceive and use personas? *Proceedings of the 2012 ACM annual conference on Human Factors in Computing Systems.* 10.1145/2207676.2208573

Mayberry, J., Hergis, J., Bolles, L., Dugas, A., O'neill, D., Rivera, A., & Meler, M. (2012). Exploring teaching and learning using an iTouch mobile device. *Active Learning in Higher Education, 13*(3), 203–217. doi:10.1177/1469787412452984

Mayes, T., & de Freitas, S. (2007). Learning and e-learning: The role of theory. In H. Beetham & R. Sharpe (Eds.), *Rethinking pedagogy for a digital age: Designing and delivering e-learning* (pp. 13–25). London, UK: Routledge.

McCarthy, J., & Swierenga, S. (2010). What we know about dyslexia and Web accessibility: A research review. *Universal Access in the Information Society, 9*(2), 147–152. doi:10.100710209-009-0160-5

McClure, D. (2007). *Startup Metrics For Pirates: Aarrr! 500 Hats.* Retrieved From: http://500hats.typepad.com/500blogs/2007/09/startup-metrics.html

McDonnell, M., & Verdes, C. (2016), Designing for Intellectual Disability users to teach Independent Life Skills. *Proceedings of the 10th International Conference on Interfaces and Human Computer Interaction,* 264-269.

McGrath, L., Jones, R. S. P., & Hastings, R. P. (2009). Outcomes of anti-bullying intervention for adults with intellectual disabilities. *Research in Developmental Disabilities, 31*(2), 376–380. doi:10.1016/j.ridd.2009.10.006 PMID:19897338

Medeiros Filho, M., Benicio, I., Campos, F., & Neves, A. (2013). The importance of prototyping in game design. *Proceedings of Brazilian Symposium on Computer Games and Digital Entertainment: Art & Design Track.*

Meixner, G., Petersen, N., & Koessling, H. (2010). User interaction evolution in the SmartFactoryKL. In *Proceedings of the 24th BCS Interaction Specialist Group Conference* pp. (211–220). Dundee, UK. British Computer Society.

Mendes, T. G. (2012). *Games e educação: diretrizes do projeto para jogos digitais voltados à aprendizagem* (Master's dissertation). Federal University of Rio Grande do Sul, Porto Alegre.

Menzies, S. W., Ingvar, C., Crotty, K. A., & McCarthy, W. H. (1996). Frequency and morphologic characteristics of invasive melanomas lacking specific surface microscopic features. *Archives of Dermatology, 132*(10), 1178–1182. doi:10.1001/archderm.1996.03890340038007 PMID:8859028

Mesquita, L., Sánchez, J., & Andrade, R. M. (2018, July). Cognitive Impact Evaluation of Multimodal Interfaces for Blind People: Towards a Systematic Review. In *International Conference on Universal Access in Human-Computer Interaction* (pp. 365-384). Springer. 10.1007/978-3-319-92049-8_27

Miah, S. J. (2004). Accessibility improvement of multicultural educational web interface by using the User Centred Design (UCD) approach. In *Proceedings of the 2004 Informing Science and IT Education Joint Conference* (pp. 25-28). Informing Science Institute.

Miaskiewicz, T., & Kozar, K. A. (2011). Personas and user-centered design: How can personas benefit product design processes? *Design Studies, 32*(5), 417–430. doi:10.1016/j.destud.2011.03.003

Michailidou, E., Harper, S., & Bechhofer, S. (2008). Visual complexity and aesthetic perception of web pages. In *SIGDOC '08: Proceedings of the 26th annual ACM international conference on Design of communication* (pp. 215-224). ACM. 10.1145/1456536.1456581

Michel, A., Baumann, C., & Gayer, L. (2017). Thank you for the music – or not? The effects of in-store music in service settings. *Journal of Retailing and Consumer Services, 36*, 21–32. doi:10.1016/j.jretconser.2016.12.008

Milborrow, S. (n.d.). *An example of a CART classification tree.* Retrieved October 12, 2018, from https://commons.wikimedia.org/wiki/File:CART_tree_titanic_survivors.png

Miller Mc Farlan, E. (2017). Blessing robots: Is a technological reformation coming? *Religion News Service.* Retrieved from https://religionnews.com

Millera, M. W., Rietschel, J. C., McDonald, C. G., & Hatfield, B. D. (2011). A novel approach to the physiological measurement of mental workload. *International Journal of Psychophysiology, 80*(1), 75–78. doi:10.1016/j.ijpsycho.2011.02.003 PMID:21320552

Miranda, G. L. (2009). Concepção de conteúdos e cursos Online. Ensino Online e aprendizagem multimédia. *Relógio D'Água,* 81-110.

Miranda, M., & Torres, M. (2009). *La plataforma virtual como estrategia para mejorar el rendimento escolar de los alunos en la I. E. P Coronel José Joaquín Inclán de Piura. Revista Digital Sociedad de la Información, 15.* Edita Crefalea.

Mishra, J., Zinni, M., Bavelier, D., & Hillyard, S. A. (2011). Neural basis of superior performance of action video-game players in an attention-demanding task. *The Journal of Neuroscience, 31*(3), 992–998. doi:10.1523/JNEUROSCI.4834-10.2011 PMID:21248123

Mislevy, R. J., & Haertel, G. D. (2006). Implications of evidence-centered design for educational testing. *Educational Measurement: Issues and Practice, 25*(4), 6–20. doi:10.1111/j.1745-3992.2006.00075.x

Mitchell, P. P. (2007). *A step-by-step guide to usability testing.* iUniverse, Inc.

Mitsubishi Electric. (2018). *ENEDIA Overview.* Retrieved from http://www.mitsubishielectric.co.jp/home/enedia/

Möller, S., Hinterleitner, F., Falk, T. H., & Polzehl, T. (2010). *Comparison of Approaches for Instrumentally Predicting the Quality of Text-To-Speech Systems.* INTERSPEECH. Retrieved from https://pdfs.semanticscholar.org/b39b/05dbfff7d21d8e9e50385c9786e6f7a9a007.pdf

Molnar, P., & Gill, L. (2018). *Bots at the gate: A human hights analysis of automated decision-making in Canada's immigration and refugee system.* Toronto, Canada: The Citizen Lab and Faculty of Law, University of Toronto.

Monteiro, A. (2012). O processo de Bolonha e o trabalho pedagógico em plataformas digitais: possíveis implicações. In *Educação online. Pedagogia e aprendizagem em plataformas digitais* (2nd ed.). De facto editores.

Moore, A., & Malinowski, P. (2009). Meditation, mindfulness and cognitive flexibility. *Consciousness and Cognition, 18*(1), 176–186. doi:10.1016/j.concog.2008.12.008 PMID:19181542

Morais, C., Alves, P., & Miranda, L. (2013). Valorização dos ambientes virtuais de aprendizagem por professores do ensino superior. In A. Rocha, L. Reis, M. Cota, M. Painho, & M. Neto (Eds.), Sistemas e Tecnologias de Informação, Atas da 8a Conferência Ibérica de Sistemas e Tecnologias de Informação. 1 (pp. 289-294). Lisboa: Associação Ibérica de Sistemas e Tecnologias de Informação.

Morais, N., & Cabrita, I. (2008). B-Learning: impacto no desenvolvimento de competências no ensino superior politécnico. *Revista de Estudos Politécnicos, 6*(9).

Moran, J. (2002). *O que é o ensino a distância.* Retrieved from http://www.eca.usp.br/prof/moran/dist.htm

Moran, J. (2006). Ensino e aprendizagem inovadores com tecnologias audiovisuais e telemáticas. In Novas Tecnologias e Mediação Pedagógica. São Paulo: Papirus Editora.

Morel, R. (2012). *Choosing The Right Business Model For Your Game Or App.* Retrieved from: https://www.adobe.com/devnet/flashplayer/articles/right-business-model.html

Morimoto, N. (2016). Energy-on-Demand System Based on Combinatorial Optimization of Appliance Power Consumptions. *Journal of Information Processing*, 25(1), 268–276.

Morise, M., Yokomori, F., & Ozawa, K. (2016). WORLD: A Vocoder-Based High-Quality Speech Synthesis System for Real-Time Applications. *IEICE Transactions on Information and Systems, E99.D*(7), 1877–1884. doi:10.1587/transinf.2015EDP7457

Moser, C., Fuchsberger, V., Neureiter, L., Sellner, W., & Tscheligi, M. (2012). Revisiting personas: the making-of for special user groups. CHI '12 Extended Abstracts on Human Factors in Computing Systems.

Moshagen, M., & Thielsch, M. T. (2010). Facets of visual aesthetics. *International Journal of Human-Computer Studies*, 68(10), 689–709. doi:10.1016/j.ijhcs.2010.05.006

Motschnig, R., & Nykl, L. (2011). *Komunikace zaměřená na člověka: rozumět sobě i druhým*. Prague: Grada.

Motschnig, R., & Nykl, L. (2014). *Person-centred Communication Theory, Skills and Practice*. Maidenhead, UK: McGraw Hill.

Moura, A., & Carvalho, A. (2010). Twitter: A productive and learning tool for the SMS generation. In C.M. Evans (Ed.), Internet Issues: Blogging, the Digital Divide and Digital Libraries. Nova Science Publishers.

Mu Studios. (2013). *Breathe Daily* [Mobile app]. Retrieved from https://itunes.apple.com/us/app/id659230503

Muhammad, K. I., Lawlor, A., & Smyth, B. (2016). A Live-User Study of Opinionated Explanations for Recommender Systems. *Proceedings of the 21st International Conference on Intelligent User Interfaces - IUI '16*, (1), 256–260. 10.1145/2856767.2856813

Murakami, L. C., Leite, A. J. M., Jr., Sabino, R. F. S., & Macedo, D. A. (2016). *Design Thinking como metodologia alternativa para o desenvolvimento de jogos sérios*. Nuevas Ideas en Informática Educativa 2014. Memorias del XIX Congreso Internacional Informática Educativa (TISE), Fortaleza, Brasil. Available in: http://www.tise.cl/volumen10/TISE2014/tise2014_submission_200.pdf

Murphy, M. C., Nau, A. C., Fisher, C., Kim, S.-G., Schuman, J. S., & Chan, K. C. (2016). Top-down influence on the visual cortex of the blind during sensory substitution. *NeuroImage*, 125, 932–940. doi:10.1016/j.neuroimage.2015.11.021 PMID:26584776

Mwakapina, J., Mhandeni, A., & Nyinondi, O. (2016). WhatsApp Mobile Tool in Second Language Learning: Opportunities, potentials and challenges in Higher Education Settings in Tanzania. *International Journal of English Language Education*, 4(2). doi:10.5296/ijele.v4i2.9711

Nagai, Y., & Noguchi, H. (2003). An experimental study on the design thinking process started from difficult keywords: Modelling the thinking process of creative design. *Journal of Engineering Design*, 14(4), 429–437. doi:10.1080/09544820310001606911

Narinen, A. (2014). *How Player Retention Works In Free-To-Play Mobile Games: A Study Of Player Retention Methods* (Bachelor's thesis). Tampere University of Applied Sciences, Finland.

Newell & Simon. (1988). The theory of human problem solving. *Readings in Cognitive Science*, 33–51.

Nguyen, H. (2014). *Monetization For A Free-To-Play Mobile Game* (Bachelor's thesis). Kajaani University of Applied Sciences, Finland.

Nichols, M., Cator, K., & Torres, M. (2016). *Challenge Based Learner User Guide*. Redwood City, WA: Digital Promise.

Niedenthal, P. M., Brauer, M., Halberstadt, J. B., & Innes-Ker, Å. H. (2001). When did her smile drop? Facial mimicry and the influences of emotional state on the detection of change in emotional expression. *Cognition and Emotion*, *15*(6), 853–864. doi:10.1080/02699930143000194

Nielsen, J. (2015). *Children (Ages 3-12) on the Web* (3rd ed.). Retrieved from https://www.nngroup.com/reports/children-on-the-web/

Nielsen, J. (1993). *Usability Engeneering. Academic Press Inc.* Boston: Academic Press.

Nielsen, J. (1994). *Usability Engineering.* Morgan Kaufmann.

Nielsen, L. (2013). *Personas - User Focused Design.* Springer London. doi:10.1007/978-1-4471-4084-9

Nielsen, L. (2018). Design personas- New ways, New contexts. *Persona Studies*, *4*(2), 1–4.

Nielson, J. (1994). *Usability engineering.* AP Professional.

Noor-Ul-Amin, S. (2013). An effective use of ICT for education and learning by drawing on worldwide knowledge, research and experience: ICT as a change agent for education (A Literature review). *Scholarly Journal of Education*, *2*(4), 38–45.

Nordin, A. I., Denisova, A., & Cairns, P. (2014). *Too many questionnaires: Measuring player experience whilst playing digital games.* Academic Press.

Nordstrøm, M., Larsen, M., Sierakowski, J., & Stegmann, M. (2004). *The IMM face database - an annotated dataset of 240 face images. Technical report, Informatics and Mathematical Modelling.* Technical University of Denmark.

Norman, D. A. (1988). *The Design of Everyday Things/Emotional Design/Design of Future Things.* Basic Books.

Norman, D. A. (2002). *The design of everyday things.* New York: Basic Books.

Norman, D. A., & Draper, S. W. (1986). *User centered system design: New perspectives on human-computer interaction.* CRC Press. doi:10.1201/b15703

Nunes, I., & Jannach, D. (2017). A systematic review and taxonomy of explanations in decision support and recommender systems. *User Modeling and User-Adapted Interaction*, *27*(3–5), 393–444. doi:10.100711257-017-9195-0

Nunnally, J. C. (1978). *Psychometric Theory* (2nd ed.). New York: McGraw Hill.

Ohman, A., Flykt, A., Esteves, F., & Institute, K. (2001). Emotion Drives Attention: Detecting the Snake in the Grass. *Journal of Experimental Psychology. General*, *130*(3), 466–478. doi:10.1037/0096-3445.130.3.466 PMID:11561921

Oliveira, J. F. (2013). The path force feedback belt. In *2013 8th International Conference on Information Technology in Asia (CITA)* (pp. 1–6). IEEE. 10.1109/CITA.2013.6637564

Oliveira, E., Rego, M., & Villardi, R. (2007). Aprendizagem mediada por ferramentas de interacção: Análise do discurso de professores em um curso de formação continuada a distância. *Educação & Sociedade. Scielo Brasil*, *28*(101), 1413–1434.

Olweus, D. (2013). School bullying: Development and some important challenges. *Annual Review of Clinical Psychology*, *9*(1), 751–780. doi:10.1146/annurev-clinpsy-050212-185516 PMID:23297789

Ophir, E., Nass, C., & Wagner, A. D. (2009). Cognitive control in media multitaskers. *Proceedings of the National Academy of Sciences of the United States of America*, *106*(37), 15583–15587. doi:10.1073/pnas.0903620106 PMID:19706386

Osaka City, Japan. (2013). *Results of questionnaire of before and after use of "visualizing equipment".* Retrieved from http://warp.da.ndl.go.jp/info:ndljp/pid/10189884/www.city.osaka.lg.jp/kankyo/page/0000148884.html

Osborne, W. J., & Farley, F. H. (1970). The relationship between aesthetic preference and visual complexity in abstract art. *Psychonomic Science, 19*(2), 69–70. doi:10.3758/BF03337424

Otsu, N. (1979). A threshold selection method from gray-level histograms. *IEEE Transactions on Systems, Man, and Cybernetics, 9*(1), 62–66. doi:10.1109/TSMC.1979.4310076

Overton, T. (2012). *Assessing Learners with Special Needs. An applied approach.* Boston: Pearson Education.

Owens, P. L., Kerker, B. D., Zigler, E., & Horwitz, S. M. (2006). Vision and oral health needs of individuals with intellectual disability. *Developmental Disabilities Research Reviews, 12*(1), 28–40. doi:10.1002/mrdd.20096 PMID:16435325

Paavilainen, J., Alha, K., & Korhonen, H. (2017). A Review Of Social Features In Social Network Games. *Transactions of the Digital Games Research Association, 3*(2).

Pachler, N., Pimmer, C., & Seipold, J. (2011). *Work-based mobile learning: concepts and cases.* Bern, Switzerland: Peter-Lang. doi:10.3726/978-3-0353-0496-1

Palinkas, L. A., Horwitz, S. M., Green, C. A., Wisdom, J. P., Duan, N., & Hoagwood, K. (2015). Purposeful sampling for qualitative data collection and analysis in mixed method implementation research. *Administration and Policy in Mental Health, 42*(5), 533–544. doi:10.100710488-013-0528-y PMID:24193818

Palloff, R., & Pratt, K. (2005). *Learning Together in Community: Collaboration Online.* San Francisco, CA: Jossey-Bass.

Panasonic. (2018). *AiSEG2 Overview.* Retrieved from http:// https://www2.panasonic.biz/es/densetsu/aiseg/aiseg2/index.html

Pandir, M., & Knight, J. (2006). Homepage aesthetics: The search for preference factors and the challenges of subjectivity. *Interacting with Computers, 18*(6), 1351–1370. doi:10.1016/j.intcom.2006.03.007

Papamichail, M., Nikolaidis, I., Nikolaidis, N., Glava, C., Lentzas, I., Marmagkiolis, K., & Digalakis, M. (2008). Merkel cell carcinoma of the upper extremity: Case report and an update. *World Journal of Surgical Oncology, 6*(1), 32. doi:10.1186/1477-7819-6-32 PMID:18328106

Papp, A. C., & Gerbelli, L. G. (2016). *Trabalhadores informais chegam a 10 milhões no país.* Available at: http://economia.estadao.com.br/noticias/geral,trabalhadores-informais-chegam-a-10-milhoes-no-pais,10000071200

Paras, B. (2005). *Game, motivation, and effective learning: An integrated model for educational game design.* Academic Press.

Park, T., Reilly-spong, M., & Gross, C. R. (2013). Mindfulness: A systematic review of instruments to measure an emergent patient-reported outcome (PRO). *Quality of Life Research: An International Journal of Quality of Life Aspects of Treatment, Care and Rehabilitation, 22*(10), 2639–2659. doi:10.100711136-013-0395-8 PMID:23539467

Parsons, M. J. (1987). *How we understand art: A cognitive developmental account of aesthetic experience.* Cambridge, UK: Cambridge University Press.

Pascual, A., Ribera, M., Granollers, T., & Coiduras, J. L. (2014). Impact of accessibility barriers on the mood of blind, low-vision and sighted users. *Procedia Computer Science, 27*, 431–440. doi:10.1016/j.procs.2014.02.047

Pasquale, F. (2015). *The black box society: The secret algorithms that control money and information* (1st ed.). Boston: Harvard University Press. doi:10.4159/harvard.9780674736061

Pathomaree, N., & Charoenseang, S. (2015). Augmented reality for skill transfer in assembly task. *ROMAN 2005. IEEE Int'l Workshop on Robot and Human Interactive Communication*, 500–504.

Pearson, C., & Hussain, Z. (2015). Smartphone Use, Addiction, Narcissism, and Personality: A Mixed Methods Investigation. *International Journal of Cyber Behavior, Psychology and Learning*, 5(1), 17–32. doi:10.4018/ijcbpl.2015010102

Pee, L. G., Jiang, J., & Klein, G. (2018). Signaling effect of website usability on repurchase intention. *International Journal of Information Management*, 39, 228–241. doi:10.1016/j.ijinfomgt.2017.12.010

Peffers, K., Tuunanen, T., Rothenberger, M. A., & Chatterjee, S. (2007). A design science research methodology for information systems research. *Journal of Management Information Systems*, 24(3), 45–77. doi:10.2753/MIS0742-1222240302

Peretz, I., Gagnon, L., & Bouchard, B. (1998). Music and emotion: Perceptual determinants, immediacy, and isolation after brain damage. *Cognition*, 68(2), 111–141. Retrieved from http://www.ncbi.nlm.nih.gov/pubmed/9818509. doi:10.1016/S0010-0277(98)00043-2 PMID:9818509

Persson, H., Åhman, H., Yngling, A. A., & Gulliksen, J. (2015). Universal design, inclusive design, accessible design, design for all: Different concepts —one goal? On the concept of accessibility — historical, methodological and philosophical aspects. *Universal Access in the Information Society*, 14(4), 505–526. doi:10.100710209-014-0358-z

Peterson, R. C., Wolffsohn, J. S., Rubinstein, M., & Lowe, J. (2003). Benefits of electronic vision enhancement systems (EVES) for the visually impaired. *American Journal of Ophthalmology*, 136(6), 1129–1135. doi:10.1016/S0002-9394(03)00567-1 PMID:14644225

Petri, G., Von Wangenheim, C. G., & Borgatto, A. F. (2016). MEEGA+: an evolution of a model for the evaluation of educational games. *INCoD/GQS, 3*.

Piaget, J. (1930). *The Child's Conception of Physical Causality*. London: Routledge & Kegan Paul.

Pintrich, P. R. (2003). A motivational science perspective on the role of student motivation in learning and teaching contexts. *Journal of Educational Psychology*, 95(4), 667–686. doi:10.1037/0022-0663.95.4.667

Pintrich, P. R., & Schunk, D. H. (1996). *Motivation in education*. Englewood Cliffs, NJ: Prentice Hall.

Pintrich, P. R., & Schunk, D. H. (2002). *Motivation in education: Theory, research, and applications* (2nd ed.). Upper Saddle River, NJ: Prentice Hall.

Plato. *(370 bc). Phaedrus 274e–275b. In Plato: Complete Works* (J. M. Cooper, Ed.).

Plaza, I., Demarzo, M. M. P., Herrera-Mercadal, P., & García-Campayo, J. (2013). Mindfulness-Based Mobile Applications: Literature Review and Analysis of Current Features. *JMIR mHealth and uHealth*, 1(2), e24. doi:10.2196/mhealth.2733 PMID:25099314

Plucker, J. A., Beghetto, R. A., & Dow, G. T. (2004). Why isn't creativity more important to educational psychologists? Potentials, pitfalls, and future directions in creativity research. *Educational Psychologist*, 39(2), 83–96. doi:10.120715326985ep3902_1

Polfliet, M., Klein, S., Huizinga, W., Paulides, M., Niessen, W., & Vandemeulebroucke, J. (2018). Intrasubject multimodal groupwise registration with the conditional template entropy. *Medical Image Analysis*, 46, 15–25. doi:10.1016/j.media.2018.02.003 PMID:29502030

Popescu, V., Burdea, G., & Trefftz, H. (n.d.). *Chapter 25: Multimodal interaction modeling*. Retrieved from https://pdfs.semanticscholar.org/68b0/fa1297635ba133e7d76489884fbc55023ec3.pdf

Porat, T., & Tractinsky, N. (2012). It's a pleasure buying here: The effects of web-store design on consumers' emotions and attitudes. *Human-Computer Interaction*, 27(3), 235–276.

Portal Brasil. (2014). *Sobrevivência e mortalidade.* Available at: http://www.brasil.gov.br/economia-e-emprego/2012/02/sobrevivencia-e-mortalidade

Pourtois, G., Schettino, A., & Vuilleumier, P. (2013). Brain mechanisms for emotional influences on perception and attention: What is magic and what is not. *Biological Psychology, 92*(3), 492–512. doi:10.1016/j.biopsycho.2012.02.007 PMID:22373657

Preece, J., Sharp, H., & Rogers, Y. (2015). Experimental design. *Interaction Design: Beyond Human-Computer Interaction, 486.*

Preece, J. (2013). *Design de interação: além da interação homem-computador.* Porto Alegre, Brazil: Bookman.

Pruitt, J. S., & Adlin, T. (2006). *The Persona Lifecycle.* Elsevier. doi:10.1016/B978-012566251-2/50003-4

Pruitt, J., & Adlin, T. (2006). *The Persona Lifecycle: Keeping people in mind throughout product design.* San Francisco, CA: Elsevier.

Pulford, B. (2011). The influence of advice in a virtual learning environment. *British Journal of Educational Technology, 42*(1), 31–39. doi:10.1111/j.1467-8535.2009.00995.x

Pu, P., & Chen, L. (2007). Trust-inspiring explanation interfaces for recommender systems. *Knowledge-Based Systems, 20*(6), 542–556. doi:10.1016/j.knosys.2007.04.004

Qualbrink, A. (n.d.). *Zukunftsbild im Bistum Essen: Initiative für den Verbleib in der Kirche.* Retrieved from https://zukunftsbild.bistum-essen.de/

Queirós, A., Silva, A., Alvarelhão, J., Rocha, N. P., & Teixeira, A. (2015). Usability, accessibility and ambient-assisted living: A systematic literature review. *Universal Access in the Information Society, 14*(1), 57–66. doi:10.100710209-013-0328-x

Queiroz, J. E. (2001). *Abordagem Híbrida para a Avaliação da Usabilidade de Interfaces com o Utilizador. Tese (Doutorado em Engenharia Elétrica).* Campina Grande, Paraíba, Brasil: Universidade Federal da Paraíba.

Quinn, C. (2011). *Designing mLearning: Tapping into the mobile revolution for organizational performance.* San Francisco: Pfeiffer.

Radoff, J. (2011). *Game On: Energize Your Business With Social Media Games.* Indianapolis, IN: Wiley Publishing, Inc.

Raman, V. (2003) Specialized browsers. In WebAccessibility: A Foundation for Research, 1st Edition. Springer-Verlag.

Ramos, F. (2007). Technology: Challenging the Future of Learning. In *Proceedings of eLearning Lisboa 2007.* Lisboa: Portuguese Presidency of the European Union.

Rastogi, S., Sharma, P., Dhall, P., Agarwal, R., Thakur, S., & Scholar, U. G. (2017). Smart assistive shoes and cane: solemates for the blind people. *International Journal of Advanced Research in Electronics and Communication Engineering, 6.* Retrieved from http://ijarece.org/wp-content/uploads/2017/04/IJARECE-VOL-6-ISSUE-4-334-345.pdf

Rekimoto, J., & Jun. (1996). Tilting operations for small screen interfaces. In *Proceedings of the 9th annual ACM symposium on User interface software and technology - UIST '96* (pp. 167–168). New York: ACM Press. 10.1145/237091.237115

Renninger, K. A., Hidi, S., & Krapp, A. (1992). *The role of interest in learning and development.* Hillsdale, NJ: Erlbaum.

Rheinberg, F., Vollmeyer, R., & Engeser, S. (2003). Die Erfassung des Flow-Erlebens. In *Diagnostik von Motivation und Selbstkonzept* (pp. 261–279). Göttingen: Hogrefe.

Ricoy, M., & Couto, M. (2009). As tecnologias da informação e comunicação como recursos no Ensino Secundário: Um estudo de caso. *Revista Lusófona de Educação, 14*, 145–156.

Rideout, V. J., Foehr, U. G., & Roberts, D. F. (2010). *Generation M [superscript 2]: Media in the Lives of 8-to 18-Year-Olds.* Menlo Park, CA: Henry J. Kaiser Family Foundation.

Ridge, E. (2007). *Design of Experiments for the Tuning of Optimisation Algorithms.* York, UK: Department of Computer Science, The University of York.

Riegel, U., Kröck, T., & Faix, T. (2018). *Warum Menschen die katholische Kirche verlassen. Eine explorative Untersuchung zu Austrittsmotiven im Mixed-Methods Design.* Etscheid-Stams.

Rikiya, K. (2011). *Issues of the penetration of Home Energy Management System-Summarizing issues by the investigation of past demonstration projects. Central Research Institute of Electric Power Industry Research Report Y 12011.* (in Japanese)

Roberts, M. N. (2007). *Complexity and aesthetic preference for diverse visual stimuli* (PhD thesis). Departament de Psicologia, Universitat de les Illes Balears.

Robinson, F. (1993). Technology and religious change: Islam and the impact of print. *Modern Asian Studies, 27*(1), 229–251.

Robinson, J. K. (2013). Project-based learning: Improving student engagement and performance in the laboratory. *Analytical and Bioanalytical Chemistry, 405*(1), 7–13. doi:10.100700216-012-6473-x PMID:23104311

Roda, R., & Krucken, L. (2004). Gestão do design aplicada ao modelo atual das organizações: agregando valor a serviços. In *Congresso Brasileiro de Pesquisa e Desenvolvimento em Design* (Vol. 6). São Paulo, Brazil: FAAP.

Rogers, C. R., & Farson, R. E. (1987). Active Listening. In R. G. Newman, M. A. Danziger, & M. Cohen (Eds.), *Communication in Business Today.* Washington, DC: Heath and Company. (Originally published 1957)

Rogers, C. R., & Roethlisberger, F. J. (1991). Barriers and Gateways to Communication. *Harvard Business Review.*

Rogers, Y., Sharp, H., & Preece, J. (2011). *Interaction Design: beyond human-computer interaction.* New York: Wiley.

Rogger, Y., Sharp, H., & Preece, J. (2011). *Interaction design: Beyond human - computer interaction.* West Sussex, UK: John Wiley & Sons.

Rohrbach, B. (1969). Kreativ nach Regeln – Methode 635, eine neue Technik zum Lösen von Problemen [Creative by rules - Method 635, a new technique for solving problems]. *Absatzwirtschaft, 12*, 73–53.

Rosa, J. G. S. (2012). *Design participativo.* Rio de Janeiro, Brazil: Riobooks.

Rosendahl, C., Cameron, A., McColl, I., & Wilkinson, D. (2012). Dermatoscopy in routine practice: 'chaos and clues'. *Australian Family Physician, 41*, 482. PMID:22762066

Rouse, R. (2001). *Game Design – Theory & Practice.* Wordware Publishing.

Rouse, W. (1988). The human role in advanced manufacturing system. In W. D. Compton (Ed.), *Design and analysis of integrated manufacturing systems* (pp. 148–166). Washington, DC: National Academy Press.

Rubin, J., & Chisnell, D. (2008). *Handbook of usability testing: How to plan, design, and conduct effective tests.* Indianapolis, IN: Wiley Publishing, Inc.

Rubin, P., Baer, T., & Mermelstein, P. (1981). An articulatory synthesizer for perceptual research. *The Journal of the Acoustical Society of America, 70*(2), 321–328. doi:10.1121/1.386780

Rueckert, D., Frangi, A., & Schnabel, J. (2001). Automatic construction of 3D statistical deformation models using non-rigid registration. In *International Conference on Medical Image Computing and Computer-Assisted Intervention* (pp. 77-84). Springer. 10.1007/3-540-45468-3_10

Ruffa, A. J., Stevens, A., Woodward, N., Zonfrelli, T., Belz, M., Hou, Z., … Blindesamfund, D. (2015). *Assessing iBeacons as an Assistive Tool for Blind People in Denmark An Interactive Qualifying Project Denmark Project Center.* Retrieved from http://www.wpi.edu/academics/ugradstudies/project-learning.html

Ruiz, J., Li, Y., & Lank, E. (2011). User-defined motion gestures for mobile interaction. In *Proceedings of the 2011 annual conference on Human factors in computing systems - CHI '11* (p. 197). New York: ACM Press. 10.1145/1978942.1978971

Rumelhart, D. E., Hinton, G. E., & Williams, R. J. (1986). Learining internal representations by error propagation. In *Parallel Distributed Processing: Explorations in the Microstructure of Cognition* (1st ed.). Bradford, MA: MIT Press.

Rumelhart, D. E., & McClelland, J. L. (1986). Parallel distributed processing: Vol. 1. *Foundations* (1st ed.). Bradford, MA: MIT Press.

Runco, M. A. (1995). Cognition and Creativity. *Contemporary Psychology*, *44*(6), 554–555. doi:10.1037/002141

Russell, A. S. (2010). Negative Potential of Video Games. *Educational Media Corporation.* Retrieved from http://www.education.com/reference/article/negative-potential-video-games/

Russell, S., & Norvig, P. (2003). *Artificial intelligence: A modern approach* (2nd ed.). Prentice Hall. doi:10.1017/S0269888900007724

Russoniello, C., O'Brien, K., & Parks, J. M. (2009). The effectiveness of casual video games in improving mood and decreasing stress. *Journal of Cyber Therapy and Rehabilitation*, *2*(1), 53–66.

Rusu, R. B., Bradski, G., Thibaux, R., & Hsu, J. (2010). Fast 3D recognition and pose using the viewpoint feature histogram. *Proceedings of 2010 IEEE/RSJ International Conference on Intelligent Robots and Systems*, 2155–2162. doi:10.1109/IROS.2010.5651280

Rusu, R., & Cousins, S. (2011). 3D is here: point cloud library (pcl). *Proceedings of IEEE International Conference on Robotics and Automation (ICRA)*. 10.1109/ICRA.2011.5980567

Ryan, R. M., & Deci, E. L. (2000). Intrinsic and extrinsic motivations: Classic definitions and new directions. *Contemporary Educational Psychology*, *25*(1), 54–67. doi:10.1006/ceps.1999.1020 PMID:10620381

Ryu, K., & Myung, R. (2005). Evaluation of mental workload with a combined measure based on physiological indices during a dual task of tracking and a mental arithmetic. *International Journal of Industrial Ergonomics*, *35*(11), 991–1009. doi:10.1016/j.ergon.2005.04.005

Sahdra, B. K., Shaver, P. R., & Brown, K. W. (2010). A scale to measure nonattachment: A Buddhist complement to Western research on attachment and adaptive functioning. *Journal of Personality Assessment*, *92*(2), 116–127. doi:10.1080/00223890903425960 PMID:20155561

Salen, K., & Zimmerman, E. (2004). *Rules Of Play: Game Design Fundamentals.* The MIT Press.

Salido, J. A. A., & Ruiz, C. Jr. (2017). Using morphological operators and inpainting for hair removal in dermoscopic images. In *Proceedings of the Computer Graphics International Conference* (p. 2). ACM. 10.1145/3095140.3095142

Sampurna Guha, M. (n.d.). *Effect of Assistive Devices on Educational Efficiency for Persons with Visual Impairment.* Retrieved from http://www.jodys.info/journal/march_2017/02_jodys_march_2017.pdf

Sánchez, J., & Aguayo, F. (2008). AudioGene: Mobile Learning Genetics through Audio by Blind Learners. In *Learning to Live in the Knowledge Society* (pp. 79–86). Boston, MA: Springer US. doi:10.1007/978-0-387-09729-9_10

Sánchez, J., & Elías, M. (2007). *LNCS 4662 - Guidelines for Designing Mobility and Orientation Software for Blind Children.* Retrieved from https://link.springer.com/content/pdf/10.1007%2F978-3-540-74796-3_35.pdf

Sánchez, J., Sáenz, M., & Ripoll, M. (2009). Usability of a multimodal videogame to improve navigation skills for blind children. In *Proceeding of the eleventh international ACM SIGACCESS conference on Computers and accessibility - ASSETS '09* (p. 35). New York: ACM Press. 10.1145/1639642.1639651

Sánchez, J. (2012). Development of Navigation Skills Through Audio Haptic Videogaming in Learners Who are Blind. *Procedia Computer Science, 14,* 102–110. doi:10.1016/j.procs.2012.10.012

Sánchez, J., Darin, T., & Andrade, R. (2015). *Multimodal Videogames for the Cognition of People Who Are Blind: Trends and Issues.* Springer International Publishing. doi:10.1007/978-3-319-20684-4_52

Sánchez, J., & Hassler, T. (2007). AudioMUD: A multiuser virtual environment for blind people. *IEEE Transactions on Neural Systems and Rehabilitation Engineering, 15*(1), 16–22. doi:10.1109/TNSRE.2007.891404 PMID:17436871

Sánchez, J., & Mascaró, J. (2011). *Audiopolis, Navigation through a Virtual City Using Audio and Haptic Interfaces for People Who Are Blind.* Berlin: Springer. doi:10.1007/978-3-642-21663-3_39

Sánchez, J., & Sáenz, M. (2010). Metro navigation for the blind. *Computers & Education, 55*(3), 970–981. doi:10.1016/j.compedu.2010.04.008

Sangiorgi, U. B. (2014). Electronic sketching on a multi-platform context: A pilot study with developers. *International Journal of Human-Computer Studies, 72*(1), 45–52. doi:10.1016/j.ijhcs.2013.08.018

Sankaran, S. R., & Bui, T. (2001). Impact of learning strategies and motivation on performance: A study in web-based instruction. *Journal of Instructional Psychology, 28,* 191–198.

Santos, A. R., Fernandes, P., Sales, A., & Nichols, M. (2013). Combining Challenge-Based Learning and Scrum Framework for Mobile Application Development. *ACM Conference on Innovation and Technology in Computer Science Education,* 189-194.

Sanz, P., & et al. (2014). Scenes and Images into Sounds: A Taxonomy of Image Sonification Methods for Mobility Applications. *Journal of the Audio Engineering Society, 62*(3), 161–171. doi:10.17743/jaes.2014.0009

Sas, C., & Chopra, R. (2015). MeditAid: A wearable adaptive neurofeedback-based system for training mindfulness state. *Personal and Ubiquitous Computing, 19*(7), 1169–1182. doi:10.100700779-015-0870-z

Sauer, S., Walach, H., Schmidt, S., Hinterberger, T., Horan, M., & Kohls, N. (2011). Implicit and explicit emotional behavior and mindfulness. *Consciousness and Cognition, 20*(4), 1558–1569. doi:10.1016/j.concog.2011.08.002 PMID:21885296

Savi, R., & Ulbricht, V.R. (2008). Educational games: benefits and challenges. *Revista Novas Tecnologias na Educa-ção–Renote, 6.*

Scanlon, E., Jones, A., & Waycott, J. (2005). Mobile technologies: Prospects for their use in learning in informal science settings. *Journal of Interactive Media in Education,* 25.

Scardamalia, M., & Bereiter, C. (2008). Pedagogical biases in educational technologies. *Educational Technology,* 3–11.

Schalock, R. L., Luckasson, R. A., & Shogren, K. A. (2007). The renaming of mental retardation: Understanding the change to the term intellectual disability. *Intellectual and Developmental Disabilities, 45*(2), 116–124. doi:10.1352/1934-9556(2007)45[116:TROMRU]2.0.CO;2 PMID:17428134

Scheggi, S., Talarico, A., & Prattichizzo, D. (2014). A remote guidance system for blind and visually impaired people via vibrotactile haptic feedback. In *22nd Mediterranean Conference on Control and Automation* (pp. 20–23). IEEE. 10.1109/MED.2014.6961320

Schell, J. (2014). *The Art of Game Design: A book of lenses*. AK Peters/CRC Press.

Schell, J. (2008). *The Art of Game Design – A Book of Lenses*. Morgan Kaufmann. doi:10.1201/9780080919171

Schenkman, B., & Jönsson, F. (2000). Aesthetics and preferences of web pages. *Behaviour & Information Technology*, *19*(5), 367–377. doi:10.1080/014492900750000063

Schikhof, Y., & Mulder, I. (2008). Under Watch and Ward at Night: Design and Evaluation of a Remote Monitoring System for Dementia Care. In *USAB '08 Proceedings of the 4th Symposium of the Workgroup Human-Computer Interaction and Usability Engineering of the Austrian Computer Society on HCI and Usability for Education and Work*. Berlin: Springer Verlag.

Schinazi, V. R., Thrash, T., & Chebat, D.-R. (2016). Spatial navigation by congenitally blind individuals. *Wiley Interdisciplinary Reviews: Cognitive Science*, *7*(1), 37–58. doi:10.1002/wcs.1375 PMID:26683114

Schlittmeier, S. J., & Hellbrück, J. (2009). Background music as noise abatement in open-plan offices: A laboratory study on performance effects and subjective preferences. *Applied Cognitive Psychology*, *23*(5), 684–697. doi:10.1002/acp.1498

Schmalstieg, D., & Wagner, D. (2018). *Mobile Phones as a Platform for Augmented Reality*. Graz University of Technology. Available at: https://data.icg.tugraz.at/~dieter/publications/Schmalstieg_135.pdf

Scott, T. J. (1970). The use of music to reduce hyperactivity in children. *The American Journal of Orthopsychiatry*, *40*(4), 677–680. doi:10.1111/j.1939-0025.1970.tb00725.x PMID:5507301

Sebrae. (2017). *Pequenos negócios em números*. Available at: https://www.sebrae.com.br/sites/PortalSebrae/ufs/sp/sebraeaz/pequenos-negocios-em-numeros,12e8794363447510VgnVCM1000004c00210aRCRD

Seckler, M., Opwis, K., & Tuch, A. (2015). Linking objective design factors with subjective aesthetics: An experimental study on how structure and color of websites affect the facets of users' visual aesthetic perception. *Computers in Human Behavior*, *49*, 375–389. doi:10.1016/j.chb.2015.02.056

Seffah, A., Vanderdonckt, J., & Desmarais, M. C. (2009). *Human-Centered Software Engineering: Software Engineering Models, Patterns and Architectures for HCI*. London: Springer Verlag. doi:10.1007/978-1-84800-907-3

Shachtman, N. (2015). In Silicon Valley, Meditation Is No Fad. It Could Make Your Career. *Wired*. Retrieved from http://www.wired.com/2013/06/meditation-mindfulness-silicon-valley/

Shahzad, F. (2017). Modern and Responsive Mobile-enabled Web Applications. *Procedia Computer Science*, *110*, 410–415. doi:10.1016/j.procs.2017.06.105

Shapiro, D. H. (1992). Adverse effects of meditation: A preliminary investigation of long-term meditators. *International Journal of Psychosomatics*, *39*(1-4), 62–67. PMID:1428622

Sharples, M., Inmaculada, A. S., Milrad, M. & Vavoula, G. (2009). Mobile Learning. *Technology Enhanced Learning: Principles and Products*. Academic Press.

Shattuck, D., Mirza, M., Adisetiyo, V., Hojatkashani, C., Salamon, G., Narr, K., ... Toga, A. (2008). Construction of a 3D probabilistic atlas of human cortical structures. *NeuroImage*, *39*(3), 1064–1080. doi:10.1016/j.neuroimage.2007.09.031 PMID:18037310

Shen, J., Jin, X., Zhou, C., & Wang, C. C. (2007). Gradient based image completion by solving the Poisson equation. *Computers & Graphics, 31*(1), 119–126. doi:10.1016/j.cag.2006.10.004

Sherry, J. L. (2004). Flow and media enjoyment. *Communication Theory, 14*(4), 328–347. doi:10.1111/j.1468-2885.2004.tb00318.x

Shinohara, K., & Kristen. (2006). Designing assistive technology for blind users. In *Proceedings of the 8th international ACM SIGACCESS conference on Computers and accessibility - Assets '06* (p. 293). New York: ACM Press. 10.1145/1168987.1169062

Shneiderman, B. (2000). Universal usability. *Communications of the ACM, 43*(5), 84–91. doi:10.1145/332833.332843

Shogren, K. A., Wehmeyer, M. L., Reese, R. M., & O'Hara, D. (2006). Promoting self-determination in health and medical care: A critical component of addressing health disparities in people with intellectual disabilities. *Journal of Policy and Practice in Intellectual Disabilities, 3*(2), 105–113. doi:10.1111/j.1741-1130.2006.00061.x

Shoval, S., Ulrich, I., & Borenstein, J. (2003). Robotics-based obstacle-avoidance systems for the blind and visually impaired - Navbelt and the guidecane. *IEEE Robotics & Automation Magazine, 10*(1), 9–20. doi:10.1109/MRA.2003.1191706

Shute, V. J. (2011). Stealth assessment in computer-based games to support learning. *Computer Games and Instruction, 55*(2), 503-524.

Sidorov, K. (2010). *Groupwise non-rigid registration for automatic construction of appearance models of the human craniofacial complex for analysis, synthesis and simulation.* Cardiff University.

Sidorov, K. A., Richmond, S., & Marshall, A. D. (2009). An Efficient Stochastic Approach to Groupwise Non-rigid Image Registration. In *IEEE Conference on Computer Vision and Pattern Recognition (CVPR 2009),* (pp. 2208-2213). Miami Beach, FL: IEEE. 10.1109/CVPR.2009.5206516

Siegel, R. L., Miller, K. D., & Jemal, A. (2018). Cancer statistics, 2018. *CA: a Cancer Journal for Clinicians, 68*(1), 7–30. doi:10.3322/caac.21442 PMID:29313949

Silva, I. C. S., & Bittencourt, J. R. (2016). Proposta de Metodologia para o Ensino e o Desenvolvimento de Jogos Digitais Baseada em Design Thinking. *Proceedings of XII Brazilian Congress on Design Research and Development, Blucher Design Proceedings, 9*(2), 2317-2328. doi:10.5151/despro-ped2016-0198

Silveira, I. (2016). A Game Development-based strategy for Teaching Software Design Patterns through Challenge-Based Learning under a Flipped Classroom Approach. *24º Workshop sobre Educação em Computação (WEI).*

Simões-Marques, M., & Nunes, I. L. (2012). Usability of interfaces. In *Ergonomics-A Systems Approach.* InTech. doi:10.5772/37299

Simon, H. A. (1978). Information-processing theory of human problem solving. In H. A. Simon (Ed.), *Handbook of learning and cognitive processes* (pp. 271–295). New York: Psychology Press.

Singh, A. (2012). Use of mindfulness-based therapies in psychiatry. *Progress in Neurology and Psychiatry, 16*(6), 7–11. doi:10.1002/pnp.254

Sliwinski, J., Katsikitis, M., & Jones, C. M. (2018b). Design and Evaluation of the Interactive Mindfulness Program and Virtual Evaluation (IMProVE) Game. *Journal of Cognitive Enhancement.* doi:10.100741465-018-0092-1

Sliwinski, J., Katsikitis, M., & Jones, C. M. (2015). Mindful Gaming: How Digital Games Can Improve Mindfulness. *Human-Computer Interaction–INTERACT, 2015,* 167–184.

Sliwinski, J., Katsikitis, M., & Jones, C. M. (2017). A review of interactive technologies as support tools for the cultivation of mindfulness. *Mindfulness*, *8*(5), 1150–1159. doi:10.100712671-017-0698-x

Sliwinski, J., Katsikitis, M., & Jones, C. M. (2018a). Design and Evaluation of Smartphone-based Training for Mindfulness and Openness to Experience. In *Proceedings of the 11th International Conference on Game and Entertainment Technologies* (pp. 177-184). IADIS.

Small, R. V. (2000). Motivation in instructional design. *Teacher Librarian*, *27*, 29–31.

Snyder, C. (2003). *Paper Prototyping – The Fast and Easy Way to Design and Refine User Interfaces*. San Francisco, CA: Morgan Kaufmann.

So, C., & Joo, J. (2017). Does a persona improve creativity? *The Design Journal*, *20*(4), 459–475. doi:10.1080/14606 925.2017.1319672

Sodnik, J., Dicke, C., Tomažič, S., & Billinghurst, M. (2008). A user study of auditory versus visual interfaces for use while driving. *International Journal of Human-Computer Studies*, *66*(5), 318–332. doi:10.1016/j.ijhcs.2007.11.001

Sohlberg, M. M., & Mateer, C. A. (1989). *Introduction to cognitive rehabilitation: Theory and practice*. New York: Guilford Press.

Sonderegger, A., & Sauer, J. (2010). The influence of design aesthetics in usability testing: Effects on user performance and perceived usability. *Applied Ergonomics*, *41*(3), 403–410. doi:10.1016/j.apergo.2009.09.002 PMID:19892317

Sonderegger, A., Zbinden, G., Uebelbacher, A., & Sauer, J. (2012). The influence of product aesthetics and usability over the course of time: A longitudinal field experiment. *Ergonomics*, *55*(7), 713–730. doi:10.1080/00140139.2012.6 72658 PMID:22506866

Sonka, M., Hlavac, V., & Boyle, R. (2014). *Image processing, analysis, and machine vision*. Cengage Learning.

Sorbring, E., Molin, M., & Löfgren-Mårtenson, L. (2017). "I'm a mother, but I'm also a facilitator in her every-day life": Parents' voices about barriers and support for internet participation among young people with intellectual disabilities. *Cyberpsychology (Brno)*, *11*(1), 43–60. doi:10.5817/CP2017-1-3

Sotelo, J., Mehri, S., Kumar, K., Santos, J. F., Kastner, K., Courville, A., & Bengio, Y. (2017). Char2wav: end-to-end speech synthesis. In *Workshop track - ICLR 2017*. Retrieved from http://josesotelo.com/speechsynthesis

Souza, M. (2011). *Expert Oracle Application Express Plugins*. Apress.

Soyer, H. P., Argenziano, G., Zalaudek, I., Corona, R., Sera, F., Talamini, R., ... Chimenti, S. (2004). Three-point checklist of dermoscopy. *Dermatology (Basel, Switzerland)*, *208*(1), 27–31. doi:10.1159/000075042 PMID:14730233

Spinsante, S., Montanini, L., Gambi, E., Lambrinos, L., Pereira, F., Pombo, N., & Garcia, N. (2017). *Smartphones as Multipurpose Intelligent Objects for AAL: Two Case Studies*. Academic Press. doi:10.1007/978-3-319-61949-1_14

Sprenger-Charolles, L., Siegel, L. S., Jimenez, J. E., & Ziegler, J. (2011). Prevalence and reliability of phonological, surface, and mixed profiles in dyslexia: A review of studies conducted in languages varying in orthographic depth. *Scientific Studies of Reading*, *15*(6), 498–521. doi:10.1080/10888438.2010.524463

Stanton, N. A., Booth, R., & Stammers, R. B. (1992). Alarms in human supervisory control: A human factors perspective. *International Journal of Computer Integrated Manufacturing*, *5*(2), 81–93. doi:10.1080/09511929208944518

Stanton, N. A., & Edworthy, J. (1999). *Human factors in auditory warnings*. New York: Ashgate Publications.

Stapenhurst, T. (2009). *The Benchmarking Book – A How-To-Guide to best practice for managers and practitioners*. Oxford, UK: Butterworth-Heinemann.

Steen, M., & Kuijt, L. (1988). *Early user involvement in research and design projects–A review of methods and practices*. Academic Press.

Steve, K. (2005). *Don't Make Me Think: A Common Sense Approach to Web Usability* (2nd ed.). New York: New Riders.

Stolz, W., Riemann, A., Cognetta, A., Pillet, L., Abmayr, W., Holzel, D., ... Landthaler, M. (1994). Abcd rule of dermatoscopy-a new practical method for early recognition of malignant-melanoma. *European Journal of Dermatology*, *4*, 521–527.

Stone, D., Jarrett, C., Woodroffe, M., & Minocha, S. (2005). *User Interface Design and Evaluation*. San Francisco: Morgan Kaufmann Publishers.

Streans, P. N. (2013). *The Industrial Revolution in World History*. New York: Taylor & Francis.

Stroop, J. R. (1935). Studies of interference in serial verbal reactions. *Journal of Experimental Psychology*, *18*(6), 643–662. doi:10.1037/h0054651

Suendermann, D., Höge, H., & Black, A. (2010). Challenges in Speech Synthesis. In *Speech Technology* (pp. 19–32). Boston, MA: Springer US. doi:10.1007/978-0-387-73819-2_2

Suri, J. F. (2003). The experience of evolution: Developments in design practice. *The Design Journal*, *6*(2), 39–48. doi:10.2752/146069203789355471

Sweetser, P., & Wyeth, P. (2005). GameFlow: A model for evaluating player enjoyment in games. *Computers in Entertainment*, *3*(3), 3–3. doi:10.1145/1077246.1077253

Sweller, J. (1988). Cognitive Load During Problem Solving: Effects on Learning. *Cognitive Science*, *12*(2), 257–285. doi:10.120715516709cog1202_4

SZ. (2018). *Data provided by Evangelische Kirche in Deutschland (EKD) and Deutsche Bischofskonferenz (DBK)*. Retrieved from https://www.sueddeutsche.de/

Szegedy, C., Liu, W., Jia, Y., Sermanet, P., Reed, S., Anguelov, D., & Rabinovich, A. (2015). Going deeper with convolutions. In *Proceedings of the IEEE conference on computer vision and pattern recognition* (pp. 1-9). IEEE.

TAI. (2017). *Hsuan-an. Design: conceitos e métodos*. São Paulo: Blucher.

Takekazu, K., Kenji, Y., & Takashi, M. (2013). Energy On Demand. *Information Processing Society of Japan*, *54*(3), 1185–1198.

Tang, Z., Jiang, D., & Fan, Y. (2013). Image registration based on dynamic directed graphs with groupwise image similarity. In *IEEE 10th International Symposium on Biomedical Imaging*, (pp. 488-491). San Francisco, CA: IEEE.

Tang, A., Owen, C., Biocca, F., & Mou, W. (2003). Comparative effectiveness of augmented reality in object assembly. In *Proceedings of the SIGCHI Conference on Human Factors in Computing Systems (CHI '03)*. ACM. 10.1145/642611.642626

Tanis, E. S., Palmer, S., Wehmeyer, M., Davies, D. K., Stock, S. E., Lobb, K., & Bishop, B. (2012). Self-report computer-based survey of technology use by people with intellectual and developmental disabilities. *Intellectual and Developmental Disabilities*, *50*(1), 53–68. doi:10.1352/1934-9556-50.1.53 PMID:22316226

Tao, Z., Cheung, M., She, J., & Lam, R. (2014). Item Recommendation Using Collaborative Filtering In Mobile Social Games: A Case Study. *Big Data And Cloud Computing (bdcloud). IEEE Fourth International Conference*, 293-297.

Thakare, P. U., Shubham, K., Ankit, P., Ajinkya, R., & Om, S. (2017). Smart Assistance System for the Visually Impaired. *International Journal of Scientific and Research Publications*, *7*(12), 378. Retrieved from www.ijsrp.org

Thaler, R. H., & Sunstain, C. R. (2008). *Nudge: Improving Decisions About Health, Wealth, and Happiness*. New Haven, CT: Yale University Press.

Thibault, C. (2013). *Game Data Analysis–Tools And Methods*. Birmingham, UK: Packt Publishing ltd.

Thimbleby, H. W. (2008). Understanding User Centred Design (UCD) for People with Special Needs. In K. Miesenberger, J. Klaus, W. L. Zagler, & A. I. Karshmer (Eds.), *ICCHP* (pp. 1–17). Berlin: Springer Verlag. doi:10.1007/978-3-540-70540-6_1

Think Gaming. (2018). *Top grossing all devices-games*. Retrieved from: https://thinkgaming.com

Thomas, D. C. (2006). Domain and Development of Cultural Intelligence The Importance of Mindfulness. *Group & Organization Management*, *31*(1), 78–99. doi:10.1177/1059601105275266

Thüring, M., & Mahlke, S. (2007). Usability, aesthetics and emotions in human–technology interaction. *International Journal of Psychology*, *42*(4), 253–264. doi:10.1080/00207590701396674

Tiddeman, B., Duffy, N., & Rabey, G. (2001). A general method for overlap control in image warping. *Computers & Graphics*, *25*(1), 59–66. doi:10.1016/S0097-8493(00)00107-2

Tiddeman, B., & Hunter, D. (2011). Groupwise Non-rigid Image Alignment-Results of a Multiscale Iterative Best Edge Algorithm. In *International Conference on Computer Vision Theory and Applications* (pp. 22-29). VISAPP.

Tintarev, N., & Masthoff, J. (2007). A survey of explanations in recommender systems. In *2007 IEEE 23rd International Conference on Data Engineering Workshop* (pp. 801–810). IEEE. 10.1109/ICDEW.2007.4401070

Tintarev, N., & Masthoff, J. (2012). Evaluating the effectiveness of explanations for recommender systems. *User Modeling and User-Adapted Interaction*, *22*(4–5), 399–439. doi:10.100711257-011-9117-5

Torrente, J., Del Blanco, Á., Serrano-Laguna, Á., Ángel Vallejo-Pinto, J., Moreno-Ger, P., & Fernández-Manjón, B. (n.d.). Towards a Low Cost Adaptation of Educational Games for People with Disabilities. *Computer Science and Information Systems*, *11*(1), 369–391. doi:10.2298/CSIS121209013T

Toshiba. (2018). *Feminity Overview*. Retrieved from http://feminity.toshiba.co.jp/feminity/feminity_eng/

Toth, K., de Lacy, N., & King, B. H. (2016). Intellectual disability. In M. K. Dulcan (Ed.), *Dulcan's textbook of child and adolescent psychiatry* (2nd ed.; pp. 105–134). Arlington, VA: American Psychiatric Publishing. doi:10.1176/appi.books.9781615370306.md07

Tracinsky, N., Cokhavi, A., Kirschenbaum, M., & Sharfi, T. (2006). Evaluating the consistency of immediate aesthetic perceptions of web pages. *International Journal of Human-Computer Studies*, *64*(11), 1071–1083. doi:10.1016/j.ijhcs.2006.06.009

Tractinsky, N. (2013). Visual Aesthetics. In M. Soegaard & R. F. Dam (Eds.), *The Encyclopedia of Human-Computer Interaction* (2nd ed.). Aarhus, Denmark: The Interaction Design Foundation.

Tractinsky, N., Katz, A. S., & Ikar, D. (2000). What is beautiful is usable. *Interacting with Computers*, *13*(2), 127–145. doi:10.1016/S0953-5438(00)00031-X

Tuch, A. N., Bargas-Avila, J. A., & Opwis, K. (2010). Symmetry and aesthetics in website design: It's a man's business. *Computers in Human Behavior*, *26*(6), 1831–1837. doi:10.1016/j.chb.2010.07.016

Tuch, A. N., Bargas-Avila, J. A., Opwis, K., & Wilhelm, F. H. (2009). Visual complexity of websites: Effects on users' experience, physiology, performance, and memory. *International Journal of Human-Computer Studies, 67*(9), 703–715. doi:10.1016/j.ijhcs.2009.04.002

Tullis, T., & Albert, W. (2013). *Measuring the user experience: collecting, analyzing, and presenting usability metrics* (2nd ed.). Waltham, MA: Morgan Kaufmann.

Turk, M. (2013). Multimodal interaction: A review. *Pattern Recognition Letters.* doi:10.1016/j.patrec.2013.07.003

Tversky, B., & Suwa, M. (2009). Thinking with Sketches. In Tools for Innovation (pp. 75–84). Oxford University Press. doi:10.1093/acprof:oso/9780195381634.003.0004

Twining, C., Marsland, S., & Taylor, C. (2004). Groupwise nonrigid registration of medical images: The minimum description length approach. Medical Image Analysis and Understanding (MIAU 04).

Twining, C., Cootes, T., Marsland, S., Petrovic, V., Schestowitz, R., & Taylor, C. (2005). A unified information-theoretic approach to groupwise non-rigid registration and model building. In *Biennial International Conference on Information Processing in Medical Imaging* (pp. 1-14). Springer. 10.1007/11505730_1

Udsen, L. E., & Jørgensen, A. H. (2005). The aesthetic turn: Unravelling recent aesthetic approaches to human-computer interaction. *Digital Creativity, 16*(4), 205–216. doi:10.1080/14626260500476564

Vago, D. R., & Silbersweig, D. A. (2012). Self-awareness, self-regulation, and self-transcendence (S-ART): A framework for understanding the neurobiological mechanisms of mindfulness. *Frontiers in Human Neuroscience, 6*(296), 1–30. doi:10.3389/fnhum.2012.00296 PMID:23112770

Valkenburg, R., & Dorst, K. (1998). The reflective practice of design teams. *Design Studies, 19*(3), 249–271. doi:10.1016/S0142-694X(98)00011-8

Van Den Oord, A., Dieleman, S., Zen, H., Simonyan, K., Vinyals, O., Graves, A., … Kavukcuoglu, K. (n.d.). *Wavenet: A generative model for raw audio.* Retrieved from https://arxiv.org/pdf/1609.03499.pdf

Van Meter, P., & Stevens, R. J. (2000). The role of theory in the study of peer collaboration. *Journal of Experimental Education, 69*(1), 113–127. doi:10.1080/00220970009600652

Van Someren, M. W., Barnard, Y. F., & Sandberg, J. A. C. (1994). *The think aloud method: a practical approach to modelling cognitive.* Academic Press.

Vatavu, R. D., Cramariuc, G., & Schipor, D. M. (2015). Touch interaction for children aged 3 to 6 years: Experimental findings and relationship to motor skills. *International Journal of Human-Computer Studies, 74*, 54–76. doi:10.1016/j.ijhcs.2014.10.007

Vekony, D. (2013). *Game Design Canvas – Seu projeto de jogo em uma página!* Available in: http://www.marketinge-games.com.br/game-design-canvas/

Ventura, P. (2017). *Entendendo definitivamente o que é um caso de uso.* Available at: http://www.ateomomento.com.br/o-que-e-caso-de-uso/

Vermeir, K. (2007). Athanasius Kircher's magical instruments: An essay on science, religion and applied metaphysics. *Studies in History and Philosophy of Science Part A, Elsevier, 38*(2), 363–400. doi:10.1016/j.shpsa.2007.03.008

Vianna, M., Vianna, Y., Adler, I., Lucena, B., & Russo, B. (2012). *Design Tshinking: inovação em negócios. MJV Press.*

Vicente, M. R., & López, A. J. (2010). A multidimensional analysis of the disability digital divide: Some evidence for Internet use. *The Information Society, 26*(1), 48–64. doi:10.1080/01615440903423245

Vilamnil-Casanova, J., & Molina, L. (1996). An interactive guide to multimedia. In Que Education and Training (pp. 124-129). Academic Press.

Virvou, M., & Katsionis, G. (2008). On the usability and likeability of virtual reality games for education: The case of VR-ENGAGE. *Computers & Education*, *50*(1), 154–178. doi:10.1016/j.compedu.2006.04.004

Visser, F. S., Stappers, P. J., Van der Lugt, R., & Sanders, E. B. (2005). Context mapping: Experiences from practice. *CoDesign*, *1*(2), 119–149. doi:10.1080/15710880500135987

Vredenburg, K., Mao, J. Y., Smith, P. W., & Carey, T. (2002, April). A survey of user-centered design practice. In *Proceedings of the SIGCHI conference on Human factors in computing systems* (pp. 471-478). ACM.

Vuilleumier, P. (2005). How brains beware: Neural mechanisms of emotional attention. *Trends in Cognitive Sciences*, *9*(12), 585–594. doi:10.1016/j.tics.2005.10.011 PMID:16289871

Vuilleumier, P., & Huang, Y.-M. (2009). Emotional Attention. *Current Directions in Psychological Science*, *18*(3), 148–152. doi:10.1111/j.1467-8721.2009.01626.x

Wachter, S., Mittelstadt, B., & Floridi, L. (2017). Why a right to explanation of automated decision-making does not exist in the General Data Protection Regulation. *International Data Privacy Law*, *7*(2), 76–99. doi:10.1093/idpl/ipx005

Wada, C., Sugimura, Y., Ienaga, T., & Kimuro, Y. (n.d.). Basic Research on the Method of Presenting Distance Information to the Blind by Means of Gait Measurement. *Journal of Medical and Biological Engineering*, *31*(4), 283–287. doi:10.5405/jmbe.793

Waddock, S. (2001). Integrity and mindfulness. *Journal of Corporate Citizenship*, *2001*(1), 25–37. doi:10.9774/GLEAF.4700.2001.sp.00006

Wallis, C. (2010). The impacts of media multitasking on children's learning and development: Report from a research seminar. In *The Joan Ganz Cooney Center at Sesame Workshop*. New York: The Joan Ganz Cooney Center and Stanford University.

Wang, H. F., Bowerman, J., & Yang, F. J. (2015). Do learning websites reflect users' aesthetic preferences? In C. Stroupe (Ed.), *Tenth International Conference on the Arts in Society 2015.* (pp. 1-5). Champaign, IL: The Arts in Society.

Wang, H. F., & Bowerman, C. J. (2012). The Impact of Perceived Visual Complexity on Children's Websites in Relation to Classical and Expressive Aesthetics. In *IADIS International Conference IADIS Interfaces and Human Computer Interaction 2012* (pp. 269-273). Lisbon: Inderscience Publishers.

Wang, H. F., & Lin, C. H. (2019). An investigation into visual complexity and aesthetic preference to facilitate the creation of more appropriate learning analytics systems for children. *Computers in Human Behavior*, *92*, 706–715. doi:10.1016/j.chb.2018.05.032

Wang, H. F., Shih, L. H., & Ke, Y. H. (2010). A study on the visual appeal of children's website with user performance and perceived visual aesthetic [in Chinese]. *The Journal of Art and Design*, *1*, 21–32.

Wang, M., Liu, C., & Pan, Y. (1991). Computer aided panel layout using a multi-criteria heuristic algorithm. *International Journal of Production Research*, *29*(6), 1215–1233. doi:10.1080/00207549108930129

Wang, X., Ling, Z.-H., & Dai, L.-R. (2016). Concept-to-Speech generation with knowledge sharing for acoustic modelling and utterance filtering. *Computer Speech & Language*, *38*(C), 46–67. doi:10.1016/j.csl.2015.12.003

Wang, X., Ong, S. K., & Nee, A. Y. C. (2016). Multi-modal augmented-reality assembly guidance based on bare-hand interface. *Advanced Engineering Informatics*, *30*(3), 406–421. doi:10.1016/j.aei.2016.05.004

Watson, G. H. (2007). *Strategic Benchmarking Reloaded with Six Sigma – Improve Your Company's Performance Using Global Best Practice.* John Wiley & Sons.

Weizenbaum, J. (1966, January). ELIZA—A computer program for the study of natural language communication between man and machine. *Communications of the ACM, 9*(1), 36–45. doi:10.1145/365153.365168

Weizenbaum, J. (1976). *Computer Power and Human Reason: From Judgment to Calculation.* W H Freeman & Co.

Wexler, R. (2018). Life, liberty, and trade secrets: Intellectual property in the criminal justice system. *Stanford Law Review, 70*(May), 1343–1429.

Wilkinson, S. (Ed.). (2015). *Qualitative psychology: A practical guide to research methods.* Sage.

Williams, J. (2012). *Applying Lessons Learned On Facebook To Mobile App Development.* Retrieved from: https://www.gamasutra.com/blogs/joshwilliams/20120117/90918/applying_lessons_learned_on_facebook_to_mobile_app_development.php

Williams, J. M. G., Mathews, A., & MacLeod, C. (1996). The emotional Stroop task and psychopathology. *Psychological Bulletin, 120*(1), 3–24. doi:10.1037/0033-2909.120.1.3 PMID:8711015

Williams, M., Burden, R., & Lanvers, U. (2002). 'French is the language of love and stuff': Student perceptions of issues related to motivation in learning a foreign language. *British Educational Research Journal, 28*(4), 503–528. doi:10.1080/0141192022000005805

Williamson, P. R. (2003). Commentary: Mindfulness in medicine, mindfulness in life. *Families, Systems & Health, 21*(1), 18–20. doi:10.1037/h0089496

Windows_Eyes. (2018). *Window-Eyes - Offer for Users of Microsoft Office.* Retrieved October 25, 2018, from http://www.windoweyesforoffice.com/

Witmer, B. G., & Singer, M. J. (1998). Measuring presence in virtual environments: A presence questionnaire. *Presence (Cambridge, Mass.), 7*(3), 225–240. doi:10.1162/105474698565686

Wittenberg, C. (2015). Cause the Trend Industry 4.0 in the Automated Industry to New Requirements on User Interfaces? In M. Kurosu (Ed.), Lecture Notes in Computer Science: Vol. 9171. *Human-Computer Interaction: Users and Contexts. HCI 2015* (pp. 238–245). Los Angeles, CA: Springer, Cham.

Wohlin, C. (2014). Guidelines for snowballing in systematic literature studies and a replication in software engineering. In *Proceedings of the 18th International Conference on Evaluation and Assessment in Software Engineering - EASE '14* (pp. 1–10). New York: ACM Press. 10.1145/2601248.2601268

Wolff, S., Stiglmayr, C., Bretz, H. J., Lammers, C.-H., & Auckenthaler, A. (2007). Emotion identification and tension in female patients with borderline personality disorder. *British Journal of Clinical Psychology, 46*(3), 347–360. doi:10.1348/014466507X173736 PMID:17535527

World Health Organization. (2018). *ICD-11 for Mortality and Morbidity Statistics.* Retrieved from 6A03.0 Developmental learning disorder with impairment in reading: https://icd.who.int/browse11/l-m/en#/http://id.who.int/icd/entity/1008636089

World Wide Web Consortium - W3C. (2017). *Filereader API.* Retrieved from https://www.w3.org/TR/FileAPI/#dfn-filereader

Wu, G., Jia, H., Wang, Q., Shi, F., Yap, P.-T., & Shen, D. (2012). Emergence of groupwise registration in MR brain study. *Biosignal Processing: Principles and Practices.*

Wu, G., Peng, X., Ying, S., Wang, Q., Yap, P.-T., Shen, D., & Shen, D. (2016). eHUGS: Enhanced hierarchical unbiased graph shrinkage for efficient groupwise registration. *PLoS One, 11*(1), 1–21. doi:10.1371/journal.pone.0146870 PMID:26800361

Wundt, W. (1897). *Outlines of Psychology*. Academic Press.

Wyche, S. P., & Grinter, R. E. (2012). Using sketching to support design research in new ways: a case study investigating design and charismatic Pentecostalism in São Paulo, Brazil. In *Proceedings of the 2012 iConference*. ACM. 10.1145/2132176.2132185

Yang, X., Deb, S., Loomes, M., & Karamanoglu, M. A. (2013). A framework for self-tuning optimization algorithm. *Neural Computing & Applications, 23*(7-8), 2051–2057. doi:10.100700521-013-1498-4

Yoshie, Y., Yumiko, I., & Yasuhiko, H. (2014). HEMS Browsing Behaviors and the Communication Effects. *Journal of Japan Society of Energy and Resources, 35*(4), 50–58.

Youssef, A., & Dahmani, M. (2008). The Impact of ICT on Student Performance in Higher Education: Direct Effects, Indirect Effects and Organisational Change. *Revista de Universidad y Sociedad del Conocimieneto, 5*(1), 45–56.

Yusuke, N., Kotaro, S., & Akimitsu, N. (2010). Development of the Environment and Energy Information System in Residential House. AIJ Journal of Technology and Design, 16(34), 1069–1074. (in Japanese)

Zain, J. M., Tey, M., & Goh, Y. (2007). Does aesthetics of web page interface matters to Mandarin learning? *International Journal of Computer Science and Network Security, 7*(8), 43–51.

Zanini, V. (2018). *How we built our user experience team (UX) at ContaAzul, Brazil*. Available at: https://medium.com/design-contaazul/how-we-built-our-user-experience-team-ux-at-contaazul-brazil-93ef648472f7

Zanker, M. (2012). The influence of knowledgeable explanations on users' perception of a recommender system. *Proceedings of the Sixth ACM Conference on Recommender Systems - RecSys '12*, 269. 10.1145/2365952.2366011

Zanker, M., & Schoberegger, M. (2014). An empirical study on the persuasiveness of fact-based explanations for recommender systems. *Joint Workshop on Interfaces and Human Decision Making in Recommender Systems*, 33–36.

Zardini, A. (2016). O uso do WhatsApp na sala de aula de Língua Inglesa – relato de experiência em um curso de idiomas. Blucher Design Proceedings, 2(6), 224-235.

Zarit, B. D., Super, B. J., & Quek, F. K. (1999). Comparison of five color models in skin pixel classification. In *Recognition, Analysis, and Tracking of Faces and Gestures in Real-Time Systems, 1999. Proceedings. International Workshop on* (pp. 58-63). IEEE. 10.1109/RATFG.1999.799224

Zarjam, P., Epps, J., & Chen, F. (2011). Spectral EEG features for evaluating cognitive load. *33rd Annual International Conference of the IEEE EMBS* (pp. 3841-3844). Boston: IEEE.

Zemel, R. S., Wu, Y., Swersky, K., Pitassi, T., & Dwork, C. (2013). Learning fair representations. *Proceedings of the 30th International Conference on Machine Learning, 28*, 325–333. Retrieved from http://jmlr.org/proceedings/papers/v28/zemel13.html

Zeng, L., Weber, G., Simros, M., Conradie, P., Saldien, J., & Ravyse, I., … Mioch, T. (2017). Range-IT. In *Proceedings of the 19th International Conference on Human-Computer Interaction with Mobile Devices and Services - MobileHCI '17* (pp. 1–6). New York: ACM Press. 10.1145/3098279.3125442

Zhang, C., Perkis, A., & Arndt, S. (2017). Spatial immersion versus emotional immersion, which is more immersive? In *2017 9th International Conference on Quality of Multimedia Experience (QoMex)* (pp. 1–6). Academic Press. 10.1109/QoMEX.2017.7965655

Zhang, C., Smith, W., Dessein, A., Pears, N., & Dai, H. (2016). Functional faces: Groupwise dense correspondence using functional maps. In *Proceedings of the IEEE Conference on Computer Vision and Pattern Recognition* (pp. 5033-5041). IEEE. 10.1109/CVPR.2016.544

Zheng, G., Li, S., & Szekely, G. (2017). *Statistical Shape and Deformation Analysis: Methods, Implementation and Applications*. Academic Press.

Zhu, B., Hedman, A., & Li, H. (2017). Designing Digital Mindfulness: Presence-In and Presence-With versus Presence-Through. In *Proceedings of the 2017 CHI Conference on Human Factors in Computing Systems* (pp. 2685-2695). ACM. 10.1145/3025453.3025590

Zimmerman, J., Forlizzi, J., & Evenson, S. (2007, April). Research through design as a method for interaction design research in HCI. In *Proceedings of the SIGCHI conference on Human factors in computing systems* (pp. 493-502). ACM. 10.1145/1240624.1240704

Zitova, B., & Flusser, J. (2003). Image registration methods: A survey. *Image and Vision Computing*, *21*(11), 977–1000. doi:10.1016/S0262-8856(03)00137-9

Zsupan-Jerome, D. (2014). *Connected Toward Communion: The Church and Social Communication in the Digital Age*. Collegeville, MN: Liturgical Press.

Zuehike, D. (2010). SmartFactory - Towards a factory-of-things. *Annual Reviews in Control*, *34*(1), 129–138. doi:10.1016/j.arcontrol.2010.02.008

About the Contributors

Ahmad Aal-Yhia is a Lecturer in the Postgraduate Institute for Accounting and Financial Studies, University of Baghdad, Iraq since 2013. He obtained his BSc in computer science from the Mustansiriyah University, Baghdad, Iraq, in 1999, and his MSc in computer science from The University of Jordan, Jordan, Amman, in 2004. Currently, he is working towards his PhD in computer science from Aberystwyth University, UK. His current research is in Computer Vision, Machine Learning and Image Processing (specifically groupwise image registration). He is the first author of two conference papers related to groupwise non-rigid image alignment.

Isabel Araújo is a Professor in the Polytechnic Institute of Viana do Castelo, where she has been since 1993 as a lecturer in the mathematics area. She received a PhD in Multimedia in Education from the University of Aveiro and a Master's Degree in Applied Mathematics - Optimization and Control from University of Porto. She has developed and coordinated several research and innovation projects, related with academic unsuccess in mathematics and has made also numerous international publications.

Carlos Arce-Lopera is an Associate professor and researcher at Universidad Icesi in Cali, Colombia. With experience teaching both undergraduate and graduate courses on signal processing, research methodologies and human computer interaction related subjects. His research interest are in the intersection of three main research fields: digital signal processing, machine learning and human perception. His research approach is inherently interdisciplinary and by combining his engineering skills on designing stimuli for psychophysical experimentation he has successfully developed and supported research projects that range from e-health and vision science to marketing and consumer research.

Ana Arboleda is an assistant professor at the Department of Marketing and International Business at Universidad Icesi. She is a psychologist, holds a M.S. in Industrial Relations from Iowa State University and a Ph.D. in Business from Tulane University. Her main research focus is on Sensory Marketing.

Daniel Atorf is a scientist at the Fraunhofer IOSB since 2004. Since then he did research on the field of Technology-Based Learning and developed several e-learning tools and applications. After graduating extra occupational studies on Educational Technology in 2010, he concentrated on Game-Based Learning. He was the project manager and lead designer of the Serious Game "Lost Earth 2307". Current work focuses on the measurement of flow while playing games.

Anne Marielle Bagamaspad obtained a bachelor's degree in Computer Science with specialization in Software Technology at De La Salle University in 2017. She later pursued her career as a software developer, mainly focusing on automotive systems and cloud-based software. Her interests include software and graphic design, IoT, and cloud computing.

Florian Brody is the managing partner at Brody & Partners, a startup business mentor, and certified life coach working with companies and individuals to develop their individual and corporate narratives. Born and educated in Vienna, he has been working for over 20 years in the Silicon Valley and co-founded four companies. He is a digital media pioneer and the co-inventor of the first electronic books. He developed digital media strategies for Apple Austria and Ciba-Geigy Novartis and created the first interactive book with Kodak. Brody has been teaching digital media theory and business management for over 30 years. He held the first chair for multimedia at the Salzburg University of Applied Sciences and was a member of the graduate faculty of Art Center College of Design, Pasadena CA and lecturer at the Universidad de Las Palmas, Gran Canaria. He is an adjunct professor at the Magdeburg-Stendal University of Applied Sciences and a senior instructor at the Johannes Kepler University in Linz, Austria. Brody is published in multiple languages and a keynote speaker at international conferences.

John Israel Caingles was born in Quezon City, Philippines. He graduated from De La Salle University in 2017 and started his career as a Full Stack Developer, creating web and mobile applications. Upon earning a Bachelor's Degree in Computer Science with a specialization in Software Technology, he continued to pursue his passion in building innovative technologies through his work and various projects.

Irene Connolly is an Educational Psychologist and lecturer in Dun Laoghaire Institute of Art, Design and Technology (IADT). She is also the Chairperson of the Department of Technology & Psychology's Ethics Committee. Irene specializes in the area of bullying and cyberbullying. She is a fellow researcher with the National Anti-Bullying Research and Resource Centre and is also the Psychological Society of Ireland's Irish representative on the European Federation of Psychologists Associations (EFPA) Consultation Group 'Psychology and Internet': which is a coalition to make the Internet a safer place for children. Irene has published in the area of bullying and cyberbullying over the past decade.

Abhishek Dahiya is a research scholar at Indian Institute of Technology Delhi. He did his bachelors in Architecture. His current area of research is investigating impact of users' information on design cognition in HCI Design.

André das Neves is an Associate Professor at the Federal University of Pernambuco. He holds a degree in Industrial Design from the Federal University of Paraíba, a Master's and PhD in Computer Science from the Federal University of Pernambuco and a Post-doctorate from UBI - Portugal. He has experience in the area of Computer Science, with emphasis on Computer Systems Design, working mainly in the research, development and application of design methods and techniques as a tool for innovation in Information and Communication Technology.

João de Menezes Neto is a designer, educator and entrepreneur. MSc. in Design. Works as a Product Design Coordinator at ContaAzul, Brazil. Has also worked as Head of UX Design in a prominent digital agency. Specialist in usability and user experience. Co-founder of IxDA Joinville and educator in courses, workshops and higher education. Transdisciplinarity and Design Management enthusiast.

Carlos Alberto de Miranda is a Doctor in Materials Engineering by REDEMAT, Master in Production Engineering and Bachelor in Industrial Design. He has experience in the area of Industrial Design, with emphasis on Product Development, acting professionally and providing consulting in the areas of Product Design, Prototyping and Design Management, Materials Management and Logistics. Professor at the State University of Minas Gerais (UEMG) - School of Design. Professor of the Graduate Program in Design - Master and Doctorate in Design of the School of Design / UEMG.

Pedro Henrique de Oliveira is a Master in Design from the State University of Minas Gerais (UEMG). Founder of Games and Software Developer JetDragon Studios. Designer UI / UX in the Livebetter Software Developer. Designer UI / UX in Sebraetech projects. Designer UI / UX and Game Designer at Developer Patada Studios. Designer UI / UX, 3D Modeler, Creative Director, Game Designer and Screenwriter in JetDragon Studios Developer.

Javier Diaz-Cely is a Faculty member and Researcher, and Director of the Master in Data Science Program at Icesi University, Colombia. His main interests are the real-world application of machine learning models and techniques, such as predictive and clustering, recommendation systems and deep learning, to finance, health, and retail problems. He holds a Ph.D in Informatics from the Pierre & Marie Curie University in Paris (Sorbonne Universités), as well as a Masters in Artificial Intelligence from the same university and a Masters in Corporate Finance from the Conservatorie des Arts & Métiers in Paris, and a B.Sc in Computer Science and Engineering from the Universidad Javeriana in Cali, Colombia.

Pedro Miguel Faria is a Professor in the Polytechnic Institute of Viana do Castelo, where he has been since 1998. He received a PhD in Computer Science from the University of Vigo in 2014. His research interests are in the areas of Human-Computer Interaction, User Experience, Mobile Systems, Multimedia and Computer Graphics. He has made numerous international publications and participates in several research, innovation and development projects.

Farley Fernandes lives in Porto, Portugal. Product manager with 10+ years experience in digital projects for startups and big corporations. Focused on designing, executing and measuring agile processes to create increasingly engaging products. Professor in design methodology, project and product management for digital products @ Universidade da Beira Interior. He also holds a PhD in Design (Universidade Federal de Pernambuco / Universidade Nova de Lisboa) with the research located within digital product methodologies and a Masters in Computer Science at Universidade Federal de Pernambuco. Certifications: Project Management Professional (PMP) - PMI Certified Scrum Master - Scrum Alliance.

Ronaldo Ferreira is a Master in Electrical Engineering from the Federal University of Amazonas - UFAM, studied Mathematics and Physics at the Federal University of Amazonas - UFAM, has experience with linear and nonlinear mathematical optimization, Operational Research, dynamical systems and algebraic topology, dynamic atmospheric meteorology, fluid dynamics, system control and automation, intelligent systems and supporters for decision making, and artificial intelligence. He is currently a professor and researcher at the Nilton Lins University, where he works on research aimed at developing intelligent systems and agribusiness models and interacting with the biosphere and atmosphere.

Joao Victor Gomide is a Doctor of Arts and PhD in Physics, has been working with digital game design, narratives for digital media, film editing and post-production supervision of television programs in the last twenty years. Coordinates the development of applications using computer vision and the fundamentals of digital imaging. Has coordinated the development of a free software for real time motion capture for animation, OpenMoCap, the first in the world with markers. Coordinates the motion capture laboratory (MoCapLab), which produced the first Brazilian digital games with this technique. Is the author of the book Applied Digital Image, published by Elsevier. Coordinates the undergraduate courses in Computer Graphics and Digital Games at Universidade FUMEC.

Carsten Greif is a lecturer for physical computing at Magdeburg-Stendal University. He completes his MA in interaction design with a thesis on a task management system based on a single-purpose device with a new approach to organize tasks in company environments. He is a professionally trained engineering draftsman and holds a BA in interaction design from Osnabrück University. Carstens group-works were on display at multiple exhibitions throughout Europe and his recent paper on the project Instant Church has been published by IADIS.

Dominik Hagelkruys is a computer-science teacher and lector at the University of Vienna. His interests include accessibility, human-centered design, interface design and the mutual influence of IT and society.

Moe Hamamoto is working for Panasonic Corporation since 2001 as a network engineer. She is a student in a doctoral course at Graduate School of Engineering, Kanagawa Institute of Technology. Her research interests include wireless networks and home network technology.

Sinah Herrklotsch is a carpenter, a user interface designer, and a university instructor. She currently finalizes her master thesis in interaction design at the Magdeburg-Stendal University of Applied Sciences in parallel to her work at Chemmedia, a leader in e-Learning solutions for continuing education serving 9 million users in 38 countries leveraging synergies in her professional work and her research interests in usability in e-learning solutions with an emphasis on the integration of analog and digital elements. In 2017 she received an IIID Student Award for the object "kîkmaa". Her publications include a paper on the project "Instant Church" published by IADIS in 2018.

Michael A. Herzog is a full professor for Information Systems Engineering. He serves as the Vice Dean for research at the Department of Economics and is a member of the Academic Senate at the Magdeburg-Stendal University. His research focuses on Technology Enhanced Learning, Interaction Systems, IoT-Technology, and IT-supported Sustainability. He founded and leads the interdisciplinary SPIRIT research group and is the chair of the study program Digital Business Management. Earlier he founded and led three software and media companies in Germany and Italy. Michael holds a PhD in information systems and M.Sc. in computer science from Technical University Berlin. He published 11 books and over 60 peer-reviewed research papers in international conference proceedings and scientific journals and is a fellow at the Alcatel-Lucent-Foundation for communication research since 2006. His research was recognized with multiple awards, including the Multimedia-Award of the University of Potsdam in 2004, and the Research Award 2018 of Magdeburg-Stendal University.

Masao Isshiki is a Professor of Kanagawa Institute of Technology since 2012. He was also as project professor of Keio University at 2009 to 2015. And also director of HEMS Inter-Operability Testing Center and Smart home researching center since 2011.

Ehm Kannegieser works as a scientist at Fraunhofer IOSB since 2008. He focusses on serious games projects, flow/immersion measurement, gamification techniques and operation of virtual reality in learning systems.

Kingston Anthony Koa studied Computer Science with specialization in Software Technology at De La Salle University where he obtained his bachelor's degree in 2017. In 2018, he started his professional career as a software engineer in Canon Information Technologies where he developed firmware drivers and image libraries. His research interest includes programming languages, software engineering disciplines, and artificial intelligence. In his spare time, he enjoys playing video games, and hanging out with friends.

Jyoti Kumar is a Professor of User Experience Design and HCI in the Department of Design at Indian Institute of Technology, Delhi, India. He received his PhD in 2009 from IIT Guwahati. He has 25+ international publications and he has been consultant to 15+ govt. and private agencies as principal investigator. His current area of research is user experience design, HCI design for Industry 4.0, usability studies and social innovation and design.

Naveen Kumar holds a PhD in HCI Design from Department of Design, Indian Institute of Technology, Delhi, India. He received post-graduation in Instrumentation Technology from NIT Kurukshetra. After post-graduation he has 3.5 years of industry experience in Embedded system development domain. His current area of research is HCI design for Industry 4.0, cognitive ergonomics, Interaction design and user experience design and social innovation.

Victor Laurenciano Aguiar holds a PhD in Education: Psychology of Education and Master in Production Engineering. Professor of the Professional Master's Degree in Design at Joinville University, Univille, where coordinates the Service Design project. Works also as a consultant and speaker.

Paul Malcolm received a BSc in Biochemistry and basic medical sciences in 1983 from Kings College, London and qualified in Medicine from the University of London in 1986. He is a fellow of the Royal College of Radiologists and currently a consultant radiologist and research lead in radiology at the Norfolk & Norwich University Hospital, UK. His clinical interests include imaging of prostate cancer and his research interests are in new MRI techniques for measurement of body compartments and function.

Nelson Marcos obtained his PhD Computer Science Degree with High Distinction in 2001 in De La Salle University (DLSU) during which he did a sandwich program in National University of Singapore. He earned his MS Computer Science with Distinction in 1994 in DLSU and did a Post-MS Research in

University of Houston, Texas in 1996. He graduated Honorable Mention with the degree BS Computer Science in DLSU in 1990. He is a full-time faculty and an Associate Professor in the College of Computer Studies (CCS). He is currently the Associate Dean of the CCS and the PhD Computer Science Coordinator of the Software Technology Department of CCS.

Joel Martin is the Director of Research and Development for Digital Technologies at the National Research Council of Canada. He leads a group of 80+ researchers and developers focusing on data analytics and machine learning applied in a variety of areas such as machine translation and computer vision. Dr. Martin spent his 25-year career both in academia and in the government investigating machine-learning techniques applied to natural language and bioinformatics. He holds an M.Sc. and Ph.D. from Georgia Institute of Technology in Artificial Intelligence (1987, 1992). He also earned a Master's degree in Cognitive Psychology from the University of Manitoba (1986).

Ana Martins is a researcher in the Medical Sciences Department of the University of Aveiro and in the Institute of Electronics and Informatics Engineering of Aveiro. She has a PhD in Health Sciences and Technology (2016), MSc in Gerontology, specialization in Management of Social Equipments (2011) and BSc in Gerontology (2009) at the University of Aveiro. Her research work is focused on technology assessment for the elderly, including Ambient Assisted Living (AAL) products and services. Her recent work includes the development of a methodology for evaluation of AAL products and services usability using the International Classification of Functioning Disability and Health in a Living Lab approach. She also developed work in the field of assistive technologies use and evaluation of human functioning and environmental factors using the International Classification of Functioning, Disability and Health.

Marian McDonnell is a researcher at the Institute of Art, Design and Technology, Dun Laoghaire, Ireland. Marian's current research interests are focused on the role of design, technology and psychology in User Experience and Interaction Design. She is particularly interested in the area of designing, developing and evaluating instructional technologies for individuals with cognitive impairments. She co-founded the Let's Go Skills (www.letsgoskill.com) research center for this purpose. She is presently working on the Stop Disabuse Erasmus + research project, designing online instructional materials to protect vulnerable adults from bullying and cyber-bullying. She lectures and supervises Masters students in the area of User Experience design.

Marisardo Medeiros Filho is a game designer and producer, with over eight years in the game industry, with experience on pc, web and mobile titles. Specializing in mechanics, mobile game design, F2P, game concept, and team leadership. Also, Marisardo is a college professor and entrepreneur, passionate about technology, innovation, and games. He has three graduations degree (computer science, graphic design, financial management), two specializations (Information Technology, Multimedia Creation) a master degree (design) and a Ph.D. in Design. He has been working on games since 2010, in laboratories and industry, and also making researches about usability, interaction design, design methodology, and game design, since the same date. Currently, he is the founder of Zug Studios, a multimedia studio focusing in provide great games to worldwide marketing. He is also the CEO and Creative Director at Zug Studios, and the Studio Head of The Game Lab Estácio Project.

Josua Meier recently finished his master's degree at the Karlsruhe Institute of Technology. As part of his thesis, he performed a study researching the relationship between flow and immersion, as well as the effect of flow and immersion on the human body. He currently continues this research as a research assistant at the Fraunhofer IOSB.

Joana Mendes received a PhD in physics in 2006 from the University of Aveiro. She is currently a senior researcher in the Institute of Telecommunications. Her current interests are centred in the use of diamond films to improve the thermal management of high power high temperature electronic components and in sensing applications in hostile environments using surface acoustic wave devices. She has participated in several national and international research projects, both as Principal Investigator and team member. She is the author or co-author of more than 30 journal and international conference papers and 4 book chapters. She is a permanent member of WOCSDICE Steering Committee.

Heather Molyneaux is an Analyst at the National Research Council Canada and has 12 years' experience in Human Computer Interaction (HCI). Interests include visual analysis of communication technologies, participatory design and user studies in education technologies, and HCI related aspects of AI, augmented reality and Cybersecurity.

Sara Morales is Senior Program Manager of Math Snacks NSF grant project. She has a Bachelors in Education with a TESOL and Spanish endorsement and a Masters in Teaching Mathematics. She has taught in diverse settings including New Mexico, Florida, and Hawaii. Sara oversees research activities by analyzing the learning environments in K-12 classrooms among other methods. Her responsibilities include supporting professional learning and leadership development, accountability reports, dissemination of data, and writing.

Renate Motschnig-Pitrik is Professor at the Faculty of Computer Science at the University of Vienna and head of the Computer Science Didactics and Learning Research Center. Until 1996, she has repeatedly been a Visiting Professor at the Computer Science Department of the University of Toronto, Canada. In 1995/96 she was on the faculty of the Computer Science Department of the RWTH-Aachen, Germany. Currently, she also teaches courses on communication for Computer Scientists at the Masaryk University in Brno/CZ.

Ana Oliveira Lima received the PhD and master's degree in Electrical Engineering from the Federal University of Campina Grande, UFCG, Campina Grande, Paraíba, Brazil, in 2012 and 2005, respectively. Recently she is working with research in post-doctoral in University of Aveiro, Portugal. She is CEO and founder of Centre for Innovation in Control and Automation and Industrial Robotics in Brazilian whit projects in course that receive funding for research in Brazilian.

Nelson Rocha is Full Professor of the University of Aveiro. He received his BSc degree in Electronics and Telecommunications Engineering in 1983 and his PhD in Electronics Engineering in 1992, from the University of Aveiro. He was the Head of Health Sciences School (2001-2011), the Head of the Health Sciences Department of the University of Aveiro (2001-2014) and Pro-Rector of the University of Aveiro

(2005-2010). His current research interests include the application of information and communications technologies to healthcare and social services, the secondary use of electronic health records, and the interconnection of human functionality and ambient assisted living services. He has been involved in various European and national funded research projects, has supervised several PhD and MSc students and has a patent and more than one hundred research publications distributed by books, book chapters, international journals and proceedings of international conferences.

Conrado Ruiz Jr. obtained his bachelor's degree in computer science with a specialization in software technology (cum laude) from DLSU in 1999. He received his master's and doctorate degrees from the School of Computing of the National University of Singapore in 2001 and 2015, respectively. His several works in the areas of computer graphics, computational art, and multimedia information retrieval have been published. He was a BPI Science Awardee in 1999 and received a special citation from the National Academy of Science and Technology during the Talent Search for Young Scientists in 2007. He is currently an associate professor at the College of Computer Studies of DLSU.

Julie Ann Salido is a PhD student in Computer Science at De La Salle University since 2016 as a recipient of CHED K-12 Transition Graduate School Scholarship for PhD in Computer Science. As a grantee of the Science and Engineering Government Scholarship Program (June 2010-May 2012) sponsored by the Commission on Higher Education, she obtained her Master of Science in Computer Science degree from the Department of Computer Studies, Algorithm and Complexity Laboratory at the University of the Philippines – Diliman. She is currently an assistant professor of Aklan State University.

Danny Schott is a lecturer for computational design at Magdeburg-Stendal University and a research assistant in the field of human-computer interaction in computer-assisted surgery at Otto-von-Guericke-University, Magdeburg where he completes his MA in interaction design with a thesis on contact-free manipulation of multi-modal imaging systems in sterile environments. He is a professionally trained digital and print media designer and holds a BA In industrial design from Magdeburg-Stendal University. Danny received the 2017 IIID Student Award and his recent paper on the project Instant Church has been published by IADIS.

Dominik Schumacher is a full professor for Interaction Design and head of the department of Industrial Design Technologies at Magdeburg-Stendal University. He leads the course of crossmedia studies and is a member of the committee for continuing studies. His research work focuses on user centered strategic design in interactive media. He is actively involved in multiple research projects including a project to provide tactile experiences for visually challenged people. Previously Prof. Schumacher taught at the Berlin University of the Arts and was an artistic associate at the Advanced New Media Class Prof. Sauter. He is the co-founder of the design studio TheGreenEyl in Berlin and New York. Their work was selected for Ars Electronica and the Japan Media Arts Festival in Tokyo. He holds a degree in digital media design from the Berlin University of the Arts, studied at the Central Academy of Fine Arts in Beijing and the Universidad Autonoma de Barcelona. He is a professionally trained engineer in industrial electronics, fluent in Spanish, German as well as English. His creative work has been exhibited internationally for over 13 years and he is published in multiple international publications on interactive and media design. Dominik won the Europrix Multimedia Award over multiple years as well as design awards in London and Tokyo.

Takumi Shida Received Development of Home Electronics of Degree from Kanagawa Institute of Technology in 2017. He Has Been a Students of Department of Electrical and Electronic Engineering, Graduate School of Engineering, Kanagawa Institute of Technology, JAPAN.

Isabel Cristina Silva holds a PhD in Computer Science from UFRGS, Brazil, and La Sapienza, University of Rome. She is Professor at UniRitter Laureate International Universities, Brazil. Her research interests are in the areas of Virtual and Augmented Reality, Interaction, Information Visualization, Visual Analytics, Semantic Web, Ontology, Linked Data, Education and Game Design.

Juan Lorenzo Simeon received his Bachelor of Science in Computer Science with specialization in Software Technology from De La Salle University in 2017. In 2018, he started his career as a full stack developer building web and mobile apps. His interests include augmented reality, virtual reality and game development.

Jacek Sliwinski received his PhD in Communication and Media Studies from the University of the Sunshine Coast, where he is part of the Engage Research Lab that focuses on research and development of interactive technologies for positive impact. He is a certified User Experience professional and works in the industry as an enabler of digital transformation.

Hiroshi Sugimura Doctor of Engineering. Associate Professor. Department of Home Electronics, Faculty of Creative Engineering, Kanagawa Institute of Technology. Department of Electrical and Electronic Engineering, Graduate School of Engineering, Kanagawa Institute of Technology, Japan.

Ana Teixeira, PhD, MSc in Electronic Engineering at the University of Aveiro, and BSc in Maths at the University of Porto. She is a Professor at the Department of Informatics in Higher Education School of the Polytechnic Institute of Coimbra, where she has taught Interactive Technologies, Web Programing, Networks and Multimedia Systems, User Interaction, Quantitative methods, User Experience and Design Usable Systems. She is a Master Coordinator of Human Computer Interaction Master. She has over 70 scientific articles in prestigious international journals and conferences. She is a member of the "Signal Processing" research group at the Electronic Engineering Institute of the University of Aveiro and of the "Applied Research Institute" of the Polytechnic Institute of Coimbra. Her research work focuses mostly in the area of Assistive Technologies and Human Computer Interaction, Signal Processing Methods and Applications. Her work has been referenced in many other author publications.

Bernard Tiddeman is a Reader and Head of Department in Computer Science at Aberystwyth University. He obtained his BSc from the University of St Andrews in 1992, MSc from Manchester University in 1994 and PhD from Heriot-Watt University in 1998. From 1999-2010 he worked as a researcher and then a lecturer at the University of St Andrews. His research interests include 2D and 3D facial image analysis and synthesis, texture modelling for age estimation and age progression, skin health analysis and medical image analysis.

Ruth Torres Castillo is a senior PhD student in the Interdisciplinary Doctorate with a concentration in Computer Science and Curriculum & Instruction at New Mexico State University (NMSU). She received a Masters degree in Management of Information Technologies from Instituto Tecnologico de

Estudios Superiores de Monterrey, Mexico in 2010 prior to joining NMSU. Her research interests include developing educational games that enhance critical thinking and help construction of knowledge rather than just the transmission of it. She is a graduate assistant in the Learning Games Lab at NMSU for the Math Snacks project funded by NSF to engage algebra-learning topics with multimedia tools.

Maria Vieira holds a Bachelor's Degree in Physics from the Federal University of Pernambuco (1975) and a Bachelor's Degree in Electrical Engineering from the Federal University of Paraíba (1981), a Master's Degree in Electrical Engineering from the Federal University of Paraíba (1979), PhD in Electrical Engineering - Bradford University (1985), UK, and post-doctorate at the University d'Aix-Marseille, France (2003-2004). She is currently a full professor at the Department of Electrical Engineering of the Federal University of Campina Grande (UFCG). She is active in the area of Industrial Automation, in Electrical Engineering. She was a Visiting Professor, 2005-2012, at the Laboratoire des Sciences de l'Information et des Systèmes (LSIS UMR CNRS 6168 France) and at the Department of Industrial Engineering at Paul Cezanne University (Aix-Marseille III) in France. She served as Honorary Senior Research Fellow in the Department of Electronic and Electrical Engineering at the University of Strathclyde, Scotland UK between 2009 and 2012. Him research interests are focused on the design and evaluation of user interfaces of automated industrial systems (hardware and software) and the development of tools to support the training of operators of automated environments, aiming at the construction of ergonomic interfaces and the consequent the occurrence of human error in the operation of these systems.

Norman Vinson conducts research in Human Computer Interaction, and leads and participates in applied research and development projects at the National Research Council of Canada. Over his 23 year career, Dr. Vinson has published in several areas including HCI, software engineering, research ethics, and epidemiology. Dr. Vinson obtained his Ph.D. in psychology at Carnegie-Mellon University, where he worked in psycholinguistics and spatial cognition, and his Bachelors of Science degree at McGill University.

Hsiu-Feng Wang is an associate professor in the Department of e-Learning Design and Management, at National Chiayi University, Taiwan. She studied for her PhD in the Department of Typography and Graphic Communication at Reading University, UK. She is interested in graphic icon design, information design, the legibility of Traditional Chinese writing and user-centred design. Her current research is concerned with how design variables influence the effectiveness of online teaching materials for children.

Reyer Zwiggelaar received his Ir degree in applied physics from the State University Groningen, Groningen, The Netherlands, in 1989, and his PhD in electronic and electrical engineering from the University College London, London, UK, in 1993. Currently, he is a professor in the Department of Computer Science, Aberystwyth University, UK. He is the author or coauthor of more than 250 conference and journal papers. His current research interests include medical image understanding, especially focusing on mammographic and prostate data, pattern recognition, statistical methods, texture based segmentation, biometrics, manifold learning, and feature detection techniques. He is an associate editor of Pattern Recognition and Journal of Biomedical and Health Informatics (JBHI).

Index

Ensure Quality Research is Introduced to the Academic Community

Become an IGI Global Reviewer for Authored Book Projects

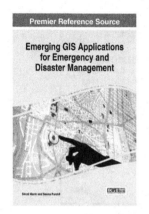

Premier Reference Source

Emerging GIS Applications for Emergency and Disaster Management

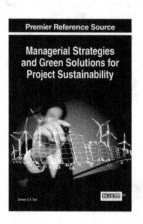

Premier Reference Source

Managerial Strategies and Green Solutions for Project Sustainability

Premier Reference Source

Comparative Approaches to Using R and Python for Statistical Data Analysis

Premier Reference Source

Solutions for High-Touch Communications in a High-Tech World

The overall success of an authored book project is dependent on quality and timely reviews.

In this competitive age of scholarly publishing, constructive and timely feedback significantly expedites the turnaround time of manuscripts from submission to acceptance, allowing the publication and discovery of forward-thinking research at a much more expeditious rate. Several IGI Global authored book projects are currently seeking highly qualified experts in the field to fill vacancies on their respective editorial review boards:

Applications may be sent to:
development@igi-global.com

Applicants must have a doctorate (or an equivalent degree) as well as publishing and reviewing experience. Reviewers are asked to write reviews in a timely, collegial, and constructive manner. All reviewers will begin their role on an ad-hoc basis for a period of one year, and upon successful completion of this term can be considered for full editorial review board status, with the potential for a subsequent promotion to Associate Editor.

If you have a colleague that may be interested in this opportunity, we encourage you to share this information with them.

Printed in the United States
By Bookmasters